OVERVIEW OF UNITED STATES LAW

OVERVIEW OF UNITED STATES LAW

Ellen S. Podgor
Associate Dean of Faculty Development and Electronic Education and
Professor of Law
Stetson University College of Law

John F. Cooper
Associate Dean of International and Cooperative Programs and Professor of Law
Stetson University College of Law

Library of Congress Cataloging-in-Publication Data

Podgor, Ellen S., 1952-
    Overview of United States Law/ Ellen S. Podgor, John F. Cooper.— 1st ed.
p. cm.
    Includes index.
    ISBN 978-1-4224-2144-4 (soft cover)
    1. Law--United States. I. Cooper, John F. (John Frederick), 1950- II. Title.
KF385.P58 2009
349.73--dc22

2009002514

NOTE TO USERS

To ensure that you are using the latest materials available in this area, please be sure to periodically check the LexisNexis Law School web site for downloadable updates and supplements at www.lexisnexis.com/lawschool.

Editorial Offices
744 Broad Street, Newark, NJ 07102 (973) 820-2000
201 Mission St., San Francisco, CA 94105-1831 (415) 908-3200
www.lexisnexis.com

MATTHEW◆BENDER

Dedication

This book is dedicated to the memory of Adam F. Cooper, the son of one of the editors. Adam was born in 1988, and died tragically in 2008. He was bright, funny, creative, artistic, generous, complicated, frustrating, angry, troubled, but always loving. He loved, and was loved, without condition.

ABOUT THE AUTHORS

Michael P. Allen

Michael P. Allen is a Professor of Law at Stetson University College of Law. He teaches courses in Civil Procedure, Constitutional Law, Federal Courts, Complex Litigation, Remedies, and Veterans Benefits Law, Practice and Policy. Professor Allen has been recognized for his classroom activities with Stetson University's highest award for teaching excellence. He has also received eight awards for his teaching voted on by students.

Professor Allen has published widely in the areas in which he teaches. He is the author of two books, *An Illustrated Guide to Civil Procedure* and the forthcoming *Federal Courts: Context, Cases and Problems*. He is also the author of over a dozen articles that have appeared or are forthcoming in publications such as the *American University Law Review*, the *Washington and Lee Law Review*, the *George Mason Law Review*, the *University of Michigan Journal of Law Reform*, the *William & Mary Bill of Rights Journal*, and the *NYU Annual Survey of American Law*.

Professor Allen is also active in professional and community groups. He is on the Board of Trustees of the Southeastern Association of Law Schools. He is also the current Chair of the Remedies Section of the Association of American Law Schools. In addition, he serves as the co-chair of the Temple Beth-El Social Action Committee.

Professor Allen received his undergraduate degree in American History and Political Science from the University of Rochester. He received his law degree from Columbia University Law School. He is married to Debbie Allen with whom he has two sons, Ben and Noah.

Thomas E. Allison

Thomas E. Allison is a Professor of Law Emeritus at Stetson University College of Law. He earned a B.S degree from Tulane University; an M.B.A. from Florida State University, a J.D. from Stetson University College of Law, and an LL.M in Taxation from the University of Florida. Before joining the Stetson law faculty in 1985, Professor Allison was engaged in the private practice of law as a partner in a St. Petersburg, Florida law firm. His primary areas of interests are in the fields of Trusts and Estates, Estate and Gift Taxation, and Property Law. He served as Associate Dean of the College of Law from 1995 to 1999, and retired from the faculty in 2008.

William Andersen

William Andersen is the Judson Falknor Professor of Law Emeritus at the University of Washington School of Law in Seattle, Washington. His degrees include an LL.B. (Denver) and an LL. M. (Yale). For 3 years, Andersen was Associate General Counsel of the then Federal Aviation Agency. He has taught the course in Administrative Law for more than three decades, has been a visiting scholar/professor at Michigan, Columbia, Chicago Kent and the University of Copenhagen. A principal draftsman of the Washington State Administrative Procedure Act, Andersen is a frequent speaker at CLE programs on the subject. Between 2003 and 2006, he was the Freeman Professor at the Johns Hopkins/Nanjing University Center for Chinese American Studies, teaching U.S. Constitutional and Administrative Law. The author of many publications in the field — including a forthcoming text on Administrative Law from Carolina Academic Press — Andersen's publications include a series of computer tutorials on Administrative Law distributed nationally by the Center For Computer-Assisted Legal Instruction (CALI).

ABOUT THE AUTHORS

Ann M. Bartow

Professor Ann M. Bartow is a professor of law at University of South Carolina School of Law. She is a graduate of Cornell University and the University of Pennsylvania Law School. She began her teaching career as an Honorable Abraham L. Freedman Teaching Fellow at Temple University School of Law, where she also received an LL.M. in Legal Education. Prior to joining the University of South Carolina School of Law in the Fall of 2000, she held visiting appointments at the University of Dayton School of Law and the University of Idaho College of Law.

Professor Bartow currently teaches Intellectual Property Survey Law, Copyright Law, Trademarks and Unfair Competition Law, and Patent Law. Her scholarship primarily focuses on the intersection between intellectual property laws and public policy concerns. Her son Casey is one of the coolest people in the known universe. She thanks Ellen Podgor for inviting her to join this project.

Paul Boudreaux

Paul Boudreaux is associate professor and (from 2008-10) the LeRoy Highbaugh Sr. Research Chair at Stetson University College of Law. He teaches property law and related topics, including environmental and natural resources law. He is a graduate of the University of Virginia School of Law.

John F. Cooper

Associate Dean Cooper joined the Stetson law faculty in 1985. While in law school, he was an editor of the *Oklahoma Law Review* and a member of the Order of the Coif. Following graduation he practiced law in the State of Oklahoma. He is co-author (with Professor Marks) of *State Constitutional Law in a Nutshell* (West, 1988) which is now in its 2nd edition and *Florida Constitutional Law: Cases and Materials* (Carolina Academic Press, 1992), which is now in its 4th edition. He is co-author (with Professor Richard Gershon of the Charleston School of Law) of *International Tax Guide: U.S. Income Taxation* (Callaghan, 1991). His teaching interests are in Taxation and State Constitutional Law.

Ronald W. Eades

Ronald W. Eades received his initial education at Rhodes College in Memphis, Tennessee where he was awarded a B.A. He then received his J.D. degree from the University of Memphis, School of Law. Professor Eades also received an LL.M. from the Harvard Law School.

The first law related position held by Professor Eades was a staff attorney for the Tennessee Valley Authority. At this agency, Professor Eades did general civil litigation. After the period of time with the Tennessee Valley Authority, Professor Eades joined the faculty of the Louis D. Brandeis School of Law at the University of Louisville in Louisville, Kentucky. While teaching at the University of Louisville, Professor Eades taught primarily in the Torts and civil litigation areas. In addition, he has written extensively in those same areas. His books include a series of Jury Instructions texts published by Lexis/Nexis and a series of Kentucky Law books published by West Publishing Company. He is currently working on three student textbooks for Carolina Academic Press. Professor Eades has also worked with the Center for Computer Assisted Legal Instruction (CALI). That work included writing computer lessons in tort law.

During his time in teaching, Professor Eades has had the opportunity to be a visiting teaching and scholar at several European Universities. He has been a teacher and scholar in Leeds, England, Mainz, Germany, and Turku, Finland.

ABOUT THE AUTHORS

Professor Eades has received numerous awards for both his teaching and research. He has received the Law School Teaching Award on three occasions and been named a Distinguished Teaching Professor by the University. In addition, for his scholarship, Professor Eades has been designated a Distinguished University Scholar by the University of Louisville.

Michael S. Finch

Professor Michael S. Finch is a professor of law at Stetson University College of Law having joined the law faculty in 1982, after practicing law in New England. He has published extensively, including articles in the *Minnesota Law Review*, the *Wisconsin Law Review*, the *Ohio State Law Journal*, and the *Business Lawyer*. His work has been cited by numerous federal and state courts, including the United States Supreme Court and the Florida Supreme Court. He is the co-author with colleague Michael Allen of the text, *An Illustrated Guide to Civil Procedure* (Aspen 2006). Together with Professors Michael Allen and Caprice Roberts, he will be publishing a text, *Federal Courts: Context, Cases, and Problems*, in 2009 (Aspen).

Steven Friedland

Steve Friedland is a Professor of Law, Senior Scholar, and Director of the Center for Engaged Learning in the Law at the Elon University School of Law in North Carolina. He has taught Evidence law for 25 years at various law schools and served as a federal prosecutor in Washington, D.C. He has written several law school text books and law review articles on Evidence. Friedland holds a J.D. from Harvard Law School and L.LM and J.S.D. degrees from Columbia University.

Peter J. Henning

Professor Peter Henning graduated from Georgetown University Law Center in 1985, where he served as a Notes and Comments Editor on the *Georgetown Law Journal*. He clerked for Chief Judge Murray M. Schwartz of the United States District Court for the District of Delaware, was a Senior Attorney in the Division of Enforcement at the U.S. Securities & Exchange Commission from 1987 to 1991, and a Trial Attorney in the Criminal Division of the U.S. Department of Justice from 1991 to 1994.

Professor Henning joined the Wayne State University Law School faculty in 1994. He teaches courses in Corporations, White Collar Crime, Professional Responsibility, Criminal Law and Procedure, and Securities Litigation. Professor Henning received the Wayne State University President's Award for Excellence in Teaching in 1998. His scholarship focuses primarily in the fields of white collar crime, constitutional criminal procedure, and attorney ethics, and he has published articles in a number of leading journals, including the *Boston College Law Review*, *Tennessee Law Review*, *Washington University Law Quarterly*, *American University Law Review*, and *University of Cincinnati Law Review*. He is a co-author of three casebooks: *White Collar Crime: Law and Practice* (Thomson West 2d Ed. 2003) (with Israel, Podgor & Borman); *Criminal Law: Concepts and Practice* (Carolina 2005) (with Podgor, Taslitz, and Garcia); *Global Issues in Criminal Law* (Thomson West 2007) (with Carter and Blakesley). Professor Henning is one of the co-authors of the *Wright & Miller Federal Practice & Procedure: Criminal Treatise*, and a co-author of *Mastering Criminal Law* (Carolina 2008) (with Podgor and Cohen).

Darryll K. Jones

Darryll K. Jones is a professor of law at Stetson University College of Law, having joined the faculty in 2007 after serving one year as a visiting professor. From 1993-2006, he taught at the University of Pittsburgh School of Law, where he also served as associate

ABOUT THE AUTHORS

dean for academic affairs from 2003-06. He has published textbooks and articles on partnership taxation and tax exempt organizations. He is the author of "K-Rations," a monthly column on tax issues published by *Tax Notes Magazine*. His scholarship on federal taxation has appeared in *Florida Tax Review*, *Virginia Tax Review*, *Brigham Young University Law Review*, *University of Pittsburgh Law Review* and several other publications. Professor Jones has been consulted by members of Congress, the Senate Finance Committee and the Internal Revenue Service on issues relating to individual income tax, partnership tax and the tax laws of exempt organizations. Before becoming a tax law scholar, Professor Jones served as general counsel at Columbia College Chicago and associate general counsel at the University of Florida. He began his legal career with the United States Army Judge Advocate General's Corps. Darryll and his wife, Karla, live in downtown St. Petersburg, Florida with their three children Simari, Sterling, and Raven. Simari and Raven are budding piano players, while Sterling enjoys soccer and is developing her skills as a concert percussionist. They have two other children, Christopher and McKenzie, both of whom live in Gainesville, Florida.

Patrick Longan

Patrick Longan is a Professor of Law at Mercer University School of Law where he holds the William Augustus Bootle Chair in Ethics. He received an A.B., Summa Cum Laude 1979 Washington University; a J.D. 1983 University of Chicago; an M.A. Economics 1980 University of Sussex. He has been a member of the Mercer Law Faculty since 2000. He teaches in the areas of Legal Profession; Judicial Field Placement; Law of Lawyering; Law and Economics; and, Introduction to Counseling. He has published extensively in the area of Professionalism. In 2005 he was selected for a National Award for Innovation and Excellence in Teaching Professionalism, by the American Bar Association Standing Committee on Professionalism, the Conference of Chief Justices, and the Burge Endowment for Legal Ethics.

Jeffrey J. Minneti

Professor Minneti holds a bachelor's in education from the University of South Florida; he taught elementary and middle school students for over five years. Professor Minneti graduated, with honors, from Cumberland School of Law at Samford University in Birmingham, Ala., receiving his J.D. and M.B.A. degrees from Cumberland's joint degree program. While at Cumberland, Professor Minneti served as editor in chief of the *American Journal of Trial Advocacy*. Upon graduation from law school, Professor Minneti clerked for Justice Thomas A. Woodall on the Alabama Supreme Court.

Professor Minneti is a member of the Florida and Alabama State Bars and the St. Petersburg Bar Association. Prior to joining the Stetson faculty, Professor Minneti was an associate with the Tampa office of Murray Marin & Herman, where his practice focused on defending London Market insurers. Professor Minneti directs Stetson's Academic Success Program and teaches in the areas of academic skills, legal analysis, legal research and writing, and legal drafting. Over the last several years, Prof. Minneti has organized and taught a two-week orientation program for Stetson LL.M. students who have graduated from foreign law schools. Prof. Minneti has also taught United States Legal Research and Writing to LL.M. students.

Ellen S. Podgor

Ellen S. Podgor is the Associate Dean for Faculty Development and Electronic Education at Stetson University College of Law, where as a professor of law she teaches courses in white collar crime, international criminal law and criminal law. She holds a B.S. degree from Syracuse University, J.D. from Indiana University School of Law at Indianapolis, M.B.A. from University of Chicago, and LL.M. from Temple University School of Law.

She is the co-author of many books and articles including: *White Collar Crime In A Nutshell* 3d. Ed. (Thomson/West 2004) (w/ Israel),*White Collar Crime: Law and Practice* 2d Ed. (Thomson/West 2003) (w/Israel, Borman, & Henning), *International Criminal Law: Cases and Materials* 2d Ed. (LexisNexis 2004) (w/Wise & Clark), *Understanding International Criminal Law* 2d Ed. (LexisNexis 2004) (w/ Clark), and *Criminal Law: Concepts and Practice* 2d Ed. (Carolina 2008) (w/ Henning, Taslitz, and Garcia). Dean Podgor served as the chair of the Criminal Justice Section of the Association of American Law Schools in 1998 and presently serves as a member of the Board of Directors of the International Society for the Reform of Criminal Law. She is a member of the American Law Institute and an honorary member of the American Board of Criminal Lawyers.

Charles H. Rose III

The Director of Stetson's Center for Excellence in Advocacy, Associate Professor Charles H. Rose III spent twenty years in the United States Army as an enlisted intelligence soldier, intelligence officer and judge advocate. He attended Notre Dame Law School and graduated in 1993, receiving his Juris Doctor Degree. Professor Rose's assignments as an Army Judge Advocate included the practice areas of international and operational law, administrative law and multiple assignments as a trial lawyer spending over five years trying cases. He is a graduate of both the Judge Advocate Officer Basic and Graduate Course, and received an LL.M. in Military Law with a specialization in Criminal Law in the spring of 2000. After receiving his LL.M. he was selected to serve as a professor of criminal law at the Judge Advocate General's School, United States Army, in Charlottesville, Virginia for three years. His primary areas of expertise included evidence, motions practice, trial advocacy, professional responsibility and various areas of constitutional and administrative law. He published numerous times on a variety of issues. He completed his Army Service as the Deputy Staff Judge Advocate at Fort Eustis, Virginia, where he retired from the United States Army in December of 2004.

Professor Rose joined the Stetson faculty in December of 2004. He teaches evidence, trial advocacy, criminal procedure and professional ethics. He has published three books, two on advocacy and one on military justice. He recently received The Florida Bar's 2008 Faculty Award on Professionalism.

Andrew E. Taslitz

Andrew E. Taslitz is the Welsh S. White Distinguished Visiting Professor of Law at the University of Pittsburgh School of Law and Professor of Law at the Howard University School of Law. He has also taught at the Duke University and Villanova University Schools of Law. He teaches Criminal Law, Criminal Procedure, Evidence, Free Speech, Terrorism and the Law, and advanced courses in those areas. He has published over 100 scholarly works, including five books. His most recent book is *Reconstructing the Fourth Amendment: A History of Search and Seizure, 1789-1868* (paperback ed. 2009), published by New York University Press, which also published his earlier book, *Rape and the Culture of the Courtroom* (1999). His other three books are co-authored and include *Criminal Law: Concepts and Practice* (2d ed. 2009); *Constitutional Criminal Procedure* (3d ed. 2007); and *Evidence Law and Practice* (3d ed. 2007), as well as a forthcoming two-volume treatise on criminal procedure. His articles have been published in such journals as the *Georgetown Law Journal*, the *Boston University Law Review*, the *Harvard Civil Rights/Civil Liberties Law Review*, *Duke University's Journal of Law and Contemporary Problems*, and *Northwestern University's Journal of Criminal Law and Criminology*.

Professor Taslitz is the Reporter for the Committee on a Model Statute for the Electronic Recordation of Custodial Interrogations of the National Conference of Commissioners on

ABOUT THE AUTHORS

Uniform State Laws and was the former Co-Reporter for the Constitution Project's Death Penalty Initiative, as well as having co-authored the monograph-length Legal Appendix to a National Academy of Sciences Report on Preventing Bomb-Blast Terrorism in the wake of the Oklahoma City Bombing. He is also currently a member of the ABA Committee on Transactional Surveillance Standards, a member of the ABA Criminal Justice Section's Criminal Justice periodical Editorial Board, and Chair of that Section's Book Committee, as well as having previously served as a member of that Section's governing Council, its Director of the Communications Division, and Chair of its Committee on Race and Racism. Professor Taslitz is also a former chair of both the Evidence and Criminal Justice Sections of the American Association of Law Schools.

Tanya Monique Washington

Professor Tanya Washington, an Associate Professor of Law at Georgia State University College of Law, is a graduate of the University of Maryland School of Law. After graduation, she clerked for Chief Judge Robert M. Bell on the Maryland Court of Appeals. Thereafter, she practiced toxic tort defense litigation in the Baltimore and Washington D.C. offices of Piper, Marbury, Rudnick & Wolfe. Upon leaving Piper, she served at Harvard Law School as both the Albert M. Sacks and A. Leon Higginbotham Research Fellows before completing her LL.M.

Professor Washington taught Civil Procedure, Contracts and Legal Research and Writing as a Visiting Assistant Professor at the University of Maryland School of Law before joining the faculty at Georgia State University College of Law. Her current teaching and research interests include adoption, affirmative action and equality; and the relationship between pedagogy and essay exam performance. Her publications include *The Diversity Dichotomy: The Supreme Court's Reticence to Give Race a Capital R*; *Loving* Grutter: *Recognizing Race in TransRacial Adoptions*; *Does Practice Make Perfect?: An Empirical Examination of the Impact of Practice Essays on Essay Exam Performance* (co-authored); *Law School and Bar Examination Performance* (co-authored); and *Throwing Black Babies Out With the Bathwater: A Child-Centered Challenge to Same-Sex Adoption Bans*.

Professor Washington also teaches as an adjunct professor at the David A. Clarke School of Law and Howard University School of Law, lending her expertise to improve law graduates' performance on the essay portion of the Bar Examination.

Mark E. Wojcik

Mark E. Wojcik is a professor of law at The John Marshall Law School in Chicago, where he has taught courses in international law, international business transactions, international trade law, international criminal law, international human rights law, torts, and legal writing. He is the Director of the Legal English Program at the International Law Institute in Washington D.C., and is the author of *Introduction to Legal English* published by that Institute. He is an adjunct professor at the Facultad Libre de Derecho de Monterrey in Mexico, and a permanent guest professor of Anglo-American and Comparative Law at the University of Lucerne in Switzerland. He previously worked as Court Counsel to the Supreme Court of the Republic of Palau (Micronesia), and clerked for the Supreme Court of Nebraska and the U.S. Court of International Trade. He is the Publications Officer of the American Bar Association Section of International Law and previously served as editor-in-chief of the *International Law News*. He has held many leadership positions within the Association of American Law Schools, the American Society of International Law, the Chicago Bar Association, and the Illinois State Bar Association.

ABOUT THE AUTHORS

Candace Zierdt

Professor Candace Zierdt joined the faculty of the Stetson University College in 2007. Prior to that, she had been on the faculty at the University of North Dakota School of Law since 1990. Professor Zierdt was the Alan Gray Professor of Law at the University of North Dakota and served as Interim Dean. In 1994, she received the Lydia and Arthur Saiki Prize for Excellence in Graduate/Professional Teaching. In addition to teaching in the areas of Contracts and the Uniform Commercial Code, Professor Zierdt has served as an academic specialist in Slovenia and Macedonia on the subjects of American Contract law, the Uniform Commercial Code. and the rule of law. Professor Zierdt practiced law for eleven years in Kansas City, Missouri where she received the Missouri Association of Social Welfare Award for Outstanding Legal Services. She also was a law clerk to Judge Doris Smith of the Pennsylvania Commonwealth Court of Appeals. She lectures and publishes about issues relating to children and the law, contracts, and commercial law.

Professor Zierdt has been a North Dakota Commissioner on the National Conference of Commissioners on Uniform State Laws (NCCUSL) since 2001. She is a member of the NCCUSL Committee on Liaison with American Indian Tribes and Nations, a member of the Joint Editorial Board for Tribal Code Development, a member of the Task Force on Implementation of The Model Tribal Secured Transactions Act, the Chair of the NCCUSL Study Committee on Tribal Legislation on Child Custody and Domestic Violence, and a member of the Drafting Committee for Uniform Notarial Acts. She also chairs the sub-committee on Article Two of the Uniform Commercial Code for the Business Law Section of the ABA and she is an elected member of the America Law Institute.

Summary of Contents

TABLE OF CONTENTS

TABLE OF CONTENTS

TABLE OF CONTENTS

TABLE OF CONTENTS

TABLE OF CONTENTS

TABLE OF CONTENTS

TABLE OF CONTENTS

TABLE OF CONTENTS

TABLE OF CONTENTS

TABLE OF CONTENTS

TABLE OF CONTENTS

TABLE OF CONTENTS

TABLE OF CONTENTS

TABLE OF CONTENTS

TABLE OF CONTENTS

TABLE OF CONTENTS

TABLE OF CONTENTS

TABLE OF CONTENTS

PREFACE

In the past few decades there has been a proliferation of LL.M programs at American law schools introducing foreign lawyers to the fundamentals of the United States (US) legal system. The website of the American Bar Association's (ABA) Section on Legal Education and Admissions to the Bar currently lists forty-nine ABA approved law schools that offer specific programs on United States Law for foreign lawyers, or international law students. Other LL.M programs with specialized subject matter are also admitting foreign lawyers in increasing numbers. The existence, and growth, of these programs, evidences the value that foreign lawyers continue to place on an understanding of US law.

Traditionally, these programs were designed as one year residential educational programs where a foreign lawyer traveled to, and studied in, the United States. The commitment, and often personal hardship, that an experienced foreign lawyer faced in leaving their employment to matriculate in these programs, acted to discourage participation.

The emergence of electronic education provided an efficient method of addressing this concern. The more recently developed programs for foreign lawyers, innovatively combine, electronic education, with more traditional course formats.

This project, which the editors affectionately refer to as "The US Law Project", is part of this evolution of programs for foreign lawyers. The project includes lectures on major US legal topics, by expert legal academics, drawn from a number of outstanding American law schools. These lectures are accessible on the Stetson University College of Law website on an asynchronous basis. The same legal experts that lecture, also author a chapter on their subject which can be used to prepare for the lecture, or to reinforce it. These same legal experts have prepared objective examinations which can be used to test a student's grasp of the instructional material.

This project was designed with foreign lawyers and international students in mind. However, it also can be used by others, including professionals interested in better understanding the US legal system. The editors hope that the accessibility of this program, will work to develop more interest in, and understanding of, the fundamental principles of US law.

This project would not have been completed without the efforts of a number of outstanding and supportive individuals. The editors would specifically like to acknowledge the input, advice and support of Darby Dickerson, the Dean of Stetson University College of Law. They also thank research assistant Lindsay A. Warner. Finally, they thank each of the individual lecturer-authors, who so generously committed their skill and knowledge to this project.

Ellen S. Podgor
John F. Cooper
December 2008

Chapter 1

AN OVERVIEW OF THE UNITED STATES LEGAL SYSTEM

By — Jeff Minneti

I.   INTRODUCTION

As you read this chapter, you embark on a journey — a remarkable journey into a unique, complex, and even elegant legal system that has drawn upon European roots to combine diverse legal elements into a cohesive whole. From England, the United States inherited a body of court decisions called the common law; from Italy, Germany, and France, the United States derived a system of legislation that has led to the codification of statutes. In fashioning its constitutionally driven representative democracy, the United States synthesized these elements and provided the world with a creative new legal system.

Your journey begins with an introduction to the American Common Law System, which focuses on how the American legal system differs from traditional civil-law systems and provides a brief history of American Common law. Next, the chapter describes the four sources of law in the American legal system: constitutions, statutes, court decisions, and administrative regulations. With an understanding of those sources, the chapter explains how an American attorney utilizes statutes and court decisions to solve legal problems. Because American attorneys spend much time working outside the court system to resolve their clients' disputes, the chapter concludes with a summary of alternative dispute resolution procedures, discussing negotiation, mediation, arbitration, and mixed processes. Armed with the content of this chapter, you will be well prepared to continue your journey into the substantive legal topics that arise in subsequent chapters.

II.   THE AMERICAN COMMON LAW SYSTEM

Like much of American society, United States law reflects a mixture of traditions, and can best be understood by examining its roots and tracing them forward. Perhaps the most significant source of American law is the common law system that arrived on American shores from England. Simply defined, the common law is a body of court decisions that has developed over centuries and spans many traditional legal topics, such as contract, property, and tort law. It is the common law system and its effect on the American legal landscape that the attorney trained in the civil system must appreciate if he or she is to comprehend how the United States legal system works. Toward that end, below, following two preliminary definitions, you will find a chart comparing a typical civil law legal system with the American system. Following the chart, you will read a brief summary of the history and forces that shaped English Common Law. Next, you will read how English Common Law has found expression in the American legal system. As you read, you will learn that the United States did not adopt the English system without modification. Instead, early American lawyers and statesmen retained portions of the English system they found valuable and set aside the rest.

A.   Preliminary Definitions

1.   Civil Law as Defined in the United States

Explanation of two common terms may eliminate some confusion as you begin your journey into the American legal system. First, in the United States, "civil law" has acquired a unique meaning. When an American attorney refers to civil law, he or she refers to a non-criminal matter. Thus, cases arising in contract, tort, property, commercial law, constitutional law or any other non-criminal field, are civil cases. In contrast, to lawyers trained in Europe, Central and South America, and a host of other countries around the world, civil law refers to a legal system built upon a civil code that encompasses private rights, duties, and obligations. Thus, to the lawyer trained in Europe, the civil law refers not to a topic of law but a comprehensive legal system. But to the American attorney, civil law is simply non-criminal law.

2.   Private and Public Law as Defined in the United States

Second, the American legal system has given unique definitions to public and private law. In the United States, private law refers to legislation enacted for the benefit of a specific individual or a specific class of persons. For example, if the federal government agrees to compensate an individual for a tortious claim against the government, Congress may enact a private law in favor of the individual that provides for appropriate damages. Such a situation developed in Oklahoma, where a farmer proved that a Federal Agency official negligently injured his 150 head of cattle. To compensate the farmer, Congress passed a federal private law providing for the farmer's recovery. In contrast, Federal public laws are those in favor of the public as a whole, operating equally on people in similar circumstances. The vast majority of enacted law in the United States is public law. The field transcends constitutional and criminal law and includes traditional tort, contract, property, and other specialized fields of law, such as health care and labor and employment law.

B.   How a Traditional Civil Law System Differs from the American Common Law System

With those definitions understood, you are ready to move into a discussion of the American legal system. But before reading the story of how the United States system developed, you may benefit from considering the similarities and differences between the civil legal system and the American legal system. As Figure 1 indicates, both systems have much in common: both acknowledge the importance of a coherent statutory scheme; both acknowledge, at least to some degree, the importance of judicial opinions in shaping the law; and both recognize the importance of lawyers in structuring the legal system. The sharpest contrasts arise in the sources of law and at trial. In the civil system, court opinions are not regarded as law, whereas in the American system, court opinions are law. In the civil system, there far less emphasis on a single-event trial; in all but some criminal cases no jury; and much less need for cross-examination, the ability to question witnesses who testify against a party, at any legal proceeding. In the American system, however, trial continues to play an integral part in shaping the law, jury trials are a constitutional right in criminal cases and many civil cases, and cross-examination is a cornerstone in the adversarial litigation process.

Figure 1: A Comparison of a Civil Law Legal System with the United States Legal System

	Civil System	American System
Sources of Law	Some civil jurisdictions have federal and state constitutions; all have a Code, a systematic and comprehensive statement of the whole field of law; typically drafted in a single event, with additions enacted as needed.	Federal and state constitutions; statutes, drafted over time as needed; court decisions; and administrative regulations, also drafted over time as needed.
Court Structure	Several independent courts, each with its own set of trial and appellate courts; the court systems include: (1) ordinary trial courts that typically specialize in an area of practice, such as labor law or commercial law; (2) administrative courts that hear disputes regarding administrative law; (3) constitutional courts that hear only questions about the constitutionality of code provisions.	Parallel system of state and federal courts of general jurisdiction; courts typically utilize three-tiered structure composed of trial court, middle appellate court, and highest appellate court. While some state and federal trial courts are specialized by subject area, all flow into the state or federal three-tiered system.

	Civil System	American System
Role of Courts	Operators of the legal system; apply the applicable code provision to the case at hand in accordance with jurisprudence, legal science and developed doctrine; less emphasis on discretion and interpretation.	Interpret and apply statutory and constitutional provisions; when case involves dispute over common law principles, discern what precedent indicates and apply precedent to the case at hand; where equitable principles are at issue, decide the case in a manner consistent with principles of fairness and justice.
Legal Effect of Court's Opinion	Resolves the matter for the parties to the dispute; less precedential value; not a primary source of law; however, modern practice recognizes judicial decisions provide a gloss on the law; the concept of precedent is starting to take root.	Resolves the matter for the parties to the dispute; becomes precedent for future decisions; possesses precedential value; source of law. In some arenas, such as criminal law, code provisions such as mandatory sentence enhancements have removed some discretion from the courts.
Dominant Style of Reasoning	Deductive; with guidance from the jurists, judges apply general legal principles to specific situations.	Inductive; courts synthesize previous court decisions to create general legal principles. Courts also use deductive reasoning when applying statutes
Equitable Principles and Remedies	Equitable principles support constitutional provisions; equitable remedies are typically not available, unless incorporated into the Code.	Available when the remedy at common law is inadequate.
Education of Judges	Enter lower-court judiciary immediately following undergraduate education in law; civil servant career; promotion based on seniority and merit; executive and legislative branches appoint higher-court judges.	Four-year undergraduate degree, law school and experience as attorney; chosen by popular vote or executive appointment based on credentials and standing in the legal community; generally considered legal experts.
Role of Jurists and Legal Scholars	Carry the title of Jurists; considered the system's legal experts; arose from universities; the creative force behind the law; publish commentaries on what the law is and how law should be interpreted and applied.	No equivalent in the American system. Legal scholars, who generally serve on law school faculties, are similar, but legal scholars do not have the authoritative impact on American law that jurists do on the civil system. Judges are also similar, but due to their ability to make law, common law judges have more power than jurists.

	Civil System	American System
Effect of Jurists' and Legal Scholars' Writings	Jurists' texts are doctrine; not a primary source of law, but a definitive view; indispensible to a systematic and comprehensive understanding of the code; molds students' minds; guides judges and legislators toward consistency.	Legal scholars' texts are persuasive to the court, but lack the compelling force of Jurist doctrine under civil law; texts critically analyze and explain the law; students and practitioners use the texts as research and reference tools.
Role of Practicing Lawyers	Private law practice is divided between Advocates and Notaries; advocates meet with and advise clients and represent them in court; notaries draft legal documents, authenticate such documents at trial, and store and maintain records on legal documents. Government attorneys represent state agencies and prosecute criminal cases. Some prosecutors also intervene in civil matters to provide the court with a sense of the public's interest in the case.	Private lawyers may serve as litigation council or transactional council or both; litigation attorneys frame parties' disputes in terms of issues for court resolution and handle case through trial and appeal; transactional attorneys draft legal documents on behalf of clients. Government attorneys represent state or federal agencies and prosecute criminal cases, though state prosecutors would never advocate in a civil matter.
Legal Education	Currently, an undergraduate five-year degree, focus is on legal theory in lecture setting; upon graduation, lawyer must elect type of practice, attorney, notary, judge, or government; such decisions are often final. Initial year or two on the job treated as apprenticeship.	Three-year graduate program that follows four-year undergraduate degree. Courses focus on substance of law, problem solving, and professionalism; some schools teach more legal skills while others teach more legal theory.
Trial	A process that utilizes a series of hearings over time. No jury; instead, inquisitorial process that elevates judge's role as questioner and finder of fact; as a result, cross-examination of witnesses is uncommon.	Single event lasting from hours to months; judge determines law; jury finds fact. Attorneys generate factual record by questioning witnesses and admitting evidence; sophisticated rules of discovery. Judges have considerable discretion over course of proceedings.
Use of Jury	Some criminal trials only; jury finds fact.	By right in criminal trials and civil trials at common law; jury finds fact.

	Civil System	American System
Appellate Review	At the appellate level, courts consider the facts and law anew, with little deference to the trial court's opinion. In limited circumstances, middle appellate courts may seek additional testimony, evidence, and expert opinions. Highest appellate courts hear only questions of law.	Appellate courts may not collect new evidence; they are bound to facts and issues preserved for appeal in trial court record. Standards of review vary, depending upon the degree to which the trial court's impressions of the evidence are material.

The preceding table has summarized differences between traditional civil systems and the American legal system. You may find that your civil system differs in some respects from the civil system presented above; if so, appreciate the unique qualities of your system and compare and contrast them with the American legal system. Below, as you continue your journey through a discussion of the history of the common law and a description of the sources of law, you will find a more detailed explanation of the characteristics of the American Legal System.

C.   A Brief History of the American Common Law System

1.   The Power and Authority of American Courts are Rooted in English Tradition

a.   Centralization of the Early English Courts

A review of the American legal system's history explains many of the differences between the civil and American legal systems. Common law developed from the early English court system established in the eleventh century. William the Conqueror had organized land ownership, taxes, and the adjudication of crimes under a central royal authority, called the Curia Regis. By 1300, out of the Curia Regis grew three courts: The Court of Exchequer, which dealt with matters affecting the treasury; the Court of Common Pleas, which dealt with suits between private citizens; and the Court of Kings Bench, which dealt with criminal and political matters. Bringing suit in the early courts was not a simple matter. First the plaintiff, the party seeking relief, had to obtain permission from the Curia Regis to bring suit. To do so, the plaintiff would purchase a writ, which was a letter from the Curia Regis directing the court at issue to hear the case. The court then required the defendant, the person from whom relief was sought, to appear in court.

b.   Origins of Civil Procedure, Jury Trial, and Appellate Review

The Curia Regis kept control of the type of actions that could be brought in the courts by controlling the types of writs it would issue. In the late twelfth century, Henry II devised a system of writs called possessory assizes. The first was the Novel Disseisin, meaning newly dispossessed. A plaintiff who felt he was wrongfully dispossessed of his land would seek this writ from the Curia Regis. Upon issuance, the writ directed the local sheriff to gather twelve men of the county where the subject land lay who would meet together to determine whether the defendant wrongfully dispossessed the plaintiff of his land. If the group so found, the land was returned to the plaintiff. Thus began the jury system as we know it today. If the defendant disagreed with the result, he could seek a writ of right from the Curia Regis to have his land restored. As the popularity of the possessory assizes grew, the Curia Regis empowered a group of judges to hear such actions on its own. The group of judges came to be known as Court of Common Pleas. Early on, the Curia Regis maintained the power of review over decisions from the Court of Common Pleas. Power over "lower" courts was also handled through writs. For example, the writ of prohibition ordered a court to stop considering a case. A writ of mandamus ordered a public body or public official to perform an act or restore a privilege. And a writ of certiorari ordered another court to send its record up for review.

The Court of the Kings Bench, as noted above, handled criminal and political matters. As this court grew out from the Curia Regis, it took with it the power to review decisions from the Court of Common Pleas. Because criminal matters often involved civil aspects, the Kings Bench retained jurisdiction over defendants to hear both criminal and civil actions arising from the same event.

c.   Emergence of the Stare Decisis Doctrine and Importance of Precedent

For the growing legal system to have legitimacy and some level of predictability, it needed some consistency. Thus was born the doctrine of stare decisis, which is Latin for the decision stands. Under stare decisis, courts sought to resolve similar cases in similar ways. For example, if two neighbors brought a boundary dispute to the court, the judge would consider not only the facts as the parties told them but also how prior courts had resolved similar boundary disputes. The decisions of the prior courts became known as precedents, which under stare decisis, a court felt compelled to follow. Implicit in the doctrine of stare decisis was the need for a judge who could understand prior court decisions and discern how to apply those decisions to the facts of the dispute before him. Because there was no formal training of judges, judges were selected from those who had experience in assisting people with legal problems. Over time, judges became better prepared to deal with people's legal problems and the body of court decisions grew and acquired widespread acceptance.

d.   Development of Equity

Writ practice became more specialized and formalized as the courts acquired more power to hear disputes. By the end of the twelfth century, the Curia Regis issued approximately seventy-five different types of writs, in the name of the King, by one of his highest officials, the Chancellor. Each legal problem developed its own writ. If plaintiff chose the wrong writ for his problem, the court dismissed his case. In addition, each writ developed its own procedure for resolution; if plaintiff failed to follow the proper procedure, the court would dismiss his case.

Before long, the public perceived the writ system to be too rigid and incomplete. A party who lost his case due to a technicality or because there was no appropriate writ to resolve his problem, petitioned the King for an order compelling the defendant to act as morality and good conscious required. The King sent the petition to the Chancellor, as the Chancellor had substantial knowledge of the writ process and the common law and, as a churchman loyal to the King, the Chancellor also had great discernment and the trust of the crown.

Over time, petitions for reconsideration were sent directly to the Chancellor, and the Chancellor developed a set of procedures and rules to address the petitions. The Chancellor's rules grew into a body of law called equity. As a legal concept, equity grew out of Greek and Roman traditions and was heavily influenced by Christianity. The classical meaning of equity was a fairness that transcended the strict application of common law, when the result of such application would lead to injustice.

In hearing the petition, the Chancellor would use a writ of subpoena to call the person named in the petition to stand before him, and him alone; formal rules of procedure and proof did not apply; no jury was involved. To resolve the petition, the Chancellor decided as he sought fit, though in time his decisions were published, and by the end of the fifteenth century, he felt as bound by precedent as the common law judges. Remedies such as injunction (the power to stop an act to prevent future harm) and specific performance (the power to compel parties to perform under a contract) grew out of the court of equity. While the Chancellor resolved a growing number of disputes, his decisions did not replace the common law; instead, they added a gloss to it by filling in and smoothing out common law's rigid and sometimes porous nature.

e.   Development of the Jury Trial

Another significant contribution of English common law was the concept of the jury. "Jury" is derived from the Norman French "juree" meaning oath and the Latin "jurare," meaning to swear. As the early courts sought legitimacy and rationality for their decisions, they found great utility in subjecting a group of people to an oath to give a true answer and then presenting the group with the case for decision. Three types of juries arose: (1) a Grand Jury, which made accusations in criminal matters; (2) a Petite or Petty Jury for criminal trials; and (3) the Petite or Petty Jury for civil trials. Grand and Petite differed by size; the Grand Jury had twenty-three persons, while the Petite or Petty jury had twelve. Initially, courts swore in jurors to find out what the jurors themselves knew about the case. Over time, however, the jury developed into a fact-finding body, one whose impartiality about the case was key. In criminal matters, the jury's decision was inscrutable, meaning that the court must accept its findings. Moreover, in criminal matters, a jury was mandatory and its decision had to be unanimous; meaning that a criminal trial required a jury and all twelve jurors had to agree on innocence or guilt. In civil matters, juries were neither mandatory nor did their decisions have to be unanimous. In fact, as noted above, cases in equity before the Chancellor required no jury.

f.   Roles of Attorneys and Judges in the Early English System

Implicit in the English common law system was the importance of attorneys and pleaders. Attorneys and pleaders were skilled in the law, and by association with one another and the courts, they established a set guilds to regulate the handling of legal matters. Attorneys were experienced business men who advised parties on the law and assisted parties with transactions in real and personal property. Pleaders were those who interacted directly with the courts, orally or in writing. The guilds established a system for training and educating new members that was built on practical experience, rather than scholarly debate. Thus, to join the legal profession, one would associate with a guild and take part in legal proceedings, appear in moots (hypothetical lawsuits), and soak up the experience of his more senior practitioner.

Judges were chosen from a small class of elite lawyers, called sergeants-at-law. The Chancellor chose the sergeants upon nomination from the judges in the Court of Common Pleas. The sergeants had regular contact with judges in and out of court. Just as their education as lawyers was rooted in practical experience, their preparation for the bench took place through conversations with current judges and assisting judges with cases. Significantly, leading judges and attorneys did not arise from the university system. Instead, the guild system promoted those to positions of authority whom it felt were the most competent and well regarded. One notable exception is William Blackstone, who after a moderate career as a lawyer went on to teach at Oxford and wrote a four-volume description of English law called Commentaries on the Laws of England. For the first time, an author provided a comprehensive and systematic summary and review of the common law. His text was tremendously successful in England and abroad.

2. American Adaptations of English Common Law

a. The Three Branch Government: A Division of Power

Even prior to American independence, the colonists agreed that the principle American law should be the English Common Law. However, as the colonies became the United States, they ratified the federal Constitution, which divided the federal law making power among three branches of government: the legislative, executive, and the judiciary. In addition to passing state constitutions that divided power in the same way, the states also passed statutes that abrogated the common law, especially in areas such as family law, real property law, and laws of succession, which perpetuated the notions of privilege and aristocracy. Through the use of a formal constitution and enacted codes, American law came to resemble a hybrid of civil and common law traditions.

b. Merging of Law and Equity Courts

For many years, courts of common law and equity coexisted in the United States. If a plaintiff sought an equitable remedy, such as specific performance of a contract, as in England, the plaintiff would file an equitable action against the defendant; conversely, if a plaintiff sought a legal remedy, such as money damages for breach of contract, the plaintiff would file suit in a court of law. In 1938, the federal government merged equity and common law pleading into one cause of action. Since that date, most of the states have followed suit and no longer require plaintiffs seeking equitable remedies to file suit in a court of equity. As you will see below, however, the distinction between law and equity is still important in American law, because, in keeping with the tradition inherited from England, claims at law may be tried before a jury, but claims at equity may not.

c. Role and Training of American Attorneys

As noted above, in the English common law system, with the exception of Blackstone, university based scholars played a minor role in the development of the law and the education of lawyers and judges. Instead, in light of precedent as argued by counsel and the court's own conscience, judges controlled the development of law. And judges learned to do so from other judges, just as lawyers learned the practice from other lawyers. The early American legal system depended upon a similar year-long training for members of the bench and bar. However, in the late 1800s, American universities began offering intensive and systematic training of attorneys. Inspired by the model of legal education that Dean Langdell developed at Harvard University, schools around the country began to offer a course of study in law. Before long, the year-long apprenticeship model of legal education became replaced with a three-year course of study that has changed little since the early twentieth century. Currently, students pursuing a degree in law must complete a four-year degree at an undergraduate institution and then enter a law school for three years of study. Practice as a licensed attorney requires sitting for a bar examination that spans two or three days. Although as much as half of the exam is a nationally normed multiple choice test, most states require that candidates who wish to practice in a state sit for that state's bar exam.

Unlike its British counterpart, the American legal system draws no distinction between attorneys and pleaders, or solicitors and barristers as they are referred to today in England. Instead, an attorney licensed to practice in the United States can choose to maintain a practice based on transactions, such as property transfers, or litigation, such as criminal cases, or both. The economic realities of large firm practice, however, often compel attorneys to specialize in either transactional work or litigation, and within each, attorneys often develop expertise in subspecialties, such as negotiating commercial property transfers or litigating labor and employment disputes.

d.　　Selection of American Judges

As in English Common Law, American judges are chosen from the ranks of attorneys. In the federal system, the President appoints a judge for life, upon confirmation by the Senate. Appointing a judge for life, at least in theory, provides freedom for the judge to decide cases in accordance with the law and his or her conscience, without the threat of being forced from office due to an unpopular opinion. The Congress retains the power to indict and impeach judicial appointees, should the need arise.

State practices vary greatly. Some states elect judges by popular elections to defined terms. Others may elect trial court judges but appoint appellate judges. Some state elections are partisan, meaning that the candidate affiliates himself or herself with a specific political party; other states' elections are non-partisan. In states that appoint judges, typically the governor makes appointments; though in a few states, the legislature appoints judges. Once elected, judges can run for re-election; if appointed, the judges typically face a retention election, where the public is permitted to accept or reject the judge with no opposition running against him or her.

e.　　Jury Trials in the United States

An enduring institution of the common law system is the use of a jury at trial. Americans believe deeply in submitting the facts of a case to a jury of their peers for resolution. And while the jury system is frequently criticized for its lack of expertise in complex cases and its excessive monetary awards in some tort cases, the system is still an integral part of United States law.

The United States Constitution provides for a jury trial in criminal cases; though the defendant may waive right to a trial by jury. The criminal trial jury's verdict must be unanimous in the federal system and in some state systems pursuant to their constitutions, and the trial court has no power to set aside a jury's finding of innocence. Juries in criminal trials are composed of twelve people. Currently, less than half of the states use a grand jury proceeding to determine whether the state has enough evidence to charge a defendant in a criminal matter. Instead, most states now use an "information"; a written document prepared by a state prosecutor that informs the defendant of the charge against him and the facts supporting the charge.

While England has abolished the civil trial jury, it continues to operate in the United States. The federal Constitution provides a right to a trial by jury for common law claims, though not for equitable claims. Civil juries may be composed of six members, as in England, referred to as a petite or petty jury, or they may be composed of twelve members. While a plaintiff may waive his right to civil trial by jury, few do so, believing that a jury of his or her peers may be more receptive to his or her story and award damages. Civil judges have the power to set aside a civil jury's verdict, if the court finds that there is no substantial basis in the evidence to support the jury's verdict.

Federal and state jurors in the United States are randomly drawn from race-neutral databases, such as state driver's licenses or voter registration rolls. If a person's name is drawn for jury duty, the individual receives a jury summons in the mail, requiring him or her to report to the courthouse on a date certain. Jurors are not expected to be experts on the facts or law. Instead, they listen to the evidence presented and receive instructions on the law from the trial judge. Because the court provides the law, all a jury must do is decide questions of fact. Questions of fact include which version of events to believe, whether a witness was telling the truth, which witness's story is more credible, and which evidence to find most significant. For example, in a civil case arising from an automobile accident, the court may instruct the jury as to the standard of care that the defendant driver should have used, such as reasonable care under the circumstances. The jury will then decide whether, based on the evidence, the driver breached that standard. In considering the facts before it, the jury may have testimony from the police or other expert witnesses as to how fast the defendant's car was travelling, or whether the traffic light was green, red, or yellow. The jury may also hear testimony from the plaintiff as to how the defendant's car struck hers, how much damage it caused to the car, and how badly the plaintiff was injured. The defendant may elect to testify as to his version of the events. In deciding the case, the jurors meet in secret to discuss the facts of the case, decide which version of events to believe, and enter their findings on a verdict form they have received from the judge. In criminal matters, they find the accused guilty or innocent; if they find the defendant guilty, the judge decides the appropriate sentence. In civil trials, jurors find the defendant liable or not liable, and if they find the defendant liable, they may award damages. Upon announcement of the jury's verdict, neither the parties nor the court may question the jury as to its deliberations. Instead, the court may only poll the jury to verify that each juror supports the conclusion of the group.

III. SOURCES OF LAW IN THE UNITED STATES LEGAL SYSTEM

The fabric of United States federal and state law is woven from four distinct threads: constitutions, statutes, court opinions, and administrative regulations. This set of sources reflects the hybrid nature of American law; the system is not exclusively common-law based, nor is it entirely civil. Instead there is a mixture and perhaps a tension among the sources that reflects the country's founders' goal to diffuse governing power among several entities.

Significantly, there is a hierarchy among the sources. Constitutions are the highest and most fundamental law. Statutes are next in line; statutes must not conflict with constitutional provisions. Where no statute is on point, common law principles as the courts have articulated them, are considered law and apply to parties' disputes. When a statute is applicable to a dispute, courts are bound to interpret and apply the statute, unless the court finds the statute unconstitutional. Courts are also bound to apply administrative regulations to parties' disputes, as long as the administrative regulations arise from power granted to the administrative agency by statute. Each branch of government has primary responsibility for one source of law. And each source of law plays a unique role in the United States legal system.

A.   The Primacy of the Constitution

A constitution is an expression of fundamental law that arises from the will of the people as a whole, unlike a statute, court opinion, or administrative regulation, each of which is the product of an elected or appointed official. Thus, a constitution is regarded a jurisdiction's highest law, and all other forms of law flow from the constitution. The fifty United States have each granted to the federal government specific powers, which are expressed in the federal Constitution. Any power not ceded to the federal government in the Constitution, remains with the states and generally finds expression in the states' constitutions.

1.   Composition of the U.S. Constitution

The United States Constitution is not a lengthy document. It is composed of seven articles and twenty-seven amendments that span roughly eighteen pages of a text such as this one. The primary focus of the document is to articulate the balance of power between three separate but related governing entities: the legislature, the executive, and the judiciary. While each entity performs a unique function, the entity's power is held in check by at least one of the other entities. For example, while the Congress has the power to enact legislation, the judiciary has the power to reject the legislation if it finds it unconstitutional. Meanwhile, the executive branch has the power to appoint judges; though the judge may not serve unless the legislature confirms the appointment. See Figure 2 for additional examples the federal Constitution's system of checks and balances.

Figure 2: Checks and Balances at Work in the United States Government

Action	Executive Branch	Legislative Branch	Judicial Branch
Judicial Appointments	Appoints federal judges	Confirms judges; may impeach judges	Serve life term as a judge
Statutes	Must accept to become law; vice-president serves as tiebreaking vote in Senate	Generates text of statutes; may override executive branch veto	Interprets and applies statutes; may find statutes unconstitutional
Military Action	President serves as Armed Forces Commander-in-Chief	May declare war	
Treaties	Makes treaties	Provides advice and consent on treaties	Interprets and applies treaties

The federal Constitution also provides basic rights to United States citizens, which are expressed in many of the twenty-seven amendments. The rights include the right to associate, the free expression of speech and religion, and the right to a trial by jury. All other governing power is left to the states, each of which is sovereign and has its own constitution.

2.   Interplay Between Federal and State Constitutions

Significantly, the states may ascribe more rights to their citizens than the federal Constitution provides. For example, consider the following case: Police suspected that Scott Malone possessed LSD, an illegal drug, so they obtained a warrant to search Malone's home for doses of the drug. Malone shared his home with Michael Graves; each man had his own separate bedroom. When police arrived at the home, Malone escorted police to his bedroom and surrendered the LSD to the police. Police then searched Graves's bedroom for additional drugs and found more LSD in his closet. At his trial for possession of the LSD, Graves argued that the court should not admit evidence of the LSD found in his closet against him. He asserted that the police should not have searched his bedroom because he was not named on the police's search warrant. The court noted that under federal law, the officer's search of Graves's closet was justified because under the federal Constitution, a search is not invalidated when an officer reasonably interprets a search warrant too broadly. However, because the Mississippi Constitution "extends greater protections of an individual's reasonable expectation of privacy than those enounced under Federal law," the Mississippi court held that the search of Graves's closet was illegal. *Graves v. Mississippi*, 708 So. 2d 858 (Miss. 1997).

3.   Ratification, Amendment, and Revision of Constitutions

While states may provide more rights to their citizens than the federal Constitution, they may not provide less; that is, the states may not restrict the rights that the Constitution grants. By its own terms, the Constitution is the supreme law of the land; it is the highest and most authoritative law. The primacy of the Constitution arises, in part, from the way in which the Constitution was ratified. Ratification of the federal Constitution required agreement by nine of the then existing twelve states' legislatures. Amendments to the federal Constitution do not come easily. An amendment is proposed when agreed upon by at least two-thirds of both houses of Congress or by at least two-thirds of states' legislatures. Ratification of an amendment requires the approval of three-fourths of the states' legislatures. The period of time between proposal and ratification varies greatly from amendment to amendment. For example, Amendment XXVI, which provides the right to vote to persons eighteen years of age or older, was proposed in March of 1971 and ratified by the states in July of 1971. In contrast, Amendment XXVII, which requires an election of Representatives to occur before changes in compensation to members of the Senate and the House of Representatives take effect, was proposed in September 1789 and ratified in May 1992.

State constitutions followed a similar process for ratification — they were a product of the people as a whole, not the legislature, executive branch, or the courts. Amendments to state constitutions typically arise from citizen initiatives and are approved through a referendum process, whereby the citizens vote to accept or reject the amendment. Should a state wish to revise its constitution, the state typically must call for a constitutional convention, which proposes constitutional revisions to the general electorate for a vote.

B.   Statutes as a Source of Law

1.   The Process of Enacting a Statute

As noted above, state and federal constitutions provide for a legislature to promulgate statutes, which a representative from the executive branch, the President in the federal system or the governor in the state system, then signs into law. The statutes are the products of bicameral or two-house legislatures. In the federal system, the legislature is composed of the Senate and the House of Representatives. The Senate is the legislature's upper body; it is composed of two representatives from each state. The House of Representatives is the lower body; a state's population determines the number of representatives it can send to the House. As illustrated in Figure 3, a statute begins its life as a bill, introduced onto the floor of either legislative body. The bill is deferred to committee where provisions are revised, edited, and refined. Note that there is no limit to the revisions and additions that can be made to a bill; thus, the product of a committee may bear little resemblance to the bill's original structure. Once the Senate or House committee approves the bill, it returns to the floor of the body for further debate and a vote. If the bill passes one body, it is introduced onto the floor of the other and undergoes the same committee process. If the second body passes the bill in the exact form of the first body, the bill goes to the president for a signature. If each body passes different versions of the same bill, the bill moves to a joint Senate and House Committee to generate a compromise bill. Should that committee agree on the bill, it then passes on to the President for signature.

Once the bill reaches the President's desk, the President may either sign the whole bill or reject the whole bill; the President has no power to reject portions of the bill and accept others. If the President rejects a bill, the legislature can override his veto with a two-thirds vote from both houses. The President may also exercise a pocket veto. Bills left on the President's desk for too long are vetoed automatically, without the possibility of an override from Congress, if the period for a veto extends beyond the current session of Congress. Should the President sign the bill, it becomes law.

Statutes in state systems follow a similar bicameral process. Each state has a body like the United States Senate where a set number of state senators are elected from each county, township, or parish, depending upon the geo-political make-up of the state. Additionally, each state also has a body like the United States House of Representatives, in which the number of representatives is based on the population of a geographic area. Legislation proceeds through state legislatures as outlined above regarding the federal system, and to become law the legislation requires the governor's signature. The federal or state legislature retains the power to amend or repeal legislation as needed.

2.   Conflict Between State and Federal Laws

Where state and federal laws conflict, the federal law controls. The conflict may be explicit, apparent from the text of the state and federal legislation, or it may implicit, arising from the way that the legislation is applied. In either case, upon a showing of conflict, the federal law preempts the conflicting state law.

C.   Court Decisions as a Source of Law

The courts play three general roles in shaping American law. First, they author decisions that make up the common law. Second, they interpret and apply statutory law. And third, they rule upon the constitutionality of statutes. No court in the United States system may, of its own accord, make a ruling on a statute. Instead, judge-made law arises when parties present issues regarding the law to the courts. As noted above, the United States legal system was at one time based largely on common or court-made law. Although state and federal legislatures have codified much of what was once common law, judicial opinions on legal questions where no statute controls carry the full force and effect of law. Under the principle of stare decisis, courts are bound by their prior decisions and by decisions of higher level appellate courts. In addition to reviewing and applying pure judge-made law, the courts also interpret and apply statutes in resolving parties' disputes. A court's interpretation or application of a statutory provision also has the force of law. When the legislature disagrees with a court's interpretation of a statute, the legislature may propose legislation that preempts the court's opinion on the matter. A court may go further than simply interpreting and applying statutory provisions; the court may also offer an opinion on a statute's constitutionality. That is, a court has the power to render a statute unconstitutional. The legislature has no power to mandate a statute's constitutionality. Thus, when a court finds a statute unconstitutional, the court effectively kills the statute.

1.   A Brief Overview of the Court System

Both the state and federal court systems are multi-layered. In the federal courts, litigation begins in a trial court generally called a federal district court. Each state and the District of Columbia have at least one federal district court. Through the trial court process, parties seek a resolution to disputes about the law and/or the facts of the case. Disputes about the law include which state or federal law should apply to the dispute, whether one party can obtain information from another party in advance of trial, and whether a piece of evidence should be admitted at trial. Disputes about the facts of the case include determining which evidence or witness to believe when conflicting versions of events are offered and whether a defendant is guilty or innocent, liable or not liable. Judges always resolve questions of law; when the case involves a jury, the jury makes determinations of fact. Juries are not permitted in all cases. Where they are not seated, the judge makes findings of facts and law.

a.   The Federal Court System and Standards of Review

If a party seeks an appeal from a federal district court opinion, the party may file an appeal with a circuit court of appeal. Geographically, the United States is divided into thirteen circuit courts of appeal. Each federal district court falls into one such circuit court. When a party appeals a case, the party prepares a record that includes the relevant facts of the case and the disputed trial court's decision. No new evidence is taken for an appeal; the circuit court of appeals bases its decision on the paper record alone. Based on the type of issue presented to it, the appellate court applies a standard of review to the trial court's decision; that is, it gives the trial court's decision a degree of deference. Questions of law receive no deference; an appellate court considers such issues anew, without taking into account why the trial court ruled the way it did. Factual determinations, however, are accorded great weight. An appellate court will not overturn a trial court's factual finding without a showing of significant error. The rationale behind this rule is that while the record on appeal can plainly convey legal issues and concerns, a paper record may not capture the characteristics of witnesses or evidence that are present in a live trial. Thus, such decisions are highly protected. Appeals to the circuit courts of appeal commonly involve oral as well as written argument. Oral argument generally provides each party with up to thirty minutes to state its case before the court and answer the court's questions about the case. If a party is unhappy with the circuit court of appeals decision, the party may appeal to the United States Supreme Court, which is the court of last resort on federal issues. The Supreme Court is highly selective about which cases it hears; thus most litigation ends at the circuit court of appeal level. Like the circuit court of appeal before it, the Supreme Court applies a standard of review to the trial court's decision.

b.   State Court Systems and Standards of Review

State courts operate in a similar way. Most states also have a three-tiered court system, with trial courts (often called county, superior, or circuit courts), middle-level appellate courts (often called courts of appeal), and a highest level appellate court (often called supreme courts). Like the federal appellate courts, state appellate courts review only a written record and accept no new evidence. In addition, state appellate courts also apply standards of review to trial court decisions. State supreme courts are the final authority on issues arising under that state's law. Implicit in the preceding statement is that the United States Supreme Court is not the final authority on all legal matters. Where an appeal involves issues of state law alone, the United States Supreme Court is bound by the law as that state's supreme court has interpreted and applied it. Oral argument is also a component of the state appellate process, with mid-level appellate courts granting oral argument more frequently than the state's highest appellate court. As in the federal courts, state appellate judges use oral argument to help them frame issues and gain a better understanding of the parties' written arguments.

2.   The Relative Weight of a Source of Law in a Court's Decision

American courts do not have a free hand in resolving parties' disputes. Each source of law is either mandatory or persuasive to the court. Mandatory law binds or controls a court in the sense that the court must apply that law to the case. Persuasive law is law that the court may, in its discretion, choose to interpret and apply to parties' claims. If the parties' claims before the court involve questions of state law, the constitution, statutes, and administrative regulations of that state are mandatory law. A court must apply that law to the parties' claims. A court may consider constitutional provisions, statutes, administrative regulations, and court decisions from other states, but such law is merely persuasive. Nothing requires a state court to follow or apply another state's law. If the parties' claims involve issues of state and federal law, state law controls the state law claims and federal law controls the federal claims.

3.   The Relative Weight of a Court's Decision

The structure of the court system itself creates additional mandatory and persuasive law. Middle level appellate court decisions bind trial courts within the appellate court's jurisdiction. Furthermore, a jurisdiction's highest appellate court binds the middle level appellate courts and the trial courts within that jurisdiction. In the federal system, for example, the United States is divided into thirteen circuit courts of appeal. Decisions of each circuit court of appeal are mandatory law for all the federal district courts within their circuit. Thus, decisions of the First

Circuit Court of Appeals are binding on all the district courts that fall within the geographic boundary of the First Circuit Court of Appeal. As noted above, the United States Supreme Court is the highest federal court. Thus, decisions of the United States Supreme Court are binding on all federal courts of appeals and all federal district courts.

The state court system works in a similar manner. In Idaho, for example, the Idaho Court of Appeals is the state's middle level appellate court. If that court issues a decision on a point of law at issue in an Idaho trial court, the Idaho Court of Appeals decision is binding on the Idaho trial court. If Idaho's highest appellate court, the Idaho Supreme Court, issues a decision on a point of law, that decision is mandatory law for the Idaho Court of Appeals and all Idaho trial courts.

If the parties call upon a federal court to resolve issues of state law, the federal court, even the United States Supreme Court, looks to the law of the state at issue, expressed through its constitution, statutes, administrative regulations, or court decisions to resolve the case. If the federal court finds the state law unsettled or unclear, the federal court certifies the case to the state's highest appellate court for an opinion on how the state would resolve the issue.

Courts on the same level do not create mandatory law for one another. Thus, no federal district court opinion is binding on any other federal district court. Nor is any federal circuit court of appeals decision binding on any other federal circuit court of appeals. Instead, under the principle of stare decisis, courts find decisions from other courts at the same level highly persuasive. The same principle applies within the state court system; state trial courts do not bind one another, and if the state divides itself into several middle level appellate courts, those courts do not bind one another. Conflicting opinions from middle level district courts in the state or federal system may trigger review of the issue from the jurisdiction's highest appellate court.

Note that whether a court publishes a decision is often within the discretion of the court itself. For example, the United States Court of Appeals for the Eleventh Circuit has adopted the following internal operating procedures regarding the publication of opinions.

> 5. Publication of Opinions. The policy of this court is: The unlimited proliferation of published opinions is undesirable because it tends to impair the development of the cohesive body of law. To meet this serious problem it is declared to be the basic policy of this court to exercise imaginative and innovative resourcefulness in fashioning new methods to increase judicial efficiency and reduce the volume of published opinions. Judges of this court will exercise appropriate discipline to reduce the length of opinions by the use of those techniques which result in brevity without sacrifice of quality.

> 6. Unpublished Opinions. A majority of the panel determine whether an opinion should be published. Opinions that the panel believes to have no precedential value are not published. Although unpublished opinions may be cited as persuasive authority, they are not considered binding precedent. The court will not give the unpublished opinion of another circuit more weight than the decision is to be given in that circuit under its own rules. Parties may request publication of an unpublished opinion by filing a motion to that effect in compliance with FRAP 27 and the corresponding circuit rules.

Federal Rules of Appellate Procedure 36, 11th Circuit Internal Operating Procedures Numbers 5–6 (2007).

4.   The Power of a Court to Hear Parties' Claims

The federal district courts are courts of limited subject-matter jurisdiction, while the state courts are typically courts of general jurisdiction. Jurisdiction here refers to the court's power to hear the case. The United States Constitution and federal statutory law set the federal district court's limits on jurisdiction. Cases involving questions of federal law, such as federal constitutional rights or federal statutes, may be filed in federal district court. Note that a state court may hear a case with federal questions, but the state court is bound by federal courts' opinions in rendering a decision. Of course, a state court may always resolve disputes involving its own law. Under a legal principle called diversity jurisdiction, federal courts may also hear cases involving state law. For diversity jurisdiction to apply, each party filing suit must reside in a different state from each party that defends the case; in addition, the case must involve an amount in controversy that exceeds $75,000. The need for diversity jurisdiction arose because the party defending a suit brought by a party from another state preferred a neutral forum to hear the dispute; one that was set apart from the state court where the party bringing the suit resided. For example, consider the following hypothetical: Classic Toys, a toy manufacturer domiciled in Kentucky, creates an interactive website that allows customers to view products, ask questions, purchase products, and provide product reviews. Classic Toys advertises on the web and in newspapers and magazines targeted at citizens of Illinois, a nearby state. While searching the Internet, a customer in Illinois sees a Classic Toys advertisement and purchases a toy from the website. Shortly after the toy is delivered, the toy grievously injures the customer's child. The customer sues Classic Toys in Illinois state court, asserting negligence claims and $95,000 in damages. If Classic Toys prefers that a federal court hear the case, Classic Toys may petition to remove the case to federal court because the customer and Classic Toys are from different states and the customer has asserted more than $75,000 in damages.

When, under diversity jurisdiction, a federal court is obligated to hear state-law issues, as in the case against Classic Toys above, the federal court must determine which law to apply, federal or state; and in some cases the courts must consider which state's law to apply. In evaluating whether to apply state or federal law, the Erie Doctrine, a set of rules that arose from a United States Supreme Court decision, *Erie v. Tompkins R.R. Co.*, 304 U.S. 64 (1938), guides federal courts. The Erie doctrine requires that the federal court apply federal law to procedural questions and the state's substantive law to the substance of the state law claims. Procedural law governs how the litigation proceeds prior to trial, at trial, and on appeal. Examples include rules of civil and criminal procedure and evidence. Substantive law, on the other hand, is law that affects parties' rights and relationships with one another and with property. Substantive law includes the state's common and enacted law on questions of contract, property, or tort law. Thus, in the Classic Toys case above, if Classic Toys removes the case to federal court, the Federal Rules of Civil Procedure will govern how the parties plead the case, the timeline for sharing information about the case, and standards for pre and post-trial motions. At trial, the Federal Rules of Evidence will govern which evidence is admitted and which is not. Illinois state law, however, will govern issues regarding Classic Toys' liability, damages, and applicable defenses.

A third form of subject-matter jurisdiction is Supplemental Jurisdiction. When a case involves federal and state law claims that arise from a common set of facts or events, a federal statute may empower a court to hear the state-law claims. Prior to Supplemental Jurisdiction, a plaintiff had to file his federal claims in federal court and his state law claims in state court, even though his claims arose from the same set of events. Under Supplemental Jurisdiction, a federal court may hear all of the claims. As with diversity jurisdiction, in hearing the state-law claims, the federal court applies state law.

5.   The Power of a Court over a Person or Entity

In addition to needing power to hear a claim, state and federal courts also require power over the defendant that the plaintiff calls into court. Such power is called personal jurisdiction. Unlike subject-matter jurisdiction, which is primarily a creature of federal statute, personal jurisdiction is largely a product of the United States Supreme Court's interpretations of federal constitutional rights. Personal jurisdiction problems arise most often when the defendant, be it an individual or a corporation, does not reside in the state where plaintiff filed suit. Current Supreme Court decisions require that such defendants have sufficient minimum contacts with the forum state such that being sued in that state does not offend traditional notions of fair play and substantial justice. Upon such a showing, the court has sufficient power over the defendant to require that he or she appear in court and defend the suit. In the hypothetical case against Classic Toys above, the customer will probably be able to show that the court has personal jurisdiction over Classic Toys because Classic Toys has sufficient minimum contacts with Illinois. Classic Toys has such minimum contacts because through its advertisements and websites, it does business with citizens of Illinois such that being haled into court there would not offend traditional notions of fair play and substantial justice.

D.   Administrative Regulations as a Source of Law

As noted above, through the publication of administrative regulations, the executive branch of the state and federal governments also contributes to the body of United States law. State and federal constitutions empower legislatures to delegate rule-making ability to state and federal agencies that fall within the executive branch. Often Congress will pass legislation with the expectation that a federal agency will create rules to enforce the legislation. The rules typically articulate legal standards and policy and procedure for statutory compliance. For example, volume 11 of the Code of Federal Regulations deals with the Federal Election Commission. Part 2.3 provides that meetings of the Federal Election Commission shall be open to public observation. Part 7 details standards of conduct for election commissioners and their staffs.

E.   The Four Sources of American Law Form a Complex by Workable Legal System

Now that you have learned about each source of United States law, you are ready to understand how the sources work together to shape the American legal system. The following example illustrates how the United States Constitution, statutes, administrative regulations, and court decisions impact a corporation's duties and obligations. Thunderbird Propellers, Inc. was an aircraft repair facility operating in Oklahoma City. In repairing an aircraft's propeller, Thunderbird recorded in its repair log that it had used a certain type of nut, called an A-2043-1. In reality, Thunderbird used an MS nut, not the A-2043-1, in its repair. Both nuts were rated as equal in quality, but the MS nut was slightly less expensive. The propeller manufacturer approved of the A-2043-1 nut in repair of its propellers, but disapproved of the MS nut. Upon learning of the discrepancy between the part Thunderbird stated it used in its repair and the part it actually used, the Federal Aviation Administration (FAA) filed a complaint against Thunderbird, claiming that Thunderbird intentionally falsified maintenance records.

Article 1, Section 8, Part 3 of the United States Constitution empowers Congress to regulate commerce among the several states. Applying that power, Congress enacted a law that enables an executive branch agency, the FAA, to promulgate regulations necessary to "promote safe flight of civil aircraft in commerce." 49 U.S.C. § 44701. In promoting the "safe flight of civil aircraft," the FAA prohibits any person from making a "fraudulent or intentionally false entry" into an aircraft maintenance record. 14 C.F.R. 43.12. The regulation, however, did not define a "fraudulent or intentionally false entry." Instead, it left that definition up to the courts. In evaluating the FAA's claim against Thunderbird, the court noted that "[i]ntentional falsification [of an aircraft maintenance record] consists of a knowing misrepresentation of a material fact," and that a fact is material when it has "the natural tendency to influence" an FAA decision.

The trial court found that Thunderbird intentionally falsified its maintenance record, violating 14 C.F.R. 43.12 when it reported the use of A-2043-1 nuts but actually used MS nuts in repairing propellers. The Tenth Circuit Court of Appeal affirmed, holding that substantial evidence supported the trial court's conclusion. *Thunderbird Propellers, Inc. v. Federal Aviation Administration*, 191 F.3d 1290, 1296 (10th Cir. 1999).

Following the court's decision in *Thunderbird Propellers*, under the common law principles of stare decisis and precedent set out above, repair shops now have a better idea about how to conduct and record repairs, and if a shop finds itself in a similar situation, it now knows how a court will define intentional falsification of an aircraft record. The preceding example also illustrates how the sources of law: the Constitution, a statute, an administrative regulation, and the court, contribute to the body of American law and govern conduct in American society.

IV.   HOW AN AMERICAN ATTORNEY UTILIZES STATUTES AND CASE LAW

Armed with an understanding of the sources of American law, you are now prepared to consider how an American attorney uses those sources in advocating for his client's interests. This section specifically discusses how United States lawyers utilize enacted law and case law.

A.   Reading Statutes

Whether you are reading a statute in a civil law country or here in the United States, the general approach is the same. Below you will find four steps that may make your statutory reading more efficient and effective.

First, understand why you are reading the statute. If a professor has assigned the statute as part of class reading or you are doing research for a class-related project, know the context in which the statute applies before you start reading it. Does your syllabus list the statute? If so, what headings or topics precede and follow the statute? If the statute is part of a class project, what are the goals of the project? Further, reflect on what you already know about the subject of the statute; consider what information you expect to find in the provision.

Next read the statute carefully. If the provision is a page or less, read the whole statute, start to finish, not just the part that directly applies to your specific needs. If the statute is longer than a page, begin by skimming the headings of the statute to get a sense of the provisions that are most applicable to your needs. Then, having found the most applicable sections, break up your reading of the statute into segments of approximately one page each. As you read, make notes of questions you have about the meaning of the text. List words and concepts that are new to you and define them with a legal dictionary.

Once you have read the applicable provision, question the context of the provision within the code. Where does the statute fall among other statutes? Is there a separate section for definitions? Do those definitions apply to the statute you are concerned with? If so, make certain to read the statute in light of those definitions. Get a sense of where your statute fits within the framework of the code. Skim the statutory provisions located before and after your provision to get a better sense of what your statute is stating and the context in which it applies. Consider whether a full understanding of the statute you are interested in requires the integration of other statutory provisions.

The third step is to evaluate what you have read. Consider whether the statute has provided the information you expected to find within it.

Once you have fully read the statute and have a good sense of its context, determine whether any courts have interpreted or applied the statute. As noted above, court decisions often involve the interpretation or application of statutes. When a court interprets or applies a statute to a dispute, the court's decision becomes part of the body of law on the topic the statute addresses. Thus, to fully understand what a statute means, you must read court cases that have interpreted or applied the statute.

Consider, for example, the following situation:

> Mr. Clyde Johnson approached the side window of a modest home. From outside the window, Mr. Johnson electronically activated the controller for a remote control device that he had placed inside the home earlier that day while at a party given by the homeowner. Mr. Johnson electronically directed the remote control device to access a list of account numbers, the device then converted the numbers to an enhanced code and transmitted them to his home computer. When he made certain he had received the data, Mr. Johnson left the home. Police later apprehended Mr. Johnson. Can the state charge Mr. Johnson with burglary?

The applicable state statute defines burglary as the entering or remaining in a structure with the intent to commit an offense therein. What does the statute say to Mr. Johnson's case? One issue is whether Mr. Johnson entered the home when he stood outside the window and operated the remote control device. The statute however, does not define "enter." Consequently, the American attorney must look to case law for a definition. The cases provide that entry must be made by some part of the body or by an instrument used not only for the breaking but also for the commission of a felony. *Stanley v. State*, 626 So. 2d 1004 (Fla. 2d Dist. App 1993). Further, "entry by instrument" is not sufficient to establish entry unless the instrument inserted into the structure is actually used to commit the contemplated crime. *Baker v. State*, 622 So. 2d 1333 (Fla. 1st Dist. App. 1993).

Based on these sources, the Attorney synthesizes the statute and the case law rules to generate a rule of law for entering:

> Under the burglary statute, a person enters a home when he enters with a part of his body or an instrument that not only breaks into the home but is also actually used to commit an offense inside the home.

And she applies that rule to the client's situation:

> The state's attorney can argue that Mr. Johnson entered the home when he used a controller to send a signal to a remote control device inside the home, which then accessed the homeowner's account numbers, because he used the controller to insert an electronic signal into the home and activated a device that was actually used to commit an offense inside the home, the theft of the account numbers.

In the following section, you will learn more about how to read court decisions; for now, appreciate that to fully understand a statute, you must also read the applicable case law.

B.   Reading and Briefing Cases

Even though statutes and regulations increasingly shape the United States legal landscape, court decisions play a significant role in traditional common law areas such as contract, tort, and property, and, as noted above, court decisions play an important role in understanding how statutes should be understood and applied. Because cases are often tightly woven together with layers of important information, they can appear intimidating or simply confusing to an untrained reader. To assist you in your journey into American case law, below, you will find a plan of attack for critically reading cases. Before engaging in that plan of attack, however, you should first consider what you will do with the information you find within the case.

To assist in reading the case and to record what is learned from the case, law students and attorneys generate case briefs. A case brief is a document that the case law reader creates as he or she reads a case. A case brief is more sophisticated than summary notes about the case; instead, the most effective briefs are analytic tools that unpack the case into discrete and useful parts. Case briefs often reflect an ongoing dialogue between the reader and the court that authored the opinion. The reader paraphrases what he or she understands the court to be stating, and the reader lists questions or concerns raised from reading text. In U.S. law classes, the law student will bring the case brief to class and edit it during class in light of the discussion and the professor's comments. The attorney will incorporate text from the brief into his legal document. As you read the case-law attack plan below, pay special attention to how you might work with the information you find within a case.

1.   Appreciate Why You Are Reading the Case

As a preliminary step to reading a case, know why you are reading it. If the case is assigned reading for a class, look at the course syllabus or the casebook table of contents to determine what topic the case addresses. Casebook chapter headings or notes are also helpful in determining the context for the case. If you are reading the case for school or work-related research purposes, make certain you have explicitly set out your research goals before engaging in a reading of a case. Once you know why you are reading the case, make some predictions about what you expect the case to tell you. Hypothesize as to what the case result will be and how the court will reach that result.

2.   Skim the Case to Determine Who the Parties Are, Why They Filed the Case, and Who Won It

Having determined a sense of context and expectation for the case, you are now prepared to read it. To gain a thorough understanding of a case you will need to read it at least three times. The first reading should be something of a "skim." Read the case to answer four questions: (1) Who sued who? (2) Why was suit filed? (2) Who won? (4) Why did the winner prevail?

a.   Who Sued Who?

As noted above, in civil cases, the person or entity filing suit is called the plaintiff; the person or entity being sued is called the defendant. In criminal cases, the prosecution (either the state or federal government) brings suit against an individual or entity, which is also referred to as a defendant. At the start of the case, the parties' names are written into the case's caption. If the decision arose from a trial court's opinion, the person or entity named first is the plaintiff, the person or entity named after the "v." is the defendant. Note that in many cases, there are multiple plaintiffs and defendants in one case. If the case you are reading is from an appellate court, the court may have listed the parties' names in the caption of the case in the order of who sought the appeal. The party filing for an appeal is called the petitioner or appellant and may be listed first; the party responding to an appeal is called a respondent or appellee and may be listed second. Thus, if the defendant in a criminal case loses his case at trial and files an appeal, as appellant, his name may appear first in the caption of the case, and the prosecution may be listed second.

b.   Why Was Suit Filed?

In civil suits, the party seeking relief files a cause of action that sounds in some legal theory, such as negligence, a contract claim, or a constitutional violation. In a criminal matter, the prosecution brings charges against a defendant; the charges initiate the court process. Understanding what legal theory or charge the case involves is essential to understanding the law of the case. So in your first reading, skim the case to understand why the case was filed.

c.   Who Won?

The nature of a court setting renders the legal process adversarial; the parties, unable to resolve the matter on their own, have enlisted the help of the court to decide who should win and lose. Thus, another key to understanding a case is understanding who has won or lost. Typically, the court's opinion indicates who wins at the beginning or the very end of the opinion. Words such as "judgment," "hold," "find," or "conclude," are often clues that the court is indicating which party it has favored.

d.   Why Did the Winning Party Prevail?

Finally, understanding why a party won is often more important than which party won the case. Thus, in your initial skimming of the case, try to get a sense of why the court ruled in favor of the winning party. In some court opinions, the judge makes the answers to the three preceding questions clear from the outset of the case. In most decisions, however, the reader must skim the whole decision before he or she gets a sense of what the opinion is about. Such a skimming of the text is integral to a firm understanding of the case. Often readers include the answers to the preceding questions in their briefs as an introduction to the case. At a minimum, for future reference, you should note your responses to the questions in the margins of the case.

3.   Analyze and Brief the Case

Once you have obtained a general understanding of the case by answering the questions posed above, you are ready to engage in your second reading — a careful, thorough reading during which you will analyze the court's decision. The process of analyzing the case will require that you sort the information in the case into discrete units: style, issue, procedural history, facts, rule, holding, and reasoning. Each unit plays a special role in the case and ultimately factors into how the case shapes the law.

a.   The Style of the Case

A case's style includes the parties' names, the court, and the date. The style functions as a title of a case; it is usually the first piece of information you will read. As noted above, understanding who the parties are is essential to understanding the case. Because judicial opinions are given different weight (mandatory or persuasive), the reader should note which court authored the decision so he or she knows the case's precedential value. The date of a court decision is also significant. In addition, to providing a sense of the case's setting in history, the date speaks to the precedential value of the case. If the case is an older decision, the reader should question whether it is still valid law. If an older case appears in one of your casebooks or is mentioned prominently in your research, it may be because the case is a landmark decision. Such decisions are generally the product of a jurisdiction's highest court, and they recite legal principles which have stood the test of time and been referred to over the years.

b.   The Issue of the Case

The issue is the legal question the parties have asked the court to decide. The issue frames the context for the court's opinion. In a trial court's opinion, the issue may be the admissibility of evidence or whether the evidence supports the jury's verdict. On appeal, the appellant has reviewed the record and found what he or she believes are errors in the lower court's decision. The appellant selects from among those errors those which it believes will provide the best chance of winning and the best relief possible. Note that the appellant may not raise an issue on appeal that the trial court has not first had an opportunity to address. Issues typically involve one of three types of questions: fact, law, or mixed fact and law. As noted above in the discussion of jury trials, questions of fact concern the events of the dispute, and questions of law concern what legal standard should apply. Mixed questions of fact and law arise when the parties ask the court to apply a given legal standard to a given set of facts and decide the result. Note that the case may involve more than one issue. In briefing the issue, the reader typically paraphrases the legal question the court addresses.

c.   The Procedural History of the Case

The procedural history indicates how the decision has moved through the courts and what disposition the case is in at the time the writing court authors its decision. Trial court written decisions may arise from pre-trial motions, such as motions to dismiss the case or for summary judgment. Appellate court decisions generally arise from final decisions of the trial court. The kind of decision the trial court has made is important because it drives the kind of review the appellate court can provide. As noted above in the discussion of the role of the courts, if the lower court's decision was one of pure law, the appellate court may decide the question de novo, without giving the lower court's decision any deference. If the lower court's decision was one of fact or mixed fact and law, such as a jury verdict or a trial court's grant of summary judgment, the appellate court gives the lower court's decision greater weight in deciding the case. Thus, as a reader of a court decision, you must take note of the disposition of the case at the time the court authors its opinion, because the disposition of the case plays a role in how the writing court decides the case. As the sample brief illustrates, you may brief the case's procedural history by summarizing the case's course through the courts.

d.   The Facts of the Case

The case's facts refer to the events that led to the parties' dispute. A full understanding of the facts is essential because courts never interpret or apply law for its own sake; instead, courts interpret or apply law in the context of a factual dispute. In a way, the factual context becomes a part of the law itself. Thus, the stories about the parties and their concerns with one another are integral to understanding the law of the case. In addition, as you will read below, the facts of a case are important tools for building analogical argument with case law. As with procedural history, you can brief the facts with bullet points. Readers also find that creating timelines and other diagrams helps them understand and recall the case events. A timeline can depict events chronologically when the court's opinion does not do so. In a diagram, you can convey complex components of the case such as the relationships between parties or the physical layout of a real property dispute in far less time and space than writing text would require.

e.   The Rule of the Case

The case rule is the legal principle that the court uses to decide the issue the parties have posed. The rule may arise from any of the four sources of American law (constitutional provisions, statutes, court decisions, and administrative regulations) or a combination thereof. In generating the legal rule for the case, the court often provides a deductive explanation of the law, moving from general legal principles to more specific. When the court looks to precedent for its rule, it often must synthesize the decisions of a number of courts to reflect the nature of the legal landscape on point. Generally, each issue a court addresses has a corresponding rule that the court applies. Thus, briefing the rule requires that you isolate the legal principle that the court applies to resolve the parties' issue.

f.   The Holding of the Case

The holding of a case is the writing court's final disposition of the case — it is the result the court reaches or the answer to the parties' issue. If the writing court is a trial court, the court typically writes in terms of granting or denying a motion. If the writing court is an appellate court, the court typically writes in terms of affirming a lower court decision or reversing. Figure 3 summarizes other expressions of holdings. To reach a holding, the court applies a legal principle to the facts of the case. Consequently, the holding becomes the law of the case — that part of the case that other courts will look to and build on, and that part of the case that attorneys can base legal argument upon. Words such as "hold," "opine," or "conclude" often signal that the court is about to state its resolution of the case. As you brief a case, look for a holding on each issue the court addresses.

g.   The Reasoning of the Case

The last part of the case to consider is the court's reasoning. Reasoning refers to the decision-making process the court engaged in to reach its decision — it is the court's analysis or an explanation of how the court arrived at its result. United States courts utilize many different forms of reasoning; a few are set out below, others are summarized in Figure 3. As in many civil law countries, when a court interprets or applies a statute, it typically utilizes deductive reasoning — that is it begins with general propositions about the law and then moves to more specific propositions. U.S. courts also engage in inductive reasoning; the courts derive general principles from a set of more specific principles. For example, when a court synthesizes the holdings of a number of courts to generate a single rule of law, which it then applies to its case, the court has inductively reasoned. In reaching its decision, a court may also choose to compare and contrast its case with that of other factually similar cases, ultimately deciding to follow an earlier case because the facts of the earlier case and the present case are significantly similar. Such reasoning is called analogical reasoning. Because analogical reasoning expressly connects current decisions to precedent, thereby invoking the doctrine of stare decisis, it is a highly persuasive form of reasoning. As noted above in the discussion of equity, courts sometimes find that a mechanical application of previous court decisions does not lead to the best result. In such situations, courts may look to principles of equity, seeking a more fair or just result for the parties, or they may also look outside the law, drawing conclusions from natural or social science data. In addition, courts may also look to public policy principles — those that affect the interests of society as a whole such as public health, safety, and welfare. When briefing a court's reasoning, look for text that explains why the court resolved the case the way it did — not the legal reason itself, which is the court's rule, but how the court developed the legal reason or why the court applied the legal reason in the manner that it did.

Figure 3: Selected forms of Reasoning

Form of Reasoning	Description
Deductive	Analysis flows from an explanation of general legal principles to more specific legal principles and application of the legal principles to the case facts to support the conclusion
Inductive	Analysis derives legal principles from a collection of legal authorities, synthesizing the authorities to generate a legal rule that the court then applies to the facts of the case before it

Form of Reasoning	Description
Analogical	Analysis first compares or contrasts the facts of a previously decided case with the facts of the case; if the facts of the previouse decision and the current case are similar, the court reaches the same result as in the previouse decision; if the facts of the previous case are different, the court reaches a result different from the previous case
Modernism	Analysis flows from considerations other than pure logic, such as concerns about the economic and social implications of the court's decision
Postmodernism	Analysis rejects the forms of reasoning above as ineffective because the forms do not provide justice to diverse populations, such as the old, weak, or powerless; analysis characterized more by critisism of other forms of reasoning than the representation of a new form of reasoning

4.   Putting the Pieces Together: A Sample Case Brief

Given the complex nature of court decisions, a passive reading of a case will profit you little. Instead, you must actively engage with the text. As you work through the case, list and define words that are new to you and write down questions that arise from your reading. As noted above, engage in a conversation with the court as you read. Make predictions and evaluate whether they are correct. Try to make connections between the case and others you have read or material you have discussed in class. Your ability to understand, recall, and use the information in the case reflects the time and effort you put into understanding it. So when a reading assignment calls for case reading, prepare your mind for an active and engaging reading session.

Below is an edited version of an actual case dealing with the burglary issue raised above in the section on reading statutes. Following the case is an annotated sample brief of the case. Note that there is no hard and fast format for case briefs. In fact, law professors stress different parts of the cases and that in practice, lawyers may only actually write down certain parts of the brief. Whatever case-brief format is adopted, it is important to leave space in the text for edits, revisions, and further notes about the case and that the format is flexible enough to accommodate the different purposes for reading the case.

Appeals Court of Massachusetts, Suffolk

COMMONWEALTH v. William COTTO
No. 99-P-928

Argued — April 5, 2001

Decided — August 2, 2001

KANTROWITZ, J.

This case presents the novel issue of whether an entering has occurred, for purposes of the burglary statutes,[1] if one[2] breaks a window and then throws an infernal device through the opening. We conclude that an entering has occurred.

Background.

The defendant, William Cotto, was charged in two sets of indictments based on two separate incidents. The January 4, 1997, charges consisted of assault with intent to murder Shirley Suarez while armed with a flammable liquid, *G.L. c. 265, § 18(b)*; breaking and entering in the nighttime with intent to commit murder, *G.L. c. 266, § 15*; and arson, *G.L. c. 266, § 1*. The January 10, 1997, charges included assault against Nilsa Wong by means of a dangerous weapon, a baseball bat, *G.L. c. 265, § 15(b)*; and kidnapping Wong, *G.L. c. 265, § 26*.

After his conviction on all counts, Cotto now appeals, claiming that the judge (1) provided the jury with erroneous instructions on the breaking and entering count; and (2) abused his discretion by joining the two sets of indictments for trial. For the reasons set forth below, we affirm.

Facts.

The Commonwealth sought to prove that the events of January 4 and 10 were connected, stemming from an ongoing feud between the defendant's family and Francisco Martinez. The jury could have found these facts.

On September 15, 1996, Francisco Martinez was allegedly shot in the abdomen by Garribel Bautista,[3] the defendant's brother. On January 3, 1997, at nine in the evening, the alleged shooter, Bautista, was found lying in a road in Milton, beaten, stabbed, and gagged. Hours later, shortly after midnight, the defendant and two others set fire to Martinez's apartment.

Shirley Suarez, who was staying at Martinez's apartment that evening, heard glass breaking. Going into the living room to investigate, she saw a white plastic bottle being thrown through the broken window. It was later determined that the

---

[1] *General Laws c. 266, §§ 14* (armed burglary of a dwelling), 15 (unarmed burglary of a dwelling), and 16 (breaking and entering).

[2] Either individually or in concert with another.

[3] Bautista is also known as Carlos Ivan Hernandez. While a warrant was issued for his arrest, the record indicates that he was never arrested.

bottle contained gasoline, and that it caused a fire in the apartment.

Frightened, she ran to the back door and saw three people outside the apartment. She recognized the defendant as one of the group of three vandals. She then ran upstairs to warn the other tenants. She heard the fire alarm go off and smelled smoke. The fire department was summoned. Ultimately, the damage to the apartment consisted of the walls of the living room and bedroom being completely covered with soot; the heat from the fire caused children's plastic toys to melt in the bedroom.

Not content with that evening's mischief, one week later the defendant kidnapped Nilsa Wong, Martinez's girlfriend. During the kidnapping, the defendant demanded to know the whereabouts of Martinez and threatened Wong with a baseball bat, stating that he should beat her "to leave Francisco Martinez another message." He also told Wong that he had set fire to Martinez's apartment.

The entering.

The defendant argues that the trial judge erred by instructing the jury that an entry occurs when an instrument or weapon controlled by the defendant physically enters the dwelling. He urges us to hold that an entry by instrument can only be found where the instrument is being used, not only to commit the felony within, but also as the means of committing the break.

Here, it is evident that the window was broken, by either the defendant or one of his two cohorts.[4] The precise manner in which it was broken is unknown. The sole evidence of entry consisted of the infernal device[5] being thrown into the living room through the broken window. We must now decide whether an entry for the purpose of the burglary statutes occurs when an instrument, used to commit the felony therein,[6] crosses the threshold.

Burglary is an offense against property. *See Nolan & Henry, Criminal Law* § 401, at 299 (2d ed. 1988). "It is the purpose of burglary statutes . . . to prohibit that conduct which violates a person's right of security in a place universally associated with refuge and safety, the dwelling house." *Commonwealth v. Goldoff*, 24 Mass. App. Ct. 458, 462, 510 N.E.2d 277 (1987). "By not defining the term [entering] in the burglary statutes, the Legislature is presumed to have intended to incorporate the common law definition of that phrase, at least in so far as it is not inconsistent with the terms or the purpose of the statute." *Commonwealth v. Ricardo*, 26 Mass. App. Ct. 345, 356, 526 N.E.2d 1340 (1988) (internal quotations omitted). *See Commonwealth v. Colon*, 431 Mass. 188, 191, 726 N.E.2d 909 (2000).

"There must be *both* a breaking and an entering to constitute the crime of burglary. They are distinct and separate acts." *Rex v. Hughes*, 1 Leach 406, 406 (1785) (emphasis in the original). At common law, "any intrusion into a protected enclosure by any part of a defendant's body was enough to satisfy the legal requirement of entry." *Commonwealth v. Burke*, 392 Mass. 688, 690, 467 N.E.2d

---

[4] Suarez heard the glass break, but did not see who broke it.

[5] An infernal device or machine is defined as "including any device for endangering life or doing unusual damage to property, or both, by fire or explosion, whether or not contrived to ignite or explode automatically and whether or not disguised so as to appear harmless." *G.L. c. 266, § 102A*.

[6] The felony intended in this case was murder.

846 (1984), citing *Rex v. Bailey*, Russ & Ry. 341 (1818); *Rex v. Davis*, Russ & Ry. 499 (1823); *Commonwealth v. Glover*, 111 Mass. 395 (1873).[7]

In cases where only an instrument crossed the threshold of the dwelling house, there is no entry where the instrument was only used for the breaking. *See Rex v. Hughes*, 1 Leach at 407. However, where the instrument is used to commit the felony within, there is an entry. *See ibid.* "And in those cases where an instrument has formed any part of the question, it has always been taken to mean, not the instrument by which the breaking was made, but the instrument, as a hook, a fork, or other thing by which the property was capable of being removed." *Ibid.*[8] *See Burke*, supra at 692.

This view is in conformity with a majority of jurisdictions, which has held that an entry can occur if an instrument, "being used to commit the felony intended," passes the line of the threshold, regardless of whether the instrument was used in the breaking. 3 Torcia, *Wharton's Criminal Law* § 323 (15th ed. 1995). *See* Nolan & Henry, *Criminal Law* § 403; Perkins & Boyce, *Criminal Law* 254 (3d ed. 1982) ("Where a tool or other instrument is intruded, without any part of the person being within the house, it is an entry if the insertion was for the purpose of completing the felony but not if it was merely to accomplish a breaking").[9] *See State v. Ison*, 744 P.2d 416, 418–419 (Alaska Ct. App. 1987); *State v. Johnson*, 587 S.W.2d 636, 638 (Mo. Ct. App. 1979).

A minority of jurisdictions hold that an entry can occur if any instrument, whether or not intended for use to commit a felony, crosses the threshold. *See People v. Davis*, 18 Cal. 4th 712, 717, 958 P.2d 1083 (1998); *Hebron v. State*, 331 Md. 219, 237–238, 627 A.2d 1029 (1993); *State v. Tixier*, 89 N.M. 297, 298–99, 551 P.2d 987 (Ct. App. 1976).[10]

Today we agree with the majority of jurisdictions and hold that an entry occurs when any part of the defendant's body, or an instrument which is used to commit the intended felony, crosses the threshold. We so hold because "by permitting an instrumental entry to satisfy this element of the offense only when the instrument is to be used in connection with the ulterior crime, we properly differentiate between attempted burglary, burglary, and the commission of the ultimate

---

[7] "It is well settled that it is a sufficient entry 'when the thief breaketh the house, and his body, or any part thereof, as his foot or his arm, is within any part of the house.'" *Burke*, 392 Mass. at 690–691, quoting from Glover, *supra* at 402. See *Commonwealth v. Lewis*, 346 Mass. 373, 377, 191 N.E.2d 753 (1963), *cert. denied*, 376 U.S. 933, 11 L. Ed. 2d 653, 84 S. Ct. 704 (1964).

[8] "Neither Coke, Blackstone, nor Hale make the distinction, though it might be implied from their examples. [Hawkins] queries whether this is not the proper distinction, and [East] states that such is the law though it was not mentioned in the earlier writings." 3 LaFave & Scott, *Substantive Criminal Law* § 8.13, at 467 n.35 (1986), citing 1 Hawkins, *Pleas of the Crown* 161–162 (1787), and 2 East, *Pleas of the Crown* 490 (1803).

[9] The origin of the distinction between entry of an instrument and a body part was due to the "ancient style of lock and key [where the key, when inserted,] went entirely through and extended a fraction of an inch on the other side. And the special rule in regard to a tool or instrument was developed to insure that the mere insertion of the key would not be held sufficient to complete the burglary." Perkins & Boyce, *Criminal Law* 254.

[10] Other jurisdictions appear to hold to a more conservative view, finding an entry only where the instrument which crosses the threshold is also used to break into the premises. *See Walker v. State*, 63 Ala. 49, 51–52 (1879).

[crime]." *State v. Ison*, 744 P.2d at 419.[11]

The position we adopt differentiates between breaking and entering and an attempt to break and enter. For example, assume in the case at bar that the defendant had broken the window, but upon seeing Suarez, dropped the infernal device and ran. In this scenario, he may be found guilty of attempted breaking and entering as well as attempted arson, but not of arson or breaking and entering.[12]

We turn to the actual instructions given in this case. The trial judge stated: "An entry is the unlawful making of one's way into a dwelling house of another. Entry occurs if any part of the defendant's body, even a hand or foot or any instrument or weapon controlled by the defendant, physically enters the dwelling house." The judge failed to state that, in the unusual facts of this case, entry can be found only where the instrument that entered is intended for use in the commission of the felony within.[13]

However, the error was harmless. There was no dispute at trial that the container thrown into the apartment contained an accelerant and that it was the cause of the fire. Since this was not a live issue at trial (the only issue at trial was identification), there was no prejudice to the defendant. *See Commonwealth v. Gagnon*, 430 Mass. 348, 350, 718 N.E.2d 1254 (1999) ("where the identity of the killer is the only live issue at trial, any error in the malice instruction is not prejudicial because the defendant's state of mind is not in dispute. The issue is the identity of the perpetrator"). * * *

Judgments affirmed.

---

[11] "Whether the insertion of an instrument or tool is sufficient (without any part of the body entering) seems to depend upon the purpose for which it is inserted. If the tool is inserted simply to accomplish the breaking, there is no entering for purposes of burglary; but, if the tool or instrument is inserted to accomplish the felony, the insertion is sufficient for the requirement of entering. If a bullet is fired for purpose of breaking the lock, though the bullet lands inside, it would probably not constitute a burglarious entering if fired solely to break the lock. If fired to kill a person inside, probably an entering could be found." Nolan & Henry, *Criminal Law* § 403 (footnotes omitted).

[12] *See Commonwealth v. Reynolds*, 10 Mass. App. Ct. 830, 406 N.E.2d 1042 (1980), wherein the defendant's conviction for attempted breaking and entering with intent to commit a felony was affirmed on evidence, in part, of a rock being thrown through the window of a pharmacy during the nighttime.

[13] Given the unusual nature of the fact scenario in this case, a judge would have to add this proviso in instructing the jury only on rare occasions.

Sample Case Brief

COMMONWEALTH
v.
William COTTO

Wide margin allows for note taking on brief during class

For clarity, I have used complete sentences and no symbols. You can shorten your briefs by using bullets and phrases and adopting a code of symbols.

I.   Who is suing who and why; who wins

The parties are the state of Massachusetts and William Cotto.

Massachusetts has filed an action against William Cotto, asserting that Cotto burgled an apartment.

Massachusetts prevailed in the case because the appellate court agreed with the trial court that the defendant entered the apartment when he threw a gas-filled bottle into the apartment that exploded and caught the apartment on fire.

II.   Style

You can use your citation manual to figure out the court's level.

Massachusetts v. Cotto
Mid-level appellate court (Mass Appeals Court)
2001

III.   Issue

Note that for both issues, the writer has included language of the law and key facts.

Whether a defendant enters an apartment under the burglary statute when the defendant throws an instrument through an apartment window and then uses the instrument to commit an offense inside the apartment.

Whether a judge's erroneous trial instruction is harmless error when the error does not prejudice the defendant.

IV.   Procedural History

Live issue at trial was identification — whether Cotto was among those who committed the burglary. A jury convicted Cotto of burglary and other crimes. Cotto appealed to the mid-level appellate court, arguing that the trial judge improperly instructed the jury on the definition of entry under the burglary statute.

V.   Facts

The case provides lots of other facts, such as an explanation for why Cotto may have burgled the apartment, but those facts are not relevant to the issue here, so the writer chose not to include them.

The state alleged that Cotto was among a group of people that broke an apartment window and threw a plastic bottle filled with gasoline through the broken window and into the apartment. The bottle of gasoline caused fire to the apartment.

The core of this case is really a legal issue — the definition of entry, so the facts here include reference to the trial court's definition of entry. Be aware of the differences between legal and factual issues, and make certain to include only the facts that connect with the issues in your brief.

The trial court instructed the jury that under the burglary statutes entry by instrument occurs when "any instrument or weapon controlled by the defendant, physically enters the dwelling house." Cotto argued that the trial court should have instructed the jury that entry by instrument also requires that the defendant use the instrument that entered the apartment to commit the intended offense.

VI. Rule

Under the Massachusetts burglary statutes, entry by instrument occurs when "an instrument which is used commit the intended felony, crosses the threshold."

Note that for each issue the writer provides a rule.

An erroneous jury instruction is merely harmless error when the instruction does not prejudice the defendant.

VII. Holding

Note that the holding encompasses the court's decision on both issues.

Although the appellate court determined that the trial court erroneously instructed the jury on the definition of entry under the burglary statute, the appellate court found that the error was harmless and affirmed the trial court's judgment.

VIII. Reasoning

The focus on this section is on explaining how and why the trial court reached its result. Notice the number of times the writer uses the word "because" when the writer explains why the court resolved the matter the way if did.

The trial court's jury instruction on entry was erroneous because the trial court's entry by instrument instruction failed to mention that the instrument must be used to both enter the space and commit the intended offense.

In generating its definition of entry by instrument, the court noted the following:

- The legislature did not define entry, presumably intending to incorporate the common law definition of the phrase, so far as the common law definition is not inconsistent with the terms or purpose of the statute.

- At common law burglary required a breaking and an entering — two separate acts.

- At common law "there is no entry where the instrument was used only for the breaking. However, where the instrument is used to commit the felony within, there is an entry." (harkens back to the notion that merely inserting a key into a lock is not burglary).

- Majority of jurisdictions now require that instrument must enter and be used to commit an offense.

- Minority of jurisdictions hold that "used to commit an offense" is not necessary to show entry by instrument.

Note that each bulleted point here is a legal rule that the court uses as a building block to explain how and why it reached its result.

- Other courts hold that instrument that enters and commits offense must also be the instrument that breaks into space.

Note that here the court changes the facts to illustrate a point; such information is dicta. The law of this case is not what happens if a defendant drops an instrument and runs away; instead, the law of the case arises from the facts of the case — what happens when a defendant throws an instrument into an apartment and the instrument causes a crime. Recall that while the dicta is not binding "law," it may be highly persuasive authority to a future court.

The court adopted the majority position because the definition best differentiates between attempted burglary, burglary, and the commission of the ultimate crime. For example, if the defendant had broken the window, seen a bystander, dropped the gas-filled bottle, and ran away, the defendant would be guilty of attempted burglary as well as attempted arson, but not burglary or arson.

The trial court's jury-instruction error was harmless because at trial, the only "live" issue was whether Cotto was among the group of people that was witnessed outside the apartment. The court noted that there was no dispute that the container thrown into the apartment was the cause of the fire. Thus, the court's failure to properly define entry did not prejudice Cotto.

V. BEYOND THE COURT SYSTEM: PROCEDURES FOR RESOLVING PARTIES' DISPUTES WITHOUT TRIAL

One of the growing areas in the American legal system is the resolution of disputes without trial. Given the cost of engaging in litigation and the uncertainty of placing the outcome of a dispute in the hands of a judge or a jury, more parties are willing to explore options that give the parties more control over the resolution process. In addition, alternative dispute resolution proceedings are typically faster and held in private, in contrast to the courts, where litigation can drag on for years at a time and filed documents are typically public records. Courts have also found that by requiring parties to meet and confer before filing some motions and ordering other parties to mediation, the courts can focus their time on disputes that the parties truly cannot resolve on their own. Given the rise of such alternative dispute resolution procedures in recent years, an overview of the US legal system would not be complete without briefly addressing the topic. Therefore this section will provide brief overview of some of the more common alternative dispute resolution forms: negotiation, mediation, arbitration, and mixed processes.

A. Negotiation

Negotiation is a process by which opposing sides resolve disputes by reconciling conflicting positions. Informal negotiations may occur between parties over procedural and substantive issues in a case. Parties may negotiate the issues they contest, the damages they claim, or the information they will share prior to trial. Negotiations may also be more formal as parties gather together to try to resolve the case in its entirety. The process of negotiation requires that each side become aware of its interests in the matter and what it would give and take to resolve the matter. Parties also give significant thought to what the other side's interests are and what the other side may be willing to give and take to resolve the matter. Once each party is prepared, they gather to discuss the case. Some negotiators take an adversarial point of view, such that they see the negotiation as an attack plan where they give as little as possible and attempt to gain as much as they can. In the minds of such negotiators, a negotiation is won or lost, much like a case at trial. Other negotiators take a problem-solving approach. These negotiators seek common ground among conflicting interests and try to create conditions where each party emerges a winner.

B. Mediation

Mediation is similar to negotiation in that the parties meet to try to resolve their dispute; however, with mediation, the parties entrust a third party with the task of facilitating a resolution. The preparation for mediation is similar to that of a negotiation. The parties identify their interests and evaluate their positions, determining in advance a range of acceptable resolutions. The parties also spend some time studying and evaluating the other side's position. In contrast to a negotiation, many mediators require the parties to submit a mediation statement in advance of the mediation session. The mediation statement summarizes the case from the party's perspective and provides a set of goals for the mediation. Mediation sessions are generally more structured than negotiations. The process often begins with each party providing an opening statement to the mediator summarizing the facts of the dispute and the party's contentions regarding the dispute. Following the opening statements, the parties engage in conversation, sometimes with the mediator alone, other times in the presence of the other party. The mediator listens carefully to both sides and questions both sides to make certain he or she understands their positions and that each side understands the other's position. Some mediators see their role as exclusively facilitative, meaning that they do not push the parties to accept a resolution; instead, through active listening and questions, they help parties understand one another so that the parties can generate their own solution. Other mediators are more assertive. They may define the issues for the parties, and they may value the case and urge the parties to accept a specific resolution. If the parties agree to resolve the case, typically the mediator drafts a mediation agreement, which the parties then sign. Such agreements are enforceable contracts. Mediations generally attempt to resolve a case in one day or less.

C.   Arbitration

Arbitration is a third form of dispute resolution that is generally more structured than those previously mentioned. A private arbitration proceeding is somewhat similar to a trial, except there is no judge or jury; instead, the parties select a neutral arbitrator to decide the case, and the arbitrator is not bound by procedural or substantive law in making his or her decision. Thus, unless the parties otherwise agree, the rules of evidence and procedure do not apply to arbitration proceedings, nor does stare decisis. Parties usually agree in advance that certain disputes will be resolved by an arbitrator, or they enter an agreement to arbitrate after a dispute arises. Unlike trial judges, arbitrators are typically experts in the field in which they arbitrate cases. Thus, to provide a greater sense of predictability, efficiency, and fairness, some parties will choose to have an arbitrator or a panel of arbitrators hear their case. The arbitrator's decision is generally binding. Courts may validate or invalidate agreements to arbitrate, and they may confirm or vacate an arbitrator's award, but courts rarely review the merits of an arbitrator's decision. The preparation for arbitration is more rigorous than the previous dispute resolution forms. In addition to making written and oral arguments before the arbitrator, parties may prepare exhibits and call witnesses. State and federal courts have mandated that certain cases be subject to arbitration. The decision of arbitrators in such cases is not binding (parties may appeal to the court); courts use arbitration to promote case settlement without trial.

D.   Mixed Dispute Resolution Processes

Mixed process resolution proceedings draw upon the elements found in negotiation, mediation and arbitration. One set of mixed processes grows out of the courts, while another set operates independent from the court system. Court-annexed mixed processes reflect the courts' creativity in trying to find a means for resolving disputes that moves cases off crowded trial dockets and out of the courthouse for resolution. Those processes include mandatory arbitration (mentioned above), summary jury trials, and procedures for dealing with mass litigation, such as asbestos claims and other toxic tort cases. Summary jury trials provide parties with an opportunity to present the merits of their case before a jury without engaging in full-scale trial. By presenting the case to a jury, the parties can get a realistic sense of the value of their case more quickly and for less expense than trial. Such proceedings are nonbinding and are designed to get the process of negotiation or mediation moving. Procedures for dealing with mass litigation include informal groupings of cases and more formal case consolidations to insure consistency in court decisions. Courts also play a role in designing settlement schemes that will cover a host of individual cases.

Private processes include use of a private mini-trial and a combination of mediation and arbitration. The private mini-trial is part negotiation, part mediation, and part arbitration. The process is typically used to resolve business disputes that have reached an impasse in negotiations. Parties agree on a neutral advisor to hear the case. The advisor's decision is nonbinding, but the advisor is generally authorized to question the parties regarding the strengths and weaknesses of their case. During the mini-trial, attorneys make summary presentations of their best case. Rules of evidence generally do not apply. Representatives of the party businesses with settlement authority typically attend mini-trial proceedings so that they can get a feel for the value of the case and the likelihood of prevailing at trial. Mediation-Arbitration is a process that provides parties with an opportunity to mediate a case before submitting it to binding arbitration. Because mediation is faster than arbitration, it is less costly. If parties can resolve their case through mediation, they can save time and money. Further, while arbitration tends to promote an adversarial approach to problem-solving, mediation attempts to help parties find common ground in their dispute and resolve it themselves. By combining the two processes, only those cases that really need the assistance of an arbitrator are subjected to arbitration. In some mediation-arbitrations, the mediator drafts an advisory opinion, suggesting how the case would be resolved if it was arbitrated. In other cases, the mediator and arbitrator is the same individual.

VI.   CONCLUSION

This chapter has equipped you with the information you need to process and understand those that follow, and perhaps it has raised questions for you as well — your pursuit of the answers to those questions will make your journey through this material a unique experience. From the comparison between the civil and American legal systems, you were introduced to terms common in the American legal vocabulary and you observed similarities and differences between the systems. The next section provided you with a historical context for understanding the concepts, principles, and tensions that shape the American legal system. You then learned how those concepts, principles, and tensions are expressed in American law by studying the four sources of United States Law. With a background in the legal sources, you observed how American attorneys utilize cases and statutes. And lastly, you learned that while the court system continues to serve as the primary forum for resolving legal disputes in the United States, a variety of extra-judicial alternative dispute resolution procedures have arisen.

Now take the knowledge and understanding you have acquired here and continue your journey into the following chapters, which will add depth, color, and substance to your understanding of the United States Legal System.

Chapter 2

CONTRACTS, OBLIGATIONS & COMMERCIAL LAW

By — Candace M. Zierdt

SYNOPSIS

I. INTRODUCTION

This chapter contains a brief overview of the law of Contracts, Obligations, and Commercial Law in the United States. It is not intended to teach analysis, be totally comprehensive, or to address the many exceptions to the general rules. Instead, it will briefly describe the major concepts in the common law of contracts and contracts for the sale of goods, which is found in Article Two of the Uniform Commercial Code. (For the rest of this chapter the Uniform Commercial Code will be referred to by its acronym — the UCC.) There are some very important differences between the common law and Article Two of the UCC. This chapter will review some of the major differences; however, it will not delineate all of the differences between the two bodies of law. Coverage of Article Two will be more brief than the common law. Although this chapter will not review the United Nation's Convention on the International Sale of Goods, also referred to as the CISG, it is important to understand that this body of law applies to certain contracts made by parties who reside in the United States. The CISG governs international commercial contracts for the sale of goods between parties who live in countries that have ratified the CISG. The United States did this in 1988.

It will cover how the common law of contracts develops in the United States, the basic elements needed for a promise to become an enforceable contract, how courts determine the meaning of a contract, how courts may add terms into contracts, how courts may allow parties (as opposed to the court) to add terms into a contract, issues that may arise during the performance of a contract, permissible excuses for breaching a contract, and remedies available to both parties after a breach of contract occurs. Additionally, there are certain situations when contracts, even though they appear to be formed correctly, may not be enforceable. This chapter will refer to the concepts used in these situations as "policing concepts." The term policing is used because the courts will monitor or "police" certain contracts for fairness, overreaching, unconscionability, age, mental competence, and other behavior or terms in a contract that are problematic. The policing concepts allow a court to refuse to enforce what appears to be a perfectly valid contract or, in some instances, modify the contract to make it enforceable.

In addition to traditional contract doctrines, there are alternative ways to enforce promises. This chapter will focus on Promissory Estoppel, which is the most prominent one. It allows the enforcement of certain promises after a party has changed his or her position in reliance on the promise. Another concept that does not require a party to meet the elements of a contract, in fact it does not even involve a promise by a party, is the doctrine of restitution. Restitution permits a court to imply a promise to pay by an individual who has received a benefit. It is based on a theory of unjust enrichment. That means that if a party was enriched and it would be unjust not to pay for the benefit the person received, a court may imply a promise to pay for the benefit. Lastly, there are a few other concepts that are important to contract law that a student should be familiar with. The two additional doctrines this chapter will review are the Statute of Frauds and the law of third party beneficiaries.

II. SOURCES OF CONTRACT LAW

In addition to the CISG previously mentioned, there are two other sources of contract law in the United States and one major source of contract theory. Those sources respectively are the common law, the UCC, and the Restatement of Contracts. First, this chapter will explain how each law or source is enacted or drafted and the differences between them. Then it will review the substance of the law.

A.   The Common Law

The common law is law made by judges instead of legislatures. It evolves over time. The law of contracts today is not the same in every state nor is it the same as it was 100 years ago. There are several reasons for this. Each state court controls its own law, so it is not unusual to find some variation among the states, although the basic rules do not differ greatly. It varies because it is judge made law and judges in different states may resolve issues in a variety of ways. Second, as you learned in the first chapter of this book, the common law is based on precedent. That means that courts are bound to follow the rule of law pronounced in previous cases in the same jurisdiction. The common law, however, allows a court to change previous rulings instead of absolutely relying on precedent if there is a sound basis in the law for the change. If the facts of a case and the attorney presenting them are persuasive enough, they may convince a court to change the law, as long as the court determines that a new rule is more appropriate. In that situation, a court will overrule previous cases and establish new precedent. That is how the common law changes.

To understand how these changes occur, consider how Promissory Estoppel, a doctrine that will be explored later in this chapter, became law and allowed courts to enforce promises outside the requirements of traditional contract doctrine. Historically, promises were only enforceable using traditional contract theory. Traditional contract theory requires parties to take certain steps before a promise will become enforceable as a contract. In the twentieth century, courts found that some promises should be enforced, even though they did not follow the usual requirements of traditional contract theory. This did not happen by statute; but instead, developed through the process of the common law. It started when a few courts were persuaded that society had reached a point where it required that some promises should be enforced, even though they did not meet all of the elements of a contract. A few courts were convinced that in certain situations promises should be enforced because a party reasonably relied on a promise and changed his or her position in a way that it would be unjust not to enforce the promise. Slowly, courts in other states also were persuaded to change. Now every state recognizes some form of this theory. This is one of many examples of how the common law changes over time.

B.   The Uniform Commercial Code

The UCC, the other main source of contract and commercial law in the United States, is statutory. That means the legislature of each state must enact the UCC before it will become law. Article Two of the UCC, which will be the focus in this chapter outside of common law, has been enacted in some form in every state except Louisiana. Although this chapter will concentrate on the original uniform law, it may not be exactly the same in every state. To understand why there are differences, you need to appreciate the uniform law process and how the UCC becomes law in each state.

The uniform law process involves three influential organizations. They are the National Conference of Commissioners on Uniform State Laws (hereinafter referred to as NCCUSL — now also referred to as the Uniform Law Commission), the American Law Institute (hereinafter referred to as the ALI), and the American Bar Association (hereinafter referred to as the ABA). To understand this process, it is helpful to know who the members are of each organization.

NCCUSL was formed in the late 1800s. The primary purposes of the organization are to draft uniform laws dealing with crucial issues important to all states, that also support the federal system, and to assist in enacting rules that are uniform from state to state. NCCUSL has also recently begun to work on international initiatives. The organization consists of more than 300 practicing lawyers, judges, state legislators, and law professors who are appointed by the states, the District of Columbia, the Virgin Islands, and Puerto Rico. The commissioners, who are all lawyers, volunteer their time to research, draft, and help enact uniform laws. NCCUSL, however, does not do this alone. It partners with the ALI in drafting the UCC and any revisions needed to the laws. The ALI's membership also consists of practicing lawyers, judges, and legal scholars from the United States and some foreign countries. Membership in the ALI is by election, and members are elected on the basis of achievements in their professional life and a demonstrated desire to improve the law. In addition to partnering with NCCUSL, the ALI publishes a variety of Restatements of the law. Those Restatements have an independent persuasive basis for courts that will be discussed in the next section. The ABA, the third organization involved in the drafting process of the UCC and other uniform laws, is the largest association of attorneys in the United States. Because of that, it is one of the most influential legal groups in the United States. These three organizations are instrumental in the uniform law process.

The first step in the drafting process occurs when NCCUSL appoints a drafting committee comprised of NCCUSL Commissioners, representatives from the ALI and ABA, and a reporter for the uniform law being proposed. The reporter is responsible for considering all of the comments from committee members, constituents, and advisors, then drafting the law with those comments in mind. In addition to drafting the law, the reporter writes commentary to the law that explains the reasoning for much of the law. Although the commentary is not the law, it is highly persuasive for courts. A variety of advisors, who have expertise relevant to the laws being drafted, also are invited to attend committee meetings. The draft of the law goes through many edits, and it often takes several years before a final draft is completed. After completion of the draft law by the drafting committee, it is read a number of times at NCCUSL's annual meeting where all commissioners have an opportunity to comment on it and to request changes. If the drafting committee does not agree with the proposed changes, the changes must be approved by a majority vote of all of the commissioners. After the final reading, every state votes on whether to approve the law. After the draft is approved by a majority of the states, it is forwarded to the ALI, so that the membership of the ALI may comment on it and eventually vote on it for approval. After approval by the ALI, the draft is presented to the leadership of the ABA, where they too have an opportunity to approve the law. Finally, after completion of all of the approvals, the enactment process begins. That process requires NCCUSL Commissioners and staff from the national office of NCCUSL to work with the various state legislatures in an effort to have the law enacted as drafted. Because there is now a new audience for the law, there may be amendments suggested by lobbyists, legislators, or other interested groups. Legislators in each state may be swayed by different arguments for or against changing the law. Because of this unique process, the laws do not remain totally uniform in every state.

C.   The Restatement of Contracts

The ALI drafts Restatements on a number of different subjects. One of the most important resources for contract law is the Restatement (Second) of Contracts, which is drafted by the ALI. Each Restatement is an effort to try to clarify the common law that exists in a majority of states. It is very helpful; but it is important to remember that Restatements are not the law anywhere. They are only a restatement by the ALI of what it believes the black letter law is or should be in the majority of states. Only the common law and the UCC are actually laws that courts must follow. However, the Restatement (Second) of Contracts is persuasive authority, and it is very good reference material for the black letter restatement of the law. With this background and these sources in mind, it is time to turn to the law of contract.

III. CONTRACT FORMATION

The law of contract is simply about how society determines which promises will be enforceable, because not all promises are or should be enforceable. The law has its own language; consequently, words used in the law may have a different meaning than their ordinary use or they may have no definition outside of their intended legal use. Take, for example, the word "consideration." What does that word mean to you? Perhaps it means that a person is supposed to be nice and to take the other person's feelings into account? While that may be its ordinary use, it is not its legal use in the law of contract. "Consideration" is a complicated concept requiring an exchange between the parties. Thus, remember that there are certain "terms of art" that have a specific legal meaning. Other terms of art in contract law include offeror, offeree, promissor, promisee, and assent. Each one of these terms has a specific meaning in the law of contract. An "offeror" is the party who makes an offer, an "offeree" is a party who is empowered to accept an offer. The "promissor" is the party who is breaking a promise, and the "promisee" is the party who is trying to enforce a promise. "Assent" is shown when a reasonable person would think the parties actually intended to enter a contract or when one of the parties actually knew that the other party intended to enter into a contact. All of these terms are important in contract law. When determining whether there is assent, courts often look for an offer and acceptance.

A.   Assent — Offer and Acceptance

Although there are certainly quite a few complicated contracts, many contracts start with a simple promise that proposes an exchange. I promise to sell you my car for $10,000, if you promise to buy my car for $10,000. The first question is how does one determine whether a promise is legally enforceable? Not all promises will be enforceable. Some are not significant, some are not seeking an exchange, and some simply do not have the requisite elements. One requirement for enforceability is that the parties must assent to contractual liability. This means that they intend to enter a legally binding contract. The process of assent generally happens through the mechanisms of offer and acceptance. The courts basically look for actions or words that indicate each party is seeking to be part of a legally enforceable agreement. The first contract forming event is usually the offer. Because not all promises or communications will rise to the level of being an offer, there has to be a way to distinguish an offer from other communications or promises. This is accomplished by looking for specific characteristics that indicate the person making the communication intended to contract, although no certain formalities are required. Typical characteristics of an offer are specificity, the number of people who have received an offer, how definite it is, how complete it is, and whether there is common language of offer. Because there may be a number of different communications involved, it is often difficult to discern when negotiations end and an offer to contract begins. The ultimate determination is whether a reasonable person would believe that the words and conduct of the person making the purported offer would lead to contractual liability. Therefore, if a communication is very specific, has definite requirements, and states all of the necessary terms to close the deal, it looks more like an offer and less like negotiation. For example, if Stella Corporation says it will sell twenty-five acres of land of a specific description to Athena Corporation for a definite price, on a certain date, with specifics about the property and terms of the sale — it looks like Stella is making an offer to sell its land. Alternatively, a general announcement from a representative of Stella Corporation at a meeting of a large group of people that it may want to sell its property would likely not have the characteristics of an offer because it would not be reasonable for a person who heard this at a large meeting to think he or she could accept and close the deal. The representative used the word "may," it is not definite, and there is not enough specific information.

Once an offer is made, how long does a party have to accept the offer and what does it take to make an acceptance? It has to be accepted within a reasonable amount of time or it will lapse, unless the offer states a specific time for it to remain open, and before a revocation occurs. The definition of a reasonable amount of time will vary depending on the type of contract, the subject matter of the contract, and other matters. For example, an offer to buy oil in a very volatile market will remain viable for a shorter period of time than an offer to buy a good that has little price fluctuation — such as a piano.

Another way the ability to accept an offer may be terminated is by a revocation. If an offer is not accepted before a revocation occurs, it may no longer be accepted. A revocation occurs when the party making the offer indicates she or he no longer wants to go through with the deal or when other circumstances indicate this. Although the easiest way to revoke an offer is to simply say, "I revoke," a revocation may occur without those words actually being spoken. The law looks for an indication that the offeror no longer intends to contract. Remember that for an offer to be effective, the offeror must intend to be legally bound by a contract or there is no offer and no assent. For example, when an offeror indicates she or he may not want to proceed with the deal, that may be sufficient to revoke an offer because it no longer shows a definite intent to contract. If an offeree hears from a third party that the offeror is trying to revoke his or her offer or attempting to enter into a contract on the same subject matter with a different party, that too may qualify as a revocation. The death of an offeror also will constitute a revocation of the offer, even if the offeree does not know about the death.

A concept similar to revocation is rejection. A rejection of an offer may occur when an offeree, the party empowered to accept an offer, states that she or he is not interested in accepting the offer. It may also occur when an offeree changes the terms of the offer. A change in the offer is a counter offer on the new terms, as well as a rejection. Once a counter offer occurs, it terminates the offeree's ability to accept the original offer, unless the offeror reinstates it. For example, Susan makes an offer to Tom that she will sell her house to him, if he promises to pay her $300,000 on January 1. Assume that the offer has all of the specifics needed to be an effective offer, such as a description of the property, closing date, and how the financing will be worked out. When Tom says he does not want to buy the house for that price, he rejects Susan's offer. That rejection terminates Tom's ability to accept the original offer to sell the house for $300,000. If, however, Tom responds by saying that he will buy the house for $290,000 on February 1, Tom has made a counteroffer because he changed the terms of the original offer. That counteroffer is a rejection, so it cuts off Tom's ability to accept the original offer. If Susan says she does not want to sell her house on Tom's new terms, Tom may not change his mind and accept Susan's original offer to sell her house for $300,000 on January 1. Further, Susan has now rejected Tom's offer.

As long as an offer has not been revoked, been rejected, or lapsed, it may be accepted by the party to whom it is directed. Once an acceptance occurs, both parties are legally bound to the contract. There are different ways for an acceptance to happen, and this will depend, to some extent, on whether the offeror was looking for a return promise or some type of performance.

An acceptance must be on the terms of the offer, and the offeree may not change the offer. This is called the "mirror image rule." Think of holding a contract in a mirror and seeing the reflection of the contract. Each term of that contract that is reflected in the mirror must be accepted as proposed or it violates the mirror image rule. If the acceptance changes the offer, that acceptance will become a counter offer. Consider the previous example of Tom and Susan, where Susan offered to sell her house to Tom for $300,000 on January 1. If Tom accepts by promising to buy her house for $300,000 on February 1, he has violated the mirror image rule because he has not accepted on her terms. He changed the closing date. Thus, Tom's communication was a counter offer instead of an acceptance, and there is no contract unless Susan accepts the counter offer.

B.   Consideration

A contract is not enforceable unless, along with an offer and acceptance, it also has consideration. The mechanisms of offer and acceptance are how parties exchange consideration in a contract. The concept of consideration is foreign to many people who have not been trained in U.S. contract law. Consideration requires an exchange, and in that exchange both parties must make a commitment or take on some type of obligation. When analyzing consideration, the common law often says that there must be mutuality of obligation between the parties. The commitments do not have to be equal. It is enough that each party actually acquires a true commitment or obligation. As stated previously, the offer and acceptance are merely a way to exchange the obligations required by consideration. The offer will usually be the consideration for the acceptance and the acceptance will generally be the consideration for the offer. A court of law will not inquire into whether the consideration for a contract is "adequate;" it is sufficient that consideration exists and that each party incurs an obligation.

Consideration requires an exchange between the parties. In addition to the requirement that each party take on an obligation in the exchange, each party must receive what he or she was seeking from the other party. In other words, there must be reciprocal commitments or obligations given in exchange for each other by both parties. If there is not, consideration is lacking, and there cannot be an enforceable contract.

To understand this concept, it may be helpful to consider some common examples where consideration is not present, as well as reviewing some examples where consideration clearly exists. First, this chapter will review situations where consideration is lacking. If a party makes a gratuitous promise, it will not be enforceable under traditional contract theory because, by the very definition of a gratuitous promise, there can be no consideration. That is because a gratuitous promise occurs when the person who makes the promise is looking for nothing in return. Often a gratuitous promise is made for a benevolent reason and not because the person making the promise wants to receive anything in exchange for the promise. If you see a homeless man on a street and you are moved to promise him $100 because of his situation, you would be making a gratuitous promise. You are not seeking anything in return from him, and you are making the promise only because you are a nice person. Since you are not trying to cause an exchange, there can be no consideration. (Please note that although a gratuitous promise is not enforceable under traditional contract theory, it may be enforceable in certain circumstances using the doctrine called promissory estoppel that will be addressed later in this chapter.)

Another common example where no consideration exists is when a person makes a promise motivated by an event that happened in the past, before the promise was ever made. There can be no consideration because, if a promise is made based on past events, the person making the promise clearly is not trying to cause an exchange. For consideration to be present, the exchange must be forward looking and that means the person making the promise is looking for something in the future. If you promise to pay your friend Karen $1,000 because she has helped you so many times in the past, that promise would not be enforceable under traditional contract theory because it lacks consideration. Why does it lack consideration? The motivation for it is based on an action that occurred in the past, and you were not looking for anything from Karen in exchange for your promise.

One last example of a promise lacking consideration is when an unsolicited action occurs. Obviously, if an action is unsolicited, it cannot be consideration because it lacks the required exchange. If you go to your neighbor's house and cut her grass without being asked, that is an unsolicited action. You will not be entitled to recoup any payment from your neighbor for the work you have completed, at least not under traditional contract theory, because you acted without a promise motivating you.

Compare the last few paragraph to several examples where there clearly is an exchange and consideration to support a promise. If Mark promises to sell Ellen a car for $20,000 in return for her promise to buy his car for $20,000, this is a promise supported by consideration. Mark is seeking an exchange from Ellen because he wants her to promise to buy his car. If she promises to buy the car, then there is an exchange of promises and consideration. Ellen's return promise is the consideration for Mark's promise to sell his car and Mark's promise to sell the car is the consideration for Ellen's promise to buy the car.

Another example of a contract with a different type of consideration might occur in a reward case. It is different because the person making the promise wants a performance and not a return promise. If Joe offers a $500 reward to Bill for the return of Joe's lost dog, he is trying to cause an exchange. He wants Bill to search for and bring him the lost dog and, if he does, Joe will pay him $500. When Bill returns the lost dog to Joe, his performance was what Joe was seeking. This is the consideration for Joe's promise to pay the reward of $500.

Although the requirements for an enforceable contract under traditional contract theory have been presented in very simplistic terms, it should be apparent that there are three main concepts involved. They are offer, acceptance, and consideration. Within each concept there are a multitude of potential issues, and this chapter has only touched on a few of those.

IV.   CONTRACT FORMATION AS GOVERNED BY THE UCC

Contract formation is much simpler for contracts governed by Article Two of the UCC than those ruled by the common law. Remember that Article Two only applies to contracts for the sale of goods. Under Article Two of the UCC, an offer and acceptance do not have to exactly match. This is very different from common law because of the mirror image rule. Under the common law, if a party wants a return promise and does not receive it, the mirror image rule would apply and there would be no contract. The UCC abolished the mirror image rule. Instead, it looks at whether the parties intended to contract. If a court finds an intent to contract between the parties, it likely will save the deal and find a contract without worrying about whether the parties jumped through the proper hoops. Even a non-conforming tender may qualify as an acceptance under the UCC in certain situations. If I order 200 computers and the buyer only sends me 175, the shipment may still be an acceptance under Article Two, subject to a few limitations. It would not be an acceptance under the common law because of the mirror image rule.

The more difficult question under Article Two is how to determine the actual terms of the contract when the offer and acceptance contain different terms. In commercial deals, it is common for buyers and sellers to use their own preprinted forms, and often these forms have terms that are exactly the opposite of each other. A seller's form will attempt to relieve a seller of liability for defective goods, and a buyer's form will attempt to make the seller liable for everything legally possible under the UCC, especially consequential damages, a concept that will be discussed later in this chapter. Consequently, when parties governed by Article Two enter contracts by sending forms back and forth, the courts often have to determine what terms will control the contract. A controversial section of Article Two, Section 2-207, deals with this "battle of the forms," and it has a complicated method for determining which terms will become part of a contract. Explaining the nuances of section 2-207 is beyond the scope of this chapter; however, you need to know the section exists and will apply instead of the mirror image rule.

V. DETERMINING THE CONTENT AND MEANING OF A CONTRACT

The next significant areas of contract law, after contract formation, center around the questions of what performance the contract requires and whether that performance has taken place. Before a court can determine whether a party is performing the contract properly, it must first decide what performance the contract actually mandates. This requires understanding three different contract concepts. They are interpretation, filling the gaps, and, if the contract has been reduced to writing, the parol evidence rule.

A.   Interpretation

Courts use the process of interpretation when there are terms or clauses in a contract that are not clear, and clarity is necessary to resolve an issue about performance between the parties. This requires a court to determine what the parties intended when they used certain words in the contract. The court will only interpret terms that are ambiguous. An ambiguous term is one that is susceptible to more than one meaning. If a term is not ambiguous, a court will use the unambiguous term in the contract. Depending on the jurisdiction, a court may interpret ambiguous terms by reading only the contract, or, in addition to reading the contract, the court may also consider the surrounding evidence and circumstances when deciding whether a term is ambiguous.

To understand this principle, it is helpful to review a hypothetical situation. If a contract calls for the sale of 300 bolts of "dark" cloth, a problem may arise when the seller delivers bolts of black, dark blue, dark gray, or even brown cloth. If the buyer was expecting all black cloth, she or he will not want to accept any other colored cloth. The resolution of this issue will depend on how a court interprets the term "dark" and that turns on the question of what the parties intended when they contracted. Regardless of what jurisdiction decides this issue, a court is likely to find that the term "dark" is ambiguous because it is susceptible to many different meanings. After determining that the term "dark" is ambiguous, the court will review all of the circumstances when the contract was negotiated in an effort to decide what the parties intended when they used that term.

In the business world, the court often will consider trade usage or how the parties actually performed the contract. If members of the trade define "dark" as black, then there is a good argument that the contract required black cloth. Alternatively, if the parties had performed the contract for six months with deliveries every month and each delivery of cloth was dark gray, with no objection from the buyer, that evidence would support an interpretation that the term "dark" meant dark gray. The court will consider whether either party had actual knowledge or should have known how the other party interpreted the term at the time they entered the contract. This consideration may include whether either or both parties should be bound by trade usage. If the buyer can show that the parties actually talked about only sending dark brown cloth during negotiations, then the term may be interpreted to mean only dark brown cloth and not any other color. You should see from this example that interpretation is necessary in many contracts because attorneys and parties do not and cannot always spell out precisely the meaning they intended for all of the terms of the contract.

B.   Filling the Gaps

In addition to interpreting any terms in the contract, the court may need to "fill the gaps." This is where a court reviews a contract to determine whether the parties omitted terms in the contract that need to be supplied to resolve a dispute between the parties. This is accomplished by a process called implication. That means that a court adds a term that is not written in the contract and was not discussed by the parties when they negotiated the contract. It does this by looking at notions of fairness, justice, and whether the parties' expectations require the court to imply a term into the contract. One common term that is implied in every contract is a term that requires the parties to act in good faith when performing the contract. A failure to treat the other contracting party in good faith may, in some circumstances, be a violation of a party's implied promise to use good faith and fair dealing. Other types of terms that may be implied in a contract have to do with the behavior of the parties. These may include a requirement to use best efforts when performing the contract or to give a reasonable amount of notice before terminating a contract.

C.   UCC as a Gap Filler

Article Two contains a series of default terms that fill gaps in a contract. With a few limited exceptions, parties may negotiate different terms instead of relying on Article Two; however, many parties simply use the gap fillers. One example is warranties. Warranties are simply promises, statements of facts about the goods, or implied promises about goods in a contract.

If actual promises are made, Article Two provides for an express warranty to become part of a contract, as long as the promise was a part of the basis of the bargain. If a car salesman tells a buyer that a certain car will get thirty-five miles per gallon, that statement may become an express warranty because it is a statement of fact about the car, and the buyer may partly rely on the statement when making the decision to purchase the car. Article Two also contains two other warranties of quality that may become part of a contract, even though a seller makes no express promises about the goods. They are the implied warranty of merchantability and the implied warranty of fitness for a particular purpose.

The implied warranty of merchantability automatically attaches to every sale of a good that is made by a merchant who deals in goods of the kind sold. If you buy a computer from a computer store or a television from a television store, this warranty will be implied in the contract unless the seller effectively disclaims it. This warranty promises, in addition to other things, that the goods will be fit for their ordinary purpose and will be of an average quality that would be expected in the trade. If you purchase a new Apple computer from an Apple store for $2,000, that sale will be governed by Article Two of the UCC and the implied warranty of merchantability would attach to the sale. If the computer fails to work after a week, it is no longer fit for its ordinary purpose and the seller has breached the implied warranty of merchantability. There are a variety of remedies available for the buyer in this situation depending on the severity of the breach and the type of contract.

The second type of implied warranty that may attach to a sale of goods is the implied warranty of fitness for a particular purpose. It is not as common as the warranty of merchantability. It is most often seen in transactions between businesses where one business needs equipment or a good for a specific purpose, so the business seeks the expert advice of the seller. The fitness warranty requires that the seller know about the particular purpose of the buyer, that the seller know the buyer is relying on the seller's skill or judgment, and that the buyer actually rely on the seller's skill or judgment when making the purchase.

Consider Steve, a veterinarian, who goes to a store that sells special diagnostic machines for sick animals and tells the seller that he wants to buy an MRI machine that may be used for both cats and dogs. The seller shows Steve a machine specifically for that purpose, tells him how it will work for his purposes, and after that conversation Steve buys the diagnostic equipment. That good is sold with an implied warranty of fitness for a particular purpose. The substance of the warranty is that the equipment will be satisfactory to diagnose both dogs and cats. The fitness warranty is sometimes confused with the merchantability warranty. The merchantability warranty only applies to the ordinary purpose of the goods as opposed to any specific purpose the buyer may need it for. If the equipment works perfectly well for dogs but not for cats because of the way it was designed, the fitness warranty would be breached; however, the implied warranty of merchantability would not be breached because the MRI was still fit for its ordinary purpose of diagnosing dogs.

As stated earlier, it is important to keep in mind that Article Two is a series of default rules. That means the terms will become part of the contract unless the parties have negotiated a different term. The implied warranties may be disclaimed by a seller in a number of ways. Although it is not appropriate to discuss the intricacies of how that is accomplished, you should know that a seller has the ability to negotiate out of most of the default rules. One rule that a party may not change is the rule on unconscionability that is discussed later in this chapter.

D.   The Parol Evidence Rule

One other concept that is important in determining what performance a contract requires is the parol evidence rule. Although it is named an evidence rule, it is not really a rule of evidence like you would see in a trial. It controls the ability of a party to add a term to a written contract in certain circumstances. The word "parol" is sometimes defined as oral, but the parol evidence rule applies to more than oral promises. It may apply to oral or written agreements or communications that occurred at the time of or before entering the contract. It does not apply to promises or communications made after the contract has been made. The reasoning behind the parol evidence rule is that once a contract is written, outside promises and agreements should only become part of the contract if it is clear that the parties intended that.

Although this brief summary cannot describe the complete analysis needed for applying the parol evidence rule, it is important to note that there are generally three issues that may present themselves when analyzing whether a term may be added by one of the parties to a written contract. They include whether the written document is integrated, whether it is a total or partial integration, and whether the evidence to be added contradicts or merely supplements the contract. These are, ultimately, all questions of the intent of the parties with respect to the writing. In modern practice, the parties who intend a written contract to contain all terms and agreements will include a "merger clause" in their contract. A typical merger clause states: "[t]his is the entire agreement of the parties; there are no other oral or written agreements." Although a merger clause is not conclusive in many jurisdictions, it may still be strong evidence that the parties did not intend to include any outside agreements or terms in the contract. Parties who do not include a merger clause in their contract run a greater risk that a court will add other promises that were made before the contract to the written agreement.

Both the common law and Article Two of the UCC enforce the parol evidence rule; however, a party has a better chance of adding a term if a contract is governed by Article Two because that law presumes that written contracts are more likely to have outside promises or terms that need to be added to the contract. Assume that Randy agrees to buy James' car, and they reduced their agreement to writing but did not include a merger clause. Randy wants out of the contract because he cannot obtain a loan to pay for the car at an interest rate lower than 7%. Randy claims that the parties orally agreed that he would not have to buy the car unless he could find financing at 6% or lower. That term is not in the written contract. A court would apply the parol evidence rule to decide whether the parties intended for that term to be included in the contract. Because there is no merger clause and this contract would be governed by Article Two (a car is a good), there is a presumption that the term should be added to the contract. The court would need to consider evidence to determine what the parties actually intended when they contracted and whether the term contradicted the contract. Although there are a few exceptions for trade usage, course of dealing, and course of performance, if a term contradicts the written contract, it must be excluded.

E.   Express Conditions

A party may protect herself or himself from having to perform a contract unless some event occurs by employing the concept of an express condition. Express conditions allow a party to be excused from performing a promise unless or until a certain event happens. In the preceding example, Randy did not want to buy the car unless he obtained an interest rate of 6% or lower. He could have drafted the contract by writing that as an express condition in the contract. Then he would not have to buy the car unless he obtained the interest rate he wanted. To do this, the contract would contain a term that says Randy promises to buy the car only on the express condition that he obtain an interest rate of 6% or lower. In contract terms, that means that Randy's duty to buy the car (a duty is created by a promise) does not have to be performed until the express condition (the event of obtaining a loan at a certain interest rate or lower) occurs. An express condition requires strict compliance. If it is not met, the promise does not have to be performed.

VI. PERFORMANCE OF THE CONTRACT

A.   Dependent Promises

Before moving to the question of breach, a court may have to make one other determination, and that is whether promises in a contract are dependent or independent. A breach of an independent promise will have different consequences than a breach of a dependent promise. As a general rule, promises in a contract are presumed to be dependent. That means each party's promises in a contract are dependent on the other party's promises. If one party does not perform, the other party will be excused from performing his or her part of the contract as a result of the dependent promise. When performance is actually due depends, in part, on the type of contract. The nature of some contracts requires that performances occur at or about the same time, such as the closing of a sale of a house. In other contracts, one party has to go first before the other party's duty to perform will arise, such as in a contract to build a house.

Consider a contract to build a house. I promise to build a house for you in exchange for your promise to pay me $350,000. A presumption that those promises are dependent means that my promise to build the house is dependent on your promise to pay $350,000 and your promise is dependent on my promise to build the house. If I do not build the house, you do not have to pay the $350,000 because our promises were dependent on each other. This is an example of a contract where one party must perform first.

Now, put the concepts of dependent promises and express condition together. If the contract also said you will buy and pay for the house on the express condition that you are able to sell your house by June 1 and you do not sell your house by June 1, your promise to buy is excused. It is excused because the condition never occurs. This is true even if the house is built.

From the previous illustrations, you should see that dependent promises and express conditions may reach the same result of excusing performance. Dependent promises in a contract are not the same as express conditions. Dependent promises do not require strict compliance and express conditions do. The amount of performance actually required of dependent promises will be addressed in the next section. The difference is very important because it allowed the common law to develop concepts that permit a party to be in breach and yet still collect some compensation from the non-breaching party.

In addition to dependent promises and express conditions, a contract may also contain an independent promise. Although it is rare to see an independent promise in a contract, this does not mean that there are no independent promises. If a party desires an independent promise in a contract, he or she needs to be very clear that this is what the parties intended because of the consequences of this type of term. If a promise in a contract is independent, it has to be performed even if the other promises are broken. Thus, if my promise to sell you a computer is independent of your promise to pay and I do not deliver the computer to you, you still have to pay. Because that is not usually what the parties intend, there is a presumption that promises are dependent.

The consequences of dependent promises, independent promises, and express conditions are significant because they may put a party in a difficult situation known as "forfeiture." In forfeiture, a breaching party may lose any money she or he spent attempting to perform the contract. For example, I promise to employ you for one month for $10,000, if you promise to work for me for the entire month. In return, you promise to work for one month. After two weeks, you quit. Because the promises are dependent, I do not have to pay you because you did not complete performance of the contract. That would put you in forfeiture, which means that you lose any time and money you put into the job. Change the contract and use an express condition. I promise to employ you for one month, only this time you and I agree that I will pay you only on the express condition that I sell my house by the end of that month. If you work the full month and I do not sell my house, you forfeit any right to be paid by me because my promise to pay you was expressly conditioned on the sale of my house.

You should see from the preceding examples that forfeiture may cause significant losses for a breaching party or for a party who agreed to allow performance to be excused if an express condition did not happen. Because of the harshness of forfeiture, several doctrines developed over the years to alleviate that harshness. Three that this chapter will focus on are substantial performance, divisibility, and restitution. These doctrines apply to dependent promises in contracts, but they do not pertain to express conditions. Although the law demands strict compliance with express conditions, it does not do so with dependent promises in contracts.

B.   Substantial Performance

Absent an express condition, a party who breaches a contract, in certain situations, may be compensated for performance even if he or she only substantially performs the contract. The doctrine of substantial performance rests on the idea that the non-breaching party received a significant amount of performance that was a benefit before the breach occurred. And, the injured party can be compensated for the injury caused by not completing performance. This doctrine is commonly used in construction contracts, although it may be used in analyzing other contracts, except for those governed by the UCC. There is no bright line rule as to how much performance is necessary before there will be substantial performance. Instead, a court will weigh a number of different factors before making this determination. They include whether the injured party essentially received the benefit of the bargain in the contract, how serious forfeiture will be if a court does not employ the doctrine of substantial performance, the innocent behavior of the breaching party, and how much of the contract has been performed.

To see how courts apply this doctrine, consider an example where you contract with Sharra Construction Company to build a house for you. The contract includes the basic plans, a time table for completion, and a price of $350,000. What happens if the house is built except for a few minor problems, such as the cabinets in the kitchen and the bathrooms are not completed? If a court cannot apply the doctrine of substantial performance because the promises are presumed to be dependent, then when the house is not built properly, you do not have to pay. That puts Sharra Construction Company in forfeiture and this will cause it to suffer a significant loss. If, however, Sharra Construction had substantially performed the contract, it could collect the amount due on the contract minus any damages caused by the breach. Because the breach in our example was very minor, forfeiture would cause a significant loss, and the injured party can be adequately compensated for the breach, it appears that Sharra substantially performed the contract. Of course, there is much more to this analysis, but in this brief overview, it is not appropriate to discuss all of the related issues. What is important to understand is that not all promises must be completely performed before payment will be due as long as they were dependent promises.

Two other doctrines that may help a breaching party avoid forfeiture are divisibility and restitution for a defaulting plaintiff. Both of these concepts are based on the same theory as substantial performance. The theory is that a non-breaching party who has received a benefit should be required to pay for that benefit, even if there is no complete or substantial performance.

C.   Divisibility

Generally, the law regards a contract as "entire." In other words, a promise to pay is based on receiving an entire and complete performance. There are some contracts, however, that may be divided easily by performance due and consideration to be paid for that performance. That type of contract may be divisible and that allows a party to collect some of the money that the injured party had promised to pay, even if there is a breach of contract. It depends on whether the parties intended for separate performances to be paid for by a corresponding consideration.

For example, I contract to build four houses and you agree to pay $350,000 for each house, with a grand total for the contract of $1,400,000. I build only one house and then I breach by refusing to build the other three houses. Although substantial performance would not apply because there has not been a sufficient amount of performance, the doctrine of divisibility may offer some relief from forfeiture. In this instance, it would be fair to apportion the $350,000 to the performance of building one house. It is easy to do that because the contract provided a separate consideration for each house and therefore the contract is divisible. As long as the injured party can benefit from one completed house, it seems equitable to hold the contract divisible and allow the breaching party to collect on the performance that benefited the injured party. If the doctrine of divisibility did not exist and forfeiture was applied instead, the breaching party may not be entitled to recover any money. Even though the breaching party recovers some money using the doctrine of divisibility, the injured party may still collect damages for the failure to build the other houses.

D.   Restitution for Defaulting Plaintiff

The last doctrine that may help a breaching party recover a portion of the money owed on a contract is restitution. The doctrine of restitution encompasses a multitude of different ideas and crosses over many subject areas. It is not possible to do justice to the entire doctrine in this short chapter; however, it bears mentioning because it may help a breaching party recover money that would otherwise be forfeited due to a breach. Some jurisdictions will allow a defaulting plaintiff to recover under restitution and recover if the injured party actually received a benefit from the breaching party's performance. Restitution is based on the doctrine of unjust enrichment. That doctrine states that when a party is enriched and it is unjust to allow that party to retain the benefit without paying for it, the court may award damages based on restitution.

Imagine a contract where Stella promises to work for one month in return for a promise by the employer to pay her $8,000. The contract provides that the employee will not be paid until the end of the month. If the Stella breaches the contract by quitting her job after one week, and no labor statutes exist that would complicate the issues, a court may apply restitution to require the employer to pay the employee for the one week of work, provided that the employer received a benefit from that one week of work. Note that neither substantial performance or divisibility would apply to this contract. Factors that a court may consider when determining whether to allow restitution include the reasons for breaching and the actual benefit received. Add the following facts to our previous example: the employee left under the mistaken notion that she would not breach her contract and the employer received a definite benefit because she really needed a skilled employee for that week. Without Stella's work, the employer would have breached a contract with another company. In that scenario it seems unjust for the employer to retain that benefit without having to pay Stella, so a court may order the employer to pay restitution. If the employer can show that he or she was damaged by Stella's breach, the employer may be compensated for that injury.

E.   Performance Under Article Two of the UCC

An important area of difference between Article Two of the UCC and the common law is how demanding the law is in relation to the type of performance required by a contract. Recall that under the common law, the courts do not always require 100% strict performance of a contract before a party may collect on a contract. Instead, as was just discussed, the law developed measures to allow parties to avoid forfeiture in certain situations even though performance had been less that what was required by the contract. The law permitted this because the non-breaching party received a benefit from the breached contract. One of these measures, the doctrine of substantial performance, is not followed in the UCC. Article Two adopted the perfect tender rule for contracts that will be completed with only one performance. This rule requires that performance comply perfectly with the requirements of the contract or the buyer may reject the goods and avoid the contract. As just mentioned, it only applies to contracts that call for a single performance, as opposed to a contract that will be completed in installments or a number of separate deliveries.

An installment contract has a different standard for breach that is similar to a material breach analysis, which this chapter discusses later. These types of contracts require that defective performance substantially impair the value of an installment and ultimately the whole contract before a buyer may cancel the contract. It also requires that, except in a few situations, a seller be given a right to cure the defect. If cure is possible, then a buyer will not have the ability to reject the goods and avoid the contract.

The perfect tender rule only applies when goods are first tendered to the buyer. If the buyer does not reject the goods when delivered, an acceptance occurs. Once there is an acceptance, it is more difficult for a buyer to avoid a contract under the UCC. Even if a buyer cannot avoid a contract, this does not mean that he or she loses the right to sue for defects in the goods. A buyer may, however, prefer to avoid the contract completely instead of bothering with a lawsuit. In that case, because there was an acceptance, the buyer must revoke his or her acceptance. In a case of revocation, the standard is more difficult than it is under the perfect tender rule. A buyer may only revoke an acceptance under certain conditions that are similar to material breach. There are other specific requirements before a revocation will be effective, including that it must occur within a reasonable time and before there has been any substantial change in the goods.

VII. BREACH

The previous discussion reviewed possible responses for a breaching party who needs to avoid forfeiture. An important consideration in this analysis requires a discussion of what actually constitutes a breach and what are the acceptable responses by the injured party.

A breach occurs when one party fails to perform her or his promise. This should be distinguished from the failure of a condition. A failure of condition excuses performance but it does not cause a breach. That is important, because a breach is needed to give rise to a claim for damages. How should or may the other party respond to a breach? May the injured party cancel the contract and walk away from the deal? These questions require an analysis of what type of breach has occurred. The first issue is whether the breach is material or insignificant. If the breach is insignificant, an injured party does not have a right to cancel the contract. Instead, the only remedy available is for the non-breaching party to continue performance and sue the other party for any damages caused by the insignificant breach. If the injured party wrongfully cancels the contract as a result of the insignificant breach, then she or he will be in breach for repudiating the contract. A cancellation of a contract is called a "repudiation."

When a breach occurs, the first issue is how serious or significant is the breach? If the breach is serious enough, it may be a material breach. If the breach is not material, the injured party must continue with the contract, although he or she still has the right to sue for damages for the insignificant breach. Even a material breach may not give an injured party the right to cancel the contract immediately and walk away from a deal. Except in very serious and limited situations, an injured party may only suspend performance after a material breach happens and he or she must give the breaching party the right to cure the material breach. If the breach is so serious that it would not be reasonable to require an opportunity to cure, then the injured party may cancel the contract instead of waiting for the breach to be cured. The problem occurs if the injured party made a mistake and should have given the breaching party the right to cure but failed to do so. In that case, cancellation of the contract would be a wrongful repudiation of the contact and the originally injured party has now committed a material breach.

Consider an example where Smith contracts to build a house for Jones, and Smith breaches after building less than 30% of the house. Upon inspection, Jones determines that the work is so shoddy and inferior that no reasonable person would want the breaching party to cure the problems and continue with performance. In that situation, it may be permissible to cancel the contract and sue on the material breach. Absent something that serious, an injured party must give a breaching party a reasonable time to cure the breach before canceling the contract. If the breaching party cures, then the contract continues and the injured party may not cancel the contract, although he or she still retains the right to sue for the breach that occurred. Alternatively, if the breaching party does not cure within a reasonable amount of time, the injured party may cancel the contact and sue for the breach. Additionally, after a material breach occurs, the injured party may suspend his or her performance while waiting for the breaching party to cure.

One other doctrine that needs to be mentioned is anticipatory repudiation. So far, the examples have illustrated canceling a contract after a breach occurs. There may also be instances when a breach occurs before performance is due. This is called an anticipatory repudiation. An example of this doctrine is when a party absolutely repudiates a contract and refuses to perform a month before performance is scheduled to start. It is important to remember when reading these rules that parties are free to negotiate different terms to govern their contract, subject to limitations imposed by the doctrine of unconscionability.

VIII.   EXCUSE

There may be occasions when a party does not perform but the breach is excused, so the breaching party does not have to pay damages. This chapter will review three concepts that may excuse a breaching party from performing a contract and having to pay damages. They are impracticability, frustration of purpose, and mutual mistake. The common thread in these doctrines is that the performance that was bargained for has changed in a way that neither party anticipated at the time he or she entered the contract. The concepts of impracticability and frustration of purpose have a common element of an unexpected event happening caused by a change in circumstances so severe that it justifies allowing a party not to perform his or her part of the contract. All three doctrines relieve a breaching party from having to pay damages.

A.   Impracticability

Impracticability, historically known as impossibility, excuses a party from performing a contract when performance has become impracticable. The first case to recognize this doctrine illustrates the concept very well. In that case, the owner of a concert hall agreed to lease the hall to a promoter so it could be used for a concert in exchange for rent. The concert hall burned before the day of the concert. The owner was sued for breach because the building was not available as promised. Because the concert hall burned through no fault of either party, performance became impossible and the breach of not renting the concert hall was excused.

Contemporary doctrine does not require the complete impossibility of performance. It is enough if performance has become impracticable and that impracticability was caused by a contingency that was not a risk assumed by the breaching party. A party assumes certain risks when agreeing to a contract, so not all performances that have become impracticable will be excused. Consider a contract to manufacture a specific type of pesticide to be used in gardening. The manufacturer requires the use of a chemical that the United States has banned because of environmental problems and the manufacturer knew that when it agreed to the contract. It was hoping the regulation would be changed before its performance was due, but it was not. Because the chemical cannot be used in the United States, the pesticide cannot be manufactured. The failure to obtain that chemical made performance impracticable, but it will not excuse performance. This is because the manufacturer assumed the risk, since it knew about the problem with the chemical at the time it entered the contract. If the manufacturer, however, had contracted before the ban on the chemical and if the manufacturer had no way of knowing that the United States would issue such a ban, a breach for non-performance may be excused using the doctrine of impracticability. An unexpected event occurred when the United States banned the use of the chemical. That event made performance impracticable because the manufacturer could not produce the pesticide legally, and it did not assume the risk because it had no knowledge that this chemical might be banned.

Many parties have attempted to use the doctrine of impracticability because the performance has become too expensive for them to perform. Although there is no blanket rule stating that a party cannot use the doctrine of impracticability in this situation, it is very very difficult to avoid a contract using the doctrine of impracticability simply because it has become very unprofitable to perform.

B.   Frustration of Purpose

Frustration of purpose essentially considers the same issues as impracticability, only from a different view point. The difference with frustration of purpose is that the only performance required under the contract is to pay, and payment may easily be made; it is not impracticable. Thus, this doctrine does not focus on whether the performance of payment is impracticable. Instead, it focuses on the purpose of the contract. Like impracticability, it is important to determine whether the party claiming excuse assumed the risk; if not, and all of the other elements of the doctrine are met, he or she may be excused, as long as the purpose of the contract was frustrated through no fault of the breaching party.

Another famous case from Great Britain illustrates this concept quite well. The events surrounding the contract occurred in 1902. Krell and Henry agreed to a written contract where Henry promised to rent a room in Krell's home during the daytime for two days. Krell and Henry expected that the flat where the rooms were to be rented would be on the coronation route of King Edward VII. Because of a serious illness of the King, the coronation procession was postponed. Consequently, Henry refused to pay rent, and Krell sued him. The court considered the defense of frustration of purpose. It determined that the doctrine required an inquiry of what the parties contracted for and whether that purpose could still be fulfilled by the contract. The court found that the purpose of the contract was to rent rooms to view the coronation procession. The facts showed that the rooms were advertised for that purpose and that Henry discussed this purpose with Krell's housekeeper at the apartment. Further, the rooms were only rented for the daytime, not the evening, and only on the days of the expected procession. The court found that the purpose of the contract was frustrated because the coronation parade could not be held on the days that the rooms were to be rented. Henry was excused from paying rent. Note that his performance was certainly possible, because all Henry needed to do to perform was to pay rent, yet that was not important to the court. Instead, the court focused on what performance both parties expected from the contract. That performance was frustrated, and there was no evidence that Henry assumed the risk of the coronation process being postponed.

C. Mutual Mistake

Mutual mistake is another way for a party to be excused from a breach of contract. A party uses the doctrine of mutual mistake when he or she is unable to perform due to a mistaken fact that neither party took into consideration at the time of contracting. Although unilateral mistake may also offer an excuse for a failure to perform, it is more problematic than mutual mistake where both parties were operating under a faulty assumption, and this chapter will not cover it. A mutual mistake occurs when, at the time of contracting, both parties shared an erroneous assumption concerning a fact. The mistaken fact must be a basic assumption on which the contract was made, and it must be so fundamental that a court can conclude that it will have a material affect on the performances required by the contract. The basic issue is whether the mistake essentially deprives one party of the performance he or she thought he or she acquired from the contract. Lastly, as with other concepts of excuse, the party attempting to get out of the contract must not have assumed a greater risk.

Consider a contract to sell land where the buyer intends to use the land for a specific purpose, such as building a golf course and club. At the time of contracting, the buyer and seller determined that the zoning laws would cause no obstacle for that specific use. Unfortunately unbeknown to the buyer and seller, the zoning laws were changed in a way that would not permit the buyer to use the property as intended. The buyer wants to be excused from performance on the theory of mutual mistake. Should a court permit the buyer to get out of the deal? First, there is a mutual mistake that goes to the basic assumption on which both parties made the contract. The basic assumption at the time of contract was that the zoning ordinances would not prohibit the buyer's desired use of the land. The mutual mistake had a material affect on the performance of the contract, because the buyer could not use the property and was not in a position to resell it. Further, it is less onerous for the seller to keep the property and sell it than to force the buyer to try to resell. One last question to consider is whether the buyer bore the risk of this mistake. The answer is no, because both the buyer and seller had investigated the zoning laws and had been told that the use would not be a problem. Therefore, the buyer should be excused from performing the contract on the basis of mutual mistake.

IX. REMEDIES

A. Common Law Remedies

If a party has not fully or properly performed and has not been excused from non-performance, the other party may sue for money damages or specific performance. As a general rule, money damages are the remedy of choice for a breach of contract. Specific performance, where a court requires a party to actually complete his or her performance, is an extraordinary remedy, and United States courts do not prefer it. This is quite different from civil law countries, where courts routinely allow specific performance as a remedy. In the U.S., specific performance may only be ordered in exceptional circumstances, where money damages will not adequately compensate the injured party. Land sales and unique goods are often considered appropriate for the remedy of specific performance. Examples of unique goods that may qualify for the remedy of specific performance are a family heirloom or a painting by a famous painter such as Vincent Van Gogh. Further, goods that are unique by definition are not fungible, so money will not allow a party to simply buy a replacement. That means the normal remedy of money damages would not be appropriate.

There are three types of money damages typically awarded in breach of contract disputes. They are expectation, reliance, and restitution damages. Courts prefer to give an injured party his or her expectation interest. This means the court attempts to put the injured party in the same place as if the contract had been performed. For example, imagine a situation where Sarah buys a car from Sam Motors for $20,000. The contract comes with various warranties, including an implied warranty of merchantability. After using the car for one month, the car breaks down due to a defective water pump. How can Sarah obtain her expectation interest in the contract if she sues Sam Motors? If a court wanted to put her in the same position as if the contract had been fulfilled with no defective performance, her damages should be the cost to repair or replace the defective water pump. Another example is where you contract to paint your neighbor's garage, and your neighbor agrees to pay you $800. Assume it would have cost you $500 in time and supplies to paint the building, and your neighbor breaches before you have taken any action on the contract. You have not purchased any supplies or done any work at all. In that case, your expectation interest would be the $300 profit that you expected to make from the contract. There are many more factors to consider on this topic, but this chapter will not explore the multitude of complex issues involved when a party attempts to obtain his or her expectation interest.

A party may have difficulty proving the amount of his or her expectation interest for a variety of reasons. If that happens, there are other options available to the injured party, although they may provide a smaller recovery. Reliance damages focus on the non-breaching party and try to put that party in the position that he or she would have been in if the contract had never been made. This doctrine can be illustrated by an employment contract where a party lives in Miami, Florida, and contracts to work for a year in New York City in exchange for a salary of $200,000. In preparation for that contract, the employee hires a moving service and pays other out-of-pocket expenses totaling $5,000. The employer breaches the contract. If the employee cannot collect expectation damages for any reason, he or she may still be eligible to recover reliance damages. Reliance damages in this example would be $5,000 — the amount of money spent by the employee in reliance on the contract. That amount would put the employee in the same position as if the contract had never been made.

The last measure of damages that may be available to an injured party is restitution damages. Restitution changes the focus from the injured party to the breaching party and attempts to put the breaching party in the position she or he would have been in if the contract had never happened. For example, imagine a contract to buy a house where a buyer agrees to buy a home for $300,000, and the seller agrees to sell the home and provide good title. The buyer also gives the seller a down payment of $1,000 at the time of contract. The seller later breaches by refusing to sell the house. Assume that the buyer no longer wants the home, so he or she would not want to ask a court for specific performance. Instead, the buyer simply wants restitution damages. Restitution damages in this example would be the $1,000 that the seller had received from the buyer as a down payment. When the court requires the seller to return the $1,000 to the buyer, the court puts the seller, the breaching party, in the same place as if the contract had never been made.

A discussion of damages must also include the concept of consequential damages. Consequential damages are losses that occur due to a breach of contract, other than those arising directly from the breach, that are foreseeable at the time the parties entered the contract. For example, James buys a new space heater from the Heater Store, takes it home, plugs it in, and goes to sleep. The heater is defective and, when it malfunctions, it causes his house to burn to the ground. Assuming that James could prove that the defective heater caused the fire, he should be able to collect consequential damages resulting from the fire that were caused by the defect. If James is not allowed to collect consequential damages, the only damages he could collect would be the cost to replace the heater and those likely would be minimal. It is foreseeable, however, that a defective space heater could cause a house fire, so the buyer should also be able to collect the consequential damages caused by the fire in this example. Two major limitations on consequential damages are that they must be caused by the breach of contract, and they have to be foreseeable to the breaching party at the time of contract. This doctrine does not inquire whether the breach was foreseeable. Instead, the question is whether, at the time of contract, assuming that a breach would occur, it is foreseeable to the breaching party that these other damages may occur. For example, go back to the heater hypothetical. Under those facts, what would happen if the damages incurred due to the fire were that James lost a big contract because he could not make it to the plane that was supposed to take him to the contract signing? Those damages would be too remote and not foreseeable, so the seller would not be responsible for them as consequential damages.

B.   Remedies Under Article Two of the UCC

In addition to warranties, other sections of Article Two that have been very influential in the area of contracts are the sections on remedies. There are separate remedy sections for buyers and sellers, and each section has a formula for computing damages. Although an injured party is not required to choose any particular remedy, the remedies that will most likely give a party his or her expectation interest are the sections on substitute transactions. After a breach by the seller, a buyer is encouraged to find replacement goods on the open market and sue for the difference in the two contracts. That means an injured buyer would contract to buy the same or similar goods after a breach by the seller. This is called "cover." Likewise, a seller will want to try to resell the goods from a breached contract to another buyer and collect the difference between the two contracts from the breaching buyer. If an injured party is not able to find a substitute transaction, Article Two has remedy sections that allow the injured party to recover based on a hypothetical substitute transaction determined by the market price for the goods.

Article Two also allows for specific performance in appropriate cases. Two other areas that changed the common law are the provisions permitting recovery of incidental and consequential damages. A party may collect incidental damages, which usually are damages resulting from a party's breach that include reasonable expenses incident to the delay or breach, such as expenses related to entering a substitute transaction, transportation and care of the goods, or similar types of damages. Additionally, sellers are not permitted to collect consequential damages.

Although some commentators believe this was just a drafting glitch, the reasoning behind the rule is that it is not usually foreseeable for sellers to have consequential damages, because sellers usually are simply expecting to be paid.

X. POLICING THE CONTRACT AND THE PRE-EXISTING DUTY RULE

Another important area of contract is sometimes referred to as "policing" the contract. Policing concepts allow a party to escape liability from a contract that appears to be perfectly valid and has no excuse for non-performance. They often deal with such issues as overreaching on the part of one party to the contract, unfairness, age, or competence. An older doctrine used by the courts to essentially do the same thing and police the contract deals with the concept of consideration and is called the pre-existing duty rule.

A. Policing When Specific Performance is the Remedy

A court may "police" a contract for fairness if the non-breaching party requests the remedy of specific performance. Recall that specific performance is an extraordinary remedy and not routinely granted. When there is a request for specific performance, it permits a court to use certain equitable rules before deciding whether to allow that remedy, because a request for that remedy goes to a court of equity instead of a court of law, which decides claims for money damages. Although a court will not normally consider the "adequacy of the consideration" (this refers to the fairness of the exchange), it may do so when a party requests specific performance. A common maxim states that a party requesting specific performance must come into court "with clean hands." This is often referred to as the "clean hands doctrine," and it allows a court of equity to look more closely (than would happen in a court of law) at the behavior of the parties and the substance of the exchange.

Consider a contract to purchase land where the seller refuses to perform. If the buyer sues for specific performance — that means to force the seller to actually sell the land — what remedy should the court order? Because the contract is for the sale of land, specific performance would normally be an appropriate remedy; however, the court may consider other pertinent facts when determining whether to grant specific performance. Now, imagine that the buyer is a sophisticated businesswoman who took advantage of an unsophisticated seller and got her to agree to sell her house for $50,000, when in fact it was really worth $500,000. The buyer knew the property was worth a lot of money, and she knew that her seller likely would not know that fact, and that the seller was desperate for money. When the seller refuses to sell the house after discovering the unfair price, the buyer sues for specific performance. Although this would normally be an appropriate case for specific performance because it involves land, the court could protect the seller by refusing to allow specific performance due to the inadequacy of the consideration and the disparity of bargaining power between the parties. The consideration is inadequate because of the $450,000 price difference. Additionally, it seems even more inequitable because the buyer knowingly took advantage of the seller. This does not mean that the buyer may not sue for money damages; it just means that she may not obtain specific performance.

B.   Pre-existing Duty Rule

Consideration doctrine has often been used in situations where pressure on a party to a contract was perceived to be excessive. That is how the pre-existing duty rule developed. According to the rule, after parties have contracted, one party may not force the other party to do more than was expected for the same consideration that was agreed upon in the original contract. For example, Hans and Bob agree that Hans will paint Bob's house for $1,500. Hans later refuses to paint the house unless Bob agrees to pay him an extra $500 for a total of $2,000, even though he will be doing exactly the same amount of work as agreed to in the original contract. Bob should be able to enforce the original contract, because Hans has a pre-existing duty to paint the house for the agreed amount. He cannot force Bob to pay more money unless performance is changed on both sides. For example, if Hans said that he would agree to paint Bob's garage, in addition to his house if Bob agreed to pay him an extra $500, and Bob agreed to pay $2,000, the second contract should be enforceable. It is not subject to the defense of pre-existing duty, because both parties changed their obligations. Bob agreed to pay an extra $500, and Hans agreed to do the extra work of painting the garage.

In addition to the two topics just addressed, there are traditional policing mechanisms which include duress, economic duress, misrepresentation, unconscionability, and public policy. Each doctrine may allow a party to escape from what appears to be a perfectly valid contract because of some behavior that the courts have determined is bad enough that it will affect the contract.

C.   Duress

To escape liability from a contract using the doctrine of duress, a party must show that certain elements have been met. Duress considers the degree of coercion placed on a party when agreeing to a contract. To prove duress, it must be shown that an improper threat was made that caused a party to appear to assent to the contract. This cannot be a simple or minor threat such as "I will not speak to you for a day." It needs to be serious enough to justify agreement to a contract because of fear of the threat. It is a matter of degree as to how much compulsion was placed on a party by the threat. For example, a threat by Ellen to Frank that she will physically harm his children if he does not agree to sell his property to her would be a serious threat that would justify agreeing to a contract against his will. If a party contracts under the threat of duress, he or she can use duress as a defense if sued or bring an action to disaffirm the contract.

In recent times, courts have expanded the concept of duress to include "economic duress." This type of duress usually involves a threat to a party's business or livelihood, and the threat is generally that a party will breach a contract unless the other party assents to the demands of the party making the threat. In these situations, courts require that the threatened party first try to obtain the goods or services elsewhere before succumbing to the threat. Additionally, to be successful in a claim for economic duress, courts have held that an action for damages must not be sufficient. This means that specific performance would be an appropriate remedy for the injured party. Remember that specific performance is only ordered in situations where paying money damages will not be an adequate remedy.

Consider the following example: Sam is the president of a small business which manufactures and sells tractors. He contracts with Beta Corporation to buy the parts that he needs to complete the manufacture of the tractors. Sam also has a contract with Alpha Corporation to sell the completed tractors to them. Sam just started doing business with Alpha, and he hopes to obtain many more contracts with them in the future. Alpha has indicated this will likely happen if the current contract goes well. Beta wants more money for the parts, so it refuses to sell the parts to Sam unless he agrees to a price increase in the original contract. If Sam does not agree to pay the extra money, he will breach his contract with Alpha. He is particularly worried about breaching his contract with Alpha because he anticipates obtaining more business from them. Sam searches for several weeks and determines that he cannot buy these goods anywhere else in the country, so he assents to the price increase. He should be able to claim economic duress to avoid paying the extra money to Beta. Note that the pre-existing duty rule may also help Sam avoid paying extra compensation to Alpha company because Alpha had a pre-existing duty to deliver the parts and nothing about their original performance has changed.

D.   Misrepresentation

Another policing concept is misrepresentation. It should be obvious that commitments that have been made based on the misrepresentation of the other contracting party may be avoided in many instances. Not all misrepresentations will be serious enough to allow a party to avoid a contract. It is sometimes difficult to discern whether a party is truly misrepresenting the facts or is simply stating a colorful or optimistic opinion. Historically, in United States sales law, the rule has been buyer beware or *caveat emptor*. Therefore, under the common law originally, if a person says nothing about a possible problem in a contract, he or she is better off than if he or she mentions something related to the contract. Although the general rule is buyer beware, courts have held that once a party discusses the facts related to a potential important fact in the contract — even if it is just a little bit — then that party is under a duty to disclose any relevant information about the subject. Some courts have held that buyer beware does not apply in all situations, and sellers should apprise buyers of any known material problems with the subject of the contract.

To state a case for misrepresentation, a number of elements must be alleged. The first is an assertion that is not in accord with the facts. In other words, it can be a statement about the facts surrounding the contract that is not exactly aligned with the truth. This may be a half-truth, as well as a blatant lie. Thus, if a seller gives a home buyer a report that shows no termite infestation in the home after the buyer has inquired about this fact, but removes a report that shows there were termites in past years, that would be an assertion not in accord with the facts which possibly could lead to liability for misrepresentation. Once a party gives information about a subject that is significant to the contract, he or she is obliged to give all of the information about the subject or face the possibility that a court may allow the other party to avoid the contract based on an allegation of misrepresentation.

Three more elements are necessary to prove misrepresentation. A party must also show that the assertion is either fraudulent or material, that the other party relied on it when agreeing to the contract, and that the reliance was justified. If the fact is not material, there is no misrepresentation. For example, in a contract to buy a house where the seller tells the buyer that the front steps are 100% marble when they are only 99% marble, that would be an assertion not in accord with the facts. It would be unlikely that a court would allow a party out of the contract based on that misrepresentation because that fact likely is not relevant to the contract. Even if the statement was material, if the buyer had done his or her own independent investigation and determined that the steps were not 100% marble, the buyer probably would not be able to later avoid the contract for misrepresentation because he or she did not rely on the seller's statement. The last element of misrepresentation requires that the reliance of the recipient must be justified. Consider the previous home sale example. If the seller stated that the steps were 100% marble and anyone could plainly see that they were wood, reliance would not be justified because the statement was obviously false. If a statement is obviously false or cannot be expected to be taken seriously, reliance is not justified, and there is no action for misrepresentation. There are a number of exceptions to this rule, but they are not covered in this brief overview. After a court finds misrepresentation, it may allow the recipient of the misrepresentation to avoid the contract and claim restitution for any money paid to the party making the misrepresentation.

E.   Unconscionability

Another important policing doctrine is unconscionability. Although this term is not easily defined, it usually involves one party who has superior bargaining power, as well as a contract that seems grossly unfair. A concept closely linked to unconscionability is an adhesion contract. This is where one party has no power to negotiate the terms of the contract. Instead, the contract is written with all of the terms expressly stated, and it has to be accepted as written; there is no room for negotiation. Adhesion contracts are economically useful because they may save both parties time and money, so there is no blanket rule against them. Just because they are permissible does not mean that a court will not scrutinize them for fairness. In fact, courts review adhesion contracts more critically to determine whether they are unconscionable.

There are two types of unconscionability — procedural and substantive. Generally, courts require that both types exist before allowing a party to avoid a contract based on this doctrine; however, there have been rare occasions where courts invalidated a contract based on only one type of unconscionability.

Procedural unconscionability involves the process of contracting or the behavior exhibited during contracting. The court considers the bargaining power of the parties and whether the stronger party pressured the other party into agreeing to the contract. The types of factors that courts may consider when determining whether there has been procedural unconscionability include age, education, ability to read, and economic circumstances, among other things. The court considers these factors in light of the bargaining process.

For substantive unconscionability, the court reviews the contract to determine whether it is grossly unfair. It may be just one term of the entire contract that is substantively unconscionable. Examples of such terms include grossly excessive prices or credit terms. Courts vary considerably in deciding these types of cases. One criticism of the doctrine is that it allows a judge to enforce contracts based on what he or she believes is morally correct. If a court determines that a contract is unconscionable, it has much leeway to decide how to deal with the problem. It may refuse to enforce the entire contract, it may refuse to enforce only the offending term or terms, or it may modify the contract to make it conscionable.

Imagine a situation where Sam, a traveling door-to-door salesman, goes to Sarah's home to attempt to sell her a computer. Although many states have specific statutes regulating door-to-door sales that might complicate the result, we will review the facts only in terms of a claim of unconscionability and without considering whether there are any specific statutes regulating door-to-door sales. Sam gains entry to Sarah's home, over her initial reluctance to allow him entry to her home, and notices immediately that she seems overwhelmed and distracted. As Sam talks to Sarah, he discovers that she is a single parent with three children who has just lost her job and is afraid that she will soon lose her home because her unemployment checks are not large enough to cover her mortgage and her daily living expenses. Sarah has three school-age children, and she tearfully tells Sam she is worried about them because of this situation. Sam appeals to Sarah's concern for her children and convinces her that her children will not do well in school unless they have a home computer. Sam tells her he has one that is a "great deal" for her and a steal at the price he is offering to her. Sam tells her it is a brand new top of the line computer that he will sell her for the low price of $2,000 and she could pay the price over three years for a nominal fee. Sarah wants Sam out of her house so, after some very heavy pressuring, she finally relents and agrees to buy the computer. He tells her that she is getting "a great deal." When the new computer arrives at Sarah's home she discovers that, although it is new and has never been used, it is four years old. She later learns that it is only worth about $300 on the market and her finance charges are over 28% per year. Sarah may have a chance to avoid the contract based on a claim of unconscionability. The procedural unconscionability would be due to the fact that Sam was in her home, knew about her dire circumstances, and used high pressure tactics to persuade her to agree to the sale. The potential substantive unconscionability is found in the terms of the contract. The mark up is astronomical, and the computer is out of date, although it is new and has not been used. Additionally, the interest rate is excessive. In this situation, a court may allow Sarah to completely escape liability under the contract, or a court could reform the contract to make it fairer and then enforce the modified contract.

F.   Public Policy

Another area where a court may interfere with a contract is if it is against public policy. There is a difference between a contract to do an illegal act and one that is against public policy. A party legally cannot contract to do an illegal act. A contract to have someone murdered would obviously be illegal and not enforceable. There also may be instances where a court refuses to enforce a contract based on public policy, even though the contract does not violate any law. The concept of public policy is not easily defined. The definition changes over time depending on the norms and social policies of the era. A court may define public policy based on its own sense of fairness, justice, and the acceptable behavior for the time.

For example, Patti agrees in her employment contract not to compete with her employer in the event that she leaves her current job. A court may look at the promise not to compete very strictly. A reasonable promise not to compete may be enforceable, whereas an unreasonable one may be void as against public policy, because public policy generally favors not restricting a person's ability to work for a living. If Patti is a veterinarian who agrees never to work as a veterinarian again anywhere in the United States for the next twenty-five years if she leaves her employment with the Animal Hospital, a court may find that contract to be overly broad and against public policy. If, however, the agreement only covered a short period of time and a small geographic area, a court may uphold the agreement as reasonable and therefore not against public policy. Another example of a contract that might be against public policy is where a mother agrees to give up her child's right to child support from the child's father in return for some benefit for herself, such as a new luxury car.

G.   Age

So far, the discussion has centered on policing the contract using doctrines that consider the behavior of the parties or the substance of the contract. There is another area of policing that focuses on the status or specific circumstances of a party to a contract. They include the age and mental capacity of the contracting parties.

The law has been concerned with the protection of minors for a long time, and the area of contracts is no exception. In the United States, minors do not have the capacity to contract, based on the reasoning that minors often need protection from themselves or others who may seek to take advantage of them. The age of majority for contracting purposes is usually eighteen, although that age may vary depending on the statutes in any given state. A juvenile who contracts may avoid that contract simply by raising age, or lack of capacity to contract, as a defense. One exception allows a juvenile to contract for "necessaries," although what qualifies as a "necessary" may vary depending upon local statute or interpretation by a court. Food, housing, and clothing have been found to fall within the exception, even though at least one court determined that housing was not a "necessary" for a minor who had a parent or guardian willing and able to provide housing. This policing mechanism is based solely on the status of being a minor. A court does not look further into the contract to determine whether the contract is fair. It may be a completely fair contract but that will not matter. As long as one party is a minor, that is sufficient to allow the minor out of the contract, even a very fair one.

H.   Mental Competency

The last area of policing concerns individuals who may avoid contracts due to mental incompetence. Two different tests exist to determine the competency of an individual to contract. The older cognitive test requires an individual to be so affected by his or her mental illness that she or he is rendered absolutely incompetent to comprehend and understand the nature of the transaction. Clearly, this is a very difficult standard to apply if a party wants to avoid a contract due to mental health issues. The cognitive test developed at a time when there was little understanding of the psychology of mental illness. It was largely based on old notions of mental illness grounded in the nineteenth century. Over the years, great strides have been made in understanding and treating mental illnesses, such that mental health professionals now understand that some individuals who appear perfectly rational may not be able to make a competent decision to contract due to mental illness. Because of this progress in the psychology field, a newer and more workable test developed. This modern test, sometimes referred to as the volitional test, allows a person to avoid a contract if she or he is suffering from a mental illness and he or she is unable to act in a reasonable manner in relation to the contract. The volitional test also requires that the other party must have reason to know of the mental illness. With either test, if all requirements are met, an incompetent person may be relieved of his or her duties in a contract.

XI. PROMISSORY ESTOPPEL

An alternative theory for recovery on a broken promise is Promissory Estoppel. So far, this chapter has reviewed the major requirements for liability under traditional contract theory. You will remember that an enforceable contract requires an offer, acceptance, and consideration. At a minimum, if those elements are not present, a party may not recover for a broken promise under a theory of traditional contract. Even if a party fails to or cannot show the existence of a contract, he or she may still have some recourse using the theory of promissory estoppel (hereinafter referred to as P/E). P/E theory holds a party liable for a broken promise when an injured party relies on a promise and that reliance causes a loss that should be compensated. To recover under a theory of P/E, an injured party must show that the other party made a promise, that the injured party acted on the promise in a way that was foreseeable to the person making the promise, and that the promise should be enforced to avoid injustice. After a court determines the promise should be enforced using P/E, the court may fashion a remedy based on notions of fairness and justice. Because this is not liability under traditional contract theory, there is no requirement that there be an offer, acceptance, or consideration.

Consider this example: After Stella receives a large inheritance, she promises her long-time friend Bill that she will give him $20,000 to help him start a new business venture. She makes this promise because she wants to do something nice for Bill. Stella gets mad at Bill and decides not to give him the money. In this situation, can Bill, using a contract theory, sue Stella for the $20,000 when she refuses to give him the money? Of course, the answer is no, because, since Stella was not trying to cause an exchange and was not looking for anything in return from Bill, her promise is merely a gratuitous promise, and gratuitous promises are not enforceable under traditional contract theory because they lack consideration. That does not mean that Stella may completely escape liability. If Bill can prove the elements of P/E, a court may order Stella to pay damages to Bill, as long as the court determines it must do so to avoid injustice.

Add some facts to the hypothetical situation between Stella and Bill, then apply them to this theory. The additional facts are that Stella and Bill had long discussed going into business together, but Stella had some misgivings due to a few other financial obligations. Her inheritance greatly improved her ability to take care of her financial obligations. Stella consistently told Bill that she would definitely help him with his business. On September 1, she promised him that she would give him $20,000 to start his business. After Stella made this promise, Bill told her he would immediately start working on setting up his new business. He contracted to lease a store, purchased products needed to open the business, and paid to advertise it in the local newspaper. Under these circumstances, should Bill recover any money from Stella using a theory of P/E? The principles of P/E may allow Bill to recover from Stella. Stella clearly promised to give Bill $20,000, and she should have reasonably expected him to act in reliance on her promise since she had repeatedly told him she would loan him the money. Also, Bill told her he intended to act on her promise so he could get the business up and running. It seems reasonable for Bill to act on the promise, especially since he knew Stella had the ability to give him the money because of her inheritance. The actions that Bill took in reliance on the promise caused him a significant loss, because he contracted for a lease and spent other money to get his business started. Arguably, the court should enforce Stella's promise to avoid injustice. Lastly, P/E allows a court to fashion a remedy that is fair.

XII.　RESTITUTION

Earlier this chapter covered the theory of restitution by a defaulting plaintiff. A party used that theory who had breached a contract and sued to recover some compensation under the contract in spite of the breach. As was mentioned in that section, the theory of restitution covers many facets of the law and many volumes have been written about the subject.

This section will cover another small part of restitution theory that may be used in a situation where there is absolutely no promise. Therefore, there can be no contract. Recall that restitution is based on a theory of unjust enrichment. The inquiry is two-fold; a party must be enriched, and it must be unjust for the enriched party not to pay for the benefit received. Not all who benefit will be forced to pay because some people are merely volunteers. For example, Susan builds a garage for her neighbor Jerry because she heard that he wanted to have a garage. In that case, is Jerry enriched? Of course, the answer is yes. But it is not unjust for him not to pay because he was in no way involved with the building of the garage, and there is no policy reason to force him to pay.

Now consider a situation where restitution would apply. Joe is in an accident in a rural road and is unconscious. Stacy, a doctor, happens upon the accident and spends a great amount of time tending to Joe and ultimately saving his life. Is Joe enriched? Clearly, he is. Is it unjust for him not to pay for the services of the doctor? Most likely, a court would conclude yes, because Stacy was acting in her professional capacity as a doctor, and we often assume an expectation of payment in those types of situations. Further, there are policy reason for finding a promise to pay, because we want to encourage doctors to help victims. In that situation, a court likely would imply a promise by Joe to pay Stacy for the reasonable value of her services.

XIII.　STATUTE OF FRAUDS

So far, the focus of the discussion has been on the common law of contracts and Article Two of the UCC. There is another law called the Statute of Frauds that, like the UCC, is passed by the legislature in every state. The Statute of Frauds makes certain types of agreements unenforceable because they are not written. This law often deals with suretyship contracts (promises to pay another person's debts), contracts to buy interests in land, contracts that will not be performed within a year, and contracts for the sale of goods which are governed by Article Two. The states often have two separate statutes — one for contracts governed by Article Two of the UCC and one for other types of contracts. This law is purely a creature of statute created by state legislatures, so it may not be uniform throughout the states, although there are common elements. For example, some states have added promises for cures or certain types of medical treatment to the Statute of Frauds. Because the statute often produces harsh results, many courts work to create exceptions. Consequently, the rule is peppered with exceptions.

This law traces its historical origins back to the 1600s in England. Although England has abolished the Statute of Frauds, it remains law in the United States. Historically, the reason for the law was to prevent parties from fraudulently claiming they had entered into an oral contract. The concern was that a person could claim he or she had agreed to an oral contract and, even though there was no written proof, a jury might find that a contract existed.

It is helpful to review a state statute as an example of what many legislatures have enacted as their state's Statute of Frauds. Following is an example of a typical Statute of Frauds from the state of Vermont. It says:

> An action at law shall not be brought in the following cases unless the promise, contract or agreement upon which such action is brought or some memorandum or note thereof is in writing, signed by the party to be charged therewith or by some person thereunto by him lawfully authorized:
>
> (1) A special promise of an executor or administrator to answer damages out of his own estate;
>
> (2) A special promise to answer for the debt, default or misdoings of another;
>
> (3) An agreement made in consideration of marriage;
>
> (4) An agreement not to be performed within one year from the making thereof;
>
> (5) A contract for the sale of lands, tenements or hereditaments, or of an interest in or concerning them. Authorization to execute such a contract on behalf of another shall be in writing;
>
> (6) An agreement to cure, a promise to cure, a contract to cure or warranty of cure relating to medical care or treatment or the results of a service rendered by a health care professional which shall mean a person or corporation licensed by this state to provide health care or professional services as a physician, dentist, registered or licensed practical nurse, optometrist, podiatrist, chiropractor, physical therapist, or psychologist, or an officer, employee or agent thereof acting in the course and scope of his employment;
>
> (7) An agreement to cure, a promise to cure, a contract to cure or warranty of cure relating to medical care or treatment rendered by a health provider, which shall mean a corporation, facility or institution licensed to provide health care as a hospital.

Vt. Stat. Ann. Tit. 12, § 181 (2007).

The above statute illustrates the basic rule that, although contracts generally are not required to be in writing, if it is the type of agreement that falls within a Statute of Frauds, there must be some form of writing before it will be enforceable. This does not mean that the entire contract has to be in writing or that the writing must have all of the terms. Usually, it is sufficient to have a written document signed by the person raising the statute as a defense, which shows that he or she had agreed to a contract. Overcoming a Statute of Frauds defense merely shows that a party has evidence of an agreement that is in writing. It does not necessarily mean that a contract exists. The necessary elements of a contract still must be proved. Now, we will look at a few common examples of several clauses in the Statute of Frauds.

A promise where one party promises to pay the debts of another person in the event that the other person fails to pay is called a suretyship agreement. For example, Cheryl is considering loaning money to Abraham so he can start a new business; but Cheryl is worried that Abraham may not be able to repay the debt when it comes due. Cheryl may require Abraham to have someone stand as a surety for him. Abraham's friend Hans agrees to repay Abraham's debt if Abraham fails to repay the money he owes Cheryl. Hans has entered into a suretyship agreement with Cheryl where he promises to pay Abraham's debt if Abraham fails to pay Cheryl when it is due. The Statute of Frauds requires this type of agreement to be in writing.

A second example of a clause often found in a Statute of Frauds requires that if performance of a contract will not be completed within a year, it has to be in writing. This category is not as broad as it seems, because it does not apply to an agreement that is capable of performance within a year, even if it may still take longer than a year. Because courts often try to narrow the application of the rule, they tend to deal with this type of clause quite literally. Jan orally agrees to pay Mark $20,000 over a period of ten years. At first glance, it would appear that the Statute of Frauds would prohibit enforcing this contract because it is not written. The agreement, however, *could* be performed in less than a year, because Jan could pay all of the money owed before a year has passed since there is no prohibition against an early pay off. In that situation, many courts would determine that the Statute of Frauds did not apply. Another example may be found in employment agreements. Courts have held that the one-year requirement does not apply to employment agreements, because death of the employee or employer can happen at any time; thus, the contract may be completed within a year. From these few examples, you should see that courts often try to find ways to avoid the application of the statute.

If there is no way to avoid the statute and it applies, the next question is what type of writing will satisfy the statute? The statute is usually satisfied if there is a writing that shows an agreement between the parties, contains the material terms of the contract, and is signed by the party who is asserting the Statute of Frauds as a defense. The courts have been very expansive in determining what suffices as a signature. It may even include a stamped name or a letterhead in appropriate circumstances.

As mentioned previously, Article Two of the UCC also has a Statute of Frauds that pertains to contracts for the sale of goods of $500 or more. It too looks for a writing signed by the opposing party that shows an intent to make an agreement. Many terms may be supplied later that are not in the writing. The one term that absolutely must be in that writing before it will satisfy the Statute of Frauds is the quantity of goods to be supplied in the contract. Additionally, it codifies a few specific exceptions to the statute including agreements between merchants, agreements where a manufacturer relies on a promise to buy specially manufactured goods and begins to substantially perform the contract, and agreements where payment has been made and accepted or goods have been received and accepted.

XIV.   THIRD PARTY BENEFICIARIES

One last problem to consider in this chapter is whether a party may sue to enforce a contract, even though he or she is not a party to the contract. The general rule is that a party must have privity of contract before he or she can sue to enforce the contract. Privity of contract simply means that the person was a party to the contract. If Randy contracts to buy ten poodles from Lee, then Randy and Lee have privity of contract because both are parties to the contract. Lee planned to obtain the poodles from Sharra Kennels. When Randy breaches the contract with Lee, may Sharra Kennels sue to enforce the contract? If Sharra attempts to enforce the contract, Randy will claim she has no rights under the contract; therefore, she can not sue to enforce it. While that is generally true, there are certain exceptions where third-party beneficiaries to a contract may sue to enforce the contract even though they are not parties to the contract. Certainly, Sharra would have benefited had the contract between Randy and Lee been performed, because she would have made a profit when she sold the poodles. Is that sufficient to allow her to sue on the contract? Not every third-party beneficiary is allowed to enforce a contract, so there most be some rules established to determine which beneficiaries will be permitted to enforce the contract.

Although this doctrine is quite complicated, for our purposes it will suffice to mention a few important principles that will guide courts when making the determination of whether to allow a third party beneficiary to sue to enforce a contract. The first important distinction is between an intended beneficiary and an incidental beneficiary. Only an intended beneficiary may use this doctrine to successfully sue as a third party beneficiary under a contract; however, not all intended beneficiaries will be able to sue. To be an intended beneficiary, the court looks to evidence to determine if it is necessary to allow the third party to sue to effectuate the intention of the parties to the contract. This determination often centers around questions of whether the promise in the contract was intended to satisfy an obligation to the beneficiary from the promisee or that the promisee intended to benefit the third party.

Return to the hypothetical contract between Randy and Lee to buy poodles. Sharra just happened to be in a situation where she was a beneficiary of the contract between Randy and Lee. Yet, neither party to the contract had a specific intention to benefit Sharra, she just happened to be the poodle supplier Lee chose. In that situation, she is not an intended beneficiary and has no right to sue to enforce the contract.

Consider another contract where a party will have a better chance of being successful at claiming third party beneficiary status. Marvin contracts with James, an attorney, to draft a will for him. Marvin wants to leave fifty acres of his estate to his dear niece, Kimberley. Marvin gives that instruction, along with others, to James, including exactly what property he wants to bequeath to his niece. After Marvin's death, Kimberley discovers that James failed to properly include Kimberley in the will. May Kimberley sue James for breach of contract? Many courts would conclude yes. Marvin clearly intended to bestow a benefit on Kimberley in his will, and James was very aware of that fact. Kimberley should have standing as a third party beneficiary of the contract between James and Marvin to sue James for breach of contract, since he failed to draft the will as directed.

Article Two has a specific provision related to third party beneficiaries, and it is section 2-318. This section is very non-uniform among the states. One reason for this is because the original draft of Article Two provided three different alternatives for states to choose from when enacting this section. This section allows certain third party beneficiaries who have been injured by a breach of warranty to sue under the contract, even though they lack privity under the contract. Because this section varies so much by state, it is necessary to check the statute in every jurisdiction before determining whether a suit will be successful.

XV. CONCLUSION

This chapter provided an overview of contract formation and how courts determine the content and meaning of a contract. It also explored possible responses to non-performance or part performance of a contract, and the remedies available for breach of contract. This included an examination of the concepts of substantial performance, divisibility, and restitution for a defaulting plaintiff. This chapter also explored concepts that allowed a court to excuse a party from paying damages even though she or he had breached a contract. Additionally, it reviewed doctrines that allowed a party to escape or reform a contract because of the behavior of a party, the status of a party, or some other fact that made the contract unfair and/or unreasonable to enforce. In addition to exploring traditional contract theory, this chapter reviewed alternatives to traditional contracts such as promissory estoppel and restitution, and it explored the doctrines of the Statute of Frauds and third party beneficiaries. Finally, the chapter highlighted a few of the differences between the common law and the UCC.

Chapter 3

TORTS & PERSONAL RESPONSIBILITIES

By — Ronald W. Eades

I. INTRODUCTION

Torts, or as it may be called tort law, is a basic area of law in the common law system. It is one of the building blocks to the English and American legal systems. In U.S. law schools, most law students take a course in torts during their first year of law school. This area of the law concerns legal actions between private citizens that seek to recover the financial costs due to injuries. Those injuries may be to the person or to property. In order to bring about that compensation for injuries, the law has developed a series of claims that an injured party may pursue. This chapter will explain what tort law seeks to accomplish and how those goals are met. In order to study tort law, several steps must be taken. First, it is necessary to review the three bases of liability that may be used. Those three bases of liability are intent, negligence, and strict liability. It is then important to view a few specialized areas of tort law that allow recovery for particular types of injuries. Those specialized areas of tort law still use one or more of those three bases of liability, but illustrate some of the more complex problems in tort law.

This Chapter will follow that basic format. It will discuss the three bases of liability that make up the major portion of tort law. It will then discuss some of the special topics that use one or more of those three bases of liability. Before getting to those major portions of the discussion, however, it is necessary to study a little background on torts.

Before discussing the details of tort law, however, the broad scope of the area should be noted. It will become clear in the following Chapter that torts is such a broad area that only the basic details can be noted in a brief period. Students in law schools in the United States take a full course devoted solely to tort law. In some law schools, that course in tort law lasts for one full academic year. Many scholars and students in the tort law field recognize that even such an extended course does not cover all of tort law. Some students while in law school in the United States will take further courses that specialize in particular topics in tort law. This material is designed to offer an overview of the topic of tort law. A complete understanding of tort law would take a lifetime of study.

II. BACKGROUND ON TORTS

A.   What Is a Tort?

The word itself, tort, is probably not capable of a good definition. The background of the word comes from Latin. The Latin root meant something like "twisted" or "wrong." Many of the claims in tort law are based upon some wrongdoing by a person. As the law has expanded, however, clear proof of wrongdoing is not required in all actions. With the broad and continuing development of tort law, stating a simple definition is not possible.

Although it is difficult to state a simple definition of tort law, it is possible to give a general description of the area. Understanding the general description will make it easier to study the individual parts of torts.

Tort law may be described as an area of law that is civil and not criminal, that imposes, by law, duties upon people, so that if a person breaches a duty and causes an injury, the law will shift the cost of that injury from the person who suffered the loss back to the person who caused the injury. In outline form, this description would have the following elements:

1. It is an area of the law.

2. It is civil and not criminal.

3. The law imposes the duty.

4. The law will shift costs of injuries from the injured person to the person who caused the injury.

Each of those items should be discussed.

By calling torts an area of the law, it helps to indicate that torts is a broad section of the law in the United States. Within tort law are numerous subsections that allow for different types of injuries and claims. Tort law is on an equal footing with such other areas of the law as property, contracts, and criminal law. Tort law, like those other named areas of the law, is one of the basic features of law in the United States.

Noting that tort law is "civil" and not "criminal" is an important distinction. By this use of the word "civil," it is not meant to denote the type of law that is usually found on the continent of Europe. When civil law is mentioned in that context, it is meant to distinguish between civil law on the continent and common law found in England. The United States adopted much of the legal system of England and tort law was a part of that adoption. As such, tort law is a part of the common law tradition. It is primarily case law. To the extent that it has a counter-part in

European Civil Law, tort law is similar to the area that many civil law systems refer to as "delict."

In the United States, however, the term "civil law" is used to distinguish between "civil" and "criminal" law. In the United States, "criminal" law is that area of the law that is imposed by government, litigated by agents of the government and the outcome of which may cause a defendant to be placed in jail. "Civil" law is that area of the law that deals with actions between private citizens that seek to resolve private disputes. Using that distinction, it can be seen that tort law in the United States is "civil" and not "criminal." It is designed to resolve disputes between private citizens.

The description noted that tort law imposes duties. A major part of tort law is the recognition that law imposes duties and responsibilities on everyone. When someone breaches such a duty and that breach causes an injury to another, that gives rise to a claim in torts.

The last feature of the description notes that when the duty is breached and the injury occurs, the law requires that the loss for that injury be shifted. The cost of the injury will be shifted from the person who suffered that loss to the person who caused the injury. This feature of tort law raises its primary purpose. That primary purpose is compensation. When such an injury occurs, the courts seek to compensate the injured party for the losses suffered. Obviously if the injured party suffered the loss of an arm or leg, the courts can not replace the arm or leg. The courts can, however, try to put the injured party in the position they should have been in had the injury not occurred. This attempt at compensation will mean that the courts will force the person who caused the injury to pay for medical bills, lost wages and pain and suffering.

Since the law is shifting the loss from the injured person to the one who caused the injury, several issues may be noticed. This area of the law is imposing responsibility on people for injuries that they cause. It also allows private citizens to sue each other to enforce those duties and responsibilities.

With that description of torts, it should be obvious what types of cases the area of law concerns. Cases in tort law tend to be those everyday accidents and mishaps that occur. Car wrecks, medical malpractice and defective products that injure people are the typical cases that arise in torts. The other sections of this chapter will try to illustrate how the law deals with the most important aspects of tort law.

B.   Short History of the Area

Before studying the specific issues of torts, a few additional items should be noted. Tort law has a long history in England and the United States. Its history goes back so far that there are some differences of opinion about the true origins of torts. It is believed that torts arose as a part of the criminal law system. As courts would punish a wrongdoer for some act, those courts would begin to also require the wrongdoer to compensate injured parties. This attempt at compensation would be the earliest indicators of a new area of the law. Some of the earliest written records of such a development appear over six hundred years ago in England.

The early development of the law, however, is substantially different from the modern practice. Those early cases would have required one person to pay for injuries without any proof of fault or wrongdoing. It would not be until more recent times that tort law began to develop many of its current distinctions.

As an area of the law that is intended to compensate injured people for injuries, tort law continues to be broad and in a state of development. It would be a mistake to assume that all torts have been developed and secured for all time. Tort law tends to be that area that allows recovery when a wrong has been committed. It is frequently the area of law that recognizes new and previously unanticipated recoveries for new and previously unanticipated injuries. Although some of the tort law may date back over six hundred years, there are some topics that emerged approximate forty years ago and remain in a state of change. Tort law tends to be the area that covers all new claims until such claims become sufficiently established to have their own area of the law.

C.   General Bases of Liability

It has been noted that tort law has some connection with wrongs and wrongdoers. It is true that many tort claims require evidence that someone did something wrong. As a broad area of the law, however, not all tort claims require that showing of wrongdoing. Although there are numerous claims that may be brought in tort law, there are three and only three bases of liability that those claims may use. All claims in torts will be based on one or more of those bases. Those three bases are intent, negligence, and strict liability. Some of the following sections in this Chapter will fully discuss those bases of liability.

III. INTENTIONAL TORTS

A.   Definition of Intent

One of the earlier bases of liability is that of intent. This area seems to have developed along with the early criminal law. With the connection to criminal law, some of these torts share names with some of the common law crimes. Although the names of these torts are the same as some crimes, the required elements are different.

With all of the intentional torts, the first element that the injured party must prove is that the defendant acted with intent. The basic definition of intent is that the plaintiff must prove that the defendant acted for the purpose of bringing about the consequences that occurred, or that the defendant acted knowing that the consequences were substantially certain to occur.

In order to understand this element, a few examples will help. Battery is one of the intentional torts. A battery requires the harmful or offensive touching of another. It also requires the intent. The intent for battery, therefore, is that the defendant acted for the purpose of bringing about a harmful or offensive touching or acted knowing that the harmful or offensive touching was substantially certain to occur. Some examples are easy. Imagine a defendant walks up to the plaintiff. The defendant then makes a fist and punches the plaintiff in the nose. Obviously the defendant acted for the purpose of bringing about the harmful touching. That would be a battery. Imagine, however, that another defendant is out shooting a rifle. This defendant shoots at a passing train while knowing that there are people riding the train. The defendant will claim that he or she did not actually want to hit anyone on the train. The courts would probably rule, however, that the defendant knew that hitting someone on the train was substantially certain to occur. It would, therefore, be a battery.

Other examples will be more difficult. If the defendant is out hunting and shooting a rifle, the defendant might hit someone else who is also out hunting in the woods. If the defendant did not see the other person and did not know the other person was there, there would be no intentional tort. The mere fact the defendant intended to fire the rifle is not enough. There would have to be proof that the defendant intended to hit the other person.

It is also important to note that there is a difference between intent and motive. It is not important as to what the defendant's motive was in acting. Imagine, for example, that a person is getting ready to sit down in a chair and the defendant quickly removes the chair from underneath the person preparing to sit. The person preparing to sit would miss the chair and hit the floor. If the defendant was sued for battery, that defendant would claim no intent to cause harm. The defendant would claim that only a joke or prank was intended. There would be an intentional tort. The defendant intended the consequences of hitting the floor and hitting the floor was a harmful or offensive touching. Although the defendant's motive was to make a joke, the intent was to cause the touching.

As noted above, all of the intentional torts require the first element of intent. The rest of this section will discuss the intentional torts individually while keeping in mind that first element.

B.   Harms to the Person

Some of the intentional torts are available to allow an injured plaintiff to recover for personal injuries suffered as a result of the actions of the defendant. These torts arise when the defendant's conduct either puts the plaintiff in the apprehension of suffering some personal injury or when he or she actually suffers that injury.

1.   Assault

A defendant may commit an assault upon the plaintiff and allow the plaintiff to recover for any injuries suffered as a result of that assault. A claim for assault requires that the plaintiff prove that the defendant had the intent to bring about the assault, put the plaintiff in the apprehension of some immediate bodily contact, committed this assault with some overt act and that the defendant had the present ability to carry out the threat.

The assault does not require that the defendant actually hit or touch the plaintiff. This tort is, instead, a claim to allow recovery for the apprehension of such a touching. Examples of this tort may be easily seen. Imagine that the defendant comes running up to the plaintiff with a big stick. As the defendant is approaching the plaintiff, the defendant is screaming, "I am going to hit you in the head with this stick!" Obviously that would be an assault. The defendant is acting for the purpose of bringing about an apprehension of being touched and that would satisfy the intent element. The defendant is also fulfilling the other elements. By carrying the stick, the defendant is making an overt act. That carrying of the stick also shows that the defendant has the present ability to carry out the threat. Finally, one could imagine that any plaintiff in this situation would be under the apprehension that the bodily contact was about to occur. The plaintiff could believe that he or she is about to be hit with the stick. Finding that all of the elements are met, the plaintiff could recover for the assault.

2. Battery

The intentional tort of battery was noted in the general description of intent. As a review, a battery requires that the defendant act for the purpose of bringing about a harmful or offensive touching or act with knowledge that the touching is substantially certain to occur. In addition, it is necessary that the plaintiff prove that the touching did, in fact, occur. In the subsection on intent, it was noted that shooting someone with a rifle could be a battery.

In order to add another example, think about the person carrying the stick and threatening to hit someone with it. While the defendant is swinging the stick around and making the threats, that conduct would be an assault as discussed above. If, however, the person with the stick hit the plaintiff with that stick, then the defendant has also committed the battery. It is possible, therefore, for a defendant to commit both an assault and battery during the same series of events. The assault would be the making of the threat to hit the person, while the battery would be carrying out the threat. Frequently, plaintiffs will bring claims for both assault and battery, as it is common for both of these torts to be present in the same case.

Although it is common for both assault and battery to be present in the same case, they may each exist independently. In fact, the critical difference between the two is seen best by examining how they differ. Battery requires the touching, irrespective of whether or not the plaintiff knew it was going to occur. Assault requires that the plaintiff be aware of the threat, irrespective of whether or not it is carried out. These two torts differ, therefore, on the need for evidence of awareness. If, for example, a defendant came up behind a plaintiff without the plaintiff knowing it, and then the defendant struck the plaintiff on the head, there would be a battery and not an assault. Since the plaintiff was not aware the event was about to occur, there would be no assault. Since the plaintiff got struck, however, there would be a battery.

3. False Imprisonment

False imprisonment, which is sometimes called false arrest, provides another intentional tort claim for recovery of personal injuries. The key element of this tort is that the plaintiff is confined within some boundaries by the defendant. This tort requires that the plaintiff prove that the defendant intended to confine the plaintiff, the plaintiff was confined, the confinement was by a physical restraint, the plaintiff was either aware of the confinement or harmed by it, and that the defendant had no legal authority for the confinement.

It is necessary that the plaintiff be actually confined in order for the claim to be valid. There may be times when a plaintiff is prevented from traveling in certain directions, but that loss of total freedom of movement is not adequate. The plaintiff must actually be confined within boundaries to have a basis for the tort of false imprisonment.

It is also necessary that the confinement be the result of some physical restraint. Locking the plaintiff in a room or cell would meet that requirement.

Chaining the plaintiff to a chair or floor would also meet the requirement. There are times that plaintiffs may decide to stay somewhere due to moral or ethical force. If, for example, someone said to the plaintiff, "I think you are a thief. If you leave my home without empting your pockets, I'll always believe you are a thief." If the plaintiff decides to stay to clear his or her good name, that would not be a false imprisonment. The confinement was due to moral pressure not physical restraint. If, however, the defendant had said, "I think you are a thief. I have locked the doors of my house and will hold you here with my gun until the police arrive," that could lead to a false imprisonment if the other elements are met, as the confinement would be by physical restraint.

The tort of false imprisonment requires that the plaintiff either know of the restraint or be harmed by it. This appears to be the law's way of making sure there is some real injury to the plaintiff. If, for example, the plaintiff was locked in a house and then the house burned down injuring or killing the plaintiff, a false imprisonment action could be brought. If, however, a plaintiff was asleep in the house and the house was first locked and then unlocked before the plaintiff woke up, there would be no false imprisonment. The plaintiff was never aware that he or she could not leave and there was no injury to the plaintiff.

Finally, it is important for the plaintiff to be able to prove that there was no legal authority for the confinement. In the area of law enforcement of criminal laws, many people are confined every day. A person may be a suspect in a murder case when he or she is arrested by the police and put in jail awaiting trial. Clearly that person is confined by physical restraint and is aware of the confinement. If, however, the police used proper arrest techniques and had legal authority to make the arrest, this would not be considered false imprisonment.

Another example of the issue of "legal authority" to make the arrest arises in the area of stores and shops where the owner or someone within the store stops a customer who he or she believes may have stolen something from within store. In the traditional case, the shop owner might see someone that the owner believes has placed an item in his or her pocket. The shop owner might then detain that person to see if something was stolen. In many cases, this would be a false imprisonment. The plaintiff had been detained and, if nothing was actually stolen, there would have been no legal authority to confine that person. Many states have now passed special statutes to allow shop owners to make such a confinement. The statutes, frequently called "Shop Keeper's Privilege Statutes" allow shop owners to detain people if there is a reasonable belief that the person has stolen something.

4.   Intentional Infliction of Emotional Distress

One of the most recently developed intentional torts is the intentional infliction of emotional distress. This tort was clearly defined by the California courts in the 1950s. As a relatively new tort, it has not been adopted by all of the states in the United States and is still being developed by the courts.

Many jurisdictions that have adopted this tort call it the tort of outrageous conduct and require that the plaintiff prove that the defendant acted intentionally or recklessly, in an extreme and outrageous manner to cause severe emotional distress. This tort, like the other intentional torts, requires that the conduct be the result of intentional actions. The defendant needed to have acted for the purpose of bringing about the severe emotional distress.

It is also important that the conduct of the defendant be extreme and outrageous. It is not every intentional insult that will lead to a claim of intentional infliction of emotional distress. The law recognizes that it is a crowded world and many people are rude and it can be hard to get along with some individuals. If the law was too lenient in this area, plaintiffs would file a tort claim every time someone said a rude or unkind word. Imagine the court system if people could sue every time a store clerk, government employee, or restaurant waiter was rude to a customer. There would be no room in the courts for anything else. In order to bring a claim for outrageous conduct, the conduct must be so severe as to be beyond the bounds allowed by ordinary society. Courts have found that cases where the defendant has made sustained and continuing threats against the plaintiff may give rise to such a claim. In addition, where the defendant has made threats or acts against the well known weaknesses of the plaintiff, successful litigation in this area is more likely. Although attorneys like to file claims for outrageous conduct, courts are not as likely to allow recovery for these claims.

The final element of the claim requires that the emotional distress that results must be severe. As with the element of outrageousness of the conduct, the harm element must be beyond the ordinary. In dealing with the outside world on a daily basis, it is common to be upset. People frequently have to deal with rude and angry people. It is not every emotional disturbance that will allow liability. The courts want proof that the plaintiff has suffered severe emotional distress that goes beyond that suffered on a regular basis. Although the plaintiff is not required to show some physical harm from the emotional distress, evidence of such physical harm from the stress would be helpful to the plaintiff's case. Plaintiffs frequently offer evidence of having to go to counseling, losing sleep, and becoming physically ill from the stress as evidence of the harm suffered from the emotional distress.

C.   Harms to Property

The above material discussed the intentional torts that could be used to recover for harms done to the plaintiff's person. Intentional torts are actually broader than merely protecting from personal injury as they may also be used to seek compensation for injuries to property. There are two types of property. Property that is connected with the land is called real property. Obviously, tracts of land and buildings attached to the land are considered part of real property. Other types of property may be referred to as personal property or chattels. Such property would include items like cars, clothes, stereos, computers and all other property that is not considered to be real property. The following subsections discuss the torts that may be used to recover for harms to property. In referring to the torts that deal with property, always be sure to specify whether the tort is dealing with land or chattels. A mere reference to "property" will leave the audience uncertain as to which category within property is being discussed.

1.   Trespass to Land

One of the early intentional torts was the claim for trespass to land. The basic purpose of this tort was to protect the exclusive right of possession. A plaintiff that had the right of possession of the land could bring a claim against anyone who intentionally entered or stayed on the land without consent of the plaintiff.

Today, the basic elements of the tort of trespass to land are the intent to be on the land and being on the land of another. The easy example is when a stranger enters upon the land of another. Although trespass to land seems easy to understand, there are a few difficult issues.

The first issue is that it is not necessary that the defendant intended to trespass. The only intent necessary is that the defendant intended to be where he or she was. If, for example, the defendant honestly believed that he or she owned the land, but in fact, the land was occupied by another, then that is a trespass. The fact that the defendant intended to be where he or she was is sufficient. It would not be trespass if the defendant was on the land through negligence or innocence. Imagine, for example, that the defendant was driving an automobile and had an accident in the road. As a result of the automobile accident, the defendant's automobile was knocked onto the land of an adjoining landowner. Clearly the driver has no right to be on that land. The entry, however, would not be a trespass. The driver did not intend to be on the land, but instead was on that land due to some negligence.

It is also important to note that there is no requirement that the plaintiff prove that there was damage to the land in order to bring the action. The intent and being on the land are sufficient. It is believed that the right to exclusive possession is so important that the plaintiff may bring the action without proof of actual harm.

2.   Trespass to Chattels

The tort of trespass to chattels is meant to protect against the intentional interference with personal property. Where someone interferes with the personal property of another, then the true owner has the right to sue for that interference. The tort requires that there be an intent to interfere with that personal property and that there be some harm to the property.

Notice that the above statement of the rule indicated that there be some harm to the property. It is important to note that the element is some harm that is short of full destruction. When the harm to the personal property amounts to a need to recover the full value of the property, then the appropriate tort is conversion.

3.   Conversion

As noted above, the tort of conversion and the tort of trespass to chattels are similar. Where trespass to chattels is designed to recover for damages to personal property that does not reach the level of full value, conversion is designed to recover the full value of the personal property. The basic elements of conversion may be stated as intent to interfere with the personal property and an interference that appears to be an exercise of dominion over the property to the exclusion of the rights of the true owner. The law has sought to explain this tort in a way that indicates that the full value of the personal property is protected.

D.   General Defenses

Proof of the basic elements of a tort does not automatically result in a judgment for the plaintiff, as there are defenses to claims of intentional torts. The defendant has the right to try to explain or avoid liability. The common law defenses provide that opportunity for the defendant.

1.   Consent

The first defense to an intentional tort is consent. It is clear that if the plaintiff consented to the commission of the acts, then there is no tort. The easy example would be where a person invites another person to his or her home to enjoy a social visit. When the "defendant" comes to the home, the plaintiff would say, "Come on in. It is great to see you." If, after the defendant then entered the home, the plaintiff sought to sue the defendant for trespass to land, the defense would be consent. This same type of consent could be used to avoid an action for trespass to chattels where a plaintiff lends a defendant a chattel. It could also be used to avoid an action for battery where two professional boxers agree to enter into a boxing match.

The use of consent by the express language of the plaintiff to allow the action is the obvious example. It is commonly used in medical treatment. When a patient goes to the doctor, the patient will frequently be asked to sign a consent form to allow the doctor to touch the patient. Before surgery, for example, the patient will have to consent to being cut by the doctor. If there was no consent, there would be a battery. The consent removes the claim for battery. This use of express consent is the easiest to see. Consent, however, may be implied.

Implied consent can arise in three ways. The consent may be implied from the circumstances, the acts of the plaintiff, or by custom. Each of those requires a short explanation.

Consent may be implied by the surrounding circumstances of the event. Frequently when a plaintiff seeks medical treatment, that plaintiff will sign an express consent form. There are times, however, when that does not occur. A plaintiff may have been injured in an accident and taken to the hospital in an ambulance. If the patient is unconscious upon arrival at the hospital, then the patient cannot give express consent. If the doctors had to wait and hope that the patient regained consciousness before treatment, many patients would die. The law, therefore, assumes that most unconscious patients would consent to treatment. It is, therefore, implied from those circumstances that the patient would have consented.

A plaintiff may also consent by his or her own acts. Where a plaintiff is visiting a doctor, implied consent by acts may also occur. Imagine that the doctor informs the patient that the patient needs a shot. The patient does not respond but rolls up a sleeve of the shirt and holds up his or her arm. The doctor may imply by those acts that the patient has consented to the shot.

Finally, consent may be implied by custom. The easy examples occur in the everyday world. Many cities are crowded places. It is not uncommon to be bumped when walking along the street, getting on buses, or entering the subway. The law will not litigate those events. It is assumed that by living in a crowded world, people consent to those usual events. There are other examples that may also be seen. Many sporting events could give rise to being touched. Football, baseball, basketball, and soccer all have times when the players run into each other. The law would assume that the players all have implied consent to the normal and usual contact that arises in such games.

2.   Self-Defense

Self-defense is another tool for defendants to use to avoid liability for intentional torts. It usually arises in claims for battery. The plaintiff will sue the defendant for a battery and the defendant will claim that the attack on the plaintiff was done by the defendant to protect him or herself. The elements of self-defense require that the defendant prove that the defendant reasonably believed that he or she was under an immediate threat and that the force that was used was reasonable under the circumstances.

The threat to the defendant must be immediate in order for the defendant to claim self-defense. That would mean that the threat must be one that the defendant feels is about to happen at the present time. This rule prevents the defendant from attacking someone in revenge for something that happened in the past. It also prevents a defendant from attacking someone from a fear of something that might happen in the future. Self-defense is designed to protect the defendant from that immediate threat. If the danger is one that has already passed or one that could only occur in the future, the law requires the defendant to seek help from the police authorities.

The defense also limits the amount of force that can be used. The force must be reasonable in light of the circumstances. When, for example, the defendant is being threatened by some mere pushing and shoving, the defendant cannot use that opportunity to shoot and kill the plaintiff. The defense force must be reasonable. If the defendant is protecting his or her own life, the circumstances may lead to the use of deadly force. Deadly force, however, should not be the first option.

3.   Defense of Others

In the same way that a defendant may protect him or herself, a defendant may use force to protect others. A defendant may see a third party being attacked by someone. The defendant may come to the aid of that third party, even if force is required. If the defendant is then sued for an intentional tort, the defendant may use the defense of that third party as a basis to avoid liability.

4.   Defense of Property

Defense of property works in much the same way as self-defense and defense of others. The defendant may use force to protect his or her property. That force, however, must be reasonable in light of the circumstances. Although there may be times when deadly force may be reasonable for self-defense, the courts would not consider deadly force reasonable for defense of property. Taking the life of another to protect property alone would not be reasonable.

The issue of reasonableness of the force has arisen in cases where the defendant has sought to put up traps to protect property. Where a person, even a thief or trespasser, was injured by those traps, the courts have ruled that the use of maiming or deadly force was not reasonable for the protection of property alone.

5.   Necessity

A final possible defense is that of necessity. This defense is available in two forms. It may be used as a public necessity or a private necessity.

A public necessity arises when an intentional tort is committed in an effort to protect a public interest. A traditional example of this defense arose in cases of large city fires. During the spread of the fire, the city officials would decide that certain buildings and homes had to be destroyed to help stop the spread of the fire. The owners of those buildings and homes would sue for the damage to property that could have been removed before the fire reached the homes. The courts ruled that the needs of the public were greater than the needs of the individual. The public necessity would act as a defense for that claim.

A private necessity arises when an individual commits an intentional tort to avoid injury to him or herself. A traditional example occurred when a ship owner would tie up to a dock to avoid a storm. The tying to the dock would be a trespass to land. The ship owner, however, will defend by claiming that failure to tie up would have resulted in the loss of the ship and possibly his or her life. That private necessity will be a defense to that claim.

There is a distinction that should be noted between pubic and private necessities. A public necessity is a complete bar to recovery. The public agency is relieved of any payment of damages. A private nuisance will relieve the defendant of the intentional nature of the act. The defendant will not have to pay punitive damages. If, however, the defendant causes an actual harm, those damages may be recovered.

IV. NEGLIGENCE

Negligence is a separate basis of liability in tort law. It arose primarily in the 1800s and was the dominant basis of liability through the twentieth century. Many of the most common tort claims use negligence as the basis of the claim. Automobile accidents and medical malpractice, for example, are both negligence claims.

The key difference between negligence and intent is the state of mind of the defendant. As noted earlier, the defendant in an intentional tort action will have acted for the purpose of bringing about the consequences or acted with knowledge that the consequences were substantially certain to follow. In negligence claims, the defendant would have acted in a way to create a risk that consequences would occur. Intent, therefore, is to act with knowledge. Negligence is to act in a way that is unreasonable. The defendant in an intentional tort claim *knew* of the consequences. In the negligence claim, the defendant did not know, but maybe the defendant *should have known.*

All negligence claims have four elements. The plaintiff must prove that the defendant had a duty to the plaintiff, that the defendant breached that duty, that the plaintiff suffered an injury and that the breach of the duty caused that injury. Each of those elements is complex and could require lengthy study. The topic of negligence makes up a substantial portion of the basic class in torts that American law students take. The important points of each of those elements will be discussed below.

A.   Duty

1.   How Is a Duty Formed?

The law imposes a duty on people in society to act in a certain way. This duty is one that is imposed as a matter of basic law and will be interpreted by the courts. In fact, the existence of the duty is considered a question of law. In the simple negligence case, it is the judge in the case that determines whether there is a duty and to whom it is owed. The judge, therefore, will consider the circumstances of the case and decide whether there is a duty.

The underlying theory of the duty is that people should act reasonably. The concept of reasonableness is that people must act the way most usual people act. Individuals are not allowed to use their own best judgment, especially when that judgment is not good. An individual will not be able to defend a negligence case by saying, "I did my best." That may not be good enough. Courts will usually require that the defendant perform as other "reasonable" people.

There are conflicting theories as to how the determination of the duty is made. Several of those may be noted.

Since tort law uses words that sound fault oriented, many assume that negligence is based on moral or ethical grounds. This would lead some to believe that negligence, fault, and reasonable care must be based upon some form of standards of conduct that might be found in moral and ethical codes.

Others have expressed a modern belief that tort law is based on rules of economic efficiency. These individuals believe that reasonable people behave the way they do because it is most economically efficient to do so. The theory would claim that reasonable people would spend money to protect against injuries, but would not spend on prevention in excess of the amount that the injury would cost. To economists, reasonable people would determine which would cost less. Reasonable people would be willing to accept an injury or pay to prevent it; whichever was less.

Regardless of the theory used to determine how the duty arises, the courts seem consistent on what that duty is. Although it will be discussed in more detail below, that duty usually requires a person to act as a reasonable person of ordinary prudence under similar circumstances.

2.   To Whom Is a Duty Owed?

Although the law assumes that almost everyone owes a duty, there is some concern on how far that duty extends. In a perfect world, one might hope that all people owed a duty to all others. That may fit moral and ethical standards, but tort law does not extend that far. The failure of an individual to feed the hungry or house the homeless will not result in the right of the hungry and homeless to bring a tort action to demand food and shelter. Tort law seeks to find a limit to how far the duty will extend.

A classic case in Tort law is called *Palsgraf v. Long Island Rail Road*. A lady, Mrs. Paslgraf, had purchased a ticket to ride a train and was waiting on the platform. Further down the platform, a man was being assisted on the train by railroad employees when a package was dropped and exploded. Palsgraf was injured in the resulting chaos and sued the railroad. The majority opinion of the court ruled that she could not recover. Although railroads might owe a duty of reasonable care, the court ruled that the duty did not extend very far. The defendant only owed a duty to those plaintiffs in a small group to whom injury could reasonably be foreseen from the negligence of the railroad porters in helping a passenger to board the train. The railroad might, for example, owe a duty to the man they were specifically assisting, but there would be no duty owed to those further down the platform. The idea of the duty extending to those reasonably foreseeable plaintiffs seems to be a common position by courts in the United States.

3.   What Is that Duty?

a.   Adults

Once the judge determines that there is a duty and it is owed to the plaintiff, the question arises as to what is that duty. As noted above, the usual duty for adults is the duty to act as a reasonable person of ordinary prudence under similar circumstances. That phrase actually contains three ideas in one.

When the court speaks of reasonable people, the issue seems to be one of how people perform. It is easier to imagine sets of facts then to speculate on the issue in the abstract. Courts would find that reasonable people drive their automobiles under the speed limits, observe traffic signs and carefully watch for other cars. Reasonable people always read all instructions and warnings on labels of products. Reasonable people carefully maintain their tools and equipment so that the equipment does not fail. Those examples are the types of things that can arise in a simple negligence case. It should be noted that the judge would instruct the jury that the defendant was required to act as a reasonable person and it would be up to the jury to decide whether the conduct was reasonable. The issue of the jury deciding that fact is discussed more fully in the section below on breach.

The usual standard of care also requires that an adult have ordinary prudence. This implies that the adult defendant must be held to the same level of intelligence and knowledge as other usual adults. When, for example, a defendant's automobile tires wore out, flattened and caused an accident, the defendant would not be allowed to say, "I didn't know I had to check for that." The defendant would be required to know those things that other usual adults would know.

Finally, the conduct and knowledge of the defendant will be measured under the circumstances of the event. It is clear that a typical adult driving an automobile would not swerve suddenly into another lane. If, however, a defendant was driving along the road and a child suddenly ran into the road, that defendant would swerve into the other lane to avoid hitting the child. If a claim arose because of that conduct, the defendant would be allowed to let the jury hear about the circumstances of the event. The jury would have to decide if the defendant acted reasonably in light of the emergency that was presented.

b.   Professionals

Although there are other categories of defendants besides adults that could be considered, professionals offer the most common issue raised in tort claims. When a professional is sued for malpractice, the issue will arise as to what duty is owed by the professional. This, for example, arises when the professional is a doctor, lawyer, engineer or some other well trained person. That professional holds him or herself out as having greater skills and knowledge then the general public. The law will, therefore, hold that professional to those greater skills.

Generally, the professional duty is to perform as other qualified professionals in that field. This will require the professional to be held to the qualifications, care, and skill of other such professionals. Physicians, for example, are held to the care and skill of other qualified physicians.

Professional malpractice cases are difficult to litigate. Since the professional will be held to the care and skill of other professionals, it is necessary to use expert testimony. Juries will ultimately have to decide the case, so the jury must be informed about what other professionals would have done under the same circumstances. Thus, the expert witness will be called to fully explain the matter to the jury.

B.   Breach

1.   Question of Fact for the Jury

Once the trial judge had determined that a duty was imposed upon the defendant, facts must be presented in order to determine whether the defendant breached that duty. The jury will be instructed by the judge that the defendant had the duty to act as a reasonable person of ordinary prudence under similar circumstances. The jury will listen to all the facts and determine whether the defendant met or breached that duty.

2.   Proof by a Preponderance of Evidence

Since the breach of the duty is a question of fact for the jury, the parties to the litigation must present evidence on that issue. In negligence cases, the burden of proof is on the plaintiff to prove every element of the claim. The burden on the plaintiff in tort claims is not as high as the burden placed on the prosecutor in criminal cases. Many people are aware that in a criminal case, the prosecution must prove every element of the crime beyond a reasonable doubt. In tort cases, however, the plaintiff must only prove the case by a preponderance of the evidence.

The courts have tried to explained "preponderance of the evidence" in many different ways. Some have said that it means that the facts must show it was more likely than not that the event occurred. Others have suggested that the plaintiff's evidence must be a little more than half. Regardless of the method used to explain preponderance, it is not just an issue of quantity. The plaintiff does not win just by having more witnesses. Preponderance of the evidence means that the plaintiff's witnesses must be more convincing. It might be by the use of more witnesses or it might be by the use of better witnesses.

C.   Injury

In the discussion of intentional torts, it was noted that the intentional torts do not require proof of actual injury. It is thought that the seriousness of the conduct and the personal or property invasion is enough to justify the action. For an action in negligence, however, there must be proof of actual injury.

The actual injury in a negligence case is usually a combination of personal injury and property damage. Using an automobile action as an example provides the opportunity to illustrate this issue. When a plaintiff has an automobile accident, both property damage and personal injury will occur. The proper damage will, of course, be the automobile. The plaintiff can recover for the loss of value of the automobile due to the accident. In addition, the plaintiff can recover for the personal injury suffered. The personal injury may include medical bills, lost wages, and pain and suffering. All of the damages would need to be proven by the plaintiff who would bring in expert witnesses who could testify as to the loss of value of the automobile and the personal injury losses.

D.   Causal Relationship

The last, and possibly the most complex, issue in negligence is that of causation. It is necessary for the plaintiff to prove that the breach of the duty was the *cause* of the injury. The issue of causation actually contains two parts. The plaintiff must be able to prove that the breach was the cause in fact of the injury and that the breach of the duty was the proximate cause of the injury. Each of those parts must be examined.

1.   Cause in Fact

Cause in fact is the easier of the two parts of causation to understand. The breach must have been the reason that the injury occurred. Many courts would use what is called a *sine qua non* test. *Sine qua non* may be roughly translated as "but for." Applying it to the issue of a negligence claim, the courts might say that the plaintiff must prove the injury would not have happened "but for" the breach of the duty by the defendant. In other words, the injury would not have happened if the defendant had not been negligent.

The theory of the "but for" test is not as complicated as it sounds. Imagine, for example, that the driver of an automobile in Paris, France is driving at an unreasonably high rate of speed. At that same time, a serious automobile accident occurs in New York City. If the plaintiff in New York City sought to sue the driver in Paris, the answer would be so obvious as to be silly — there would be no claim against the driver in Paris. Although the driver in Paris was negligent, that negligence had nothing to do with the accident in New York City.

For a more reasonable example, imagine a driver in New York City driving his or her automobile just slightly above the appropriate speed limit. Suddenly a person steps out in front of the automobile and is struck before the driver can stop. Clearly the driver was negligent. Driving at a rate of speed above the posted speed limit would be negligence. The driver, however, will claim that the actual speed had nothing to do with the accident. The driver will claim that even if he or she had been driving at the speed limit, the automobile could not have been stopped in time. The claim would be that the carelessness of the person stepping into the road was the cause in fact of the accident and not the fast driving. It would be a question of fact for the jury to determine whether the fast driving was the cause of the accident.

2.   Proximate Cause

Proximate cause is the more difficult of the causation issues. Proximate cause is not really a question of factual cause, but is, instead, a question of policy. There are times that the conduct of the defendant did, in fact, cause the injury. The defendant will claim, however, that the injury was so bizarre or different that liability should not attach. Courts may, at times, agree with that position.

A good way to understand the issue is to use an example that is probably myth or legend in the United States. In 1871, the City of Chicago caught on fire and, within three days, most of the city had burned down. The rapid expanse of the fire was due to high wind and the fact that much of the city was made of wood. There is a myth that the whole fire was started by a woman by the name of Mrs. O'Leary. Legend claims that Mrs. O'Leary went out to milk her cow, the cow kicked a lantern over into some hay, the hay caught on fire and the fire spread throughout the city.

Using that hypothetical example, it is easy to understand how causation works. If those facts had been true, clearly Mrs. O'Leary was the cause in fact of the burning down of Chicago. She was negligent with the use of the lantern and the negligence caused the whole city to burn down. The question of proximate cause would be more difficult. The question of proximate cause that is asked is, "Even though she would be the cause in fact of the fire, do the courts want to hold her liable for the whole city?"

Over the years, the courts have developed a series of rules that tend to limit the extent of liability even where the defendant was the cause in fact of all of the injuries. The typical rule is that in order to be liable for the injuries, the defendant must have foreseen the possibilities that those injuries would have occurred. It is frequently discussed that the risk needs to have been "reasonably foreseen" in order to hold the defendant liable. In our example of Mrs. O'Leary, she would not have been able to foresee the burning down of Chicago and would not, therefore, be liable for the full extent of that fire. She might have been liable for the immediate damage to the surrounding area where she started the fire.

The issue of proximate cause continues to be a serious one in U.S. tort law. As toxic chemicals and large disasters tend to occur, the courts have to ask whether the ultimate injury was reasonably foreseeable from the initial negligence of the defendant. Cases arise where a defendant corporation pollutes a stream with chemicals. Those chemicals can last many years and tend to cause disease among a large portion of the surrounding population. It is possible to show that the pollution was the cause in fact of the injuries, but proximate cause is more difficult. The courts will want to see that the injuries were reasonably foreseeable from the initial negligence.

E.   Defenses

As with intentional torts, there are defenses to negligence claims. Thus, proof of negligence on the part of the defendant does not guarantee the plaintiff a recovery. The defendant has the opportunity to offer evidence in defense. The most commonly used defenses are based upon the acts or conduct of the plaintiff. Where the plaintiff was also negligent, the liability of the defendant may be reduced or eliminated.

1.   Contributory Negligence

The defense of contributory negligence arose along with the original development of the negligence claim itself. The theory behind the defense was simple. Where the defendant was negligent, the defendant should pay for harm to the plaintiff. Where, however, the plaintiff was also negligent, the defendant should be excused from paying for any harm to the plaintiff. Using that basic theory, the defense of contributory negligence had the following elements. The defendant could prove that the plaintiff failed to use reasonable care for his or her own safety and that the injury that the plaintiff suffered was within the risk that the plaintiff created.

An easy example of using contributory negligence can be seen with another automobile accident. Imagine that the defendant is driving along the road at a speed higher then the posted speed limit. The plaintiff suddenly comes out into the road in front of the automobile. The plaintiff is struck by the automobile and sues the defendant for injuries. The defendant was negligent for driving over the posted speed limit. The defendant would claim that the plaintiff engaged in contributory negligence. The plaintiff failed to use reasonable care by not looking before stepping into the road and that negligence caused the accident. If the jury believed the defendant's evidence, the claim against the defendant would be barred.

2.   Last Clear Chance Doctrine

Courts were not happy with the all or nothing approach with contributory negligence. It seemed possible that a negligent defendant was avoiding liability when a seriously injured plaintiff may have contributed to the accident. Courts created a doctrine known as last clear chance to avoid some of the harshness of contributory negligence. This doctrine provides that even though the plaintiff engaged in contributory negligence, if the defendant had the last clear chance to avoid the accident, the defendant will still be liable.

3.   Assumption of Risk

Another traditional defense to negligence is assumption of risk. This also provides that the defendant will not have to pay for the injuries to the plaintiff, but on proof of different elements. This defense requires that the defendant prove that the plaintiff knew and understood the risk and voluntarily encountered it. Where contributory negligence is a situation where the plaintiff carelessly and unknowing creates risks for him or herself, assumption of risk is where the plaintiff understands the risk and voluntarily encounters it. There are times, for example, when a plaintiff might get into an automobile with a driver that the plaintiff knows is not fully competent to drive. This might occur when the plaintiff is trying to help a new driver learn to drive or where the plaintiff is accepting a ride from a driver the plaintiff knows to be impaired by drugs or alcohol. Under either situation, the plaintiff would be held to have assumed the risk. The plaintiff knew of the risks and voluntarily encountered them.

4.   Comparative Fault

As noted earlier, courts have not been completely supportive of the idea of negligence and defenses being an all or nothing proposition. It did not seem appropriate that a defendant who was at fault should avoid all liability when the plaintiff was even partially at fault. Due to this concern, the vast majority of United States jurisdictions have moved away from contributory negligence and adopted comparative fault. Under comparative fault, the defendant can still prove that the plaintiff was also negligent, but that negligence by the plaintiff will not completely bar the defendant's liability. Under comparative fault, the defendant's liability will be reduced by the plaintiff's percentage of fault.

As jurisdictions have adopted comparative fault, they have chosen one of two types. Jurisdictions may use "pure" or "modified" comparative fault.

Pure comparative fault allows the plaintiff to recover damages from the defendant regardless of the extent of the plaintiff's fault. In such a jurisdiction, if the plaintiff was 10% at fault, the plaintiff would recover 90% of his or her damages. If the plaintiff was 90% at fault, the plaintiff would recover 10% of his or her damages.

Modified comparative fault allows the plaintiff to recover, less his or her percentage of fault, so long as the plaintiff's fault does not exceed the fault of the defendant. If the plaintiff's fault exceeds the fault of the defendant, then the plaintiff recovers nothing. In such a jurisdiction, if the plaintiff was 10% at fault, the plaintiff would recover 90% of his or her damages. If, however, the plaintiff was 90% at fault, the plaintiff would recover nothing.

V. STRICT LIABILITY

Strict liability is the third and final basis of liability. Intent required that the defendant knew of the consequences. Negligence required that the defendant failed to use reasonable care to create the risk. Strict liability allows recovery against the defendant even though the defendant neither knew of the consequences nor acted unreasonably. The defendant may be thought of in such cases as an innocent party. It may seem to some to be unfair to require a defendant to pay for injuries when the defendant was innocent. The theory, however, is that there are certain types of conduct or undertakings that are so dangerous that the defendant must be ready to pay for damages when they occur. It does not matter that the defendant used all possible care to avoid the injuries.

A.   Animals

One of the earliest forms of strict liability arose from the keeping of animals. The issue of animals may be divided into two types. Strict liability may occur due to escaping animals and it may also occur due to attacking animals.

When defendants keep barnyard animals, such defendants will be liable when those animals escape and cause harm. This could occur when cows in a pasture move into a neighbor's corn field and start eating the corn. It would not matter that the defendant used all possible care to keep the cows in the field. It should be noted that there is no strict liability for non-barnyard animals escaping. If, for example, a defendant's cat escapes, goes into the neighbor's flower bed and digs up the tulips, this is not considered to be strict liability. The plaintiff would have to prove negligence on the part of the defendant.

The rules for escaping animals developed in the early common law system. Although those rules are well known, many states have passed statutes modifying the rules. For barnyard animals, many states have "fencing statutes" that specify exactly the duties owed for keeping animals. In addition, many areas have leash laws that regulate non-barnyard animals.

When animals attack humans, there may be strict liability. Where someone keeps wild animals, for example, that person is liable if the animal escapes and attacks someone. Attacks by domestic animals, such as dogs, create more difficult problems. The old rule for attacking dogs was that the owner of the dog would be strictly liable if the owner had "scienter" of the dog's vicious tendencies. Because of this rule, it has frequently been said that all dogs were entitled to one bite. Since the owner needed to know of the vicious tendencies of the dog, the owner would claim no such knowledge unless the dog had bitten someone before. Although clearly a previous attack by the dog would prove the scienter, the "one bite" rule is not really accurate. It is possible for a dog owner to know of the vicious tendencies of the animal without the dog having ever bitten anyone before. The owner could have trained the dog to be vicious or observed the dog trying to bite someone. As with escaping animals, many states have passed statutes extending strict liability for animal bites. Some of these statutes apply strict liability in the absence of "scienter."

B.   Abnormally Dangerous or Ultrahazardous Activities

Another area of strict liability may be grouped under the heading of "abnormally dangerous" or "ultrahazardous" activities. Text writers have used both terms over the years to try to describe the types of activities that will lead to liability without proof of fault on the part of the defendant. The current trend appears to indicate that there are two elements to prove to bring the conduct within this theory. The plaintiff can recover without proof of fault on the part of the defendant if the plaintiff can prove that the activity was one that created a risk of harm that could not be eliminated by the exercise of utmost care and the activity was one that was not of common usage.

Examples of activities that may give rise to strict liability may be seen in companies that must use blasting materials in their work. Major construction companies and mining companies may frequently need to have dangerous blasting materials. It has been common in the United States to apply strict liability to blasting. Thus, a construction company that uses dynamite to blast a hole in the ground for new construction, could have rocks being thrown into the air that hit someone's house. The company would be strictly liable for the harm. The plaintiff would not have to prove that the company intended to hit the house or even acted unreasonably. The business of blasting is considered to be so dangerous that the company must cover the costs.

VI.   PRODUCTS LIABILITY

All of the above discussion covered the basics of tort law. It was intended to point out the three bases of liability that are used. The rest of the material in this chapter notes some of the larger additional issues that arise in torts. The following topics are not additional bases of liability. As noted several times, there are three bases of liability and only three. Those three are intent, negligence and strict liability. The following claims all use one or more of those three bases. Products liability, for example, is a type of claim that uses, primarily, negligence and strict liability.

A.   Negligence

Products liability is an area of tort law that has expanded rapidly since the 1960s. It was, however, an area that has generally been available since the early part of the twentieth century. The early development was concerned with the use of negligence. As the marketing of products began to change in the late 1800s, long chains of distribution opened up. Consumers did not purchase products directly from manufacturers. Manufacturers would sell to wholesalers who would then sell to retailers. Consumers would then purchase the product from retailers. The early part of the twentieth century saw the creation of actions by injured consumers against anyone in that chain of distribution. When a consumer purchased a product and was then injured by it, that consumer would sue the manufacturer, wholesaler or retailer. The difficulty, however, was that the consumer had to prove the elements of negligence. The consumer would have to prove that the defendant failed to use reasonable care in the manufacturing and marketing of the product. Imagine, for example, the difficulty in proving negligence on what would appear a simple products liability case. A consumer might purchase a soft drink in a grocery store. When the consumer gets home and tries to open the drink, the bottle might explode and injure the consumer. If the consumer wanted to sue for negligence, that consumer would have to prove which parties in the manufacture or sale of the drink were negligent. For a soft drink, that might include trying to prove that the manufacturer of the bottle, the company that fills the bottles, the delivery company, or the grocery store failed to use reasonable care. Such a case is very difficult to prove. In the 1960s, the law created a form of strict liability to ease the plaintiff's burden in seeking recovery for injuries due to defective products.

B.   Strict Liability

Courts began to discuss the idea that manufacturers of products were making substantial profits from those products but were not being required to pay all of the costs associated with them. When a product failed and caused an injury, costs were generated. If the manufacturer could avoid paying those costs, then the injured party would have to cover his or her own injury costs. Some courts began to speculate that injury costs ought to be considered a cost of doing business. In order to ease the injured party's burden in proving such a case, the courts and scholars recommended a new claim.

In the 1960s courts began to adopt strict liability for defective products. If an injury occurred, a plaintiff could recover upon proof that:

1)   The injury was due to a product,

2)   that was in a defective condition,

3)   unreasonably dangerous,

4)   to users or consumers,

5)   reached the consumer in an unchanged condition, and

6)   caused physical harm to the person or property.

The new doctrine of strict liability for product injuries was widely accepted in the United States. This area is new and continues to grow and change. It is important to look at some basic concepts while keeping in mind that this area of the law may change further in the future.

This claim is limited to injuries that arise out of products. It is not designed to cover claims for injuries due to real property or the dispensing of services. Where, for example, a person is injured due to medical malpractice, the claim remains one of negligence in that it is a service and therefore not subject to strict liability. In addition, if a person trips in a hole in the ground while visiting an outdoor garden shop, the claim must be for negligence.

It is required that the product be defective. The courts have realized that there are three possible types of defect. A product may have a design defect. The design defect claims are the most difficult. The product would have been manufactured in exactly the condition that the manufacturer intended. The plaintiff, however, is claiming that it could have been made using a better design. Typically, the plaintiff will have to offer expert evidence that a feasible alternative design is available. Upon the initial introduction of strict liability for product injuries, design defect cases were considered a part of that doctrine. As the law has continued to develop, however, courts seem to be returning design defect cases to negligence.

The second type of possible defect is a failure to warn. In such cases, the plaintiff has identified a danger that the product has and claims that there were inadequate warnings on how to use the product in a safe manner. It should be obvious to any modern consumer that most products now come with extensive warnings and instruction. Much of this has been brought about by the fear of lawsuits. As with design defect, warning cases appear to be moving away from true strict liability. Courts seem to be placing the failure to warn cases back into negligence.

The third type of defect is the failure to properly manufacture the product. These cases were and remain the true strict liability claim. In these cases, the plaintiff is claiming that something was done to the product during the manufacturing process that was not consistent with the original design. Such a claim may be that parts were left off or improperly installed. Typically, the plaintiff can offer evidence that the product that caused the injury is different then all of the other products made by that manufacturer.

Once it is possible to identify the type of defect, it is also necessary to prove that the defect is unreasonably dangerous. Strict liability is not intended to be insurance. The manufacturer is not liable for every injury caused by a product. Imagine, for example, a consumer cuts his or her hand with a knife. Knifes are sharp and intended to be so. There is no way to make them safer. It would not be an appropriate action to sue for such an injury. If, however, the knife blade broke during normal use and injured the plaintiff, a strict liability claim may be appropriate. If the plaintiff could show that the blade was made with inferior metals, the plaintiff might be successful. Courts had to create tests to try to explain how those types of examples could be interpreted.

One of the first tests developed was the consumer expectation test. In order to prove unreasonably dangerous, courts would ask if the product performed in a manner as would be expected by the ordinary consumer. This allowed the jury to focus on the product and not the conduct of the manufacturer. There was some concern that the consumer expectation test would not work with complex products. Consumers would not be able to have expectations about products that were too complex. Some courts began to move to a risk-utility test. Such a test would ask the jury to compare the risks with the utility of the product. Using the knife example, the test seems clear. A knife that cuts a finger is reasonably safe. There is a risk of injury, but the utility of having knives in the modern world outweighs that. A knife that breaks apart is too risky for its own utility. Other similar tests have been developed by courts, but those two seem to capture the spirit of the majority of jurisdictions.

An additional test, for example, may be referred to as a knowledgeable manufacturer test. The jury is instructed that they are to assume that the manufacturer had knowledge of the defect and then decide whether a reasonable, knowledgeable manufacturer would have placed the product on the market. This test is merely asking the jury to perform a risk/utility analysis under a different format.

In applying strict liability, courts have had to decide how far the liability would extend. Modern products may injure not only the buyer, but members of the family and even total strangers. An automobile that is defective may jump a curb and hit a bystander. In reviewing products cases, the courts have determined that "users or consumers" may recover for such injuries. This includes, for example, the buyer, family members, and even other users and bystanders. The ultimate test for the proper plaintiff is similar to the "foreseeable plaintiff" test discussed in the section on negligence.

It is necessary that the product has reached the injured party in a substantially unchanged condition. The manufacturer would be liable for defects that the manufacturer created in the product. The manufacturer would not be liable for defects that arose due to changes or alterations made by others to the product.

The injuries for which recovery may be sought are limited to physical injuries to the plaintiff's person or property. The purpose of this limit is to avoid using strict liability for economic loss damages. When a product fails, it may cause personal injury to the user and it may damage other property. An automobile defect may cause a wreck that injures people and other cars. Those damages would be recoverable. That same wreck, however, may result in the automobile not being available for use in a business. The automobile, for example, may have been used for package delivery or as a taxi. By being damaged, the automobile would cause lost profits for that business. The lost profits would not be available in a claim for strict liability. The plaintiff would have to use other types of claims. Contract remedies and warranty claims, for example, would have to be used for those economic losses.

C.   Other Types of Claims

It should be noted that this discussion of products liability is merely an overview of the topic. Negligence and strict liability are the primary claims in tort for product injuries, but other types of claims may also be brought. As noted above, it is common for claims based on contract and warranty to also arise when a product causes an injury.

VII. DEFAMATION

An interesting area of tort law is the claim for defamation. This claim has an ancient history that arose initially in England, but it continues to change in the United States. The basic theory of the claim is that people have a right to protect their good name. People should not have to suffer others telling lies about them. The action for defamation allows recovery for the harm done to a person's reputation.

A.   Common Law Elements

There are two types of defamation claims. The claims may be for libel or slander. Libel actions are for those defamatory statements that are in writing. Slander actions are for those defamatory statements that are oral. The plaintiff must prove the nature of the defamatory statement by showing why it is defamatory.

The plaintiff must also prove that the defamatory statement was heard or read by some third party. This element of the claim is called publication. Passing the defamatory statement to others is what harms the plaintiff's reputation.

The plaintiff must also be able to prove that the statement was understood by others as actually applying to the plaintiff. This element is called the requirement that the statement be "of and concerning" the plaintiff.

Those elements would have been the basic claim for relief for a common law tort of defamation. It was also recognized at that time that the defendant could avoid liability by proving that the statements that were made were true. It was commonly stated that, "truth was an absolute defense." It is the issue of truth as a defense that has seen the greatest change in twentieth century United States.

B.   The Impact of Free Speech Requirements

The United States Constitution has a provision known as the First Amendment. This amendment protects the right of freedom of speech. It is designed to make sure there is free and open debate on all issues. The law concerning the First Amendment is quite complex and covers a range of topics. This chapter will not try to cover the full law of the First Amendment, but must note some of the ways in which the First Amendment has had an impact on the law of defamation.

In the 1960s, in a case called *New York Times v. Sullivan*, the United States Supreme Court began to recognize that a large tort judgment against a defendant could have the impact of creating a fear of speaking. This fear of speaking, frequently known as a "chilling effect on free speech," was raised as a reason to limit the broad scope of defamation cases. In the *New York Times* case and additional subsequent cases, the United States Supreme Court added some rules of limitation on claims for defamation. Those limitations would be in addition to the other elements that had existed at common law.

First, the Court recognized that public officials and public figures had great access to the public to clear their own good names. In addition, actions by public officials and public figures were the ones that needed to be discussed fully in newspapers and by the public at large. If a public official could sue and recover a large judgment, there could be a chilling effect on the free and open debate about public issues. To limit that impact, the Court added the first limitation. In order for a public official or public figure to bring an action for defamation, the public figure would have to prove that the defendant knew the statement that was being made was false. This element of the claim is referred to as "actual malice." Notice that this raised the defamation claim to one of intent.

Second, the court recognized that private figures do not have such great access to clear their names. In addition, there is less need for the public to debate issues about private figures. The Court ruled that private figures could sue for defamation, but states had to adopt a basis of liability that was not strict liability. This meant that states could adopt the same standard as the one used for public figures or the states could adopt a negligence standard.

It is interesting that it has now been recognized that the Court had indirectly changed the burden of proof on truth. In the past, the defendant had to prove that a statement was true in order to avoid liability for defamation. Today, the plaintiff has to first prove that the statement is false in order to recover for defamation.

These changes in defamation law have made it more difficult for plaintiffs to recover for such statements. It has been thought that the increased difficulty was necessary to protect the guaranteed right to free speech.

VIII. PRIVACY

An area of tort law that is similar to defamation is the area for protection of the right of privacy. Where defamation protects an individual from harm to his or her reputation, privacy claims are designed to protect the general right to a person's identity. Tort law in this area has developed four separate types of actions.

The first type of action is to protect a person from commercial appropriation. Where a defendant uses a plaintiff's name or likeness for commercial purposes, the plaintiff has a claim. Clearly this is a claim that protects the rights of celebrities to sell the rights to use their names and pictures in advertising campaigns. Companies cannot use such names without paying fees. Attempts to use such a name or picture would lead to a claim. The right of privacy protects others, however, and not just celebrities. Even unknown people may, at times, find their name or likeness used without consent. Such use is protected by this claim.

A second type of privacy claim is for the intrusion into the seclusion or solitude of an individual. If a defendant intrudes into the home or privacy of another, a claim is available. This claim can be used when law enforcement enters a home without a proper search warrant. It can also be used, however, for much broader activities. If someone is using hidden cameras or looking into someone's home, the action for this type of right of privacy can be used to recover for the harm done.

A third type of right of privacy is for placing the plaintiff in a false light. Where a defendant makes false statements about a plaintiff, that plaintiff may bring an action to recover for the harm done by those statements. This claim appears to be very similar to defamation. The primary difference is that the statement does not have to be defamatory. There may be times when a defendant makes a statement about a plaintiff that does not harm his or her reputation. In fact, those that hear the statement may feel pity for the plaintiff. That is sufficient for this claim. Since this claim needs a publication to a third party in order for the action to exist, the constitutional issues that were discussed in the defamation section arise. The plaintiff would have to prove those special elements as either a public figure or a private figure in order to recover for the false light claim.

The final type of right of privacy claim is for the public disclosure of private facts. Where a defendant reveals private facts to the public that are highly offensive, the plaintiff may seek a claim. This part of the right of privacy is in a state of change. Because of the constitutional issues discussed in the defamation section, some believe that statements made must be false in order to be actionable. The traditional claim for public disclosure was allowed for making true information public. This might mean that there can no longer be an action for public disclosure where the statements are true. There are some issues that are clear. Since the action only lies when private facts are made public, the repeating of public facts does not give rise to a claim. In addition, revealing information about public figures is probably not actionable. The fact of being a public figure opens up the person to public discussion. It appears, therefore, that if this action still exists, it only exists in limited form. Private figures may be able to bring actions for public disclosure of private facts.

IX. BUSINESS TORTS

Tort law has a wide variety of uses. It may, for example, appear that when actions arise protecting business interests, that those actions are based on contract, partnerships, or corporations. In fact, many such actions are tort claims. The following will point out some of the basic business torts.

A.   Misrepresentation

The making of a false statement upon which someone relies, is a tort. The tort of misrepresentation has a series of elements that the plaintiff must prove. An examination of those elements will reveal the details of the tort.

First, the plaintiff must prove that there was a false representation of a material fact. This element requires proof that there was some outward expression of the fact. That expression may have been oral, written, or by conduct. In addition, the falsity must have been of a fact. The tort of misrepresentation will not lie for statements of opinion.

Second, misrepresentation is one of the torts that may be based on intent or negligence. The plaintiff may recover if the statement was made with knowledge that it was false or if the defendant failed to use reasonable care to determine whether it was true or not.

Third, the defendant had to have the intent to induce the plaintiff to rely upon the statement. The statement was made in an attempt to gain the plaintiff's reliance.

Fourth, there must have been justifiable reliance on the statement. The plaintiff can only bring the claim if the plaintiff actually relied upon the statement. If the plaintiff acted for his or her own reasons or for other reasons, then no action will lie.

Finally, there must be harm as a result of the reliance on the false statement. The plaintiff may be able to point to some personal injury or property damage. In addition, this is one of the few torts that would also allow the plaintiff to recover for pure economic losses.

B.   Interference with Contracts

There is also an action for interference with a contract. Clearly when two parties enter into a contract and one of the parties breaches the contract, the other party to the contract would have a claim. That claim would be based on contract law. Where, however, some third party stranger to the contract induced one of the parties to the contract to breach it, the injured party would have a tort claim against the third party. In order to bring this claim, the plaintiff would have to prove just a few elements. It would have to be proven that the third party knew about the existence of the contract and intentionally induced the breach.

Other similar claims can also be brought. There are times when two parties have a long history of business relationships. The relationships may be defined by periodic contracts or may just be a course of doing business. During this relationship, the parties may have developed the expectation that the relationship will continue. If a third party stranger to the relationship induces one of the parties to break the relationship, then there may be a claim for intentional inducement to breach an advantageous relationship. These claims are much more difficult to prove then the inducement to breach a contract. Where there is no existing contract, the third party will allege that he or she was merely engaging in a free market economy in an effort to gain new business. The free market economy does expect open and competitive markets. It also expects "fair" markets. The claim for inducement to breach an advantageous relationship is designed to promote the "fair" competition. In order for a plaintiff to be successful, some evidence of unfair dealings will probably be required. It may be necessary, for example, to prove something like a monopoly, misuse of trade secrets, or other such unfair trade practices.

C.   Beginnings of Intellectual Property

Tort law is also the home for the beginnings of intellectual property. The interference with privately owned intellectual property is a wrong that can be remedied with a tort. Copyrights, trademarks, patents, and other trade secrets are merely forms of "property." When others take those forms of property for use without consent, the claim is one in tort. Much of this area of the law has now been regulated by statutes and government agencies. The early beginnings, however, saw the creation of these rights as forms of torts.

X.   OTHER TORTS

The topics discussed in this Chapter were designed to give an overview of the law of torts. The initial material covered the three bases of liability which are the only bases of liability in torts. Some of the other sections were designed to highlight the more important areas of tort law, such as products liability or defamation, which apply to one or more of the three bases of liability. The law of torts, however, is a broad and complex area. There are numerous other areas of tort law that could also be discussed. Actions to protect civil rights or to protect the use and enjoyment of land, for example, are also tort claims. It is even recognized that there are torts that do not have names. When an injury occurs due to the conduct of another, the law of torts will create a remedy to compensate that injured party. This Chapter, therefore, was designed to give merely an introduction to the study of torts.

XI.   STRUCTURE OF A LAWSUIT IN TORT ACTIONS

Torts claims are, of course, litigated in the civil courts in the United States. Since tort law is primarily a matter of state law, the claims are regularly handled by the state civil courts. It is possible to bring a state claim for tort in federal court, but the law to be applied will be the state law. The procedure that is followed in tort claims is similar to all other civil matters. There are, however, a few differences that are noteworthy.

A. Judge and Jury Roles

The judge and jury play specific roles in tort claims. The judge, as noted in some of the sections above, is in the case to decide questions of law and then explain that law to the jury. In addition to deciding questions of admissibility of evidence, the primary issue that the judge must decide is the duty question. The judge will decide whether there is a duty and the extent of that duty. The jury will decide the facts of the case. This means that the jury will have to decide whether the duty has been breached, whether there is an injury, the extent of the injury and whether that injury was caused by the breach. It should be clear that the jury has an extensive role in tort cases. Because of this, much of the litigation with tort claims concern problems related to proving the facts. Tort lawyers spend much of their time preparing fact witnesses and expert witnesses to give evidence at trials.

B. Roles of Attorneys

With the critical importance of convincing the jury of the facts of the case, the role of the attorneys in a tort case is to prepare and question witnesses at trial. A complex tort case may take several years of preparation. The attorneys will have to question and prepare fact witnesses. Those same attorneys will have to find and prepare expert witnesses for trials. With the great use of expert witnesses, attorneys frequently find that they too must develop a good level of expertise in specialized areas where they litigate regularly. A trial attorney that conducts numerous medical malpractice cases, for example, may find that gaining a substantial medical knowledge is critical. The role of the attorney is to present that evidence and make arguments to show the case to the jury in the best light favorable to his or her client.

C. Fees for Attorneys

Fees for attorneys in tort cases are somewhat different in the United States than many other countries. Attorneys that handle the defense of cases are paid in the usual way. They will accept a client and state a contract amount for handling the representation. That amount will usually be based upon an hourly fee. The defendant client will then be billed on a regular basis for the time that has been spent on the case.

Attorneys that represent plaintiffs, however, may have a different type of fee structure. Plaintiff's attorneys may work on what is called a contingency fee. The attorney will agree to represent the client and work the entire case, but will only be paid if the plaintiff is successful and recovers a judgment. The plaintiff's attorney will then take a percentage of that final judgment. The usual percentage charged is about 33%, but the figure may be higher or lower depending on the case. Using this fee arrangement, the plaintiff does not have to provide any money to begin the case. The attorneys for the plaintiff are only paid if the plaintiff recovers a judgment.

XII. CONCLUSION

It was suggested in the beginning of this chapter that the study of tort law could occupy a lifetime. This overview should illustrate the basic rules of tort law while suggesting the broad areas that are still open to review. The basic principle of tort law can be seen as simple. It is that area of the law that provides for compensation to an injured party when another person is responsible for that injury. The earliest years of tort law that were concerned with the simple punch in the nose or the trespass on land could deal with simple rules. Because of the numerous conflicts, confrontations and injuries that may arise in a modern society, that simple principle has expanded to include a multitude of differing fact situations. Modern tort law must concern itself with medical malpractice, products liability, rights of privacy, and intellectual property to name just a few. Since society continues to grow and change, tort law must also continue to grow and change to keep up with the types of circumstances and injuries that may occur in the future. It is difficult to predict what new conflicts and injuries will occur in the future. It is possible to say, however, that tort law will form the rules to allow for peaceful resolution of those conflicts and injuries.

Chapter 4

OVERVIEW OF U.S. LAW: CRIMINAL JUSTICE

By — Andrew E. Taslitz

I. CRIMINAL JUSTICE SYSTEM BASICS

There is no such thing as a single "American" system of criminal justice. Each of the fifty states has its own set of procedures and substantive crimes, as does the federal government. There are also separate criminal justice systems for the military and for juveniles, and even local ordinances can render some conduct criminal in one city but not another in the same state. Each of these systems is in some ways unique, yet the systems may overlap as well. For example, some conduct may violate both federal and several state laws, each level of government having jurisdiction over the respective crimes. Inter-jurisdictional compacts and negotiations among prosecutors are often necessary to resolve jurisdictional conflicts over particular cases. Moreover, there can be multiple systems run by the same governmental entity. Thus there may in a single jurisdiction be courts of general jurisdiction for adult criminal cases, but, with a defendant's consent, a parallel alternative system of "specialty" courts, generally reserved for first-time offenders, such as a court for drug abusers, and another court for drunk drivers.

Yet there are also substantial similarities among these jurisdictions, and it is mostly these similarities on which we will focus here. Some of these similarities are mandated by the United States Constitution, most of its Bill of Rights provisions regulating criminal justice having nationwide application. The federal Constitution sets a floor on these rights, but state constitutions can apply, at times, even greater protections. Other similarities result simply from historical, cultural, economic, and political forces common to most of the nation. The federal Constitution in particular guarantees freedom from unreasonable searches and seizures in the Fourth Amendment, from compulsion to be a witness against one's self (also known as "self-incrimination") in the Fifth Amendment, and from excessive bail and cruel and unusual punishments in the Eighth Amendment. The Sixth Amendment also guarantees an accused rights to the effective assistance of counsel, including counsel's being paid by the State when clients are indigent; compulsory process for witnesses in the accused's favor; confrontation (primarily meaning face-to-face cross-examination) of the witnesses against him; and notice of the charges against him. Virtually every American jurisdiction has a public prosecutor's office, usually meaning full-time state employees who represent the State's interest in court and in aspects of pre-trial investigation. Jurisdictions vary, however, concerning the procedures for providing defense counsel. Some jurisdictions have state-funded public defender's offices of full-time defense lawyers for the indigent; others appoint private lawyers to represent individual clients at state expense; and still others combine both approaches. Defendants who can afford to hire counsel are expected, however, to do so on their own.

II. STEPS IN THE CRIMINAL PROCESS

Most criminal cases, particularly street crimes, begin with investigation by the police. The police might receive a report of a crime and catch a suspect in flight or might focus further investigation on particular individuals based upon perpetrator descriptions. The police administer lineups (several persons are placed in a line, and the victim or eyewitness is asked to select whom, if anyone, he or she recognizes as the assailant), photospreads (similar to lineups but using photos rather than live persons), interrogations, and scientific tests, such as DNA identification — tests generally done by professional police laboratory analysts. The police may also engage in searches and seizures, including, in important cases, electronic surveillance. Once the police conclude that they have identified the correct person as the offender, they will arrest him or her, something that requires a warrant if done in a home but that can be warrantless when done on the street. After arrest, the suspect is brought to the police station for "booking" — the taking of his or her photograph and fingerprints and the collection of information relevant to assessing the amount, if any, of this individual's bail and the conditions of release while awaiting trial. The formal process then begins with the filing of a complaint.

In large urban areas, the complaiant will be drafted by local prosecutors based upon police-submitted paperwork summarizing the evidence and perhaps upon brief interviews with one or more officers. The prosecutor must decide what charges the evidence supports; whether to give notice of an intention to seek special remedies, such as mandatory minimum sentences or the death penalty; whether to pursue alternatives to the formal processes, such as "pre-trial probation," allowing the suspect to avoid prosecution entirely if he or she successfully completes, for example, drug-counseling programs, job-training programs, or a high school equivalency diploma; and what bail to seek or whether to oppose pre-trial release entirely.

The suspect next proceeds to the initial appearance, also known as a preliminary arraignment, before a judge or magistrate, an appearance that, barring unusual circumstances, is constitutionally mandated to occur within forty-eight hours of arrest. At that appearance, the court informs the suspect of the charges and of his or her basic constitutional rights; determines whether, if the allegations made are assumed true, the evidence recited in the complaint supports each of the charges alleged; and sets bail of a specific amount, which is designed to ensure the accused's appearance at trial, or, instead of bail, the court may order preventive detention of the suspect on the grounds that he will be a danger to himself or to others. In misdemeanor cases, a date will be scheduled for trial or a guilty plea. In felony cases, a date will be set for a preliminary hearing.

A preliminary hearing serves as a moderately more vigorous mechanism than the initial appearance for screening baseless charges out of the system. Evidence supporting the charges must be presented sufficient to show probable cause to believe the charges are true or to show a prima facie case (enough evidence to enable a reasonable jury to find the truth), the precise standard of proof varying with the jurisdiction. Unlike with the initial appearance, the mere allegations made in the complaant are insufficient. On the other hand, witness credibility is not in dispute, and the standard of proof is far lower than at trial, so proof might be quite informal and fairly minimal. Thus many jurisdictions may require a small number of percipient witnesses but permit them to testify to varying amounts of hearsay. Other jurisdictions permit unlimited hearsay, so that the hearing may be little more than an officer reading his (or another officer's) police report into evidence. If the hearing judge finds sufficient evidence to proceed to trial, the court may issue an "information," a new charging document to replace the complaint, particularly doing so in jurisdictions where there are no grand juries.

In the federal system and some states, the preliminary hearing will be followed by a grand jury hearing. Such hearings generally occur in secrecy and are ex parte, for neither defense counsel nor judge, but rather only prosecutors, witnesses (one-at-a-time), a court reporter, and the grand jurors, are present. The grand jury decides whether to "indict," that is, to file a new charging document called an "indictment" to supersede any complaint, doing so if they find probable cause to support the charges. The grand jurors might indict on some, all, or none of the charges. However, given that they are alone with the prosecutor, who has de facto if not de jure authority to call witnesses and who instructs them on the law, most grand jurors defer to a prosecutor's recommendation, leading to the well-known, if acerbic, saying that "a grand jury will indict a ham sandwich." But "runaway" grand juries, who are not so compliant, do occur, and some grand juries choose as well to exercise their inherent power of "presentment," permitting them to investigate certain matters they deem of public interest and to prepare a report on them. Grand juries may also be used as an alternative to police investigation as a way to start a case. This may happen because grand juries have a power that police and prosecutors acting on their own do not: the power of the subpoena. A subpoena is a court order for documents, other physical evidence, or testimony to be brought before a grand jury. The documents and the witness transcripts may give the State powerful evidence with which to indict that they otherwise would have lacked, while pinning down witness stories in case they try to tell another tale at trial. Even jurisdictions that do not routinely use grand juries usually permit them to be enlisted into action where special investigation is needed, thus the moniker, "investigating grand juries." Furthermore, where grand juries are routinely mandated, a defendant might sometimes waive his right to a grand jury, especially if he plans to plead guilty. Other times, however, an accused will insist on a grand jury but file motions "to quash," to invalidate many or all the subpoenas, a ploy that, if successful, may deny the State sufficient evidence to indict.

After indictments, the case proceeds to an arraignment. At the arraignment, a defendant again pleads guilty or not guilty. If he pleads guilty, his plea may be taken either at the arraignment or at a separate date scheduled for taking the plea. It is not enough for a defendant simply to say, "I plead guilty." He must engage with the judge in a guilty plea "colloquy." A colloquy involves the court, with the assistance of the prosecutor, in advising the defendant of all his relevant constitutional and statutory rights; ensuring that he waives them knowingly, intelligently, and voluntarily; and advising him of the facts alleged and ensuring that his admission to the truth of those facts is also done knowingly, intelligently, and voluntarily. A plea may be open (no agreement between the defense and the prosecution) or negotiated (an agreement that the prosecution will recommend, or that the defendant will in fact receive, with judicial approval, a particular sentence or sentence range ("sentence bargaining") or will plead only to some charges but not others ("charge bargaining")). Negotiated pleas usually occur only if each side has something to gain. With "cooperating defendants," the defendant agrees to assist the prosecution in proving another criminal case, perhaps by testifying against a bigger fish, in exchange for sentencing or other concessions. With non-cooperating defendants, no such agreements are involved, but a prosecutor might have proof problems, making the prosecutor worry about the ability to prove many of the charges at trial, or the prosecutor may want to free up resources to use in more serious cases, so the prosecutor agrees to accept reduced charges or sentences to limit the risk of loss or increase resource availability elsewhere. The vast majority of criminal cases, in the federal system 96% of all convictions, are resolved by guilty pleas. The various American criminal justice systems combined, however, are so vast that the small remaining percentage of cases that do go to trial overburden the courts, frequently causing long delays between arrest and trial and causing still longer delays in civil cases, which, given constitutional speedy trial rights in criminal cases, must defer to criminal justice needs.

For defendants who do not plead guilty at arraignment (technically, defendants can choose to plead guilty at virtually any time — either before or after arraignment — that the court's schedule permits), a date will be set to hear pre-trial motions, such as motions to suppress evidence obtained unconstitutionally or violative of written evidence codes; motions to compel discovery; and motions to dismiss, perhaps on speedy trial or double jeopardy grounds. The losing side on such motions might re-evaluate the risks of going to trial and agree to further negotiations in the hope of finally achieving a guilty plea.

The next stage, trial, may either be before a judge (a "bench trial") or a jury. The defendant usually has a constitutional right to a jury, and there can be strategic advantages to exercising that right. For example, conviction generally requires a unanimous vote by all (usually twelve) jurors. If only eleven jurors agree on a verdict, the jury is "hung" and a mistrial is declared, permitting prosecutors to re-try the cases. Having lost once, however, prosecutors may not think it worth their limited time to try again. Additionally, jurors have the power, though, depending upon the jurisdiction, not the right, of "nullification," meaning that they can nullify or ignore the law to seek the verdict that they deem just. They have this power because jury deliberations (where the jurors debate the law and the evidence and decide what the verdict will be) occur in secret, so they cannot, with rare exceptions, be held to account for ignoring the law. There is a debate over whether they have the right to nullify, some arguing that it permits lawlessness, others arguing that it provides an important check on unjust laws or vindictive or incompetent prosecutors. Defendants in jury trials also gain some control over who will determine their fate because of the process of voir dire, of posing written and oral questions to jurors to ensure that they can be fair to both sides. Each side can move to strike a juror "for cause" on the theory that he or she cannot be fair, but each side is also entitled to a limited number of "peremptory strikes" — strikes that can be made without offering any justification for doing so. Short of a few constitutional limitations, such as an equal protection prohibition on striking jurors primarily because of their race, ethnicity, or sex, peremptory strikes can thus be made for entirely tactical reasons. Defendants may also sometimes prefer juries to judges because jurors do not become jaded by repeatedly hearing similar cases and collectively may bring a wealth of life experience, technical knowledge, and common sense to the table that may sometimes seem to favor the accused.

But bench trials can have their advantages too. Through the luck of the draw, a case might be assigned to a judge whom the defendant believes will be more sympathetic to his or her plight than the jury or more skeptical of police testimony and behavior. Judges often, consciously or not, give defendants a sentencing break if convicted after a bench trial because it saves an enormous amount of time and money relative to a jury trial. Some judges may also be more likely to believe certain defense witnesses or be more receptive to technical defenses than will a jury.

Once a petit jury (also known as a "trial" jury, as opposed to the investigating or indicting "grand" jury) is empanelled, the format of the trial proceeds much like a civil trial, though the liability rules, burdens of proof, and some of the grounds for objection may differ. The prosecutor presents his or her case-in-chief — his witnesses and other evidence — first. When done, the prosecutor "rests." If the case survives a defense motion for acquittal on the grounds that no reasonable jury could find that the prosecution has met its burden of proof, then the defense is free to present its case, if it so chooses, though it need not offer any proof whatsoever. After the defendant rests, the prosecution might offer rebuttal witnesses; then the defense may have a sur-rebuttal, if requested and if permitted by the court. The prosecution then makes its closing argument to the jury, seeking to explain why its witnesses should be believed and why the law mandates conviction, followed by the defense closing argument, which seeks to do the opposite. The judge, after a hearing debating the wisdom of jury instructions proposed by each side, instructs the jurors on the law, who then deliberate. If they unanimously acquit the defendant, the Double Jeopardy Clause of the Fifth Amendment of the United States Constitution bars the defendant being re-tried. No appeal is permitted from an acquittal. If they unanimously convict on any charges, a date will be set for post-trial motions, either for a new trial on the grounds that some aspect of the proceeding was so unfair as to potentially have altered the verdict, or for a motion in arrest of judgment (in effect, an order of acquittal) on the ground that no reasonable jury could have found each of the elements of each of the crimes proven beyond a reasonable doubt, which is the burden of persuasion placed upon the State as to all elements of crimes. Absent these motions, or assuming they are denied, a date is set for sentencing.

Much happens before sentencing. There are two broad types of sentencing jurisdictions: guidelines and non-guidelines. In guidelines jurisdictions, the legislature has crafted numerical rules to guide the sentencing judge's choice of punishment. Usually there will be one score based on the number and severity of any prior convictions and another score based on the severity of the current offense. The legislature creates a grid, each square in the grid specifying a range of punishment in terms of months and whether that range will be served on probation or in jail (for misdemeanants) or prison (for felons). In mandatory guidelines jurisdictions, barring special circumstances, the judge *must* sentence within the specified range, while in advisory jurisdictions he or she is not required to do so, although the judge must consider the guidelines and justify departures therefrom. In mandatory guidelines jurisdictions only, the federal Constitution requires a jury trial as to any facts (other than a prior criminal record) that might raise the guidelines sentence. A probation officer will also prepare, or arrange for the preparation of, both a pre-sentence report suggesting the proper guidelines ranges and recommending where the sentence should sit within those ranges and a psychologist's report. Lawyers on both sides might seek to offer input on the wisdom of the probation officer report's calculations and sentencing recommendations and on the accuracy of the facts the report recites, including the number and nature of prior convictions, the defendant's life history, character, and mental health, and the circumstances of the current offense. Plea bargaining may also have resulted in an agreement to set (with judicial approval), or to recommend, particular prior record and offense severity scores.

In non-guidelines jurisdictions, statutes specify the minimum and maximum penalties for each offense and the factors that the sentencing judge must consider in choosing the appropriate punishment. So long as the judge considers each factor and reasonably justifies how he or she weighs it, the judge's decision to choose any sentence within the statutorily-specified range will receive great deference from appellate courts. In any jurisdiction, guidelines or not, a defendant has a right of "allocution" — a right to address the court on matters relevant to sentencing. The sentencing options include probation — a sentence of no confinement but subject to such reasonable conditions as the judge might specify, including committing no new offenses, getting drug treatment or job training, or entering a sexual offender therapy program. A defendant who violates probation can be sentenced to any term of incarceration up to the maximum permitted by the statute defining the offense. For example, if a burglary statute permitted sentencing an offender in a non-guidelines jurisdiction to up to twenty years in prison but the judge in fact sentenced the offender to only five years probation on condition that the offender complete a drug abuse program, the defendant's failure to complete the abuse program entitles the judge to re-sentence the defendant to up to twenty years incarceration on the probation violation. If the suspect violated parole by committing a new burglary, upon conviction, he or she could be sentenced to up to twenty years in prison for that crime *on top of* the sentence of up to twenty years for the probation violation on the first offense.

Many jurisdictions also permit parole or its analogues to be part of a sentence. Parole is analogous to probation but may be served only after a term of incarceration is completed. Parole might be part of the original sentence ("I sentence you to five years in prison, followed by five years of parole"), in which case the term "supervised release" is generally used in place of the "parole" label. Or parole may result from a parole board recommending a prisoner's early release before a term of incarceration is completed, serving the remainder of this term as a parolee rather than a prisoner. (The only important distinction between "supervised release" and "parole," therefore, is that the judge determines the former, whereas a parole board of supposed specialists initially determines the latter.) Parole differs from probation in one other important respect: a parole violator in most jurisdictions may only be required to serve the remaining time on an original sentence in imprisonment. Imagine a defendant sentenced to ten years imprisonment but eligible for parole in five, who is in fact then paroled for a crime, such as burglary, for which the individual could originally have received up to twenty years in prison. If the defendant serves the resulting five-year prison portion of his or her sentence, then, after one year on the outside, violates parole, he or she can be required to serve the remaining four years of the sentence in prison. However, unlike probation, the defendant cannot be re-sentenced to serve the full maximum twenty years in prison to which he or she could originally have been condemned.

If a motion to reconsider a sentence is made and denied, the defendant may appeal either the sentence or the conviction itself. Usually the defendant will have at least one appeal as of right to an intermediate court, any later appeal to a still higher court sometimes also being of right but often being discretionary. Concerning the conviction, the defendant can seek the equivalent of an order of acquittal for the jury's unreasonably concluding that the state had proven its case beyond a reasonable doubt or for a new trial on the grounds that unfair procedures tainted the conviction, remedies similar to those sought at the trial level in post-verdict motions. Defense success is hard, however because the standard of review on appeal requires the appellate court to assume the truth of all the verdict-winner's (the prosecution's) witnesses, to make all reasonable available inferences in the prosecution's favor, and to be highly deferential to the verdict. Appellate courts will also apply the "harmless error" doctrine, refusing to reverse even a conviction based on error absent defense proof beyond a reasonable doubt that the error altered the verdict. Appeals of the wisdom of sentences also face an uphill battle, unless the record reveals that the sentencing judge did not consider all statutorily mandated factors, did not declare on the record reasonable justifications for his or her decision, did not properly compute the guidelines range, or did not provide sound reasons on the record for departing upward or downward from the guidelines' dictates.

If all appeals fail, defendants can file petitions for post-conviction relief, often called habeas corpus petitions, in a trial court, followed by an appeals process on those petitions. The post-conviction process is complex but generally requires a defendant to prove claims that he or she did not and reasonably could not have raised earlier, such as the ineffectiveness of his or her trial and appellate counsel.

III.   THE SUBSTANTIVE CRIMINAL LAW

A.   The Purposes of Criminal Law and Punishment

American substantive criminal law is generally understood to serve a number of sometimes conflicting purposes. These include primarily deterrence, retribution, isolation, rehabilitation, and education.

There are two forms of deterrence: specific and general. Both are future-oriented, seeking to prevent tomorrow's new crimes rather than respond to yesterday's old ones. Specific deterrence aims to discourage the individual punished from committing further crimes. General deterrence aims to discourage others contemplating crime from acting on those desires. The discouragement stems from their fear of suffering the penalties that they see visited upon current lawbreakers. In this sense, general deterrence sanctions use the punished individuals as a mere means for general crime prevention rather than as an end in themselves. Deterrence depends upon an economic vision of human nature: rational, informed persons will commit fewer crimes as the certainty of capture and the harshness of punishment rise. Critics question whether humans are in fact quite so rational and whether most persons are ordinarily aware of the penalties they face or of the true likelihood of their being caught. Resource and other constraints also mean that the chance of capture in the real world is low, so penalties must compensate by being so high as to frighten would-be criminals away from even the smallest risk of being caught — a logic that can lead to penalties out of all proportion to the seriousness of the crime committed. Tort law also serves as a deterrent, so critics find it hard to see how deterrence rationales justify the liberty-deprivation and stigma of criminal punishment.

Retribution is cousin to revenge — seeking to "get even" — but is different too in important ways. Revenge is wrought by the individual to right wrongs done to him. Retribution is done by the community, via the mechanisms of the State, to sanction harms done to the public. Both revenge and retribution are, however, backward-looking, seeking justice for harms done rather than discouragement of harms yet to be. However, because revenge is done by individuals, who may over-react, they may do more than "get even," seeking to hurt their assailants more than the harm they have suffered at the latter's hands. Retribution must instead be proportional, an eye-for-an-eye, a tooth-for-a-tooth, but no more.

There are many theories for what makes certain harms public ones, but two stand out: the debt-to-society and communicative retributivism approaches. The debt-to-society idea is that each member of society sacrifices his or her freedom of action in some ways to gain security for persons and property. Thus an angry man foregoes punching the victim of his ire and a covetous man foregoes stealing his heart's desire, and they do so so that they too will be freed from the fear of assault or of theft. Society exists only because of this security. When one man breaks the social contract, for example, getting the satisfaction of attacking someone he despises while himself remaining free from attack, he gets one benefit — the pleasure of the punch — denied to the rest of us; retains security that he will not suffer similar bodily harm; and does so without paying the price that the rest of us pay for restraining our impulses. In this small way, a single offender steals from society some of the security that makes it possible and angers its members, who rage at his breach of the social contract's bonds of reciprocity.

Communicative retributivism focuses instead on the messages expressed by criminal conduct. If I shoot you or steal your property, I send the message that you are less deserving of physical safety, property ownership, regard for rights, and simple respect than I. You humiliate me and must be brought down a peg. If society fails to sanction you, it tolerates, even reaffirms, this message of my diminishment. But society in a democratic republic must recognize the equal worth of all human beings. It must thus humiliate you in a way, and to a degree, that will unequivocally lower you in both your victim's eyes and society's more generally, toppling you from the higher status you wrongly assumed, thus humbling you into recognizing that you are worth no more (but also no less) than me. Only punishment can send this message effectively.

At its best, retributivism places a side constraint on deterrence, barring any penalty exceeding what the individual wrongdoer "deserves," even if a higher penalty would be a more effective deterrent. The criminal is thus no longer merely a means — though he may partly be so — to deterrence's end. However, gauging the amount of "humiliation" required to compensate for the amount of "insult" inflicted upon the victim is an amorphous and difficult task. Proportionality may thus prove elusive. At its worst, therefore, retributivism becomes an excuse for venting public rage via hugely excessive penalties, proportionality served in word but not deed.

The remaining purposes of punishment are far easier to explain. Under specific deterrence, an offender "isolated" in prison cannot harm others — at least not others outside the prison — while there. "Rehabilitation" refers to using punishment to make the offender into a better citizen, for example, sober instead of stoned, educated rather than ignorant, industrious rather than lazy. "Education" refers to the way in which the special stigmatizing effects of criminal punishment mark some moral principles as at the heart of society's identity, reaffirming and strengthening those principles in the public's eyes.

B.   Common Law Versus the Model Penal Code

Before moving from the purposes of the criminal law to studying some specific crimes and the structure of American criminal liability, some terms must first be defined. The term "the common law" generally means "judge-made law." Today, however, virtually all American criminal law is statutory. Some jurisdictions have, therefore, codified what was originally judge-made law. For ease of reference, these will be called "common law jurisdictions." Other jurisdictions have instead largely followed a model code prepared by the prestigious American Law Institute and called the Model Penal Code ("MPC"). Most real-world jurisdictions in fact draw on aspects of both the common law and the MPC approaches, adding further provisions unique to the particular jurisdiction. Because one cannot study all the many American jurisdictions in this chapter, for simplicity the world is divided into two ideal types: the common law approach or the MPC approach. Where the common law and the MPC, are similar there will simply be no mention of any distinction between them.

C.   Elements of Crimes

Each statutory crime defines a series of facts that must be charged and proven by the State in each individual case to convict that person of that crime. Each statutory fact-to-be-proven is an "element" of the crime. There are four basic types of elements: acts (or omissions to act where there is a duty to do so), mental states, attendant circumstances, and results. Not every crime contains all four types of elements, but almost every crime contains the first two types — acts and mental states.

An "act" is a voluntary bodily movement. Thus a defendant drinking himself into a stupor in his bedroom but thereafter dragged into the street must be acquitted of the crime of public drunkenness. He did voluntarily drink to excess but did not voluntarily do so in a *public* place.

A mental state is either subjective — what was actually in the offender's mind — or objective — what the community says should have been there. There are numerous types of mental states required by the voluminous criminal codes of the states, territories, military, and federal governments, but the four most common or "core" mental states are these: purpose (wanting something to be true), knowledge (being aware of its truth or of a practical certainty that it will occur), recklessness (conscious awareness of a risk of its existence), and negligence (should have been, but was not, aware even of any risk that it existed, prompting action whose social costs exceed its social benefits).

An attendant circumstance is a fact that must exist to obtain a conviction but that a defendant need not cause to exist. Common law burglary thus requires a trespassory breaking and entering of the dwelling house of another in the nighttime with intent to commit a crime therein. Lack of consent to enter ("trespassory"), residential use, by another, and the presence of nighttime are all facts that must be proven to convict an offender, but they need not have been caused by the offender — that is, the offender does not make day turn into night or others to reside in the home entered.

A result, by contrast, is a fact that must exist *and* must be caused by the defendant's voluntary act. The classic example is homicide, which has death as an element. If death does not result, or if defendant's action was not the cause of the death, there is no homicide, though the State might proceed by charging attempted homicide or aggravated assault.

Two of these four types of elements — acts and mental states — merit further elaboration because of their central roles in American criminal justice.

D.   Acts

The act requirement reflects the idea that no one should be punished for evil thoughts alone. Those thoughts must cause voluntary behaviors with real-world impacts before criminal liability may be imposed. Moreover, those actions must be voluntarily chosen or they are not really the *defendant's* actions.

Inaction can also be the basis for liability but only rarely. American culture is highly individualistic, so American law frowns upon creating too many affirmative obligations to others. There are exceptions to this rule, the most common being: (1) where a statute expressly creates a duty to act; (2) where there is a special status relationship, such as a mother owing a duty to protect her young child from harm; (3) where you contractually assume an obligation to act, as a nurse might in agreeing to care for an ill patient; (4) where you create a risk, for then you must act to prevent its being realized (for example, if you open a chemical plant near a residential neighborhood and thus create a risk of leeching toxic substances into the water supply, you must make reasonable efforts to prevent that from occurring); (5) where you voluntarily undertake to aid another in a way that isolates him or her from others' providing help (for example, saying to concerned onlookers that you will take an ill man to the hospital, leading them to abandon their efforts to do so, you must follow through on your promise); and (6) where you invite others onto your land, you must take reasonable steps to protect them from danger.

One sort of act — possession — has mental-state-like elements. The act of "possession" occurs when you are aware that you have dominion and control over something, even if you do not know its nature. Thus, if a friend asks you to hold a cigarette and you do so, you have committed the "act" element of the crime of possessing marijuana, even if you believed that the cigarette contained only tobacco. That does not mean that you are guilty of that crime — whatever mental state the statute requires must also be shown — but the act element has been met.

E.   Mental States

One of two factual disputes characterize most criminal trials: whether the defendant or someone else did the criminal act and, if he did, whether he had the mental state required for the crime. The more serious the mental state, the more culpable the offender. There can be fine lines between some mental states. Thus, whether a suspect wanted to kill someone is, at common law, more serious than when he was simply aware of a practical certainty that he would do so. For example, a tavern owner deep in debt might blow up his tavern at night to collect the insurance money. Immediately before doing so, however, he notes to his surprise that his favorite employee is inside working late. He blows up the tavern anyway. Did he do so regretting the death that he was aware would almost certainly result — after all, this was his favorite employee — thus being a mere knowing killer, or did he at that moment *want* to kill the employee, precisely reasoning that no one would suspect him of the crime, a crime he nevertheless had to commit to prevent any witnesses to the arson, thus making the tavern owner a truly purposeful killer? These are tough judgments to make, and they are necessarily imbued with values and dependent upon hard credibility determinations. Partly for reasons like this, the Model Penal Code avoids this distinction entirely in this area, making purposeful and knowing killing subject to the same maximum penalties.

Some mental state determinations are even more values-infused. Notably, one form of first degree murder in common law jurisdictions requires that the killing be willful, deliberate, *and* premeditated, roughly meaning that the defendant wanted to kill, did so with full appreciation of the enormity of his choice, and planned it. In one sub-set of these jurisdictions, premeditation requires a significant amount of time to think about the killing beforehand. But in another sub-set, any amount of time can be sufficient for premeditation. To capture the emotional and moral sense of the crime, a willful, deliberate, and premeditated killing is said to be done in "cold blood."

Yet the same killing done in the "heat of passion" — that is, while subject to a high, overwrought emotion, like anger — would merely be second degree murder. Such passion is thought to stifle the deliberation required for first degree. The consequences of the cold versus hot blood decision are grave, for only the first degree murderer faces the prospect of the death penalty or of a life sentence.

But if the killer was reasonably provoked into the heat of passion by the victim and reasonably did not cool off by the time of the act causing death, the killer is not guilty of murder at all. Rather, he is guilty only of voluntary manslaughter, for he is thought to merit compassion, though not to be forgiven, for his understandable but still undesirable loss of self-control. The original common law approach was to declare only a few specified victim actions as reasonably provoking, generally meaning: (1) a serious assault and battery; (2) a crime committed against a close relative; (3) mutual combat; (4) illegal arrest; or (5) adultery by or with the defendant's spouse. The requirement that the provocation be *by the victim* implicitly reflects a concern with shared fault — a concern rare in other corners of the criminal law. But the modern trend is to reject these limited categories of reasonable provocation, leaving the jury to decide what is "reasonable," unless strong policy reasons militate against doing so in a particular case. This approach in effect leaves it to the jury to choose whether to show compassion for the offender.

There are other common law distinctions in the law of homicide that equally leave the ultimate decision in practice to the moral conscience of the community. Involuntary manslaughter requires mere criminal negligence in some of these jurisdictions but recklessness in others. Yet if recklessness is of a special type, one showing a "depraved heart," then it becomes a form of second degree murder. Jurisdictions differ over what distinguishes ordinary from depraved heart murder, but relevant factors may include the size of the risk (the bigger, the more likely it is murder), the degree of awareness of the risk (more awareness of the actual size of the risk, more culpability), and whether the risk was created because of an anti-social motive. An example best explains this last factor. If a man has a pit bull trained to kill tied to a stake on a twenty-foot leash in his backyard, and living next to a family with a three-year-old child who wanders onto his property, the dog fatally biting the child, but the man trained his dog to violence to discourage burglary, then the man did not act from an anti-social motive. But if he trained the dog to guard the marijuana growing in the backyard from poachers, then he did indeed act from an anti-social motive.

The Model Penal Code simplifies this scheme for grading homicide and favors dryer, more abstract language but nevertheless still requires the factfinder to make highly moralistic judgments. Thus, while it rejects the first degree, second degree murder distinction, making all serious homicides "murder," one type of murder it retains is nearly identical to depraved heart murder, though the MPC labels the crime differently: an unlawful killing is murder if done with such "extreme recklessness as to show an indifference to the value of human life." One form of manslaughter under the MPC is far broader than the common law "heat of passion," requiring "extreme mental or emotional disturbance" for which there is no "reasonable explanation or excuse." The reasonableness determination is, once again, largely left up to the jury. But the MPC requires the jury to judge the reasonableness of the defendant's state of mind under the circumstances as he or she believed them to be. In other words, the MPC creates an empathy requirement. The jury must step into the defendant's shoes. Once there, it must decide whether, given what the defendant believed and felt, there was a "reasonable explanation" for the mental or emotional disturbance and resulting action. This analysis seems as difficult and value-laden as common law voluntary manslaughter, though the MPC rejects the common law's shared fault notions, jettisoning *any* requirement of provocation, whether by the victim or someone else.

Rarely is the victim's mental state, as opposed to the defendant's, at issue in a criminal case, but there are some exceptions, most notably whether the victim "consented" in a rape case. Technically, lack of consent in the common law definition of rape — forcible, nonconsensual sexual intercourse by a man with a woman not his wife — is an "attendant circumstance." Rarely, however, are jurors given a definition of "consent." In practice, they will frequently treat it as a state of mind — whether she "wanted it," that is, desired to have sexual intercourse, rather than as an action constituting a grant of permission to the man to proceed. Gender, class, and racial stereotypes can infect the jury's consent determination, and various jurisdictions have struggled with ways to alleviate the problem, including expert testimony on those biases, cautionary jury instructions, and "rape shield laws" generally of prior consensual sexual conduct by the victim with persons other than the accused. Some jurisdictions have even eliminated "lack of consent" as a formal element, but jurors tend informally to re-insert consent as a central issue in finding rape or its absence.

F.   Inchoate Crimes

"Inchoate" crimes are those that seek to prevent some harm thought highly likely to occur if not nipped in the bud. "Attempt" and "conspiracy" are among the most important inchoate crimes.

"Attempt" is a failed crime. The difficulty with attempt is distinguishing "mere preparation" from a firm commitment toward achieving the criminal goal. If mere preparation but no more is punished, we risk stigmatizing merely evil thoughts or tentative actions that may ultimately pose no danger to anyone. The common law therefore struggled with just how to define when an act is sufficient for attempt, with varying jurisdictions crafting no fewer than six different formulations. Some formulations stressed how close the acts came to those required for the completed crime, for example, whether the actions were in "dangerous proximity" to being completed, while others stressed how far the actions moved beyond mere contemplation. The Model Penal Code's formulation is that the offender must take a "substantial step" toward completing the crime, a term defined as acts "strongly corroborative" of criminal purpose. The necessary mental state for an attempt is generally a purpose to bring about all the elements of the completed crime.

Sometimes the failure to achieve the desired crime occurs for reasons other than not completing the planned acts. There are two particular types of attempts that indeed occur despite completing every act necessary for the underlying crime: a mistake about an attendant circumstance or a failure to achieve a desired result. Thus common law larceny is the trespassory taking and carrying away of the personal property of another with intent to deprive that other of the property permanently. A would-be pickpocket who sticks his hands in a woman's purse believing that there will be a wallet inside but instead finding the purse empty has not committed larceny because he did not succeed in taking any personal property. He was mistaken in his belief that the attendant circumstance of the property's presence in the purse existed. Nevertheless, he wanted to bring about all the elements of larceny, and he in fact committed all acts necessary for the completed crime.

Likewise, an offender who pulls the trigger of a gun pointed at the intended victim's head hoping to kill him but misses is not guilty of homicide. He has not caused anyone's death. But he wanted to cause that result and committed all acts he believed necessary to achieving that outcome. He is guilty of attempted homicide.

"Conspiracy" is an agreement to commit a crime with the purpose of its occurring. The mere agreement with the prohibited mental state generally constitutes conspiracy even if the completed crime never occurs. Thus, if John and George agree to rob Mary, but she unexpectedly leaves town before they can do so, the two men have committed no robbery, but they have engaged in a conspiracy to rob. Some jurisdictions require not only the act of agreeing to commit the crime but also that at least one of the co-conspirators engaged in an overt act in furtherance of the conspiracy. In the John and George example, therefore, their merely agreeing to rob Mary would not suffice to prove the conspiracy. However, if George brought a gun to use in committing the robbery, that would be an overt act by one of the co-conspirators, so both men would be guilty of conspiracy.

Conspiracy prosecutions serve two major goals. First, they enable the State to stop a crime before it occurs. Second, the more people who are involved in a crime, the greater the danger, in society's eyes, that the crime's harms will be realized.

What constitutes an "agreement" for the purposes of conspiracy law also varies by jurisdiction; again, there are two major approaches: "bilateral" and "unilateral." A bilateral approach requires a subjective "meeting of the minds." Even though this sounds like a mental state, the law views this requirement that at least two persons intend to agree to commit a crime as an "act" requirement. Unilateral jurisdictions instead find agreement even if only one person acts *as if* he is agreeing to commit a crime, it being irrelevant whether the other person wanted to do so. In this sense, a single person can "agree." Thus, if Andy and Boris say that they will kill Rudolph but, unbeknownst to Andy, Boris is an undercover police officer, there is no liability in a bilateral jurisdiction because there was no "meeting of the minds." Andy thought he was agreeing with Boris, but Boris wanted only to get grounds to arrest Andy. In a unilateral jurisdiction, by contrast, Andy is a conspirator precisely because he thought he was agreeing with Boris and acted as if he were doing so.

One of the most difficult mental state problems with a conspiracy charge is distinguishing knowledge from purpose. Assume that Mr. Big hires Annie's Phone Answering Service to take phone messages for Mr. Big in the days before electronic answering machines. Annie quickly realizes, however, that all messages for Mr. Big are from men wanting Mr. Big to arrange appointments for the men with prostitutes. Annie keeps taking Mr. Big's money anyway. This evidence is sufficient to show that Annie knew that Mr. Big was involved in a prostitution ring but not that Annie wanted Mr. Big to do so. In most jurisdictions, mere knowledge is insufficient to make Annie a co-conspirator. But now assume that Mr. Big's business rises to constitute eighty percent of Annie's income and that Mr. Big voluntarily offers to pay Annie twice the fee per call that she ordinarily charges her customers. On this evidence, Annie arguably has a motive to want Mr. Big's prostitution ring to succeed and to agree to be part of his criminal project, for if Mr. Big's prostitution business fails, Annie's business collapses, and she may be rendered destitute. On these additional facts, many jurisdictions will allow a jury to conclude, if it wishes, beyond a reasonable doubt that Annie had the purpose (the desire) to agree with Mr. Big to commit the crime, thus making Annie a co-conspirator.

G.   Complicity

Accomplice liability, also known as "complicity," is not a crime. Rather, it is a doctrine that makes one person liable for the criminal acts of another. At common law, one is an accomplice if he aids another in committing a crime with the purpose that it be committed. The aid can be psychological or material, and it need not be true that without the aid, there would have been no crime. All that is necessary is that the aid make it easier, even just psychologically easier, to commit the crime. If A gives B a gun in the hope that B will use it to kill C, and B does just that, A is guilty of homicide for B's action because A aided B in the crime. Even if B already had a knife, the gun made it easier for B to kill C. Likewise, if B already had a gun but A told B that C "deserved" to die, salving B's conscience about the killing that B planned to do anyway, A would still be an accomplice, thus guilty of homicide for B's actions.

The MPC goes further by requiring only an attempt to aid, even if the attempt fails, though the accomplice is then guilty only of the *attempted* crime. Similarly, if the intended principal receives the aid but merely attempts to commit the crime, or even if he never even attempts it, the aider is, under the MPC, an accomplice guilty of attempting the particular crime. For example, if A anonymously mails a gun to B, which B never receives, hoping that B will kill C, which B never even tries to do, A is guilty of the attempted murder of C under the MPC's approach to accomplice liability, and this is so despite B's having committed no crime whatsoever.

H. Defenses

There are two primary sorts of defenses to crimes.: failure of proof defenses and affirmative defenses. A "failure of proof" defense, in common-sense terms, is an argument that the defendant has some evidence — and only *some* evidence is generally needed — that raises a reasonable doubt about whether one or more elements of the crime existed. The most well-known such defense is mistake of fact, which concerns the mental state element of a crime. Some jurisdictions, for example, require proof of a reckless state of mind as to whether a woman consented to sexual intercourse to convict an accused of rape. If a rape defendant testifies that it never occurred to him even for a second that there was a risk that his alleged victim did not consent, he seeks to raise a reasonable doubt about whether the State has proven his recklessness, that is, whether he was consciously aware at the time of a substantial and unjustifiable risk that she was not consenting.

The second major type of defense is an "affirmative" defense. In common sense terms, this is a defense of the following form: "Yes, perhaps you can prove the elements of the crime beyond a reasonable doubt, but you still must acquit me because I have an excuse (I was not fully responsible for my actions) or a justification (my actions were in fact a socially good thing under the circumstances)." Common excuses, with their elements colloquially stated, are duress (someone threatens physically to harm you if you do not commit the crime) and insanity (because of mental disease or defect, you either did not know what you were doing or that it was wrong or, in some jurisdictions, you were acting under an irresistible impulse). Common justifications are self-defense (I had to kill him to stop him from imminently or immediately killing me or causing me serious bodily injury) and necessity (I avoided a greater imminent harm by my crime than by doing nothing — a vague and last-ditch defense that appeals to first principles). The key point to understand is that, even when the State can prove the elements of a crime, the accused may still be acquitted because he had good reason for what he did or just cannot fairly be held responsible for it.

IV. CONCLUSION

There is both a procedural and substantive aspect to the study of the criminal justice system. The procedure often examines issues related to the U.S. Constitution's Bill of Rights. The substantive examines crimes. But it is important to remember that unlike many countries that have one system, there are several systems that can provide criminal laws in the United States.

Chapter 5

JURISDICTION AND CIVIL PROCEDURE

By — Mark E. Wojcik

SYNOPSIS

I. INTRODUCTION

This chapter introduces the subjects of jurisdiction and civil procedure. A chapter of this size cannot cover these topics in depth, but it can introduce them to you. The goal here is to increase your familiarity with those aspects of jurisdiction and civil procedure that you will most likely encounter in your further studies (both in this book, and elsewhere) and that you will likely encounter in practice, even if you are not going to be a lawyer practicing in the United States.

The previous Chapter in this book dealt with criminal matters. This Chapter is limited to civil matters.

The first half of the Chapter focuses on jurisdiction, with particular emphasis on the jurisdiction of federal courts in the United States. The second half of the Chapter deals with civil procedure. It will also introduce the steps of civil litigation, so that you can better understand litigation in the United States but also have a better understanding of appellate cases that describe judicial proceedings. Even if you never find yourself in court, the information in this Chapter will still be quite valuable.

II. JURISDICTION

A preliminary question in deciding any dispute is to determine which court or tribunal has the power to hear a case.

The word "jurisdiction" has several meanings. The term is sometimes used in a geographic or territorial sense to refer to other states within the United States. For example, a court may note that other jurisdictions, such as New York and California, have already ruled on a particular point of law. If most states in the United States have adopted a particular rule of law, you may see a court describe that rule as being adopted by a "majority of jurisdictions" (a "majority rule"). Those states not in the majority may follow the "minority rule" or may not yet have had a chance to rule on the particular issue.

The term "jurisdiction" can also refer to the power, authority, and ability of a court or other tribunal to decide a case. For example, you may see a sentence that says: "The federal court found that it had jurisdiction [or subject matter jurisdiction] to decide the case." You may also see that a court has "jurisdiction to adjudicate" a case, which means simply that the court has jurisdiction to decide that case.

The term jurisdiction can also sometimes apply to legislative or executive acts or powers. For example, you may see a sentence like this: "The state legislature should not pass a law on immigration; immigration laws are within the exclusive jurisdiction of the U.S. Congress." In other contexts you might hear something along the lines of "this case is no longer one for the state police, it falls within the jurisdiction of the Federal Bureau of Investigation (FBI)."

The term jurisdiction may be used to show that a court or other tribunal has power over a certain person or business: for example, "the court had jurisdiction [or personal jurisdiction] over the distributor as well as the company that manufactured the product." The court must have personal jurisdiction over the defendant in order to decide the case.

The most common uses of jurisdiction for purposes of this book will be (A) subject matter jurisdiction and (B) personal jurisdiction.

A.   Subject Matter Jurisdiction

Courts in the United States can hear cases only when they have both subject matter jurisdiction and personal jurisdiction. "Subject matter jurisdiction" requires that the court be empowered to hear a certain type of case. The term "subject matter jurisdiction" refers to the court's power to hear a case, rather than to the substantive or procedural rules that will apply during a trial.

Subject matter jurisdiction for federal courts in the United States falls into two categories: (1) federal question jurisdiction and (2) diversity jurisdiction. The federal court must have jurisdiction in one of those two categories. If does not have jurisdiction, the court simply cannot hear the case. Even if the parties agree to have the federal court hear their case, the federal court cannot do so where it lacks subject matter jurisdiction.

The question of whether a federal court has subject matter jurisdiction is so important that the federal court will raise the issue on its own if the parties fail to address it. If a federal court finds that it lacks jurisdiction (again, either federal question jurisdiction or diversity jurisdiction), the court will then dismiss the case. (It is then up to the plaintiff to find another forum where the case could be heard, for example in a state court proceeding or perhaps some form of alternative dispute resolution such as arbitration or mediation.)

The following sections explore subject matter jurisdiction in more detail.

1.   Federal Question Jurisdiction

Federal courts have jurisdiction to hear cases arising under the U.S. Constitution. Federal courts also have jurisdiction over federal statutes. (Federal statutes are those passed by the U.S. Congress and signed by the President of the United States). Federal courts also have jurisdiction over questions that arise under treaties where the U.S. is a party. The reason for giving federal courts jurisdiction over both federal statutes and treaties was to keep those cases out of state courts, which people thought might sometimes show favoritism to local citizens.

Federal courts have original jurisdiction over "all civil actions arising under the Constitution, laws, or treaties of the United States." 28 U.S.C. § 1331. Under this federal statute, parties who want to bring a case in federal court must show that their case is one "arising under" the U.S. Constitution, a federal statute, or a treaty where the United States is a party. Federal courts also have jurisdiction to hear cases arising under federal regulations, which implement the federal statutes.

In order for a federal court to have federal question jurisdiction, the federal question must appear in the plaintiff's complaint. If the only federal issue is one that the defendant will raise, there will not be federal question jurisdiction. A plaintiff cannot claim federal question jurisdiction by predicting that the defendant will raise a defense or counterclaim under federal law.

2.   Diversity Jurisdiction in Federal Courts

Federal courts have "diversity jurisdiction" when two factors are satisfied. First, there must be "complete diversity" of citizenship between the parties. Second, the actual amount in controversy must be more than $75,000. 28 U.S.C. § 1332(a).

a.   Complete Diversity of Citizenship

To have diversity for purposes of federal diversity jurisdiction, the case must fall into one of the following four categories. The case must be between: (1) citizens of different U.S. states; (2) citizens of a U.S. state and citizens or subjects of a foreign state; (3) citizens of different U.S. states where citizens or subjects of a foreign state are additional parties; or (4) a foreign state (where the foreign state is a plaintiff suing citizens of a state or different states). 28 U.S.C. § 1332(a).

Because those categories can be confusing, here is an easier way to learn the rule: the plaintiffs have to be from a different jurisdiction than the defendants. If any of the plaintiffs is from the same state as any of the defendants, there is no diversity. There must be "complete diversity."

But where is a person from? Is it the state where they were born? Is it the state where they own property? Is it the state where they work? Is it the state where they live? The modern rule is that for individuals, a person's citizenship for purposes of determining federal diversity jurisdiction is based on the person's domicile. "Domicile" is the place where the person has a permanent home. The person has generally chosen to live there and expects to live there for some time. It is reasonable to be able to sue a person in the place where they have chosen to live.

What about corporations? For purposes of diversity jurisdiction, a corporation can be considered a citizen of both the state of incorporation (such as Delaware) and the place where the corporation has its principal place of business. To figure out where a corporation has its principal place of business, some courts will look to where the corporation has its corporate headquarters. Other courts might look to where the corporation has most of its production or service activities.

What about other entities that are not incorporated? There might be an unincorporated partnership, for example, with six partners — each from different states. For purposes of federal diversity, that unincorporated partnership will be considered to have the citizenship of each of the partners.

Can you have two plaintiffs (or two defendants) from the same jurisdiction? Yes. You can have two plaintiffs from Mexico and two defendants from New York, for example. The only requirement is that none of the plaintiffs be from the same jurisdiction as any of the defendants.

What happens if a foreign national is living in the United States but is not a U.S. citizen? Will the federal court treat him or her as a citizen of the foreign country, or of the state where he or she is living? Here is the rule: if foreign nationals are permanent residents of the United States, the federal diversity statute will treat them as if they were citizens. This means that if a U.S. citizen living in New York sues someone from Germany who is a permanent resident living in New York, there will not be diversity of citizenship. There would not be federal diversity jurisdiction. (They would have to bring the case in state court.)

What happens if the cases do not involve any U.S. citizens at all? If that happens, the federal court will not be able to hear the case. One of the parties in the case must be a U.S. citizen in order for the federal court to have diversity jurisdiction. (There may be some kind of federal question jurisdiction, however, such as a claim under the Alien Tort Statute, 28 U.S.C. § 1350, or another federal statute.) Unless there is a federal statute or some other basis of federal question jurisdiction, the federal court will not be able to hear the case, even if the actual amount in controversy is over $75,000. Diversity jurisdiction does not extend to cases involving only aliens.

b.   Amount in Controversy

For a federal court to have diversity jurisdiction, the case must be sufficiently important. Importance has been measured by money: the case must be one where "the matter in controversy exceeds the sum or value of $75,000, exclusive of interest or costs. . . ." 28 U.S.C. § 1332(a). The dispute could involve more than $75,000 in cash, or it could involve something actually valued at more than $75,000. If the amount in controversy is not at least $75,000 plus a penny, then the federal court will not have diversity jurisdiction. (The state court might hear the case instead of the federal court.)

What happens if at the end of the case when the judge is entering a verdict in favor of the plaintiff, the amount awarded by the jury is less than $75,000? Does this mean that the federal court no longer has jurisdiction over the case? No. The federal court will still have jurisdiction, but the court can assess costs against the plaintiff. 28 U.S.C. § 1332(b). In practice, this does not happen very often, but the court can assess costs if it finds that the plaintiff acted in bad faith when he or she first filed the case and claimed that the amount in controversy was more than $75,000.

3.   State Court Jurisdiction

If a federal court does not have subject matter jurisdiction over a dispute (either federal question or diversity jurisdiction), the case may instead be heard in state court (as long as the state court has personal jurisdiction over the defendant). For example, if the amount in controversy is only $70,000, the federal court will lack diversity jurisdiction and the case must instead be heard in state court.

The state courts are sometimes said to have "plenary jurisdiction." This means that state courts will have jurisdiction over most matters except for a few things specifically reserved to federal courts, such as the validity of a federal patent to protect intellectual property rights.

State courts are not prohibited from hearing cases where a federal statute or the U.S. Constitution is at issue. For example, a defendant might raise a defense under the U.S. Constitution or a federal statute. And state courts can hear cases where the amount in controversy is more than $75,000. Just because there is federal diversity jurisdiction for a particular case does not mean that it must be brought in federal court. The state court can be equally competent to hear the case.

4.   Supplemental Jurisdiction

What will happen if there are multiple claims, and not all of the claims individually satisfy the requirements of federal jurisdiction? For example, what would happen if a plaintiff sues a defendant from another state for $85,000, and the defendant has a counterclaim for $10,000 based on the same facts as the plaintiff's complaint? That $10,000 claim does not independently satisfy the minimum amount required for diversity jurisdiction. Must the defendant file a separate action for that $10,000 claim, or can it be part of the pending federal action?

Federal courts have "supplemental jurisdiction" over all of the state law claims that are part of the same case or controversy as the federal claims. 28 U.S.C. § 1367(a). In older cases, you might see references to "ancillary jurisdiction" or "pendent jurisdiction," which were doctrines that the federal courts developed to be able to hear state law claims as part of the federal case. These doctrines were developed to avoid multiple trials (in federal court and state court). To determine if the federal court should hear the state law claim, the courts traditionally used a two-part test. First, the court looked to see if the state law claim has a "common nucleus of operative fact." For example, there may be a claim under a state unfair trade practice statute and the federal antitrust statute. If both claims involve the same business practices, the federal court can find that there is a "common nucleus of operative fact" and hear the state law claim as part of the federal case. In the second part of the test, the court had to decide whether it would be fair to the parties to hear the state law claim, and whether it would promote judicial economy to do so. If the federal court decided that it should not hear the state law claims, it would dismiss those state law claims and allow them to be heard instead by the state court.

When you study this issue further, you will learn about how the issue of supplemental jurisdiction can become more complicated when additional parties and additional issues are brought into the litigation. For example, what will happen if a plaintiff sues a defendant under diversity jurisdiction, but the defendant then seeks to add another defendant who is from the same state as the plaintiff? The answer can be complicated, and the answers may depend on factors such as whether the claim against the additional defendant is based upon the same facts as are in the original complaint. It is not necessary to get into these additional issues in this introductory text, but just be aware that special rules may apply when additional issues or additional parties are sought to be added to federal litigation.

5.   Removal

A plaintiff may file an action in state court against a defendant. If there is a clear federal claim made in the plaintiff's complaint or if jurisdiction is based on diversity, the defendant can remove the state court action to federal court. 28 U.S.C. § 1441.

A defendant cannot remove a case based only on a federal defense. The federal issue must arise in the plaintiff's complaint.

Similarly, the plaintiff cannot remove the case to federal court, even if the defendant raises a federal defense to the plaintiff's complaint.

6. Other Matters

a. Original Jurisdiction of the U.S. Supreme Court

When learning about the U.S. Supreme Court, you may hear someone mention its "original jurisdiction" under Article III of the U.S. Constitution. The term means that under the U.S. Constitution, the U.S. Supreme Court (and only the U.S. Supreme Court) can hear certain specific cases. This limited number of cases includes jurisdiction to hear disputes between states (for example, a case brought by the state of New York against the state of New Jersey), or cases involving consuls or ambassadors. Because of the foreign policy implications of having the official representative of another country on trial, the U.S. Supreme Court (rather than a lower federal court) is the one that has "original jurisdiction" over trials involving consuls and ambassadors. Thankfully, there are very few (if any) of those trials.

b. "In Rem" Jurisdiction

As you advance in your study of U.S. law, you may find cases that discuss "in rem" or "quasi in rem" jurisdiction. You do not need to worry about these terms now, but here is a short explanation of each.

"*In rem* jurisdiction" refers to the court's power to decide competing claims over a specific piece of property (rather than a person or corporation). The court will have jurisdiction over the property because is it physically located within the state where the court is sitting. The court is asked to rule on the ownership of property in that jurisdiction, and the court's ruling as to ownership of that property will be binding on everyone else.

"*Quasi in rem* jurisdiction," on the other hand, applies to personal suits against the defendant where the property is not the source of the conflict, but the plaintiff wants to get the defendant's property as compensation. The court's authority in a "quasi in rem" case is limited to determining the defendant's interest in that property.

Again, you need not worry about these terms right now. When you see them again in your future studies, you will have more context to understand the difference between these terms.

c. Exclusive Jurisdiction

Some federal courts have "exclusive jurisdiction," meaning that a case must be heard in that particular court or not at all. For example, the U.S. Court of International Trade is a federal court sitting in New York. That court has exclusive jurisdiction over matters such as appeals from denials of protests against the Customs Service's tariff classification of imported merchandise.

Until now, we have been speaking of "Article III" federal courts — these are courts established under Article III of the U.S. Constitution. There are also some courts under Article I of the U.S. Constitution (which addresses executive powers of the president). Examples of these courts include Bankruptcy Courts (which have exclusive jurisdiction over bankruptcy petitions) and Immigration Courts (which are not independent courts, but are part of the U.S. Department of Justice).

d.   Arbitration Clauses

Many international contracts contain arbitration clauses that provide for arbitration of disputes rather than litigation. If the dispute involves a contract with an arbitration clause, federal and state courts in the United States will respect that clause and will usually refuse to hear the case. They will honor the decision that the parties made when they entered into their contract, and the court will dismiss the court action in favor of the arbitration.

Contracts may specify that a dispute be decided by arbitration rather than litigation. Other contracts may instead be fine with the idea of litigation, but may designate a particular state as the forum for that litigation, or a particular state's laws as the controlling law for the dispute. Courts in the United States will generally give effect to these contractual choices wherever possible.

B.   Personal Jurisdiction

In addition to having subject matter jurisdiction, a court in the United States must also have personal jurisdiction (*in personam* jurisdiction) over the defendant. This means that a court will have power to order the defendant to appear in court. (If a defendant does not appear in court as ordered, the court may enter a "default judgment" for the full amount of damages alleged in the plaintiff's complaint.)

1.   Individuals

Traditionally, a court could only have jurisdiction over a defendant who resided in the state where the lawsuit was filed. But if the defendant can be personally served while in the state, even a "momentary presence" in the state will be enough to establish personal jurisdiction. If the defendant can be located anywhere in the state, the court will have personal jurisdiction over that defendant; physical presence is sufficient to establish personal jurisdiction.

The physical presence rule is a simple requirement, but it can also be controversial when applied to foreign defendants who do not normally live in the jurisdiction where they have been sued. Take, for example, the situation of business owner who is travelling from Europe to Central America. The traveler might have to change planes in the United States along the way. If that traveler is personally served with a summons and complaint while waiting in Chicago or Miami for the next flight, the court will have personal jurisdiction over that defendant. Under those facts, physical presence is enough to establish personal jurisdiction, even if the defendant was going to be in the United States for only a few hours.

Most of the problems in the area of personal jurisdiction arise with defendants who are not physically within the state. Where a defendant lives in a different state or even a different country, the court must look to two tests. First, the court must look to see if there is a statute that authorizes the assertion of personal jurisdiction over individuals who do not live within the state. A long-arm statute, for example, might provide the statutory basis for asserting personal jurisdiction over a non-resident defendant. Second, the court will have to consider whether the application of the particular statute would be constitutional as to that particular defendant. If applying the statute would violate due process guarantees under the U.S. Constitution, the court will not apply the statute.

When discussing whether a court has jurisdiction over a non-resident defendant, you may see that the discussion focuses on whether the defendant has sufficient "minimum contacts" with the state. This means that the defendant has done something more than incidental travel to the state. (However, remember that if the defendant can be physically served with the summons and complaint while in the jurisdiction, that physical presence is enough. We are talking here about what the situation is when you cannot physically serve the defendant in the jurisdiction with notice of the lawsuit.)

Under the long-arm statutes of various jurisdictions, a defendant may be found to be subject to the personal jurisdiction for transacting business in the state, committing a tort within the state (for example, causing a car accident while driving through the state), or owning property within the state. State statutes (called "long-arm statutes") will set out the specific rules for each state.

2.   Businesses

Corporations that are doing business within a state may have designated a registered agent who can accept process on behalf of the corporation. The specific activities of a non-resident business may fall under the activities listed in a particular long-arm statute.

3.   Consent

Although the parties cannot confer subject matter jurisdiction upon a court, a defendant can always consent to the exercise of personal jurisdiction. This means that the defendant will appear voluntarily in court and will not assert any defenses to the exercise of personal jurisdiction. The defendant can also consent to the particular venue where the case will be heard.

C.   Actual Case or Controversy (Requirements for Standing)

In addition to subject matter jurisdiction and personal jurisdiction, another requirement for a federal lawsuit is that the plaintiffs have "standing." To show standing, the plaintiff must show three things.

First, the plaintiff must show an actual injury (sometimes this is called an "injury in fact"). The injury cannot be speculative or hypothetical. It must be concrete, particular, and actual or imminent. *See, e.g., Long Term Care Partners, LLC v. United States*, 516 F.3d 225, 231 (4th Cir. 2008). The reason given for this rule is to guarantee that the plaintiff is someone with a sufficient personal stake in the dispute, rather than someone who has merely a "generalized interest" in the dispute. Persons with a real stake in the outcome of a controversy may be more likely to be forceful and effective advocates in court. In an adversarial system of justice, the court can reach a good decision only when both sides are presenting strong cases.

Second, the plaintiff must show that the injury suffered is "fairly traceable" to actions of the defendant. If the actions of that defendant are not related to the injury suffered, that defendant should not have to defend the action in court.

The third requirement of standing that the plaintiff must show is that a favorable decision would likely resolve the injury. If the court order will not provide relief for the plaintiff's injury, the plaintiff will lack standing.

The plaintiff must show standing at the beginning of the case. The plaintiff cannot fix a standing problem later. Additionally, the plaintiff's standing must continue throughout the proceedings, including on appeal. *See, e.g., Williams v. Boeing Co.*, 517 F.3d 1120, 1128 (9th Cir. 2008). If something destroys the plaintiff's standing, the federal court will have to dismiss the case.

D.   Venue

Venue is the term used to describe the proper place where a lawsuit should be heard, because that place has some meaningful connection to one of the parties or to the events involved in the lawsuit. The term "venue" may be confused with "jurisdiction," and even experienced lawyers and judges sometimes forget the difference between those two terms.

Determining whether the court has jurisdiction is determining whether the court has the power to act. Determining whether venue is proper is determining whether the case should go forward in a particular place, or whether it should be transferred to another place that might have a stronger connection with the case or with the parties.

You should also keep in mind that whether a court has authority to hear a case (in other words, whether it has jurisdiction) is something that must be based on something other than the agreement of the parties. The same is not necessarily true of venue: the parties to a case can often decide between themselves where venue will be proper. In fact, many contracts contain "choice of law" provisions that dictate both where any disputes will be decided (this may also appear in a separate "choice of forum" clause in a contract), as well as which state's law will apply to resolve controversies between the parties (for example, the law of New York).

Venue is not a constitutional issue, but a statutory one. Although each state may have different laws establishing where venue is proper, many states will generally look to where the defendant resides, where the cause of action arose, where the plaintiff resides, or where the property in dispute is located.

III. CIVIL PROCEDURE

A.   Introduction

Civil procedure, most simply, are the procedural rules that a court will follow in a civil case. The rules for civil cases in federal courts are contained in the *Federal Rules of Civil Procedure*. Specific procedural rules for civil trials in state courts may differ from state to state, and it will always be important to consider that different states may use different terms or have slightly different rules of procedure in their own state courts.

This section will go through the steps of a civil trial in federal court. It will then describe the process of appeals and enforcing judgments.

B.   An Overview of a Civil Trial

A citizen of Italy living in Italy wants to sue a company that was incorporated in the state of Illinois and that has its principle place of business in Chicago, Illinois. The actual amount in controversy is $1.3 million dollars, much more than the minimum jurisdictional amount of $75,000 that is required for federal diversity jurisdiction. Will the Italian plaintiff be able to file a lawsuit in the United States District Court for the Northern District of Illinois? Should the Italian plaintiff instead sue in the Circuit Court for Cook County, Illinois (the state court)?

1.   Picking a Forum

The plaintiff must select a court with jurisdiction to hear the case. The court selected must have both subject matter jurisdiction over the action and personal jurisdiction over the defendants.

The Italian plaintiff could file the suit in either federal court or state court. It is the plaintiff's choice here, because both courts would have subject matter and personal jurisdiction. The federal court would have diversity jurisdiction (because the amount in controversy is more than $75,000, because the parties are from different jurisdictions, and because at least one of the parties — the Illinois corporation — is a "citizen" of the United States). The federal court sitting in diversity in Illinois will apply the substantive state law of Illinois (unless there is some reason to apply the law of another state or jurisdiction).

The case begins when the plaintiff files the complaint. As stated in Rule 3 of the Federal Rules of Civil Procedure, "[a] civil action is commenced by filing a complaint with the court."

2.   Giving Notice of the Suit — Service of Process

The plaintiff must let the Illinois corporation know that it has been sued. If the defendant is not given notice of the lawsuit, the failure to provide notice would violate due process of law, which is guaranteed by the Constitution.

How does a defendant learn about the lawsuit? Notice is usually given by serving a *summons* and a *complaint*. The summons is a document that identifies the court and the parties, and which tells the defendant to appear and defend the lawsuit before a specific date. The complaint is the document that lists out the "causes of action" for which the defendant is being sued, such as breach of contract. The complaint is also sometimes called the *pleading*.

Delivering the summons and complaint to the defendant is called *service of process*. If the defendant is served, the defendant must appear in court within the time identified in the summons. If the defendant fails to appear to defend the action, that failure may result in a *default judgment* against the defendant for the relief demanded in the complaint. Fed. R. Civ. P. 4(a).

Service of process is usually by *personal service*. This means that a copy of the summons and complaint must be personally delivered to the defendant, or a person of suitable age living at the defendant's home. A public official such as a sheriff or marshal may do this service of process, or a private process server may do it. (If the dispute involves a contract, that contract may contain specific provisions for service of process, including (for example) that the parties agreed to service of process by register mail, regular mail, fax, or even by email. Which method will be allowed will of course depend on what the specific contract actually says. An agreement to an alternative method of service of process is a "waiver of service" under the Federal Rules.)

If the defendant lives in another jurisdiction, service of process may done by registered mail or by serving an agent within the state. In some extreme cases where the defendant cannot be located for personal service, the court may also allow service by publication of a notice in a newspaper. The method of notice chosen must be reasonably calculated to give the defendant notice of the suit. Actual notice by personal service is the best way to show that the defendant has notice of the lawsuit.

Rule 4(f) of the Federal Rules of Civil Procedure contains specific rules for serving individuals who live in foreign countries. Look at that rule if you need to know more about serving a foreign party. To serve a corporation, a copy of the summons and complaint must be delivered to an officer, a managing or general agent, or to another agent authorized to accept service. Look at Rule 4(h) of the Federal Rules of Civil Procedure if you need to know more about serving a corporation.

What happens if the defendant cannot be found? If service of process is not made within 120 days after filing the complaint, the federal court will generally dismiss the case "without prejudice." The phrase "without prejudice" means that the plaintiff can refile the case later.

3. The Complaint

The complaint lists out the plaintiff's claims against the defendant. If there is more than one claim, they will be listed as "counts" of the complaint. For example, Count I might allege a breach of contract action, Count II might allege consumer fraud, and Count III might allege some other tort.

Rule 8(a)(2) of the Federal Rules of Civil Procedure requires a complaint to contain "a short and plain statement of the claim showing that the pleader is entitled to relief." The purpose of this rule is to "give the defendant fair notice of what the claim is and the grounds upon which it rests." *Davis v. Coca-Cola Bottling Co.*, 516 F.3d 955, 974 (11th Cir. 2008). The allegations in the complaint must be more than speculative.

Within each count there will be numbered paragraphs containing the *allegations* against the defendant. The allegations will attempt to state a *cause of action* against the defendant.

The complaint will also include a *prayer for relief.* In that prayer for relief, the plaintiff tells the court what relief it is seeking, such as money damages or injunctive relief.

4. Responding to the Complaint

A defendant may respond to the plaintiff's complaint by moving to dismiss it (for any number of reasons, such as those discussed below). The defendant may answer the complaint (and must do so if the motion to dismiss was unsuccessful). The defendant may have a claim against the plaintiff (a counter-claim). And the defendant might want to bring in another defendant to share the burden of defending the case and paying any judgment that might be awarded at the end.

This section discusses each of those possible responses.

a.   Motion to Dismiss

The defendant may respond to the complaint by filing a motion to dismiss. The motion to dismiss might be based on a number of different reasons, including these:

- A challenge to the service of process (for example, that the defendant was not personally served with the summons and complaint);

- A challenge to the court's exercise of personal jurisdiction over the defendant;

- Failure to state a cause of action (meaning that even if all of the allegations of the complaint are accepted as being true, the complaint does not state a cause of action upon which the court could grant relief);

- The complaint is so general or so confusing that the defendant cannot be expected to defend the case; or

- A statute of limitation bars the suit (meaning that the plaintiff waited too long to file the suit).

If the court grants the motion to dismiss, the court may allow the plaintiff an opportunity to fix the problem and try again with an amended complaint. (The plaintiff will ask the court for an opportunity to "cure the defect" in the complaint by asking the court for "leave to amend the complaint.") It may not always be possible to fix the problem. Where the complaint cannot be amended to fix the problem, the motion to dismiss ends the case and the defendant does not have to do anything else.

The defendant may also file a motion to challenge venue, or may file a motion to change the location of the court action based on the doctrine of *forum non conveniens*. Such a motion states that the forum is inconvenient, and that the proceeding should be transferred to a different court.

b.   Answer

If the court does not dismiss the action, the defendant must file an answer to the plaintiff's complaint. The defendant must admit or deny the factual allegations of the complaint. The defendant may admit some of the allegations of the complaint and deny other allegations.

If the defendant has an affirmative defense to the complaint, the defendant must mention it in the answer to the complaint.

c.   Counterclaim

In addition to filing an answer to the complaint, the defendant may file a counterclaim against the plaintiff. For example, a lawyer might sue a client for non-payment of legal fees. The client, in turn, might countersue for negligence in the performance of the legal services.

Most courts will hold that the failure to raise a counterclaim will bar the defendant from raising the issue later.

d.   Other Responses

A defendant may think it unfair to be the only person defending the suit. If someone else might also be held responsible for the plaintiff's alleged injury, the defendant may bring other defendants into federal court. This process is sometimes called "impleader." It gives defendants a better opportunity to defend themselves.

There are two requirements for bringing in a third-party defendant. The first requirement is that the person sought to be brought in as an additional defendant is not already a party to the lawsuit. The second requirement is that the person "is or may be liable" to the defendant if the defendant is found to be liable to the original plaintiff.

5.   Discovery

Pre-trial discovery can be a nightmare. It is complicated, expensive, and time-consuming. But it is also the main way that parties exchange information about the claims that they are making in the case and the defenses to those claims. There are several "tools" of discovery, including written interrogatories, demands to produce documents, depositions, and requests to admit.

a.   Interrogatories

Interrogatories are written questions that one party serves on the other, and that the other party must answer. The answers may be things that the party already knows (what is your full name, where do you live, when was the company incorporated, and similar questions) or it may be information that the party may have to collect before answering (how many claims were made against your company last year).

Under Rule 33 of the Federal Rules of Civil Procedure, a party can ask another party to answer no more than twenty-five written interrogatories. If the party wants to ask more than twenty-five questions, he or she can only do so by agreement with the other side (a "stipulation") or by order of the court. The party upon whom the interrogatories are served must serve its answers (or objections to the questions) within thirty days, unless the parties agree to a different date or if the court orders a different date.

b.   Production of Documents

A party may require another party to produce business or personal documents related to the litigation. A document can be more than a piece of paper — it can include electronic documents (such as email messages, or electronic files). It could also include photographs, diagrams, blueprints, and other items that might not necessary come to mind when you hear the word "documents."

The age of electronic discovery has changed document production and review tremendously. It is not uncommon in a large case to see dozens of associates reviewing thousands of email messages and other electronic documents.

A document must generally be produced unless it is somehow privileged or exempt from disclosure. For example, a document prepared by an attorney for pending litigation may be protected as "attorney work product." And a letter from an attorney to a client might be protected under the "attorney-client privilege."

c.   Depositions

A deposition is the process of taking testimony of a party or a witness out of court. The testimony is usually written down (or "transcribed") by a court reporter. It is now also common for these depositions to be videotaped or recorded in some fashion. The lawyers may ask the person being deposed to explain written answers given in the answer to the complaint. The lawyer may ask questions about documents produced in the litigation. The lawyer may ask questions that may lead to other relevant evidence for the case.

Many foreign attorneys are surprised to learn that these depositions are not taken in court. They may be taken in the lawyer's office, or at some other location. The judge is not present, only the lawyers, the witness, and the court reporter.

Depositions are useful for finding out relevant information and for getting leads on other witnesses who might have evidence about the case. Parties will generally take the deposition of the other party.

If the party or witness who was deposed later testifies in court in a way that is different from what was said in the deposition, the lawyer might use that earlier deposition testimony to "impeach" the credibility of that witness.

d.   Requests to Admit

A party can ask the other party to admit certain facts (such as that the company was incorporated on a specific date) or to admit that a particular document is genuine (such as admitting that the signature on the contract is that of the company's president). These requests to admit are part of the discovery process, and they can make the trial proceed faster on points that are not in dispute.

If a party fails to admit a certain fact by the date given, that fact may be deemed admitted.

6.   Summary Judgment

In a motion to dismiss, the court must accept the allegations of the complaint as being true — even if it is likely that they are not.

In a motion for summary judgment, a party can provide the judge with documents that prove that one or more of the allegations in the complaint are not true. A party might, for example, submit the *affidavit* of a witness in support of the motion for summary judgment.

Under Rule 56(c) of the Federal Rules of Civil Procedure, a moving party is entitled to summary judgment "if the pleadings, the discovery and disclosure materials on file, and any affidavits show that there is no genuine issue as to any material fact and that the movant is entitled to judgment as a matter of law."

If the court grants the motion for summary judgment, it may be on the entire case or on only part of it, such as a single issue within the case. If summary judgment is not granted on all issues, the case will proceed and be set for trial.

7.   Trial

Many cases never make it to trial. Most of them are settled, often during the discovery period when many parties realize the time and cost of producing thousands of documents. But cases do proceed to trial when they do not settle and when a dispositive motion (such as a motion to dismiss or a motion for summary judgment) does not otherwise resolve the case.

A trial is the examination in court of the witnesses and evidence. It is an adversarial proceeding, usually meaning that each side's own lawyers will represent their side. (A party can also represent himself or herself *pro se*, but it is usually a much better idea to hire a lawyer.)

If the trial is before a judge without a jury, it is called a *bench trial*. If the trial is going to be held before a jury, it is called a *jury trial*.

a.   Selecting a Jury

A jury will decide the factual issues in the case. It is important to select jurors who do not have pre-conceived notions about the case or prejudices that would keep the jurors from making an impartial decision.

Juries historically had to be made up of twelve persons, and verdicts had to be unanimous. But federal and state courts now allow smaller juries (composed of less than twelve persons) and verdicts in civil cases that are not unanimous. The smaller juries are thought to make the trial go faster (at the very least, it will take less time selecting the members of jury). And allowing the jury to give its verdict even when the result is not unanimous is thought to reduce the chances of having a "deadlocked" jury and having to conduct the trial all over again with a new jury.

If there is a right to have a jury in a particular case, and if one of the parties demands to exercise that right to have a jury, the first task is to pick the jury. This process of jury selection is called *voir dire*. Jurors will be asked questions to see if they can be fair and impartial.

b.   Opening Statements

The trial begins with an opening statement from the attorney for the plaintiff and, usually, an opening statement from the attorney for the defendant. These statements are not evidence but give the jurors (and the judge) an idea of what the case will be about and what evidence will be presented.

c.   Examination of Witnesses and the Introduction of Evidence

The plaintiff will present its witnesses and other evidence in support of its case. The plaintiff's attorney will ask questions of the witnesses on direct examination. The defense attorney may then cross-examine the plaintiff's witnesses.

The introduction of evidence will be governed by the rules of evidence. In federal courts, those rules are the *Federal Rules of Evidence*. Those rules generally require that the evidence introduced be reliable and relevant to the issues in the case.

d.   Motion for Judgment as a Matter of Law (the "Directed Verdict")

When the plaintiff has finished presenting its case, the defendant may move for judgment as a matter of law. Previously, and in some state courts still, this motion was called a motion for a "directed verdict." This motion asks the court to find that the plaintiff has not proven its case and asks the court to find in favor of the defendant. The court must look at the evidence in the light most favorable to the plaintiff (the "non-moving party") when deciding whether to grant a motion for judgment as a matter of law. These motions for judgment as a matter of law are in practice rarely granted. If the judge denies the motion, the trial will continue and the defense will present its case.

e.   The Defense

If the defendant does not move for a directed verdict, or if that motion for a directed verdict is denied, the defense will then present its own witnesses and evidence. The plaintiff may cross-examine the defense witnesses (just as the defense attorney cross-examined the witnesses for the plaintiff). The plaintiff may be allowed to introduce additional evidence to rebut evidence presented by the defendant.

f.   Submitting the Case to the Jury

When both sides have finished, the attorneys will make their closing arguments to summarize their version of the case and the evidence supporting it. The attorneys will suggest to the jury how they should view the evidence in the case. The lawyers can speak only about the evidence that was presented at trial — the lawyers cannot present new evidence that has not been introduced at trial.

The jury will receive "jury instructions" from the judge to help it reach a verdict. The judge will summarize the facts and issues, give some general instructions about the credibility of witnesses, and state who has the burden to prove a particular fact in each issue. Usually this burden will fall upon the plaintiff.

g.   The Jury's Verdict

After the jury finishes its deliberations, the jury will reach a verdict.

The verdict may be a general verdict, deciding only who won the case and, if that winner is the plaintiff, the amount of damages awarded. A general verdict setting forth these conclusions is the most common type of verdict. In some cases, the jury may also be asked some additional questions, to test whether the jury properly understood the case. If the answers to those additional questions show that the jury did not understand the case, the judge will not enter judgment on the verdict.

8.   Post-Trial Motions

After the jury returns its verdict, the losing party may move for judgment notwithstanding the verdict. This is also sometimes called a motion for a judgment n.o.v. (the Latin phrase, "non obstante veredicto"), but in federal courts, it is called a renewed motion for judgment as a matter of law.

The losing party may also move for a new trial, alleging that errors in the trial are so severe that the parties should litigate the matter all over again. As you might imagine, these motions are not often granted, particularly in civil trials. The judge is more likely to allow the losing party to appeal than to grant a new trial.

9.   The Judgment

A judgment is the "court's final determination of the rights and obligations of the parties in a case." *Black's Law Dictionary* 858 (Bryan A. Garner ed., 8th ed. 2004). The judgment may be a default judgment (if the defendants failed to appear after being given notice of the suit), or it may be a judgment entered by the court after granting a motion to dismiss or a motion for summary judgment. The judgment could be that entered by a judge who heard the case without a jury, or it could be one entered by the judge after a jury returns its verdict following a jury trial. It is the final stage of the case . . . unless there is an appeal.

C.   Appeals

A party who is unhappy with the judgment entered by the trial court can file an appeal of that final judgment. A party who is the losing party at the trial court level may file an appeal. (That party will be the appellant, and the other party will be the appellee.) But even parties who win their cases below may appeal if they did not win as much as they had hoped. (For example, they sued for a million dollars but the judgment gave them only one thousand dollars; they will likely file an appeal even though they "won.")

The appellate court will look at the transcript of the trial below. It will hear arguments ("appellate arguments") on the points of error that are alleged to have happened in the proceedings before the trial court. New issues that were not raised or litigated in the court below cannot be raised for the first time on appeal.

To see if there is reversible error, the appellate court will apply an appropriate *standard of review*. On appeal, the court looks only to the record. It will defer to many factual findings of the trial court, because that court had an opportunity to observe the witnesses.

The appellate court will usually include in its written decision the standard of review it used to decide the case.

In the United States federal courts, a party generally has a right to petition the federal appellate court to review the case. Further review by the U.S. Supreme Court by writ of certiorari is discretionary; four of the nine U.S. Supreme Court Justices must vote to hear the case. The U.S. Supreme Court takes only a small number of cases each year.

D.   Enforcing Judgments

A judgment might require a defendant to pay an amount of money to the plaintiff. The judgment might order the defendant to do some action. If the defendant pays the money owed or does the act ordered, there is no further need to enforce the judgment. The defendant had his or her day in court, lost, and paid the damages owed or did the thing required.

Other judgments might not require enforcement at all. For example, if the case was a declaratory judgment action (to declare the rights and duties of the parties to the case), the declaration of rights was the judgment sought and no further enforcement action is necessary.

But if the judgment is one that needs to be enforced, there will be specific rules about how that can be done. For example, if the plaintiff wins a judgment against the defendant to pay a specific sum of money, the plaintiff can bring a copy of that judgment to the sheriff, who will go after property owned by the defendant to satisfy the judgment. The sheriff might take the judgment debtor's car, for example, and sell it at an auction to satisfy the judgment.

If the judgment is one from another state, it will be necessary for the judgment holder to bring an action in the local court to enforce the judgment. The debtor must be served with notice of the action and be given an opportunity to be heard. It will not be necessary to re-litigate the case, however. Under the United States Constitution, a state must give "full faith and credit" to the judgments entered by other states. U.S. Const. art. IV, § 1. There are only a very limited number of ways to avoid the judgment.

The constitutional requirement to recognize judgments of sister states in the United States does not extend to the recognition of judgments from foreign countries, however. The Constitution requires only that states enforce the judgments of sister states. But judgments from other countries have been enforced in U.S. courts on the basis of comity. U.S. courts enforce foreign judgments in part on the hope that foreign countries will likewise recognize and enforce judgments of federal and state courts in the United States. But foreign courts have not widely enforced U.S. judgments, in part because the judicial systems in other countries may not recognize punitive damage awards (which can often be many times the amount of actual damages suffered by the plaintiff).

E.   Attorneys' Fees

In other countries, the losing side may have to pay the attorney fees of the winning side. But in the United States, the "American Rule" for litigation provides that each side in a case must pay their own attorneys.

As with most rules, there are some limited exceptions to the "American Rule." A court can order the losing side to pay attorneys' fees if a statute specifically authorizes the court to do so. Such statutes might be called "fee-shifting statutes," because they shift the burden of paying the fees for one party's attorney to the other side.

Another way that the court might order the losing side to pay the attorneys' fees of the winning side may happen if the case was brought in bad faith, or if it was frivolous, or if there were abuses committed during discovery. Awards can be made for these reasons, but such awards are uncommon. The parties generally have to pay their own attorneys' fees.

One final exception may arise where the dispute concerned a contract and a provision in the contract obligated the losing side to pay the attorney's fees for the winning side.

F.   Final and Binding Effect of Judgments

If a claim is litigated, the losing party should not be able to go to another court to re-litigate the matter again. A party who attempts to do so will face the doctrines of *res judicata* or *claim preclusion*. These doctrines will preclude other courts from hearing the case where (1) there was an earlier decision on the issue; (2) a final judgment on the merits; and (3) the involvement of the same parties, or parties who have some relationship to the parties in the original litigation. *See, e.g., Black's Law Dictionary* 1336–1337. The doctrine of claim preclusion will apply even if the new lawsuit attempts to raise a new cause of action based on the same facts. The party has already had a day in court and should not be able to argue a new theory of the case. The idea is that individuals should not have to face a constant string of litigation, and courts should not be burdened with having to hear the same case again. Even if the first action was "wrongly decided," the remedy is to appeal that wrong decision rather than to file a new lawsuit in another court.

IV. CONCLUSION

This Chapter has introduced the subjects of jurisdiction and civil procedure. There is certainly more that could be said on each of the topics discussed in this Chapter. The purpose of this Chapter is to help you go more deeply into the substantive issues raised in other chapters and that you will encounter in further study or law practice.

The first part of the Chapter focused on jurisdiction, with particular emphasis on the federal courts in the United States and their federal question and diversity jurisdiction. It also explored personal jurisdiction, requirements for standing, and venue. The second part of the Chapter dealt with issues of civil procedure and provided an overview of steps in the litigation process. Even if you never find yourself in court, it is helpful to understand the litigation process in the United States.

Chapter 6

EVIDENCE

By — Steven I. Friedland

SYNOPSIS

I. AN INTRODUCTION TO EVIDENCE LAW

A. What Is Evidence?

Evidence is generally required to win a dispute in the American legal system. This evidence is called "proof." To win a lawsuit, a party must offer a sufficient amount of proof to persuade the trier of fact, namely a judge or a jury. There are different kinds of proof. To illustrate, growing up as children, we learned about evidence and proof when a parent asked about homework. The parent might have relied on our oral assertion, which is equivalent to witness testimony. The parent might have wanted more than that, namely the tangible proof of the homework itself, or the parent might have relied on our grades as indirect or circumstantial proof that we completed the homework.

In addition to the stuff that constitutes proof in a hearing or trial, the term "evidence" also refers to the rules that govern what proof is allowed and what proof is not allowed to be considered by the trier of fact. These rules set forth all of the foundations or prerequisites required for the admission of evidence.

All states have their own rules of evidence that govern what can be admitted at trial. There are also rules in federal courts. The federal rules are called the Federal Rules of Evidence and govern the admission of evidence in all federal courts. Most state laws are patterned after the Federal Rules of Evidence, although there are significant differences from state to state upon a closer look. This overview will focus mostly on the Federal Rules of Evidence, since they have the broadest applicability — federal courts and their facsimiles in many state courts.

The Federal Rules of Evidence were adopted less than forty years ago, in 1975, to replace the common-law rules that had long governed in federal courts. The common law is composed of rules of law that have been created by judges. The Federal Rules of Evidence are just like statutes — they were codified by Congress after considerable input. The Rules were proposed and formulated by a special Advisory Committee. The Advisory Committee wrote a series of notes explaining why they proposed the rules they did. These Notes are similar to legislative history. Thus, when trying to figure out what the Federal Rules of Evidence mean, one easy and important reference is the Advisory Committee Note to the particular rule.

B.   Evidence Categories: Real, Representative, and Testimonial Evidence

There are many ways of categorizing evidence. One such division involves categorizing evidence as real, representative, or testimonial. Real evidence means the tangible objects offered as proof in court. In an auto accident case, the tangible objects may be the hubcap from a car or even its steering wheel or engine. In a breach of contract action, real evidence may be the written paper on which the contract was formed. In a slip and fall case, the real evidence might be the banana peel on which the plaintiff allegedly slipped. All of these objects are submitted as proof in a case and may be admitted as real evidence.

In addition to real evidence, there is representative evidence. As the word "representative" indicates, this category involves evidence that represents something else. If you look at a driver's license, the photo on it represents the person who owns the license. Diagrams and charts also represent other things. For any building, a blueprint is representative of that building. In today's age, there is a wide variety of representative evidence that is useful in deciding cases.

A third category is perhaps the most popular — witness testimony. "Viva voce," Latin for "by voice," involves witnesses testifying about various facts through what they saw, heard, smelled, felt, and the like. These fact witnesses are also accompanied by expert witnesses who may give their opinions about what facts mean or how scientific evidence or technical evidence relates to the case at hand. At every trial, there are usually one or more witnesses.

C.   More Categories: Direct and Indirect Evidence

Another way of dividing up the world of evidence is into direct and indirect evidence. Direct evidence requires no inferences for it to be useful to the trier of fact in a case. Indirect evidence, on the other hand, requires at least one inference for the evidence to be used by the trier of fact. Another name for indirect evidence is circumstantial evidence. A terrific example of circumstantial evidence involves an alleged perpetrator of a crime who runs from the scene when confronted there. The inference to be drawn from a person running from the scene of a crime is that the person is guilty. That may not be true, of course, but it is a helpful inference for the trier of fact. Eyewitnesses often supply direct evidence of what they saw or heard. If a person is alleged to have committed a crime, an eyewitness who saw the crime would be offering direct evidence.

II.   EVIDENCE IN CONTEXT: THE LAWSUIT

Evidence can best be understood in context, namely through a lawsuit, because that is when evidence is offered. In essence, evidence does not take place in a vacuum; it is the fuel that makes the lawsuit run. Thus, it is helpful to understand how lawsuits occur in the American system.

A.   The Stages of a Lawsuit

In the American justice system, cases are generally divided up into two types — civil and criminal. A civil action is generally typified by what kind of remedy it seeks, such as damages, injunctive relief (telling someone to do or not to do something), other equitable relief like specific performance (especially in contract actions), and still other relief such as a declaratory judgment action. A criminal case differs from a civil case in that the criminal action generally seeks incarceration (jail time), fines, and even death. While the burdens of proof are different — the burden is much higher in a criminal case because of the greater consequences — the general stages of a lawsuit are similar. These stages will be tracked below.

Stage #1:   The Charging Instrument.

A civil case starts with a complaint, a formal document providing notice of the suit. The complaint includes the parties, the jurisdiction of the court, and the legal basis for the complaint, as well as what remedy the parties seek. In a criminal case, charging documents primarily include informations or indictments. An information is a paper filed by the prosecutor, and an indictment is brought by the Grand Jury, a special jury convened to determine if continuing the case is appropriate. All of these documents provide notice that a crime allegedly has been committed, that it was committed by the defendant, and that it was committed in a certain place and time.

Stage #2:   **Responsive Pleadings.**

The second step in a civil case involves a response to the complaint by the opposing party, generally called an answer to the complaint. This is where the opposing party indicates what is conceded and what is opposed in the complaint. In a criminal case, there is no such equivalency. In fact, in a criminal case, it is often more important what happens to the defendant during the pre-trial proceedings, because he very well could be detained or subject to physical restrictions. For the criminal defendant, the initial concern is release from jail. This may occur in what is called a first appearance, which is a first hearing before a neutral magistrate who decides such issues as release and, if appropriate, the appointment of counsel.

Stage #3:   **Pre-Trial Motions.**

In a civil case, the next step for either plaintiffs or defendants may include a series of motions, from a motion to dismiss the case to a motion for summary judgment, both seeking to end the case. In criminal cases, there are also various motions available to the parties, which can claim the indictment or information is defective, ask for an advance copy of the indictment or information, or for a statement of particulars about the time and place of the alleged crime. Other motions include a motion for continuance and for a change of venue. In addition, there may be a request to remove the judge for a lack of impartiality. This is called a motion to recuse the judge.

Stage #4:   **Discovery.**

The next step is common to both civil and criminal cases and is called discovery. This is an attempt to find out more about the case from the opposing party to reduce the level of surprise. Discovery serves a variety of purposes, including understanding how strong one's case is for the purposes of settlement or plea bargaining. While some information possessed by the opposing party is not subject to discovery — see the attorney-client privilege or what is known as the work product privilege — much information is available to each party.

Stage #5:   **Additional Pre-Trial Practice.**

More motions may be made after discovery ensues. These motions result from the additional information obtained during discovery. The motions may include a motion to sever or join the parties or to sever or join claims. There are very specific rules about such requests that are argued to the judge. In criminal cases, there is an additional motion called a motion for speedy trial rights. This right emanates from the Constitution and requires that prosecutors try criminal defendants without excessive delay, so a criminal defendant does not languish in prison or have a case open indefinitely. In a criminal case, the defendant is also arraigned. This is where the defendant enters a plea to the charges. The plea can either be guilty, not guilty, or nolo contendere. The nolo plea means no contest and is the functional equivalent to a guilty plea but is less damaging to the defendant because it means the defendant is simply not contesting the charges and not admitting guilt.

Stage #6:   **Settlement Negotiations or Plea Bargaining.**

The next step in the process involves avoiding a trial through either settlement in civil cases or plea bargaining in criminal cases. This step may be occurring throughout the pre-trial process but occurs more heatedly on the "courthouse steps." This means as trial approaches, with parties having completed discovery and with considerable information, many try to avoid going to trial. The trial process occurs only in about five to ten percent of civil or criminal cases. There is great use of mediation and arbitration on the civil side and much plea bargaining in the criminal arena.

Stage #7:   **The Trial.**

Finally the trial takes place. There are different stages within the trial process.

a.   Jury Selection

The first part of the trial process is selecting the jury. Voir dire, to tell the truth, really involves jury panel de-selection and not selection. Based on questions of the jury panel, many people are discharged due to cause or through preemptory challenges, basically for no reason at all. If preemptory challenges are made, the Constitution limits such challenges on the basis of race, gender, national origin, and religion.

b.   Opening Statements

In opening statements, the attorneys tell the jury what the evidence will show. This means the attorneys get to tell the story of the case in chronological order, in a way that might not occur with the witnesses at trial. The attorneys tend to present the evidence that will lead to the jury finding for their clients. But the attorneys must limit their statements to only the evidence they intend to offer in court, and not talk about evidence that is inadmissible or is not something they will offer to the jury through the proper channels.

c.   Prosecutor's/Plaintiff's Case-in-Chief

After opening statements, the party with the burden of proof, either the prosecutor (criminal) or the plaintiff (civil), presents his or her case-in-chief. This is done through real or representative evidence and witness testimony. With witnesses, the party calling the witness does the direct examination, followed by a cross-examination from the opposing party, and then sometimes redirect examination from the original party. While the opportunity to cross is required, the opposing party is not required to actually do so. A redirect examination following the cross-examination sometimes occurs to follow up on information elicited during the cross-examination. The redirect examination is another type of direct examination.

d.   Defendant's Case-in-Chief

The defense gets to offer its own case-in-chief. Since the prosecution/plaintiff generally has the burden of proof, the defense often need not offer any evidence at all. This is especially true in a criminal case, where the defendant has the constitutional right to remain silent throughout the trial. If the defense does offer a case though, the prosecution or plaintiff then may follow with its rebuttal case. This rebuttal contests things raised by the defense. If the prosecution or plaintiff offers its rebuttal case, the defense is then allowed one last attempt to rebut the prosecution or plaintiff's case. This is called the surrebuttal.

e.   Jury Instructions Conference

Before the closing arguments, the parties talk about the jury instructions and have a conference with the judge to discuss them. Most jurisdictions have standard instructions, but each party attempts to have these instructions altered in their own favor.

f.   Closing Arguments

The parties then get to argue to the jury one last time about what the evidence meant and why that evidence should be construed in the party's favor. After the parties have completed their closing arguments, which is not evidence, the judge then will instruct the jury and send them off to deliberations.

g.   The Verdict

The jury comes back with a verdict on each count. In civil cases, juries sometimes answer specific questions of fact as well. Occasionally, the jury is polled to determine if each juror agrees with the verdict. The jury will deliberate based on the evidence and return a verdict on each count offered. If the jury cannot agree on an outcome and does not reach a verdict, it is called a hung jury and a mistrial occurs. Sometimes, cases will be retried and sometimes they will not.

h.   Post-Verdict

If there is a verdict of guilty in a criminal case, sentencing must occur. The judge often gets a pre-sentencing report. After the pre-sentencing report, the judge finally sentences the defendant in a criminal case.

In a civil case, after a verdict, motions occur. The defendant may move for reconsideration by the trial judge and then move for an appeal at a later time.

III.   THE FUNCTIONS OF THE RULES OF EVIDENCE AND THE ROLES OF JUDGES, ATTORNEYS, AND JURORS

A.   The Functions of the Rules of Evidence

The Rules of Evidence have been enacted for various reasons. There are three primary functions: accuracy; fairness; and policy. The accuracy rules are designed to ensure accurate verdicts and confidence in the legal system. Much has been made about inaccurate verdicts and how those verdicts undermine the system, ranging from rogue prosecutors, such as the infamous Duke lacrosse case, where the prosecutor maintained a case even though the evidence indicated there was no basis for the prosecution, to verdicts that look like partisan justice. The system strives for impartiality and accuracy. Rules such as relevance and unfair prejudice ensure that the evidence considered by the jury will be helpful and not misleading.

Fairness rules ensure that both sides have an opportunity to present their positions, giving each side their day in court and ensuring an even playing field. Thus, if one party raises an inference, the other side is often allowed to rebut that inference.

Also included in the fairness rules are traffic rules, meaning rules that help expedite the case. Rule 403 excludes evidence that is a waste of time. Under Rule 611, the judge can control the case to ensure that it develops fairly, but expeditiously at the same time. This fairness objective sometimes contradicts accuracy, since a more accurate verdict may result from endless testimony and a countless number of witnesses, but given the amount of time and cost, would be too burdensome for the system.

Finally, there are policy rules that balance larger public policies against the need for evidence in a particular case. These public policy rules primarily advance privileges (e.g. attorney-client, clergy-penitent) and the quasi privileges of excluding subsequent remedial measures, offers to compromise, plea bargaining, and liability insurance, as well as offers to pay medical expenses. These rules generally consider policies to be greater than the need for the evidence in the case. The policies sometimes sacrifice accuracy in a particular case for the greater good overall.

B.   The Roles of Judges, Attorneys, and Juries

1.   Judges

Judges have several main responsibilities at trial. It is their job to admit or exclude evidence and to make sure the case functions smoothly and fairly. In determining whether to admit evidence, judges must decide if evidence is relevant and meets the other requirements of the rules. Their general decision-making is discretionary, and judges can consider just about anything except for privileged evidence — even inadmissible evidence — in their admissibility determinations. The threshold for admissibility is fairly low, given that it is up to the trier of fact to make the final determination of whether the evidence meets the proof requirements for causes of action, claims, or defenses.

The judge decides whether there is enough evidence to go forward with a case to reach the jury or trier of fact. This is called the burden of going forward. The judge also decides when witnesses may testify and how long they may testify for, thus determining the duration of trials and how cases are presented to the jury. Judges rule on objections to evidence, generally sustaining or overruling the objections. "Sustained" means it is a proper objection and the evidence is excluded or the question is disallowed. "Overruled" means the objection is not valid and the attorney may ask the question or offer the evidence.

2.   Juries

Juries generally act as the trier of fact. (In trials without juries, the judge is the trier of fact.) This means juries determine what the facts are and, after being given the law by the judge, effectively determine the outcome of the case. That is, a jury generally will determine whether the plaintiff wins in a civil cause of action and whether a defendant is guilty in a criminal case. Jurors must decide whether the evidence meets the applicable burden of proof or persuasion. In a civil case, the burden of persuasion is generally "by a preponderance" of the evidence, meaning more likely than not. Another way of describing this burden is that there must be more than fifty percent of the evidence weighing in a party's favor. In some civil cases, there is a higher standard of proof, called "clear and convincing" evidence. There is no quantitative number attached to this level, just that the evidence must be clear and convincing. (This occurs in defamation actions, namely libel or slander.) In a criminal case, the defendant has much more to lose, possibly his or her life, and the burden is much higher. The burden is described as "beyond a reasonable doubt." This also is not quantified, but really means that there is no doubt to which a juror can give a reason in order to find the defendant guilty. The theory behind this very high level of proof is that it is better to let ten guilty people go free than convict one innocent person.

Note: Sometimes, innocent people are convicted. This fact is being uncovered by the Innocence Projects that exist around the country. These projects use DNA and other evidence to show that people who have been convicted of crimes are actually innocent of the crimes for which they are serving time. These people are being freed now by pardons and other measures.

3.   Attorneys

The attorneys' job is to represent his or her clients zealously and offer evidence on the clients' behalf, especially if the clients have the burden of going forward with evidence. It is also the attorneys' job to object when evidence is inadmissible and offered by the other side. If the attorney does not object, generally the evidence will be allowed. Unless it is plain error, an appellate court will not hear an issue about which the attorney failed to object.

Sometimes the judge excludes evidence the attorney believes is admissible. An attorney must then make a "proffer," meaning explain to the court for the record what the evidence would have been, so the appellate court could consider it if an appeal is taken at a later time. Thus, attorneys not only object to evidence that is being offered, but make proffers about excluded evidence.

The attorneys also are responsible for developing strategies on their client's behalf and arguing the case to the jury. Attorneys may offer evidence for one purpose, such as impeachment or for proving an issue in the case or both. Attorneys generally are allowed to control their own cases, and it is up to them to determine what and when evidence is offered.

IV.   AN OVERVIEW OF THE STRUCTURE OF EVIDENCE LAW AT TRIAL

It is important to understand that evidence at trial can be offered for different purposes. Sometimes, evidence can be offered just to impeach a witness, meaning attack the witness's truthfulness or accuracy. Evidence also is needed as proof of the cause of action, claims, or defenses. That is, if a person files suit based on negligence, the plaintiff must show that there was a duty, a breach of that duty, an injury caused by the breach, and resulting damages. This is all shown through evidence or proof. Similarly, if a criminal case is brought against a defendant for selling drugs, the prosecution would have to prove the elements of drug distribution and the defendant also could offer proof of a defense such as entrapment. If a defendant claims entrapment, such as the famous automaker John Delorean did when charged with selling cocaine, the defendant would have the burden of offering some evidence. Thus, the initial question that must be asked when evidence is offered at trial is, "What is the evidence offered to prove?"

> *Important Evidence Question #1:* What is the evidence offered to prove?
> *Answers:* (1) To prove the case;
> (2) To impeach a witness; or
> (3) Both (1) and (2) above

If evidence is offered to prove an issue in the case, there are seven major areas which may prevent it from being admitted. That is, there are seven major obstacles to the admission of the evidence. Admission of the evidence means the jury can consider it, not that the evidence will be weighed fully by the jury or will be dispositive of an issue in the case. The seven major areas include: relevance; character evidence; opinions; hearsay; privileges; witnesses; and writings.

A.   Offered to Prove an Issue in the Case

> *How is the evidence offered to prove an issue in the case?*
> Relevance
> Character Evidence
> Opinion Evidence
> Hearsay
> Privileges
> Witnesses
> Writings

Each of these areas has its own set of rules within the Federal Rules of Evidence and in state evidence codes as well. A brief overview of these areas follows.

1.   Relevance

Relevance is the minimum requirement for admissibility for all evidence in federal and state courts. Essentially, if evidence is irrelevant or unhelpful to the case, it will be excluded. The initial step then, is determining if evidence is in some way helpful to the trier of fact. The test for relevance is very low, meaning evidence only has to connect to the case in one way, and will be considered relevant even if there are many inferences from the evidence that do not connect to the case.

It is the judge who decides whether evidence is relevant and is therefore the gatekeeper of evidence. If the judge opens the gate, the evidence will live to be tested again by other objections to admission.

In addition, not all relevant evidence is admissible. Evidence that is unfairly prejudicial, even though helpful, will be excluded because it misleads the jury and distorts the evidence. Relevant evidence that is cumulative or a waste of time also will be excluded.

2.   Character Evidence

Character evidence is special evidence about a party, victim or witness. A witness's character often is restricted to truthfulness and is dealt with separately in this Chapter under impeachment. It does not deal with whether a party committed the incident in question, but is a generalized description of a trait or disposition. Whether a person tends to be happy, sad, peaceful, violent, hardworking, or lazy are all character traits. While this is very helpful evidence, it is also extremely prejudicial and consequently, usually excluded.

3.   Opinions

Generally, witnesses must have personal knowledge of the facts in order to help the jury or judge decide the case. While lay witnesses are allowed to give some opinions, they are mostly restricted to "facts only." A large exception to witnesses giving opinions involves experts. Experts trained by experience, education, technical training, or other means may answer hypothetical questions and provide their opinions in court so long as it helps the trier of fact. There are other limitations as well, most notably, that the expert's opinion must be based on data reasonably relied on in the field, and the theory on which the expert is relying must also be reliable. The judge decides whether the expert's theory is sufficiently reliable to testify based on multiple factors. Without reliability, the aura of expertise, which already exists, would be too great and would mislead and distort the ultimate results.

4.   Hearsay

Hearsay is perhaps one of the largest obstacles to the admissibility of evidence. Hearsay means any out-of-court statement (assertion) by a declarant (the person uttering the statement) offered for the truth of the matter asserted. This legalese is difficult to understand, even by law students and lawyers. If all four hearsay elements are met, the evidence is presumptively excluded from trial. If evidence is not hearsay, that doesn't mean it necessarily will be admitted because it still must overcome other objections, such as relevance, character, privilege, etc. It just won't be excluded as hearsay.

Hearsay is excluded because it is considered unreliable evidence. This theme of unreliability is especially prevalent in hearsay. These out-of-court statements cannot be assessed by the trier of fact as a testifying witness's statements are. The statements are not subject to cross-examination. The trier of fact cannot see the demeanor of the declarant when the statement is being made and the declarant is making a statement out-of-court, which means it is often not under oath. Without these big three safeguards, the evidence is considered unreliable.

5.   Privilege

Privileged evidence means that otherwise relevant evidence will be excluded from trial due to a larger policy. Privileges often protect relationships such as attorney-client, clergy-penitent, husband-wife, or psychotherapist-patient. Constitutional privilege also protects individuals, including the Fifth Amendment privilege against self-incrimination. Privileges can be waived and have a variety of exceptions.

6. Witnesses

All witnesses must be competent, which means they must be able to understand what it means to tell the truth. Thus, very young children and perhaps some elderly and infirm seniors may be excluded from the stand if they do not understand what it means to tell the truth. Otherwise, even people who have a tendency to be untruthful will be allowed to testify. That means a person who has ten perjury convictions will be allowed to go for number eleven. The fact that witnesses are competent to testify, however, does not mean the jury will believe them or credit their testimony. It is up to the trier of fact to evaluate the testimony and weigh it.

Also, there are form limitations on how questions may be asked by attorneys and how witnesses may answer. For example, no leading questions are allowed on direct examination as a general rule. While there are exceptions to this rule, a leading question, meaning one that suggests an answer, is usually permitted on cross-examination of a witness.

7. Writings

Writings are prevalent in many trials. When offered, they commonly suggest three objections — hearsay, authentication, and the Best Evidence Rule. While hearsay has been covered above, authentication is something that is required of all writings and, in fact, of all testimony. It generally means that the thing is what it purports to be. Writings can be forgeries and have subsequent additions or subtractions that necessitate authentication prior to being received in evidence. The Best Evidence Rule simply requires writings whose contents are to be proven at trial to be the original, if possible, to minimize the likelihood of forgery. There are numerous exceptions to the Best Evidence Rule when it applies — and it does not apply all that often.

B. Offered to Impeach a Witness

The second major reason why evidence is offered, next to proving an issue in the case, is to impeach a witness. Impeachment is a mini-trial, solely about a witness's truthfulness or veracity. A better way to understand impeachment is that it is about attacking a witness's truthfulness or veracity. These attacks occur in two ways, either directly, by asking the witness questions and expecting the witness to answer, or by circumventing the witness and offering evidence directly to the court or by calling a new witness. When a witness is asked questions, this is called intrinsic impeachment. When the witness is circumvented and new evidence is offered, this is called extrinsic impeachment. There are only a limited number of ways to impeach a witness intrinsically or extrinsically. For example, certain kinds of convictions, such as felonies or crimes of fraud, can be used to impeach the witness on the stand. If the witness denies being convicted of these crimes, the attorney is allowed to use a certified copy of conviction and offer that copy directly to the trier of fact as extrinsic impeachment.

All of these evidence topics will be covered in greater detail below. The coverage will be accompanied by examples.

V. RELEVANCE

Relevance is a good place to start any discussion about evidence. Relevance technically means "probative of a fact in issue in the case." Probative means "relates to" and fact in issue means "a fact properly provable in the case." Thus, relevance is really about a relationship, how the evidence relates to impeachment of a witness or an issue in the case. Evidence may require many inferences to be connected to a fact properly provable in the case. Thus, a pen found at the scene of the crime may be linked to the type of pen the defendant uses at work, which makes it a little bit more likely that the defendant was there. If it is a little bit more likely the defendant was at the scene, it makes it a little bit more likely the defendant might have committed the crime. While this inference chain may be long and somewhat tenuous, if it connects to a fact in the case, the evidence is relevant. The fact that evidence is relevant, however, does not mean it is admissible at trial. It just means it passes the first hurdle and can face the other hurdles, such as privilege, unfair prejudice, character, hearsay, and the like.

Example # 1: Paul Revere, a famous member of the Revolutionary War army, who warned Bostonians about the British attack "one if by land, two if by sea . . . ," was in actuality a dentist. Was that relevant to identifying soldiers who had died on the field of battle? The answer is Yes. Revere was able to identify a soldier by his dental work, one of the first to ever do so.

Example # 2: Jones is accused of robbing the First National Bank in Tampa, Florida. Is it relevant that he is divorced and is late on alimony payments? The answer is Yes, because the lateness on alimony payments helps to show that he may need money, and if he may need money, it may be more likely that Jones obtained the money by robbing the bank.

Example # 3: In the same case in which Jones is charged with robbing the First National Bank above, it has been shown that Jones was convicted of selling cocaine eight years ago. Is that relevant? Of course, the real question is, relevant to what? The conviction is relevant to many things, from "Jones may need money" to "Jones is a criminal." If it is used to show Jones is a criminal, one inference can be that once a person is a criminal of any kind, that person will always be a criminal. Because Jones committed a crime earlier, he is more likely to commit a crime later, even if it is somewhat unrelated. In addition, the fact that he was selling cocaine may mean he uses drugs and has a drug habit, and to support that drug habit, he needs money. So there are many ways to connect this alleged fact to the case. Of course the inferences may be weak and the evidence still may be excluded as unfairly prejudicial, which in all likelihood would be the case if offered as substantive evidence to prove he robbed the bank.

A.   Unfair Prejudice

A significant exclusion is unfair prejudice. This means that even if evidence is relevant to the case, it may be excluded as unfairly prejudicial. The unfair prejudice test requires a balancing of the probative value and the prejudicial impact of the evidence. Because of a need for evidence, the evidence will only be excluded if the unfair prejudice substantially outweighs the probative value. That means that evidence will still come in if the prejudicial impact equals the probative value (helpfulness) of the evidence.

Example # 4: Tammy is charged with shoplifting. The prosecutor wishes to offer the fact that Tammy has been convicted of shoplifting on two other occasions. This evidence is not admissible, because while the evidence is relevant, meaning helpful to proving whether Tammy shoplifted here (once a shoplifter, always a shoplifter is the pertinent inference), it is unfairly prejudicial. The jury will likely look at the prior convictions and not look at whether Tammy in fact shoplifted here. Thus, the unfair prejudice impact is very high, even though there is significant probative value. The probative value is substantially outweighed by the danger of unfair prejudice, and the evidence should be excluded.

Example # 5: In the Scott Peterson case, Scott Peterson was convicted of killing his wife and unborn child. During the trial, it emerged that he was having an affair with another woman. Is this evidence unfairly prejudicial? While the defendant's infidelity indicates he is not a faithful person, it is much more relevant to the case to show his motive for why he would kill his wife. Thus, it is extremely probative of the fact he killed his wife, and while prejudicial in some respects, the probative value is not substantially outweighed by its prejudicial impact. The evidence was allowed in the actual trial.

B.   Relevant Evidence Excluded for Policy Reasons

Some relevant evidence is excluded because of policy reasons unrelated to the facts of the case. Major examples are subsequent remedial measures, plea bargaining and offers to compromise, and completed compromises. Offers to compromise, for example, promote the settlement of civil actions, which are to be encouraged. There must, however, be a disputed claim before the exclusion of evidence will occur.

Example # 6: A gets into an auto accident with B. As they are talking on the side of the road, A spontaneously blurts out to B, "I must have been looking for my cassette tape when my car swerved, I am so sorry. How about if I pay you $10,000 right now and we settle the whole thing?" B responded by saying, "No way," and brought suit, looking at his damaged Rolls Royce and figuring that the damage was much greater than $10,000. At trial, B offers A's statements. Are these statements excluded by the offers to compromise rule? While it appears that A and B had a dispute, there must have been some threat of a dispute before the settlement negotiations would be excluded. Indications of a dispute depend on what the future plaintiff says, not what the defendant spontaneously offers. Thus, the conversation that occurred before the plaintiff threatened the lawsuit is not excluded by the offers to compromise rule.

Example # 7: A and B are in the same accident. The police come to investigate, and the parties later leave the scene. A gets a letter from B's lawyer the next day saying that he would be filing suit in a week. A calls up B and tries to settle the case. Are A's statements excluded by the offers to compromise rule? The answer here is Yes. Because the plaintiff, B, threatened suit first, these statements by A are all shielded under the offers to compromise rule. The goal of the rule is to promote settlement negotiations leading to compromises and avoid unnecessary trials.

C.   Sexual Assault Cases

In our society, there are numerous highly charged sexual assault cases. Many such cases, in fact, are not reported at all because of the fear the victims have of being put on trial themselves. The evidence rules are fashioned to protect the victim who becomes a complaining witness. For example, the prior sexual history of a complaining victim is generally excluded, with only few exceptions.

Example # 8: Warwick was prosecuted for sexual assault. At trial, the defense offered the fact that the victim had a child out of wedlock and dressed in a miniskirt on a regular basis. Is this evidence admissible? The answer is that the evidence will be inadmissible at trial. The fact that the complaining witness had a child out of wedlock is exactly the type of history of a sexual assault victim that is not admitted at trial. The evidence of how the victim dressed is not directly dealt with by the rule excluding prior history, but will be excluded as unfairly prejudicial. How the alleged victim dressed is intended to incite the jury and play on cultural biases and would be inadmissible at trial.

Other Acts of Sexual Assault Defendants. In recent years, there has been a growing body of literature about the recidivist nature of pedophiles. Because pedophiles tend to repeat their crimes, the rules have been adjusted to allow into evidence, at least on the federal level, evidence of other similar acts involving sexual assault defendants. This rule applies to both criminal and civil cases and is intended to stop the bias against child complainants and sexual assault victims who make a complaint against an apparently upstanding member of the community.

D.   Character Evidence

Character evidence, as touched on briefly in the overview above, is evidence of a generalized trait or propensity used at trial to help paint the picture of a party, victim or witness. With respect to a party or victim, it helps to prove an issue in the case, whether they did what was alleged. As for a witness, trait evidence is used to show the witness's character for truthfulness, a single trait that relates to his credibility or believability. The character of witnesses is dealt with in impeachment, separately from the character of a party or victim.

The general rule for character evidence offered to prove a trait or disposition of a party or victim is to exclude it. In a sense, this exclusion can be attributed to unfair prejudice. While the evidence is probative, it is also highly prejudicial — a jury will likely misuse this evidence by relying on it too much to prove an issue in the case.

Example # 9: Winona was convicted of shoplifting. If she is charged with shoplifting again, would the prior conviction be permitted to prove she did it the second time? While the evidence may be helpful and indeed relevant, it is unfairly prejudicial and would be excluded. People can change, and this type of evidence convicts people for who they are, not for what they have done. That is contrary to how the American system operates.

Character Evidence Exceptions

There are exceptions to the general character evidence exclusion. If character is an *essential element* in the case that must be proven by a party to prevail, such evidence is permitted. This occurs, for example, in defamation actions or when the entrapment defense is raised. In addition, character evidence is admitted in cases where a criminal defendant "puts it at issue" to help his case or either side in criminal or civil cases offers "other act" evidence, which is evidence which could show character but is relevant for a non-character purpose like motive, intent, or common scheme or plan.

Example # 10: In a public gathering, Jim says Sarah is a "lazy thief." Sarah sues Jim for defamation. At trial, Sarah offers evidence that she stays in the office and works from 8 a.m. to 8 p.m. regularly. Sarah also offers five witnesses to say Sarah has a reputation for being truthful and not a thief. Jim, in response, offers evidence that Sarah takes naps at the office and the opinion of a neighbor that Sarah is a thief. All of the above evidence would be permitted, because in a defamation action, character is to be proven as an element. If Sarah does not prove that Jim's statement has hurt her reputation, meaning defamed her, she will lose the case. If Jim proves that the allegation is truthful, that would be a defense. Thus, all forms of character evidence are permitted here.

Example # 11: Peter is charged with perjury. At trial, Peter offers his mother and sister-in-law to testify that Peter has a very truthful reputation in the community. This evidence would be allowed, because in criminal cases, the defense is given a special dispensation to offer character evidence of a pertinent trait. The form of the evidence must be reputation or opinion only and not specific acts. Thus, the evidence in this case would be permitted, because both witnesses are testifying about Peter's reputation in the community for a pertinent trait, his truthfulness.

VI. OPINIONS

People often communicate their opinions in normal conversations. This observation can readily be seen on television, where pundits offer opinions about everything. Trials are permeated with witnesses giving opinions as well, but there is an attempt to limit these opinions to specific circumstances. Lay persons can give their opinions if it is within their common experience and helpful to the jury. Thus, opinions such as height, weight, speed, time, distance, and the like are all within common knowledge and are permitted. Opinions beyond common knowledge, however, are generally excluded from evidence unless a foundation is laid that the person is an expert and has the competence to give such an opinion. Expert witnesses require several foundations before they are allowed to answer hypotheticals or simply give opinions outright.

One required foundation is that the science on which the testimony is based must be considered reliable. Reliability is based on a series of factors and determined by the judge. Also, the expert must be qualified. To qualify an expert, the attorney asks the expert about her training, experience, education, and any other background fact that might assist in determining if this person is an expert in the field. Thus, the expert is often asked about his or her publications, whether he or she has testified as an expert in the field before, for which side, and whether he or she has been an officer in any of the organizations in that field as well. Before the expert is accepted, the opposing side is permitted to voir dire the witness about his or her qualifications. Once accepted as an expert, the witness can give an opinion and then is subject to cross-examination. (While it can be asked whether the witness is being paid for testifying, that question often does not work, because the expert often says I am not being paid for my testimony, just for my time, in fact, just like counsel.) While opposing counsel may stipulate to the qualifications of an expert, meaning agree to them so they do not have to be presented, the proponent of the witness often wants these qualifications presented to the jury so that the aura of expertise attaches to the person's opinion.

Example # 12: Jennie was an eyewitness to an auto accident. She saw two cars approach an intersection and one of the cars go through a stop sign. At trial, she stated, "I saw the red car approach the intersection at about thirty-five miles per hour and it proceeded to put its brakes on for about fifteen yards without stopping before it crashed into the blue car." Are Jennie's opinions about the speed of the red car, and how long it put its brakes on, permitted? The answer is Yes. Jennie can give her opinion, because it is within common knowledge about the speed of a car and also distance, if she did have some personal knowledge for saying one car was using its brakes. These lay opinions are permitted under the Federal Rules of Evidence and in most state rules as well.

A.   Foundations for Expert Witnesses

In order to lay a foundation for experts, there must be a reliable theory and a reliable application of that theory. The reliability is left to the judge to decide, so the judge is not only the gatekeeper of all relevant evidence, but the gatekeeper of which experts get to testify. Reliable theories can be scientific theories or technical theories.

Example # 13: Madame Leo is an astrologer and probably the best in the country. She is called to testify in a criminal trial concerning whether the defendant committed burglary. Madame Leo uses her astrological expertise to determine that the defendant would not have been in the condition or location to commit the burglary. Is this testimony allowed? The answer is clearly No. Since the theory on which Madame Leo is basing her testimony, astrology, is not accepted sufficiently in the scientific community and is not subject to peer review, testing, or a known rate of error — all factors that are considered by courts in determining reliability — it would not be deemed reliable by a judge.

Example # 14: Dr. Marx is called to the stand to testify that she gave the defendant a lie detector test and he passed with flying colors. Is Dr. Marx's testimony admissible? Whether this is a civil or criminal case, such testimony is generally excluded at trial because it is considered unreliable. While lie detectors are commonly used in the employment arena and even by police departments, such devices are not considered to be sufficiently reliable by courts using the expert screening factors such as testing, peer review, replication, known rate of error, and generally accepted in the scientific community. Some experts say that lie detectors can be ninety percent accurate, while other experts say the devices are based on no more than mere chance. Thus, lie detector evidence is generally excluded at trial.

Example # 15: The defendant is charged with grand theft auto. The defendant claims that she did not steal the car and it must have been someone else who stole the car. At trial, the prosecution calls a fingerprint expert who compares the defendant's fingerprints with a fingerprint found on the car. The expert says that the two prints were the same, in her expert opinion. Is this opinion allowed? This opinion likely will be allowed, because fingerprint analysis is considered a sufficiently reliable science in federal courts. So long as the expert applied that science accurately and reliably, the opinion will be allowed to be received by the jury. This does not mean, however, the jury must believe the opinion; it will be up to the jury to weigh the evidence and determine how much weight to give it.

VII.   HEARSAY

Hearsay is perhaps the most monumental obstacle in evidence, both to law students and lawyers. Hearsay basically covers an area of evidence that is not only difficult to understand, but is permeated with subcategories and nuances. The hearsay rules exclude special statements from evidence. The Federal Rules of Evidence, like many states, have a single rule of exclusion for hearsay statements, with numerous exemptions and exceptions. Hearsay is excluded because it is unreliable, meaning the jury will not be able to properly evaluate it. An utterance is only hearsay, however, if it is a statement made out-of-court, by a declarant, and is offered for the truth of the matter asserted. These hearsay elements will be reviewed below.

A.   Hearsay Definitions

1.   Out-of-Court

This really means off of the witness stand, not necessarily out of the courtroom. If the witness is testifying under oath, it is not out-of-court, but if the witness made the statement while walking into the courtroom, a previous hearing or even a deposition, all will be considered out-of-court.

2.   Statement

This means an assertion by a declarant generally of fact or opinion. The statement, "The sky is blue," is asserting or contending that the sky is a particular color. The statement, "I think my shoes are the nicest in the room," constitutes an opinion about shoes by a declarant. While most utterances are statements, some are not. Many questions do not have assertive content, and most nonverbal conduct does not contain any assertions, meaning, the conduct is not primarily intended to communicate to others. However, nonverbal conduct can become an assertion when it is primarily intended by the actor to communicate.

Examples of Nonverbal Assertions. Some significant illustrations include: A person nodding her head "yes"; a sports umpire signaling a foul; a person signaling thumbs up when asked, "Are you okay?"; a person who sits down when asked, "Can you sit down?"; and a person who gives another a "high five" when asked if she was successful.

3.   Declarant

A declarant must be a human being, not an animal or a machine. Thus, talking parakeets and radar guns do not qualify as declarants.

Example # 16: Sarah entered a contest in which all drives hit within 100 yards of the pin would receive a prize in a local golf tournament. Sarah hit the ball just about 100 yards to the pin and then holed it out, giving her a car if she was eligible to compete by having the drive less than 100 yards to the pin. The tournament official said she hit her drive just outside of 100 yards, while her friend Suzy's distance yardage machine, the Kelpro Yardage Machine, measured her ball as only 99.2 yards from the pin. At a later trial brought by Sarah against the golf tournament sponsor, she offered the printout of the ball yardage machine that said she was 99.2 yards from the pin. Is this printout hearsay? The answer is No. While the printout, a writing, was made out-of-court and is in fact a statement because it asserts how far Sarah was from the pin, there is no declarant making the statement. Therefore, it is not hearsay. The declarant making the statement must be a human being, and this is simply a yardage measuring device, a machine. The real obstacle to admission would be authentication, not hearsay. The ball machine must be shown to be calibrated properly and accurately.

4.   Offered for the Truth of the Matter Asserted

This is perhaps the most difficult element of hearsay. The statement must be offered for its content, its substance, not simply because it is said. While most statements are offered for their content or substance, some statements are offered and are still relevant even if they are not true. For example, a prior inconsistent statement is still relevant regardless of whether the out-of-court statement is true or the in-court statement is true. The prior statement is offered to show the witness is inconsistent and therefore, less credible. Also, operative facts, those statements that create legal relationships, are offered because they are said, not necessarily because they are true. These include the contents of a contract, trust, will, and other legal documents. In addition, warnings or notices are permitted because of the effect on the listener, not because they are true. The statement, "Watch out, there is ketchup on the floor ahead of you," should impact the listeners to be more careful as they walk ahead, regardless of the statement's truth.

Example # 17: James and Arlene entered into a written contract to sell James's computer to Arlene for $500. James later refuses to sell, and Arlene sues him. At trial, Arlene wants to offer the contract in evidence and James objects, claiming hearsay. Is he correct? The answer is No, because while a contract is an out-of-court statement by declarants, it is not offered for the truth of the matter asserted, but merely because it was entered into, creating a legal relationship between the parties. Once signed, there are legal rights and responsibilities created for both of the parties.

Example # 18: Mital gets into a car crash with Mohammad. Just before the crash, Mital's passenger, Lindsey, yelled to him, "Watch out, there is a sharp curve ahead!" If Mital is called to the witness stand by Mohammad to testify to this statement, is it hearsay? The answer is No, because while this is out-of-court, by declarant Lindsey making a statement or an assertion of fact, it is not being offered for the truth, that the road in fact curved sharply, but rather that Mital heard it and should have driven more responsibly and slowly.

B.   Admission by Party Opponent

Admissions by a party opponent are a major category of hearsay statements that are considered by the Federal Rules not to be hearsay, despite the fact that all of the elements are met. An admission is a statement by a party offered against the party by an opposing party. The party need not be admitting anything per se, so the word "admission" is really a misnomer. These statements also are not admitted because they are reliable, but because of the adversarial system. If a party made a statement, the party should be able to explain it. Thus, admissions are allowed, even if the party had no personal knowledge of the facts being asserted and the statement is otherwise an improper opinion. In essence, even if a party speculated as to what occurred, the party should be able to explain why they were doing so.

Example # 19: A sues B for breach of contract. B denies entering into a contract with A. A wants to offer B's statement, "You know I like this other mower better, but I want to buy your mower instead." Is this statement permitted at trial? The answer is Yes, because it is an admission by a party opponent. A is offering a party statement, namely B's. Because A is the opposing party, that means element number two, the party statement must be offered by the opposing party, is met. Therefore, it constitutes an admission and likely is admissible, if it can overcome other objections, such as relevance, unfair prejudice, and the like.

Example # 20: The prosecutor charges Jim and Bill with larceny by trick. Jim wants to offer Bill's out-of-court statement as an admission that, "I'm going to commit this crime whether you're with me or not." Is this permissible? The answer is No. Jim cannot offer the statement as an admission by a party opponent because Bill is not a party opponent. Bill is a co-defendant, and that does not qualify. The only person who can offer Bill's statement as an admission is the prosecutor, and the prosecutor may indeed want to offer that statement.

C.   Hearsay Exceptions

While hearsay is excluded as unreliable evidence, there is some hearsay that is sufficiently reliable to send to the jury. These forms of hearsay have sufficient indicia of reliability; that is, there is something about them that makes it less likely the statements are inaccurate or fabricated.

1.   Spontaneous Statements

The first group of reliable hearsay statements is admissible because they are spontaneous and, therefore, offer less opportunity for fabrication and inaccuracy. These statements include present sense impressions, describing things that are occurring at the time or immediately thereafter, excited utterances, which are made under the stress of excitement, and present state of mind statements, which are statements reflecting current feelings or future intentions. All of these statements arrive mostly contemporaneously with the events that are occurring or are still impacted by the startling nature of the event and, therefore, offer less opportunity for deliberation and fabrication.

Example # 21: Ellen, a newscaster, says to the news anchor, Darby, "And the parade is coming up the street now. The big balloon is Snoopy. It is passing by and being held by five people, although it is fairly windy and they are struggling with the balloon." This statement is a present sense impression because it is contemporaneous and spontaneous, and it is likely admissible as a hearsay exception. Ellen is doing a "play-by-play," which is describing an event as it is occurring. Thus, while Ellen's statements are hearsay, they are reliable hearsay and, if they meet other objections, could be admitted at trial.

Example # 22: Alana sees Patina slip and fall on a banana peel in the local convenience store. An hour later, Alana says to her friend Sherry, whom she is meeting for lunch, "I saw Patina slip and fall on a banana peel! That peel looked like it had been on the floor for hours." If these statements are offered as evidence in a subsequent trial brought by Patina against the convenience store, they would be considered reliable hearsay. These are excited utterances, made under the stress of excitement and relating to the event in question. While the statements occurred an hour after the event, if the stress of excitement still exists, it is believed that there is less chance of fabrication. Of course, the lapse of time could impact Alana's memory of the event; and the fact that it was a startling event in and of itself could mean that Alana likely was not as accurate about the event. However, under the rules of most states and the Federal Rules, these statements would be considered sufficiently reliable to allow the jury to evaluate their weight.

Example # 23: In *United States v. Timken*, Sally is on trial for a murder that occurred at the Outback Bar and Grill on October 16. If the prosecution offers a statement Sally's best friend, Penny, had made on October 12 saying, "I plan on going to the Outback Bar and Grill on October 16," that statement would be a permissible statement of intent to do something. The statement is forward looking and reliable because it expresses Penny's intent as of the time she is making the statement. If Penny intends to go to the Outback Grill on that day, it makes it a little bit more likely that she will indeed go, and that she indeed went at that time in question. Thus, the statement is reliable enough to be admitted into evidence (assuming, of course, it is relevant).

2.   Statements Made for the Purpose of Medical Diagnosis or Treatment

These statements also are considered sufficiently reliable to be admitted in evidence. Because of the gravity of the circumstances, it is believed there is a much lesser chance that someone would be fabricating an illness or injury.

Example # 24: Betty appears in the emergency room of a hospital and says, "My right foot has been hurting me for a week. I stepped in hole. I think I broke my ankle." These statements would be allowed in a later trial if Betty sues the landowner of the property containing the hole in the ground. These statements are reliable because Betty is seeking medical aid and treatment, not furthering her litigation.

3.   Business Records

The area of business records is perhaps one of the most significant hearsay exceptions. It exists for both private records and public records. Private records have reliability, because they are relied on in business all of the time to make businesses work and run smoothly. Without records, businesses would not have the foundation needed to see what the bottom line was and how they could improve it. Public records are reliable in a somewhat similar fashion. It is presumed that government employees do their jobs and that their records make the government operate smoothly as well.

There are limits as to the kinds of records that can be used in both private and public contexts. Private records that are about litigation are not as reliable because they are partisan and prepared to benefit the company, not to be objective. These records are not trustworthy and are likely subject to exclusion. Public records that are used in criminal cases offer a too-easy substitute for live testimony for the prosecution. These records generally consist of police reports and the like. Because of a need to have convictions based on live testimony, there is a general prohibition on using police reports and other public records by the prosecution in a criminal case.

Example # 25: An ophthalmologist, after seeing a patient, writes down a comprehensive record about what the visit entailed. At a later trial, can the record be offered into evidence? The answer is Yes, because even though it may involve a diagnosis, the record is a reliable part of the ophthalmologist's business — reliable enough to give to the jury.

Example # 26: The State Meteorological Service keeps copious records about rainfall during the month of February. At a trial involving an auto accident, the question was whether it was raining at all that day. Can the public records be offered into evidence? The answer is Yes. These records are reliable, since they are about what the public agency does regularly.

Example # 27: Jane's Mail Order Service accepts phone orders seven days a week, twenty-four hours a day. The general routine used is to have a person take the order, check off on a sheet what is ordered, and pass that to a supervisor, who reviews it, okays it, and writes up directions on how the order shall be accomplished. A third person enters the order into a permanent record indicating when it was received and the delivery date. The order is then sent out within three days. In a suit by one of Jane's customers against the company, can Jane use one of these business records as evidence? The answer is Yes. Even though several people compile the record, they are all in the chain of the business and are performing their regular functions about a regular business activity. That is precisely the kind of record the Federal Rules of Evidence and many state rules permit. To lay a foundation for the record requires someone with knowledge, usually a business custodian, even though the custodian may have no personal knowledge of the individual record. It is the record process, and not the individual record, that matters.

4.   Other Exceptions

Other hearsay exceptions include learned treatises, on which experts often rely, ancient records, such as old newspapers, which are reliable because of their antiquity, and statements about marriages, divorces, baptisms, and other family events.

5.   The Confrontation Clause

The Confrontation Clause is part of the Sixth Amendment to the United States Constitution and guarantees criminal defendants the right to confront the witnesses against them. The Clause has served to limit what kinds of evidence can be used by prosecutors in criminal cases. Until recently, this Clause did not have much significance and really paralleled existing hearsay exceptions. In 2004, in a case called *Crawford v. Washington*, 541 U.S. 36 (2004), Justice Scalia indicated that any evidence considered testimonial and involving an unavailable declarant would need an opportunity for either previous or current cross-examination in order for that evidence to be considered sufficiently reliable under the Confrontation Clause. Testimonial statements are any statements that had an objective likelihood of being utilized in a later court proceeding when made. This category of testimonial evidence includes criminal interrogations, affidavits, and even some 911 calls, covering a wide variety of evidence.

VIII. PRIVILEGE

Privileged evidence excludes otherwise relevant evidence from consideration by the trier of fact. There are different types of privileges, from attorney-client, to clergy-penitent, to psychotherapist-patient, to the constitutional privilege of a criminal defendant's right to remain silent. Sometimes, in what are called diversity cases, the state law of privileges may govern in federal courts.

Privileges are all based on policies larger than any individual case, mostly about relationships that are important and need preserving. All of these privileges have exceptions. The privilege may be expressly or impliedly waived by the holder, for example, or may not cover all situations. For example, the attorney-client privilege does not cover situations when the client is using the attorney to commit a future crime. The husband-wife privilege does not cover when the husband and wife are committing a crime together or there is a crime being committed by them against their children. Also, in many jurisdictions, there is no doctor-patient privilege. This means that while a doctor has confidentiality requirements and cannot disclose any patient confidences off of the witness stand, a doctor sometimes can be forced to testify through a subpoena at trial. This illustrates that the privilege at law really is pervasive and includes a right not to disclose even if asked to do so in a court of law. There is a psychotherapist-patient privilege, but, if the patient raises a claim of insanity at trial as a defense, that privilege is considered waived. Many states have a wide variety of privileges that go beyond the federal privileges. These may include accountant-client privilege, child abuse victim-therapist privilege, sexual assault victim-sexual assault therapist privilege, domestic abuse counselor-patient privilege, and more.

Example # 28: Clyde told his longtime girlfriend Bonnie that he robbed banks for a living and had just robbed one three days ago. If Clyde is later prosecuted for bank robbery of the previous bank, will Bonnie be able to testify? If the prosecution calls Bonnie to testify, she can be forced to testify against Clyde because they were not married at the time the statement was made or at trial. A husband-wife privilege generally requires a marital relationship, not a couple who is merely engaged to be married or boyfriend-girlfriend.

Example # 29: Bonnie and Clyde get married, and Clyde then tells her in detail about all of his bank robberies. They soon get divorced. In a later trial against Clyde, can Bonnie be forced to testify? There are actually two husband and wife privileges. One is a confidential communication privilege that requires that the couple be married at the time of the communication. The other is a spousal immunity privilege that requires the couple to be married at the time of the trial. Since Bonnie and Clyde are not married at the time of the trial, the only privilege he can rely on is the confidential communication privilege. Any confidential communications Clyde had with Bonnie while they were married are still privileged, even though the pair has subsequently obtained a divorce. So the statements in question indeed may be privileged.

IX.   WITNESSES

Witnesses often serve as the main form of evidence in a trial. They use all of their senses — sight, hearing, smell, and touch — to explain what happened at a previous time or place. All witnesses must be competent in order to testify. While at common law there were many incompetencies, such as for persons interested in the outcome of a case, anyone who had been convicted of a felony, and anyone who lacked religion, the current law generally restricts those limitations to simply requiring that witnesses be able to understand what it means to tell the truth. If witnesses can raise their right hands and swear (or affirm) to tell the truth and understand what that means, they are allowed to testify.

There are form limitations on the testimony, however. This means witnesses generally cannot be asked leading questions, those questions that suggest an answer, on direct examination, but can be asked leading questions on cross-examination. Other objections include asked and answered, compound, argumentative, and assuming facts not in evidence. While these objections generally are not contained in the rules of evidence, they have been well accepted in courts of law.

Example # 30: Jones calls her first witness in a tort action for conversion. The eyewitness, Molly, is asked, "Did you see the defendant take the plaintiff's tennis racket?" The defendant objected, claiming the question was leading. How should a judge rule? The judge sustained the objection, finding that it was leading, because it suggested an answer, namely that the defendant took the tennis racket. The plaintiff rephrased the question. The new question was, "What did you see at 3:15 p.m. on March 16?" The witness answered, "I saw the defendant, Molly, take the tennis racket." If this question was objected to as leading, how should a judge rule? This question was not leading because it did not suggest the answer and was allowed because the witness supplied the answer to the question.

X. WRITINGS

While this category has been covered in part in the section on hearsay, there are three common objections to writings. These are hearsay, authentication, and the Best Evidence Rule. Authentication and the Best Evidence Rule will be discussed below.

A.   Authentication

Authentication means that the thing is what it purports to be. If a person holds up a newspaper and says, "This is the *New York Times*," there needs to be some confidence that what is held up is in fact the *New York Times*. If another person holds up a written letter and says it was written by Sally Jo, there needs to be some confidence that, indeed, that letter was written by Sally Jo. Authentication means to lay enough of a foundation so that there can be a reasonable basis for believing that the writing is what it purports to be. This again is decided by the judge in determining admissibility.

Example # 31: At trial, the issue was whether a letter from Denmark was written by Josephine Gertrude Stein. The plaintiff called Josephine's brother, Max, to the witness stand to testify that the letter was written in Josephine Gertrude's handwriting. To lay the foundation for authentication purposes, the attorney asked Max, "I show you what's been marked as Plaintiff's Exhibit #38 for identification purposes. What is it?" The witness answered, "It is a letter from my sister." The attorney then asked, "How do you know?" The witness answered, "I have seen her handwriting before." The attorney asked, "How many times before?" The witness responded, "Oh, I'd say at least thirty to fifty times before." In this way, the attorney has laid a foundation for the witness's testimony, and Max Stein was able to give his opinion that this was a letter from his sister, Josephine Gertrude.

B.   The Best Evidence Rule

The Best Evidence Rule arises when some writings are offered in evidence. It only applies to those situations where the parties are trying to prove the contents of a writing. The party is attempting to prove the contents when the writing is either central to the case or is the only basis for the witness's knowledge. This rule does not apply when the writing is being used merely to corroborate action (like the notes of a law school class).

Example # 32: In a breach of contract action, Jamaal attempted to testify about the written contract between himself and Arthur. Arthur objected, claiming a violation of the Best Evidence Rule. In this situation, the Best Evidence Rule would apply, since the parties are trying to prove the contents of a writing, a contract, at trial. A substitute for the original would be permitted, however, under many circumstances.

Example # 33: In a criminal case, Officer Friday is called to describe what happened when the defendant was arrested. Officer Friday gave a terrific recitation of exactly what happened during the arrest. On cross examination, the officer was asked, "Officer, isn't it true that you were not there at the scene when the defendant was arrested and that you are testifying only based on your fellow officer's police report?" Officer Friday responded, "Yes, that is true." The Best Evidence Rule would apply in this case as well, since the officer is testifying only based on a writing. That is, the officer's knowledge is solely based on the writing, and it is better to have the writing rather than to have the officer's dramatic rendition of it.

The Best Evidence Rule does not apply in a lot of cases, though, and the words "best evidence" are a misnomer since the rule does not really require the best evidence generally. Even when the rule applies, substitutes, such as Xeroxed copies, are generally permitted.

XI. IMPEACHMENT

Impeachment of a witness is a significant and often exciting part of a lawsuit and is prominently characterized in popular culture as a result. It involves attacking a witness' credibility, also known as the witness' character for truthfulness or accuracy. In a sense, impeachment is a mini-trial, dealing solely with the weight of the witness' testimony. It generally does not directly deal with proving the issues in the case. There are only a limited number of ways a witness can be impeached. The two main categories are intrinsic and extrinsic. Intrinsic means the witness is being asked questions and is expected to respond. Extrinsic means the witness is being circumvented and either new evidence is offered, such as a new witness, or a document is directly submitted in evidence. Extrinsic evidence often follows unsuccessful intrinsic impeachment.

A. Intrinsic Impeachment

A witness can be impeached intrinsically in the following ways: contradiction; bias; some convictions; prior untruthful acts; testimonial defects; and prior inconsistent statements.

1. Contradiction

This form of impeachment involves disputing the facts presented by the witness.

Example # 34: Attorney on cross-examination: "Ms. Witness, you have testified that you came from Fourth Street to get to the movie theater in question, when in fact you really came from Third Street, isn't that right?"

This question disputes part of the witness's testimony and indicates that if she is wrong on this point, she may be wrong on other points as well. The question elicits proper contradiction testimony.

2.   Bias

This type of impeachment indicates the witness is not neutral, but rather interested in the outcome or is otherwise corrupt.

Example # 35: Attorney question: "Ms. Witness, isn't it true that you owe money to the defendant?" Opposing Counsel: "Objection!" How should a court rule?

If this question is indeed true, the witness is biased, at least as for the perception of not being neutral in her testimony. It is thus a proper question.

3.   Convictions of a Crime

Convictions sometimes directly indicate the truthfulness of a witness, such as those involving fraud, dishonesty, or false statement, and sometimes somewhat less directly relate to honesty, such as those that are felony convictions. Both types of convictions are usually allowed as impeachment, suggesting the witness who has been so convicted is likely less truthful.

Example # 36: Attorney question: "Isn't it true, Mr. Witness, that you were convicted of grand theft auto in 2006?" Opposing Counsel: "Objection!" How should a court rule?

This question likely would be allowed under the Federal Rules of Evidence, since grand theft auto is a felony. However, if this question is unfairly prejudicial, it may not be allowed.

4.   Bad Untruthful Acts

This category is the functional equivalent of fraud convictions. The questions are about the underlying fraudulent acts. The only thing missing is the conviction itself, that is to say the witness has committed the act, but may not have been convicted of it.

Example # 37: Attorney question: "Isn't it true, Ms. Witness, that you committed perjury three years ago?" Opposing Counsel: "Objection!" How should a court rule?

This question would be permitted as a prior untruthful act, and if she had been convicted of perjury, she could be asked about that as a prior conviction. This untruthful act category directly relates to a witness's truthfulness or veracity.

5.   Testimonial Defects

Witnesses who testify may often have defects in perception, memory, or narration and thus may be inaccurate and less believable. Perception defects are those involving the senses, such as degenerative eye disease or a loss of the sense of smell. Memory defects may include amnesia, Alzheimer's Disease, or other forms of dementia. Narration defects concern how a person communicates with others.

Example # 38: In the film, *My Cousin Vinnie*, defense counsel cross-examined several earnest and well-intentioned witnesses who all have various testimonial defects. One witness needed thicker glasses and was not able to see accurately. Another witness could not see through thick trees. This is proper impeachment of a witness by testimonial defects.

6.   Prior Inconsistent Statements

This is really an example of self-contradiction, where the witness has made other prior statements that are inconsistent with the statement she is making on the witness stand. It is not important which statement is truthful, just that an inconsistency is occurring.

Example # 39: Attorney asks: "Ms. Witness, you have testified that you observed the accident after leaving your torts class, but you did say last week to your friend that you observed the accident after leaving your contracts class, isn't that right?" Opposing Counsel: "Objection!" How should a court rule?

While it may not be important to the case as to which class the witness left before she observed the accident, it can make it a little more likely that she would not be believable as she was inconsistent on which class she was attending first. In other words, one inconsistency indicates a witness may be inconsistent in other places as well.

B.   Extrinsic Impeachment

If the witness is asked whether she has committed a crime, been convicted of a crime, been biased, uttered a prior inconsistent statement, or has a testimonial defect, among other things, and the witness denies all of it, the examining attorney may be able to go further and impeach that witness extrinsically. Extrinsic impeachment, however, is limited to only those subjects that are considered important to the case. This is known as the Collateral Issue Rule — only those matters that are considered important, or non-collateral, are allowed to be inquired into through extrinsic evidence. This limit is designed to avoid distracting the jury from deciding the major issues in the case. The important matters are fewer than those allowed intrinsically. They include bias, testimonial defects, convictions of a crime, and a new reputation or opinion witness attacking the truthfulness of a previous witness. All of these subjects permit extrinsic impeachment as well as impeachment that coincide with an issue in the case.

Example # 40: If a witness is asked whether he was convicted of grand theft auto and the witness says no, the attorney will be allowed to offer directly in evidence a certified copy of the witness's grand theft auto conviction. This is permissible extrinsic impeachment.

Example # 41: If the witness is asked whether he has dated the defendant's sister and he says no, the defendant's sister, or someone else with knowledge of their relationship, can be asked to testify, indicating bias. This also is permissible extrinsic impeachment.

Example # 42: If the witness is asked whether she needs a hearing aid and she says no, an audiologist can be called to testify that the witness indeed needs a hearing aid under the testimonial defects section of extrinsic impeachment.

Example # 43: If a witness testifies as an eyewitness to an auto accident and then leaves the stand, the other side can call in its own case a new witness who will testify based on reputation or opinion that the previous witness has a bad reputation for truthfulness or, in the witness's opinion, is untruthful. That is, a new witness can extrinsically impeach the prior witness based on reputation or opinion evidence.

XII. CONCLUSION

Evidence is used at trial to paint a picture of what happened and to prove the elements of a claim or defense. It is a special picture, because it is limited by many rules and traditions. Good attorneys use the rules to paint their pictures well. Because the Rules of Evidence lie within the cradle of trials, learning about one is important to understanding the other.

Chapter 7

CONSTITUTIONAL LAW

By — Michael P. Allen

I. INTRODUCTION

The United States Constitution contains only about 4,500 words. Yet, it has spawned hundreds of thousands of pages of commentary. Given this reality, the reader can appreciate that what follows in this Chapter will be at a high level of generality. However, even at such a general level, the Chapter provides an important overview of the United States Constitution both as it was originally drafted and how it has been interpreted in contemporary times. In addition, this Chapter must be read in conjunction with many other chapters in this book touching on matters of constitutional law. These chapters include Chapter Four (Criminal Law and Procedure); Chapter Five (Jurisdiction and Civil Procedure); Chapter Six (Evidence); Chapter Eight (Property); Chapter Fourteen (Family Law); Chapter Fifteen (Administrative Law); and Chapter 16 (Conflicts of Law/ Choice of Laws/Enforcement of Judgments).

The Chapter has four sections in addition to this introduction and a brief conclusion. Section II discusses the history behind the adoption and development of the Constitution. It also describes the structure of the document both as it was initially ratified as well as how it developed over time through the amendment process.

Section III focuses on the various means of interpreting the Constitution. Many of the Constitution's provisions are phrased in general, open-textured language. Over the years, interpreters of the document have developed a number of techniques — some contradictory — by which to give concrete meaning to these general provisions. The Section briefly catalogues and describes the major techniques. This Section also discusses how the various parts of American government play a role in constitutional interpretation. A major focus of this Section is on "judicial review" by which courts wield significant power to authoritatively interpret the Constitution.

Section IV focuses on the power structures created and recognized by the Constitution. It principally deals with the powers of the national (or federal) government as a whole as well as the division of those powers among the three branches of the national government (the legislature, the executive, and the judicial). This Section also considers the Constitution's impact on the powers of the states of the union.

Finally, Section V deals with the individual rights provisions of the Constitution. In particular, it focuses on the protections of religious freedom and free speech under the First Amendment, the prohibition against the deprivation of life, liberty, or property without "due process of law" under the Fifth and Fourteenth Amendments, and the requirement that no person be denied "the equal protection of the laws" under the Fourteenth Amendment. This Section will also briefly mention other liberty-protecting provisions of the Constitution.

II. HISTORY AND CONSTITUTIONAL STRUCTURE

A.   The Ratification of the Constitution

After the thirteen colonies that had been governed by Great Britain succeeded in securing their independence in the American Revolutionary War, they faced the question of how a newly independent United States should be governed. After debate, the newly independent states adopted the Articles of Confederation for this purpose. Under the Articles, the national government was essentially comprised of a single body that exercised legislative, executive, and (to a limited extent) judicial power. In reality, however, the national government under the Articles had little power. Any decision of significance required either the unanimous approval of the states or at least a super- majority of them. For a number of reasons, it soon became clear that if the United States was to succeed as a free nation, there would need to be a significant change in its governmental structure.

In 1787, delegates from the states gathered in Philadelphia, Pennsylvania, to form what would become known as the American Constitutional Convention. The Convention's purpose was to draft the new document to govern the United States. The product of the Convention was the United States Constitution, which contained seven parts denominated Article I through Article VII. The Constitution came into force on June 21, 1788 after having been ratified by a sufficient number of states. Eventually all thirteen states would ratify the document.

B.   The Structure of the Original Constitution

What did the Constitution look like when originally ratified? The answer is that it looked materially different than it looks now. Today, the document contains twenty-seven amendments that alter or expand the structure set forth in the original document. Many of these amendments focus on the individual liberty rights for which the United States is known today, such as protections of freedom of speech and religion and guarantees of due process and equal protection. The original document had very few direct liberty protecting devices. Indeed, it provided certain protections for institutional slavery, an idea that is fundamentally at odds with personal liberty.

Yet, the fact that the Constitution as originally ratified did not contain liberty protecting devices does not mean that liberty was not an important concept to the framers of that document. Protection of liberty was, in fact, a central concern of the framers and ratifies of the Constitution. However, they sought to protect liberty indirectly through the adoption of a governing structure that was both more effective than the one under the Articles of Confederation but that was organized in such a way that the stronger national government would not invade the rights of the people. The balance of this sub-part describes the governmental structure the Constitution enshrines.

The fundamental principle underlying the Constitution is one of dividing power among different centers of political authority. The idea was to ensure that no one governmental entity was powerful enough to trample on the liberties of the people. This division of power was accomplished through two devices generally known as "federalism" and "separation of powers."

1.   Federalism

Federalism refers to the division of power between the national government and the various states. The Constitution creates a national government that would exist in addition to the states, all of which would continue as governmental units in the United States under the Constitution. In other words, federalism refers to a division of power that operates on a vertical level — there would be both a national — or federal — government in addition to the governments of the states.

The framers recognized, of course, that creating separate sovereigns (i.e., a national government in addition to the governments of the states) raised the danger of creating confusion about which sovereign could act in a given situation. They addressed this danger in two principles ways. First, the national government was made one of enumerated powers. That is, the national government would *not* have power to act unless there was a specific grant of power in the Constitution. If there was no such grant of authority, the states retained the exclusive power to govern in that field. This requirement stands in contrast to the powers of the states. One does not need to find a grant of power to the states in the Constitution. Instead, the Constitution only constrains the power of the states. We will highlight how that is possible in various parts of this Chapter. Some important examples include the Constitution's prohibitions on the states entering into treaties with foreign nations, coining money, keeping troops without Congress's consent or, again without Congress' consent, entering into agreements with other states. U.S. Const. art. I, § 10.

Second, when there was a specific grant of power to the national government and the national government in fact exercised that authority, the Constitution provides that the action of the national government displaces any contrary action taken by the states. Article VI of the Constitution provides in relevant part that

> This Constitution, and the Laws of the United States which shall be made in Pursuance thereof; and all Treaties made, or which shall be made, under the Authority of the United States, shall be the supreme Law of the Land; and the Judges in every State shall be bound thereby, any Thing in the Constitution or Laws of any State to the Contrary notwithstanding.

This provision, known as the Supremacy Clause, is an incredibly important part of the Constitution because it ensures that when the national government acts, its laws (as well the Constitution itself) provide the final word. You should also be able to see that interpreting how broad a particular grant of authority to the national government is takes on additional importance because of the Supremacy Clause.

An important corollary to the Supremacy Clause is the doctrine of "preemption." When Congress acts pursuant to a valid grant of authority in the Constitution, its actions are said to preempt or displace certain state laws. Preemption occurs by virtue of the text of the Supremacy Clause itself when the federal law is inconsistent with the state law or when Congress says expressly that it wishes to preempt state law in a given area. However, the Supreme Court has also held that preemption may be implied from congressional action. Thus, a state law may be preempted when that law is an obstacle to federal policies more generally or when Congress has, by pervasive regulation, marked out a certain field for federal regulation alone.

The Chapter considers the particular division of power between the states and the federal government in the next Section. For now, simply recognize that one important structural feature of the Constitution is federalism. In addition, you should know that each state has its own Constitution providing for the structure of state government and protecting individual rights. The Supremacy Clause ensures that nothing in the state constitutions can take away from the individual liberty guarantees in the United States Constitution. However, state constitutions can provide greater protection than that afforded under the federal Constitution. This Chapter does not consider state constitutions.

2.   Separation of Powers

The second device by which the framers divided governmental power is referred to as separation of powers. This concept concerns the division of power among the parts or branches of the federal government. It thus operates on a horizontal level as opposed to the vertical orientation of federalism.

The Constitution establishes three branches of the federal government dealing with, respectively, legislative power (Article I), executive power (Article II), and judicial power (Article III). The Constitution then assigns certain powers to each of these branches. In the balance of this sub-part, the Chapter first lays out in general terms the powers of each of these braches. A more specific discussion of many of these powers appears in Section IV. Thereafter, this sub-part discusses the ways in which the Constitution ensures that no one branch has too much power even with respect to those areas in which it may act. This latter concept is referred to as "checks and balances."

a.   Article I

Article I of the Constitution deals with the legislative power or, in other words, the power to make law. That power is assigned to the Congress of the United States. Congress is divided into two houses, the House of Representatives and the Senate. Most of the specific powers of Congress are contained in Article I, section 8. We will discuss the specific legislative powers of Congress in Section IV. In general, the House and the Senate have the shared authority when acting pursuant to an enumerated power to enact laws, provided that the two Houses of Congress agree on the exact language of the law to be enacted.

The House of Representatives was intended to be the most democratically representative body in the new federal government. Its members were to be elected directly by the people every two years. Each state was ensured at least one representative. Otherwise, the number of each state's representatives would be determined by population. In order to be elected a member of the House, a person must be at least 25 years old and have been a citizen of the United States for at least 5 years. The person must be a resident of the state he or she is to represent at the time of election. There are currently 435 members of the House.

The Senate as originally constituted was meant to be less democratically accountable than the House. Each state has two senators regardless of a state's population, meaning that there are currently 100 members of the Senate. One-third of the Senate is chosen every two years. To be chosen a senator, a person must be at least 30 years old and been a citizen of the United States for at least 9 years. At the time of election, the senator must be a resident of the state he or she is to represent. Under the original Constitution, senators were chosen by the legislature of their state. As we will see in the next sub-part, that is no longer the rule.

b.   Article II

Article II discusses the executive power. The Constitution vests the executive power of the United States in a single President of the United States. The Constitution also provides that there is to be a Vice-President of the United States. In addition, the Vice-President serves as the President of the Senate. As expressly provided in an amendment, should the President be unable to serve, the Vice-President becomes the President.

A person must be at least 35 years old to serve as President. In addition, a person must be a natural born citizen of the United States and have been a resident of the United States for 14 years. The President is elected to a term of 4 years. The original Constitution did not limit the number of times a person could be elected President. This changed as we will see later in this Section.

The President is not elected directly by the people. Instead, the President is formally elected by a body called the Electoral College. The Electoral College is made up of electors appointed in a manner directed by the legislature of each state. Each state has a number of electors equal to the combined number of members of the House and the Senate representing the state. Thus, it is possible for a person to be elected President with a majority of the Electoral College but with a minority of the popular vote in the United States. This happened most recently in 2000 when George Bush won a majority in the Electoral College but Al Gore had a majority of the popular vote. Under the Constitution, George Bush became President of the United States.

The President is required to "take Care that the Laws be faithfully executed." This means that the President is empowered to enforce the laws Congress passes. In addition, the President — a civilian — is the Commander in Chief of the Armed Forces of the United States. The President is also assigned the power to appoint federal judges, including Justices of the Supreme Court, ambassadors, as well as other officers of the United States. These appointments must be confirmed by the Senate. The President also has the unconditional power to grant pardons for violations of federal law. Finally, the President has significant powers in connection with foreign affairs. He or she has the power to recognize foreign governments and to make treaties on behalf of the United States (although the treaties must be ratified by two-thirds of the Senate).

The Constitution provides that the President may be removed from office for "Treason, Bribery, and other high Crimes and Misdemeanors." U.S. Const. art. II, § 4. The House of Representatives impeaches the President, and the Senate is charged with convicting the President by a two-thirds margin. Two U.S. Presidents have been impeached: Andrew Johnson in the late 1860s, and Bill Clinton in the late 1990s. Both were acquitted by the Senate.

While this Chapter will discuss presidential power more later, one thing is important to keep in mind at this point. The modern American President is far more powerful than reading the Constitution would suggest. The President is a single individual who can monopolize the world stage merely by making a speech on the White House lawn. This power is dramatically increased by modern communications technology.

c.   Article III

Article III of the Constitution concerns the judicial branch. The Constitution requires that there be a Supreme Court. It granted Congress the power to determine whether there would be inferior federal courts. The first Congress created such inferior courts, and they have existed ever since. The framers were concerned with ensuring that federal judges were sufficiently insulated from politics that they would be independent. They sought to provide such independence by providing that federal judges serve for life ("during good Behaviour") and that their salaries could not be reduced.

As you have seen in Chapter Five, the federal courts have limited jurisdiction. The scope of the potential jurisdiction of the federal courts is set forth in Article III, section 2. In addition, the Supreme Court has held that the federal courts cannot issue advisory opinions but, instead, may act only when there is an actual "case or controversy" between or among litigants with actual stakes in the matter (a concept referred to as "standing").

d.   Checks and Balances

This sub-part has discussed separation of powers at the federal level. However, in some respects at least, the phrase separation of powers is somewhat misleading. A better conception of the framers' design on the national level is one of intertwined powers or checks and balances. The framers made sure that in many ways the power exercised by one branch was dependent on the actions of other branches. A summary of some of the important checks and balances in the Constitution follows:

- Congress has the power to enact laws within its enumerated powers. However, those laws must then be presented to the President. U.S. Const. art. I, § 7. The President has the power to veto (or disapprove) of the law. If he or she does so, the bill at issue will only become a law if both Houses of Congress override the President's veto. To override a veto, each House must pass the vetoed bill by a two-thirds margin.

- Once Congress passes a bill and the President signs it into law, the President then must enforce the law. However, that enforcement is dependent in many situations on the actions of the Article III courts as well as the governments of the states.

- The President has the power to appoint federal judges, ambassadors, and other officers of the United States. However, these appointments do not become effective unless they are confirmed by the United States Senate.

- The President is assigned the power to negotiate treaties on behalf of the United States. However, those treaties must be ratified by a two-thirds vote in the United States Senate. In addition, to be effective, many treaties require that Congress pass laws so that the treaty obligations have domestic effect. Finally, the terms of ratified treaties are often determined by Article III judges.

- As we will see later, Congress is assigned the power to "declare war" on behalf of the United States. However, the President is the Commander in Chief of the Armed Forces. Yet, Congress has the power to appropriate funds for those forces.

As the foregoing discussion demonstrates, the framers created an elaborate system of government in the United States. The states would continue to exist with their powers intact unless specifically restricted in the Constitution. There was also a federal government created that would have only those powers enumerated in the Constitution. That federal government was itself broken into branches with powers that were separate from the other branches but which also required the actions of the other branches in important respects. All of this was done to ensure that there was not only an effective government for the United States but also that the government would not invade the rights of the people. The next part considers some important changes to the Constitution after it was originally ratified.

C.   Significant Structural Constitutional Changes

The framers needed to walk a fine line when they drafted the Constitution. They were well aware that they were creating a document that needed to endure for generations. At the same time, they recognized that they could not envision all the needs of the United States in the future. They balanced these points by creating a Constitution that was binding and enforceable but also included within it a means for change.

Article V of the Constitution sets forth the means by which the document may be amended. The process is a difficult one. In fact, in the over two hundred twenty years in which the Constitution has been in force, there have been only twenty-seven amendments ratified and only five in the past fifty years. Article V provides two means by which the Constitution can be amended. First, it is possible to amend the Constitution by means of another constitutional convention. No such convention has ever been called. Second, the Constitution can — and has been — amended when two-thirds of each House of Congress proposes an amendment and that amendment is ratified by the legislatures of two-thirds of the States.

While many specific amendments to the Constitution will be discussed in the balance of this Chapter, it is useful to have an overview of some major structural developments that have resulted from amendments. This sub-part briefly discusses five such amendments or groups of amendments.

1.   The Bill of Rights

As mentioned above, the Constitution as originally ratified contained few direct liberty protecting devices. In fact, the absence of specific protections for individual liberty was a significant obstacle to ratification. It was only with a promise that there would be a "Bill of Rights" added to the Constitution that ratification was possible. The first ten amendments constitute the Bill of Rights. They were added to the Constitution in 1791. We will discuss several of these amendments when we consider individual liberties below. You have also read about some of them already when you considered the Fourth, Fifth, and Sixth Amendments in Chapter Four.

When the Bill of Rights was added to the Constitution, it applied only to the federal government. In other words, state governments were not restricted by the various matters set forth in the Bill of Rights. As you will see, this largely changed with the ratification of the Fourteenth Amendment after the Civil War.

2.   The Civil War Amendments

It is a gross understatement to say that the Civil War was a pivotal event in American history. For our purposes, it was also an incredibly important event for American constitutional law. In the wake of the Civil War, three amendments were added to the Constitution that had a significant impact on both individual liberty and the structure of government. While we will discuss at least one of these amendments in much greater detail below when we consider individual rights, a brief summary follows:

- The *Thirteenth Amendment* was ratified in 1865. It prohibits slavery and involuntary servitude. Congress also has the power to enforce the amendment.

- The *Fourteenth Amendment* was ratified in 1868 and did a number of things. First, it specifically prohibited the states from denying any person in their jurisdictions the equal protection of the laws or from depriving any person in their jurisdictions of life, liberty, or property without due process of law. Second, it gave Congress the power to enforce these provisions, thus, as with the Thirteenth and Fifteenth Amendments, providing another source for an enumerated federal power. Third, the Supreme Court has interpreted the Fourteenth Amendment as "incorporating" at least some of the Bill of Rights, thereby making them applicable to the states. Therefore, most of the rights mentioned in the Bill of Rights of which people are aware (e.g., the First Amendment's freedom of expression and religion, the Fourth Amendment's prohibition on unreasonable searches and seizures, the Fifth Amendment's double jeopardy and self-incrimination provisions, the Sixth Amendment's right to a jury trial and lawyer in a criminal case, and the Eighth Amendment's prohibition on cruel and unusual punishment) now apply to the states as well as the federal government.

- The *Fifteenth Amendment* was ratified in 1870. It prohibited discrimination in voting on the basis of race. Congress was also given power to enforce the amendment.

3.   The Seventeenth Amendment

The Senate as originally constituted was elected by state legislatures. The Seventeenth Amendment, ratified in 1913, provides that the Senate, like the House of Representatives, is to be elected by the people of the states. This change was a continuation of the shift discussed concerning the Civil War Amendments away from a focus on strong state power under the Constitution.

4.   The Nineteenth Amendment

The Fourteenth Amendment was a significant expansion of the right to vote in the United States. However, section 2 of that Amendment also enshrined discrimination against women in terms of voting rights. All too late in the history of the United States, gender-based discrimination in voting was prohibited by the Nineteenth Amendment, which became effective in 1920.

5.   Amendments Concerning the President

There have been several amendments concerning the election of the President altering the original constitutional structure discussed above. Some of the most important changes include: limiting a person to being elected President twice (the Twenty-Second Amendment); providing for how the voting for President and Vice-President in the Electoral College proceeds in case of ties (the Twelfth Amendment); and stating how presidential incapacity should be handled (the Twenty-Fifth Amendment).

III.   CONSTITUTIONAL INTERPRETATION

As you will have recognized already, there are parts of the Constitution that do not require any serious interpretation. For example, all one needs to do is read to "interpret" the Constitution concerning the number of senators to which each state is entitled in the Senate (two) or the minimum age of a person elected President (thirty-five). But there are also many open-textured constitutional provisions that could mean any number of things: What is an "unreasonable" search under the Fourth Amendment? What is "commerce among the several states" over which Congress is given legislative power? What does the phrase "equal protection of the laws" mean? For these types of questions, one does need to engage in constitutional interpretation.

This Section considers two issues. First, it discusses who interprets the Constitution. As you will see, all governed actors interpret the Constitution. However, there is a special role for the courts when they exercise the power of judicial review. Second, this section considers the various devices courts (and other government actors to a lesser degree) use to interpret what the Constitution means.

A.   Who Interprets the Constitution?

Every governmental actor in the United States on the state, local, and national level is called upon to interpret the Constitution. When a state legislator or member of Congress decides whether to vote for a bill, he or she may base the decision on an assessment of a law's constitutionality. When the President decides whether to veto or sign a bill, he or she may make the decision in part based on the Constitution. Thus, it is not correct to say that constitutional interpretation under the United States Constitution is assigned solely to judges. As we will see in the balance of this sub-part, the courts play a highly significant role in constitutional interpretation, but it is often not an exclusive one.

One of the most important powers of courts — both state and federal — in the United States is the power of "judicial review." Judicial review is, as stated in the famous case of *Marbury v. Madison*, the power to "say what the law is." This power includes declaring that a given law enacted either on the national or state level is unconstitutional. Thus, in this respect, the judiciary, and ultimately the Supreme Court, is the ultimate arbiter of the meaning of the Constitution. When the Supreme Court states what the Constitution means, that interpretation can be changed only by a constitutional amendment or by a later Supreme Court decision.

The notion of judicial review is controversial largely because the courts, particularly on the federal level, are not democratically accountable institutions. This issue is often referred to as the "counter-majoritarian difficulty" because a non-elected judiciary can overturn the actions of the democratically elected branches of government. That criticism is descriptively accurate. However, it may very well be that such an anti-democratic feature was precisely the type of check and balance the framers wanted to build into the constitutional structure. In any event, whatever the merits of the criticisms of judicial review, it is an integral part of the American constitutional system.

B.   Interpretive Devices

A wide array of devices is used by courts (in particular) and other actors when interpreting the Constitution. This sub-part briefly describes several of these devices, but we do not purport to provide a list of all the devices that could be used to interpret the Constitution. While there are some judges (and other actors) who argue that a single interpretive device "answers" all questions, most people engaged in interpreting the Constitution use more than one of the various devices.

- *The Text:* The starting point for all interpretation is the words of the Constitution itself. As mentioned above, there are times when the text alone answers the question. But the text is often only the starting point.

- *Original Intent:* Some people argue the intention of the drafters of the Constitution is a critically important piece of information when deciding what the Constitution means. This information is surely relevant to the interpretive enterprise. However, a significant problem is determining precisely what the framers of the original Constitution or the amendments meant.

- *Original Understanding:* A different variety of "originalism" focuses not on the drafters but rather on the ratifiers of the Constitution or its amendments. Thus, one is not concerned with what the drafters of the document meant. Rather, one is concerned with what the ratifiers would have understood the terms used to mean at the time. So, for example, the meaning of the word "commerce" in 1788 when the Constitution was ratified would be important under the original understanding interpretive device in deciding the scope of congressional power to regulate "commerce among the several states." While not easy, there are fewer difficulties in determining the meaning of words at a given point in time than there is in finding the intent of the drafters of a document. However, one could still argue against using this interpretive device because it ties the Constitution to the understanding of people long since dead and buried.

- *Constitutional Structure and History:* Another interpretive device is to use the structure of the Constitution and the historical development of the document as guides in determining the meaning of ambiguous provisions. For example, the Constitution contemplates both federalism and separation of powers. These structural considerations could guide the interpretation of the document. Moreover, the Civil War Amendments historically shifted power in important respects from the states to the federal government. This historical reality could also serve as an interpretive device.

- *Constitutional Values:* Closely associated with constitutional structure is using constitutional values as a means to interpret the document. For example, while the document does not use the word "democracy," there is no question that democratic values are an important part of American values. Thus, one could keep that commitment in mind when interpreting ambiguous provisions of the Constitution.

- *Non-United States Sources of Law:* An enormously controversial area in constitutional interpretation concerns the use of non-United States legal sources to interpret the document. Some people argue that decisions of the courts of other nations as well as international legal bodies provide an important source of information when interpreting the meaning of at least some parts of the United States Constitution. Other people assert that such sources should play no role in deciding the meaning of the Constitution. One expects that this disagreement — which is reflected on the Supreme Court itself — will continue for some time.

- *Precedent:* As you learned in Chapter One, precedent is an important part of the American legal system generally. This is no less true in constitutional law. When the Supreme Court declares that a certain portion of the Constitution means something, that holding will be significant in later cases facing similar issues.

IV. GOVERNMENTAL POWERS UNDER THE CONSTITUTION

This Section considers the powers the Constitution grants to the various branches of the federal government. Recall, one does not need to find a source of state power in the United States Constitution. The Constitution can only serve to limit state power. But because the federal government is one of enumerated powers, it is essential that one find a specific grant of authority to sustain a given action on the national level.

This sub-part considers first congressional power and then presidential authority. In addition, it considers certain areas in which state power is limited precisely because of the grant of authority to the federal government.

A.   Congressional Power

While there are several sections of the Constitution that grant power to Congress, the two main areas are Article I, section 8 of the original document and provisions of certain amendments providing that Congress has power to enact legislation to enforce a newly added amendment. One such provision is section 5 of the Fourteenth Amendment. In this sub-part, the Chapter describes certain of the major congressional powers and then briefly mentions some of the other powers of that body.

Before addressing the specific powers the Constitution grants to Congress, one preliminary point is important to note. The Constitution bestows all the legislative power of the federal government on Congress. Under the so-called "anti-delegation principle," Congress cannot transfer its legislative powers to another body. At one point in American constitutional history, the Supreme Court rigidly enforced the anti-delegation principle. However, those days are long passed. As you will consider in more detail in Chapter 15 (Administrative Law), a part of the advent of the modern era of administrative agencies has been a great relaxation in the anti-delegation principle. So long as Congress gives sufficient direction to an administrative agency, courts are willing to allow that agency to take actions that in an earlier era would have been unconstitutional as an improper delegation of legislative power.

1.   Power to Regulate Interstate Commerce

a.   Congressional Power

A deceptively broad grant of authority comes from the Constitution's provision that Congress has power to "regulate Commerce with foreign Nations, and among the several States, and with the Indian Tribes." U.S. Const. art. I, § 8, cl. 3. This constitutional provision, referred to as the Commerce Clause, has provided the basis for a wide variety of federal laws, particularly over the past seventy-five years.

The Commerce Clause has three parts. Congress has the power to regulate commerce with foreign countries. Congressional power in this respect is quite broad as one might expect given the federal government's primary role in international relations. We will consider foreign affairs more generally in other parts of this Section. The Clause also allows for the regulation of commerce with Native American tribes. That too is not surprising, because the Constitution assigns to the federal government the primary role in dealing with Native Americans. It is the third prong of authority — to regulate commerce "among the several States" — that has proven to be the most important part of the Clause. It is on this portion that we will focus.

As an historical matter, the Supreme Court narrowly interpreted the scope of Congress' authority under the Commerce Clause until about the mid-1930s. In the midst of the Great Depression in the United States, the Court began to expand its conception of congressional power over interstate commerce. That expansion continued until the mid-1990s, when the Court issued several decisions that placed greater limits on Congress' powers over interstate commerce. How meaningful these limitations are is not entirely clear. There certainly are greater limits than existed for much of the past 70 years, but they ultimately may not actually limit Congress' power. Only time will answer this question. What follows is a description of the current state of the law in this area.

The Supreme Court has held that Congress has the power to regulate under the interstate prong of the Commerce Clause in four situations. First, Congress may enact laws dealing with the channels of interstate commerce, or, in other words, the arteries through which commerce passes between and among states. Thus, the Commerce Clause allows Congress to pass legislation concerning things such as roads, railroads, canals and other waterways, as well as airspace.

Second, Congress may regulate people or things in interstate commerce. Thus, Congress may enact laws concerning the movement of individuals and goods from state to state. So, for example, under this prong of the Commerce Clause, Congress could enact a law requiring that certain chemicals be shipped in a specific way to avoid the danger of explosion or that truck drivers engaged in interstate commerce rest for at least eight hours per day. In addition, the Supreme Court has held that the authority to regulate things in interstate commerce includes the power to ban such items from interstate commerce. This power — referred to as the "commerce prohibiting technique" — allows Congress to, for example, prohibit the shipment of lottery tickets in interstate commerce. The reason Congress acts is irrelevant under the Commerce Clause. Keep in mind, however, that while the Commerce Clause might give Congress the power to act, the liberty protecting devices in the Constitution, discussed in the next Section of this Chapter, might make such an action unconstitutional. For example, the commerce prohibiting technique would provide the power to ban the shipment of Bibles in interstate commerce but the First Amendment's protection of the free exercise of religion would make such an action unconstitutional.

Third, Congress has the authority under the Commerce Clause to regulate the instrumentalities of interstate commerce. This prong of the analysis allows Congress to pass legislation concerning things that do not themselves move in interstate commerce but that are part of interstate commerce nonetheless. For example, airports and port facilities do not move in interstate commerce but Congress may regulate these facilities because they are instrumentalities of interstate commerce.

The most controversial and far-reaching power under the Commerce Clause is the fourth one. Congress may regulate those activities that "substantially affect" interstate commerce. The reason that this prong of the Commerce Clause is so controversial is that in an integrated economy such as exists in the world today, many things that are entirely local in character could very well be said to have an impact on interstate commercial activity. Wary of expanding the enumerated powers of Congress beyond recognition, the Supreme Court has attempted to craft a test that simultaneously gives Congress sufficient power under the Clause while reserving for the states the power to act alone in truly local matters. Whether the Supreme Court has been successful in its efforts is a matter of great dispute in American constitutional law.

The Supreme Court has articulated two ways in which to judge whether a given congressional action is sustainable as regulating an activity that substantially affects interstate commerce. The first of these tests starts by identifying the specific activity that Congress is regulating. This can usually be done by looking at the face of the statute, although occasionally one may need to look at legislative history to make the determination. Once that activity has been identified, the court then asks whether the activity is "economic." If it is not economic, Congress lacks authority to regulate it. What is "economic"? The Supreme Court found its definition of economic in a dictionary, holding that economic meant something that refers to the production, distribution, and consumption of a commodity. This definition is quite broad and, if applied literally, does not appear to be much of a check on Congress' power over interstate commerce.

Assuming that a given activity is economic, that may be the end of the analysis if the activity at issue is said to "*substantially* affect" interstate commerce. However, there are many economic activities that, standing alone, will not substantially affect interstate commerce. Thus, a farmer growing wheat on his or her farm in Kansas standing alone would likely not have a substantial effect on interstate commerce. Yet, if every farmer grew wheat, there would certainly be an effect on interstate commerce. The Supreme Court recognized this reality and adopted the "aggregation principle." Under the aggregation principle, if an activity has been deemed economic, Congress may regulate the activity under its interstate commerce power if that activity in the aggregate would substantially affect interstate commerce.

If the approach outlined above sustained congressional action, no further analysis would be required. However, if it did not, the Supreme Court has articulated a second approach to judge congressional action. Congress may also regulate under its interstate commerce power when there is in place a complex regulatory scheme in the relevant area. If that scheme regulates an economic enterprise and if the specific regulation at issue is sufficiently important to the functioning of that scheme, Congress may regulate that activity under its commerce power. Thus, Congress has in place a complex web of regulations concerning the production, distribution, and consumption of illegal drugs. The regulation of markets for drugs is an economic activity, the Court tells us. As such, Congress may regulate the personal cultivation and use of marijuana (even if that activity is not itself economic) because regulation of that activity is essential to the functioning of the overall regulatory scheme.

In the end, one simply cannot overestimate the importance of the scope of the federal power over interstate commerce. Many of the laws that are a hallmark of the legal culture in the United States have their roots in the Commerce Clause. Such laws include, but are by no means limited to, environmental regulations, drug laws, minimum-wage and maximum-hour regulations, many civil rights laws, and workplace safety rules. It is not an overstatement to say that American law would look quite different today if the Commerce Clause had not been interpreted as it has been over the past seventy-five years.

Before leaving the Commerce Clause, there is one important qualification to note. The Supreme Court has held that Congress may not utilize its Commerce Clause power in such a way that it "commandeers" state government. That is, Congress may enact a law directly under the Commerce Clause but it could not order a state to enact that law. Nor could Congress commandeer state officials to carry out a federal program even if that program itself was within Congress' powers to enact. The Supreme Court said that allowing such actions by Congress would be fundamentally inconsistent with the federal system of government in which the states remain as sovereigns in their own rights in many respects.

b.   Limitation on State Power

There is a final point to be made about the Commerce Clause. The Supreme Court has developed a doctrine under which the Commerce Clause acts not only as a source of power for Congress but also as a limitation on the power of the states to enact certain laws. Of course, such a limitation can exist when Congress exercises its power under the Commerce Clause and thereby preempts state law under the terms of the Supremacy Clause. However, the Supreme Court has held that the Commerce Clause limits state authority in certain situations even when Congress has not acted. This doctrine is known as the "dormant" or "negative" Commerce Clause.

The key to understanding the dormant Commerce Clause doctrine is economics. The Supreme Court has stated that the inclusion of the Commerce Clause in the Constitution was meant to imbue in the document a commitment to a free market economy. In other words, the Court has said that the framers meant to prohibit the imposition of barriers to commerce that had existed among the states under the Articles of Confederation. The United States was, in essence, to be a free trade zone for the states of the Union.

The Court has implemented this economic philosophy by holding that state regulations that either discriminate against or significantly burden interstate commerce are unconstitutional under the dormant Commerce Clause. Congress could always allow such regulations by consenting to such state action. However, in the absence of such consent, state actions in this area are not allowed. What follows is a brief description of the doctrine the Supreme Court has fashioned to implement the dormant Commerce Clause.

First, state laws that discriminate on their face against interstate commerce will almost always be invalidated under dormant Commerce Clause principles. Such laws are presumed to be unconstitutional. An example of such a law would be a regulation prohibiting in-state land fills from taking trash for disposal if the trash at issue came from out of state. Unless a state can show that it has a legitimate interest (apart from economic protectionism) and that what it has done cannot be served by any less discriminatory means, the law at issue will fail. It is extraordinarily difficult for a state to satisfy this constitutional test.

Second, if a state law is neutral on its face (that is, it does not discriminate against interstate commerce formally) but in effect the law at issue discriminates against interstate commerce, the law will fail almost as surely as one that did facially discriminate. An example of such a statute would be a requirement that all apples sold in the state only be advertised with a grade or classification issued by the United States Department of Agriculture. That law is facially neutral — it applies to all apples. However, it turns out that Washington State apples — the industry leader — had a stronger classification system. Thus, the effect of the law would be to limit only Washington State apple producers in their advertising. While the Court has been inconsistent in stating the specific test it will use to judge such effects-based laws, the end result is almost universally invalidation. The same is true if the Court determines that a state had the purpose of discriminating against interstate commerce.

Finally, there are laws that are facially neutral with respect to interstate commerce, that are not prompted by an illicit motive to effect interstate commerce, and that do not have a discriminatory effect on interstate commerce (that is, they actually have an impact on both in-state and out-of-state commercial actors). These laws are presumed to be constitutional. However, they may still be struck down under dormant Commerce Clause principles if a challenger can establish that the burden on interstate commerce substantially outweighs the legitimate local benefits the law at issue seeks to achieve.

2.   Power to Tax and Spend

A second practically important set of congressional powers concerns the collection and spending of money. First, the Constitution provides that Congress may "lay and collect Taxes, Duties, Imposts and Excises." U.S. Const. art. I, § 8, cl. 1. The Constitution was amended in 1913 to specifically grant Congress the power to tax incomes. U.S. Const. amend. XVI. These powers are practically important because they provide the means by which Congress can generate revenue for the United States. Taxing measures will almost always be upheld if they are facially consistent with being a revenue producing device.

Second, Congress has the power to spend "for the common Defence and general Welfare of the United States." U.S. Const. art. I, § 8, cl. 1. The Spending Clause power is independent from other congressional powers. That is, Congress can spend even when it would lack the power to directly regulate in a given area. So long as the spending at issue is for the common defense or general welfare of the United States, the regulation is within Congress' power. It is difficult to imagine that any court would ever hold that a congressional determination that something is, for example, for the general welfare of the United States is unlawful under the Spending Clause.

The real issue under the Spending Clause comes when Congress uses its spending power with respect to the states. This occurs when Congress attaches conditions to its spending. For example, Congress might enact a law under its spending power to give money to the states for public education purposes. As part of the law, Congress might require the states to take certain actions concerning public education. In other words, the federal funds will come with strings attached. The Supreme Court has held that such conditional spending is constitutional so long as (1) Congress satisfies the Spending Clause requirements (which as mentioned above is easy to do); (2) Congress makes its conditions sufficiently clear to the states; (3) Congress' action does not violate some other provision of the Constitution (such as an individual liberty protecting device); and (4) the condition is sufficiently related to the funds being spent. The Court has not articulated how closely related the condition needs to be, but it was sufficient that funds given to states for building highways were conditioned on raising the drinking age to twenty-one years. Thus, it seems fair to say that the nexus between condition and funds is not terribly close.

3.   "War" and Related Powers

The Constitution assigns to Congress important powers concerning war and peace. For example, Congress has the power to "declare War." U.S. Const. art. I, § 8, cl. 11. This grant of power was significant at the time of the framing. It may be less so in a world in which at least industrialized nation-states are less apt to go to war to settle differences. However, the power is still important because the Supreme Court has held that the power also includes the lesser power to authorize military action short of a formal declaration of war. Thus, authorizations for the use of military force in the Vietnam conflict as well as the "war on terror" ultimately spring from the Constitution's war power grant to Congress.

In addition to the power to declare war, Congress also has the power to "raise and support Armies," U.S. Const. art. I, § 8, cl. 12, and to "provide and maintain a Navy." U.S. Const. art. I, § 8, cl. 13. Along with these powers comes authorization to enact regulations for such military forces. U.S. Const. art. I, § 8, cl. 14.

The bottom line is that Congress has significant authority in the domain of war-making and the formation and regulation of United States Armed Forces. The real issues in this area come not from disputes between the federal government and the states, as they do say when considering the Commerce Clause, but rather in disputes between Congress and the President. As we describe later in this section, the President also has significant powers in the field of war and peace.

4.   Power to Enforce the Terms of the Fourteenth Amendment

As described above, the Civil War led to significant amendments to the United States Constitution. One of the most important of these amendments was the Fourteenth. Among other things, and as we will explore in Section V of this Chapter, section 1 of the Fourteenth Amendment provided that states could not deny persons the equal protection of the law or deprive persons of life, liberty, or property without due process of law. But the framers of the Fourteenth Amendment recognized that these guarantees could amount to empty words if there were not means to enforce them. The framers of the amendment addressed this concern with section 5 of the Fourteenth Amendment, which provides "[t]he Congress shall have power to enforce, by appropriate legislation, the provisions of this article."

Section 5 of the Fourteenth Amendment is an important grant of authority to Congress. Under it, Congress has the power to enact legislation with the aim of enforcing the due process and equal protection provisions of section 1, as well as the provisions of the Bill of Rights said to be made applicable to the states through incorporation. Congress has used this power to enact many important civil rights statutes dealing with matters such as employment discrimination, maternity leave, voting rights, and religious freedom, among other things.

Congress' power under section 5 is not unlimited. The Supreme Court has held that the word "appropriate" in section 5 acts as a limitation on the legislation Congress may enact. The Court has developed a test under which a piece of legislation will be upheld if it is deemed to be "congruent and proportional" to the problem Congress has sought to address. This test is highly fact specific, and one would need to read a number of the Court's decisions to understand fully how it applies. Generally speaking, however, the reference to congruence means that what Congress has done has a sufficient relationship to the problem it has identified; it is a qualitative analysis. The reference to proportionality means that Congress has acted in a way that is not overkill given the scope of the problem it has identified; it is a quantitative question. As a practical matter, the congruence and proportionality test has served as a significant check (at least at times) on the power bestowed on Congress under the Fourteenth Amendment.

5.   The Necessary and Proper Clause

The powers that we have discussed above are specific to certain topics. That is, Congress has the power to regulate interstate commerce or to declare war. However, the framers understood that they could not anticipate all the needs of the national government in terms of the implementation of the enumerated powers. They sought to address this issue by including in the Constitution what is known as the "Necessary and Proper Clause." Article I, section 8, clause 18 provides that Congress has the power to "make all Laws which shall be necessary and proper for carrying into Execution the foregoing Powers, and all other Powers vested by this Constitution in the Government of the United States, or in any Department or Officer thereof."

The Supreme Court set the bounds of the Necessary and Proper Clause in the early days of the United States in the important decision of *McCulloch v. Maryland*. The starting point is to ensure that Congress has a legitimate end. In other words, Congress must be seeking to advance some enumerated power. If that is the case, the Necessary and Proper Clause becomes relevant as a way to judge whether the means Congress has utilized are appropriate. The Court has held that so long as the means Congress uses are (1) not prohibited by the Constitution and (2) are rationally connected to the end (i.e., the enumerated power), the Necessary and Proper Clause provides the basis for action.

McCulloch v. Maryland provides a useful example. Congress had passed a statute creating a Bank of the United States. Maryland challenged the statute as beyond Congress' enumerated powers. The Supreme Court rejected the challenge. First, the Court identified numerous enumerated powers that Congress might have sought to advance by creating a national bank, including the power to coin money or provide for the maintenance of the army and navy. Therefore, there was a legitimate end. What means did Congress use to advance that end — the creation of a bank? The Court stated that nothing in the Constitution prohibited the creation of a national bank. In addition, the Court reasoned that Congress could have rationally concluded that having a national bank would advance its interests in using certain of its enumerated powers.

As the example with the national bank suggests, the Supreme Court has interpreted the Necessary and Proper Clause in a way that gives Congress great latitude. This power has become a practically important one in American constitutional law.

6.   Other Powers

This sub-part has described a number of the most significant powers given to Congress under the Constitution. These powers are in addition to those described earlier, such as the requirement that the Senate confirm presidential appointments and ratify treaties. In addition, there are many others that are also important. We cannot cover all of these powers but merely list them below for your information:

- Congress has the power to make rules concerning bankruptcies. Congress has utilized this power to create a comprehensive system for bankruptcies in the United States. U.S. Const. art. I, § 8, cl. 4.

- Congress has the power to make rules of naturalization and citizenship for the United States. Congress has utilized this power to enact the many rules concerning immigration that are applicable in the United States today. U.S. Const. art. I, § 8, cl. 4.

- Congress has important powers concerning copyrights, patents and trademarks about which you will have learned in Chapter Nine concerning intellectual property. U.S. Const. art. I, § 8, cl. 8.

- Congress has the power to legislate concerning the delivery of mail. This power has been practically significant in the United States. U.S. Const. art. I, § 8, cl. 7.

- Congress has the power to coin money and establish uniform weights and measures in the United States. U.S. Const. art. I, § 8, cl. 5.

- Finally, Congress has the practically important power to "borrow Money on the credit of the United States." U.S. Const. art. I, § 8, cl. 2.

B.   Presidential Power

As described above, the executive power of the federal government is vested in the President of the United States. The President's powers are defined with less detail than are those of Congress. The more general phrasing of the President's powers have often led to disputes between the President and Congress. In this sub-part, the Chapter considers the scope of presidential authority with a particular emphasis on the ways in which disputes between the President and Congress are resolved.

While there are many ambiguities in presidential authority under the Constitution, there are also certain powers that are fairly easy to state. We have mentioned most of these before. To review, the President has the power to (1) appoint, pursuant to approval of the Senate, federal judges, ambassadors, and other officers of the United States; (2) veto legislation Congress has passed, subject to override in Congress; (3) unconditionally pardon people in connection with the violation of federal law; (4) recognize foreign governments; and (5) enter into treaties on behalf of the United States, subject to treaty-ratification in the Senate.

Presidential power is augmented, however, through more generally worded clauses such as the constitutional directive that the President is the commander in chief of the United States Armed Forces, U.S. Const. art. II, § 2, and that the President "shall take Care that the Laws be faithfully executed." U.S. Const. art. II, § 3. These general powers are by no means self-defining and can often put the President and Congress on a collision course when the two branches each seek to exercise their respective constitutional powers in inconsistent ways.

Historically, the Supreme Court has ruled that the President has greater latitude to act unilaterally (that is, without Congress) in the foreign arena than he or she would when acting domestically. That state of affairs remains true in theory, but the reality is that the distinctions between foreign activity and domestic matters are blurry to say the least. Take the fight against terrorism as an example. Is that a domestic matter or a foreign one? The answer is that it is both. Therefore, the trend has been to use essentially the same approach discussed below to assess presidential power whether or not one classifies a given situation as involving foreign or domestic matters.

The Supreme Court articulated the means for testing presidential actions in the *Steel Seizure Case* decided during the Korean War. President Truman had nationalized several steel mills to avert a labor strike. The President took the action, he asserted, to keep the mills running so that steel used for military purposes would still be available. The steel mill owners challenged the President's authority to take the action. The Court sided with the mill owners. The key opinion in the case was a concurrence by Justice Robert Jackson. Jackson's opinion has since been adopted by a majority of the Court.

Justice Jackson articulated a spectrum on which one was to judge presidential action. On one end of the spectrum were situations in which the President acted with the express or implied blessing of Congress. In this situation, the President acted at the apex of his or her authority. This was the case because the President was essentially acting with all of the power of the federal government. He or she had all the Article II executive power *plus* the Article I power given by Congress. Thus, if the President could not act in this situation, the federal government itself could not act.

On the other end of the spectrum were situations in which the President acted against the express or implied will of Congress. In this situation, the presidential authority was at its lowest ebb. All the President could rely on to act was his or her own power under Article II, less whatever Congress had taken away when exercising its Article I powers. (It was in this category that Justice Jackson placed President Truman's seizure of the steel mills.)

This leaves the area of the spectrum between the two ends, what Justice Jackson called the zone of twilight. In this area, Congress has not acted either to endorse or prohibit presidential action. Here, presidential power under, for example, the Commander in Chief or Take Care Clauses carry greater weight than when Congress prohibits actions but not as much as when Congress approves of the action. Precisely how much power the President has in this zone of twilight depends on the precise facts of a given case.

What one takes from the *Steel Seizure Case* fundamentally is that the President does have independent constitutional authority under Article II to take action but that this authority is intertwined with the authority of Congress to act under Article I. The precise contours of the President's independent power are not clear, and much depends on judicial interpretation of what Congress has meant to authorize or to prohibit.

V. PROTECTION OF INDIVIDUAL RIGHTS UNDER THE CONSTITUTION

With the addition of many of the amendments, there are many liberty protecting devices now included in the Constitution. In this Section, the Chapter describes some of the more important of those devices with a focus on those that have not been covered in other chapters of this book. Before addressing the specific devices, there are two important general concepts to keep in mind.

First, there are few if any absolutes in American constitutional law. The First Amendment says that Congress shall make "no law" concerning, among other things, prohibiting the free exercise of religion. But the Supreme Court has never read this language literally. Instead, it has adopted various means by which to test whether a given law touching on the free exercise of religion is nonetheless constitutional. We will see the same general pattern in other areas concerning the protection of individual liberty. Thus, much of what we will discuss in this section concerns the Supreme Court's development of a series of tests under which the courts balance the government's need to act against the individual liberty interest the Constitution recognizes. Such balancing has been the subject of fierce criticism, but balancing remains an integral part of constitutional law.

Second, in most respects, only governments or government officials can violate the Constitution. This concept is referred to as the "state action requirement." In most situations, state action is clear. Congress or a state's legislature passes a law claimed to be unconstitutional. Or, perhaps, the President or a state's governor acts in an unconstitutional respect. You should be aware, however, that there are situations in which a private entity can be so cloaked with governmental authority that its conduct counts as state action. The rules here are complex, and we will not delve into this area. However, you should at least be aware that it is possible for a non-governmental entity to be held to constitutional standards, although it is a rare event.

A.   Due Process of Law

There are two identical Due Process Clauses in the Constitution, one in the Fifth Amendment and the other in the Fourteenth. The Fifth Amendment clause binds the federal government while the Fourteenth Amendment concerns the states. Each clause prohibits the government from depriving persons of life, liberty, or property without due process of law. The Supreme Court has interpreted the Due Process Clauses to have two components, one procedural and one substantive. We consider these two facets of due process separately below.

1.   Procedural Due Process

As its name suggests, the procedural component of due process concerns the process by which the government may deprive a person of life, liberty, and property. It is important to note at the outset that the Constitution does *not* prohibit the government from depriving a person of life, liberty, or property. Rather, the government can only do so after providing due process of law. Also, the Supreme Court has held that the term "person" in the Due Process Clauses includes legal entities such as corporations as well as natural persons.

There is a two step process under the procedural prong of due process. First, one must determine whether there is a life, liberty, or property interest at issue. If there is none, or if there has been no deprivation of such an interest, the clause has no bearing. Second, assuming there is such an interest and there has been a deprivation, one must determine what process is due before a person can be deprived of that interest. This sub-part considers both of these issues in turn.

a.   Life, Liberty, and Property Interests and Deprivation

The first step is to determine if there is a life, liberty, or property interest at stake. Life interests tend to be easy to spot. The true difficulty comes in terms of liberty and property. Beginning with liberty, certain matters are clear. When a government attempts to imprison or confine you, there is no question that your liberty has been infringed. The difficulty comes when the state takes an action short of confinement that has some impact on you. The Supreme Court has indicated that one judges the liberty interest in this situation by asking whether the government's action had changed your legal status in some way. If it has, there is a constitutional liberty interest at stake. If it has not, there is no such interest.

One can see the test in action by comparing two situations. Assume that there is a state law that allows a local sheriff to brand someone as a habitual drinker. If someone is labeled a habitual drinker, a state law provides that he or she cannot purchase alcohol for one year. In this situation, there would be a liberty interest at stake, because the state action changed the person's status. Before the branding they could buy alcohol, but they cannot do so after the fact.

Contrast the situation of the habitual drinker with this scenario. The local police are authorized by law to distribute to stores the pictures of people arrested for shoplifting. The pictures are distributed before trial on the shoplifting charges. A person eventually acquitted of shoplifting sues the police for distributing his or her picture. In this case, there is no constitutional liberty interest at stake, because the state action does not result in the change of legal status.

In terms of property, the Supreme Court has held that one looks to the relevant state or federal law to determine whether a property interest exists. Thus, one might consider the intent of a state legislature or Congress when enacting a certain program (such as a welfare program). Similarly, one might look to state common law to find a property interest. While the determination of whether a property interest does, in fact, exist, the question of whether there is a reasonable expectation under law of a property interest is ultimately one of federal constitutional law.

A couple of examples might help. Assume that a teacher employed by a state university works under a contract that expressly states that the contract is for one year and may be renewed at the sole discretion of the university. In this situation, the teacher has no property interest in a renewal of the contract. On the other hand, assume that the contract provided that the teacher's contract would be presumptively renewed so long as the teacher fulfilled his or her responsibilities. In this latter case, there would be a property interest. The key difference is that in the latter case, the person would have a reasonable expectation that his or her employment contract conferred a property right.

Finally, under this prong, one must determine whether there has been a deprivation of the relevant interest. In many cases, this will be clear beyond doubt. However, in other contexts there can be significant questions. For example, can a negligent act count as a deprivation? In most cases the courts have said no, even if there is a life, liberty, or property interest at stake.

b.   What Process Is Due?

Assuming there is a life, liberty, or property interest at stake, the next question is what process is due a person before they may be deprived of that interest. The Supreme Court held in *Mathews v. Eldridge* that a court should use a three-part balancing test to answer the question. The Court has consistently reaffirmed the *Mathews v. Eldridge* test in a number of contexts concerning the procedural component of due process.

The first factor to consider is the private interest at stake. In other words, the Court makes a judgment as to how important the life, liberty, or property interest is in a general sense. Sometimes this assessment is easy. The deprivations of life or the liberty interest associated with confinement are clearly important. Sometimes, however, the determination is not so clear cut. For example, the Court has held that the receipt of welfare benefits is very important while the continued receipt of disability payments under the Social Security Act is not as significant. Accordingly, one would need to consider the full scope of relevant precedent in many cases to assess the importance of the individual interest at stake.

The second factor concerns the government interest in connection with the deprivation. The more important the government interest, the more leeway there will generally be in the procedures utilized. For example, if the government's only interest is limiting the time or expense of additional procedures, there will be less leeway than if there is an interest in national security.

The final factor focuses on the risk of error in the procedure currently in place, and the likelihood that the error rate will be reduced by utilizing a different procedure. The higher the error rate and the more that rate would be reduced, the greater the chance that the court will require enhanced procedures.

As one can surmise from this brief discussion, the procedural due process analysis is highly fact specific. In certain situations, fairly elaborate pre-deprivation proceedings will be required, including in some cases quasi-trial like adjudication. In others, a prompt post-deprivation hearing will suffice. And in still others, some far less formal procedure will be constitutional. But the end product of all of these matters will only specify the procedures a government must follow before depriving a person of a life, liberty, or property interest. It will not mean that the government is prohibited from acting at all. This latter point concerns substantive due process to which this Section turns next.

2.   Substantive Due Process

As described above, the procedural prong of due process is concerned with the means by which the government deprives a person of life, liberty, or property. The substantive component of due process is concerned instead with the reasons the government has for acting. Essentially, in a substantive due process review, a court assesses whether the government's actions are sufficiently strong to justify a given action.

As you may notice, there is a danger inherent in a substantive due process review. If a court substitutes its own judgment for that of a legislature by saying that the government's reasons (or means) of acting are not "good enough," the non-elected courts (at least in the federal system) will be substituting their judgment for that of the political branches. Courts are aware of this danger and have developed a system of tiered review. Under this type of review, which we will describe in more detail below, a court will generally defer to legislative judgments and use a deferential standard of review. However, when a given right is deemed important enough, a court will employ a heightened standard of review requiring that the government show more in order to sustain the law at issue.

There are two tiers of review under substantive due process. The default standard of review is the most deferential to the judgment of the political branches. This standard of review is called "rational basis review." Under rational basis review, a given law is presumed to be constitutional and will be upheld so long as (a) the government has a legitimate interest and (b) the means the government has used in the law in question are rationally related to serving this interest. Most laws will be upheld under the rational basis standard of review.

The second tier of review is far less deferential. It is called "strict scrutiny." Under strict scrutiny, the law in question is presumed to be unconstitutional. It will be upheld only if the government can demonstrate that (a) it has a compelling interest and (b) the means the government has used in the law in question are narrowly tailored to serve that compelling interest. Most laws will be struck down under strict scrutiny.

Both rational basis review and strict scrutiny require the assessment of the reason the government has acted as well as the means the government has used to act. So, in this respect, the tests are similar. However, the tests are applied in quite different ways. Therefore, it is important to determine which test should be used. The courts do so based on the nature of the right that a plaintiff claims is being infringed by a government action. If that right is deemed to be "fundamental," strict scrutiny is the appropriate test. If the right is not fundamental, rational basis review is utilized. (Of course, if there is no infringement, it does not matter whether the right would be fundamental or not.)

Determining whether a right is fundamental for substantive due process principles is a difficult task. The modern formulation — which is not all that helpful, to be honest — provides that a right is fundamental if it is "implicit in the concept of ordered liberty." A court determines whether something is implicit in the concept of ordered liberty by looking to history and tradition. However, the Supreme Court has recognized that history and tradition are not static. They grow and develop, and, therefore, what is fundamental can shift. In reality, it often seems that one of the most significant touchstones for determining whether a right is fundamental is precedent. In other words, a court will look to earlier decisions and compare the right at issue with those that have been found to be fundamental in the past.

For a significant period of time, economic liberties, such as the right to enter into contracts were deemed to be fundamental. This period of American constitution history is referred to as the *Lochner* era after a famous case. (*Lochner v. New York*). However, in the mid-1930s, the Supreme Court rejected *Lochner*, and, today, economic rights are not considered fundamental.

Instead, fundamental rights have been reserved for more personal and intimate matters. Such rights include: (1) the right of persons — married or unmarried — to possess and use contraceptive devices; (2) the right of a woman to obtain an abortion, at least prior to the point at which the fetus is viable outside the womb; (3) the right to marry (although the scope of "marriage" was not defined, leaving the impact on same-sex couples uncertain); and (4) the right to participate in certain familial relationships such as controlling a child's upbringing and living with certain of your extended family. The Court has also suggested that one has a fundamental right to refuse medical treatment, but has not *formally held* that this is the case. The Court has affirmatively rejected that one has a fundamental right to have assistance in ending one's life (so called assisted suicide).

Recall, however, that saying that something is a fundamental right merely tells you what test to use to judge the government action at issue — strict scrutiny. The government can still prevail if it shows it has a sufficiently important interest (one that is compelling) and that what it has done is narrowly tailored to serve that interest. The latter provision — narrow tailoring — is highly fact specific. The assessment of the compelling character of the interest is more abstract. Some interests that have been deemed compelling are (1) national security; (2) protecting the health of a pregnant woman; (3) preserving potential life; and (4) having a generalized commitment to preserving existing life.

Just as it is possible — albeit difficult — for a law to pass strict scrutiny, it is also possible — although difficult — for a law to fail rational basis review. This can occur in one of two ways. First, the state's interest may not be legitimate. This state of affairs does not occur often, but it is possible. For example, the Supreme Court has held that it is not a legitimate interest for the government to impose its own moral code on citizens, at least if that is its only basis for acting. This was one of the reasons the Supreme Court struck down laws against sodomy between consenting adults in a case called *Lawrence v. Texas*. It is also not a legitimate interest for the state to have a "bare desire to harm" an identifiable group. Second, a law may fail rational basis review if there is no rational connection between the government's purpose and what it is done. Few laws fail this prong of the analysis.

As one can see from this brief discussion, substantive due process is both complex and controversial. This Section has only been able to touch on the richness of the law in this area.

B.   Equal Protection of the Laws

The Fourteenth Amendment provides that states may not deny persons within their jurisdiction the equal protection of the laws. There is no parallel provision applicable to the federal government, but the Supreme Court has held that the Fifth Amendment's Due Process Clause contains an equal protection component. Thus, what follows is applicable to all governmental actors.

The Equal Protection Clause does not require that everyone be treated the same as an absolute matter. As with substantive due process, equal protection doctrine is one of tiered review. The question a court asks is whether the government has a sufficient reason for treating separate groups differently. Thus, it is perfectly okay under equal protection doctrine for the government to say, for example, that only a person with a law degree may be a lawyer. But it is inappropriate for the government to say that only a white person (or only a man) may be a lawyer. Your intuition would probably have led you to this conclusion. This sub-part provides the constitutional foundation to justify your intuition.

The default standard of review under the Equal Protection Clause is the rational basis test. It is the same rational basis review applied in substantive due process. A law will be upheld as constitutional so long as the government (1) has a legitimate interest for its actions and (2) what it has done is rationally related to serving this interest. As with substantive due process review, most laws evaluated under the rational basis standard of review will be upheld. The exception to this conclusion usually is when the government acts with a "bare desire to harm" a particular group or bases its actions on irrational stereotypes about a group.

There are certain situations in which the courts will apply a higher level of scrutiny for laws challenged under the Equal Protection Clause. This is most often the case when the law at issue classifies with respect to certain groups such as race, national origin, birth status (i.e., legitimacy), or gender. The law has developed to require a greater government justification for laws classifying on these bases, fundamentally because we are suspicious about whether the traits defining these groups can be a sufficient reason for government action. The danger of invidious discrimination is simply too high.

There are two levels of scrutiny above rational basis review under equal protection doctrine. The highest level of scrutiny is called strict scrutiny and is the same test as the strict scrutiny approach under substantive due process. The government must show that (1) it has a compelling interest in acting and (2) what it has done is narrowly tailored to serving that interest. As with substantive due process, most laws to which strict scrutiny applies will be found unconstitutional. Strict scrutiny applies to laws that classify on the basis of race, alienage, and national origin. These groups are referred to as "suspect classes."

The strict scrutiny test applies whether the government action at issue is meant to harm a particular group or whether the government seeks to help the group in question. So, for example, the test would clearly apply when state government intentionally segregated public education prior to the Supreme Court's landmark decision in the early 1950s in *Brown v. Board of Education*. The test also applies, however, to affirmative action programs under which the government seeks to help disadvantaged groups. The reason this is so, the Supreme Court tells us, is that in both situations the law at issue classifies by race. The Court is unwilling to delve into the reasons the government acts and, instead, relies on the fact of classification itself.

As mentioned above, it is very difficult for a law to be sustained under strict scrutiny. It is, however, possible. For example, during World War II, the Supreme Court upheld the internment of Japanese Americans because it concluded that national security was a compelling state interest and what the government had done was sufficiently narrowly tailored to serve that interest. Similarly, the Supreme Court has upheld certain affirmative action programs in college and university admissions programs. The Court concluded that diversity in education was a compelling state interest. So long as the university gave an individual review to each applicant (what the Court termed a holistic review), such an affirmative action program was deemed sufficiently narrowly tailored to serving the interest in educational diversity. But do not be deceived by these examples of laws surviving strict scrutiny review. They are very much the exceptions.

Unlike substantive due process, there is a level of scrutiny between rational basis review and strict scrutiny called "intermediate scrutiny." Under intermediate scrutiny, the law at issue will be deemed unconstitutional unless the government can show (1) that it has an "important" interest and (2) what it has done is substantially related to serving that interest. A law that classifies on the basis of sex or the legitimacy of one's birth is subjected to intermediate scrutiny. These groups are referred to as "quasi- suspect classes." Most laws subject to intermediate scrutiny will fail, but it is easier to satisfy this tier of review than it is strict scrutiny.

Why should there be an intermediate level of review? The Supreme Court has indicated that there is something special about quasi-suspect classes that makes them different than the groups considered suspect classes. Specifically, the Court has said that while classification on the basis of, say, sex is suspicious, there are certain situations in which we need not be as suspicious because there are real biological differences between men and women. When the Court views a given classification as being based on such biological differences, it is far more likely to uphold a law. In contrast, if the Court views the classification as being based on stereotypes about the sexes, the law is far more likely to fail.

Before leaving equal protection doctrine, there are two final points to consider. First, it is possible that other groups could be added to the list of suspect and quasi-suspect classes. A court would likely consider factors such as how similar a given group was to the groups already in these classifications, whether that group has political power, whether the traits defining that group are immutable or by choice, and whether the group has been subject to discrimination in the past. One group that is likely to be subject to consideration for heightened scrutiny in the future is gays and lesbians. The Court has to date avoided deciding this classification issue.

Second, as you can see, it is important for equal protection analysis to determine the basis on which a law classifies. After all, it is the classification that triggers the appropriate level of scrutiny. In many cases, this question is easily answered, because the law on its face classifies according to one of the suspect or quasi-suspect classes. It is equally easy to determine when a neutral law is applied in a manner indicating a classification on a suspect or quasi-suspect basis. But what happens when the law is facially neutral but has a disproportionate impact on one of the groups? The answer is that such an impact standing alone is not enough to trigger heightened scrutiny. The Constitution's guarantee of equal protection is violated only by *intentional* action. Therefore, in order to trigger heightened scrutiny in a situation of disproportionate impact, one must find evidence that, despite the law's facial neutrality, the government actually meant to use a suspect or quasi-suspect class as a classification device. This can often be a difficult task for a person challenging such a facially neutral law.

C.   First Amendment Rights

The First Amendment is one of the most important liberty protecting devices in the Constitution. It protects a bundle of rights going in many ways to the heart of freedom in the United States. In this Section, the Chapter focuses on two particular aspects of the First Amendment, its protection of freedom of expression and of religious liberty. In addition to these matters, you should also be aware that the First Amendment protects the important rights of the people to "peaceably assemble" as well as to "petition the Government for a redress of grievances," as well as what has been termed the right of freedom of association. These matters could be considered as part of the freedom of expression under the amendment but they also go beyond that classification. In addition, the First Amendment also provides certain special protection concerning the freedom of the press. These freedoms are closely associated with the more general protections afforded to freedom of expression. Space limitations do not allow us to address these important rights further.

One final introductory word is important. As you know, this book is meant to be an overview. This Chapter has thus far been faithful to that goal in connection with American constitutional law in general. You should keep in mind when reading what follows that First Amendment doctrine is extraordinarily complex and varied. Entire classes are taught just on this portion of the Constitution. Thus, this Section is even on a more general level than others.

1.   Freedom of Expression

The First Amendment protects the freedom of individuals to express themselves and the corresponding right not to do so. It reflects one of the values at the core of American democracy. In other words, democracy works in large measure because citizens are free to express their views largely in the time and manner they choose. It is for this reason that a significant part of First

Amendment doctrine has focused on the rights of those engaged in the political process, including candidates for office as well as their supporters and opponents. This line of doctrine has not only protected the obvious political activities such as making speeches but also less obvious "speech" such as making political contributions.

The First Amendment also reflects a truth finding function often articulated in connection with the metaphor extolling the virtues of the "marketplace of ideas." The concept here is that the truth is most likely to see the light of day in a free and robust exchange of various points of view. It is for this reason that prior restraint of speech is almost never allowed. Finally, the First Amendment embodies a strong individualist component. That is, it reflects a belief that an important part of personhood is the ability to autonomously decide what views to express and correspondingly when to remain silent.

Despite these goals — or perhaps, at least, in part because of them — there are certain categories of speech that have been held to be outside of the ambit of the expression the First Amendment protects. These areas of speech are said to have such little value while correspondingly causing significant harm that government can ban the speech outright. Important examples of such categories of speech are obscenity (judged by contemporary community standards), child pornography (even if somehow not obscene), true threats of imminent harm, and fighting words (words intended to provoke physical violence and likely to have such an effect on a reasonable listener).

Beyond such categorical exclusions, however, the First Amendment protects speech generally. In other words, while some might say that the speech at the core of what the framers sought to protect was political, the First Amendment has also been interpreted to protect matters far beyond that core, including but not limited to artistic speech and commercial speech. In addition, the First Amendment has been interpreted to protect expressive *conduct* as well as speech itself. Thus, if a person has the intent to communicate a message through conduct and a reasonable observer would understand that a message was being communicated, the conduct will generally be assessed as speech.

But as this Chapter has attempted to make clear at various points, there are few absolutes in American constitutional law. Instead, most constitutional doctrine concerning individual rights has focused on the development of balancing tests used to judge whether a particular governmental infringement of a right should be sustained given the specific interest and means at stake. We saw such tests in both substantive due process and equal protection. First Amendment law follows the same basic doctrinal approach.

Most often, the central question for determining the appropriate level of scrutiny under the First Amendment's freedom of expression component is whether the government regulation is content-based or content-neutral. When the government regulates based on the content of speech, its regulations are subject to strict scrutiny (i.e., the government must have a compelling interest and its regulations must be necessary to serve that interest). Content-based laws are presumptively invalid and will usually be struck down under the First Amendment. This result is not surprising, because the purposes behind the First Amendment outlined above are most endangered when the government seeks to regulate speech precisely because of its content.

There is less danger of undermining core First Amendment values when the government's regulation is not based on the content of speech. Accordingly, when a government regulates in a content-neutral manner, the courts apply a form of intermediate scrutiny, which is easier to satisfy. Specifically, a regulation will be upheld if it is narrowly tailored to serve a significant government interest and leaves open a sufficient number of other channels of communication. These types of content-neutral regulations are often described as reasonable time, place, and manner restrictions on speech.

There is one final issue to consider. The place in which the government regulates speech has been considered to be important in assessing the constitutionality of the regulation. There are certain places deemed "traditional public fora" in which the government may not ban all expressive activity. Such places include streets and parks. On the other end of the spectrum is the "non-public forum," which is property that has not traditionally been used for expressive activity. Here, a government regulation of speech will generally be upheld if it is content-neutral and reasonable. Finally, there are certain places that would not be a public forum but the government has designated the place as such for a limited purpose. These locations are referred to as "limited" or "designated public fora." When a government creates such a limited public forum, regulations of speech will be assessed on the same basis as would regulation of speech in a traditional public forum.

2.   Religious Freedom

The First Amendment protects two aspects of religious freedom. First, it provides that the government will not "establish" a religion — the Establishment Clause. Second, it protects an individual's right to freely exercise his or her religion — the Free Exercise Clause. In many respects, government neutrality concerning religion is at the core of both these rights. However, you should see that there is often a tension between the Establishment Clause and the Free Exercise Clause. The government may not "establish" a religion but must also ensure that a person may freely exercise religion. So, for example, if a state provides scholarships to qualified college students, must it provide a scholarship for someone otherwise qualified who wishes to use the scholarship to pursue a religious degree? On the one hand, providing a scholarship could be seen as a violation of the Establishment Clause. On the other hand, failing to provide the scholarship could be seen as inhibiting the student's ability to freely exercise his or her religion. Courts wrestle with the tension between these Clauses on a case-by-case basis. By the way, in a case dealing with the basic facts discussed in the paragraph, the Supreme Court held that the state was not required to provide the scholarship to the student.

In the balance of this sub-part, the Chapter considers first the Establishment Clause and then the Free Exercise Clause.

a.   The Establishment Clause

Harkening to the metaphor attributed to Thomas Jefferson, people often refer to the central principle underlying the Establishment Clause as one of a "wall" built between church and state in America. That description is accurate in the general sense that there is a division between these entities. However, the metaphor can be taken too literally in suggesting an impermeable barrier. Instead, the doctrine concerning the Establishment Clause suggests that the "wall" between church and state is more permeable than one might think.

It is clear that the Establishment Clause precludes the creation of a national religion. However, the Clause does far more than that. It deals with a broad array of situations in which the government may be seen to be acting to support one religion over another or even religion in general over a lack of religion. In short, the Clause is also concerned with the appropriate neutrality of the government towards religion.

Although it is much maligned, the Supreme Court has developed a test to judge whether a given government action violates the Establishment Clause. This three-part test is referred to as the "*Lemon* test" after the case in which it was articulated. In order for a government action challenged under the Establishment Clause to be sustained, three conditions must be satisfied: (1) the government must have a secular purpose for acting; (2) the primary effect of the government's action must not be to advance or inhibit religion; and (3) the government's action must not lead to an excessive entanglement between the government and religion. Although a majority of the Supreme Court continues to adhere to the *Lemon* test, some Justices have also used a supplemental test in which the central question is whether the government's action is an "endorsement" of religion. If it is, then the action is unconstitutional.

Establishment Clause cases arise in a number of contexts. We will highlight two of the more important ones. One quite common situation in which the Court has dealt with the issue involves government support for religion in public schools or the related issue of government support of religious schools. The cases are not entirely consistent, but some things are clear. First, the government may not compel students to pray in school or, in most cases, provide direct support to religious educational institutions. However, in recent years, the Supreme Court has been more willing to uphold certain types of more indirect support for such institutions including the use of vouchers to pay for private education even if religiously based. This field is in many ways in flux.

A second common Establishment Clause situation involves government displays that include religious symbols. Such displays include monuments including the Ten Commandments as well as displays around holidays such as Christmas. Here, the Court has allowed such displays when it is convinced that the government is not acting with an overt religious motive or otherwise endorsing religion. The downside of the approach the Court has taken, however, is that it is difficult to predict in advance which displays will pass constitutional muster.

b.   The Free Exercise Clause

The free exercise component of the First Amendment is in some respects a counterpart to the freedom of expression provision. In particular, one can think of the Free Exercise Clause, at least in part, as protection for autonomy and free choice in the specific area of religious belief. Thus, while the Freedom of Expression and Freedom of Religion Clauses are separate, there is a strong connection that also binds them together.

A central component of free exercise doctrine is that the government is absolutely barred from judging the sincerity or truth of religious beliefs. However, beliefs can also be manifested through conduct. The Free Exercise Clause does not prohibit the regulation of conduct. The trick is distinguishing when the regulation of such religiously-motivated conduct is appropriate and when it is not.

Roughly speaking, one can divide conduct regulation into two categories: (1) regulation of religiously-motivated conduct flowing from generally applicable laws; and (2) regulation of religiously-motivated conduct as the result of a law targeted at such conduct in particular. With respect to conduct regulated as a result of generally applicable laws, it had been the case until 1990 that courts evaluated such regulation under a heightened standard of review (meaning courts engaged in a searching review of the government action). In 1990, the Supreme Court changed course, holding that an incidental burden on religious practices flowing from a generally applicable law would essentially be subjected only to rational review. If, however, the Court concluded that the government actually meant to target religious conduct, strict scrutiny would be employed.

Two situations serve as useful examples. Assume a state has a generally applicable law allowing state employees to be fired for drug use. A state employee is a Native American who smokes a certain drug as part of religious ceremonies. That employee may be fired for violating the no drug policy because the state's interest is legitimate and its means are rationally related to serving that end. Since the law is generally applicable, and there is no evidence of an intent to target religious conduct in particular, the government need show no more.

In contrast, assume that a city enacts an ordinance prohibiting the slaughter of animals. A religious group in the city slaughters animals as part of its ceremonies. There is also evidence that the generally applicable ordinance was adopted in response to complaints about the religious group and its animal sacrifices. In this case, the Court would employ the strict scrutiny standard we discuss below. This is the case even though the ordinance is generally applicable.

As opposed to generally applicable laws, the courts are inherently suspicious concerning laws that are targeted at religiously-motivated conduct and in fact place a significant burden on such conduct. Courts will uphold such laws only if the government is able to establish that it has a compelling interest for acting and that what it has done is narrowly tailored to serve that interest. As with other versions of strict scrutiny we have discussed, most laws evaluated under this test will be found to be unconstitutional.

D.   Other Liberty Rights

This Section has discussed three of the most important liberty protecting devices in the Constitution: the First Amendment, the Due Process Clause, and the Equal Protection Clause. There are other such devices, many of which you will read about in other Chapters in this book. We briefly highlight some of these additional liberty protecting devices here.

- The Second Amendment provides in part that the "right of the people to keep and bear Arms shall not be infringed." The Supreme Court has had little opportunity to interpret this amendment, and it remains (for now) unclear the extent of the liberty it protects.

- The Fourth, Fifth, and Sixth Amendments provide important protections for those accused of crimes and those people the police (or other government actors) investigate for criminal activity. You have learned about these amendments in Chapter Four (Criminal Law and Procedure).

- The Fifth Amendment also prohibits the taking of private property without just compensation. You will learn about the Takings Clause in Chapter Eight (Property).

- The Seventh Amendment provides in part that a person is entitled to a jury trial in federal court in a civil case if that person would have been entitled to have a jury in 1791 and the case has a value of greater than $20. This amendment applies only in federal courts, and was covered in the Chapter on Civil Procedure.

- The Eighth Amendment in part prohibits the imposition of cruel and unusual punishment. This amendment embodies a proportionality requirement. In other words, the punishment must at least roughly fit the crime. The Supreme Court has held that one assesses the constitutionality of a punishment by considering the "evolving standards of decency" in society.

- The main body of the Constitution prohibits laws that criminalize past conduct (the Ex Post Facto Clause) as well as a legislative "conviction" of a crime (a Bill of Attainder). U.S. Const. art. I, § 9, cl. 3 (federal government) and U.S. Const. art. I, § 10, cl. 1 (state governments).

- The federal government may not suspend the writ of habeas corpus "unless when in Cases of Rebellion or Invasion the public Safety may require it." U.S. Const. art. I, § 9, cl. 2. The writ of habeas corpus is the means by which a person may challenge the legality of his or her continued detention by the government.

- A state may not deny to the citizens of other states certain "privileges and immunities" of its own citizens. U.S. Const. art. IV, § 2, cl. 1. This is an equalizing clause, in that a state is not required to provide anything to a person. Rather, it simply must treat state citizens and non-state citizens equally unless it has a very good reason for not doing so. The Supreme Court has held that three rights are implicated by this clause: (1) the right of access to courts; (2) the right to own and dispose of property; and (3) the right to engage in a trade or business.

- A state may not enact a "Law impairing the Obligation of Contract." U.S. Const. art. I, § 10, cl. 1. While this clause (referred to as the Contracts Clause) could have been interpreted to impose significant limitations on state conduct, in fact it has not been. Instead, courts largely defer to legislative judgments when the Contracts Clause is implicated.

- Finally, the Ninth Amendment provides that "[t]he enumeration in the Constitution, of certain rights, shall not be construed to deny or disparage others retained by the people." One might imagine that this amendment is the font for innumerable constitutional rights. However, it has not been interpreted in this way. Indeed, many people would argue that the Supreme Court essentially has read the Ninth Amendment out of the Constitution.

VI. CONCLUSION

As should be clear from this Chapter, American constitutional law is a rich and complex field. Both the governmental structure the Constitution provides and the protections of individual rights it affords touch millions of people everyday. Our fundamental goal was to provide you with a basic overview of the Constitution in the hope that your interest will be spurred to find out more.

Chapter 8

PROPERTY LAW

By — Paul Boudreaux

SYNOPSIS

I. INTRODUCTION

Property law concerns the ownership, use, and resolution of disputes concerning land, buildings, and things. In the United States, as in most societies in history, most property is owned by private persons or organizations. What benefits does private ownership have over communal ownership — an idea that many societies adopted (and then many abandoned) in the twentieth century? One argument is that the desire to own private property is a natural aspect of human behavior. Another argument is that encouraging private control of property — and the private receipt of profits from using that property — encourages the productive use of resources. This encouragement of productivity is one the themes that runs through U.S. property law.

Most of U.S. property law is made by state courts, through the case-by-case *common law* process. Much of property law stems from old English law, which was transferred to North America by English settlers. Sometimes, state or local statutes have overridden the common law, especially in instances in which modern public policy favors the protection of unsophisticated citizens. Only rarely, however, does national law intrude into the rules concerning private property.

United States law generally recognizes three types of property. The first is *real property*, which includes land and buildings. The second type is *personal property*, which includes moveable objects, such as books, cars, money, and intangible but unique property, such as stocks and bonds. The third type is *intellectual property*, which includes the creations of the mind.

II. "FIRST OWNERSHIP" — GAINING TITLE TO PROPERTY THAT NO ONE OWNS

Let's start with the question of how a person — let's call her Olive — can gain *title* (which is another word for ownership) to property that nobody already owns, such as a wild animal. The most common and simplest way is simply to *capture* it. A famous early nineteenth century case in New York held that, between two young men who were hunting a fox, the capturer got the title, not the man who had been chasing the fox without success. Today, the capture rule is still used in some cases for property such as minerals, oil, and gas. Under traditional law, law awarded the title to such resources to the person who had the initiative to capture them. The rule is also straightforward and simple, and thus easy to understand. Courts often adopt legal rules because they that are straightforward and easy to administer. During the twentieth century, however, a trend was for courts to adopt property rules that were more complicated because they yielded, as a whole, fairer results.

Another way to gain title to property that nobody already owns is to *labor* on the property. Let's say that Andy mistakenly takes a piece of firewood that actually belongs to Olive, and Andy carves the wood into a valuable sculpture. A court probably would allow Andy to keep the sculpture, over Olive's objections, because of Andy's labor, although Andy probably would have to compensate Olive for the value of the piece of firewood.

The idea of encouraging useful labor is evident in the law of *intellectual property*. If Olive writes a novel, invents a machine, or creates computer software, the law gives her the exclusive right to use and sell these creations. No one else can legally copy these creations without Olive's permission. Because these forms of intellectual property are so easy to copy, and because copying is easily accomplished across state lines, however, the U.S. Congress has enacted statutes that set forth procedures for registering and enforcing these intellectual property rights. The U.S. Constitution authorizes Congress to enact these laws. The statutes protect *copyright* (which covers written works, such as books, songs, or software), *patents* (including inventions), and *trademarks* (images used in commerce). Because of these federal laws, few states courts today recognize any additional "common law" intellectual property rights. There is no property right in simply a "good idea," for example.

Because of the rapid growth in technology-related intellectual property, this topic is one of property law's most rapidly changing areas. Some of the stormiest controversies in intellectual property include the following questions: whether facilitating others to copy intellectual property, such as through an Internet music-downloading site, is itself a violation of law; whether a celebrity holds a property right to his or her likeness or voice; and whether scientists can gain the exclusive right to life forms created in a laboratory.

III.   TRANSFERRING TITLE

The most common way for Olive to transfer property to another owner is, of course, to sell it. The special rules for selling land through a written *deed* are discussed below, in Section VII of this Chapter. This current section addresses other ways in which the title to property can be transferred.

A.   Death

When Olive dies, her property is distributed according to her written *will*. State laws try to ensure that an interpretation of a will reflects the true desires of the decedent. But rarely today does the law allow a person to distribute his or her property on the deathbed, as used to be common in the days before most people were literate. If Olive dies without a will, the state law of *inheritance* determines the distribution of her property. These recipients are called *heirs*; properly, only persons who inherited property not through a will should be called heirs. Olive's children, if any, inherit her property first; if she had no children, it then goes to her other relatives.

B.   Gifts

Transferring personal property typically isn't accomplished by a written document (with the exception of state laws for automobiles); it is usually done simply by an oral statement, or by an action. The law concerning the making of a *gift* is surprisingly complex. Because law wants to avoid ambiguities over whether the original owner truly intended to make a gift, traditional law required the owner to hand over *manually* the property in some way (or, for something that can't be moved easily, such as a locked chest, to hand over manually the keys). Only slowly are courts allowing a gift to be accomplished (and thus irrevocable) solely by a piece of paper, such as a latter saying, "I'm making a gift to you." All courts still hold that a mere *promise* to make a gift (such as a letter stating, "I will give you my gold necklace for your birthday") is not binding until the gift is delivered manually. Likewise, promises to make a gift at death are invalid because law wants to encourage people to make wills.

C.   Bailment

An owner may allow another person to have temporary possession of the property; this is a *bailment*. Giving one's car to a valet to park, leaving a suit at the dry cleaner, or having a shop repair one's truck are examples of bailments. Under modern law, a *bailee* (the person temporarily possessing the property) has a duty not to act negligently (in effect, to take reasonable precautions) against harm or damage to the property of the *bailor*; if the bailee does act negligently and the property is harmed, the bailee must compensate the bailor.

D.   Lost property

An owner can give up title by abandoning the property, in which case the property is up for "capture," just as with the wild animal example. But if the owner simply *misplaces* or *loses* the property, the law does *not* follow the old saying of "finders keepers, losers weepers"! To the contrary, courts recognize that everybody misplaces things; traditional law held that the original owner keeps the title to lost property, theoretically, forever; a person who loses property holds the right to demand its return from a finder. But the *finder* also has rights. If Andy finds a jewel that Olive has misplaced, Andy holds the right to possess the jewel (and act like the owner in other ways, such as recovering it if *he* misplaces it) until Olive recovers it. In many states, Olive has a fixed period time in which to recover the lost property, after which time the full title shifts to Andy.

E.   Adverse possession

It may seem strange to speak of real property (land and buildings) as becoming "lost." But law provides a means for a landowner, in a sense, to "lose" the title to land. If a landowner such an Olive fails to pay attention to a trespasser on her land, such as Andy, and she fails to use the legal process to *eject* him from the land, Olive can, over many years, lose the title of her property to Andy. This unusual and complicated process is called *adverse possession,* and it arose in centuries past, when boundaries were often uncertain and families often lived for years on farms without knowledge of the true ownership. Courts found it unfair to eject a family that might have been living and working on the land for decades.

Although state laws on adverse possession vary, nearly all states require the trespasser to accomplish the following steps: (1) occupy the land exclusively; (2) do so openly (that is, not to hide when the original owner comes to check on the land); (3) use it in a manner as if the trespasser owned it (to live in the house, if it's residential property, or farm it, if it's farmland); and (4) continue the occupation for a certain number of years (traditionally twenty years — one generation). After this time, if Olive has "slept" on her rights to eject Andy for twenty years, the court probably will hold that Andy (or his child) has "earned" the title to the land. In the fast-paced modern age, many states have decreased the time for adverse possession to as little as five or seven years, for certain types of property.

Although most adverse possession cases today involve boundary disputes, one can also adversely possess personal property (such as, for example, a valuable painting) if the original owner fails to act to recover it through a legal action against the possessor for *replevin* (to recover the painting itself) or for *trover* (to recover the value of the painting). Because, unlike with land, the original owner might have difficulty locating a lost painting, the adverse possession "clock" does not start to tick in many states until the original owner knows precisely *who* possesses it.

IV. SPLITTING OWNERSHIP OVER TIME: ESTATES AND FUTURE INTERESTS

Title to property can be shared by more than one person. This section addresses how people can share property over time. Section V addresses how people can share ownership at the same time.

Sharing property over time is very common with land. Because ownership of land over generations was of paramount importance in pre-industrial England, many owners tried to control the use of land after they sold their land, or after they died. For example, an owner might want to allow his only child, who had no children of her own, to live on the land while she is alive, but then to transfer the land to the eldest of his nephews. To handle these arrangements, English courts developed complicated rules and terminology. These rules and terminology still complicate U.S. law today.

Sharing property over time works like the following: One person can possess the property today, but at some point in the future the person must give up possession to another person. The key concept to understand is this: Both the current possessor and the future possessor are considered to be "owners" of the property right now. This is the concept of owning an *estate* in property. The current possessor holds a *possessory estate*, while the future possessor holds a *future estate* (which more commonly is called a *future interest*). Because a future interest is an ownership interest right now, even before possession, the owner of a future interest can sell it, split it up, make a gift of it, or do almost anything else that the owner of the possessory estate can do. When the owner of a future interest dies, the future interest goes to the person named in the decedent's will, or to the decedent's heirs. But each estate owner can control or transfer only the estate that each owns. Thus, the owner of the possessory estate can control and transfer only the possessory estate, while the owner of the future interest can control or transfer only the future interest.

There are a number of types of possessory estates. The most common is the *fee simple*, which entitles the owner to possess the property forever. (Real property lawyers often shorten this to simply the "fee.") Another type is the *life estate*, which entitles the owner to possess the property only during the person's life.

How are these estates created? If Olive owns the fee simple for a parcel of land, she can create a written deed that transfers the land "to Andy for life, then to Benita." After Olive signs and delivers the deed, Andy owns a life estate, while Benita owns a future interest called a *remainder*. When Andy dies, possession shifts to Benita, whose future interest (the remainder) transforms into a possessory estate (the fee simple). If the deed specified that Olive would get back the land after Andy's death (or didn't specify anything, thus retaining the future interest with Olive), Olive would hold a *reversion* during Andy's life, which would transform at Andy's death back into the fee simple.

If Olive wants to deed her fee simple to Andy, the traditional language in a deed is a grant the property "to Andy and his heirs." The term "and his heirs" doesn't actually give Andy's heirs anything; the term is simply the traditional way to signify that a fee simple is being transferred.

Olive could desire to give Andy the title to the land, but that the use of the property be restricted. Consider a grant by Olive "to Andy and his heirs, but only if the owner keeps the land as a farm; if the owner tries to build houses or stores on the land, the land transfers back to Olive." In this case, Andy would hold a *fee simple subject to a condition subsequent*, while Olive keeps a future interest called a *power of termination*. Because Olive's farm-only restriction was imposed on Andy's fee simple, it would restrict any owner in the future, including someone who bought the land from Andy or inherited it from him. If any future owner violated the farm-only restriction, Olive (or whoever then owned her power of termination) would be entitled to act affirmatively to take back the land.

If Olive's deed stated that violation of the farm-only restriction would trigger a transfer to Benita, Benita would hold an *executory interest*. In both of these examples, Olive's or Benita's future interest might ripen into the possessory estate of the fee simple if they took the land after violation of the farm-only restriction.

By allowing restrictions to be imposed on future landowners, the law enables one owner to control the land for many years, even after the person's death. In the example above, Olive's farm-only restriction would, as written, restrict the land forever, and might make the future ownership uncertain for many years. Such an outcome would conflict with another principle of property law. The principle of *free alienability* of property means the ability to buy and sell property easily. If land is freely alienable, resources are more likely to flow to productive uses and the community is likely to be better off. Long-term restrictions hamper alienability and place the future ownership of land in doubt. Consider that fifty years after Olive's death, the land might become far more valuable as land for housing. Why should future owners be hamstrung by the desires of the long-dead Olive?

In order to restrict the reach of the "dead hand," old English judges imposed some limits on the ability of an owner, such as Olive, to restrict land use by future owners. The most important limit is the complicated *Rule Against Perpetuities*. The general idea was to allow Olive to control the property while her children were alive, and until her grandchildren reached maturity (twenty-one years old), but not after that. Because the judges wanted to be able to issue a thumbs up or thumbs down concerning a grant as soon as it was written, they developed a general set of rules for evaluating grants (deed and wills). A grant is valid if its restriction on land use is guaranteed to last less than twenty-one years. It is also valid if the restriction lasts only during the lifetimes of any relative who was alive when the grant was made. But if it is possible that a restriction would linger on, leaving the future of the property in doubt, beyond the life of any of Olive's relatives who were alive when the grant was made, and more than twenty-one years into the future, the grant is invalid as written.

Consider, for example, a grant of land by Olive "to my brother Peter and his heirs, but if the property is ever sold to a housing developer, then the title shifts to my sister Rhonda and her heirs." Such a restriction might linger on for many generations (more than twenty-one years after both Peter and Rhonda are dead), creating a long-term "cloud" over the title. Such a restriction would violate the traditional Rule Against Perpetuities. Under this rule, the restriction would be wiped out, and Rhonda would receive the fee simple, with no restriction.

Because applying the traditional Rule Against Perpetuities is so complicated, many states have changed the rule by statute. Many states have adopted a revised form that allows a restriction to last for up to ninety years. In such states, a grant such as the one to Peter and Rhonda above would be re-written by law to impose a restriction that lasts only ninety years. Some states have abolished the Rule altogether.

In part because the laws of future interests are so complicated, they are used less often than in years past. If Olive wants to leave her property after her death to her young son Andy but she wants to restrict what he does with it, a more common technique today would be for Olive to set up a *trust*. The trust document provides that *legal ownership* of the property is transferred to a *trustee* (often a bank), while the *equitable ownership* goes to Andy, who is the *beneficiary*. While the trustee controls the property, it must do so solely to help the beneficiary; the trustee owes the beneficiary a *fiduciary duty*.

For example, if the property is a portfolio of stocks, the bank trustee can trade the stocks, but it must consider only Andy's interests in doing so. Such a duty might require the trustees to invest in moderate risk stocks that provide Andy with a moderate income stream. Courts typically allow a trustee to use its judgment as to whether an investment decision is reasonable. It would be a violation of the fiduciary duty, however, for the trustee to make investments only in stocks in which the trustee has a financial interest. If the fiduciary duty is violated, the beneficiary can sue the trustee.

With young children, trusts often terminate when, for example, the child turns twenty-one years old, at which time the child gets the entire fee simple. Such a grant could be worded as follows: "I grant all my property to the First National Bank as trustee for the benefit of Andy, until Andy reaches twenty-one years of age, at which time the property will transfer to Andy and his heirs."

V. CO-OWNERSHIP

Title to property also can be split by having two or more people share possession. This is co-ownership. Again, American law is stuck with some old English terminology. Each co-owner is called a *tenant* (which, in this sense, does *not* refer to someone who is leasing property). There are three types of co-ownership. First, and most common, is a *tenancy in common*. This is a fairly loose relationship; each co-owner can sell its share, split it up, or leave it in a will. If a share is transferred, the new owner becomes a new tenant in common.

The second type of co-ownership is *joint tenancy*. The chief distinction is that one joint tenant cannot transfer its share through a will; when one joint tenant dies, the other assumes the full ownership, through the *right of survivorship*. Because a joint tenancy restricts alienation, the law imposes a burden on a person who wants to create a joint tenancy to specify that a joint tenancy with the right of survivorship be intended; if a grant does not make this clear, it will create a tenancy in common. Moreover, although a share in a joint tenancy may be transferred while the owner of the share is alive, the transferee will become a tenant in common with the other owner.

The final type of co-ownership is the oddly named *tenancy by the entirety*, which is available only for married couples in some states. The couple can choose to have property acquired during marriage held as tenants by the entirety, or to be held separately by the two spouses. A tenant by the entirety can transfer a share only with the permission of the other spouse. Thus, if a married couple owns their house as tenants by the entirety, neither spouse can sell or "lose" the house without the other's permission. For example, if Olive and Andy are married, and Olive runs up large gambling debts in Las Vegas that she can't pay back, her creditors can't seize the house, because Andy did not agree to place the house at risk. This rule protects the marital home. This significant benefit of a tenancy by the entirety is one reason that same-sex couples desire the legal right to be "married."

Co-ownership among non-married persons is often precarious when the co-owners disagree how the use the property. If the co-owners can't agree, any one of them can go to court and demand a *partition* of the property, which dissolves the co-ownership. If the property is land that is easily split up, a court will order a physical partition, or a *partition in kind*. The co-ownership is partitioned into a number of smaller parcels owned by single owners. However, if the property is not easily split up — such as with a jewel or a house owned by three siblings — then a court will order a *partition by sale*, with each co-owner entitled to a share of the proceeds of the sale. Accordingly, when three children inherit a house as co-owners, the children most often work out some arrangement for one of them to become the sole owner (often for a payment to the others) or for the house to be sold. Lawyers who specialize in wills often discourage their clients from creating co-ownership in children.

When a married couple divorces, special rules govern the distribution of the spouses' property. In most states, each spouse gets to keep for himself or herself the property that he or she acquired before the marriage. Property obtained during the marriage, however, is considered *marital property* (regardless of whether it was purchased by one spouse alone). Such marital property is *equitably distributed* by the court, using a variety of factors; this is a striking example of a flexible but complicated system of law that often leads to contention between the parties. Some cases have held that one spouse's successful career, if developed with the assistance of the other spouse, is marital property to be equitably distributed.

In most western states, a system of *community property* (adapted from Spanish or French law) provides even more equality among spouses. Each spouse is deemed to own an equal share of all *earnings* of each spouse during the marriage; accordingly, both spouses must agree to any transfer of assets or large expenditure. At divorce, this community property is equitably distributed.

In most states, a surviving spouse also holds the right to a share of the decedent spouse's property, regardless of the will. Under these laws, the surviving spouse gets to *elect* to reject the will and *force* a share to be delivered to him or her. Such a rule protects a spouse from the late-in-life whims of the decedent spouse. In community property states, the surviving spouse is entitled to half of the community property; the other half may be transferred by the will.

When a couple moves from a state with community property to a state without it (or vice versa), the ownership rules do not change. Thus, if Olive and Andy are married and live in California (which has community property), earnings acquired there remain community property even if they move to Florida, although earnings acquired after the move belong to each spouse separately.

VI. LANDLORD-TENANT LAW

A separate system of law governs the *lease* (or *rental*) of property. In one sense, the *lessee* (or *tenant*) holds a possessory estate, while the *lessor* (or *landlord*) holds a future interest. But the *leasehold* relationship typically is governed by a long contractual document called simply the *lease*; this document makes leasehold law a combination of contract and property law.

The most common type of leasehold is for a fixed period of time, such as for one year, six months, or two years. This is called a *term for years* (even if the term is for only one month). A *periodic tenancy* automatically renews for another term, unless either party notifies the other ahead of time that it wants to terminate the leasehold at the end of the current term. Similarly, a *tenancy at will* continues until one party decides to terminate it. Many states require advance notice of the desire to terminate a periodic or at-will tenancy.

Because a typical residential tenant is not a sophisticated contractual negotiator, a primary theme of landlord-tenant law is the protection of the tenant against terms in the lease that might be misunderstood or be unfair to the tenant. During the twentieth century, much of landlord-tenant law was transformed from being simply a matter of enforcing contractual terms in the lease contract, to a series of statutes designed to give protection to tenants.

Under the federal *Fair Housing Act*, a landlord (or the seller of a house) generally cannot discriminate against a prospective tenant (or buyer) on the basis of race, national origin, or handicap, or against a family with children. Moreover, a landlord is required to make reasonable exceptions to rules to facilitate handi- capped persons. Some states and cities have adopted laws that further restrict a landlord's ability to discriminate on other bases, such as, for example, sexual orientation. A landlord remains free, however, to discriminate on bases not covered by any statute, such as tenants who have been convicted of a felony.

If a tenant violates a term of the lease, such as by not paying rent, most states require that the landlord go to court to obtain an order to *evict* the tenant; the law prohibits a landlord from simply using *self-help* to lock out the tenant. State laws typically set up a "summary" process for landlords to obtain eviction orders more rapidly than it typically takes to litigate a civil case. In many big cities, however, the landlord-tenant court system remains slow and cumbersome. Laws vary as to whether tenants are permitted to raise problems with the premises in such proceedings.

Likewise, even if a tenant is lawfully evicted or abandons the leasehold, the landlord has a duty to use reasonable efforts to try to re-lease the property, as part of a general duty in contract law to mitigate damages. If the landlord succeeds in doing so, the landlord can't sue the first tenant for further rent money.

Finally, most states have adopted laws that impose on a landlord a duty to maintain the physical quality of the leasehold property. The *implied warranty of habitability* requires the landlord to provide services that are essential for a "habitable" leasehold, such as working electricity, plumbing, and heat. In many states, a tenant cannot waive this right; if the lease contract contains a waiver, it is unenforceable. This form of legal paternalism is designed to protect unsophisticated tenants. Many states have extended the landlord's duty to include maintenance of commons areas, such as hallways and parking lots.

If the landlord fails to maintain these services, the tenant has a number of options. First, the tenant may terminate the lease and leave (in many states, the tenant may argue that it has been *constructively evicted* by the physical defect). Second, the tenant may stay but *withhold* some or all of the rental payments. In some jurisdictions, the tenant is required to pay the rent money into a court account, which is returned if the tenant prevails in a lawsuit. The option of withholding rent payments gives the tenant a potentially powerful lever against the landlord, by putting the burden on the landlord to file a lawsuit if the landlord believes that it is in the right.

Some free-market-oriented critics argue that the pro-tenant laws adopted in the twentieth century have had the perverse effect of discouraging the availability of low-cost rentals for low-income residents. For example, they argue, a law that allows tenants to withhold rent payments increases costs to landlords, which costs are then passed on to all tenants. Criticism has been especially pointed with regard to *rent control*, a legal system by which a government agency sets maximum rental rates and the amount by which they may rise over time. Critics argue that such laws decrease the amount of low-cost housing, by making the business of being a landlord of such housing less profitable. In response, many jurisdictions have abandoned or modified their rent control laws.

VII. THE SALE OF LAND

The purchase or sale of land with a house is the most important transaction that a typical citizen engages in. Indeed, in centuries past, only land was considered "real" property — a term that we continue to use today. Because of the importance of this transaction, law once again imposes many special rules, often designed to avoid potential disputes or to protect unsophisticated buyers.

A valid transfer of land must be accomplished through a written *deed*. This rule, which originated in the old English *Statute of Frauds*, is designed to avoid complications and uncertainties that might arise from a merely oral agreement. A valid deed does not have to take any specific form; it only has to identify the property, refer to an agreement as to price, and be signed. A purely oral agreement, by contrast, does not create a valid contract; any party can back out of such an agreement. The two significant exceptions to the deed requirement are (1) when one party *relies* on an oral agreement to its detriment (such as when an oral home buyer sells its existing home in reliance on the new purchase), and (2) when the parties take steps to *partially perform* the contractual duties, such as moving in and out of the house.

Most often, a house — or any parcel of land, for that matter — is sold through a two-step process. The process takes two steps because of the many duties that each party has to perform. In the first step, the prospective seller and buyer agree on a price and sign a document called a *contract of sale*. This document does not complete the transaction, but rather sets forth duties for each party to fulfill, in order to finish the sale. If the duties are accomplished successfully, the deal moves on to the second step. If not, the deal may fall through and no transfer of the land occurs.

A.   The First Step

First, the seller holds a duty to show that he or she holds *marketable title* — that is, that he or she truly is the sole owner of the house. If someone else has a major claim to the house — such as the government's holding a lien for nonpayment of taxes or a creditor's holding a mortgage on the house — such an *encumbrance* on the house makes the title unmarketable and the prospective buyer can back out unless the seller "cures" these problems rapidly. Encumbrances include liens, mortgages, future interests (see Section IV above), easements and covenants (see Section IX below), and any other claims to the property. They typically are discovered through a search of the public land records (see Section VIII below). Similarly, the seller usually agrees to a physical inspection of the house by a licensed home inspector and agrees to fix any significant physical problems.

Usually, a borrower will agree to pay a small amount in *earnest money* with the contract of sale, to show that the borrower is "earnest" about proceeding with the deal. More significantly, a typical buyer will have to get a *mortgage loan* in order to pay for the house. The typical contract of sale imposes on the buyer a duty to apply for such a loan with reasonable terms soon after the contract of sale. The contract also typically provides that if the buyer can't obtain such a loan, the buyer can back out of the transaction. In the year 2000, lenders routinely approved mortgage loans to families with even modest incomes, in return for the buyer's agreement to pay a high interest rate. In light of the enormous problems with such "subprime" loans a few years later, many lenders became much tighter in the lending of mortgage credit.

The mortgage loan itself can be a complicated contract (the term *mortgage* means that the borrower pledges the house as *security* in case he or she doesn't pay back the loan). Back in the year 1950, most mortgage loans were simple, with fixed rates that lasted for fifteen or thirty years. By the year 2000, however, lenders often wrote complicated loans in which the rate fluctuated. After an initially low "teaser" rate, for example, the rate might rise dramatically, under a complicated formula, a few years into the term. Many unsophisticated first-time homebuyers agreed to such loans without full knowledge of the costs to them after the first few years, often because of the encouragement of aggressive lenders. By 2008, hundreds of thousands of recent homebuyers risked losing their homes because they faced higher monthly mortgage payments than they could afford. Both the federal government and state authorities were debating new legislation to restrict the ability of lenders to encourage modest-income buyers to accept loans that they could not afford.

If a borrower fails to pay back the loan on time, the loan agreement allows the creditor (which might be the lender or, more often today, another party that has bought the loan) to *foreclose* on the property. The foreclosure process allows the creditor to sell the house at an auction, in order to satisfy the mortgage debt from the proceeds of the sale. Again, statutes give borrowers some protections. First, the creditor must give notice by mail to the borrower that it is in risk of foreclosure, and the creditor must accept late payments. Next, the creditor typically must go to court obtain an order to allow it to conduct a foreclosure auction. Then, the creditor must use good faith and diligence in getting a high price for the house at the auction. Creditors typically must notify the public of the sale (through newspaper or Internet notices, for example) and must conduct the sale at a convenient time and place.

Consider a case in which the borrower owes the creditor $100,000 on the mortgage loan. If the foreclosure auction results in sale of the house for $120,000, the creditor takes $100,000, and the extra $20,000 goes to the borrower. If the house is sold for $90,000, however, the borrower still owes the creditor $10,000. Some states prohibit a mortgage creditor from suing the borrower for such a *deficiency*. Even in states where such suits are allowed, many creditors do not sue because borrowers in foreclosure often do not have assets to pay the deficiency.

In any event, the prospect of a foreclosure often encourages a borrower/homeowner simply to abandon the house. As of 2008, many abandoned homes were magnets for vandalism and criminals, which further decreased the value of homes in low-income neighborhoods. Local governments were struggling with ways to keep these abandoned homes from becoming blights on the community.

Returning to the duties under the contract of sale, the outcomes may vary if a party fails to meet its duties under the contract. If the seller tries to back out of the deal, a buyer can go to court and demand *specific performance* of the contract — that is, a court order that the seller must complete the sale. By contrast, a court will rarely order a buyer to complete a sale; more often, a seller will have to be satisfied with keeping the buyer's earnest money or with suing for monetary compensation for the time and effort needed to put the house up for sale again.

B.   The Second Step

If all goes well with the duties imposed by the contract of sale, the parties move to the second step. This step is the *closing*. On one side, the borrower will hand to the seller a check for the *down payment* (typically, around ten percent of the purchase price, although the percentage can vary), sign the mortgage loan contract (through which the lender pays the remainder of the purchase price to the seller), and pay taxes. On the other side, the seller typically will sign documents that pay off any old mortgages or remove other encumbrances, and will sign and deliver the deed to the buyer.

Although the seller should have already shown that no encumbrances stay with the land, most borrowers will demand the further assurance of a *warranty deed*. These warranties obligate the seller to reimburse the borrower if any third person asserts a valid claim to the land at any time in the future. For example, if Olive sells her house to Andy with a warranty deed, and Benita shows up two years later with a lien on the house, Olive will have to pay Andy to have the lien removed.

By contrast, a *quitclaim deed* includes no such warranties. It is most often used when the buyer understands, and agrees, that there may be serious complications with the title to the property. For example, if Olive and Andy are engaged in a legal quarrel as to who owns the house, Benita might accept a quitclaim deed from Olive for a low price.

Finally, the homebuyer is further protected by *title insurance*, which typically is demanded by the mortgage lender. In return for a single payment at closing, the insurer agrees to pay the buyer for any future claim to the property. A typical buyer wants this assurance because it is not always easy to find and recover from a former seller, even if the seller signed a warranty deed. Insurers protect themselves by doing a search of the public land records (discussed in Section VIII).

The two-step home-buying process does not necessarily protect the borrower against hidden physical defects with the house — such as a cracked foundation, a leaky roof, or termite damage — that might not be noticed during a quick inspection. The old rule of law was *caveat emptor*, which is Latin for "buyer beware." Over time, courts concluded that such a rule was unfair to buyers, especially in cases in which the seller knew about defects with the house.

Today, most states have imposed on a seller *a duty to disclose* any important physical defect that the seller knows about. Some states require the completion of a form in which the seller must disclose information about leaks, termites, etc. If the seller fails to disclose the defect and the buyer discovers it before closing, the seller can try to cure the defect. If it is not cured, the buyer can back out of the sale. If the defect is not disclosed until after closing, the buyer can demand compensation from the seller to fix the defect.

Courts are struggling with how far to extend this duty, and whether to cover information that a typical buyer would want to know about problems *off* the property. For example, a few courts have held that a seller must inform a potential buyer about very noisy neighbors or an unusually acute crime problem in the community. Some states have reined in the courts with statutes clarifying that sellers do not have to reveal "stigma" information, such as the fact that a murder once occurred in the house. These laws are prompted by policy judgments that some information is better forgotten.

VIII.   THE RECORDING SYSTEM

A typically buyer — or more precisely, the buyer's title insurer — will search the public land records before the closing. These records are created by local governments to clarify ownership and avoid conflicting claims. If Olive receives a deed to a house, she is not required to record her deed, but she can and should record it, in order to give *notice* to everyone else that she now owns the house. Indeed, the owner of *any* interest in land — including the owner of a lien, mortgage, or future interest — can and should record his or her interests. But the recording system does not avoid all complications. Sometimes people fail to record their interests, and sometimes the records themselves contain errors. A body of law seeks to resolve these dilemmas.

The fundamental rule is this: If a person fails to record properly his or her interest in the property, that person may lose the interest to a *subsequent good faith purchaser* of the same interest — that is, to someone who doesn't know about the earlier interest. This rule encourages people to record and sometimes punishes those who do not. For example, let's say that Olive agrees to a second mortgage loan from a bank to build an extension on her house. The mortgage loan gives the bank an interest in the house — the right to foreclose. The bank fails to record its mortgage. If Olive then sells the house to Andy and he doesn't know about the mortgage (which isn't recorded), Andy and the bank have conflicting claims. The bank wants to keep its right to foreclose, but Andy doesn't want the bank to retain this right. Because the bank, by failing to record its interest, created this confusion, the bank loses this conflict. The bank loses its interest to Andy, the good faith purchaser. If the loan had been recorded, however, the bank would keep its interest, even if Andy failed to notice the record, because it was there for Andy to see.

Many states, including Florida, follow a simple rule of "notice," under which a subsequent good faith purchase extinguishes any previous unrecorded interest, unless the subsequent purchaser knew of the earlier interest in another way. Other states, including California, follow a more complicated "race-notice" rule, under which the subsequent good faith purchaser prevails only if it records its subsequent interest before the holder of the earlier interest records its interest. This rule gives an added incentive to record quickly.

In an effort to make title searching quicker and easier, many states, including Florida, have a *marketable title act*, under which an old interest in the land, such has a old deed, can be extinguished unless the owner re-records the interest at least once every thirty years. Such a rule allows a prospective buyer to limit its search to the previous thirty years. In most jurisdictions, searches are done through a time-consuming search of names in an index of interests; the searcher starts with the name of the current owner, works back through the line of former owners, and then searches for any interests that these owners might have sold to others. In a growing number of jurisdictions, all the interests in a single tract of land are recorded in a single tract index.

When there are a number of potential claimants to the same property, a number of different types of claims, and a number of different recording dates, the resolution of the conflict may become extraordinarily complex and uncertain. Fortunately, better public records, facilitated by computers, are decreasing the number of instances in which subsequent purchasers are unaware of earlier interests.

IX. RELATIONS AMONG PROPERTY OWNERS AND NUISANCE

A common saying is that one's home is one's "castle." This means that, for the most part, an owner can *exclude* anyone that he or she doesn't want, and can allow onto the land anyone that is desired. But this doesn't mean the owner can *do* everything that he or she wants with the land. An owner cannot unduly annoy the neighbors, and an owner must abide by government regulations. Relations among neighbors are addressed in this section; Section XI addresses government regulation.

A landowner risks a lawsuit under tort law if he or she creates a *nuisance*, which is defined as using land so as to unreasonably interfere with another's use or enjoyment of his or her land. A landowner who constantly plays window-shaking music at 3 a.m. or burns tires in the backyard probably creates a nuisance to nearby landowners. But determining what is "unreasonable" is up the court; nuisance lawsuits against polluting factories in the nineteenth century usually failed because it was then considered a reasonable activity to pollute, considering the jobs and wealth that industry brought to a community. Pollution in a growing industrial city was a fully "reasonable" activity, these courts held. These cases showed the importance of *context* in deciding nuisance cases. Nuisance law is most often used today in relations among neighbors. But a court will not recognize a nuisance simply because the complaining neighbor is abnormally sensitive.

In addition to the discretion of the court in deciding whether annoying conduct is an actionable nuisance, the court also holds great flexibility in ordering a remedy. The most traditional remedy is for the court to issue an *injunction* — that is, for the court to order the offending party to stop creating the nuisance. In some cases — such as when the nuisance is fairly minor and holds some social value — the court may order only that the defendant compensate the plaintiff for the nuisance. Such compensation is, after all, the usual remedy for a violation of tort law. The availability of this lower-level remedy makes courts more likely to find that a nuisance has occurred. Next, a court can order that the nuisance may continue, but that the offending defendant must pay the plaintiff to move away. In a famous case from rural New York, a cement plant company was ordered to compensate a homeowner so that the homeowner could move further away from the vibrations and smoke that created a nuisance. Finally, and most creatively, a court can order that the plaintiff must pay the defendant to move away. In another famous case, a real estate developer outside Phoenix built a community for retirees very close to an existing cattle feeding operation that produced a million pounds of manure per day. Because the cattle operation was there first, the court held that the developer had "come to the nuisance" — conduct that usually bars any remedy. But because the future of the Phoenix area clearly was destined for suburban sprawl, and because allowing the cattle operation to stay would be unfair to the retirees who had moved there, the court ordered the developer to pay the cattle business to relocate.

X. SERVITUDES: EASEMENTS AND COVENANTS

A landowner's use of property also can be restricted by private agreements. One landowner may agree, for payment, to do something with the land, or to refrain from doing something with the land. In this sense, the land "serves" the interests of another person. Accordingly, these restrictions are called *servitudes*. The restricted land is "burdened" with the servitude. A servitude is an encumbrance that can and should be recorded. Accordingly, a buyer of the burdened land with a recorded servitude must obey the restriction. If a servitude is *not* recorded, a good faith purchaser who buys the land without notice of it will be relieved of the restriction. There are two types of servitudes: *easements* and *covenants*.

A.   Easements

An easement allows one party to *use* the land of another. The most common example is to physically enter the burdened land. For example, Olive may sell to Andy an easement to enter onto her property. Unlike an informal *license* or *permission* (which can be revoked), a formal easement almost always must be created in writing and cannot be revoked, unless the written agreement so provides. Olive's burdened property is called the *servient* property. An easement does not give the owner the exclusive right to use the property; Olive may still use her land, but may not use it in a way to hinder Andy's easement.

If the easement helps Andy in enjoying his own property — for example, if he is a neighbor who crosses Olive's land as shortcut to get to a bus stop every day — Andy's land is the *dominant* property. The easement is *appurtenant* (meaning "attached to") to Andy's land. If Andy sells his land to Benita, the right to the easement on Olive's land goes with it. If, however, the easement simply helps Andy personally without regard to land ownership — such as, for example, if Andy lives across town but uses the easement to watch birds on Olive's land — then the easement is *in gross*. Although older cases held that an in gross easement could not be sold, today most courts hold that easements of any kind can be sold.

Although an easement typically must be created in writing, there are a few exceptions. If Olive splits up her property into four sections, for example, and sells Benita a part with no ground access to the outside world, a court may give a Benita an *easement by necessity* over another of the sections. In addition, if Andy crosses Olive's property every day for many years, and Olive does nothing to stop him, he may earn an easement by adverse possession — an *easement by prescription*.

B.   Covenants

A covenant is a very flexible form of servitude that makes it, today, the most common private method of controlling the use of land. A covenant is simply a legally enforceable promise; a covenant that concerns land is a *real covenant*. The landowner promises to do something, or to refrain from doing something, on its land.

If Andy doesn't want Olive to plant trees on her land because they would block sunlight from reaching Andy's backyard, Andy can purchase a real covenant from Olive that restricts her from planting the trees — a *negative* covenant. Alternatively, Andy could buy a covenant that required Olive to trim existing trees — an *affirmative* covenant.

Real covenants are especially popular in the creation of planned housing communities, in which all homeowners are bound by a series of covenants that require each to, for example, mow the grass, keep the house painted, not hang laundry in the back yard, and not have loud parties after midnight. These covenants make such communities attractive to prospective residents who want assurances that their neighbors will be "good" neighbors. In the past few decades, about half of all new houses in the United States were built in developments with deeds that contain a set of restrictive covenants.

While some commentators believe that the growth of covenant-restricted communities reflects the voluntary desires of modern Americans for assurances about their communities, other commentators assert that these covenants too often enforce social conformity that stifles individualism. Real-estate developers have been especially vigorous in recent years in imposing very intrusive covenants — for example, covenants against placing signs in the yard or against having pets. Most courts have rejected arguments that homebuyers hold a "right" not to obey certain covenants. In a famous case from California, the state Supreme Court held that a condominium buyer had to obey a no-pet rule, despite her argument that her cat was an indoor feline that bothered no one. To allow such a cat-by-cat review of the application of a covenant in courts would create an unacceptable uncertainty for both developers and neighbors, the court reasoned.

In some instances, however, courts may strike down a covenant for violating a statute or other public policy. For example, it used to be very common for deeds in a community to include a racist covenant that prohibited owners from selling to anybody except white people. The U.S. Supreme Court held in 1948 that enforcing such a covenant would involve government participation in racism, and thus would violate the U.S. Constitution. Similarly, covenants that prohibit group homes for people with disabilities may violate the federal Fair Housing Act.

At the state level, legislatures have enacted statutes to make other specific types of covenants unlawful — for example, a covenant prohibiting the display of any flag, including an American flag. Indeed, public outcry over the cat case encouraged the California legislature to enact a law making no-pet covenants unenforceable in certain circumstances. Some commentators have encouraged legislatures to enact a homeowner's right to engage in free expression by, for example, putting up political signs in the front yard. Environmentalists argue that residents should have the right to engage in environmentally friendly practices, such as drying laundry on a clothesline (something that is barred by most residential development covenants) or replacing grass with less thirsty plants in order to conserve water.

XI. GOVERNMENTAL LAND USE LAWS

Finally, a landowner's use of land can be restricted by government statutes. Most local governments have enacted a series of *land use laws* that constrain the private use of land in order to further some public interest or desire.

A.   Zoning Laws

For centuries, governments have enacted land use laws to protect the public — for example, by prohibiting that houses be made of wood in a dense, fire-prone city. But starting in the twentieth century, governments expanded the reach of their land use laws. Governments now create zoning maps under which land in one zone can be used only for housing, in another zone only for commerce, and in another zone only for industry. Governments also restrict the size and height of buildings in certain zones. Early zoning laws targeted the juxtaposition of incompatible land uses, such as a housing development next to a smelly factory; in effect, these laws prevent some nuisances from occurring. Because of the power of these zoning restrictions, the entire set of land use laws is often called the *zoning law*.

Land use laws are justified as maintaining property values for the majority of the landowners in the community, even if some landowners might benefit from another land use. In a famous case from the 1920s involving the new zoning law of Euclid, Ohio, the U.S. Supreme Court upheld the general power of a local government to restrict land uses through zones. The court rejected the argument of a landowner in Euclid — which asserted that land zoned for houses was more valuable as commercial property — that it held a constitutional right to use its property as it wished. Interestingly, one reason that the court upheld the zoning power was the benefit to homeowners in the community of keeping out apartment buildings — a somewhat elitist rationale that continues to haunt governmental land use laws.

Most zoning laws contain some exceptions. First, a landowner whose existing land use would conflict with a new zoning law — such as a small store owned by Olive in an area now zoned for houses — may be permitted to continue its *nonconforming use*. To require Olive to close or sell her business would unfairly disrupt her expectations, many governments conclude. Next, the zoning law may provide for a *conditional use*, which enables a landowner to make a special application to build an otherwise unpermitted use in a certain area, upon a showing that the proposed land use would be compatible with its neighbors. Building a small hospital in a residential area is a common example of such a conditional use. Finally, if a landowner can prove that its specific parcel of property cannot be used profitably under the zoning laws, it can sometimes obtain a *variance* to use the land differently, as long as it does not conflict with neighbors.

Zoning laws cannot violate a landowner's constitutional rights. Thus, a town cannot lawfully enact a land use that prevents a homeowner from placing a political sign in the front yard, even if such a law might benefit the community at large by reducing clutter and improving visibility. Americans hold a First Amendment right to engage in free speech by placing signs in their yards. Notice the contrast here between mandatory governmental laws (which cannot restrict free speech) and private community covenants, which can restrict free speech, because the residents presumably have chosen voluntarily to live in a covenant-bound community. In contrast to the sign example, however, many state courts have held that governments can restrict the appearance of buildings for aesthetic reasons — which in turn might increase the values of neighboring properties — especially if the law is part of a historic preservation plan or a program to maintain a unique appearance, such as the laws restricting the appearance of buildings in New Orleans' distinctive French Quarter.

Some critics argue that local governments, especially in suburbs, abuse their land use powers by, in effect, "zoning out" low-cost housing. This harkens back to the anti-apartment reasoning in the famous case from Euclid, Ohio. By "zoning out" apartment buildings, mobile homes, modest townhouses, and even small single-family houses, a suburb can in effect bar poor people from moving to the suburb. This effect concentrates poor people in the small number of communities where low-cost housing is permitted. Although suburbanites traditionally have resisted the movement of poor people into their communities, in recent years advocates have changed some minds by arguing that many moderate-income citizens — such as schoolteachers, police officers, and garbage workers — are necessary for the success of even the most affluent communities. The New Jersey courts were the first to hold that a town's system of *exclusionary zoning* laws violated principles of the state constitution; some states now require each town and city to make some effort to provide for their "fair share" of low-cost housing. Requiring new private developments to set aside a share of the new construction for low-cost housing has proven to be an effective way of moving towards this goal.

Similar disputes simmer over laws that restrict the composition of households. In a case from the 1970s that many now disparage, the U.S. Supreme Court held that a town near a university could lawfully prohibit more than two unrelated persons from living in a house, thus in effect banning college group houses. The benefit to the community of peace and quiet overcame the argument of freedom of association, the Court held. But the same Court has struck down, citing the sanctity of the family, a law that limited the number of related persons who can live in one house.

B.   Takings

Perhaps the most prominent controversy in land use law concerns a property owner's right, through the Fifth Amendment of the U.S. Constitution, not to have the property "taken for public use without just compensation." Sometimes referred to as the "taking" right, this short provision encompasses many issues.

First, the right implicitly refers to the government's power of *eminent domain*, through which government has for centuries held the power to "take" the title to private property and put it to public use. The government must provide the landowner with "just compensation," which is usually the fair market value of the taken property. Governments often exercise eminent domain in order to expand a highway, build a public school or public park, or construct a new sewage plant. In recent years, however, local governments have used eminent domain to facilitate public-private partnerships to, among other things, revitalize old commercial downtowns. In a recent case, the U.S. Supreme Court held that a town meets the Constitution's "public use" requirement even if transfers land taken by eminent domain to private hands, as long as the town does so to further its view of the public interest. The public outcry over this decision in 2005 prompted many state governments to enact laws to prohibit their local governments from using eminent domain in this manner.

More common are claims by a landowner that a government land use law imposes such a heavy financial or regulatory burden that the law should be considered a "taking," requiring the payment of just compensation. Interestingly, there is no evidence that the framers of the Fifth Amendment believed that a regulation of land use, without taking of the title, could ever be a compensable "taking." Nonetheless, both the federal courts and state courts have developed a body of law on the issue of *regulatory takings*.

The U.S. Supreme Court has held that if government regulates private land so intensively that it removes "all economically beneficial use" of the land, the government conduct constitutes a taking, unless the regulation was in effect regulating a common-law nuisance. Thus, if Olive purchased a three-acre beachfront property with the reasonable expectation that she could build a dozen valuable houses on the land, but the local government then prohibited her from building anything or running any business on the land, then Olive would have a strong case that the government must pay her for the diminished value of the property.

If the land use restriction allows Olive to retain some economically beneficial use of the land — such as the ability to build one house on the three acres — she probably would not be able to demand compensation, even though the value of the land might have been diminished by more than half because of the land use restriction. To allow a landowner to demand compensation for any diminished value of land would, in effect, cripple the power of government to zone.

A variant of takings law addresses situations in which the government conditions the approval of a land use permit on the landowner's providing some payment — either in the form of a monetary *impact fee* or through the *exaction* of title to land — to compensate for the expected harmful impact to the community of the landowner's planned construction. If Olive is a developer who wants to construct a large new housing development, the government can lawfully condition the permit on Olive's paying for a share of the police station, sewage service, and public road construction that the new development might necessitate. Because governments might abuse this power, however, courts have held that the government must make a case-by-case determination of the need for such compensation and the extent of the required compensation. The question of how widely governments should be permitted to use these regulatory tools is one of the most contentious questions of property law in the early twenty-first century.

XII.   CONCLUSION

In summary, we can see that the American law of property reflects principles of wider modern American legal policy. Most often, law allows owners to do what they want with their property. In some instances, however, law tilts the legal landscape — in cases such as adverse possession, the Rule Against Perpetuities, foreclosures, and zoning statutes — to try to ensure that owners use the property in ways that serve the larger public interest.

Chapter 9

INTELLECTUAL PROPERTY LAW

By — Ann Bartow

I. INTRODUCTION: THERE ARE THREE INDEPENDENT AREAS OF INTELLECTUAL PROPERTY LAW: PATENT LAW, COPYRIGHT LAW, AND TRADEMARK LAW

The term "intellectual property" can refer to a patent, a copyright, or a trademark. Each is a unique area of the law. The authority to regulate trademarks stems from Article 1, Section 8, Clause 3, known as the Commerce Clause. Legislative power to promulgate patent and copyright laws comes from Article I, Section 8, Clause 8. of the U.S. Constitution. The so-called Intellectual Property Clause vests Congress with the following enumerated responsibility:

> To promote the Progress of Science and useful Arts, by securing for limited Times to Authors and Inventors the exclusive Right to their respective Writings and Discoveries;

Patents help provide monetary incentives for technological innovation. Patents usually last for about twenty years, and they provide legally enforceable monopoly rights over newly invented products or processes. Copyrights help provide monetary incentives for creative works such as novels, plays, paintings, photographs, sculptures, musical compositions, sound recordings, audiovisual works such as movies and television shows, architectural works, and computer programs. Copyrights usually last the entire life of the author plus an additional seventy years, or for a flat period of time ranging from 95 to 120 years, depending on how the work was created. Trademarks are usually words or symbols that identify the source of goods or services in commerce. They can be used in association with creative or innovative goods or services that are patented or that are copyrighted. Trademark rights last as long as the trademark continues to be used in commerce, so it is possible for a trademark to last forever.

The focus of this chapter is on U.S. intellectual property law. It is also important to know that the U.S. is a signatory to various international treaties that attempt to regulate aspects of international trade that are affected by intellectual property laws, and differences in these laws across nations. For example, the Agreement on Trade Related Aspects of Intellectual Property Rights (TRIPS) is an international agreement administered by the World Trade Organization (WTO) that sets down certain minimum standards of intellectual property protections that signatory nations must meet, to facilitate international trade.

II. PATENT LAW

There are three different kinds of patents: utility patents, plant patents, and design patents. The Patent Act is the main body of statutory law for all three. Plant patents are available to inventors (or the inventor's heirs or assigns) who invent and asexually reproduce a new variety of plant, other than a tuber propagated plant or a plant found in an uncultivated state. A plant patent lasts for 20 years from the date of filing the application, and it protects the inventor's right to exclude others from asexually reproducing, selling, or using the new plant.

A design patent is available to inventors of visual ornamental characteristics that are embodied in, or applied to, an article of manufacture. The subject matter of a design patent application may include the configuration or shape of an article, surface ornamentation applied to an article, or the combination of configuration and surface ornamentation. Examples might include a snow shovel with a decoratively shaped handle, or a stapler with a decorative element welded to it. Patents for designs last for a term of fourteen years from the date of the patent grant.

When people discuss patents, they are usually referring to utility patents. The defining characteristic of a utility patent is that it provides its owner with the exclusive rights to an idea. The idea may be very "high technology" and complex, or it may be quite simple and straightforward. The specific legal privilege conferred by a patent grant is the right to exclude others from making, using, offering for sale, or selling the invention. A patent does not confer an affirmative right to make, use, or sell or import an invention, and patent owners are sometimes precluded from exploiting their patented inventions by laws, contractual obligations, or other adverse circumstances. To illustrate: a pharmaceutical company might patent a new drug, but be unable to actually sell the drug until its safety and efficacy was demonstrated; or it may have previously agreed to license new drugs to another entity; or making and selling the drug might infringe another patent owned by someone else; or the drug could be illegal.

A.   The Effects of Patents

Companies, and sometimes individuals, obtain utility patents to "protect" their ideas. A patent gives a patent owner the exclusive right to use (or license others to use) the patented invention for a limited period of time, currently twenty years from the date of application in the United States and a similar length in many other industrialized nations. This exclusivity enables a patent owner to charge monopoly prices for the invention. Patents enable patent owners to charge consumers more for patented products than they could if others could compete with them. A patentee can reap high monopoly profits if it is the only source of a product for which there are few satisfactory alternatives. However, often a patented invention will be in competition with other products or processes that are patented by someone else, or not covered by patent protections at all. Competitors may be able to offer similar products or processes, but they cannot make or use a patented invention without being vulnerable to legal action by the patent owner.

In theory, the monopoly prices a patent owner can charge allow the patent owner to recoup the research costs and resources that were expended when the invention was developed. Monopoly profits acquired by patent owners are also available to invest in new research projects. Not every patent generates monopoly profits, however. Some patented inventions are unsuccessful in the market place, and some patents are never commercially exploited at all. Because filing a patent application and advocating for the patentability of the claimed invention (called "prosecuting a patent") can be time consuming and expensive, most companies do not file patent applications for inventions unless they expect to either make a profit or prevent a competitor from commercially exploiting a product or process. Individual (or "small") inventors will sometimes patent inventions for vanity reasons, or in hopes of attracting investors, or of selling the invention to a larger company.

Companies that invent and patent these products have the exclusive right to make and sell their inventions. Any entity that wants to make or use these particular inventions legally must obtain permission from the patent holder. Typically, the parties negotiate a license, under which the licensee remits the designated royalty to the patent owner in exchange for permission to make the patented product or use the patented process.

B.   Patent Requisites

The first step in obtaining a patent, to state a fairly obvious point, is to develop a patentable invention. When someone invents something they believe is new, searching through scientific literature and pre-existing patents in the same technological areas is necessary to determine whether the invention is eligible for a patent. This search should include patents and publications all over the world, not just in the United States.

Many inventors apply for patents in many countries simultaneously, so that their inventions are protected in as many markets as possible. There is no such thing as a "worldwide" patent, so separate patents must be obtained. In the United States, a patent application is filed with the U.S. Patent and Trademark Office. This is called prosecuting a patent. Patent examiners read the applications, often make recommendations to the applicant about making productive changes to the applications, and eventually decide whether or not a patent should issue. This process can take three years or longer. The term of a patent is twenty years from the date the patent application is filed, so the faster a patent issues, the longer it is in effect and fully enforceable.

Under Article 27 of TRIPS, signatory nations must grant patent protection to "any inventions, whether products or processes, in all fields of technology, provided that they are new, involve an inventive step, and are capable of industrial application." TRIPS has thus attempted to establish an international definition of patents. However, no two countries have identical patent laws, and the degree to which they share fundamental concepts about patentability varies. So the process for obtaining a patent in a foreign country may be very different than what was described above.

In the United States, a patentable invention can be a product, such as a new machine to clean floors, or a process, such as an inventive method of removing impurities from water. Once an invention is operable, the inventor, or anyone the inventor has assigned rights to the invention, can apply for a patent. A patent application must contain a full description of the invention that is adequate to teach others how to make or use the invention. Based on disclosures in the patent application, a government agency then makes a determination about whether the invention is sufficiently novel, useful, and nonobvious.

1.   Novelty

In the patent context, "novel" means new, something that was never made or used before in public. The reason for the novelty inquiry to is insure that no one patents a product or process that is already part of the public domain. A patent is a monopoly that must be earned. An inventor or her or his assignee earns a patent by publicly disclosing (in the patent application) a product or process that has never been made or used before, and is therefore deemed to advance scientific development for the benefit of society. TRIPS requires that a patentable invention be novel, as do most national regimes.

2.   Utility

"Useful" means operable, in the sense that the product or process achieves the result that it is supposed to. One couldn't patent a perpetual motion machine, for example, even if its design was highly novel, unless the patent applicant could prove that the machine actually worked (a dubious prospect, at least according to current scientific understanding). At one time, patent applicants had to demonstrate some sort of beneficial usefulness for the invention, but that is no longer the case. Even if the invention is so expensive and inefficient that no rational person would ever make or use it, the invention may still be eligible for a patent as long as it is capable of performing the function ascribed to it, and meets the other requirements of patentability such as novelty and nonobviousness. Usefulness is also required as a condition of patentability by TRIPS and most national patent regimes, though standards and tests for utility vary.

3.   Nonobviousness

The "nonobvious" requirement is the most difficult to describe, predict, or ascertain, because it is subjective and rooted in relativism. To be deemed nonobvious, an invention must not only be new, but must also reflect some degree of creativity and cleverness. A new invention that appears to be something anyone could have thought up without much effort would be considered "obvious" and therefore unpatentable. If the invention was rather simple, like a uniquely shaped paperclip, the specific query would be whether people ordinarily skilled in the art of designing paperclips would find the new shape obvious, or concede that the new paperclip shape was an unanticipated (and therefore nonobvious) advance in the art of using small pieces of metal wire to temporarily join sheets of paper. For a more sophisticated invention, the threshold question would remain the same, but the evaluative benchmark would be elevated. For a novel invention related to genetic engineering, the test of obviousness might be whether or not the invention was something that a PhD-holding molecular biologist of ordinary skill might have stumbled across with little effort or imagination. Alternatively expressed, to be sufficiently nonobvious, an invention must differ from the state of the pertinent art enough so that it would not have been obvious to a person having ordinary skill in that field. Inventions deemed "obvious" are said to represent mere technical tinkering or journeyman modifications of existing inventions, and are not patentable.

C.   Patent Disclosures

To be valid, a patent must explain the claimed invention clearly and specifically enough that a person with an ordinary level of skill in the pertinent science or field could understand how to make or practice it. This is called enablement. It must also disclose any information known by the inventor about the best mode for making or using the invention. Only by fully disclosing all pertinent information can an inventor earn a patent. Inventors who intentionally omit important details about their inventions are said to have engaged in misconduct, and this can render an otherwise valid patent unenforceable.

Once a patent issues, the information contained within the patent application becomes available to anyone who is interested. Sometimes patent applications are published and accessible after a set period of time (e.g., 18 months) even before a patent issues. It is through disclosure of information contained in a patent application that the technology embodied in an invention is dedicated to society. The patent provides the invention owner with exclusive rights to make and use the invention for a set period of time, but after a patent expires anyone is free to use whatever they have learned from a patent application.

D.   Patent Scope

The claims of a patent set forth the metes and bounds of what the government has granted to the patent owner, describing the scope of the invention and what the patent owner can prevent others from making, selling, or using. Claims that describe an invention very generally are referred to as broad claims, and are used to try to construct a large scope of exclusivity. However, if claims are drafted too broadly, they may overlap with knowledge and technology that already exists, beyond that which has been newly conceived of by the patent inventor. Claims that do this are said to "read on the prior art," and are not enforceable. Narrowly constructed claims are less likely to read on the prior art, but because they carve out a more slender scope of exclusivity for a patent owner, are usually viewed as less valuable.

If two inventors independently come up with the same invention at about the same time, the person who can prove they thought of it first wins the right to patent it, as long as they diligently reduced their idea to practice. In the rest of the industrialized world, however, the first person to file a patent application would win the priority contest, even if they were not the first to conceive the patentable idea.

E.   Patent Infringement

If another entity makes or uses a patented invention without the permission of the patent owner, this entity is said to be an infringer. Patent owners can enforce their exclusive patent rights by asking courts for injunctive relief (typically a court order requiring the infringer to stop engaging in infringing activities) and for monetary damages. Patent infringement suits tend to be very complicated and expensive. In addition to denying that they are infringing a patent, an accused infringer can attack the validity of the patent at issue. If it can convince a court that a patent is invalid, an accused infringer prevails whether its conduct was putatively infringing or not. Bringing an infringement suit therefore can put a patent at risk.

Exact copying of an invention is called literal infringement. When copying is close to exact, with a few minor changes or substitutions, infringement is characterized as being via the doctrine of equivalents. A patentee who wins an infringement claim is usually eligible for injunctive relief as well as a monetary damages award.

III. COPYRIGHTS

The primary source of statutory authority on copyright law in the United States is the Copyright Act. This is a long and complicated statute that contains a wide array of statutory provisions. One copyright school has described it as "mind numbing in its complexity." It is frequently amended, and should be consulted at the start of any research project involving copyright law.

A.   Copyrights Defined: A Limited Monopoly on Expression

Copyright protection generally extends to original works of authorship including literary works, musical works (a song's melody and lyrics, if any, can be covered by separate copyrights), scientific and technical texts, computer programs, dramatic works, pantomimes and choreographic works, pictorial, graphic and sculptural works, motion pictures and other audiovisual works, sound recordings, and architectural works. Copyright protection does *not* extend to any idea, procedure, process, system, method of operation, concept, principle, or discovery, regardless of the form in which it is described, explained, or illustrated, as ideas are the province of patents.

1.   Obtaining Copyright Protection

Copyright protection is secured automatically when the work is created, and a work is "created" when it is fixed in a copy or phonorecord for the first time. "Copies" are material objects from which a work can be visually perceived either directly or with the aid of a machine or device, such as books, sheet music, film, videotape, or microfilm. "Phonorecords" are material objects embodying fixations of sounds such as cassette tapes, CDs, and MP3 files. No publication or registration or other action in the Copyright Office is currently required to secure copyright. There are advantages to registering a copyright, as well as to affixing a copyright notice on each copy of a work, but neither is necessary to secure copyright protection.

Copyright formalities such as registration and notice were eliminated in the United States when it signed onto the Berne Convention. As with patents, there is no such thing as an "international copyright" that will automatically protect a copyrightable work throughout the entire world. The Berne Convention, originally enacted in 1886, is an international treaty establishing minimum substantive standards for protection of copyrights in literary and artistic works. It defines literary and artistic works broadly as "every production in the literary, scientific[,] and artistic domain, whatever may be the mode or form of its expression." This definition was adopted as part of TRIPS, and applies to all TRIPS member nations regardless of whether they are Berne Convention signatories.

Any original work of authorship is generally copyrighted from the moment of its creation. Observing voluntary formalities, such as registering a copyright with a government entity or placing a notice of copyright on copies embodying the protected work, may be advantageous for commercial or litigation purposes, but is generally not necessary to obtain a valid, enforceable copyright in any Berne signatory nation.

2.   Copyright Ownership and Duration

Simply being the author of a copyrightable work generally makes one a copyright owner, unless the creator is an employee who has produced the work during the course of her or his employment. In the United States, under the "work for hire" doctrine, the employer is deemed both the author and the owner of the copyright in any work created by an employee. In other countries, an employer may own the copyrights in the works created by her or his employees, but the employees are still recognized as the authors of the works. This right of recognition (or attribution) of authorship is sometimes called a "moral right." A second, related moral right is the right of integrity, meaning that work should not be destroyed or changed, so that the artistic vision of the work's creator is preserved. Moral rights get only limited recognition in the United States under copyright law, but authors can sometimes secure rights of recognition and integrity through negotiated contract provisions, or by utilizing certain aspects of trademark law pertaining to "false designations of origin."

Before 1978, copyright was secured either on the date a work was published with a copyright notice or on the date of registration if the work was registered in unpublished form. The copyright endured for a first term of 28 years from the date it was secured, and the copyright was eligible for renewal for a second 28 year term. The Copyright Act of 1976 extended the renewal term from 28 to 47 years for copyrights that were subsisting on January 1, 1978.

A work that was created on or after January 1, 1978, is automatically protected from the moment of its completion, and copyright protection lasts for the author's entire life plus an additional 70 years after the author's death. In the case of a joint work, the term lasts for 70 years after the last surviving author's death. For works made for hire, and for anonymous and pseudonymous works, the copyrights last 95 years from the date of publication or 120 years from creation, whichever is shorter.

3.   Copyright Scope: Protection of Expression, But Not Ideas

Copyrights protect expression, but not underlying ideas. In other words, copyright protection encompasses the expression of a concept, rather than the concept itself. To ascertain what elements of a work are copyrighted and protectable, it is necessary to cognitively separate creative expression from the underlying idea that is expressed. To provide a very rough illustration: The cliché "When in Rome, do as the Romans do," is an expression of the idea that one should observe local customs. The exact wording of the phrase is copyrightable expression. The idea that one should observe local customs, however, would still be freely expressible using alternative language. The sentence, "If you are in Athens, behave like an Athenian," might communicate the same concept, but it would not infringe a copyright in the "When in Rome" axiom. (It should be noted, however, that short words or phrases are often considered unworthy of copyright protection altogether.)

Consider how many "cop buddy movies" that have been made which follow the same basic formula: Two police officers with very different backgrounds are put together as partners against their will. One is very straight-laced, and the other is a bit of a screw up. At first they are at loggerheads, but eventually they come to appreciate each other as they solve crimes and apprehend nefarious bad actors against a backdrop of improbable car chases, gun fights and explosions. Dozens of popular action films fit that pattern or "idea," but each is executed with unique expressive attributes, and those are the copyrightable parts of the endeavor.

In the visual context, the idea/expression dichotomy can be illustrated as follows: A photographer may take a photograph of a mountain, turn the photo into a poster, and sell thousands of copies. She has a copyright in her photograph, which no one can copy without infringing her copyright unless she gives them permission to do so. However, she cannot use her copyrights to prevent someone else from taking an independent photograph of the same mountain, and making and selling competing posters featuring the alternate, competing photograph. Each photographer has a copyright in his or her own photographic work, but neither has any exclusive rights pertaining to the mountain itself, and neither can prevent the other from exploiting photographs of the mountain, even if photographs are similar (which they are bound to be, given that they depict the same subject!).

4.   Facts Are Not Copyrightable

Copyright law protects creative expression only, and is not supposed to provide exclusive rights with respect to facts or information. However, works comprised of facts are copyrightable. By way of illustration, a newspaper story consisting exclusively of factual information is protected by copyright, and cannot be copied without permission. However, all of the information contained within the story can be extracted from the article and "re-expressed" by an independent party without permission, and without infringing the copyright in the original story. The copyright protects the expression of the facts (such as word choices and the structure and tone of the piece), but the facts themselves are in the public domain, and can be freely used by others. Biographies and histories can be copyrighted, but copyrights do not give anyone the exclusive right to the factual information contained therein. However, sometimes it is so difficult to separate information from expression, individuals are afraid to use uncopyrighted (and uncopyrightable) information contained in copyrighted works for fear of being accused of copyright infringement. For this reason, some people believe that aggressive protection of copyrights, particularly in informational works, undermines and inhibits our capacity to communicate with and learn from each other.

5.   Exclusive Rights

A copyright owner has a range of exclusive rights with respect to the copyrighted work, including the right to reproduce the work, distribute copies of the work, perform or display the work publicly, and to make derivative works based upon the copyrighted work. The copyright owner can choose to exercise these exclusive rights herself, or to license some or all of these rights to others. Emerging electronic technologies, which permit the transmission of copyrighted works over networks, raise complicated questions about what constitutes a copy or performance in the digital environment, since computers necessarily make copies of everything they display, and can save or transmit everything they receive. Meaningful protection of copyrights requires copyright owners to be able to detect and stop the unauthorized dissemination of digital copies, but this is difficult to achieve both legally and technologically.

a.   Anti-Circumvention Laws

Certain provisions of the Copyright Act render illegal technology that could circumvent other technology that is used to restrict and control the dissemination of copyrighted works. Such "anti-circumvention laws" are aimed at reassuring copyright owners who fear that no matter how much they invest in technological means to protect their works from unauthorized use or reproduction, they are vulnerable to the ingenuity of hackers and thieves. Copyright owners that feel they will be able to manage and control dissemination of their works online are more likely to engage in electronic commerce.

Anti-circumvention laws can be problematic, however. Making certain technologies illegal without repressing and discouraging innovation of new technologies in general requires artful drafting of the pertinent legislation. Additionally, some technologies can be employed for both positive, productive applications and negative, "circumventing" purposes simultaneously. Efforts must be made to prohibit only the destructive uses of a technology, rather than the technology itself.

b.   Automated Rights Management

Some transactions involving copyrighted works can happen automatically, through use of electronic data attached to a copyrighted work, which identifies the owner, and sets terms and conditions for use of the work. Automated rights management can benefit from (and be encouraged by) consistent legal standards with respect to the interpretation and enforceability of automatic rights management contracts.

6.   Fair Use

Copyright protection does not provide an absolute monopoly. Not every unauthorized use of parts of a copyrighted work, or even of the entire work, is an infringement. Even if a work is "fact free" and comprised entirely of creative expression, sometimes the work (or at least small portions of the work) can still be used by others without the copyright owner's permission, but without constituting an act of copyright infringement. This is because of the doctrine of fair use, which is explicit in copyright law. One can make "fair use" of someone else's copyrighted work if the use is scholarly, or for purposes of news reporting or criticism, or for many other reasons, as long as the use is deemed fair and reasonable, given the applicable circumstances.

A court weighing whether an unauthorized use was fair will consider factors such as the purpose of the use, how much of the copyrighted work was taken, how much of that portion was protectable, and whether the use will have a negative effect on the market value of the original work. Non-permissive uses that are transformative and lead to the creation of other new works are more likely to be deemed fair than straightforward acts of copying.

The Berne Convention defines fair uses narrowly. Fair use varies from nation to nation, and individual countries are likely to have internally inconsistent fair use policies as well. Whether or not an unauthorized use is a fair one (and therefore neither infringing nor monetarily compensable) is a subjective determination that is made by a court after the use has been made, and after an infringement suit has been brought against the user by the copyright owner. As a result, "fair use" can be a very expensive and risky right to assert, even if the unauthorized user prevails with a fair use defense at trial.

Some copyright owners use licenses to force individuals to contract away any rights to use a copyrighted work that they might otherwise have as a consequence of the doctrine of fair use. For example, an online publication could require aspiring readers to agree via a license not to quote from the publication as a condition of gaining access to it. Any reader who subsequently quoted in a limited way from the work would probably not be a copyright infringer because limited quotation is usually deemed to be within the scope of fair use. However, the quoting reader would be in breach of its contract with the copyright-owning publisher.

7.   Transfers

Copyright is a personal property right, and it is subject to the various state laws and regulations that govern the ownership, inheritance, or transfer of personal property as well as terms of contracts or conduct of business. A copyright owner can transfer one or more of the exclusive rights that copyright protection confers, but the transfer of exclusive rights is not valid unless that transfer is in writing, and that writing is signed by the owner of the rights conveyed. Transfer of a right on a nonexclusive basis, however, does not require a written agreement. Recordation in the Copyright Office of transfers of copyright ownership is not required to make a valid transfer between the parties, but it does provide certain legal advantages and may be required to validate the transfer as against third parties.

8.   Computer Software

For many years computer programs could not be patented, and by default, copyrights were used to provide intellectual property protection for computer programs. Copyright legislation, originally and primarily intended for creative works, is not easily adapted to computer software, which leaves some uncertainty about how to define the scope of copyright protection in these works. Often, entities that develop or license computer software will try to imbue their computer source code with both patent and copyright-based protections. Alternatively, sometimes software developers will eschew formal intellectual property protection altogether and use licenses and technological means to keep their source code secret and proprietary. Both are responses to the uncertainty inherent in using copyright principles to protect computer software.

9.   Databases

Copyright is also the primary type of intellectual property protection that is currently available for databases. While an individual datum is "information" and therefore uncopyrightable, compilations of data can be protected by copyright if the data have been selected, compiled, or arranged with some small amount of originality or creativity. Copyright protection is available for (e.g.) maps and guides and directories, but the scope of the copyrights is narrow and does not extend to the information imbedded in these works. Databases that represent significant effort and investment may be jeopardized by readily available copying technologies. Entities have successfully asserted copyrights in database documents such as customer lists, but uncertainties about the scope of copyright protection has led many companies that own or license databases and other information products or services to lobby governments for "stand alone" intellectual property protection for databases that is not bound by the copyright law, and not subject to its limitations. Those in favor of a *sui generis* database protection argue that such a framework is necessary to protect substantial investments made to collect and organize large data collections. Opponents, who are often "downstream" data users, assert that this will compromise public access to information, and lead inexorably to perpetual monopolies for the entities that are first to collect data, to the disadvantage of other commercial entities then forced to pay high prices for the data if they are allowed to have access at all.

Database protection independent of copyright strictures is available in European Union nations via the European Communities Directive on the Legal Protection of Databases and is encouraged by Article 10 of TRIPS.

10.   Protection of Online Artistic and Literary Content

Visual, textual, and aural works are protectable by copyright even if they are freely available online. One should assume that the artistic and literary components of any given website are copyrighted, even if the site does not carry a copyright notice. Many websites use technological mechanisms to prevent or at least inhibit content copying, perhaps believing that copyright laws (or levels of adherence to copyright laws) do not adequately protect their copyrighted works.

Many websites have interactive components, and allow site users to add site content. Absent an agreement to the contrary, when someone posts something to an online forum, the author of the posting retains copyright in his or her posting. Many forum providers therefore require users to agree ahead of time to cede copyright ownership (or at least control), so that they can freely copy, edit, and delete all of the content on their sites. However, it is virtually impossible for an entity to ensure that no one makes unauthorized postings of a third party's copyrighted works on a website. A site user could, for example, post a poem she claimed to have authored that was actually written by someone else who did not authorize the posting. The person who posted the poem without the copyright owner's permission might very well be a copyright infringer. A more difficult question is whether the "innocent" website to which the poem was posted was guilty of infringement. Some countries have addressed this issue by passing laws that protect websites from liability as long as they promptly remove infringing materials from their sites when requested to do so by copyright owners.

The capabilities of the Internet to spread copyrighted works of any variety throughout the world are extensive and unparalleled. The transmission of text, sound, images and computer programs over the Internet is commonplace, and transmission of audiovisual works is becoming more widespread as networking technology improves. Cyberspace offers substantial benefits to copyright owners because it offers wide exposure and broad distribution capabilities for copyrighted works. Information and entertainment products protected by copyrights represent a significant portion of the subject matter of electronic commerce. For commerce involving digitalizable products such as music, software, films, and books, the Internet can serve both as a medium in which to advertise and promote sales, and as a system to effectuate delivery. However, it also poses dangers, such as the risk that a copyrighted work will be copied without permission and then extensively dispersed, ruining the market for the work and making it impossible for the copyright owner to profit from the work, or even recoup investment costs.

In the fall of 1998, the Digital Millennium Copyright Act ("DMCA") took effect. This legislation was intended to discourage the unauthorized use and copying of copyrighted intellectual property in cyberspace. Congress passed the DMCA primarily to implement World Intellectual Property Organization (WIPO) treaties and to provide some protection from liability for Internet and Online Service Providers (ISPs). The DMCA amended U.S. copyright laws so as to exempt all ISPs from liability for copyright infringement claims that are based solely on the

ISPs having transmitted, routed, or provided connections for information or material via a system or network controlled by the ISP or by reason of its having stored such material in the course of transmitting or routing it. It limits the liability of Internet service providers for online copyright infringements that occur as in incident of information transmission, caching, and hosting, if the service provider does not have knowledge that the material is infringing. Copyright owners can formally notify service providers of claimed infringements, whereupon the service provider must promptly remove the offending material or disable access to it. This notification-and-takedown procedure allows copyright owners to stop infringing acts without having to obtain injunctive relief from a court.

Some commentators believe that the DMCA encourages the creation and distribution of new copyrighted works by reducing the risks of online infringement. Others are concerned that it restricts the free flow of information, which hampers creativity, and protects currently existing copyrighted works at the expense of new works that now will never be originated. An ISP will be motivated to take down any material claimed to infringe a copyright, and the burden may then be on an author to get accused material reinstated. The entire process can also be abused in efforts to control or prevent certain types of online speech, or to censor particular speakers.

IV. TRADEMARKS

A.   Trademarks: Source Identifiers in Cyberspace

A trademark is a word, short phrase, symbol, picture, design, or other feature that is used in trade in conjunction with specific goods, to indicate the source of the goods and distinguish them from the commercial offerings of competitors. Though often referred to as a form of intellectual property, trademarks are more accurately described as intangible commercial property. Marks that identify the source of services (such as the name of a travel agency or dry cleaner) are most correctly denominated "service marks," but are treated virtually identically to trademarks as a matter of law. Trademarks usually appear on a product or on product packaging, while service marks appear in promotional material for services. However, service marks are therefore commonly incorporated within the general "trademark" rubric, and "trademark" or "mark" will be used to denote both trademarks and service marks below, in conformity with common practice.

Trademark owners have the right and ability under trademark law to prevent others from using confusingly similar marks. However, trademark rights do not provide a right of exclusivity with respect to the underlying products and services that are identified by the marks. Trademarks do not protect the outcomes of creative undertakings, and are never substitutes for or alternatives to copyrights or patents.

Federal trademark law is laid out in the Lanham Act, which is sometimes called the Trademark Act. Unlike patents and copyrights, which are almost exclusively creatures of federal law, trademarks can be affected by state laws. States are preempted from passing their own copyright and patent laws, but they can independently regulate trademarks, just as they do other aspects of commerce. Trademarks can be registered with the U.S. Patent & Trademark Office, but even if they aren't, they can be protectable as common law trademarks.

1.   Trademarks Are Intangible Property, But Not "Intellectual"

Though popularly referred to as a form of intellectual property, there is very little that is "intellectual" about trademarks in the sense that protectable marks do not need to reflect any effort, uniqueness, or creativity whatsoever. Patent owners receive a finite term of monopolistic control over their inventions to reward them for inventing (or investing in the invention) of new, useful, and nonobvious products and processes and making the technology behind the inventions available to the public. Copyright owners also receive a finite term of monopolistic control over copyrighted works, though of course a copyright is enforceable far longer than a patent, and the nature of a copyright monopoly is somewhat different and narrower than the exclusivity conferred by a patent. Copyright owners are given their bundle of exclusive rights to reward them for creating original works of authorship. By contrast, trademark owners can assert and retain ownership of their marks in perpetuity, and are not even theoretically obliged to provide anything creative, unique, or of value to the public.

2.   Source Identification

Part of the original justification for recognizing enforceable rights in trademarks was the idea that trademarks would protect consumers by performing source identifying functions. If the Coca-Cola Company was the only entity allowed to use the Coca-Cola(name and logo, consumers could be confident that when they bought a beverage bearing Coca-Cola(marks, it would comport with Coca-Cola Company standards (whatever they are perceived to be), and that they could contact the responsible party if they had questions about, or experienced problems with, a product or service associated with the Coca-Cola Company mark.

Companies also benefit from trademark protection to the extent that they enjoy a good reputation with consumers. Corporate interests often view protected trademarks as one mechanism for insuring that they receive the full benefits of their investments in producing quality goods and services. Trademark protection also strengthens the ability of commercial advertising to promote brand identification. Sometimes effective advertisements will even substitute for investments in quality: Research has demonstrated that consumers often prefer one brand of a product over another (even though the underlying products are identical) based on their subjective feelings about a trademark.

Marks that are virtually identical may not been deemed confusing to consumers if the goods or services they identify are very different. This is how the Dell Publishing Corporation, which makes Dell books, and the Dell Computer Corporation, which makes Dell computers, can both assert trademark rights in the word Dell.

3.   Infringement

Accusations of trademark infringement are generally made when one entity makes use of a mark that is the same or similar to a mark that is owned by another. If the competitor uses an intentionally confusing mark, such as putting a tan "Levy's" label on a pair of blue jeans to fool consumers, the "Levy's Jeans" maker is likely to be accused of trying to pass off its products as the goods of Levi Strauss & Co., and of "trading on" the Levi's(trademark. Whether something is infringing is assessed via an inquiry into whether consumers are likely to be confused. A judicial fact finder will look at how strong the mark is, and how similar the mark accused of infringing is, and make some assessment about how likely it is that the goods or services will be in direct competition or in overlapping channels of trade. The fact finder will also consider whether the accused infringer had bad motives, whether any actual consumers have been confused, and what degree of care a consumer might use when choosing the product. After considering all the evidence, a determination will be made about whether there is a likelihood of confusion. If there is, the plaintiff can usually obtain an injunction that prevents the defendant from continuing to use the confusingly similar mark. Confiscation or impoundment of offending merchandise and an award of monetary damages may be appropriate remedies as well.

The most extreme form of trademark infringement is counterfeiting, whereby one entity makes an exact copy of the trademark of another and markets the goods or services as if they were authentic. Counterfeiting is a crime, as well as a violation of civil trademark laws. If a competitor makes unauthorized use of another's exact trademark, such as by putting the "Microsoft®" logo on boxes of computer programs that were not manufactured or licensed by the software giant, that rival may be accused of counterfeiting as well as trademark infringement.

People or companies who facilitate counterfeiting or other forms of trademark infringement can be guilty of vicarious or contributory infringement. This could include landlords who rent space where counterfeit or infringing items are manufactured or flea markets or swap meets where counterfeit or infringing items are sold.

4.   Dilution

Holders of famous trademarks may also be able to assert a statutory right to prevent others from "diluting" their marks. Famous marks are generally defined as those that are widely used and broadly recognized. A judge will consider the duration, extent, and geographic reach of advertising and publicity associated with a mark, the amount volume and geographic extent of sales of goods or services offered under the mark, whether the mark is registered, and the extent of actual recognition of the mark, as measured by consumer surveys, in determining whether a mark is famous enough to warrant protection from dilution.

Trademark dilution is use of a mark by an unauthorized entity that does not fit traditional notions of infringing conduct because there is little risk that consumers will be confused or misled by the use. For example, consumers viewing a blue bicycle bearing the word "Kodak" in silver might not assume that the bicycle was manufactured by the Eastman Kodak Company, famous for producing cameras and film, and recognized by its yellow and red "K" logos and packaging. However, the Eastman Kodak Company could argue that unauthorized use of the word Kodak(by the bicycle manufacturer diluted the mark, undermining the mark's uniqueness, and unfairly usurping the goodwill associated with the mark that the Eastman Kodak Company had worked hard to generate.

There are two primary forms of actionable dilution, denominated "blurring" and "tarnishment." Blurring is an association that impairs a mark's distinctiveness. In determining whether blurring has occurred, a court will look at how similar the accused mark is to the famous mark, how distinctive the famous mark is, how exclusive and widely recognized it is, whether there is an actual association between the marks, and the defendant's motivations. Tarnishment is defined as an association arising from a similar mark that harms the reputation of the famous mark. If the use of a similar mark is found to dilute a famous mark, the use can be enjoined. Confiscation of offending merchandise and an award of monetary damages may be appropriate remedies as well.

By giving famous mark owners the ability to prevent dilution, some people assert that these mark holders are given improperly expansive property rights in words and symbols. Customarily, a mark could not be registered unless it was in use, or the registration applicant asserted an intention to begin using the mark in commerce shortly. Under anti-dilution principles, mark owners gain the ability to "reserve" marks for a wide variety future uses, even if they have no intention of ever utilizing the marks in alternative ways. For example, the General Motors Corporation may have no interest in making or marketing Chevrolet(ice cream, but it can bring a trademark dilution suit against any dairy company that attempts it.

5.   No Extra-Territorial Effect

Trademark registration does not have extraterritorial effect, and if the owner of a mark in one country wants to protect the mark abroad, she must seek available protection in each country separately under the relevant laws.

B.   Domain Names

Entities that own trademarks have recently had a great deal of success arguing that their trademark rights extend to domain names on the Internet. For example, Panavision, a movie industry company, was deemed to have trademark-based rights in the "panavision.com" domain name, even though the domain name had been purchased by someone else (who was later dubbed a "cybersquatter"). The trend both nationally and internationally is for courts to award trademark owners rights to domain names that comprise or incorporate their marks.

C.   Links, Frames, and Meta-Tags

The overwhelming amount of information available on the Internet makes it essential to have efficient methods for identifying and accessing specific sites and content. Hyperlinks (hereinafter "links"), frames, and meta-tags are very useful tools for Internet navigation, but can impact upon the intellectual property rights of others.

1.   Linking

Deep hyperlinks are links that bypass the website's home page and provide direct access to corresponding text on interior pages deep within the website. These deep hyperlinks have been the subject of several controversies in recent years. Hyperlinks which provide direct access (deep hyperlinks) to the text that is published on a website make it unnecessary for a user to go through a site's home page, where the site's advertising may appear. As a result of deep hyperlinks, a site's advertisements would never be seen by visitors arriving through the linking site, arguably leading to a potential loss of advertising revenue by the site that is linked to.

Linkers often take the position that they do not need written permission to provide links because the principle of the Internet is free access. Courts, however, have found that hyperlinks may raise trademark infringement and dilution issues, as well as constitute unfair competition when links do not send the user to the website's home page but rather directly to the relevant interior page of a website. Though deep links may make it easier and more efficient for users, links that enable Internet users to bypass a home page that contains paid advertising may deprive sites of advertising revenue. Use of an entity's marks as links may also lead consumers to believe that there is an affiliation between the linking and linked-to sites that does not exist.

Some websites attempt to prevent non-permissive linking by placing "terms and conditions of use" on their home pages that ask users not to link to these sites without authorization. However, courts may be reluctant to entertain breach of contract claims arising from violations of these "terms and conditions of use," as they are unlikely to be construed as binding contracts if visitors are not required to assent to it or even to read it in order to access content at these sites. A complaining site might have the best prospects for success if it could prove that a linker knew or should have known about the terms or conditions prohibiting hyperlinks.

In the context of trademark suits, courts are being asked to find a compromise between protecting intellectual property rights while at the same time not hindering the growth of the Internet by limiting the use of arguably its most important asset — the hypertext link. Given that the potential loss of advertising revenue has been a consistent complaint by plaintiffs in controversies based on deep-linking and framing, courts may decide to give relief to linked-to sites with respect to loss of advertising revenue if damages are proven. However, the nature of the relief may be based on legal principles in the business tort area rather than on trademark principles.

2. Framing

Framing is a relatively new technology that allows a web page to be divided up into a number of sections or "frames" that work independently of one another and which display separate information. Like linking, framing has raised trademark infringement and dilution concerns, especially when framing and linking are used in tandem.

The defendant in a framing case in the U.S. operated a website which was designed to act as a gateway to other new services available on the World Wide Web. A visitor to its site would see displayed on the screen of her or his browser three frames: a frame containing buttons labeled with the names of the news services which could be accessed via the site; a frame in which the news stories were displayed; and a frame containing the framer's advertising. When the user elected a particular news service, the web pages from the server operating that service were displayed in the news story frames while the other two frames remained visible. For example, you could read a news story from an online newspaper, but would continue to see the framer's advertising rather than the advertising on the newspaper's website. This particular dispute was ultimately settled out of court, but similar conflicts are likely in the future.

3.   Meta-Tags

Meta-tags are invisible codes embedded in the hypertext language used to create websites. Meta-tags are not visible to the viewer but are read by the viewer's computer. Meta-tags are intended to describe the contents of the website, and Internet search engines use meta-tags to find sites with information related to the search request. The more often a term appears in the meta-tags, the more likely it is that the web page will be "hit" in a search for that keyword. Meta-tags can serve the useful purpose of describing the content of the HTML page. However, in some cases, the meta-tags do not accurately reflect the content of the relevant HTML page, but rather are inserted solely for purposes of attracting Internet users to their website.

Causes of action based on meta-tags have primarily been in the areas of trademark infringement and dilution with additional claims of unfair competition. Companies have claimed that use by one entity of another entity's trademark in the context of a meta-tag is likely to cause confusion and an erroneous belief that the goods and services provided by one entity were authorized or sponsored by another, when in fact there is no relationship between the two. Entities that portray themselves as victims of meta-tags argue that their marks are intentionally being used by others who trade off their reputation and goodwill.

Courts have also reflected that they must be careful to give consumers the freedom to locate desired sites on the World Wide Web while at the same time protecting the integrity of trademarks and trade names.

4.   Possible Alternatives: Disclaimers, the Linking License, and Technological Approaches

a.   Disclaimers

Many believe that no permission should be required to link from one website to another, because obtaining permission would be at odds with the concept of the free flow of information on the Internet. However, if a site in any way falsely suggests an association with the linked site or incorporates trademarks or materials having copyright protection without a license, linking can lead to legitimate claims of trademark infringement and dilution, copyright infringement, and unfair competition.

Disclaimers may provide a simple and inexpensive preventive measure against a trademark or copyright claim. If one plans to use the trademark of another in her or his website, the name of the trademark owner should be included with the trademark to designate the source. Also, the disclaimer should state that the website and the owner of the website are not sponsored by, or affiliated in any way with, the owners of the specific trademarks used on the website or any hyperlinks including those trademarks. Any disclaimer should be prominently displayed. If one is using a hypertext link in a commercial context and plans to bypass the advertising of the owner of the linked site, or if one uses frames, to avoid litigation she or he should consider a simple agreement reflecting permission to link, such as through a web-linking agreement.

b.   Linking Licenses

While it is not clear whether an agreement is necessary to link, frame, or use meta-tags, it is clear that an agreement can define liability, establish business relationships, and provide for reciprocal links. Some of the issues that should be considered when drafting a web-linking agreement include: First, a determination of the purpose for which the parties are establishing the web links, such as advertising or sharing information. Next, one should consider the nature of the site's content, the nature of the links to other sites, and the conditions of use. If the web link incorporates copyrighted images or text, and/or a trademark of the linked party, the parties should make provision for the scope of the intellectual property rights granted. The express limitations of the grant and the rights reserved by the owner should be noted. For example, if one party does not want its content to be framed, it should be specified. If web links are established for commercial reasons, the parties should clearly make provisions for payment for the link and for sharing the revenue generated by the link. Finally, in light of the certainty of technological advances, any linking agreement should include language relating to changed circumstances due to advanced technology.

c.   Technological Approaches

A website owner can take a pro-active approach and set out a linking policy on the home page of her or his website. This policy statement should set out guidelines for third-party websites that may want to link to her or his website. Further, the owner should assert a policy restricting access to only those users who first visit the home page. In the event that written policies are ignored, however, technological remedies can stop unwanted links. First, one could use tracking methods to find out which websites are linking to them; then incorporate computer coding to block users from linking to or framing internal pages from other sites. Also, an alternative way to block uninvited guests from linking to a web page is to create a filter by specifying a list of URLs from which the owner does not wish to be accessed. There is also technology called dynamic paging in which the reference point of the web page changes, depriving the linking site of a fixed point to which to link. Further, the website owner could adopt a "pay for access" to limit access by hyperlinking or framing or request a password for access. These solutions are relatively simple but not widely used because most websites are created for the purpose of attracting visitors and technological remedies soon become obsolete.

5.   Conflicts With the First Amendment

Comparative advertising is one unauthorized use of trademarks that can be very beneficial to consumers. As long as it is neither confusing not deceptive, comparative advertising is usually not considered to be an infringing use of trademarks. It is instead an exercise of free speech. Parodying trademarks, using them in criticism or social commentary, or otherwise using trademarks to communicate information not directly related to commercial transactions are also ways that non-permissive uses trademarks can be protected by the First Amendment.

V.   CONCLUSION

All three areas of intellectual property law set up frameworks for defining the scope and content of intangible property. Without laws, patents, copyrights and trademarks would not exist. The U.S. Congress had written statutes that establish legal monopolies, and give the holders of intellectual property certain rights and privileges. Courts then mediate conflicts between intellectual property holders, and those they come into conflict with, with an eye towards keeping a balance that continually facilitates fair and healthy competition, and incentivizes the creation and distribution of new and useful goods and services

Chapter 10

PROFESSIONAL RESPONSIBILITY

By — Patrick E. Longan

SYNOPSIS

I. INTRODUCTION

Lawyers in the United States have responsibilities to their clients, to former clients, to opposing lawyers and parties, to the system of justice, and to third parties generally. Lawyers also are limited in the ways in which they can organize themselves to deliver legal services. These obligations and limitations arise from a variety of sources. Our primary focus will be on the obligations and limitations imposed by the American Bar Association Model Rules of Professional Conduct, which serve as a model for the states to use in promulgating their own rules.

In these materials, we will survey these various responsibilities. We will begin with a discussion of how the delivery of legal services is regulated. The next few subjects will concern the relationship between the lawyer and the client, with particular emphasis on the lawyer's duties of confidentiality and loyalty. We will then turn our attention to the duties that lawyers owe as advocates to the system of justice, and we will conclude with an examination of the duties that American lawyers owe to third parties.

II. THE DELIVERY OF LEGAL SERVICES

American lawyers work in a variety of settings. Some work for the government, while others serve as in-house counsel for corporations and other entities. Most, however, work as solo practitioners or in law firms, and that is the setting with which we will be concerned. The Model Rules of Professional Conduct regulate how lawyers in private practice can organize themselves in several ways. All of these rules are intended to protect the public by safeguarding the independence of lawyers and by ensuring the competence of lawyers.

A. Rules Regarding Independence

American lawyers are expected to exercise independent professional judgment on behalf of their clients. The rules strive to protect that independence by forbidding lawyers from forming partnerships with non-lawyers if any of the activities of the partnership consists of the practice of law. The fear is that the non-lawyer partners in such an enterprise, known around the world as a multi-disciplinary practice (MDP), could exercise economic control of the lawyer to the detriment of service to the client. More generally, the rules also prohibit lawyers from practicing in a firm for profit if any non-lawyer owns any interest in the firm, is an officer or director of the firm, or could otherwise direct or control the activities of the lawyer. Again, the purpose of this rule is to ensure that the lawyer is not making judgments for the client under circumstances that compromise the lawyer's independence. In or outside the context of a firm, a lawyer is not permitted to allow someone who recommends, pays, or employs the lawyer to regulate or direct the lawyer's judgment, nor is a lawyer permitted to share legal fees with non-lawyers.

These rules are subject to criticism as being self-serving and as unduly limiting the capital structure of U.S. law firms. Lawyers write the rules, and these particular provisions ensure that only lawyers receive legal fees and only lawyers own law firms. Nevertheless, the stated purpose of the rules is not to line the pockets of lawyers but to ensure their independence. It is also true that limiting ownership in law firms to lawyers prevents firms from raising capital through the sale of shares or other methods of investment. These limits constrain the size of law firms and to some extent curb competition from new firms. Again, however, these costs are deemed to be acceptable in the name of the greater good of protecting lawyers' independence.

B.   Rules Regarding Competence

The Model Rules of Professional Conduct also limit the ways in which legal services can be delivered in order to ensure that clients receive competent assistance. The relevant provisions concern the unauthorized practice of law (UPL) and multi-jurisdictional practice (MJP).

Only lawyers are permitted to practice law in the United States, although there is some variation among the states regarding what it means to "practice law." For example, in some states an attorney must be present to close a real estate transaction, whereas in some other states non-lawyers can perform this task. Putting aside those few local variations, the important rule for lawyers is the requirement that they not assist a non-lawyer in UPL. A typical scenario would be the following. The lawyer might set up a practice where non-lawyer staff members are not merely assisting the lawyer with his or her practice of law — that is permitted — but instead are operating so independently that they are in fact the ones practicing law. Because these staff members do not have the training that a member of the bar has, they are assumed to be less competent and thus a threat to the client's interests.

Another way in which a lawyer's competence might be suspect is for the lawyer to practice law in a state where the lawyer is not licensed. Lawyers are admitted to the bar on a state-by-state basis, and laws of the various states differ in significant ways. Lawyers are not generally permitted, therefore, to take a license issued in one state and establish an office or other permanent presence in another state. The concern is that the lawyer might simply not know what he or she is doing in that other state. In recent years, lawyers have been granted permission to engage in a number of temporary activities in other states, including representing clients if the local court permits it, assisting clients with the assistance of a local lawyer, and even helping clients with transactions that "arise out of" the lawyer's home-state practice. Lawyers for corporations are permitted to practice even on a permanent basis for their one client in a state where the lawyer is not licensed, on the assumption that the entity is sophisticated and can protect itself from incompetent lawyering. The general rule remains, however, that a lawyer licensed in one state cannot practice on any kind of permanent basis in another state.

III.   THE LAWYER-CLIENT RELATIONSHIP

The Model Rules of Professional Conduct heavily regulate the relationship between lawyer and client. They specify the duties that lawyers owe to clients, and they delineate how authority is divided between lawyer and client. The rules also identify the circumstances under which lawyers must or may withdraw from the representation of a client.

A.   The Basic Duties of Competence, Diligence, Communication, and Candid Advice

Lawyers owe clients a basic set of duties that includes competence, diligence, communication, and advice. Clients typically come to lawyers with problems that the client cannot solve for himself or herself because the problems require specialized legal knowledge or skill. It should be no surprise, therefore, that the first rule of professional conduct (other than a set of definitions) is that a lawyer shall render competent representation to a client. Competence includes knowledge, skill, thoroughness, and preparation. These last two components of competence are examples of diligence, and the rules separately specify that a lawyer owes a duty of diligence to his or her clients. The basic duties of the lawyer also regulate interactions between the lawyer and the client. Lawyers have a duty of communication that includes consulting with clients about how to achieve the client's objectives (we will see more on this when we discuss the division of authority between lawyer and client), keeping the client reasonably informed about the status of the client's matter, and promptly complying with requests for information. A particularly important example of the duty of communication is the requirement that the lawyer tell the client about every offer to settle a matter, unless the client has already informed the lawyer that such an offer is unacceptable. In addition to the general duty of communication, lawyers also owe clients their independent judgment and candid advice, even when the judgment and the advice may not be palatable to the client. Lawyers are permitted, but not required, to advise clients about non-legal aspects of the client's problem such as the morality of a client's proposed course of action. These duties of competence, diligence, communication, and advice are fundamental to the lawyer-client relationship.

B.   The Division of Authority between Lawyer and Client

Beyond these basic duties, the rules deal with a series of issues that concern the division of authority between the lawyer and the client. Some decisions belong to the client alone. The client decides the objectives of the representation and also has the power to decide whether or not to settle a matter. In criminal cases, clients also have the exclusive power to decide what plea to enter, whether to demand a jury trial, and whether or not the client will testify.

The rules specify that other matters are a shared responsibility between the lawyer and the client. With respect to the means by which a client's objectives are to be achieved, recall that a lawyer is required to reasonably consult with the client. The rules do not further specify what belongs to whom. It is expected that clients will usually defer to the lawyer on matters that are more within the lawyer's area of expertise, such as litigation or negotiation tactics, and that the lawyer will usually defer to the client about such matters as how much particular means will cost or how they will affect third parties. In the event of an impasse, however, the rules do not allocate final authority to either lawyer or client with respect to means, other than to suggest that the client can discharge the lawyer or the lawyer can seek to withdraw from the representation.

The rules are more specific, however, with respect to things that the lawyer is not permitted to do. An American lawyer is not permitted to counsel or assist a client in the perpetration of a crime or fraud. Although the lawyer can and should discuss with the client the consequences of any such action, the lawyer has to draw the line at rendering any assistance.

C.   Duties Regarding Fees

Lawyers in private practice understandably expect to be paid for their work. The financial arrangements between a lawyer and a client are not, however, matters purely of contract. Lawyers may not make an agreement for, charge, or collect an "unreasonable" fee. Because it is difficult to specify in a rule what makes a fee unreasonable, the rules simply list a number of factors to be considered in the evaluation of any particular fee. Of particular importance to this determination are the time and labor required for the services, the novelty and difficulty of the matter, the skill needed, the customary fee for such services in the community, the stakes, the result, the experience, reputation, and ability of the lawyer, and whether the fee is fixed or contingent. All other things held equal, a reasonable contingent fee will be higher than a reasonable non-contingent fee to account for the risk that the lawyer undertook. Lawyers in the U.S. can charge contingent fees for matters other than divorces and criminal defense.

D.   The Duty of Confidentiality

1.   The General Duty

Lawyers owe a general duty of confidentiality to clients. Although many think of this duty as the "attorney-client privilege," the duty is actually much broader. The privilege protects communications between lawyer and client made in confidence for the purpose of obtaining or giving legal advice. The ethical duty of confidentiality protects all such communications and much more. It protects all "information relating to the representation." For example, information that a lawyer obtains from third parties would not be privileged but as long as it relates to the representation the lawyer will be constrained, with certain exceptions discussed below, to keep it confidential.

2.   General Exceptions to the Duty of Confidentiality

The rule that creates the lawyer's duty of confidentiality contains some general exceptions. There are also four specific special cases that require separate treatment.

Lawyers are permitted to reveal the confidential information of clients with their express, informed consent or with "implied authorization." Informed consent here, as elsewhere, requires that the lawyer explain to the client the risks of and alternatives to the proposed course of conduct. For example, to borrow from a famous case, lawyers who have learned that their client murdered a young girl and buried her body could obtain their client's consent to revealing that information only if they explained the risks. Those risks certainly would include the probability that the client would be charged with the murder and that the police likely would recover evidence against the client when they recovered the body. "Implied authorization" is a much more routine concept. For example, one would expect lawyers within a firm to share a client's confidential information among themselves and with staff in the interest of better serving the client. Unless the client directs otherwise, such routine revelations of confidential information made for the purpose of helping the client are permitted.

The general rule on confidentiality also contains six exceptions that might result in harm to the client. It is important to note that each gives the attorney the option to reveal confidential information, but none requires the lawyer to do so. The first circumstance under which the lawyer is permitted to reveal confidential client information is if the lawyer reasonably believes it is necessary to prevent reasonably certain death or substantial bodily harm. For example, if a client threatens to kill an opposing party, and the lawyer takes the threat seriously, the lawyer would have the option but not the obligation to warn the intended victim. Two exceptions permit the lawyer to reveal confidential information if the client is using or has used the lawyer's services to cause substantial financial injury to another through a crime or a fraud, if revelation of the information can prevent the crime or fraud or can prevent, rectify, or mitigate the harm. Lawyers are also permitted under this general rule to reveal confidential client information to obtain advice about compliance with the rules of professional conduct, to defend themselves or to collect a fee, or to comply with other law or a court order.

3.   Four Special Cases

There are four special circumstances under which a lawyer either may or must reveal a client's confidential information. They relate to a lawyer's role in representing an entity, the possibility that the lawyer's services are about to be used to perpetrate a crime or a fraud, the giving of false evidence, and, more generally, the perpetration of a fraud on a court.

Lawyers who represent entities such as corporations are expected to act to protect the entity. If the lawyer learns that someone within the entity is acting in a way that is illegal and that will cause substantial injury to the entity, then the lawyer is expected to bring the matter to the attention of the appropriate corporate officers including, if necessary, the board of directors. If the board refuses to act, the lawyer has the option to reveal the confidential information if the lawyer reasonably believes that doing so is necessary to prevent substantial injury to the entity.

A second special case is more intricate and is best understood with an example. Suppose that a lawyer has innocently prepared documents for a transaction. Before the transaction closes, the lawyer learns that it is part of a fraudulent scheme. One concern that the lawyer may have is that, through the preparation of the documentation, the lawyer will be deemed to have "assisted" the client with a crime or a fraud, which we know that lawyer is not permitted to do. The lawyer here must withdraw from the representation and may choose to inform the other party to the transaction of the fact of the lawyer's withdrawal. That news should make the other party sufficiently suspicious that the transaction does not occur, and the lawyer need not worry that the lawyer has "assisted" in a fraudulent transaction. However, if the other party does not take the hint, it may be necessary for the lawyer to reveal the fraud in order to avoid assisting in it. Under such circumstances, the lawyer is required — not just permitted — to reveal the confidential information.

Two other special cases concern the lawyer's duties as an advocate, about which we will learn more later. First, a lawyer is not permitted to offer evidence that the lawyer knows to be false, but the lawyer might learn of the falsity of the evidence only after it has been offered. Under these circumstances, the lawyer is required to undertake "reasonable remedial measures," and if other measures fail the lawyer ultimately is required to reveal the falsity of the evidence to the tribunal. More generally, a lawyer might learn that someone has engaged in criminal or fraudulent activity related to the proceeding. For example, the lawyer might learn that someone has threatened or bribed a witness or a juror. Under these circumstances, the lawyer is also required to undertake "reasonable remedial measures," and these measures include, if it becomes necessary, the obligation to inform the tribunal of the activities.

E. The Duty of Loyalty

Another fundamental aspect of the lawyer-client relationship is the lawyer's duty of loyalty. The rules surrounding the duty of loyalty are among the most detailed of all the rules of conduct. To understand them better, we will discuss them in three parts: concurrent conflicts of interest, former client conflicts, and rules on the imputation of conflicts among members of a firm, including some special rules regarding so-called "migratory" lawyers who move from one firm to another.

1. Concurrent Conflicts of Interest

A lawyer has a concurrent conflict of interest under two circumstances. One is that the representation of one client will be directly adverse to another client. The second is that there is a significant risk that the lawyer's representation of a client will be materially limited by the lawyer's obligations to another client, a former client, a third person, or the personal interest of the lawyer. A lawyer cannot represent a client if the lawyer has a concurrent conflict of interest unless the lawyer is permitted to seek, and obtains, informed consent to the conflict.

A "direct adversity" conflict is what the name implies. If the lawyer is representing a client and then is asked to undertake a new matter in which the lawyer would be suing, or negotiating against, the first client, then the lawyer is being asked to do something that is directly adverse to an existing client. It is important to note that the two matters need not be related. If, for example, the lawyer is representing a client in a negotiation to purchase real estate, and the lawyer is then asked to represent a new client in a lawsuit against that client concerning some unrelated business deal, the first client is likely to feel betrayed. The lawyer cannot undertake that new, unrelated representation without obtaining the informed consent of the first client (an unlikely prospect).

A "material limitation" type of conflict can come in an almost infinite variety of circumstances. The basic principle is that there is a significant risk that the lawyer will "pull a punch" in representing his or her client because of some other interest. For example, suppose that a lawyer is asked to represent a client in a lawsuit in which the opposing party will be represented by the lawyer's spouse. This is not a "direct adversity" type of conflict because the lawyer does not represent two clients who are adverse to each other in a lawsuit or a negotiation. However, there is a significant risk that the lawyer might not litigate against the lawyer's spouse in the same way as the lawyer otherwise would litigate, because the lawyer has a competing interest in domestic harmony and the professional welfare of the spouse. This is just one example. The basic point is for the lawyer to be sensitive to any circumstance that would cause the lawyer to have competing allegiances.

Lawyers sometimes are allowed to represent clients despite a concurrent conflict of interest, if the lawyer is permitted to obtain and actually obtains informed consent of the client. There are several circumstances in which a lawyer may not seek the consent of the client, and the most important of these is when the lawyer concludes that the lawyer cannot render competent and diligent representation for the client because of the conflict. Consider the example of the lawyer asked to litigate against the lawyer's spouse. Even with client consent, it might be impossible to set aside the lawyer's concern for the spouse and represent the client competently and diligently. If that is so, the lawyer cannot seek consent to the conflict. However, if the lawyer is permitted by the rules to seek consent, then the lawyer must ensure that the consent is informed, which means that the lawyer must explain the risks involved in the representation and reasonably available alternatives, such as retaining other counsel.

2. Former Client Conflicts

Lawyers owe duties to former clients as well as to current clients. A lawyer has a conflict of interest if the new representation would be materially adverse to the interests of the former client if the new matter is the same as, or is substantially related to, the matter for which the lawyer represented the former client. Note that the scope of this conflict is narrower than the scope of the conflict for current clients. The old matter and the new one must be the same or "substantially related." The primary purpose of this limitation is to make sure that the lawyer does not take advantage of the prior representation and use the former client's confidential information against the former client in this new matter. Obviously, a lawyer who switches sides in a dispute is in a position to use the former client's confidential information. When the two matters are not the same, the inquiry becomes more difficult, but it still focuses on the potential misuse of confidential information. Matters are "substantially related" if there is a substantial risk that the type of confidential information that the lawyer ordinarily would obtain in such a matter would materially advance the new client's position in the second matter. The inquiry is not what the lawyer actually learned from the former client, because that inquiry would require revelation of the very information that the rule is seeking to protect. Rather, the relevant question is what confidential information the lawyer ordinarily would have learned in such an engagement.

3. Imputation of Conflicts: General Rule and the Special Problems of Migratory Lawyers

When lawyers practice in a firm, it is important to know when a conflict of one of the lawyers will be imputed to the others. The general rule is that concurrent conflicts and former client conflicts are imputed to all lawyers in the firm. It is not generally enough, therefore, to "screen" a lawyer who has a conflict from involvement in the matter that is causing the conflict. If one lawyer has a conflict, they all do.

This general rule creates some particular problems for lawyers moving between firms. For example, suppose a lawyer is in a firm that is on one side of a large case for Client A. Suppose further that the lawyer has no involvement in the case and knows nothing of Client A's confidential information. If that lawyer receives an offer to move from his or her current firm to the firm on the other side of this huge case, the lawyer runs a risk (absent a special rule) that the move will disqualify the new firm, even though Client A's confidential information is not at risk. A special rule permits the lawyer to move freely in this situation. Conversely, suppose a lawyer leaves a firm and takes a client along. No lawyer in the firm left behind knows any of that client's confidential information. Without a special rule, the firm could not undertake a substantially related matter against the former client even though no lawyer left in the firm has any confidential information to use against the former client. A special rule also permits the firm in these circumstances to take on the new matter.

F.   Termination of the Lawyer-Client Relationship

The termination of the lawyer-client relationship is also heavily regulated. Lawyers must withdraw (subject to court approval if the matter is in litigation) if they are fired, if they are no longer physically or mentally capable of carrying out the representation, or if continuing the representation would require the lawyer to violate the rules of professional conduct. Lawyers are permitted to withdraw (again, subject to court approval in a litigated matter) for a variety of reasons. These include a failure of the client to fulfill an obligation to the lawyer, a client's insistence on taking actions that the lawyer considers to be repugnant or with which the lawyer has a fundamental disagreement, and an unreasonable financial burden that will befall a lawyer if the lawyer does not withdraw. After termination of the relationship, a lawyer has the obligation to take steps to reasonably protect the client's interests.

IV. THE LAWYER'S DUTIES AS AN ADVOCATE

Lawyers owe duties not just to clients but also to the system of justice. When lawyers act as advocates, their obligations include gatekeeping, diligence, candor to the tribunal, fairness to the opposing party and counsel, maintenance of the impartiality and decorum of the tribunal, and limits on publicity. Advocates also may be witnesses only in limited circumstances, and criminal prosecutors have special obligations as "ministers of justice."

A.   Gatekeeping and Diligence

There is a general perception that litigation in the United States takes too long. The rules of conduct address this concern in two ways. First, lawyers act as gatekeepers to the judicial system. Because the United States does not have a "loser pays" system in which a losing party to a civil case has to pay the other side's attorneys fees, the rules of procedure and the rules of professional conduct put burdens on the lawyers not to clog up the system with frivolous disputes. Under the rules of conduct, lawyers are not permitted to bring or defend a civil case, or to assert or controvert an issue in such a case, unless there is a non-frivolous basis in fact and law for doing so. Lawyers are not entirely bound by the current state of the law, however, because they are permitted to make good faith arguments for the reversal, modification, or extension of existing law. Lawyers are, however, given more latitude to defend criminal cases in such a way as to require the prosecution to prove every element of the alleged offense.

Another rule directly addresses the question of diligence. Lawyers must make reasonable efforts to expedite litigation, consistent with the interests of the client. Obviously, there are many legitimate reasons why an advocate might take action that slows down the resolution of a proceeding. Taking the time necessary to gather the relevant evidence is an example. However, lawyers are not permitted to delay proceedings when there is no substantial purpose other than delay.

B.   Candor to the Tribunal

Tribunals in an adversary system are heavily dependent upon the advocates. As a result, the rules impose obligations on the lawyers to be candid with the court so that the court can trust what the lawyers present. For example, lawyers are not permitted to make false representations of fact or law to a tribunal, and they must correct any previous misstatement if they come to learn that one has been made. Lawyers also must be careful in citing legal authority. If there is a case from a controlling court that is directly on point, and the other side has not cited it, the lawyer must do so, even if it hurts the lawyer's client. Lawyers also are not permitted to present evidence that they know is false. As mentioned in a previous section, if a lawyer presents evidence and later learns that it was false, the lawyer must undertake "reasonable remedial measures," up to and including if necessary telling the court about the false evidence. These rules presuppose that the lawyer actually knows of the falsity of the evidence. If the lawyer reasonably believes that the evidence is false, but does not know, the lawyer has the discretion to present it or not, with one exception. A lawyer who is defending a criminal case and who believes, but does not know, that the client intends to testify falsely, must permit the defendant to testify. Recall that the decision to testify as a defendant in a criminal case is one of the decisions reserved for clients to make, albeit after consultation with counsel. Recall that lawyers also have the more general responsibility to undertake "reasonable remedial measures" if the lawyer knows that anyone has engaged, is engaging, or intends to engage in criminal or fraudulent conduct (such as bribing or threatening a witness or a juror) related to the proceeding.

C.   Fairness to Opposing Parties and Counsel

Lawyers owe duties to opposing counsel and to opposing parties. These duties include obligations related to evidence, to the rules of procedure, and to the conduct of the trial.

1.   Evidence

Cases of course should be decided upon the evidence, and lawyers are not permitted unlawfully to obstruct another's access to evidence or unlawfully to alter, conceal, or destroy material with potential evidentiary value. The key word here is "unlawfully." The rules of conduct do not define what is lawful and what is unlawful. One must look elsewhere, such as to statutes that define obstruction of justice, to determine that. In the same spirit of open access to evidence, lawyers are not permitted (with some narrow exceptions) to ask third-party witnesses not to cooperate with the opposing party. Also, lawyers are not permitted to falsify evidence, to counsel or assist a witness to testify falsely, or to give a witness an unlawful inducement to testify.

2.   Rules of Procedure

Litigation is governed primarily by rules of procedure, such as the Federal Rules of Civil Procedure. Advocates must abide by such rules or face the sanctions provided for in those rules. Violations can also, however, become matters of professional responsibility. The rules of professional conduct provide that it is misconduct to knowingly disobey an obligation under the rules of a tribunal, except for an open refusal based upon the assertion that no valid obligation exists. In effect, the rules of conduct incorporate all the rules of the tribunal and make them rules of conduct. More specifically, the rules of conduct have special provisions regarding discovery. It would be difficult to overestimate the importance of the discovery process to the resolution of civil litigation in the U.S. More than ninety-five percent of civil cases are disposed of without trial, and the motions and settlements that take care of the rest are driven in large part by the information gained in discovery. In recognition of the importance of discovery and the frequency with which discovery obligations are flouted, the rules forbid lawyers from making frivolous requests in discovery and from failing to make a reasonably diligent effort to comply with a proper discovery request from an opposing party.

3.   Trial

For the few cases that make it to trial, the rules of conduct impose limitations on unfair tactics that lawyers might try to employ. Cases are supposed to be decided on the evidence, and lawyers may not allude to some inflammatory fact if the lawyer does not reasonably believe it is relevant, nor may the lawyer refer to a relevant fact that, for whatever reason, will not be supported by admissible evidence. Lawyers are also prohibited from asserting personal knowledge of facts at issue in the proceeding (except when the lawyer is a witness) or giving the lawyer's personal opinion regarding the justness of a party's cause, the credibility of a witness, or the culpability of a party.

D.   Impartiality and Decorum of the Tribunal

The rules of professional conduct protect the impartiality of the tribunal by forbidding lawyers from seeking to persuade a judge, a juror, or a prospective juror in ways that are prohibited by law. As one means of preventing such actions, the rules specifically ban any ex parte contact (conduct between the court and counsel without the presence of opposing counsel) with any such person unless the lawyer has due authorization. Even after the proceeding is over, the rules limit the contacts between counsel and the jurors. The lawyers might want to contact the jurors simply to get tips on how to do better next time, or the lawyers might be looking for evidence of juror misconduct. Either way, the contacts are regulated and may not continue if the juror expresses a desire not to communicate. Finally, lawyers are generally not permitted to engage in conduct that is intended to disrupt a tribunal. Importantly, this duty extends not just to activities in trial but also to activities in depositions. Few cases go to trial, while most cases involve depositions. The temptation to engage in disruptive conduct at a deposition, where usually no judge is present, proves too much for some lawyers. This rule is intended to curb such activities.

E.   Trial Publicity

It may come as a surprise in an era of cable television and recent celebrity trials to learn that there are limits on what lawyers are supposed to say about their cases to the media. However, there are such limits, and they are intended to prevent lawyers from tainting a jury pool by trying the case in the media. Generally, a lawyer who is participating in a proceeding (as opposed to a lawyer who is commenting on someone else's case) may not make public statements outside of court if the lawyer knows or reasonably should know that the media will report the statement and the statement has a substantial likelihood of materially prejudicing the proceeding. The rule provides some "safe harbors," statements that can be made without fear of discipline. For example, a lawyer can recite information that is contained in a public record. There are also statements that are usually improper, such as statements regarding whether a party or witness passed a lie detector test. If the opposing lawyer makes statements that violate the rule, a lawyer has some limited freedom to respond in kind. It simply must not go further than necessary to mitigate the harm of the other side's statements.

F.   Lawyer as Witness

In general, lawyers are not supposed to be witnesses in cases in which they are also acting as advocates. The fear is that jurors will not be able to keep straight which statements made by the lawyer came from the witness box (evidence) and which statements came during opening or closing statements (not evidence). If it turns out that a lawyer is a necessary witness, then the lawyer personally is disqualified from acting as an advocate. As long as the lawyer's testimony is favorable to the client, then the lawyer's firm is not also disqualified. Presumably, the jurors can distinguish between the statements made from the witness box by one lawyer and the other statements made by that lawyer's partner elsewhere. However, it is possible for the entire firm to be disqualified. If the lawyer's testimony is harmful to the client, then there is a concurrent conflict of interest because the lawyer advocate is placed in the uncomfortable position of cross-examining his or her partner. In that circumstance, it may be that the entire firm, and not just the witness, will be disqualified.

G.   Special Responsibilities of Prosecutors

Prosecuting attorneys in the U.S. are deemed to be "ministers of justice" whose obligation is to seek justice, even if that means an acquittal of the defendant. The rules of conduct accordingly place some special responsibilities on prosecutors. The prosecutor is not supposed to prosecute a case that is not supported by probable cause. Nor is the prosecutor to seek the waiver by the defendant of important pre-trial rights. The prosecutor is expected to take steps to make sure that the defendant knows about the right to counsel and how to exercise that right, and the prosecutor also must turn over to the defense evidence or information that tends to negate the defendant's guilt or mitigates the offense. In an era of exonerations that have followed the testing of DNA evidence long after convictions have been obtained, it is important to note that the rules place special, affirmative obligations on prosecutors who learn of evidence creating a reasonable likelihood that a convicted defendant did not commit the offense. If the prosecutor learns of clear and convincing evidence of a wrongful conviction, the prosecutor must seek to remedy the conviction.

V. THE LAWYER'S DUTIES TO THIRD PARTIES

In this section, we will examine the duties that lawyers owe to third parties. These duties include a duty of truthfulness, a general duty not to contact another lawyer's client, limits on interactions with unrepresented parties, and more general rules regarding fairness to these parties.

A.   The Duty of Truthfulness

Lawyers have a general duty not to make a false statement of material fact or law to a third person. The issue may arise routinely in negotiation. If a lawyer representing a plaintiff is negotiating a settlement of a personal injury case with a lawyer representing an insurance company, one crucial material fact will be the limit of the insurance policy. If the defense lawyer misrepresents the limits of the policy, that lawyer has engaged in professional misconduct by making a false statement of material fact. It is important, and much more efficient, for lawyers to be able to trust each other, and this rule promotes that trust.

The rule is more subtle than it appears, however. In our culture, it is common for negotiators to "huff" and "puff" as part of the process. For example, a lawyer might make disparaging remarks about how the other lawyer's client came across in deposition, even if that lawyer believed the witness actually was effective. Or a lawyer might represent that his or her client could not settle for any less than a certain figure, even though the lawyer is authorized actually to accept a lower amount. Outside the litigation context, it is routine for sellers to purport to place a higher value on property than they really believe is appropriate. The problem is to square these routine expected negotiating ploys with the duty to be truthful. The way the rules do so is by classifying certain statements not as "statements of fact." These include, but are not limited to, statements regarding value and a party's intentions regarding settlement of a matter. More generally, what is a statement of fact depends upon generally accepted conventions in negotiation. In other words, it is not a violation of the rule against lying if the statements are made in a context in which, under our culture of negotiating, they ordinarily would not be taken as statements of fact.

B.   The "No-Contact" Rule

When a lawyer knows that the opposing party is represented by counsel in a matter, the lawyer is not permitted to have direct contact with that party without the permission of opposing counsel. The purpose of the rule is to protect that party from overreaching, particularly insofar as a lawyer might use such a contact to interfere with the other party's lawyer-client relationship (by, for example, disparaging the other lawyer) or to obtain privileged information. The rule applies even if the opposing party is the one who initiates the contact. The lawyer who is contacted by a represented opposing party must immediately terminate the conversation. Only the other party's lawyer has the authority to waive the protection of the rule.

Application of this rule is more complicated when the opposing party is an entity such as a corporation. The rule would be simpler if it provided either than all corporate constituents can be contacted or none of them can. Instead, the rule is applied to permit contacts with all corporate constituents except those who fall into one or more of three categories. Those categories are people who supervise, direct, or regularly consult with the entity's counsel regarding the matter, who have the authority to obligate the organization with respect to the matter, or whose acts or omissions may be imputed to the organization for purposes of civil or criminal liability in the matter. Importantly, it is permissible for lawyers to have contact with former employees of an organization, even without the organization's lawyer's permission (although there are some dangers, as discussed below).

C.   Dealing with Unrepresented Parties

When the other party is not represented, a lawyer has no alternative but to deal with them. There are still some dangers, however. The other party might be confused about the role of the lawyer. In particular, the unrepresented party might believe that the lawyer is disinterested in the matter or is in a position to give legal advice to them. The rules require the lawyer in this circumstance to be careful and clear. The lawyer cannot state or imply that the lawyer is disinterested, and if the lawyer has reason to believe that the unrepresented party misunderstands the lawyer's role the lawyer is expected to correct the misunderstanding. The lawyer is not to give legal advice except the advice to secure counsel. This admonition is troublesome for the lawyer who is attempting to effect some kind of settlement or other agreement with an unrepresented party who asks what a particular provision means. Interpreting a provision sounds like legal advice, yet a refusal to comment may make settlement with an unrepresented party much more difficult. What the lawyer is permitted to do in this delicate situation is to give the lawyer's view with a warning that the lawyer represents an adverse party and is not representing the unrepresented party.

D.   Respect for Rights of Third Persons More Generally

The rules also contain some general provisions for respecting the rights of third parties. One is a prohibition on using means that have no substantial purpose other than to embarrass, delay, or burden a third person. It is important to note that lawyers, especially in litigation, will frequently use methods, such as a withering cross-examination that impeaches the witness with prior inconsistent statements, that will embarrass, delay, or burden a third person. The rule only prohibits those that have no substantial purpose other than such embarrassment, delay, or burden. The rules also prohibit lawyers from using methods of obtaining evidence that violate the rights of third persons. For example, a lawyer is permitted to have direct contact with a former employee of a corporate adversary. If that person delivers privileged corporate documents to the lawyer, however, the lawyer has circumvented the privilege and used a method of obtaining evidence that violates the rights of the corporate adversary. The lawyer is expected to use only proper channels to obtain evidence.

The rules of conduct also contain one general rule about the use of information that is inadvertently sent to the lawyer. Opposing counsel might, for example, accidentally fax a letter intended for his or her client to the lawyer, or the opposing lawyer might inadvertently send a copy of a confidential e-mail. Such actions may or may not waive the attorney-client privilege or other protections for the information that has been inadvertently revealed. All that the rules require of the lawyer who has received such an inadvertent communication is that the lawyer must notify the sender. What happens to the information after that is a proper subject for discussion or even litigation, but all that is required by the rules of conduct is that the receipt of the information not be kept a secret.

VI. CONCLUSION

As we have seen, the professional responsibilities of lawyers are many. Lawyers owe duties to clients, former clients, opposing parties, opposing lawyers, the court system, and third parties more generally. This chapter has been a brief introduction to the basics of these duties. Although much detail necessarily has been omitted, this discussion should give you the background necessary to understand the fundamentals of the professional responsibilities of lawyers in the United States.

Chapter 11

BUSINESS ASSOCIATIONS

By — Peter J. Henning

I. INTRODUCTION

Private businesses in the United States are organized in a variety of different ways. If a person walks into a store, that business may be owned by the person working behind the counter (sole proprietorship), by two or more persons who jointly own the operation (partnership), or be organized under the applicable rules of a state (corporation or limited liability company). The law of business organizations is diverse, covering enactments by states and the federal government. These rules cover the legal relationship among the owners of a business, the obligations of those who oversee its operations to those owners, and how third parties are affected by the business.

This Chapter will review the development of the law of business organizations and the structure of the predominant form of business organization, the corporation. Within a corporation, the duties of the different corporate constituents will be analyzed, and particular attention will be paid to smaller businesses, called the "close corporation," and newer forms of organization. The relationship of the corporation, which is a *legal person*, will be discussed in connection with third-party claims against it. The method by which a corporation can fundamentally change its structure and ownership presents special considerations. Finally, the role of federal law in the regulation of business organizations, primarily those corporations whose shares are traded on the public markets, will be reviewed.

II.   FORMS OF BUSINESS ORGANIZATIONS

There are four primary organizational forms for a business operating in the United States that covers the vast majority of enterprises. While these are the basic means to organize a business, there are permutations on these forms, and even a few different types that are not commonly used but are available for particular specialized transactions or industries. The four forms are:

- Sole proprietorship
- Partnership
- Corporation
- Limited Liability Company (LLC) and Limited Liability Partnership (LLP).

A.   Sole Proprietorship

The simplest business organization is the *sole proprietorship*, in which one person owns the entire business. The sole proprietor is responsible for the management of the business, and need not justify or answer to another person. As with any business, the individual owner bears the entire risk of the enterprise (in other words, all liabilities fall on that person) and reaps all of the rewards from a successful operation.

The principle legal rules that govern a sole proprietorship come from the law of *agency* if there are employees of the business. An agency relationship is a consensual agreement between two parties in which one (the *agent*) acts on behalf of another (the *principal*). A key aspect of the law of agency is that the agent owes a *fiduciary duty* to the principal, which means the person must place the interests of the principal, such as an employer, ahead of his or her own selfish interests when acting on behalf of the principal. The fiduciary duty of an agent will also be critical to other types of business organizations.

B.   Partnership

A partnership is a business organization created when two or more persons join together to operate a business for a profit. Partnerships were the dominant business form in the nineteenth century in the United States. While less prevalent today, the partnership remains as one type of enterprise that is appealing because of the ease with which it can be created. Unlike the more complex business forms, like a corporation or LLC, a partnership does not require any formality in order to be created as a legally valid organization. A partnership may exist even if the participants never call it by that name and never discuss how the business should operate. So long as there is an agreement, even an implicit one, to operate the business together for a profit, then it can be a partnership subject to the rules for such organizations adopted by the State.

The law provides a set of rules, embodied in two Uniform Acts, that supply the basic structure for the relationship between the partners, its obligations to third parties, and how the business can be ended. Importantly, these "off-the-rack" legal rules can, in most cases, be varied by the partners if they so choose, but otherwise apply if an affirmative choice has not been made to adopt a particular rule. In 1994, the National Conference of Commissioners on Uniform State Laws adopted the Uniform Partnership Act (UPA), which almost every state enacted as its governing partnership law. In 1994, the Revised Uniform Partnership Act (RUPA) was adopted, and a number of states have begun the process of revisiting their partnership laws to update them following the new Uniform Act. While there are some important differences between the two laws, they are similar in many important ways.

The basic default rule for partnerships is one of *equality*: each partner has an equal say in the management of the organization, and each shares equally in the profits or losses of the business. As noted above, this rule can be changed by an agreement among the partners. It is common for a partnership agreement to delegate the day-to-day management of the business to a committee, or even a single partner who may be selected from among the partners. For example, many larger law and accounting firms have a "managing partner" who is effectively the chief executive officer for the organization.

Profits from the business can be divided in different ways, and provision can be made to retain a certain percentage of the earnings to allow the business to grow. Partners may be required to contribute capital to the business, either in the form of assets or through their individual labor. A partnership will usually create a *capital account* for each partner to represent that partner's claim on a portion of the business that reflects the assets contributed and the value of work done on its behalf. Absent such an agreement, however, the equality rule governs.

A partnership can be *at-will*, which means that it will exist for as long as the partners want to remain members of it, or for a *term*, which can be for a specific period of time or until a particular event, such as repayment of a bank loan. Because it is a joint undertaking, the partners cannot be forced to remain as members. However, if one partner withdraws in violation of the partnership agreement, then that person may have to pay damages to the other partner(s) and could be precluded from continuing the partnership business. A partner's interest in the business cannot be sold to a third party absent the agreement of the other partners, who cannot be forced to accept a new partner.

The partners are jointly liable for the debts of the partnership. For example, if a creditor sues a partnership for repayment of a debt, and the partnership's assets are insufficient to repay the liability, then the creditor can sue the individual partners on the obligation. While the partners may agree to apportion liability for a debt among themselves, they cannot limit their liability to a third party absent an agreement as part of the debt. Therefore, if a partner is insolvent, then the other partners will have to pay that partner's portion of the debt and then seek to recover against that partner in a subsequent proceeding. This is an individual liability of each partner, which can place their personal assets at risk for the obligations of the partnership. Each partner is fully liable for all the debts of the partnership. Under the RUPA, partners are jointly and severally liable for all debts of the partnership, but the creditor must seek satisfaction from the partnership first before suing the individual partners.

Partners owe one another fiduciary duties. In the well-known New York Court of Appeals decision of *Meinhard v. Salmon*, 164 N.E. 545 (N.Y. 1928), Chief Justice Cardozo stated that partners owe one another "[n]ot honesty alone, but the punctillio of an honor the most sensitive." More specific rules prohibit a partner from using the assets of a partnership for personal purposes and restrict acting in a way that competes with the business of the partnership. The RUPA allows partners to vary the scope of their fiduciary duties to some extent in an agreement.

In dealing with third parties, partners are viewed as agents of the partnership for the purpose of binding the partnership to perform contracts or creating liability for wrongful or negligent conduct. The partnership and, indirectly, the individual partners are *vicariously liable* for the wrongs committed by a partner acting within the scope of partnership's business. For example, if a partner in a stock brokerage partnership stole money from a client's account, that partner plus the partnership — including each individual partner — would be liable for losses because the money was held by the partnership during the ordinary course of its business. Each partner is jointly and severally liable for the damages even if the wrongful partner was forbidden from acting in that way and the other partners had no idea about the misconduct.

Under the UPA, a partnership continues until it is *dissolved*, at which point it enters into a process of *winding-up* its affairs. A dissolution occurs when one or more partners ceases to be a member of the partnership. For example, if a partner decides to withdraw from the partnership, dies, or retires, then the partnership is dissolved unless the agreement provides for it to continue in existence. The RUPA does not require the partnership to be automatically dissolved when a partner *dissociates* from the partnership, so the remaining partners may be able to continue the business.

The UPA divided dissolutions into two categories: *wrongful* and *non-wrongful*. A non-wrongful dissolution is one in which the partner's withdrawal or termination of participation in the partnership is permitted by the agreement or authorized by law, such as withdrawal from an at-will partnership. If it is a partnership for a term, then withdrawal before the completion of the term or in violation of the partnership agreement constitutes a wrongful dissolution. The importance of a wrongful dissolution is that the valuation of the partnership interest of the wrongful partner is limited to the value of the partnership's assets less its *goodwill*, *i.e.* the value of the enterprise over its physical assets. In addition, the remaining partner(s) can continue the partnership business after paying the wrongfully dissolving partner for his or her share of the business. The RUPA does not use the term wrongful dissolution, but provides that a partner who *wrongfully dissociates* in violation of the partnership agreement will be liable to the remaining partners for damages, who can continue to operate the partnership business.

Upon the non-wrongful dissolution of the partnership or a partner's non-wrongful dissociation, again subject to an agreement otherwise, the UPA and the RUPA require that the business be liquidated. After liquidation, the partnership first pays off any creditors, then pays any debts owed to partners, and finally distributes any remainder to the partners in proportion to their share of the profits. Importantly, if it is an at-will partnership, then the distribution must be *in cash*, except in limited circumstances when a distribution of the fair share of the property can be made. This means that a withdrawing partner can demand that the business be sold at an auction or in some other sale arrangement so that prompt payment is made. While the partnership is winding up, it remains in existence and partners continue to owe a duty to complete the process fairly.

C.   Limited Liability Company and Limited Liability Partnership

While a partnership allows each partner to participate in the management of the organization and share in its profits, the significant downside to this form of organization is the liability of each partner for the debts of the business. If the assets of the partnership cannot satisfy the creditors, then the individual partners are *jointly and severally* liable for the debts. This means that a partner's personal property, including a home, brokerage account, and the like can be seized by a creditor to satisfy the partnership's remaining debts. A corporation, on the other hand, has the shield of *limited liability*, which means that only the assets of the corporate entity can be reached by creditors, and shareholders are not liable personally for the debts of the business (unless the doctrine of *piercing the corporate veil* applies as discussed below).

Two newly developed business organizations wed the benefits of corporate limited liability with the flexibility of the partnership: the *limited liability company (LLC)* and the *limited liability partnership (LLC)*. These organizations have become the predominant form for organizing a range of small to mid-size businesses, and every state has statutes governing the creation, operation, and termination of these entities. The first state to adopt an LLC statute was Wyoming in 1980, but these organizational forms became widespread in the 1990s when the Internal Revenue Service changed its tax rules by adopting the "check the box" regulation. This regulation allows LLCs and LLPs to have the benefits of the partnership taxation rules while using the limited liability shield of the corporation to protect the assets of the owners of the enterprise. Under the tax laws, the income of a partnership flows directly to the partners and is not taxed separately as income of the organization, as is done for a corporation. Allowing an LLC or LLP to opt into this form of tax treatment while retaining the benefits afforded by limited liability encouraged lawyers to have their clients choose this form of organization over the traditional partnership and even the corporation.

The owners of an LLC are called "members," and the management of the organization is divided into two types: the *"member-managed"* LLC and the *"manager-managed"* LLC. In order to form an LLC, the members must register with the State and choose the management structure for the firm in an *"operating agreement."* Unlike a partnership, which may be dissolved upon the dissociation of a partner, an LLC continues in existence regardless of whether a member withdraws from it or sells the ownership interest to a third party, much like a corporation which has perpetual existence.

LLPs are an even more recent creation that allows traditional partnerships, such as those found in the legal and accounting professions, to obtain the benefits of limited liability while maintaining the basic structure of a partnership. The scope of the limited liability depends on the state statute. A majority of the states provide for a *full shield* from liability from the partnership's debts, so that a partner's personal assets are not at risk if the LLP cannot repay all its debts and obligations. A smaller number of states only allow a *partial shield* that protects a partner from personal liability for another partner's torts, most importantly malpractice in a professional firm; the partners remain personally liable in these states for other debts, such as bank loans or leases that the partnership cannot repay completely.

The LLC and LLP should not be confused with another type of organization with a similar name, the *limited partnership*. Today, this organization is largely an investment vehicle by which investors purchase "limited partnerships" in a business that is run by a "general partner." Like a regular partnership, the limited partnership can take advantage of the more favorable partnership tax rules, but the limited partners have no say in the management of the partnership, which is controlled by the general partner (which may itself be a corporation, LLC, or other type of firm). Limited partnerships are most commonly used for certain types of investments, such as in the oil-and-gas industry, as a fund for investing in other companies, such as a hedge fund, and to pass assets between generations in a family, such as a family limited partnership. The limited partners are not liable for the debts of the business, while the general partner is liable in the same way that a partner in a regular partnership is responsible for the obligations of the business.

III. DEVELOPMENT OF CORPORATE LAW

Until the late nineteenth century, the predominant business organization was the partnership, along with the limited partnership as a specialized investment vehicle. Corporations could only be organized by a special act of the state legislature or Congress, and then they could only be formed for specified functions for the common good, such as operating a ferry, building a railroad, or providing banking and insurance services. With the advance of the industrial revolution in post-Civil War America, there was great demand for an organization that would allow for the pooling of the large amounts of capital needed to fund manufacturing facilities along with the transportation infrastructure (railroads, canals, ports) needed to support these enterprises. In the late nineteenth century, the states amended their laws to allow anyone to freely incorporate by means of a few simple administrative steps. In addition, corporations were permitted to have *perpetual existence*, rather than just a limited term as required at one time. As such, the corporation become the primary form of business organization, and remains the principal organizational form of larger businesses, especially those whose shares are traded on the public securities markets.

The shift away from partnerships in the late nineteenth century was due in large part to the limited liability shield the corporation offered to investors. The concept of limited liability means that the owners of the corporation, its *shareholders*, do not have any personal liability for the debts of the organization. Therefore, a claimant can only be satisfied by the assets of the corporation and cannot look to the individual owners to repay a debt. A second advantage of the corporation is the *free transferability of shares*, which means that a shareholder can sell his or her ownership interest without any effect on its continued existence. This is the opposite of partnership law, which requires dissolution when a partner seeks to withdraw from the business.

As the rules for creating a corporation were relaxed, one of the nation's smallest states, Delaware, became the primary jurisdiction in which larger businesses chose to incorporate. The reasons for this are not entirely clear. There is one school of thought that argues Delaware won the so-called "race to the bottom" by adopting laws most favorable to managers of these larger enterprises, who chose the state that would give them the most protection. Another analysis, offered largely by those applying economics to legal analysis, argue that Delaware offers the best balance between the rights of shareholders with those of management, making it the optimal jurisdiction to maximize the value of the corporation rather than the one that will disfavor investors. Regardless of which analysis is correct — if indeed either is — the fact is that Delaware is the home to a majority of the largest corporations in the United States.

Delaware's corporate laws are among the most influential in the United States because of its preeminence as the jurisdiction of choice for a wide range of larger corporations. It retains its position not just because of its widely-influential corporate code but also because its judicial system is attuned to the needs of businesses for quick, clear decisions resolving disputes. The Delaware Chancery Court is famed for judges who understand how businesses operate and provide well-reasoned decisions on a range of issues. There is no intermediate appellate court in Delaware, and the state Supreme Court has been similarly willing to resolve appeals in a fairly short window of time. Thus, a dispute may be resolved by the Delaware courts in as little as two months, almost the speed of light compared to litigation in other jurisdictions. Moreover, because of its continuing role in corporate law, Delaware has the most developed jurisprudence in the corporate field, which allows businesses to plan accordingly based on relatively clear legal principles.

When a corporation is formed, the organizers must file an application with a state office, often the Secretary of State, to register the organization and provide an agent for service of process. There is no requirement that a corporation choose any one particular state in which to incorporate. The organizers or managers can decide which state's law they want to apply by choosing the state of incorporation, which can include changing states if the law is particularly favorable. A company need not have any physical presence in the jurisdiction, such as an office or other facility, and most corporations incorporated in Delaware have no operations or employees in the state.

Any disputes about a corporation's *internal affairs* — the relationship between a corporation's shareholders and its managers and directors — are governed by law of the state of incorporation. The Supreme Court stated in *CTS Corp. v. Dynamics Corp.*, 481 U.S. 69 (1987), that "[n]o principle of corporation law and practice is more firmly established than a State's authority to regulate domestic corporations, including the authority to define the voting rights of shareholders."

While the internal corporate governance rules for a corporation are set by the State, the codes generally provide substantial flexibility in how a company can choose to structure itself. For example, state corporation codes allow a company to give greater voting rights to certain classes of shares, eliminate the board of directors, or restrict the right of shareholders to sell or otherwise transfer their shares. Thus, while the State's laws govern disputes, there is substantial room to vary the basic rules provided by a corporation code to adapt the corporation to the needs of its shareholders and managers.

While there is no general federal corporation code, the laws regulating the securities markets can exert a substantial influence on how a corporation is governed. These laws were adopted in response to the Great Crash in 1929 and subsequent economic depression, and they provide an extensive set of rules for corporations whose shares are traded on the public securities markets, such as the New York Stock Exchange. These laws require corporations to disclose a broad array of information to their shareholders, as discussed below. For example, under the Securities Exchange Act of 1934, a corporation whose shares are traded on a public market must provide certain information to its shareholders on a regular basis, and if it is going to ask them to vote on a matter then it must provide specified information within certain time periods. In order to meet the disclosure requirements of federal law, a company will have to hire an outside auditor to review its books and records and provide reports on how it protects itself from fraud and other abuses. Thus, larger corporations whose shares are available for purchase on the public securities markets are subject to the law of its state of incorporation and the federal government.

IV. THE STRUCTURE OF THE CORPORATION

Corporations range in size from those with a single owner, which is not much different from a sole proprietorship, to multinational enterprises with thousands of shareholders and revenues in the billions. The law of corporations does not provide different rules based on the size of the business, although states have adopted some special rules for smaller corporations that the owners can opt into if they choose. The core attribute of a corporation is the separation of ownership and management. Unlike a partnership, a corporation is not necessarily managed by its owners, the shareholders, but instead operates under the direction of a board of directors and is managed on a day-to-day basis by officers appointed by the board. Thus, shareholders have a more limited say in the direction of the business.

A.   Directors

The directors of a corporation are given the authority to oversee the organization. The Delaware provision on the board of directors is typical: "The business and affairs of every corporation . . . shall be managed by or under the direction of a board of directors. . . ." Del. Gen. Corp. L. § 141(a). In a smaller corporation, the board usually consists of the major owners of the business, similar to a partnership or member-managed LLC. Once the business achieves a certain size, the role of the board is separated from the day-to-day operations of the company, so that the directors are responsible for the overall direction of the corporation and leave it to the managers to implement their directives.

The board is elected by the shareholders, and can range in size from three members to as many as twenty. Most directors are elected annually, although the law allows a corporation to provide for a term of up to three years. Unlike some European companies, which reserve a certain number of directorship positions to employees or a union to select, in a United States corporation only shareholders elect directors. The board normally nominates those who will run for a board position, although an outsider seeking to gain control of the company can nominate a slate of directors and seek shareholder votes to put them in charge of the company. This is known as a *hostile proxy* in which shareholders will select among two (or more) slates of board candidates. Recently there has been pressure from large institutional investors, such as pension funds, to allow shareholders of publicly traded companies to nominate candidates rather than having to engage in a hostile proxy solicitation to elect candidates other than those chosen by the board. Companies have largely resisted this move to open up corporate elections to outside candidates.

Board members are often divided into two categories: *"inside"* and *"independent"* (or outside) directors. The rules of the major stock exchanges require companies to have a majority of independent directors. The assessment of a director's independence is based on the person's ties to the company, for example whether the director was an employee of the corporation within the past five years or received a certain amount of compensation. Typical inside directors are officers of the corporation, and virtually every Chief Executive Officer of the corporation is a member of the board, frequently serving as its chair. Longevity of service does not make one an inside director, even though the person may have close personal ties to the company's management.

In a larger corporation, the board will delegate certain responsibilities to committees that will do the main work on a particular topic. Among the most important committee of a board is the audit committee, which is responsible for overseeing the corporation's compliance with an array of laws and ensuring that the financial figures it reports to the public are accurate and reliable. Other typical committees found at corporations are an executive committee, which can make certain decisions on behalf of the board between directors' meetings, the compensation committee that decides on executive pay, and a nominating committee to consider candidates for directorships.

B.   Officers

The typical corporation will have officers who serve as the Chief Executive Officer, referred to as the CEO, a Chief Administrative Officer, sometimes designated the president, a Chief Financial Officer (CFO), and a general counsel. These positions are not mandated by state corporations codes for the most part, but have evolved as the preferred means of managing a larger business. The duties of an individual officer are determined by the board of directors, which has the ultimate responsibility for oversight of a corporation's managers. The board or one of its committees may work directly with an officer, such as the audit committee receiving reports directly from the CFO about the corporation's financial statements and system of internal controls.

The internal corporate "culture" or tone is set largely by the CEO and other senior officers, with lower-level managers often following the lead of a company's officers in dealing with customers and adhering to the requirements of the law. An important issue in any company is how it will deal with wrongdoing, and the company's senior management has a key role to play in ensuring that any reports of misconduct are dealt with promptly and appropriately. An important federal law, the Sarbanes-Oxley Act of 2002, includes a provision requiring the CEO and CFO of a publicly-traded corporation to certify the company's financial statements. A violation of the provision can result in a criminal prosecution if the officers know the financial statement was incorrect.

C. Shareholders

The basic unit of ownership of a corporation is a share of *common stock*, which is a fractional proprietary interest in the corporation. The owners are called *shareholders* or *stockholders*, and they are investors in the business. The fundamental characteristics of common stock is that it gives its owner the right to vote on certain matters concerning the corporation, most importantly for members of the board of directors, and a *pro rata* claim on the assets of the corporation after the payment of its obligations if it is dissolved. Because a corporation has no limit on its existence, the shareholders will receive a return on their investment in the corporation by receiving dividends, which are paid out of the profits of the business, and capital gains from selling the shares at a greater price than they were acquired, assuming its value has increased since the purchase of the shares. If the corporation is dissolved, the shareholders are the *residual claimant* on any remaining assets of the corporation, which means they are the last ones to be paid upon a dissolution after all other creditors. If a corporation were to declare bankruptcy, it is often the case that the value of the stock is wiped out completely.

At one time, shares were represented by a *stock certificate*, a formal document that showed the number of shares owned and could be transferred to another person by sale, bequest, gift, or any other transaction. Today, shares are maintained through a *book entry system* in which actual physical certificates are only rarely used, and companies (along with brokerage firms) maintain electronic records of share ownership. A company must maintain a list of its shareholders, although it may not include many individual investors because the actual holder of the shares is a nominee company that holds the shares on behalf of others.

The usual forum for shareholder voting is at the corporation's *annual meeting*. Individual shareholders rarely appear at the meeting, and the voting is done by *proxy*, in which the shareholders deliver their votes to a nominee who will comply with the instructions on the proxy form for voting the shares. The use of paper proxies is declining as more voting is done over the Internet or by other electronic means. In addition to electing directors, shareholders may be asked to approve certain management compensation plans, appointment of the company's auditors, and on proposals made by other shareholders regarding the operation of the company. In addition, a company or, in certain states, a shareholder owning more than 10% of the shares, can call for a *special meeting* to consider issues that need to be addressed immediately. Special meetings are fairly rare, and usually take place to consider an extraordinary issue facing the company, such as an offer to buy the corporation or other fundamental change. Another means by which shareholders can vote is through a *consent solicitation* in which shareholders are asked to approve an action without having a formal meeting.

Most corporations use *straight voting* by shareholders for electing directors, which means that each share has one vote. Thus, if a person owns one hundred shares of stock, then that person may vote one hundred times for a candidate for the board. Another type of procedure utilized in a few corporations is *cumulative voting*, which allows a shareholder to aggregate the votes and apply them to a single or smaller number of candidates seeking election to the board. For example, if there were five directorships on the proxy and a person owned one hundred shares, then the person would have five hundred votes (5 directors x 100 shares). Under a cumulative voting scheme, the shareholder could give all five hundred votes to a single candidate, or two-hundred and fifty to two of the candidates. The benefit of cumulative voting is that it allows shareholders owning a minority of the company's shares to pool their votes and elect at least one or more candidates to the board. Under straight voting, if one shareholder (or a small group of investors) owns 50.1% of the shares, then all of that person's board candidates will be elected, while cumulative voting allows other shareholders to put at least a one representative on the board, who will presumably guard their interests.

In addition to voting for directors, shareholders have the power to remove them from office. A director can be removed for cause, or without cause if allowed to by statute or the corporation's articles. If a director is to be removed for cause, then the company must afford the director the opportunity to present his or her position on the issues and to argue against removal, if the director so chooses. If a cumulative voting scheme is used, then in most states a director cannot be removed if the number of votes against removal would have been sufficient to elect the director to the board in a regular election. In other words, removal of a director chosen through cumulative voting requires a substantial majority of the votes.

D.   Structure of the Corporation

The two basic documents that establish the structure of a corporation are the *articles of incorporation,* sometimes called the charter or certificate of incorporation, and the *by-laws.* The articles are sometimes described as the constitution of the corporation, while the by-laws serve as its legislation, although some issues can be addressed in either. The articles are filed with the state in which the company is incorporated, and usually must contain provisions addressing specified topics, such as the name, duration of existence, the number of shares, including whether they will be divided into classes or have any special rights, number of directors, the name of the company's agent for service of process, and the names of the initial directors and incorporators. Form articles are readily available, and for small companies they can provide the basic information necessary to comply with state law incorporation requirements. The articles can be amended in a two-step process, with the board of directors first approving the amendment and then the shares entitled to vote approving the change. A corporation can require that a supermajority approve an amendment if the articles so provide, otherwise amendments only require a majority vote of the shares.

The by-laws of a corporation usually provide the internal corporate governance rules, such as the rules for elections, the date of the annual meeting, quorum requirements, the size of the board, and any restrictions on the right to transfer shares. In most states, the by-laws can be amended by the board or the shareholders, although in some jurisdictions the articles may reserve that right exclusively to the shareholders.

Corporations require *capital* in order to operate, which is the money and property that it obtains from investors and by borrowing funds from creditors. An *equity investment* is capital contributed in exchange for an ownership interest in the company, usually in the form of common shares. *Debt* involves obtaining funds based on a promise to repay that amount over a certain period of time along with additional money as *interest* on the obligation. A shareholder's return on the investment depends on the profitability of the business, while a creditor of the corporation receives a fixed return on the amount lent. If a corporation suffers financial reversals, including bankruptcy, the creditors will be paid before any distribution of remaining assets, if there are any, to the shareholders.

The mix of equity and debt is called the *capital structure* of the corporation, and each form of capital has advantages as a means to finance the business. Selling shares usually does not involve any obligation to make future payments to the shareholders, so this form of capital is often cheaper than debt, which requires interest payments on a regular basis. A company can choose to distribute a portion of its profits in the form of *dividends* to its shareholders, while creditors only receive the amount agreed to as interest. The decision whether to pay a dividend to the shareholders is made by the board of directors. State laws limit the amount that can be paid out to shareholders, requiring the corporation to have sufficient funds available on its balance sheet to pay its other obligations in addition to the dividend. When a corporation sells shares, however, it *dilutes* the holdings of its current owners, who will have a smaller share of the company unless they purchase additional shares, which means they commit even more capital to the company.

While borrowing money obligates a company to repay the creditor with interest, those payments are tax-deductible, while dividend payments are not. Taking on debt does not dilute the ownership of current shareholders, so it may be a preferable way to obtain capital, especially if significant sums are required for the business. Industries that are *capital-intensive*, such as utilities or large manufacturers, tend to rely more heavily on debt, while the high-tech industry is known for using equity, including options to buy shares at a fixed price, in the future, to reward employees and acquire other companies.

V. FIDUCIARY DUTIES

A cornerstone of corporate law is that the directors and officers of a corporation owe a fiduciary duty to the organization to ensure that the interests of shareholders are protected and the business is managed properly. Given the broad power and discretion they have to operate the business, fiduciary duties operate as a means to police directors and officers through judicial action. The duty to protect and further the corporation's interest is traceable to the law of agency, which requires the agent to put the principal's interests first. In most circumstances, the directors and officers owe their fiduciary obligation to the corporation and not the shareholders themselves, but in certain situations the shareholders may be the direct beneficiary of the fiduciary duty. Similarly, while shareholders do not owe a fiduciary duty to the corporation, when one shareholder controls the organization then a duty may be owed to the minority shareholders in addition to any obligation to the corporation.

There are two primary fiduciary duties owed to the corporation: the duty of due care and the duty of loyalty. In addition, the Delaware courts have recognized a third obligation, the duty of good faith.

A. Duty of Due Care

The directors of a company are responsible for determining the general course and direction of the business. In fulfilling this obligation, the board must make its decision based on adequate information, and take the time to deliberate before choosing a course of action. This responsibility is called the *duty of due care*, and it imposes on directors the obligation to discharge their functions in a reasonable manner. Section 8.30(a) of the Model Business Corporation Act describes the basic requirements for meeting the duty of due care: "Each member of the board of directors, when discharging the duties of a director, shall act: (1) in good faith, and (2) in a manner the director reasonably believes to be in the best interests of the corporation." Directors may rely on information provided to them by management and outside advisers in making their decisions.

Directors can make decisions that turn out badly, such as an unwise investment or pursuing a course of action that triggers widespread negative publicity. The duty of due care requires that directors act reasonably, but there is no guarantee that a good result will occur. Does a director breach the duty of due care if a decision turns out badly? The answer is "No" because courts apply the *"Business Judgment Rule"* when a shareholder challenges a decision of the board based on a negative result. As described by the Delaware Supreme Court, the Business Judgment Rule "is a presumption that in making a business decision the directors of a corporation acted on an informed basis, in good faith[,] and in the honest belief that the action taken was in the best interests of the company. Absent an abuse of discretion, that judgment will be respected by the courts." *Aronson v Lewis*, 473 A.2d 805 (Del. 1984). In effect, if the directors appear to have acted reasonably in reaching a decision regarding the operation of the business, the courts will not second-guess that or find a director liable for violating the duty of due care. Thus, absent additional facts showing that the directors were grossly negligent or the decision was tainted by a conflict of interest, the board's decision cannot be challenged.

To establish a violation of the duty of due care, the courts apply the standard of gross negligence, which means that a board's decision must rise to a high level of misconduct. Very few cases have been successful in alleging a breach of the duty of due care. In the well-known decision in *Smith v. Van Gorkom*, 488 A.2d 858 (Del. 1985), the Delaware Supreme Court found that the board of a company violated the duty of due care because it engaged in virtually no review of an offer to buy the corporation, never informing itself regarding the value of the business or whether the offer was the best one that could be obtained. This case illustrates that to be successful on a claim that the duty of due care was breached, the plaintiff-shareholder must show an almost complete failure in the process by which the decision was reached, not just that the result was questionable.

If the directors are liable for a breach of the duty of due care, then they could be required to pay damages to the corporation for the harm it suffered. In *Smith v. Van Gorkom*, the board could have been liable for over $100 million in damages due to the breach. In response to such potentially draconian liability, Delaware and almost every other state adopted an amendment to their state corporation codes that allows a corporation to eliminate or limit the liability of a director for a breach of the duty of due care. Most larger corporations now have an *"exculpation" provision* in their articles of incorporation that prohibits shareholders from recovering money damages from directors for a breach of the duty of due care. If a law suit is filed claiming a breach of the duty, and the only relief sought is damages, then the case will be dismissed because that remedy is unavailable even if a violation of the duty of due care could be established.

B.   Duty of Loyalty

While the duty of care focuses on the process by which a decision is made, the duty of loyalty protects the corporation from conflicts of interest that might taint a decision that is detrimental to the company. In the nineteenth century, courts held that all contracts in which a director or officer had a conflicting interest were void and unenforceable. Over time, courts softened the doctrine because there may be many instances in which it can be in the corporation's best interest to deal with a member of its board in a transaction. For example, a manufacturer may have an officer from a local bank on its board of directors, and use the bank for its accounts and loans. The law allows these types of transactions so long as the terms are fair and the other board members know of the arrangement and approve it.

There are two main types of conflicts of interest governed by the duty of loyalty: *usurping a corporate opportunity* and *self-dealing*. A usurpation claim arises when a director or officer takes a business opportunity that rightfully belongs to the corporation, and benefits personally from it. For example, a director may be contacted by a real estate agent who says that a valuable parcel of land is available for purchase. The director knows the company would like to purchase the land to build a new factory, but instead of informing the company the director acquires the land personally. The company can argue that the director violated the duty of loyalty because the information about the land came to the officer in his or her capacity as a representative of the corporation, and should have offered the opportunity to the company first before undertaking the transaction.

It is not always clear whether an opportunity is one that a corporate fiduciary should offer first to the corporation before taking advantage of it for personal gain. Courts have developed different tests that look to a range of factors to determine whether a transaction constitutes a corporate opportunity. In Delaware, the court looks to whether the company has an *interest or expectancy* in the opportunity, and whether it was within the company's *line of business*. The corporation's financial status is also important because it must be able to undertake the transaction for it to be a corporate opportunity. *Guth v. Loft*, 5 A.2d 503 (Del. 1939).

Other courts look to a broader fairness analysis that considers how the director or officer learned of the opportunity and use of corporate resources in addition to whether the transaction was within its business and financial abilities. The American Law Institute adopted a test that focuses primarily on whether the fiduciary disclosed the opportunity to the corporation and offered it to the company to allow the board to make the initial decision whether to pursue the transaction. If a company decides not to pursue an opportunity, then a director or officer should be allowed to pursue it because there is no breach of fiduciary duty to the corporation.

A conflict of interest also arises when a director or officer is on both sides of a transaction involving the corporation. For example, a director may own property that was acquired before joining the board that the company wants to purchase for a new facility. If the director sells the land to the corporation, then that person is on both sides of the transaction, and is gaining a personal benefit from the sale. This is described as *self-dealing* because the benefit comes at the expense of the company. Absent some special benefit to the fiduciary that is not realized by other shareholders of the company, then a conflict of interest would not violate the duty of loyalty. It is the personal gain from the transaction that raises a question about whether a fiduciary duty was violated.

A self-dealing transaction is not automatically prohibited, but there are certain steps that must be followed to prevent it from constituting a breach of fiduciary duty. State corporation codes authorize the board of directors or the shareholders to approve a self-dealing transaction involving an officer or director so long as it is fair to the corporation. The procedures established in most states require that there be complete disclosure of the terms to the directors. Those directors approving the transaction should be both *disinterested*, meaning they do not have any financial or other stake in the deal, and *independent* of the person involved, meaning they are not beholden or otherwise subservient to the officer or director.

Issues regarding the independence of the board approving a transaction arise most often when there is a controlling shareholder who wields a powerful influence over the other directors such that it is questionable whether they are acting in the company's best interest. Shareholder approval does not involve the same inquiry into independence and disinterestedness, although if a majority of the votes are controlled by an interested party to the transaction then the approval may not be sufficient to avoid a challenge. If there is appropriate approval of the transaction, in some states shareholders can still challenge it as not being fair to the corporation, but they will bear the burden of proof on that issue, and courts generally presume that the transaction is protected by the business judgment rule.

While fiduciary duties are usually owed only by officers and directors, a controlling shareholder may also owe a duty to the corporation even if the person or entity does not hold any formal position in the company. This issue arises most often when one corporation owns a majority of the shares of another company, so that it is considered to be the *parent* and the controlled company is the *subsidiary*. It is common for the parent to name the officers and directors of the subsidiary, and to exercise significant control over its operations, although the subsidiary's separate existence as a legal entity must be respected (see *Piercing the Corporate Veil* below). In its dealings with the subsidiary, the parent is viewed as having a fiduciary duty to treat the minority shareholders fairly, and not to engage in self-dealing transactions. This means that the parent corporation cannot gain a benefit from the subsidiary that is not also provided to the other shareholders of the subsidiary. For example, if the subsidiary pays out dividends, each share must receive the same amount. If the parent contracts with the subsidiary, the terms of the transaction must be fair, and the requirements of the agreement adhered to so that the parent does not gain an undue advantage from its control.

## C.	Duty of Good Faith

The Delaware courts have started to develop a third fiduciary obligation of directors and officers of a corporation: the *duty of good faith*. This new duty incorporates aspects of both due care and loyalty, and applies when a decision or transaction shows an almost complete disregard for the best interests of the corporation. Unlike the duty of due care, which is based on gross negligence, a violation of the duty of good faith occurs when a director or officer intentionally acts with deliberate indifference for the potential harm to the company. As described in *In re Walt Disney Co. Derivative Litigation*, 906 A.2d 27 (Del. 2006):

> A failure to act in good faith may be shown, for instance, where the fiduciary intentionally acts with a purpose other than that of advancing the best interests of the corporation, where the fiduciary acts with the intent to violate applicable positive law, or where the fiduciary intentionally fails to act in the face of a known duty to act, demonstrating a conscious disregard for his duties.

This is a recent development in Delaware law, and the courts are still developing the parameters of the duty.

D.   Shareholder Derivative Suits

Directors and officers owe fiduciary duties to the corporation, and not to the shareholders except in limited circumstances where there is a controlling shareholder. At the same time, directors are responsible for the oversight of the corporation, and so may be tempted to have the company ignore a breach of fiduciary duty by a fellow director — or even themselves — by declining to pursue a claim for damages to the company. To resolve the dilemma of requiring a director to decide whether to pursue a claim, the courts developed a procedural device called the *shareholder derivative suit* that allows shareholders to being an action on behalf of the corporation. Because the shareholders are the ultimate owners of the corporation, it is in their interest to protect it from harmful actions, including those by directors and officers.

The shareholders do not sue for their own benefit because only the corporation would be harmed by a fiduciary duty breach, so any recovery goes to the corporation itself, to be shared by all owners of the company. The derivative suit is actually two lawsuits: one against the corporation to compel it to pursue a claim, and one against the directors or officers for harming the corporation. This results in the rather odd situation in which the corporation is both a defendant in the action and effectively a plaintiff who will recover any damages. Most states require the shareholder named as the plaintiff to have owned the corporation's shares at the time of the fiduciary duty breach, and to maintain ownership throughout the derivative suit in order to have a sufficient interest in the outcome.

The reality of these suits is not the usual model of an individual seeking compensation for a personal injury. The real force behind shareholder derivative suits are the law firms that specialize in bringing these cases in the hope of receiving a portion of an award as attorney's fees, which in some situations can amount to millions of dollars. There is a natural fear of strike suits against a company, in which lawyers file an almost frivolous claim in the hope of gaining a quick settlement and the resultant attorney's fees from a corporation that wants to avoid the nuisance of a law suit that may engender significant costs during discovery.

In order to protect against these types of strike suits, the law requires a shareholder to make a *demand* on the board to pursue the action for the alleged fiduciary duty breach before filing the derivative claim in court. The board then has a chance to evaluate the claim to decide whether it is in the company's best interests to have a law suit filed on its behalf. The board will consider whether the likelihood of any recovery is outweighed by the costs of the legal proceeding, including the attorney's fees it will pay on behalf of any officers or directors sued in the case. If the board determines that the claim should be brought, then the case is filed in its own name and there is no derivative action because the company pursues the case directly. If the chance of recovery is remote, or the amount to be realized insignificant, a board may rationally determine that the suit should not be pursued. At that point, the demand is refused, and the petitioning shareholder notified about the board's decision.

While a demand refusal would seem to spell the end of the case, there is again the problem that the board of directors may well be deciding whether to sue itself, the same dilemma that spawned the development of the derivative suit. Many states have a *universal demand* requirement, that before filing a derivative suit the complaining shareholder must file a demand with the board. If the board refuses the demand, then the shareholder can file a suit challenging the decision to reject the demand on the ground that the board's decision is not a reasonable exercise of its business judgment. In Delaware and a few other states, a shareholder can file a derivative suit and plead *demand futility*, that the exercise of filing a demand would be useless because the board could not make a reasoned business decision on it. In either situation, the first issue in the derivative litigation will be whether the board could properly review a demand, or whether it is disabled because of a conflict of interest or lack of independence.

To determine whether the board's decision was proper, or in Delaware whether demand was futile, the court must determine whether a majority of the directors are *disinterested* in the transaction at issue and *independent*. A director is interested if the person has a financial or other personal stake in the transaction. A director is not independent if the person is beholden to the director or officer who engaged in the challenged transaction, such that it is unlikely the director could exercise an untainted business judgment on whether to pursue a suit for breach of fiduciary duty. Among the ties that have been found to undermine a director's independence include: (1) a college president who solicited large gifts from the company's CEO for his institution; (2) a director who received significant compensation from the company, either directly or to the director's employer, such as a law firm or financial management company; (3) family ties with an officer, such as parents, siblings, or marital partners; and (4) in one case, the CEO of the company was a significant contributor to the university where two directors were professors. If a majority of the board is not both disinterested and independent, then the board is presumed to be unable to make a reasonable decision on the demand, and it is excused (in Delaware) or the refusal is rejected (if demand is required).

Even if the derivative suit is permitted to proceed, that does not necessarily mean the corporation is powerless to seek dismissal of the case at a later point. In *Zapata Corp. v. Maldonado*, 430 A.2d 779 (Del. 1981), the Delaware Supreme Court recognized that the board of directors retains the ultimate authority to decide whether a suit in the company's name should continue, or whether it is in its best interests to dismiss it. The court noted that directors may still be tainted by a desire to protect fellow directors — the court noted a "there but for the grace of God go I" attitude is possible — and so the decision to dismiss after the case has been properly initiated is subject to greater scrutiny. The Delaware courts require a company seeking dismissal of a properly filed derivative suit to establish a committee of independent directors to review the case and present their findings to the court. That committee, often called a *special litigation committee*, must provide the court with a written report showing an objective and thorough investigation of the derivative claims and the reasons for recommending dismissal. The committee then bears the burden of proof to show its independence and good faith, at which point the court may apply its own business judgment to determine whether to dismiss the suit. The third step is discretionary, and it is up to the judge to decide whether to allow the suit to proceed or dismiss it.

VI. CLOSELY-HELD BUSINESSES

The state corporation codes developed as a "one size fits all" approach, so that a corporation with a single shareholder was subject to the same statutory provisions as a multinational corporation with thousands of shareholders. The basic premise of a corporation is that ownership is separated from management, and within the business the board of directors has the ultimate authority to decide on the direction of the corporation. For the shareholders, if they do not like how the company is being managed, they can sell their shares in the public market. While this model works well in the larger corporation, a small company — usually called a *close corporation* — often has only a small group of shareholders who also serve as the managers of the enterprise. Importantly, there is no available market for the shares because they are not listed on an exchange, and it is difficult to find buyers who might want to purchase a minority stake in an ongoing business. Thus, the rules designed to govern large corporations do not work as well for closely-held businesses.

A.   Close Corporations

The fundamental principle that the board is responsible for the management of the corporation led to decisions by the courts that the shareholders could not enter into an agreement that "sterilized" the authority of the directors to oversee the management of the corporation. Thus, an agreement among the controlling shareholder and two minority shareholders that they would ensure that each was elected a director and had a position in the company's management was declared unenforceable because it impermissibly restricted the power of the board to manage the business, a responsibility granted by the state corporation code. *McQuade v. Stoneham*, 189 N.E. 234 (N.Y. 1934). Courts were hostile to efforts to modify the structure of the corporation to accommodate the interests of the owners and operators of closely-held businesses until the 1960s.

The problem with applying the general corporate law to a close corporation is that minority shareholders have no means to protect themselves from *opportunism* by controlling shareholders. That is, a controlling shareholder may decide to *freeze out* (or *squeeze out*) a minority shareholder by refusing to employ the person, denying any dividends or profit-sharing, and increasing the salaries of those in control of the business. The minority shareholder is powerless to vote against such changes, and without a market to sell the shares the investment is effectively rendered worthless.

In response, the states have adopted provisions that allow shareholders of a closely-held corporation to modify the operational structure of the organization to limit or even eliminate the power of the directors, to require distribution of profits, protect the job security of specified shareholders, and trigger the repurchase of shares pursuant to a specified formula if certain events occurred. These provisions are often in the form of a *shareholder agreement*, which may be placed into the articles of incorporation or by-laws. Some states require a corporation to opt into a special close corporation code by registering their status with the state, otherwise the general corporate laws apply.

Even if a corporation has not been structured to provide specific protections to minority shareholders, the fiduciary duties of due care and loyalty still apply to the directors and officers of the organization. Self-dealing by a controlling shareholder can be the subject of a suit by other shareholders to recover any improper benefit.

These duties are relatively narrow, and would not restrict a controlling shareholder from freezing out a minority shareholder. The courts have developed a special doctrine for closely-held corporations that restricts the power of a controlling shareholder who engages in conduct that constitutes *oppression* of a minority shareholder. This special fiduciary duty is drawn from partnership law, which requires that partners treat one another with complete fairness in their dealings. This duty is owed by one shareholder to another, and not just the corporation, as is the case with the duties of loyalty and due care.

In the well-known case of *Donahue v. Rodd Electrotype Co.*, 328 N.E.2d 505 (Mass. 1975), the Massachusetts Supreme Judicial Court found that the similarities between a closely-held business and a partnership meant that each shareholder must be treated the same, and no one owner could receive a benefit that was denied another shareholder. The court held that an offer to purchase the holdings of the controlling shareholder for $800 per share but denial of that offer to a minority shareholder was a breach of fiduciary duty, requiring either repurchase of the shares or extending an identical offer to the other shareholder.

Massachusetts softened the rule of strict equality in a case decided a year later, *Wilkes v. Springside Nursing Home, Inc.*, 353 N.E.2d 657 (Mass. 1976), that adopted a new test for determining whether the controlling shareholder breached a fiduciary duty to the minority. The court analyzed the conduct of a controlling shareholder that harmed a minority shareholder by asking whether (1) there was a legitimate business purpose for the actions against the minority shareholder and (2) whether the minority shareholder could show a less harmful alternative could have been pursued even if the controlling shareholder had a legitimate reason for the course of conduct. The court found that the controlling shareholders had violated their fiduciary duty by forcing the minority shareholder out of his job at the nursing home, thus depriving him of a salary, not re-electing him to the board of directors, raising their own salaries, and making an offer to purchase his shares at a price that one director said he would not have accepted, in other words, a low-ball offer.

Not all states have adopted the more liberal Massachusetts approach to protecting minority shareholder rights. In *Nixon v. Blackwell*, 626 A.2d 1366 (Del. 1993), the Delaware Supreme Court rejected the equality requirement of *Donahue*. The court found that a corporation's long-standing practice of affording employee-shareholders a means to sell their shares that was denied to the plaintiffs who were not employees — they received their shares by gift — was not a breach of a fiduciary duty. Importantly, the company in *Nixon* had not opted into Delaware's special close corporation code, and the policies followed by the company had been in place for years and were provided for in the corporate articles and by-laws.

In *Donahue* and *Wilkes*, there was no special shareholder agreement governing the relationship of the shareholders and their rights, so the Massachusetts courts used fiduciary duty as a means to protect the minority. In the absence of a shareholder agreement or other documentation showing how the owners decided to treat one another, a court will use its own judgment to determine the fairness of a controlling shareholders actions. In *Gimpel v. Bolstein*, 477 N.Y.S.2d 1014 (N.Y. Sup. 1984), for example, the New York Court of Appeals required a corporation to implement a dividend or share repurchase to protect the interests of a minority shareholder, even though the controlling shareholders had done nothing wrong and the minority shareholder had left the company a few years earlier after embezzling money from it. The court applied its equitable powers to protect a minority shareholder who faced the prospect of owning shares that were entirely worthless, with no recourse to obtain some benefit from the company in which he was a minority owner.

The courts will enforce a shareholder agreement over claims of unfairness by a minority shareholder if the terms are clear. Agreements regarding the right to repurchase shares, exercise of voting rights, or valuation of the firm can effectively limit a claim of breach of fiduciary duty because, by entering into the contract, the shareholders acknowledge how they will deal with one another. In *Gallagher v. Lambert*, 549 N.E.2d 136 (N.Y. 1989), the New York Court of Appeals held that a share repurchase agreement with an employee who was terminated right before the shares would increase substantially in value was not a breach of fiduciary duty. The court held that "[t]hese agreements define the scope of the relevant fiduciary duty and supply certainty of obligation to each side. They should not be undone simply upon an allegation of unfairness."

B.   LLC Governance

The legislation authorizing the formation of the limited liability company (and limited liability partnership) is one of the most significant changes in the organization of business in the last fifty years. The LLC combines limited liability, the hallmark of a corporation, with the ability to participate in management while enjoying flow-through taxation, something once limited to partnerships. This important change in how businesses can be organized is notable for the speed with which it occurred — in less than a decade this type of organization went from being authorized by only two states and only applied in limited circumstances to being adopted in every state and used by thousands of businesses.

In order to form an LLC, the members must file *articles of organization*, which are similar to a corporation's articles of incorporation, with the state. Unlike corporate articles, this document contains only limited information about the LLC, such as the name of the LLC, its purpose, the address of its principal office, and the name and address of its resident agent. The key document for an LLC is its *operating agreement*, which sets forth the structure of the organization, how it will be operated, and how the interests of the members can be sold or valued. Courts are fond of stating that "a limited liability company is as much a creature of contract as of statute," so the emphasis is determining the intent of the members in structuring the LLC to decide how to resolve disputes. Members may enter into an operating agreement that provides great detail regarding the operation of the LLC and the relationship of the members to one another, such as (1) the financial obligations of members; (2) control of management; (3) sharing of profits, losses, and distributions; (4) withdrawal from the LLC and its dissolution; and (5) assignment or forfeiture of interests. Unless the articles of organization mandate a written agreement, the members' operating agreement need not be in writing, although it is highly prudent to commit to writing such an important agreement. Most states have default provisions in their LLC statutes that permit members to form and operate an LLC without a formal operating agreement.

An LLC's articles of organization can specify one of two structures for the firm: as a *member-managed* or *manager-managed* LLC. In a member-managed LLC, all of the members have apparent authority, comparable to that of partners in a partnership, to make managerial decisions on behalf of the LLC and to bind the LLC to the extent that the members are carrying on the usual and ordinary business of the LLC. In contrast, in a manager-managed LLC, it is the managers, who are not necessarily members or who may be only a limited number of members, who have authority to bind the LLC and make most day-to-day operating decisions. Those members who are not managers in a manager-managed LLC are not considered agents of the LLC, and their power to control the firm is generally limited to involvement only in major decisions, such as whether to engage in a merger or dissolve the LLC. The manager-managed LLC is more akin to a close corporation, while a member-managed LLC is more like a traditional general partnership, although each retains the benefit of limited liability. Courts tend to use the oppression analysis from close corporations for LLCs, at least where the owners are also the managers of the business.

VII.   THIRD-PARTY LIABILITY

A.   Limited Liability

Limited liability is among the most important reasons to organize a business as a corporation or LLC. The Model Business Corporations Act provides that "a shareholder of a corporation is not personally liable for the acts or debts of the corporation except that he may become personally liable by reason of his own acts or conduct." Thus, while the corporation may incur substantial indebtedness through borrowing or through other liabilities, such as contractual or tort obligations, the individual shareholders are not responsible for repayment, so their personal assets cannot be reached to satisfy corporate debts. The shareholders can only lose the amount of their investment in the business.

If a potential creditor wishes to have an individual shareholder responsible for a debt or obligation, the creditor should obtain a personal guarantee or other acknowledgment of the shareholder's individual liability for the corporate obligation. Sophisticated creditors dealing with a closely-held corporation or LLC know the effect of limited liability on collecting what is owed on a debt or other obligation. Therefore, prudent businesses protect themselves by charging a higher price for goods or services, or higher interest on a loan, to compensate for the risk that the corporation or LLC will default and the obligation cannot be collected. In addition, they will often require a personal guarantee from a shareholder who will be responsible personally to repay the debt.

B.   Piercing the Corporate Veil

The protection of limited liability precludes shareholders from being compelled to repay the corporation's or LLC's obligations that it cannot satisfy unless a court applies the equitable doctrine called *piercing the corporate veil* to hold an individual shareholder owner liable. The law has never recognized an absolute protection for shareholders from any liability by incorporating a business if that would work a substantial injustice on creditors. The effect of limited liability is to leave creditors of an insolvent corporation unpaid, and the judicial doctrine of piercing the corporate veil allows a court to remedy an injustice in a particularly egregious situation. When a creditor seeks to pierce the veil of limited liability, it is seeking to hold an individual personally liable for the corporation's debts because the corporate form has been misused by the shareholder.

While courts state that piercing should only be applied in the "rare" case, the doctrine is one of the most frequently litigated issues in commercial and tort law because it is a means by which a creditor can seek payment on an obligation that would otherwise be denied because of the corporation's or LLC's insolvency — the business usually is in bankruptcy, and it is unlikely creditors will receive even a small recovery in that forum. The decision whether to pierce is highly fact specific, so while there are many reported cases on the doctrine, they are of limited use as precedents that can help predict how a court will rule in a particular case. It would seem that a tort creditor who has suffered a personal injury from the corporation's conduct should have a stronger claim to pierce the limited liability veil, especially when the shareholder who controls the corporation personally engaged in the harmful conduct. Studies show, however, that courts employ piercing just about as often in contract cases as tort claims, even though the contract creditor should have been able to negotiate greater protection through a personal guarantee.

In analyzing the creditor's piercing claim, courts usually rely on the *alter ego* or *instrumentality* test, which involves establishing three elements: (1) domination and control of the corporation by the shareholder sought to be held liable for the obligation; (2) injustice from the use of the limited liability shield; and, (3) proximate cause. While easily stated, the test provides no real guidance on how a court should decide the issue. Particularly for close corporations and member-managed LLCs, the shareholders will almost always dominate and control the organization, so the bare fact of a controlling interest should not be a determining factor. Instead, courts look for certain indicia that indicate the controlling shareholder engaged in deceitful conduct.

Among the factors a court will consider are whether the business was undercapitalized so that it was likely to fail, ignoring basic corporate formalities, commingling of corporate and personal funds or assets, diversion of corporate funds by a dominant (or sole) shareholder for non-corporate expenses, continuing to incur indebtedness despite insolvency, and the absence of business records to show whether funds were expended properly. Note that these factors are going to be present in a case to a greater or lesser degree, and no one of them will be determinative on whether a court pierces the corporate veil. In effect, the creditor seeks to portray the shareholder seeking to avoid liability as engaging in conduct that appears to be fraudulent so that the loss should be shifted away from the creditor to avoid what would appear to be an injustice by the shareholder. So far, both statutory and case law have borrowed piercing standards from the corporate area to determine whether to pierce the limited liability offered by LLCs.

C.   Promoter Liability and Defective Incorporation

While the shareholders of a corporation are not responsible for its debts unless the court pierces the limited liability shield, neither are its agents — such as the employees — liable for debts or contracts entered into on its behalf. In limited circumstances, however, individuals who act on behalf of a business that is not yet formally incorporated may be personally liable for its obligations in limited circumstances.

A *promoter* of the corporation is a person who works to set up the business, and enters into contracts before the corporation is technically formed. Promoters frequently make contracts on behalf of the as-yet unformed corporation. The types of transactions a promoter will engage in often includes retaining attorneys to organize the corporation, attempting to sell stock or obtain loans, hiring employees for the business, obtaining technical assistance, and leasing or purchasing property or an office.

When a promoter makes a contract for the benefit of the corporation in aid of its future business, but before the corporation is formally organized, the general rule is that the promoter is personally liable on the agreement. The parties can agree that the promoter will not be personally liable on the contract, but the intent of the parties to release the promoter from the obligation must be clear. Where a promoter is personally liable on a contract executed before the formal creation of the corporation, he or she is not discharged from liability merely because the corporation is later organized and receives the benefit of the contract. Even if the subsequently formed corporation adopts or ratifies the contract, the promoter will remain liable unless the parties clearly agree to discharge the promoter from any obligation to perform the contract. Absent such an agreement, the creditor has the added protection of being able to hold the promoter liable if the corporation fails to perform.

Along the same lines, a corporation may not be in existence as a legal entity because of a flaw in its creation or because its authority to operate has been suspended due to a failure to pay taxes or required annual fees. Similar to the liability of a promoter entering into a contract on behalf of a non-existent corporation, those who sign an agreement purportedly on behalf of the corporation that is defectively incorporated or suspended are liable for the obligation. The Model Business Corporation Act limits liability in this situation to those agents who act with the knowledge that the corporation is not a legal entity.

VIII.   EXTRAORDINARY TRANSACTIONS

A corporation can expand its business by acquiring other firms in transactions that can be structured in a number of different ways. One of the areas in which corporate lawyers can formulate creative solutions is by adapting the different means by which one corporation acquires another to address a variety of concerns, including tax issues, potential liability problems, regulatory concerns, and protecting the interests of shareholders. Extraordinary transactions are those in which one company is acquired by another. These deals can take place in two ways: as a *friendly* transaction, in which the two sides agree on issues such as price and the form of the transfer, or as a *hostile* transaction, in which an offeror seeks to overcome the resistance of incumbent managers and directors to the deal by appealing directly to the shareholders.

A.   Friendly Transations

One of the most common ways in which one corporation acquires another is through a *merger*. In its simplest form, Corporation A acquires Corporation B by combining the two businesses together. Corporation A is usually the *surviving* corporation, and once all the assets and liabilities of Corporation B have been transferred then it is dissolved and no longer exists. Another form of merger is a *consolidation*, under which both Corporation A and Corporation B will merge into a new entity, Corporation AB, so that both of them dissolve and Corporation AB is the surviving entity.

In negotiating a merger, a key issue will be the *consideration* that will be paid to the acquired corporation's shareholders. Under modern corporate statutes, a company can offer shares in the surviving corporation, cash, a bond or other hybrid security, or a combination of these as the payment for the shares. It is up to the management and the board of directors of the acquired corporation to negotiate the best deal possible on behalf of its shareholders.

A second key component in a transaction is whether the shareholders of the corporations involved in the transaction have voting rights. As a general matter, the shareholders of the acquired corporation have the right to vote to approve the merger or consolidation. Similarly, because a merger affects the value of the acquiring corporation, those shareholders often have voting rights in the transaction. However, a number of states deny the acquiring corporation's shareholders voting rights if their company will only issue a relatively small number of new shares to complete the transaction. Delaware, for example, does not grant voting rights to the shareholders of the corporation that issues less than twenty percent of its currently issued and outstanding shares to complete the transaction. This usually means that when the acquiring corporation is much larger than the acquired corporation, only the acquired corporation's shareholders have voting rights. However, if the transaction requires a change in the acquiring company's articles of incorporation, then the shareholders of that company must approve it, which could give them an effective veto over the transaction.

If a shareholder has voting rights in a merger or consolidation, then there may be *appraisal rights*, which are sometimes called *dissenter's rights*. If a shareholder does not believe the consideration offered in the friendly transaction fairly values the shares, that person may be able to file a judicial action to have the court determine the value of the shares. This allows shareholders to challenge management's determination that the offering price was a fair exchange. Most states only give appraisal rights to shareholders who have voting rights, and do not allow an appraisal action if the shares of the company are traded on a public stock market or the person receives publicly-traded shares. This *market-out* option means that if a shareholder does not like the transaction, the person can simply sell the stock on the open market, which presumably is valuing the shares fairly, rather than requiring a judicial proceeding to determine the value.

In addition to a merger or consolidation, one corporation can gain control of another through a *sale of assets*. Under this form, Corporation B sells all of its assets to Corporation A in exchange for cash or Corporation A shares, or both, but remains in existence as a separate entity. In most such deals, Corporation B then distributes what it received in the asset sale to its shareholders and then dissolves. While the end result is essentially the same as a merger, like when Corporation A acquires Corporation B's business, the form is different because it is a two-step transaction in which only the assets, but not necessarily the liabilities, of Corporation B have been transferred. The voting and appraisal rights of the shareholders of the two corporations are different from a merger. In a sale of assets, only the *selling corporation* shareholders can vote to approve the transaction and may be able to assert an appraisal right; the acquiring corporation's shareholders have no voting or appraisal rights. In Delaware, the shareholders of the selling corporation are denied appraisal rights.

The lawyers may choose a sale of assets over a merger for a number of reasons, and often the primary ones are to avoid paying higher taxes or to keep the liabilities of the acquired corporation away from the acquiring corporation. Under a sale of assets, the selling corporation technically remains in existence and only transferred its assets, so if it has certain liabilities, such as for environmental contamination, those would not necessarily be transferred in the deal.

Because a sale of assets has many of the attributes of a merger but only limited voting and appraisal rights, some states recognize the *de facto merger* doctrine. Under this analysis, a court looks to the substance of the transaction and not just the legal labels used by the corporations to determine if the outcome of the deal is one in which a corporation's shareholders would have voting rights but are denied because of the structure used. Courts state that they will not "blind" themselves to the economic reality that the shareholders' investment will be radically different after the transaction but they have no voting rights. Thus, courts applying the *de facto* merger doctrine order a corporation to gain shareholder approval and allow for appraisal rights that might otherwise be denied. Delaware explicitly rejects the *de facto* merger doctrine, holding that the structure chosen by the participants for the transaction governs the rights of the shareholders under what is termed the *equal dignity doctrine. Hariton v. Arco Electronics, Inc.*, 188 A.2d 123 (Del. 1963).

While the decision of a board of directors to agree to be acquired is normally protected by the business judgment rule, when a controlling shareholder undertakes a transaction to buy out the minority shareholders the courts apply more rigorous scrutiny to the terms of the transaction. The concern is that the controlling shareholder will not offer a fair price for the minority's shares, and because of the control over the voting process will undervalue the stock to get complete control at a bargain price. In a controlling shareholder *cash-out* merger, some courts first apply the *business purpose test* to determine whether the controlling shareholder undertook the transaction for a legitimate business purpose or just for his or her own personal benefit. In *Coggins v. New England Patriots*, 492 N.E.2d 1112 (Mass. 1986), the court stated that "[j]udicial scrutiny should begin with recognition of the basic principle that the duty of a corporate director must be to further the legitimate goals of the corporation" and not merely to enrich the controlling shareholder in the transaction.

Other states, including Delaware, focus solely on the fairness of the transaction to determine whether the controlling shareholder breached a fiduciary duty. That requires an assessment of whether the transaction involved both *fair dealing* and a *fair price* for the minority interest. Because of the presence of a controlling shareholder, the court asks whether independent directors were able to engage in meaningful bargaining in order to procure the best deal possible for the minority shareholders. If a court is satisfied that the negotiation process was conducted in a fair manner that simulates arms-length bargaining, then it is likely to find the price offered to be fair and reject a shareholder challenge to the transaction. Note that if there is a breach of fiduciary duty, the remedy will be essentially the same as that available in an appraisal action: payment of the fair value of the shares.

B.   Hostile Takeovers

A *hostile takeover* occurs when an outside party gains control of a corporation over the objection — and often active opposition — of the incumbent board of directors and management. Recall that for a friendly transaction, such as a merger or sale of assets, the board of each constituent corporation must agree to the terms of the transaction. A friendly transaction may result in the current officers of the acquired corporation keeping their jobs, although it may be that the acquirer will remove current management. The possibility of a hostile takeover is viewed as a means to police those running corporations by making the threat of losing their jobs a motivation to ensure that the company is run efficiently and does not take inappropriate risks. If a company is not run properly, then a hostile offeror may see an opportunity to take control and operate more profitably. If every extraordinary transaction required the approval of the board of the company to be acquired, then there would be no external market pressure on managers to seek the highest returns for shareholders — they could only be removed in a friendly deal.

There are two means by which a hostile takeover of a corporation whose shares are publicly traded can occur. The first is through a *tender offer*, in which the bidder bypasses management completely by making an offer directly to the shareholders to sell their ownership interest for a specified consideration. The offer is usually to exchange stock of the offeror or cash, or a combination of the two, in exchange for the shares of the target corporation. The bidder will usually include certain conditions in the offer, such as a particular number of shares being tendered for the transaction to be completed or management taking certain action to allow for the acquisition of a substantial block of shares. There are a number of requirements for a tender offer imposed by federal law that are discussed below, and state law does not regulate the conduct of the offeror to any significant degree.

The second means to take control of a corporation over management's opposition is by a *hostile proxy solicitation*. The person or entity seeking control will nominate directors for election to the board at the next annual meeting with the intention that the nominees will be more favorable to negotiating a transaction. In some cases, the organizer of the proxy solicitation does not plan to bid for the company but only wants it sold to the highest bidder to realize a gain on shares owned. In either case, the directors will seek to displace the current board by obtaining the majority of the votes from shareholders.

A board of directors can take *defensive measures* to thwart a hostile tender offer. For example, a company might sell one of its divisions, or declare a special dividend payable to current shareholders, that might make the company a less attractive target. A company might seek a "white knight," which is another company that will enter into a friendly transaction on better terms, or even make an offer for the hostile offeror.

The Delaware Supreme Court established a heightened standard of review for the actions of directors who seek to prevent a bidder from gaining control of the company by buying shares in a tender offer that goes beyond the requirements of the business judgment rule. Under the decision in *Unocal Corp. v. Mesa Petroleum Co.*, 493 A.2d 946 (Del. 1985), a board can undertake defensive actions to thwart a hostile offer if (1) the offer poses a *threat* to the corporation's business, shareholders, other constituencies, or long-term plan, and (2) the response is proportional to the threat. In *Unocal*, the offeror sought to acquire a bare majority of the shares with a cash offer and then proposed to buy out the remaining 49.9% of the shares with junk bonds at a price the board did not consider as adequately reflecting the true value of the company. In response, the board authorized certain acts, including a competing tender offer for a majority of the shares, to prevent the shareholders from being pushed into a deal that did not constitute fair value for the company. The Delaware court upheld the defensive measures under the heightened scrutiny standard, finding that the threat was significant and the response reasonable to protect shareholders from an undervalued offer.

After *Unocal*, a number of corporations adopted defensive measures to discourage hostile offers from even being made. One of the most potent anti-takeover devices is the *poison pill*, which seeks to deter a takeover by making it prohibitively expensive. Under this device, if a hostile bidder acquires more than a specified number of the target company's shares, usually from ten to twenty percent, then all shareholders *except the hostile offeror* can exercise a right to purchase additional stock at a fifty-percent discount — effectively two shares for the price of one. The effect of triggering a poison pill — whose name is derived from spy novels in which the agent would kill himself by swallowing a cyanide tablet if threatened with capture — is to significantly dilute the offeror's ownership stake in the target corporation. If the threshold for triggering the pill is crossed, then the company issues more shares at a discount, which lowers the value of the hostile offeror's shares.

Since first coming into widespread use in 1985, poison pills have proven to be among the most effective means of thwarting a hostile takeover. In addition, a number of states adopted anti-takeover laws to prevent local companies from being acquired, which would likely result in the loss of jobs when the headquarters was closed and other ancillary services were moved to the acquiring company's location. While these statutes have been less effective in deterring hostile offers because companies can opt out of them in most instances, they are another roadblock to mounting a successful hostile offer.

The *Unocal* analysis does not apply if a company responds to an offer by putting itself up for sale or otherwise takes steps that will result in the break-up of the enterprise. In *Revlon, Inc. v. MacAndrews & Forbes Holdings, Inc.*, 506 A.2d 173 (Del. 1986), the Delaware Supreme Court held that directors who responded to a hostile offer by seeking to sell the company to a different favored bidder violated their fiduciary duty. While a company can take defensive measures to protect the corporation from an unwanted bid if it poses a threat to the business, once the board decides to sell then it must get the most money for the shareholders. As described by the court, "[t]he directors' role changed from defenders of the corporate bastion to auctioneers charged with getting the best price for the stockholders at a sale of the company." If a company takes steps that effectively put it up for sale, then its actions are no longer governed by *Unocal* and instead the board comes within the *Revlon* auction duty.

A second means to gain control of a company is through a *hostile proxy solicitation* to elect new members to the board. The nominees are likely to be more favorable to negotiating a transaction than the current directors who have resisted any friendly overtures and perhaps even rejected a hostile offer for the company. A board may respond to an attempt to elect new directors by taking actions to make it more difficult to gain control of the company by this method. The Delaware courts have adopted a much more stringent test when a board seeks to diminish the ability of the shareholders to elect new directors, requiring that the board show a *compelling justification* for its actions. In *Schnell v. Chris-Craft Industries, Inc.*, 285 A.2d 437 (Del. 1971), the Delaware Supreme Court invalidated a board's decision to move up its annual meeting shortly after the announcement of a hostile proxy solicitation to replace the current directors. The court found that changing the date of the annual meeting "for the purpose of obstructing the legitimate efforts of dissident stockholders in the exercise of their rights to undertake a proxy contest against management" was "inequitable" and "may not be permitted to stand." In response to the company's argument that changing the date of the meeting was fully within the board's power under Delaware law, the court stated that "inequitable action does not become permissible simply because it is legally possible." Once a shareholder shows that a board of directors has acted for the primary purpose of interfering with or impeding the effective exercise of shareholder voting rights, then the board "bears the heavy burden of demonstrating a compelling justification for such action." *Blasius Industries, Inc. v. Atlas Corp.*, 564 A.2d 651 (Del. Ch. 1988).

IX. FEDERAL SECURITIES LAW

The law of the state of incorporation governs the internal affairs of a corporation, and the federal government oversees the securities markets along with the conduct of professionals in the investment industry — in common parlance, Wall Street. Thus, while there is no federal corporate law, the federal government exercises considerable control over larger corporations whose securities — stocks, bonds, and hybrid securities — are traded on the *public securities markets*. The two largest, and most prominent, securities markets in the United States are the New York Stock Exchange and the NASDAQ market. While there are differences in how the two markets operate, their function is to facilitate the trading of securities through markets in which anyone can see the current price of a security and readily buy or sell shares (or other types of securities). The value of the securities traded publicly in the United States is in the trillions of dollars, and companies can gain or lose billions of dollars in their total valuation in a single day.

The two primary federal laws governing the securities markets and the companies who issue them are the Securities Act of 1933 (called the 1933 Act) and the Securities Exchange Act of 1934 (called the 1934 Act). These laws were adopted in large part to address issues in the stock markets that were perceived to have contributed to the collapse in stock prices symbolized by the Great Crash of 1929. The objectives of the 1933 Act are to require that investors receive financial and other significant information concerning securities being offered for public sale, and to prohibit fraud in the initial distribution of securities. This law focuses on the process by which corporations issue securities to finance themselves, and the goal is to provide investors with sufficient information about a company so that the benefits and risks of an investment can be fairly assessed.

The 1934 Act prohibits certain types of conduct in the markets and gives the Securities & Exchange Commission (SEC) disciplinary powers over regulated entities, such as brokerage firms and investment banks, and persons associated with them, such as investment advisers. Importantly, the 1934 Act furthers the goal of providing shareholders with information about investments by requiring companies with more than $10 million in assets whose securities are held by more than 500 owners to report information about their business, finances, and current operations. These reports must be filed quarterly, and then on an annual basis the companies' financial statements must be audited by a major accounting firm to ensure their completeness and accuracy. The overarching objective of the securities laws is disclosure and then more disclosure. The SEC does not evaluate whether something is a good investment — that decision is left up to investors — but instead seeks to ensure that there is enough information available for one to make an informed investment decision.

The 1934 Act also governs two other important areas related to securities and the affairs of corporations. First, the law mandates the type of information that must be included in any solicitation of shareholder votes at an annual or special meeting. This information, contained in proxy materials, must be filed with the SEC in advance of any solicitation to ensure compliance with the disclosure rules. Proxy solicitations, whether by management or shareholder groups, must disclose all important facts concerning the issues on which shareholders are asked to vote, such as the election of directors or approval of an extraordinary transaction. While the rules regarding who has voting rights in a corporation come in the state corporate codes, the content of the proxy solicitation is regulated by federal law.

Second, the 1934 Act requires disclosure of important information by anyone seeking to acquire more than five percent of a company's securities by a tender offer. Such an offer may be extended in an effort to gain control of the company, often as a hostile measure to take control of a company over management's objection. As with the proxy rules, the disclosure rules allow shareholders to make informed decisions on whether to tender their shares. In addition, the tender offer provisions ensure fairness to shareholders so that they are not stampeded into accepting an offer that might undervalue the company. For example, the law requires that all shareholders receive the same price for their shares, so that an offeror may not provide a higher price for those shareholders who tender earlier or agree to provide a greater number of shares. Similarly, if the offer is for less than all the corporation's shares, then the shares will be taken on a pro rata basis upon completion of the tender offer, so that each shareholder will have the same percentage of shares purchased by the offeror.

The 1934 Act also contains a broad antifraud prohibition in Section 10(b), making it illegal to engage in any "manipulative or deceptive device" in connection with the purchase or sale of a security. The SEC has implemented this prohibition through Rule 10b-5, which prohibits fraud, and any misstatements or omissions, in securities transactions. Both the SEC and private parties can file civil actions alleging a violation of Section 10(b) and Rule 10b-5. The Rule has been the subject of a number of private class actions alleging that companies issued false or misleading information on which investors relied by purchasing or selling shares in the public securities markets. For example, a class action by purchasers of Enron stock and bonds filed securities fraud actions that resulted in the payment of over $7 billion in settlements by the company and a number of its outside advisers, primarily investment banks, for the false information issued about its finances and operations prior to the company's collapse into bankruptcy.

Rule 10b-5 and its counterpart in the 1933 Act, Section 17(a), are used to police a wide variety of investments and not just those involving common stock and corporate bonds. Under Section 3(a)(10) of the 1934 Act, the term "security" is defined broadly to include a number of investment vehicles, including anything that constitutes an "investment contract." The Supreme Court has taken a flexible approach to analyzing what can be an investment contract, holding in *SEC v. W.J. Howey Co.*, 328 U.S. 293 (1946), that an investment comes within that term if there is (1) an investment of money (2) with an expectation of profits arising from (3) a common enterprise (4) which depends solely on the efforts of a third party. The courts do not require that the investor have no involvement in the enterprise, so that the fourth element only requires that the generation of a profit come in large part from the effort of third parties. Courts have found that investment contracts were involved in purchasing interests in orange groves and pay telephones, and even raising worms to be used as fishing bait. This broad approach to what can be a security means the federal securities law is used to combat a wide variety of schemes, such as pyramid or "Ponzi" schemes in which investors are duped into sending money to operators who will use the funds from later investors to repay some of the earlier investors while taking the lion's share for themselves.

Another type of securities fraud under Rule 10b-5 involves insider trading, which is when a person trades a security while in possession of material nonpublic information in violation of a duty to keep the information secret and refrain from trading on it. Insider trading cases can be brought as civil enforcement actions by the SEC, under which a defendant can be required to disgorge profits from the trading and pay up to a triple penalty, and as criminal prosecutions that can result in a jail sentence and fine. The federal government can pursue both avenues, so it is frequently the case that an individual or group will be charged with a crime and sued by the SEC for the same trading on inside information.

Insider trading requires proof of a breach of a fiduciary duty, or other duty of trust and confidence, through the use of the confidential information for personal gain. For example, a partner in a law firm took information about an impending hostile tender offer from the office of another partner and brought stock and options of the target of the offer, reaping over $4 million in profits. He was convicted and sentenced to jail, and sued by the SEC to recover his profits. The Supreme Court held that taking the law firm's information, which was entrusted to it by a client, was a *misappropriation* that breached the lawyer's fiduciary duty, so that his trading on the information was a fraud in violation of Rule 10b-5. *United States v. O'Hagan*, 521 U.S. 642 (1997). Similarly, a corporate employee using information about the company to trade in its securities would also breach the person's fiduciary duty to the corporation to maintain the secrecy of its information and not gain from its use. *Chiarella v. United States*, 445 U.S. 222 (1980). In addition, the insider trading prohibition also covers tipping, in which one person tells another about material nonpublic information for the purpose of that person trading on the information. *Dirks v. SEC*, 463 U.S. 646 (1983).

X. CONCLUSION

Businesses can be organized into a variety of different legal forms. The predominant types of business organizations are corporations and partnerships, and the recently developed LLC and LLP, which combine features of both. The States provide the legal structure for organizing a business, and each business can choose its own internal governance rules for how its owners will be involved in its day-to-day operation. In conducting the business, those responsible for running it are subject to fiduciary duties, which require that they put the organization's interests ahead of their own and to ensure that it is operated in a reasonable manner. Federal law governs the securities issued by a business, such as its stock or bonds sold to investors, and the markets in which those instruments are bought and sold.

Chapter 12

FEDERAL INCOME TAXATION

By — Darryll K. Jones

SYNOPSIS

I. INTRODUCTION

Many areas of United States law directly impact the lives of large groups of persons on a daily basis. For example, tort provisions — the set of non-penal laws that provide compensation for harm caused by one person to another, or another's property — apply to many people every day. Other areas of United States law apply relatively infrequently to smaller groups of people. Family law — the law that regulates significant or extraordinary occurrences in domestic relationships — applies infrequently, as those significant or extraordinary events occur. The United States law of federal taxation ("the tax code" or "the code") is one of the few bodies of law that directly affects each and every person within the United States on a daily basis. It is therefore a broad and detailed articulation of requirements meant to apply to every single person within the U.S. jurisdiction. The code is a generally applicable body of very specific rules meant to address the entire universe of financial transactions in which persons ordinarily engage. Understandably, then, the United States tax code can be further described as a morass of convoluted and cross-referenced rules, regulations, exceptions, and even admonitions. The code is said to perpetually lurk in the vicinity of the daily lives of U.S. persons (i.e., all persons within the U.S. legal jurisdiction) even if U.S. persons are only fully cognizant of the tax code's influence once each year when called upon to account for their financial gains and losses.

Although the code is indeed long, detailed, and convoluted, there are identifiable principles recognizable in all of its various and seemingly infinite subparts. This Chapter identifies, summarizes, and explains those principles. The Chapter begins in Part I with a consideration of the purposes of the code. Obviously, and as in every other country, the most significant purpose of the code is to raise revenue to support the acquisition of public goods and services. Public goods and services include things that are not adequately supplied by the private sector, such as roads, highways, armies, and utilities. The latter recognition implies one philosophical approach to U.S. taxation; taxes are to be imposed only in amounts sufficient to provide goods and services not adequately supplied by the private sector via the capitalist market. Taxation is not intended to supplant or otherwise "distort" the market by, for example, raising revenue to provide goods and services that are sufficiently available in the marketplace. The government would not impose taxes in an effort to provide an automobile to every U.S. person because the marketplace is the preferred provider and presumably supplies those goods in adequate supply. As will be shown, however, the United States tax code manifests several other purposes. The use of the code to achieve those other purposes often provokes complaints by some people.

The purposes to which the tax code is directed relates to the broadly intended effects of the code as a whole. A closely related topic concerns the goals of the individual statutes and regulations that comprise the tax code. Part III will describe the four goals that affect the drafting of each statute or regulation comprising the code. The people who write tax statutes and regulations, and the people who interpret those statutes and regulations, usually seek four sometimes mutually exclusive outcomes described in greater detail in Part III. First, a tax statute or regulation should be "efficient," in the sense that it does not impose unnecessary financial costs on individuals or businesses (i.e., "taxpayers"). Second, a tax statute or regulation should be "equitable" or fair, in the sense that it does not create illogical distinctions between taxpayers and fairly distributes the cost of public goods and services across society. Third, a tax statute or regulation should be "administrable," in the sense that it should be easily complied with by taxpayers and easily enforced by government. Fourth, a tax statute or regulation should be "neutral" with respect to financial transactions. In that sense, tax statutes should not unintentionally "distort" the market by causing taxpayers to favor one type of financial transaction over another when they would not otherwise do so. It is the rare case that all four goals are actually achieved in any single statute or regulation. More often, one or more of the goals is sacrificed for the sake of one or more of the other goals.

Part IV of the overview begins a discussion of the six substantive fundamentals that characterize the tax code. Part IV describes the "tax base," the first fundamental aspect of U.S. taxation. The tax base refers to how the pool of private wealth from which the government extracts revenues to pay for public goods and services is measured. In the United States, the tax base is referred to as "income." In other countries, the tax base is described as "consumption." The differences between taxing income and taxing consumption are explained below. Part V describes a second fundamental aspect of U.S. taxation; not all income is the same. If you are familiar with American politics, you might already be aware that the code recognizes two legal types of income. The majority of most people's income is labeled "ordinary"; some people earn capital income. Part V explains the rationale for taxing ordinary income more heavily than capital income, as well as the criticisms of the distinction.

The tax code, for various reasons, entirely exempts certain types of income from taxation. The most common exemptions are explained in Part VI. The purely economic theory that underlies the legal definition of "income" would not allow for any such exemption, once it was determined that a taxpayer has actually experi enced "income." As Part VI demonstrates, however, the legal definition of "income" is not synonymous with the generally recognized economic definition. Instead, legal definitions are influenced by politics, powerful constituencies, notions of social justice, and economic efficiency, among other considerations. Neither does the economic definition of "income" contemplate the concept of deductions. The code, however, allows for certain deductions in the calculation of a taxpayer's income. Many deductions, described in Part VII, exemplify the various non-revenue raising purposes to which the code is put.

Part VIII discusses the "taxing unit" — another fundamental aspect of the United States tax code. The taxing unit is the person or group of people upon whom U.S. law imposes a legal obligation to pay a tax. The three primary taxing units recognized in the United States are (1) the individual, (2) the family, and (3) certain business entities. The recognition of taxing units is significant in U.S. tax law because many intended tax benefits, burdens, procedures, or obligations are specifically denied to or imposed upon certain taxing units. The two most often discussed controversies with regard to the definition of taxing units involve the question of what constitutes a "family" and the extent to which a tax imposed on a business should entitle the business owners to a credit against taxes imposed individually on the owners with respect to the same income.

The final substantive tax principle considered in this Chapter concerns the methods by which taxpayers must account for their financial gains and losses. So called "timing methods" are important because a particular timing method may effect the measurement of a taxpayer's income in a manner that is inconsistent with the economic measurement of the taxpayer's wealth. As noted earlier, the Code's definition of income sometimes deviates from the economic definition of income, but those deviations are usually the result of deliberate decisions made in pursuit of a goal other than raising revenue. The laws relating to timing methods, on the other hand, are adopted and imposed primarily in an effort to prevent *unintended* deviations from the legal definition of income. In essence, the code's timing rules seek to require taxpayers to pay their tax liability in the precise year in which the taxpayer is richer, and to prevent taxpayers from claiming a deduction, if a deduction is otherwise authorized, until the taxpayer has actually incurred the cost for which a statute provides a deduction. Self-interested taxpayers often instead seek to delay, for as long as possible, the imposition of a tax even for income the taxpayer has already received. They might also attempt to claim a deduction before actually incurring the cost giving rise to a deduction. These timing strategies create the necessity for a body of law that regulates timing methods.

Thus, this Chapter will provide an overview of the broadly applicable tax principles that apply to every person engaged in economic activity within the United States jurisdiction. There is, of course, much more intricate detail that simply cannot be included or explained in book designed to survey U.S. law. Nonetheless, an understanding of the principles described in this Chapter is absolutely essential and, indeed, will allow readers to predict the proper tax outcome of most any given financial transaction even without reading the particular statute or regulation, if any, specifically applicable to the financial transaction.

II. PURPOSES OF THE TAX CODE

The initial and most prominent purpose of the code is to raise revenue for general public purposes. The United States Constitution authorizes the legislative branch of government — the Congress — to levy and collect taxes to provide for the "general welfare." Since the adoption of the Sixteenth Amendment in 1913, the tax code has grown from merely a few pages of statutes to over 40,000 pages of statutes and regulations. These statutes and regulations are supplemented by an infinite number of administrative rulings and publications all having the force of law. Thus, the tax code broadly measured easily exceeds one million pages. Many observers believe that if the Congress limited the code's purposes strictly to the raising of revenue, the code would be greatly shortened and simplified. Others believe the code is legitimately used for purposes other than simply raising money and that its length and complexity are justified by the pursuit of those other goals. While there are differing opinions as to the legitimacy of those other goals, it is safe to conclude that there is unanimous consent that the tax code is properly used to raise revenue for public goods and services.

Perhaps the most controversial of the other purposes to which the tax code is put is redistribution of income from wealthier persons to poorer persons. Under what is referred to as a "progressive" rate structure, individuals and other taxing units are taxed at a higher rate as their income increases. For example, an individual whose income is only $8,025 in a taxable period will pay 10% of that amount to the government as taxes. As her income increases, however, the individual will begin to pay a progressively higher rate. An individual whose income for the taxable year is $400,000 for the taxable year will pay taxes at the rate of 10% of the amount up to $8,025, 15% percent on the amounts between $8,025 and $32,550, 25% of the amount between $32,550 and $78,850, 28% of the amount between $78,850 and $164,550, 33% of the amount between $164,550 and $357,700; and 35% of the amount of taxable income over $357,770. Progressive rates mean that as an individual obtains more income, his or her proportionate tax liability increases. Wealthier individuals will therefore pay a higher percentage of their income to the government as taxes than poorer individuals. Similar progressive rates apply as families and business entities obtain greater amounts of income. Congress continually adjusts progressive rates, either in response to inflation or in reaction to changing political philosophies. As a result, the rates may be different from year to year.

Progressive rates have two primary effects. First, they cause income of wealthier persons to be redistributed to poorer persons. As a very general matter, wealthier persons will not benefit as greatly from government social programs as poorer persons. Since those social programs are funded via taxation, progressive rates result in redistribution of income to poorer individuals who benefit more from social programs than do wealthier people, at least from a strictly financial standpoint. Another impact of progressive rates, though, relates to the goal of fairness — ensuring that every taxpayer suffers a roughly equal share of the cost of public goods and services. Another way of stating this proposition is that a taxpayer's liability should be commensurate with the benefits the particular taxpayer derives from public goods. Many theorists assume that wealthier taxpayers benefit to a greater degree from police protection, for example, and therefore should pay more taxes than poorer taxpayers.

Some critics of progressive tax rates argue that it would be fairer to eliminate progressive rates and instead impose a constant or "flat" rate of tax. For example, the tax code might simply impose a tax equal to 20% of all income, regardless of the amount of income obtained by an individual. Proponents of progressive taxation argue that a flat tax would be unfair because poorer people — to whom a single dollar might be more important — would suffer a higher physical and psychic burden than would wealthier persons. For example, we may assume that it is less of a personal sacrifice for a person who earns $400,000 to pay the government $80,000 (20% of total income) than it would be for a person earning only $8,025 to pay the government $1,605 (20% of total income). The person with $400,000 will still have $320,000 left after taxes, while the person with only $8,025 will have $6,420 left. In other words, the poorer person will feel a greater impact from the payment of 20% than will the wealthier person who also pays 20%. Progressive rates are therefore set at amounts that cause wealthier people to suffer the same financial impact as poorer persons, according to some proponents.

A third purpose of the tax code is to encourage or discourage certain types of spending in an effort to influence the societal structure, encourage or discourage individual behavior, or reduce the use of scarce resources. For example, the tax code attempts to raise the educational level of U.S. persons by lowering taxes for persons who spend money on higher education. The tax rate is lowered essentially by excluding the amount from a taxpayer's income or reducing tax liability by all or a percentage of the money spent on higher education. Similarly, individuals and business units that spend money on scientific research that may lead to the cure of a disease is supported when the code lowers the taxes on persons who engage in such spending. A related example of the tax code's effort to encourage or discourage individual behavior is seen when the code reduces taxes for people who save money for future health care costs or retirement needs. In either instance, the code grants a deduction or credit when the taxpayer saves money, thus discouraging immediate consumption and encouraging long-term investment. An example of the tax code's attempt to preserve scarce resources is seen via provisions that lower taxes on individuals, families, or business entities that purchase automobiles that are powered by electricity rather than gasoline. Gasoline is a scarcer resource than is electricity, and thus the tax preference granted to electricity consumption rather than gasoline consumption encourages the former over the latter.

Another purpose of the tax code is to stimulate economic activity, particularly when the economy is functioning poorly, or in areas where investment is thought to be insufficient to support the economic needs of a surrounding population. One prominent example involves the code's allowance of "accelerated deductions" for certain types of business investment. As briefly mentioned above, deductions are usually granted only as a taxpayer incurs certain costs for which deductions are otherwise granted. Thus, a taxpayer who purchases a long lasting business asset will usually be granted a deduction as the asset is consumed or depleted in a business activity. A deduction will be granted for the amount paid for the asset, but only as the asset declines in value from its business use. In poor economic times, business owners tend to reduce the amount of money spent on long lasting assets, thereby perpetuating the poor economic cycle. In an effort to discourage this tendency and stimulate business spending, the tax code allows business owners to claim deductions sooner than the deductions would otherwise be authorized. For example, a taxpayer who purchases a computer system that is expected to generate income for five years or more may elect to deduct the full amount of the purchase price in the first year rather than as the computer system declines in value over a period of five years or more. The hope is that by allowing an accelerated deduction, the code will encourage business owners to make larger purchases sooner, thereby stimulating the economy. A related effort involves lowering taxes, via the authorization of a deduction or credit, for investment in certain areas neglected or overlooked by taxpayers. Thus, when Congress identifies an area in which there is insufficient economic activity to support the surrounding population, it may effectively lower the tax paid by people who invest financial or human capital in that underserved area. Prominent examples include provisions that lower taxes for real estate developers who build affordable homes in areas for which the market provides insufficient housing, and tax provisions that lower taxes for doctors who agree to work in certain areas where there are an insufficient number of doctors to meet the needs of the population. Lower tax rates essentially encourage economic activity that might otherwise not occur.

The primary criticism of the non-revenue-raising purposes of the tax code is that such purposes significantly increase the length and complexity of the code. Length and complexity are not merely inconveniences; they also divert financial and human capital from economic activity to regulatory activity. For every tax provision related to some purpose other than simply raising revenue, there are usually two or three other "policing" provisions designed to ensure that the tax benefit is obtained only by those persons who are engaging in the desired activity or who meet the criteria of persons intended to be assisted by the provision. A provision designed to encourage taxpayers to purchase automobiles powered by electricity rather than gasoline, for example, would normally include or be accompanied by provisions precisely defining the types of automobiles and taxpayers eligible for the tax benefit, provisions relating to actual ownership of the automobile, "recapture" provisions requiring subsequent repayment of the foregone taxes in the event the automobile is converted to one that runs solely on gasoline, and a host of other provisions, in all likelihood, designed to prevent taxpayers from taking advantage of the tax benefit without actually engaging in the desired activity. The cost of complying with and enforcing these policing provisions — most of which would be unnecessary in the absence of a statute whose purpose was other than to raise money — diverts money from other uses, such as the relief of the poor or the purchase of undeniably public goods or services such as highways or military equipment. Ultimately, if the compliance and policing costs become greater than the benefits derived from the non-revenue-raising goal, it makes no sense to use the tax code for that non-revenue-raising goal. The non-revenue raising goal might be better pursued via some form of direct expenditure rather than via the tax code.

III. TAX STATUTE AND REGULATION METHODOLOGY

The purposes described above relate to what the Congress intends to accomplish via the code in general. This section describes the more specific goals of particular tax statutes and regulations. In essence, the drafters and interpreters of tax statutes and regulations seek one or more of four outcomes. Ideally, an articulated rule of tax should be (1) efficient, (2) equitable, (3) easily administered, and (4) neutral. Rarely, however, will any one statute or regulation achieve all four outcomes. More often, an articulation of a tax rule will sacrifice one or more of the outcomes for the sake of one or more of the other outcomes. Achieving an equitable outcome, for example, might come at the expense of simplicity. That is, the drafters or interpreters of a tax statute may determine that fairness is more important than simplicity and thus articulate lengthy and complicated rules that eliminate the possibilities of unfairness. In other instances, simplicity might be viewed as more important that fairness. Thus, drafters might intentionally tolerate some degree of inaccuracy — and thus unfairness — for the sake of simplicity. This section will briefly describe what is meant by the four intended outcomes. The sections that follow will indicate the extent to which one or more goals are given precedence over others in the articulation of particular tax rules.

None of the four goals related to the articulation of a tax rule is considered more important than any other. Hence, the order in which they are discussed is not intended to suggest any particular prioritization. The term "efficient" often has different meanings to different observers or scholars. Generally, though, a tax requirement is thought to be efficient if the revenues collected via the requirement exceed the costs associated with compliance or enforcement of the requirement. To the extent an articulation costs more money than it derives, it is inefficient. For example, income normally includes all wealth derived from the performance of services by an employee for an employer. Oftentimes, that wealth may come in the form of "fringe benefits" — financial benefits an employer makes available to an employee in the course of the employer/employee relationship. Thus, a tax articulation might require that an employee include the free use of employer's copy machine as income. The amount of money it would take for the employer to keep track of each employee's use of the copy machine and the government to monitor the proper reporting of such use would likely be greater than the amount of money collected by the requirement to do so. It should therefore be concluded that such a requirement would be grossly inefficient; it would be more efficient to relieve the employer and the government of the obligation to keep track of and report as income an employee's occasional free use of the employer's copy machine.

As a relative matter, it is easier to make the determination that a tax requirement is efficient or not than it is to determine whether a tax statute is "equitable." Whether a particular requirement is fair ultimately depends on subjective considerations that differ from person to person. Still, a second goal of drafters and interpreters is that a tax statute be equitable. The phrase "horizontal equity" is often used to describe the effort to treat similarly situated taxpayers in the same manner, while the term "vertical equity" is used to describe efforts to make fair distinctions between taxpayers with different characteristics. The latter phrase, for example, is often used to justify the imposition of progressive tax rates as taxpayers earn more income. On the other hand, proponents of a flat tax argue that it is inequitable to impose higher rates of taxation on taxpayers who simply work harder to earn more income. Opponents also argue that progressive taxation is inefficient because it punishes taxpayers who work harder, resulting in lost labor when taxpayers decide not to work harder to avoid the higher tax rates that will apply. The allowance for a deduction for interest paid on indebtedness used to purchase a home, as well as the deduction for taxes on owned homes, exemplifies a context in which horizontal equity is debated. Because the deduction is allowed only to owners, rather than renters, some people argue that the deduction treats similarly situated taxpayers differently and is therefore inequitable. According to the argument, renters essentially pay the interest on mortgage indebtedness and real estate taxes in the form of rental payments but are nevertheless denied a deduction granted to owners simply because the former are labeled "renters" rather than "owners."

The third goal in the drafting and interpretation of tax rules is that tax rules should be "easily administered," both by the taxpayer or the tax collector. This goal is logically related to the efficiency goal except that it does not necessarily require a comparison of the costs and benefits of a particular rule. The "realization" doctrine, discussed in Part IV, is largely based on the desire to impose only easily administered tax rules. The economic definition of income, from which the tax base is derived, includes the increase in the value of a taxpayer's property. Tax rules, however, do not require a taxpayer to include the increase in her property value as income until the property is sold and the increase is "realized." Although some observers consider a property owner's ability to defer taxes on increased property values unfair, relative to a taxpayer whose income is derived primarily from labor, the unfairness is viewed as justified by the administrative burden that would result if taxpayers were forced to pay taxes on the increased property value before the property were sold. The administrative burden would arise from the need to determine the precise amount by which a taxpayer's property increased (or decreased) in value between two points in time. It is easier, as a relative matter, to await the sale of the property before imposing taxes because valuation is definitively determined by the parties to the sale.

The final goal with respect to the articulation of tax rules relates to a desire not to interfere with the capitalist market. In that regard, drafters and interpreters seek "economic neutrality." Economic neutrality is similar to the notion of horizontal equity except that the former concept means that the government should treat all economic transactions, rather than similarly situated taxpayers, in an identical manner so as not to encourage or discourage certain economic transactions at the expense of others. In some instances, tax rules are intentionally imposed in a non-neutral manner. A credit for the purchase of an electric powered vehicle, for example, intentionally distorts the market in an effort to encourage the manufacture and purchase of such vehicles. In such cases, there is a political consensus that favors the market intervention via the tax code — the need to preserve scarce resources (gasoline) is viewed as sufficient justification for favoring the purchase of electric powered vehicles over the purchase of gasoline powered vehicles. The notion of economic neutrality therefore relates to the notion that tax rules ought to be articulated so as to avoid *unintended* or *unsupported* market distortions.

IV. THE TAX BASE

The phrase "tax base" refers to the calculation of the pool of wealth from which the government extracts revenues in the form of taxes. In the United States, the tax base is "income," a term that requires elaboration. During the early history of the United States, income was said to occur exclusively from the performance of services. Increases in the value of property over time — i.e., appreciation — were not considered income. The economic justification for this point was based on the assumption that increases in property value occurring merely from the passage of time resulted from inflation and did not increase a taxpayer's ability to consume because inflation affects all other assets as well. In short, inflationary gain did not enrich a taxpayer and therefore should not be considered income. This view was later discarded, and income came to be defined as "gains derived from labor, capital, or both combined." This definition, too, was later discarded because it did not include other types of enrichment such as found property, gifts, or money obtained by a judicial order requiring one person to pay punitive damages to another person.

Ultimately, income came to be defined as any and all forms of financial enrichment, whether received in the form of money, property, services, or anything someone might sell or purchase.

The technical, economic definition generally viewed as the precursor for the legal definition of income is the sum of receipts (in whatever form, as noted above) plus the increase or decrease in value of property received in a prior taxable year. For example, assume a taxpayer is provided $10,000 cash, twelve free car washes which are normally provided at a cost of $10.00 each, a car that normally sells for $25,000, and a bond issued by the city council (i.e., a municipal bond) that currently sells for $1,000. Assume that prior to these transfers, the taxpayer owned nothing. Under the technical economic definition, the taxpayer's income would be $36,120 — the total value of all her receipts. Since she owned no property prior to this year, there are neither increases nor decreases in her property received in a prior year. Assume that in the next year, the taxpayer receives another $10,000 and her car's value decreases by $5,000 from her personal use. In addition, municipal bonds like hers are currently selling for $1,100. Her income would be $10,100. Her receipts include the $10,000 cash and the $5,000 from the value of her personal use of her car (otherwise referred to as "imputed income"). Her total receipts would therefore be $15,000. The value of her car decreased by $5,000 and her municipal bond increased in value by $100. Her "stored" property would therefore have decreased by $4,900. Her total income would therefore be $15,000 minus $4,900, or $10,100. Note that the calculation of the taxpayer's economic income is unaffected by the source or use of the income. Her income would be the same regardless of whether she spent or saved any portion of the income and regardless of whether she worked for or found the $10,000 cash.

The legal definition of income begins with the economic definition and is then altered by other specific rules in the code designed to achieve some purpose other than raising revenue. One particularly important exception is that the legal definition of income does not include imputed income — the amount of money saved from using one's own property or providing services to oneself. The concept of imputed income is one that helps measure a taxpayer's income by reference to his or her ability to contribute to the cost of public goods or services. Imputed income is quite illogical to most Americans but an accepted notion in many other countries. If income is regarded as a function of a taxpayer's ability to contribute to the cost of public goods or services, imputed income should logically be taken into account. Using one's own property or providing services for one's own benefit increases a taxpayer's ability to contribute by the value he or she did not have to pay to someone else for the use of such property or services. Another exception relates to the increase or decrease in the value of a taxpayer's property. The economic definition would include the increase or decrease in the determination of the tax base, but as mentioned earlier, increases or decreases in property values are not often easily determined. Thus, the legal definition would exclude the $100 increase in the value of the municipal bond. The result applies even though in this particular case, it might be very easy to determine the change in the value. Instead, the taxpayer would include $100 only if the increase is "realized" from the sale or exchange of the bond. A third distinction between economic income and legal income results from Congress' power to define income so as to achieve a purpose other than raising money. In the facts described above, even if the taxpayer collected $100 interest, she would nevertheless be allowed to exclude the $100 from her income because Congress has enacted a statute authorizing the taxpayer to exclude from income interest paid by government agencies that lend money to taxpayers. The purpose in this instance is to encourage taxpayers to lend money to government agencies.

The primary criticism of the U.S. definition of the tax base is that it doesn't encourage taxpayers to save. In fact, it might even be fair to say that the U.S. tax base discourages savings. As noted above, even if the taxpayer in the first year set aside $15,000 for retirement or future health care costs, her income would still be $36,120. On the other hand, a consumption tax is essentially an income tax combined with a deduction for receipts that are set aside for later spending. Tax liability is imposed under a consumption tax only when the receipts are withdrawn from savings and spent for current consumption. Critics of the U.S. income tax argue that a consumption tax would discourage unbridled consumption some think is the hallmark of the U.S. market. In fact, the U.S. tax code incorporates consumption tax principles in limited circumstances. Certain provisions, for example, authorize a deduction when taxpayers save money for retirement. The money set aside for retirement is instead taxed when it is withdrawn from the retirement savings account. Thus, deductions for retirement savings reflect a limited consumption tax in the U.S. tax code.

V. TYPES OF INCOME

As a statutory matter, the concept of income is a purely numerical construct and does not take into account the economic phenomenon of inflation. In one regard, then, the code endeavors to tax all numerically determined increases in a taxpayer's wealth. Thus, a taxpayer who performs services and is paid $100 is treated as having $100 income because she has a numerical increase in wealth equal to $100. The value of the taxpayer's human investment is, under this construct, assumed to be zero, and the entire amount is viewed as an increase in wealth. If the taxpayer purchases property for $80 — using the amount remaining after payment of taxes on the $100 compensation, for example — the tax code uses a device called "basis" to keep track of the fact that the wealth used to purchase the property has already been taxed. Thus, human services are considered to have a basis of zero; property is generally considered to have a basis equal to the amount of income used to purchase the property. If the taxpayer later sold the property for $100, she would be treated as having a $20 increase in wealth; the increase would be the difference between the amount invested in the property and the amount for which the property was later sold.

As an economic matter, however, it may be that the property owner who sold her property for $100 a few years after purchasing it for $80 may not have any greater ability to consume than she did when she originally purchased the property. Because of inflation, the $100 in hand as a result of the sale may allow the taxpayer to consume only what she could have consumed with $80 a few years earlier. If that is so, then as an economic matter, the taxpayer is no richer than she was when she purchased the property. Her numerical increase is purely "inflationary" and does not increase her ability to consume. Nevertheless, the tax code treats the taxpayer as though she was in fact richer and imposes a tax on the $20 numerical gain.

Some economists view the treatment of gain from the sale of property as both unfair and inefficient. They consider it unfair to impose a tax on a person who is no richer than before; they also believe the imposition of a tax to be inefficient, because a tax on capital acts to discourage long term savings or investment. In the hypothetical above, the taxpayer would have been better off immediately consuming the $80 rather than saving it, because immediate consumption would have allowed her to avoid the later tax on the sale of the property. The only other way to have avoided the second tax would have been for the taxpayer to never sell the property. Hence, the second tax generates an additional inefficiency by discouraging the sale of property when perhaps economic factors would dictate such a sale.

Congress has essentially accepted the notion that the conversion of property held long term into cash does not actually enrich the taxpayer, at least to the extent that inflation caused the increase in the property's cash selling price. It might have addressed the economic objections by allowing taxpayers to increase the basis of property by the annual rate of inflation. Thus, on the sale of the property, the taxpayer's nominal increase in wealth would be decreased by the total inflationary increase that occurred during the taxpayer's ownership. Rather than allow for such an "indexed" basis, Congress instead decided to impose a lower rate of tax on income from the sale of capital assets.

Congress has decided to subject income from the sale of long term assets to a 15% tax rate in an effort to account for the asserted unfairness and inefficiency of fully taxing capital gain. Thus, income from labor and short term assets (such as inventory) — referred to as "ordinary income" — is taxed at rates up to 35%, while income from capital — referred to as capital gain — is taxed at rates less than half that amount. The disparity between the tax rates applied to labor income and tax rates applied to capital income has provoked arguments that the tax code favors wealthy taxpayers because wealthy taxpayers are more likely to derive income from property than are poorer taxpayers. Proponents on both sides of the debate variously win and lose, depending on the extent to which they can garner political support for their views. Thus, as the political composition of Congress changes from year to year, so too do the tax rates applicable to capital gain.

VI. EXCLUSIONS FROM INCOME

The lower tax rate applicable to capital gains is, effectively, a partial tax exemption. Indeed, in years past, the Congress did not use a lower tax rate to address the economic issues asserted with regard to capital gain but simply allowed taxpayers to exclude 50% of all capital gains from taxation. For many different reasons, Congress has also seen fit to exclude other incomes from taxation. The reasons include the view that (1) the transaction has not really involved two separate taxing units, (2) the taxpayer is not really richer because of a physical loss resulting in a financial payment, (3) the taxpayer's receipt of income was involuntary and should not be taxed, (4) the desire to allow taxpayers to immediately reinvest the proceeds from the sale of property without taxation, (5) the desire to assist taxpayers who experience a significant financial crisis and (6) the imposition of a tax is inconsistent with the popular, as opposed to economic or legal, view of income. Congress, of course, is entitled by the U.S. Constitution to tax all income without any exclusion; likewise, it may exclude certain income without any consistent reason. Most exclusions, though, are motivated by an implicit consensus that it would simply be unfair or inefficient to impose a tax in a given circumstances. This part describes six types of exclusions that exemplify the primary reasons for exclusions in the tax code.

The economic definition of income described in Part IV tolerates no exemptions. All increases in a taxpayer's ability to consume constitute income, regardless of the source or reason causing the increase. The legal definition allows for many exemptions, the most popular of which is the exemption from taxation of gifts or income received by inheritance. Although the statute authorizing the exemption does not require that the income come from a particular source, the exemption is generally understood to exclude from taxation transfers from one family member to another. There are three commonly asserted reasons for the exclusion. The first relates to the belief that the transfer of wealth from one family member to another logically involves the same "taxable unit." As will be discussed below, the taxing unit is an individual, family, or business upon which a tax is imposed. If the family is viewed as a single taxable unit, then it makes sense not to tax intra-family exchanges. Family wealth is viewed as owned by all members of the family and therefore a transfer from one member to another is not viewed as a transfer at all. The second reason for exempting income received by gifts or inheritance is the assumption that tax laws should not interfere with the love and affection expressed between family members. The third reason, one particularly applicable to inherited wealth, is that the recipient may have been financially dependent upon the deceased relative who gave the property upon death, and the tax code should allow the recipient a one-time exemption to account for the loss of that relative's financial support.

A second exclusion exemplifying a common reason for exempting income is that the taxpayer has suffered an incalculable loss such that taxing her receipt of income received on account of that loss is inappropriate. Thus, a taxpayer who receives payment for physical harm caused by another person is not required to pay taxes on the amount received. It is difficult to conclude, for example, that a taxpayer who loses a limb as a result of someone else's fault is actually "richer" even if the person at fault is ordered to pay her a significant amount for the lost limb. The exclusion for amounts paid for physical injury is best described as one based on sympathy for the taxpayer.

The third exclusion is a bit harder to justify but nevertheless present in the tax code. A taxpayer who is required to accept income, in the form of housing or food as a condition of her employment, for example, is usually allowed to exclude the amount from taxation. Thus, a taxpayer who is required to live on an employer's premises free of charge is treated as if the free room and board is not income. The essential reason is that most people find it unfair to impose a tax on a person whose consumption was "involuntary." Another example of the exclusion of "forced consumption" arises when taxpayers are allowed to exclude the value of meals and lodging consumed while the taxpayer is away from home in the pursuit of business. One objection to this exclusion is that it allows taxpayers to avoid taxes on consumption that is not necessarily forced. If the taxpayer had not been traveling on business, he or she would have consumed meals and lodging in any event. It is probably true, though, that the business travel requires the taxpayer to incur greater expenses than normal (because of the need to eat in restaurants or reside in hotels). Rather than impose the administrative burden of forcing the taxpayer to calculate and exclude only the increased costs, the Congress simply allows the taxpayer to exclude the entire amount.

A fourth example involves the desire to allow taxpayers to freely invest their wealth without interference from the tax code. Investment (or saving) is viewed as beneficial to society because investment prevents immediate consumption and generates jobs and other economic activities. Various provisions in the tax code exclude gain from the sale of property if the gain is immediately reinvested in different property rather than immediately consumed. In some instances, the immediate reinvestment requirement is coupled with the "forced sale" rationale and both result in exclusion. For example, if the government forces a taxpayer to sell his or her property to the government, the gain from the forced sale will not be taxed if the taxpayer immediately purchases similar replacement property.

A fifth example involves a taxpayer who borrows money. The tax code does not include borrowed money as income because the taxpayer has an obligation to repay the money. Thus, the borrower is not considered richer because he or she will have to pay the income back at a later date. In some instances, a taxpayer does not repay the borrowed money. If the lender agrees to forgive the debt, the taxpayer is then richer because he or she no longer has to set aside money to repay the debt. If the taxpayer is a family member, the forgiveness of the debt might likely be viewed as a gift and therefore excluded from taxation under the gift exclusion described above. In other instances, the forgiven debt must be included in income.

Some debtors simply owe too much money to ever repay their debts. U.S. law allows those debtors, in certain instances, to be entirely forgiven of their debts and to "start all over again." In those circumstances, the tax code assists the taxpayer in achieving a "fresh start" by excluding the forgiven debt from taxation. The motivation for this exclusion is that the fresh start the Congress wants to provide for these debtors would be denied if the debtor had to pay taxes.

The final "exclusion" is not really a legally stated one, but is based on U.S. tradition. In some countries, the value of property or services that a taxpayer provides to him- or herself is viewed as taxable income. Taxation, in such instances, results from the view that a taxpayer who need not purchase necessary goods or services is better able to financially contribute to society than is a taxpayer who must purchase those goods and services. Thus, a taxpayer who owns and lives in her home is relieved of the obligation to rent a home from another person and is thought to have greater ability to contribute to the common welfare than a taxpayer who must rent her home. The taxpayer is said to have "imputed" income from the use of her own property. The U.S. tax code does not tax imputed income, an indication that taxation in the United States is not entirely determined by one's ability to pay. The failure to tax imputed income is also a function of the individualist ethos that prevails in the United States. Imposing a tax on an individual's imputed income would be viewed as an unwarranted infringement on individual freedom.

VII. THE TAXABLE UNIT

As noted earlier, the taxable unit refers to the individual or individuals responsible to pay a tax. The taxable unit is also the recipient of specific tax benefits and burdens under the U.S. tax code. For example, every individual constitutes a taxable unit under the tax code. Thus, federal taxes are imposed on every single person who has income over a bare poverty amount. In certain other circumstances, the family is also considered a single taxable unit. In those cases, the tax is not imposed separately on individuals but rather on the group of individuals comprising the family. For that reason, for example, a transfer of property from one family member to another will usually not be treated as a taxable transaction because a single unit cannot conduct business with itself. In addition, tax benefits such as credits against taxes for children and exemption from taxes for the support of relatives are generally granted to groups of individuals — rather than separately — who fit the definition of family. Congress grants benefits to "families," incidentally, rather than unrelated groups of people because it believes families are more beneficial to society than are unrelated groups of people who reside together or otherwise function in the same manner as a family.

Directing benefits to "the family," as the tax code does, causes complexity and controversy in the tax code because the Congress must define "family" and make distinctions between those who fit the definition and those groups of people who very closely resemble the definition. The word family, as used legally in the United States, generally refers to a group of people centered around a heterosexual married couple. The laws of most states deny homosexual couples the right to marry — and thus the status of "family" — despite the fact that homosexual couples often maintain households identical to those maintained by heterosexual couples. Thus, the United States has generally excluded (to one degree or another) homosexual couples, their children, and other relatives from the definition of "family," and this exclusion prevents the payment of tax benefits to those groups of individuals.

The third taxable unit under U.S. tax laws is referred to as "C corporations." The treatment of these usually large, publicly owned businesses is not mutually exclusive with the treatment of individuals as taxable units, as is the case with individuals and families. Thus, under U.S. law, an individual who owns a C corporation is generally subjected to "double taxation." When the C corporation earns income, it is treated like a separate individual and taxed on the income. In effect, the individual owners are taxed on the income when it is earned by the C corporation. When the remaining income is divided amongst the individual owners, the individual owners are taxed again, though usually at the lower rate applicable to capital gains. The imposition of tax at both the "entity" level (i.e., on the corporation) and the individual level is one hallmark of U.S. business taxation, though not all businesses are subject to the entity tax. Some businesses, like partnerships or what are referred to as "limited liability companies," can avoid the entity tax by electing not to pay the tax.

Most publicly owned corporations are not allowed to elect not to pay the entity tax. As in many countries, there are some large corporations that pay no taxes at all. Tax exempt corporations are treated as taxable units only for accounting purposes. Otherwise, they are treated as though all of their income is tax exempt, as long as the income is derived from the pursuit of charitable activities. The phrase "charitable activities" is broadly defined to include any legal activity engaged in by individuals who do not seek or obtain personal profit from the activity. Although these corporations are generally owned by the public, their income is not subject to taxation because they strive to achieve the public good rather than personal profit. Thus, tax exempt corporations are not taxable units in the sense they must pay a tax.

VIII. DEDUCTIONS

Exclusions allow a taxpayer to reduce their tax on certain *received* income; deductions provide for a reduction of tax when the taxpayer *pays* income for certain goods or services. There are generally three reasons Congress grants deductions. First, deductions are granted in order to properly measure a taxpayer's increase in wealth. For example, a taxpayer who purchases property for $80.00 and then later sells it for $100.00 is allowed to deduct $80.00 from the sale price to determine her actual increase in wealth. Without the deduction, the taxpayer would be treated as though her wealth increased by $100 when it actually only increased by $20.00. For similar reasons, a taxpayer who pays $80.00 to buy supplies with which to manufacture property she later sells for $100.00 is entitled to $80.00 in deductions. In essence, the first occasion upon which Congress grants deductions is for expenses paid in the pursuit of profit.

A second reason Congress grants deductions, one noted above, is to encourage one type of spending over other types of spending. There may be many reasons why Congress wishes to encourage taxpayers to spend money on certain things rather than other things. For example, the deduction for amounts paid to charities might be motivated by the desire to encourage individuals to share their wealth with less wealthy persons. The deduction granted upon the purchase of an electric-powered car encourages taxpayers to spend less money on gasoline powered vehicles, while the deduction for amounts paid into a retirement savings account encourages taxpayers to set aside money for their retirement so that the government will not need to support them when they are no longer earning income.

The final reason Congress grants a deduction is in an effort to assist taxpayers who wish to purchase certain goods or services. For example, Congress wishes to support or "subsidize" taxpayers who pay tuition at colleges, universities, or trade schools. The tax code therefore grants a deduction for such payments. When deductions are motivated by the desire to support the purchase of certain goods or services, the deduction is usually referred to as an "indirect subsidy." One criticism of indirect subsidies is that they favor those who are able to purchase the goods or services over those who are not able to purchase such goods or services. That is, the indirect support embodied in the tax deduction is available only to those who are able to initially make the purchase in the absence of the subsidy. Those who cannot make the purchase receive no government help.

IX. ACCOUNTING METHODS

The final topic considered in this Chapter are the rules regulating the methods taxpayers adopt to account for their income. Congress regulates "accounting methods" in an effort to prevent taxpayers from adopting methods that either understate their income or overstate their deductions. The understatement of income and the overstatement of deductions can illegitimately reduce a taxpayer's tax liability. A proper accounting method will ensure that a taxpayer's taxable income is consistent with his or her economic increases in wealth.

The two most common accounting methods are referred to as (1) cash method and (2) accrual method. Under the cash method, taxpayers have income upon actual or "constructive" receipt. They are entitled to a deduction when payment for which a deduction is legally granted is actually made. Constructive receipt means that money or other forms of income are set aside or otherwise made available to a taxpayer, and the taxpayer can take hold of the income at any time. Under the accrual method, taxpayers have income when they are legally entitled to receive a definite amount of income, even if they have not yet received the income. For example, an accrual method taxpayer who agrees to perform services in exchange for $100 has $100 income as soon as she performs the services even if the payment is not made until a later date. Taxpayers must use the same accounting method for both income and deductions.

Because the tax code seeks to be neutral with respect to business transactions, it does not require taxpayers to select any particular accounting method. Instead, the tax code allows taxpayers to use whatever accounting method they use in their business transactions, as long as the accounting method "clearly reflects" the taxpayer's economic income. When a taxpayer's tax accounting method does not clearly reflect his or her economic income — and the distortion is not condoned by a statute or regulation — the Internal Revenue Service can determine the taxpayer's income using an accounting method that more accurately reflects his or her economic income.

The final point with regard to accounting methods is the accepted belief that a taxpayer's accounting method should "match" income with expenses. Under this rule, a taxpayer who purchases a long lasting asset for use in her trade or business cannot deduct the entire cost of the asset in a single year (unless the Congress grants her that right in an effort to stimulate the economy, as discussed above). Instead, the taxpayer must spread the entire cost of the asset over the time the asset will generate income. Thus, a taxpayer who spends $100,000 for equipment that will be used to generate income in a business is not allowed to deduct $100,000 in the year she purchased the equipment. Instead, she must deduct a portion of the cost over the number of years the equipment is used in her business. If the equipment is predicted to last five years, the taxpayer may deduct $20,000 per year. By this method, the deductions will be more closely matched to the income generated from the use of the machine.

X. CONCLUSION

The United States Tax Code, defined to include the statutes, regulations, administrative pronouncements and judicial opinions, comprises a voluminous body of law. This is perhaps by necessity since the Code is intended to apply to every single taxable unit within the United States jurisdiction. In addition to the goal of raising revenue, the tax code also purports, in certain limited circumstances, to reward certain economic behaviors (such as the purchase of a fuel efficient vehicle or the conduct of scientific research), subsidize other behaviors (such as the pursuit of higher education) and create a more egalitarian society (as, for example, via progressive tax rates). Although long and convoluted, the tax code is nevertheless characterized by a finite set of identifiable principles described in this chapter.

Chapter 13

WILLS, TRUSTS, & ESTATES

By — Thomas E. Allison

I. INTRODUCTION

This is a very practical area of the law. It deals with a question that affects every person and every family: What happens to a person's property when the person dies? We look at some actions the person might take during life, such as writing a Will or a Trust, but the main focus is on how property passes upon death. Some of the concepts we apply are ancient, but as the nature of people's property and wealth have changed, so has the law.

A.   Basic Concepts

There are a few basic ideas that are extremely important to remember as you learn about this area of the law.

1.   Always Deal with an Individual

We always focus on a single person — the individual who died. The person might be married and might have children, but it is always that person, and that person's property, that are the focus of our attention.

2.   Deal with Property "Item by Item"

When determining what happens to the person's property, we always look at individual items of property. We start by asking whether the ownership of the property passes automatically to someone else because of the nature of this property or the manner in which it was owned. If so, then the property is given to that other person. (This type of property is referred to as "non-probate property." It is discussed in Part II.) If not, then the property passes through the court system in a process known as "probate," or "estate administration," so we can determine who should receive that property.

3.   Only Living People Can Own Property

When a person dies, the ownership of the person's property either passes automatically to someone else or goes through the probate process. The property must pass to a living person, however; a dead person cannot receive property.

B.   Terminology

Here are some of the basic terms that are used in this area:

1.   Decedent

The person who died. If the decedent had a valid Will, the person is referred to as dying testate (and the person who wrote the Will is sometimes referred to as the testator). If the decedent did not have a valid Will, we refer to the person as having died intestate.

2.   Beneficiaries

The recipients of the decedent's property. Usually, they are individuals, but they could be corporations or organizations, such as charities. Beneficiaries come in two basic types:

a.   Heirs

People who receive property when a decedent dies without a valid Will. The heirs are determined pursuant to state statutes.

b.   Devisees

People who receive property because they are named as beneficiaries in a decedent's Will.

3.   Non-Probate Property

The ownership of this property passes automatically. Other than proving that the decedent died, there is no need for any legal proceedings. This property is discussed in Part II below.

4.   Probate Property

This property does not pass automatically. Upon the death of the decedent, we need to determine who the proper beneficiary of the probate property would be, so this property passes through a legal proceeding called probate administration, or estate administration.

C.   Dealing with a Decedent's Property

As we identify probate property and take it through the estate administration process, we are accomplishing three basic goals. First, the court appoints someone (usually known as the personal representative, or the executor of the estate) to take care of and protect the decedent's property. Second, we give the creditors of the decedent an opportunity to be paid. As you will see in Part VII, this requires some diligence on the part of the creditors, but at least they have the opportunity to have their debts paid by the estate. Third, the personal representative distributes the remaining property (after creditors and estate expenses have been paid) to the appropriate beneficiaries of the estate.

II. NON-PROBATE PROPERTY

This is the property that passes automatically upon the death of the owner. It might pass because of the manner in which the property was owned, or it might be because of the nature of the property itself. Non-probate property falls into three basic categories, with some detailed variations within each category.

A.   Joint Ownership

Property might be owned by more than one person, rather than being owned by a single individual. If an item of property was owned by the decedent along with others, then upon the death of the decedent, we need to determine whether the decedent's interest in the property passes automatically to the other owners, or whether the decedent could name the person who takes the decedent's interest. The answer to this question depends on how the property was owned.

The most basic form of co-ownership of property is the tenancy in common. In this form of ownership, each of the co-owners owns a share of the property. That share belongs to that individual, and the individual co-owner can deal with his or her individual share. Upon the death of the individual co-owner, the share that belonged to the decedent does not automatically pass to the surviving co-owners. Instead, the decedent's share passes through estate administration to the beneficiaries of the decedent's estate. An interest in property held in a tenancy in common is probate property. In most states, this is the default form of ownership; if land is owned by "Alice Barnes and Charles Dunn," for example, in most states, Alice and Charles are tenants in common.

Property may also be owned as joint tenants. This form of ownership is also sometimes known as "joint tenants with the right of survivorship." This is a little more difficult to establish, as there are some special rules that must be followed. Those rules are discussed in the Property chapter of this book. In most states, in order to own property as joint tenants, you must add additional language to the title, such as "Alice Barnes and Charles Dunn, as joint tenants with the right of survivorship," or some such similar language.

Because of the right of survivorship, joint tenancy is non-probate property upon the death of the first joint tenant. Using the example of the previous paragraph, upon Alice's death, Charles automatically owns the entire property by himself. This is inherent in the joint tenancy form of ownership; no legal proceedings would need to ensue unless someone challenged the joint tenancy itself. Notice, however, that Charles now owns the entire property, in just his name. If he were then to die without doing anything to change the form of ownership, the property would need to pass through the probate administration of Charles' estate.

Another form of co-ownership of property is the tenancy by the entireties. Tenancies by the entireties are recognized by about half of the states in the United States. Essentially, this is a joint tenancy between a husband and wife. The details of the rules in the states that allow tenancies by the entireties differ, but generally, this is the form of ownership that would automatically result if property is owned in the names of the spouses. Using the example of property being titled in the names "Alice Barnes and Charles Dunn," if the state recognizes the tenancy by the entirety form of ownership and Alice and Charles are married to each other, then they probably own the property as tenants by the entirety. Upon the death of Alice, Charles is the sole owner of the property, just as he would be if they owned the property as joint tenants. (Note that if Alice and Charles are not married to each other, they probably own the property as tenants in common. If this were true, then upon Alice's death, her interest in the property would pass through estate administration.)

B.   "Pay on Death" Arrangements

This is a relatively recent form of ownership that is specifically permitted by the statutes of many states. The details differ from state to state, but the basic concepts are the same.

Many states permit accounts in financial institutions to be owned as (for example) "Alice Barnes, P.O.D. Charles Dunn." The "P.O.D.," of course, stands for "pay on death." While Alice is alive, the property is exclusively hers. She can do with it as she pleases; neither Charles nor anyone else has any interest in the bank account as long as Alice is alive. Upon Alice's death, though, the P.O.D. designation takes over, and the ownership of the bank account automatically passes to Charles. No probate proceedings would be needed. Charles must survive Alice in order to take the balance of the bank account, though; if Charles fails to survive, then the P.O.D. designation fails. The account would then be treated as if it was solely owned by Alice, and the bank account would pass through estate administration.

In many states, corporate securities and stock brokerage accounts can be held in a "payable on death" (P.O.D.) or "transfer on death" (T.O.D.) form of ownership. The rules for the securities accounts mirror those for bank accounts.

This concept may also be applied to other contracts. If Alice is entering into a contract with Charles, for example, they could insert a provision in the contract to the following effect: "If Alice dies before Charles has completely paid her pursuant to this contract, then the balance remaining due upon Alice's death shall be paid by Charles to Evelyn." In this situation, if Evelyn survives Alice, then Evelyn would be entitled to the payments from Charles. No legal proceedings would be necessary to establish Evelyn's right to payment; that right was given as a provision of the contract.

C.   Life Insurance and Other Contracts

At its simplest, a life insurance policy is a contract with an insurance company that upon the death of the insured, the insurance company will pay the face value of the policy to the beneficiary named in the contract. If the named beneficiary survives the insured, the insurance company will pay the beneficiary directly; no legal proceedings are necessary. If the named beneficiary fails to survive the insured, then the insurance company will pay the proceeds to the alternate beneficiary named in the policy, if there is one. Again, no legal proceedings are needed. If none of the named beneficiaries survive the insured, then the printed terms and conditions of the insurance policy will determine who receives the insurance proceeds. In all likelihood, the taker of last resort would be the probate estate of the insured. That is the only situation in which the insurance proceeds should be subject to the estate administration process.

III. INTESTATE SUCCESSION

If the decedent dies without leaving a valid Will, then the decedent is described as having died intestate, and decedent's property will be distributed to the decedent's surviving spouse and heirs. This process is known as "intestate succession," "intestacy," "succession," or "descent and distribution." If the decedent has a valid Will but the Will does not dispose of all of the decedent's property, then the portion of the property that is not disposed of under the Will is also subject to the rules of intestate succession. Remember that it is the net amount of the property that is subject to these distribution rules; the creditors of the decedent and the expenses of the estate administration process are paid before the beneficiaries receive any property from the estate.

A.   The Distribution Plan

State statutes determine who receives the decedent's property under the rules of intestate succession. Ideally, these statutes would mirror what the average resident of the state would want to happen to his or her property after the property owner's death. The statutes of the state in which the decedent was residing at the time of death would control all of the decedent's personal property and real property located in that state. If the decedent owned real property located in another state, then the statutes of that other state would govern the disposition of that real property.

The state statutes typically provide first for the surviving spouse of the decedent. The amount passing to the surviving spouse might be all of the estate or a fractional share, depending on whether the decedent was also survived by lineal descendants or parents.

After the surviving spouse's share is determined, the remaining property typically passes to the blood relatives of the decedent. The blood relatives who are entitled to receive the decedent's property are referred to as the decedent's heirs. Different states follow different patterns, but a typical approach is to distribute the remaining property to the decedent's lineal descendants (children, grandchildren, et cetera). If there are no surviving lineal descendants, then the property would pass to the decedent's parents. If neither parent survives the decedent, then the property would pass to the decedent's siblings and their descendants (nieces, nephews, et cetera). If no surviving relative has yet been found, the property would then be divided in two, with one half passing to the decedent's maternal grandparents and the other half passing to the decedent's paternal grandparents. If there are no surviving grandparents on one of the particular sides, then the property would be distributed to the lineal descendants of those grandparents (aunts, uncles, first cousins, et cetera); if there are none, then the decedent's property would normally pass to the other grandparents (or their descendants). If you've gone through this point of the family tree and there are no living relatives at all, then the property typically would pass to the state government. This last step is referred to as "escheat."

After identifying who is entitled to the rest of the decedent's property, the next step is to determine how much of the property each heir is entitled to receive. The share of each beneficiary is determined pursuant to the state's "per stirpes" (pronounced "stir-peas") rules. Again, the details differ from state to state; only general rules can be given here.

This explanation will assume that the decedent's heirs are lineal descendants, but the concept would be the same if you were dealing with other heirs. Start by making a chart with the decedent at the top, and with lines going down from the decedent to each of the decedent's children. (These are referred to as "bloodlines.") If a particular child survived the decedent, then the line ends with that child. If the child predeceased the decedent, however, then continue that line down to that child's children (the decedent's grandchildren). Again, if a particular grandchild survived the decedent, then the line that went to that grandchild stops. Continue this process until each line ends with a lineal descendant who survived the decedent. The descendant at the end of each line is an heir of the decedent. If a particular bloodline ends without finding a lineal descendant who survived the decedent, then that bloodline is ignored; just eliminate it from the chart.

Next, go back to the chart and identify the first level down from the decedent at which someone actually survived. In all likelihood, that will be the level of the decedent's children, but it could be the decedent's grandchildren or even a more remote generation level. At that generation level of the first actual survivor, count the number of individuals who survived the decedent and the number of individuals who predeceased the decedent but left lineal descendants who survived the decedent. In essence, you are counting the number of active bloodlines. Divide the property equally at that point, assigning one share for each active bloodline. The descendants at that level who actually survived the decedent each receive one fractional share. A share that is attributed to a descendant who predeceased the decedent but left descendants who survived the decedent flows down that descendant's bloodline, with the share splitting at each point the bloodline splits. Since each bloodline ends with a person who survived the decedent, all the property will be distributed.

Here is a numerical example: Assume the decedent had three children, A, B, and C. Child A survived the decedent; B and C predeceased. B left two children (D and E) who survived the decedent, and C left three children (F, G, and H) who survived. Charting the family tree, you end up with bloodlines that end at A, D, E, F, G, and H. Go back up the chart to the first level at which you have a person who actually survived the decedent; that is the level of A, B, and C. There are three active bloodlines at this point. Child A receives 1/3 of the property. Child B was entitled to one-third, but since you cannot give property to a dead person, B's share passes down B's bloodline to D and E. Grandchildren D and E each receive one-sixth of the decedent's remaining property (B's one-third share, divided in two). Similarly, child C's share passes down C's bloodline to F, G, and H; those grandchildren each receive one-ninth of the decedent's remaining property (C's one-third share, divided in three).

Some states modify the normal per stirpes distribution rules if you are dealing with siblings or more remote heirs and some of those heirs are related to the decedent by the whole blood (sharing two common ancestors) and others are related by the half blood (sharing one common ancestor). In those states, each heir of the half blood would receive half as much as each heir of the whole blood. Most states, however, treat all heirs the same, regardless of whether they are related to the decedent through the whole blood or the half blood.

B.   Identifying the Members of the Family

One of the issues that must be decided is whether a person is entitled to a position in the family tree as a potential heir of the decedent. Sometimes the issue arises because of action taken by the potential heir, sometimes because of actions taken by others, and sometimes simply because of fate.

1.   Adoption

English common law, which forms the basis for the system of law in the United States, did not recognize the concept of adoption. Instead, in the United States, adoption is a creation of the legislatures in the various states. As a result, the rules for adoption vary from state to state, and the adoption will be legally recognized only if the statutory requirements have been followed. An explanation of the concept of adoption can be found in the Family Law chapter of this book.

A common thread that runs through the adoption statutes is that if a legal adoption occurs, the family relationship that is created by virtue of the adoption under the state statute replaces the natural blood relationship between the adopted person and his or her natural parents. As a result, the adopted person now belongs in the family tree of the adopting individual and is removed from the family tree of the natural parents. There is an exception to this rule in the situation of a step-parent adoption; if a child is adopted by the new wife of the child's natural father, for example, the adopted child is still considered a child of the natural father. In this situation, the child is now a member of the family of the natural father and of the adopting mother; depending on the particular state, the child may or may not still be considered a member of the family of the natural mother.

2.   Children Born Out of Wedlock

It usually is not difficult to determine who is the mother of a child. As such, most states simply provide that a child is the lineal descendant of the mother and is a member of the mother's family, regardless of whether the mother was married at the time the child was born.

If a child is born to a woman who is married, the child is also presumed to be the child of the mother's husband. This is a very strong presumption, recognizing the status of the intact family. As a result, the child belongs in the family trees of both the wife and the husband. It is possible that another man could prove that he was actually the father of the child, but the strength of the presumption makes this very difficult.

In contrast to proving maternity, it is often rather difficult to prove the identity of the father of a child. Because of this, states often provide different standards for determining whether a child is the legal child of a man. A typical statutory approach is to provide that a child is a lineal descendant of a man and a member of the man's family only if the man acknowledged paternity in writing, or if there were an adjudication of paternity, or if the natural parents participated in a marriage ceremony, even if the attempted marriage was void.

3.   Simultaneous Death

One of our basic principles is that a person must be living in order to receive and own property. As a result, a person must survive the decedent in order to inherit property from the decedent. If the decedent and a prospective heir of the decedent die under circumstances in which it is difficult to determine the order of death, then how do we determine whether the prospective heir survived the decedent and, therefore, was entitled to receive the decedent's property? Further, if the heir dies shortly after the decedent, should the decedent's wealth pass to the heir and then to the beneficiaries of the heir's estate, or should the wealth remain in the bloodlines of the decedent?

States respond to these issues in two basic ways. The first approach provides that a person is not considered to have survived the decedent unless the person is living 120 hours (5 days) after the death of the decedent. This rule eliminates the first question raised in the previous paragraph, and answers the second question by imposing the arbitrary 120-hour rule before the decedent's wealth will pass to any beneficiary.

The second approach answers the second question by providing that a beneficiary is entitled to receive property from a decedent's estate if the beneficiary simply survives the decedent. The survival time need not be long; a fraction of a second is sufficient. If an heir survives the decedent by five seconds, for example, then the property passes from the decedent to the heir, and then from the heir to the beneficiaries of the heir's estate. This approach then focuses on the first question by stipulating that if there is insufficient evidence that the decedent and the heir died other than simultaneously, then the heir is deemed to have predeceased the decedent. The consequence of this rule is that if the court cannot determine whether the decedent or the heir died first, then the decedent is considered to have been the survivor; the decedent's property therefore remains in the decedent's bloodline, passing to the other heirs of the decedent.

4.   Killer Statutes

A person should not be able to profit from doing something wrong. If you kill the decedent, therefore, you should not be able to inherit the decedent's property. This basic premise is applied throughout the United States, though the details of the rule naturally vary from state to state. A typical phrasing of the rule is that an heir is prevented from receiving any property from the decedent if the heir "feloniously and intentionally" killed the decedent. If that test is met, then the heir is considered to have predeceased the decedent, and the decedent's property therefore passes to the decedent's other heirs.

IV. WILLS

Under the laws of intestate succession, the state determines who is entitled to receive the decedent's property. The state legislatures determine what they believe most people would want to happen to their property, and then they enact statutes making that the law. Obviously, the "big picture" approach used by a state legislature is not going to fit every person's situation. There is a simple response to that issue — if Carol Davis would prefer to choose the beneficiaries who receive her property upon her death, then Carol can write a Will, devising her property to those whom she wants to benefit. Note that different terminology is used here: Carol, the testator (the person signing the Will), devises her property (leaves the property in her Will) to the devisees (the takers under her Will). A codicil is an amendment to a Will and is governed by the same rules as a Will.

A.   Your Right to Make a Will

For historical reasons, a person's ability to execute a Will is considered to be a matter of "legislative grace." You have no constitutional right to execute a Will designating the people who will receive your property; the legislature has rather granted you the privilege of doing so. As a practical matter, it would be political suicide for a state legislature to ever try to eliminate the right to devise property, but the legislature certainly has the right to establish reasonable rules on who can execute a Will, the formalities that must be met for a Will to be valid, and so forth.

In order to execute a Will, a person must have the capacity to do so. There are two aspects of capacity. First, the person must have "legal capacity" to execute a Will. Typically, in order to sign a Will, a person must have reached the age of majority (age eighteen in most states); in some states, an emancipated minor can also execute a Will.

The second aspect of having the capacity to execute a Will is "testamentary capacity." This requirement is imposed in order to make certain that the testator understands what he or she is doing. Testamentary capacity is a four-part test. Suppose, for example, that Ted Thompson wants to execute a Will. First, Ted must be capable of understanding the natural objects of his bounty; in other words, the family members to who most people would expect that Ted wants to leave his property (or, "who" Ted has). Second, Ted must be capable of understanding the nature and extent of his property; in other words, the property he owns and its approximate value (or, "what" he has). Third, Ted must understand the disposition that he is making (or, "where" Ted is leaving his property). Finally, Ted must understand the fact that signing this Will effectuates Ted's intent (or, "why" he is signing this document). Note that under the first two elements of the test, the testator must be "capable of understanding" the particular element. If Ted is capable of understanding his relatives, for example, but is mistaken as to the number of his grandchildren and their names, then he meets this aspect of the test; his mere mistake will not cause him to fail the test of capacity.

B.   How Do You Make a Will

The procedures that must be followed to execute a Will differ from state to state. Since these execution formalities are statutory requirements, it is extremely important that the procedures mandated in a particular state be followed precisely. If the statutory formalities are not met, then by definition, the document is not a Will.

The ability to devise property in a Will dates from ancient times. As a result, the statutory requirements of some states are rather antiquated and formalistic. Most states, however, have modernized their statutes and treat the execution of a Will much like that of any important document.

In a state with a modern statute, the execution of a Will is very straightforward — the Will must be in writing, it must be signed by the testator, and the testator's signature must be witnessed by at least two witnesses (referred to as "attesting witnesses") who also sign the Will. In some states, if the entire Will is handwritten by and signed by the testator, then the Will is valid even without witnesses. (This type of document is known as a "holographic Will.") In a state with an older, more formalistic statute, a Will might need to be writing, signed at the end by the testator, and signed by the testator in the presence of at least two attesting witnesses, each of whom signs the Will in the presence of the testator and in the presence of the other attesting witness.

The witnesses to the Will should not also be beneficiaries under the Will; in some states, a devise to an interested witness could invalidate either the devise to that interested beneficiary, or the entire Will.

Under the laws of most states, the testator and the attesting witnesses can appear before a Notary Public and sign an oath that the proper statutory procedures were followed in the execution of the Will. A Will that has this separate affidavit is known as a "self-proving" Will. Because of the affidavit, a self-proving Will is presumed to have been properly executed, and the procedures for admitting the self-proved Will into probate after the death of the testator are much simpler than the procedures for other Wills.

C.   How Do You Change or Revoke a Will

A Will is referred to as an "ambulatory document." The testator signs it, but it does not become effective for purposes of disposing of the testator's property until the testator dies. Until then, the Will can be changed or completely revoked by the testator, for any reason. It is only the "Last Will" of the testator that determines what happens to the testator's property.

There are three basic methods by which the testator's Will might be altered or revoked. First, the Will can be revoked or changed by the testator in writing. Here, the law normally imposes formality requirements that are based on a symmetry concept — if the state requires certain formalities in order for a writing to constitute a Will, then the same formalities are usually required in order to change or revoke the Will. This method for modifying or revoking a Will is the one that is most typically used by attorneys, because it is the clearest manner of expressing the testator's desires. Most Wills prepared by attorneys, for example, begin with a sentence that includes a phrase such as "and I hereby revoke all of my prior Wills and Codicils." When the new Will is signed by the testator, the clause has the effect or revoking all of the testator's prior documents, so that this new document contains the testator's entire estate plan. A Codicil is an example of a written alteration to a Will and begins with language that reaffirms the Will, except for the changes contained in the Codicil. When the testator signs the Codicil, the original Will is still valid, except to the extent it has been changed by the language in the Codicil.

The second manner in which the testator could revoke or modify a Will is for the testator to take an action on the Will that indicates that the testator no longer wants the document to be effective. The requirements for revocation by act vary from state to state, but they typically require that the testator take a legally-sufficient action with respect to the written Will (such as burning it, tearing it, or obliterating or destroying it), and that the action be taken with the intent and for the purpose of revoking the Will. This method of revoking a Will is not often used by lawyers but unfortunately is regularly used by testators. The difficulty with this method is that the action itself is inherently ambiguous, and it often isn't discovered until the testator has died. The testator is therefore no longer available to explain the action.

Suppose I want to revoke my Will, for example. I know that I can do so by burning it, so I light a fire in the fireplace so I can burn up the Will. I look for my Will in my office, and locate it under a pile of books. In pulling the Will out from under the books, the Will tears. I know that tearing the Will is a sufficient act to revoke it, so I just leave the Will in pieces on my desk. Has my Will been revoked? Legally, no. I took a legally sufficient act, and I had the necessary intent to revoke my Will, but I did not do the act (tear the Will) for the purpose of revoking it. Instead, it was an accident. The Will therefore has not been revoked by act. If I were to die, however, my Will would be found in pieces on my desk. Would the court consider the Will revoked? Quite possibly; no one would be available to relate the circumstances under which the Will was torn, and a reasonable interpretation of the facts would lead to that conclusion. That is the problem with revocation by act — the act itself is inherently ambiguous, and usually there is no one who can explain what happened. This difficulty has led to the adoption of a legal presumption: If the testator had the original Will and that Will cannot be located upon the testator's death, then the presumption arises that the testator destroyed the Will with the intent and for the purpose of revoking it. The Will is presumed to be invalid. The presumption is revocable; the proponent of the Will can present evidence offering an explanation of what happened to the Will, and why the Will was not revoked.

The third mechanism by which the Will might be revoked or modified is through the operation of a state statute — a concept that is often referred to as "revocation by operation of law." Typically, this involves a change in the family circumstances — marriage, divorce, or birth or adoption of a child. Suppose, for example, that Rachel is married and has a Will devising essentially all her property to her husband, Paul. If Rachel and Paul were to divorce, it is quite likely that Rachel would no longer want her property to go to Paul. The legislatures of many states responded to this situation by enacting statutes providing that if a married person executes a Will that contains provisions in favor of a spouse, then upon divorce, the provisions in the Will that favored the former spouse are void. Under these statutes, the former spouse is legally considered to have predeceased the testator. Note that the Will itself is still valid; the ex-spouse is simply treated as dead for purposes of interpreting the Will.

How does the revocation of a Will or Codicil affect the disposition of the person's property upon death? The answer depends on the particular factual situation and the state in which the person resided. If Jenny had executed only one Will during her lifetime and she revoked it before she died, then her property would be distributed to her heirs pursuant to the rules for intestate succession. If she had executed one Will and revoked it by executing a second Will a few years later, and then revoked the second will, the result might be different. The rules vary from state to state, but in most states, if the first Will was still in existence, then we would presume that Jenny wanted her property to pass pursuant to the first Will. If she had destroyed the first Will, however, then her property would probably be distributed to her heirs. If Jenny had a Will and then amended it by executing a Codicil, then her later revocation of the Codicil is generally presumed to reinstate the provisions of the original Will, as if the Codicil had never existed.

D.   How Can Your Will Be Challenged

There are three primary grounds under which the validity of a testator's Will can be challenged after the testator's death, and several variations on the three basic concepts. These arguments are often made together, with each ground constituting one count in the petition filed by the person challenging the Will. This challenge is often referred to as a Will Contest.

The first ground relates back to the formality requirements for signing the Will. If the contestant can show that the document was not properly executed, then the Will is invalid. In actuality, the document never was a Will; the legislature established the formality requirements that had to be met in order for a document to constitute a Will, and this document did not meet those requirements. A variation on the formality argument would be to contest the Will on the grounds that the Will was revoked by the testator and therefore was not valid upon the testator's death. This is an example of a situation in which the presumption of revocation by act discussed in the previous section would become relevant if the testator had the original Will, and it could not be found upon the death of the testator.

The next two grounds for bringing a Will contest are somewhat related. They deal with the ability of the testator to form and freely express how the testator wishes to dispose of property at death. The first argument is that the testator lacked the capacity to execute a Will. This argument might involve issues of legal capacity, such as the age of the person when the document was signed, but it is more likely to question the testator's testamentary capacity. In order to be successful, the contestant must demonstrate that at the time the testator signed the Will, the testator did not meet the four-part testamentary capacity test. The contestant therefore must show that the testator either was not capable of understanding the natural objects of his or her bounty, was not capable of understanding the nature and extent of his or her property, did not understand the disposition that he or she was making, or did not understand the fact that signing this Will effectuated the testator's intent. This is somewhat difficult to do, as the test of testamentary capacity is fairly minimal, and the Will is not invalidated because of an innocent mistake. If Marie is wrong about the number of her grandchildren, for example, is that the result of a simple mistake (in which case the Will should be valid) or her inability to remember the natural objects of her bounty (in which case the Will is probably invalid)?

The second argument is that the testator was being influenced by someone who wanted the Will to contain certain provisions. This type of influence is perfectly natural. For example, Martie, Carol's daughter, might tell Carol how much she loves Carol's emerald necklace and how she would love to have it someday. As a result of the conversation, Carol might devise the necklace to Martie. There is nothing wrong with this. At some point, however, the "influence" could become "undue influence," resulting from Martie pressuring her mother to devise the necklace to her. If it reaches the point at which the words on the page do not reflect the free will of Carol (and instead reflect Martie's imposed desires), then it is really not Carol's will, and the devise would be invalid.

Undue influence traditionally required a four-part test. The contestant to the Will had to show that someone else (Martie, for example) had the opportunity to exert influence on Carol and had the motivation to do so, that Carol was susceptible to the influence, and that the devise in the Will was the result of Martie's influence rather than Carol's free will. The "susceptibility" element is what makes the undue influence argument related to the capacity issue — the testator who would be susceptible to being unduly influenced usually is the testator who had weakened capacity.

It is difficult for the contestant to meet the burden of proving this four-part test, primarily because the contestant must demonstrate the result. How would someone contesting Carol's devise of the necklace to Martie prove that the devise was the result of Martie's undue influence rather than Carol's simply being nice to Martie? It is hard to prove the result for several reasons, one of which is that Carol is dead and therefore cannot explain what motivated her devise. When all is said and done, who knows what Carol really wanted to do? The difficulty of proving that the Will was the result of undue influence has caused most states to develop a modern rule that is applied in certain factual situations. If the facts of the case fit the pattern of the modern rule, then it is applied; if they do not fit the pattern, then the traditional rule is applied.

The modern rule is based on the premise that a person should not profit from abusing a confidential relationship. Under this rule, if the contestant to the Will can demonstrate that a devise in the Will was actively procured by a substantial beneficiary of the Will who was in a confidential relationship with the testator, then that devise is presumed to be the result of undue influence. Essentially, the three elements of the modern rule (active procurement, substantial beneficiary, confidential relationship) are analogous to the first three elements under the traditional test of undue influence. "Active procurement" relates to the opportunity to exert the undue influence, "substantial beneficiary" establishes the motivation, and "confidential relationship" references the susceptibility issue under the premise that the testator might have heeded the wishes of a person in whom the testator placed trust and confidence. The modern rule penalizes this possible abuse of the confidential relationship by presuming the result. The contestant does not have to prove that the Will was the result of undue influence; it is instead presumed under the rule. The effect of the presumption is that the proponent of the Will now has the burden of proving that the language in the Will was the result of the free wishes of the testator, rather than the undue influence exerted by the person in the confidential relationship.

Who has the burden of proving issues in a Will contest? Nationwide, we have two basic rules and two exceptions to those rules. The first basic rule is that the proponent of the Will has the burden of making a "prima facie case" that the Will was properly executed. This means that the proponent must prove that the formality requirements of the state were followed. This is not usually done in a court hearing; instead, we simply get an oath from one or more of the witnesses to the Will as to the formalities that were followed, and we assume that they are being accurate and honest. The second basic rule is that the contestant has the burden of proving any other grounds for contesting the Will. These two basic rules favor the validity of the Will — once the proponent has presented the oath of the witnesses to the Will, it is presumed to be valid, and the contestant must prove that it is not. The contestant could, for example, argue that the statutory formalities were not met, but since the witnesses have sworn that the proper procedures were followed, the validity of the Will is presumed, and the contestant has the burden of proof.

The two exceptions to the basic rules deal with specific factual situations. The first exception deals with the modern rule for undue influence that was discussed above. If the contestant presents evidence that a substantial beneficiary under the Will was in a confidential relationship with the testator and was active in procuring the Will, then the Will is presumed to be invalid because it was the result of undue influence, and the burden of proof shifts to the proponent of the Will. The proponent now must prove that the Will was not the result of undue influence. The second exception deals with a Will that was executed by a person who had been adjudicated incompetent by a court. In that situation, the testator is presumed to lack testamentary capacity because of the adjudication. A person who has been adjudicated incompetent can sign a valid Will, however; the proponent simply must prove that the testator met the test for testamentary capacity at the time the testator signed the Will.

E.   How Is Your Will Interpreted

The Will becomes effective for the purpose of disposing of the testator's property when the Will is admitted into probate after the death of the testator. At that point, of course, the testator is no longer available to explain what the testator really wanted to do or what the testator really meant by the language that was used in the Will. How do we interpret the language of the Will? Suppose a potential beneficiary believes that the testator made a mistake; can that mistake be corrected? Can the purported mistake even be proved?

The law in this area is slowly changing. The modern trend is to leave the questions of the interpretation of the document and the correction of mistakes to the discretion of the court. If the personal representative or an interested person had a question about the meaning of the Will, then the judge (or possibly a jury, in some states) would construe that language and render a decision. In essence, the court would be determining what the testator really wanted to do with his or her property. This is the current trend, but it is not yet the majority rule.

In most states, the judge would initially apply the "plain meaning rule." This is a rule of construction that you often see used in the interpretation of contracts and other written documents. If the words on the page have a plain meaning and are used in a normal manner, then pursuant to this rule, the judge would determine that the words mean exactly what they say. That is, the "plain meaning" of the words would control. No evidence would be allowed to indicate that there was any sort of mistake, or that the testator really intended to say something other than what is written on the page. In applying this rule, the court is protecting the Will (and thereby the testator's wishes) from someone trying to create a fictitious mistake in order to alter the testator's estate plan. Applying the plain meaning rule might mean that some actual mistakes are not remedied, but the philosophy is that this approach is preferable to allowing fictitious mistakes to alter a clearly written estate plan. Under this majority rule, the court would consider the possibility of a mistake only if the plain meaning rule does not apply.

The next major issue in the area of construction or interpretation of a Will is what happens if the court determines that the language in the Will is ambiguous. There are two types of ambiguities, and their treatment has differed over the ages.

The first type of ambiguity is a latent ambiguity. In this situation, the words in the Will are clear and make perfect sense. When you try to apply the language in the Will to either the property in the estate or the estate beneficiaries, however, you discover an ambiguity. For example, my Will devises $100,000 to "my sister-in-law, Linda," and I have two sisters-in-law named Linda. (One is my brother's wife, and the other is my wife's sister.) Which one gets the money? The devise in the Will is perfectly fine on its face, but when you try to apply the language to the estate beneficiaries, you discover the problem. Another example of a latent ambiguity is my devise of "my car" to my brother, Bill. At the time of my death, I own two automobiles. Which one does Bill get, or does Bill get them both? Again, the Will itself is perfectly clear on its face, but when you try to apply the Will language to the estate assets, you discover the problem.

If you notice, the latent ambiguity was discovered only when the language of the Will was applied to the estate property or beneficiaries. These are facts outside the face of the Will. In responding to the latent ambiguity, therefore, the courts have always allowed extrinsic evidence to be admitted. After all, the ambiguity arose because of extrinsic facts, so it only makes sense to allow outside evidence to be considered in resolving the problem.

The second type of ambiguity is the patent ambiguity. In this situation, the language of the Will simply does not make sense. Note that the words might have a plain meaning, but that meaning just is not logical. For example, I might devise all my property "one-half to each of the following: Angie, Barbara, and Carole." What does that mean? Did I really mean to give each of them one-third of my property? Did I really mean to give my property to just two of the three named persons? If the latter, which two? The language of the Will itself just does not make sense.

The treatment of patent ambiguities has changed over the years. Traditionally, the courts simply left the situation as it found it. The judge read the words of the Will, and if they made sense the judge applied the language as written. If the words did not make sense, then the devise would fail. The judge would disregard the patently ambiguous language, and the testator's property would pass pursuant to the remaining language of the Will; if the remaining language did not dispose of all of the testator's property, then that remaining property would pass pursuant to the rules of intestate succession. No extrinsic evidence would be allowed to try to explain the ambiguous language of the Will. This approach is still followed in many states.

The more modern approach for patent ambiguities attempts to salvage the language of the Will and the effectiveness of the devise. It deals with the patent ambiguity the same way as the latent ambiguity; extrinsic evidence is allowed in an effort to explain away the ambiguity and determine the true intent of the testator. Under the modern approach, therefore, if the court determines that the Will is ambiguous, then extrinsic evidence is admissible, regardless of the nature of the ambiguity. The court will consider both the language of the Will and the extrinsic evidence in an effort to determine and effectuate the testator's intent.

As you can see, it is entirely possible that a devise in a Will might fail because the language of the Will cannot be determined with certainty. The devise could also fail because the devisee fails to survive the testator. Remember, the Will controls the disposition of property upon the testator's death, and only living persons can receive and own property. If the devisee predeceases the testator, then the named devisee cannot receive the property. We describe this situation as a "lapse." In an effort to prevent lapses and to salvage devises, most states have passed statutes providing that if a devise is made in favor of a person who is related to the testator (typically through a common grandparent or a closer relative) and the named devisee predeceases the testator but leaves lineal descendants who survive the testator, then the devise will be paid to those surviving lineal descendants, per stirpes. This type of "anti-lapse statute" reflects what the legislature believes the average testator would want; if the testator indicates in the Will that the testator would not prefer this rule, then the anti-lapse statute would not apply.

If a devise fails due to lapse or because an ambiguity cannot be resolved, then what happens to the property? If the devise was one of either specific property or a sum of money, and not one of part of the residue, then upon the failure of the devise, the property becomes part of the residue of the estate. If the failed devise was one of a portion of the residue, then the property would be divided among the remaining residual beneficiaries. If we have the failure of the entire residual devise, however, then the property no longer can pass pursuant to the Will, and the property will pass to the testator's heirs pursuant to the rules for intestate succession. Suppose, for example, that Cindy devises $10,000 to Linda, and the rest of her property to Adrian and Charlotte. If the devise to Linda fails, then the $10,000 becomes part of the residue that will go to Adrian and Charlotte. If the portion of the residue that should go to Adrian also fails, then Charlotte will get the entire residue of the estate, including the $10,000. If the portion that should go to Charlotte also fails, then the entire residue of the estate, including the $10,000, will pass to Cindy's heirs.

A devise might also fail because the devised property was not owned by the testator at the time of the testator's death. This could occur if the devise was of specifically described property. If Cindy devises her antique rosewood couch to David, for example, but then sells the couch, the devise to David will fail because the property did not belong to Cindy when she died. This concept is referred to as "ademption by extinction," or sometimes simply as "ademption." (The verb form of this word is "adeem.")

V.   TRUSTS

A trust is a marvelously imaginative tool for managing property. The flexibility of the trust concept allows you to do virtually anything with property, so long as it is legal and you are not violating public policy. A trust is a concept — a relationship among people with respect to property. Unfortunately, that makes it rather difficult to define. To some extent, a trust is like a dog; you learn what it is from experience. You know what a dog is because you have seen them all your life. You probably cannot define the word, though, in any way that would help a person identify the animal when walking down the street!

As you go through this material, realize that trusts are creatures of common law. Their origins are ancient, and they have been defined by the courts over the centuries. In an effort to increase the level of certainty in the field, many state legislatures have begun codifying trust law, taking the common-law concepts and reducing them to statutory form. In doing so, they sometimes change the common-law rule to reflect modern commercial procedures. Naturally, we can only give you general rules here; you would need to look at the specific law of any individual state to determine how an issue would be treated in that jurisdiction. Our goals here are simply to familiarize you with the concept of the trust and to give you the basic rules for the operation of a trust. We will also show you some of the situations in which a trust might be used. The only limitations of how a trust might be designed and used, though, are public policy, illegality, and your own imagination. It is truly an amazing vehicle for owning and controlling property.

A.   What Is a Trust

The trust concept begins with a person who owns property. As you learn in the property chapter of this text, owning property in fee simple means that you have full rights, privileges, and responsibilities over the property. Your rights are subject to some limitations that are necessary for us to live in an orderly society, but in essence you can do whatever you want with the property. If you set up a trust, you can separate these rights, privileges, and responsibilities, spread them among several people, and specify the circumstances under which the rights and privileges can be enjoyed.

Suppose, for example, that Charlie and Elaine are married. Charlie has a daughter, Lois, from a prior marriage, and Elaine has a son, David, from a prior marriage. Lois and David are both adults, living on their own. Charlie wants to make certain that Elaine would have plenty of money to support herself if Charlie should predecease her, but Charlie also wants to ensure that his money eventually goes to Lois and stays in his blood line. He does not want Elaine to be able to control the money and give it to David. One way in which Charlie could satisfy his goals would be to set up a trust in his Will and devise his property to the trustee of this trust. The trustee would be the legal owner of the property; would have the power to convey it, manage it, and deal with it; and would have the responsibility of maintaining the property, paying the taxes on it, and so forth. The trust would provide that the income that is earned on the trust property is to be paid to Elaine on a regular basis for the rest of her life, and that the trustee could make additional distributions to Elaine if she needed them. Upon Elaine's death, the trustee would distribute the remaining trust property to Lois, in fee simple.

There are two very important ramifications to Charlie's establishing this trust. First, if you notice, when Charlie (as the "settlor," "grantor," or "donor" of the trust) conveys the property to the trustee, Charlie is splitting the ownership and benefits of the property. Prior to the conveyance, Charlie was the sole owner of the property, in fee simple. After the conveyance, the legal title to the property is held by the trustee, and the beneficial (or "equitable") ownership of the property is held by Elaine and Lois. Elaine has a present interest in the trust property (usually referred to as the "income interest"), and Lois has a future interest (usually called the "remainder interest") in it. The critical issue is that the legal title, held by the trustee, has been separated from the equitable interest in the property, which is now held by the beneficiaries. There are now three people who have interests in the property, and the interest of each person is different. Since the trustee is the only person who has the legal title to the property, though, the trustee has the sole decision on how the property should be managed. The trustee can sell the property, improve it, rent it, or do any of the other things the legal owner of property might want to do.

The second ramification of Charlie's establishing the trust is that the trustee is now the owner of property in which other people, the beneficiaries, have an interest. One of the core concepts of trust law is that the trustee has an obligation to hold and manage this trust property for the exclusive benefit of the beneficiaries. In equity, the property belongs to the beneficiaries; the trustee is simply managing the property for them. Everything the trustee does with respect to the trust property must be for the beneficiaries. The trustee may not benefit from the trust property, other than by receiving a reasonable fee for the work the trustee performs in managing it.

The situations in which a trust might be used are limited only by the boundaries of legality, public policy, and the settlor's imagination. I might use it, for example, to provide for the protection and management of my property during my dotage, or to provide for my disabled spouse or child after my death, or to keep the property out of the hands of my child who is too reckless and immature to handle it. Regardless of the specifics of the factual situation, the trust concept will always encompass these two elements — the ownership interests in the property are being split between legal and equitable interests, and the trustee, as the holder of the legal interest, owes a fiduciary duty to the holders of the equitable interests, the beneficiaries.

B.   How Is a Trust Created

One of the basic requirements for a trust is that it must contain an interest in property. The property interest must be transferred into the trust in order for the property to become subject to the trust terms. Remember, the trustee is holding the legal interest in the trust property. Technically, the property is not owned by the trust; it is rather owned by the trustee, pursuant to the terms and conditions of the trust. There are two aspects to this requirement that the property be transferred to the trustee. First, who is the trustee? Is the trustee also the settlor of the trust, or is it a different person? Second, what is the interest in property? Is it real property, or is it personalty?

Generally, if the trust contains real property, then the trust must be evidenced by a written instrument. This written instrument might be a Will, in which case the trust is referred to as a "testamentary trust," or it might be a separate trust declaration or trust agreement signed by the settlor during the settlor's life, in which case the trust is described as an "inter vivos trust" or sometimes as a "living trust." The formalities required for the written instrument vary from state to state and depend on the factual situation under which the trust is being created. The law might simply require that there be some writing that indicates the terms and conditions of the trust, or it might require that the trust be executed with the formalities of a Will.

If the trust contains only personal property, then the trust usually could be oral. Some states, however, require that the trust be in writing and executed with certain formalities if the duration of the trust extends beyond the death of the settlor.

The property must also be transferred to the trustee, to hold pursuant to the terms of the trust. If the trustee is the same person as the settlor, then your formality requirements for this conveyance are minimal. After all, how do you convey property to yourself? If the settlor is also the trustee, then we normally describe the trust relationship as a "declaration of trust" — the settlor is declaring that he or she is holding this property in the trust. Most personal property is conveyed very informally, so an oral declaration of the fact that this property is held in the trust is viewed as being sufficient. Some personal property, though, such as shares of corporate stock or automobiles, are evidenced by certificates of ownership; in those situations, the certificate would need to be changed to reflect that the owner is no longer "Amy Brown," but rather is now "Amy Brown, as Trustee of the Amy Brown Trust dated March 17, 2008," or words to that effect. If real property is held in the trust, then the formality requirements are increased slightly; the trust must be evidenced by a writing, showing that Amy, as Trustee, now holds the land.

If the trustee is a different person than the settlor, then the requirements are stricter. If the trust contains real property, the terms of the trust generally must be in writing, and the property must actually be conveyed to the trustee in a written instrument meeting the requirements of a deed or a Will. Similarly, personal property must also be transferred to the trustee. The written trust is usually called a "trust agreement" when the settlor is not also the trustee.

C.   How Is a Trust Changed or Revoked

The law has recognized revocable trusts for centuries. So, if the trust states that it is either revocable or irrevocable, the status is clear. If the trust is oral or does not contain any provisions stating whether it is revocable or irrevocable, though, which is it? The real question is what is your starting point? We need a presumption.

As you might expect, the presumption differs from state to state. In most states, a trust is presumed to be irrevocable unless the settlor has specifically retained the right to alter, amend, revoke, or terminate the trust. This presumption relates to the fact that the law generally prefers absolute transfers. In a few states, though, most notably California and Florida, the presumption has been reversed by state statute; in those states, a trust is presumed to be revocable unless the terms of the trust provide that it is irrevocable. The logic behind this approach is that it prevents the settlor from unwittingly making a gift to the trust beneficiaries, which could create an unexpected gift tax liability on the settlor.

If the trust is revocable, how does the settlor exercise the power to alter, amend, revoke, or terminate the trust? If the trust is in writing and is well drafted, the document should specify the manner in which the settlor's rights may be exercised. If it does, then that is what must be done. After all, if the settlor makes the rules, the settlor should be required to follow them. If the settlor does not comply with the specified requirements, then any attempt to change the trust would be void.

If the trust is oral or does not specify how the rights may be exercised, then anything the settlor does that indicates that the trust is altered, amended, revoked, or terminated could be sufficient. As you might expect, this is a rather ambiguous standard. Such a situation could lead to litigation, and it therefore should be avoided if possible.

There are a number of other ways in which a trust might be altered, amended, revoked, or terminated, though these mechanisms have limited practicality. For example, if all of the beneficiaries of an irrevocable trust join with the settlor of the trust, then the trust can be modified in any manner whatsoever. The philosophy here is that if all these parties agree to a course of action, there is no controversy so the court should not prevent them from doing as they desire. If the settlor is dead, of course, this option is not available. A trust would also terminate if the trustee were to distribute all the trust property to the beneficiaries, and most states have statutes permitting a trustee to distribute the trust property and terminate a trust if the value of the trust property falls below an amount fixed by statute. This is a cost/benefit test, in which the legislature is recognizing that the costs of continuing to administer the trust can exceed the benefit of continuing the trust for a small amount of property.

There are two modern developments that relate to changing or terminating a trust. The first is to increase the authority of the court to modify or terminate a trust in order to allow the court to correct mistakes on the part of the settlor, to achieve tax benefits for the trust, or to respond to situations that were not foreseen and provided for by the settlor. These rules enable the court to change the trust so as to allow it to achieve the goals of the settlor. The second trend is to permit a settlor to appoint a person who can direct the trustee in its actions or actually modify the provisions of the trust itself. If a statute permits this power to direct, the person would need to be appointed in the trust instrument.

D.   Relationships Involved in a Trust

As indicated above, a trust is a relationship among people with respect to property. As a result, a great deal of trust law involves the details of these relationships. There are three groups of people within the trust itself — the settlor, the trustee, and the beneficiaries. These people must deal with each other and then also deal with outsiders who might be interested in the trust or the trust property.

The first major relationship to consider is that between the settlor and the trustee. The primary concern here is whether the settlor has the power to alter, amend, revoke, or terminate the trust. If the settlor has that power, then the settlor really has the power to control the trustee. After all, if the trustee does not do what the settlor wants, then the settlor could simply amend the trust and replace the trustee. As a result, the law generally treats the settlor as the controlling party in a revocable trust. The trust income is taxed to the settlor, and the duties that would otherwise be imposed on the trustee are minimized or eliminated. Although the trustee must still comply with the terms and conditions of the trust, the trustee's duties essentially are owed to the settlor.

The next relationship is that between the trustee and the beneficiaries. This relationship deals with the general fiduciary duties of the trustee in administering the trust; those duties are discussed in the next section. The relationship also pertains, however, to the powers and duties of the trustee in distributing trust property to the beneficiaries. This issue involves a wide variety of situations that may be described as points on a continuum. The two extremes of the continuum can be pinpointed and defined, but the point at which the trustee may (or must) operate within those two extremes is a matter that is controlled by the language of the trust.

One extreme of this continuum is the mandatory trust. In this situation, the trustee is required to distribute property to a beneficiary. The trust might provide, for instance, that the trustee "shall distribute all the trust income to my son, Ben, in monthly installments." Here, the trustee simply must execute the trust, follow the mandatory terms, and make the required distributions. Notice that this language gives Ben, the beneficiary, substantial rights that he could enforce against the trustee.

At the other extreme, the trust might provide that the trustee "may distribute to my son, Ben, so much of the trust income as the trustee, in the trustee's sole and absolute discretion, determines to be appropriate." In this situation, the trustee has a wide area of discretion; so long as the trustee is operating within this broad latitude, the beneficiary cannot force the trustee to distribute anything. If you compare this to the example of the previous paragraph, you will notice the inverse relationship that is inherent in this area of trust law; as you move from the mandatory trust to the "sole and absolute discretion" trust, the flexibility and discretion of the trustee is increased and the ability of the beneficiary to force the trustee to act is correspondingly reduced. At this discretionary extreme on the continuum, the trustee is considered to be acting properly (and the beneficiary cannot force a distribution) so long as the trustee is acting honestly, in good faith, and with the proper motivation. If the trustee's actions are an attempt to follow the instructions of the settlor, the trustee probably is acting properly.

The language relating to distributions to the beneficiaries may place the trust at either extreme of the continuum, or anywhere in between. There is a considerable area between those two extremes, and the trustee and the beneficiaries must carefully examine the trust to determine their respective rights. One typical trust provision would provide that the trustee "may distribute to my son, Ben, so much of the trust income as the trustee, in the trustee's discretion, determines to be appropriate." Notice that the "sole and absolute" language has been deleted here; if the trust simply provides that the trustee may exercise discretion, and then the trustee must act reasonably in doing so.

The third major relationship that must be considered is that between the trustee, or the trust beneficiaries, and third parties. The person serving as trustee holds the legal title to the trust property, and the beneficiaries hold the equitable interests in that property. Can a third party, such as a creditor, come in and seize the interest of the trustee or the beneficiary? Can the creditor seize the trust property itself? With respect to the creditors of the person serving as trustee, the answer is "no." The courts recognize that this person really does not have any equitable interest in the trust property; the trustee is merely holding the legal title to the property for the beneficiaries. Since the beneficiaries are really the ones who own the interests in the property, the personal creditors of the individual serving as trustee cannot touch the trust property. If the trustee incurs a debt as trustee, in a fiduciary capacity, then the creditor would be able to reach the trust property. The trust property cannot be reached, though, to satisfy the personal debts of the trustee.

The beneficiaries, on the other hand, do own an equitable interest in the trust. Their interest in the trust is property, and it is subject to the normal property rules — they can transfer their interests, and creditors can seize their interests. If a creditor seizes a beneficiary's interest in a trust, then the creditor is entitled to the same rights that the beneficiary enjoyed. The language of the trust dealing with the trustee's obligations to distribute trust property could become critical at this point. If the trustee is not obligated to distribute income or property and is within his or her area of discretion in refusing to do so, then neither a beneficiary nor a creditor that has seized the beneficiary's interest in the trust may force a distribution out of the trustee.

If the settlor established the trust because of concerns that the beneficiary would be unable or incapable of managing the property, then this rule that a beneficiary can sell his or her trust interest (or that a creditor could seize the beneficiary's interest) creates a problem. It enables the beneficiary to liquidate the interest in the trust and then go on an improvident spending spree with the proceeds, or for the beneficiary to spend excessively and then have the creditors involuntarily seize the beneficiary's interest in the trust. This, of course, is contrary to the settlor's goals. Is it possible for the settlor to restrict the beneficiary's ability to alienate the trust interest, either voluntarily or involuntarily? In the United States, it is. The settlor of the trust may insert a "spendthrift clause" into the trust. This clause provides that the interest of the beneficiary may not be transferred by the beneficiary and is not subject to being involuntarily taken from the beneficiary by a creditor. This type of provision is a very popular mechanism by which the settlor can, for example, restrict the beneficiary's access to the wealth held in the trust until the beneficiary reaches a specified age or accomplishes some other goal that the settlor wishes to encourage, such as graduating from college. This controlling restriction is sometimes referred to by estate planning professionals as "the dead hand of the settlor."

Although spendthrift provisions are recognized in the United States, they do have limitations. These limitations vary from state to state, but they generally provide that certain creditors can supersede the restrictions of a spendthrift trust. These creditors might include a child of the beneficiary trying to collect child support, an ex-spouse of the beneficiary trying to recover unpaid alimony, or a creditor of the beneficiary who provided items necessary to sustain the life of the beneficiary. In these situations, the courts have held that it would be unfair and against public policy for the beneficiary to be able to hide behind the provisions of the spendthrift clause.

Another public policy exception to the spendthrift trust is that most states prevent a settlor from setting up a spendthrift trust that operates for the benefit of the settlor. This is viewed as an attempt by the settlor to defraud his or her creditors. In this situation, the creditors are generally permitted to demand that the trustee distribute to them whatever the trustee could distribute to the settlor.

Another aspect of the relationship between the trustee and third parties involves the willingness of outsiders to deal with a trustee. For example, a third party that is purchasing something from a trustee has no idea whether the trustee is forbidden from selling the property under the terms and conditions of the trust. The outsider wants to be certain that it receives good title to the property, and it does not want to subject itself to potential liability to a beneficiary who was wronged by the trustee's actions. The third party therefore is reluctant to deal with the trustee. The law responds to this issue by protecting the marketplace. An outsider who is dealing with a trustee is permitted to assume that the trustee has the legal authority take the desired action and is protected from liability so long as the outsider did not know that the trustee was violating its authority.

E.   Administration of a Trust

The central concept of a trust is that the trustee, as the owner of the legal title to the trust property, is holding that property for the benefit of the beneficiaries, the owners of the equitable interests in the property. The trustee is a fiduciary, who owes a duty to the beneficiaries in all the trustee's dealings with the trust property. State statutes give the trustee the power to deal with the property; normally, these powers can be exercised by the trustee without having to obtain court orders authorizing the trustee's actions. Instead, the trustee is simply expected to manage the trust property and to exercise the powers and authority that an owner of property normally would have with respect to property. The statutory powers may be modified by the provisions of the trust itself; as such, the settlor can customize the powers of the trustee to fit the needs of the settlor's situation.

An example of the trustee's power to deal with the trust property is the investment authority that is granted to the trustee. This investment authority has changed significantly over the years. Throughout much of the 1900s, the trustee was permitted to invest only in certain assets specified by the state statutes or the trust itself. In the latter part of the twentieth century, the investment powers of the trustee were broadened as the states enacted statutes permitting the trustee to invest in virtually anything, so long as the trustee determined that each investment was reasonable and in the best interest of the trust beneficiaries. In recent years, the states have been enacting statutes requiring trustees to consider the trust's investment portfolio as a whole and to diversify their investments in an effort to minimize the risk exposure of the trust. Under this portfolio approach, the trustee may still invest in virtually any asset, but the trust should include a variety of assets. If a settlor is uncomfortable with this investment authority, of course, the settlor may modify or narrow the authority by inserting restrictive provisions into the trust instrument.

As a fiduciary, the trustee must exercise its powers only for the benefit of the beneficiaries. The trustee's powers are coupled with duties. These duties have been developed by the courts over the centuries and, in many states, have been at least partially codified by the legislatures.

The fundamental duty of the trustee is the duty of loyalty. Everything the trustee does must be for the exclusive benefit of the beneficiaries; the trustee may not profit from dealing with the trust property, except by receiving a fee for the trustee's services. An example of this duty of loyalty is the prohibition against conflicts of interest and self-dealing on the part of the trustee. The trustee may not purchase property from the trust, sell property to the trust, or make personal investments that are contrary to those of the trust. Doing so would permit the trustee to profit from the trust's losses, and that is a violation of the duty of loyalty.

Another major duty imposed on the trustee is the duty to account to the beneficiaries. When the trustee first takes possession of the trust property, the trustee must notify the beneficiaries and give them information about the trustee and the trust. This notification alerts the beneficiaries to the existence of the trust and the identity of the trustee, and it enables them to protect their interests. The trustee is then required to account to the beneficiaries on a regular basis, usually annually, informing the beneficiaries of all of the actions taken by the trustee during that time period. If the trustee makes full disclosure of the trustee's actions, then the beneficiaries have a very short time period (usually in the neighborhood of six months or so) within which they can question what the trustee has done. The courts would become involved only if a beneficiary objected to an action taken by the trustee and filed a lawsuit contesting it. If none of the beneficiaries object, then there is no controversy and therefore no need for the court to review the trustee's accounting.

F.   Trust Litigation

Certainly, things may go wrong, and a trust might get involved in litigation. The trustee might commit a tort or breach a contract, for example, or a third party might breach a contract entered into with the trustee. These cases involving outside parties are handled just like any other civil litigation, with the trustee either filing or defending the lawsuit in its fiduciary capacity. The litigation would be brought, for example, by "Rebecca Jones, as Trustee of the Richard Jones Trust dated July 31, 2004." It is the trustee that is the party to the lawsuit, not the trust itself.

Litigation could also arise involving only those who are part of the trust relationship. A typical example of this would be beneficiaries suing the trustee, claiming that the trustee made inappropriate investments that caused the trust to suffer a loss. If the litigation involved a matter that was fully disclosed on the trustee's accounting, then the action would have to be brought within the very short statute of limitations period (six months, in my example) referred to in the previous section. If the litigation involves something that was not disclosed on an accounting, then the general statute of limitations would apply; this is usually four to six years.

Trust litigation normally invokes the equitable jurisdiction of the court. The court therefore may exercise its power to achieve justice for the wronged party, fashioning its remedy to fit the particular factual situation. For example, the beneficiary might ask the court to force the trustee to account for the trustee's actions, to trace and recover trust property that was improperly distributed by the trustee, and to surcharge the trustee for the loss suffered by the trust. The surcharge count is an effort to hold the trustee personally liable for the loss caused by the trustee acting in a fiduciary capacity. If the trustee engaged in a conflict of interest or self-dealing, then additional damages might be appropriate.

G.   Special Types of Trusts

The concepts described above apply to private express trusts — those that are established by a person to provide for the management of property for the benefit of specific individuals. Trust concepts might be used in other situations though, and the rules applicable to these special situations might differ from those described above.

The first special type of trust is the charitable trust. People for the benefit of society establish them. They must be established for the purpose of relieving poverty; advancing the arts, sciences, education, or a religion; promoting health; or for governmental purposes. These types of trusts are encouraged as a matter of social policy, and they are granted special benefits under the law. In many states, for example, private trusts are subject to the rule against perpetuities; as a matter of public policy, they must terminate within a certain time period. Charitable trusts, however, are exempt from this rule. Since they are providing a benefit to society, we want them to continue for as long as possible, and we require them to benefit society rather than specific individuals. Charitable trusts are also exempt organizations under the federal income tax law.

Another type of trust, the constructive trust, really is not a trust at all. Instead, it is an equitable remedy that might be invoked by a court in order to prevent unjust enrichment. Suppose, for example, that John and Rachel were divorcing, and as part of their settlement agreement, John was required to maintain a $100,000 life insurance policy on his life, payable to their son, Robert. John bought the policy. A few years later, though, John married Wanda and changed the beneficiary of the life insurance policy from Robert to Wanda. When this is discovered after John's death, the court might determine that allowing Wanda to retain the $100,000 would result in her being unjustly enriched, to the detriment of Robert. The court therefore might invoke the constructive trust remedy, declare that Wanda is holding this money as a constructive trustee for Robert, and order Wanda to convey the $100,000 to him. The constructive trust really is not a trust at all, in the normal sense of the term; it is simply a tool that the court uses to right a wrong. Since wrongs can arise in a variety of situations, the constructive trust is a powerful tool for the court.

The third special type of trust is the resulting trust. Like the constructive trust, it really is not a trust at all; it is rather a mechanism for correcting the ownership of property and returning property to its rightful owner. The resulting trust can arise in three situations. First, suppose David conveyed property to Kate, to hold as trustee for the benefit of Cindy, but David's trust was invalid for some reason. Since the trust is invalid, David is the real owner of this property, but it is titled in Kate's name. A resulting trust may be imposed by the court to return the property to its rightful owner, the attempted settlor, David.

The second situation in which a resulting trust might arise involves a trust established by the settlor that is valid, but the purposes of the trust have been accomplished and there is excess property left in the trust. Who gets the leftover property? Suppose, for example, that David conveyed property to Kate, to hold as trustee and to use for paying for Cindy's college education. Cindy completed college, and there is still $5,000 in the trust. If the trust does not specify who should receive the $5,000, then a resulting trust might be imposed, returning the $5,000 to David, the settlor.

A resulting trust may arise in one other situation. Suppose David paid $200,000 for a house, but he told the seller to put the deed in Cindy's name. What is your result? Well, you have three possible results. First, David might have been making a gift to Cindy. If so, your normal donor/donee relationship would result. Second, David might have been making a loan to Cindy; if so, a debtor/creditor relationship would be the result. The third possibility is that Cindy is holding the title to the property for the benefit of David. If this is your actual situation and Cindy refuses to return the property to David when she is directed to do so, then the court might impose a resulting trust ordering her to return the property to David, the person who paid for it and actually owns it.

VI.   PROTECTIONS FOR THE FAMILY

One of the basic concepts of the private property system is that the owner of property can convey that property to whomever the owner desires. If the transfer is made during the owner's lifetime, it would be made by deed; if the transfer is made at the owner's death, then it would be made by Will. If the property owner is a member of a family, however, it might be appropriate for public policy to restrict the owner's ability to transfer property. For example, should Patrick be permitted to devise all his property to Becky, his mistress, leaving nothing for Debbie, his widow?

This conflict between private property rights and public policy forms the basis of this section. Here, we summarize the benefits that society provides to the surviving family for their protection. The greatest protection is provided to the surviving spouse; lesser protections are provided for children. The details of these safeguards vary widely from state to state, so this is intended only as a summary of the basic concepts.

A.   Protecting Against Unintentional Omission

Arlene, a single woman with no children, has a Will devising all her property to Barbara, her sister. The Will is valid, and Barbara should receive Arlene's property upon Arlene's death. Suppose, though, that years after writing the Will, Arlene fell in love with and married Carl. If Arlene were to die with Carl surviving her, should Barbara still receive all Arlene's property? Should Carl be left with nothing?

We need to recognize the possibility that Arlene really wanted to provide for Carl, but just never got around to writing a new Will. In that situation, we should protect Carl from being inadvertently omitted from Arlene's estate plan. We do so through a statute providing that if a person marries after executing a Will and the spouse survives the testator, then the surviving spouse receives an intestate share in the estate of the deceased spouse. The survivor is referred to as a "pretermitted spouse." Arlene's property would be inventoried, and the total value of the property would be determined. The court would then calculate what the share of a surviving spouse would have been if Arlene had died intestate and award Carl property that equals the value of that intestate share. The rest of Arlene's property would then be disposed of pursuant to Arlene's Will.

This result is based on the conclusion that Arlene really wanted to benefit Carl, and his omission from her Will was unintentional. If the facts indicate that Carl was intentionally omitted, however, then he is not a pretermitted spouse, and this rule does not apply. The details related to the evidence that would be permitted to show Arlene's intent vary from state to state.

A similar rule applies to the situation of the pretermitted child — a child born to or adopted by a person who has previously executed a Will. Again, the purpose of these statutes is to protect the pretermitted child from being inadvertently omitted from the parent's estate plan, and the pretermitted child is awarded an intestate share of the parent's estate. If the facts indicate that the parent intentionally excluded the child or otherwise provided for the child, then the child is not considered to be pretermitted, and the statute does not apply.

B.   Community Property

There are eight community property states in the United States (Arizona, California, Idaho, Louisiana, New Mexico, Nevada, Texas, and Washington), and one other state (Wisconsin) that follows the community property concept but uses different terminology. In those nine states, if a married person acquires property other than by gift, devise, or inheritance, then that property is community property and is owned by the husband and wife in equal shares. This rule applies regardless of how the property is titled. If one spouse brings property into the marriage, or receives property during marriage by gift, devise, or inheritance, then that property is considered to be the individual property of that spouse; it is not community property so long as its separate status is maintained. Upon death, a spouse is permitted to transfer his or her separate property and his or her one-half interest in the community property to anyone. That transfer does not affect the interest of the surviving spouse in the community property; the survivor retains the one-half interest that the survivor owned from the acquisition of the community property.

Suppose, for example, that John and Donna, husband and wife, lived in Texas. John owned property worth $50,000 when he married, and inherited $100,000 from his mother while he was married to Donna. During their marriage, John and Donna acquired property that was worth $500,000 at the time of John's death. That $500,000 is community property. Upon John's death, he can devise $250,000 of the community property and his $150,000 separate property to whomever he desires;

his ability to convey this property is unrestricted. As the surviving spouse, Donna is protected through the community property system in that she retains her one-half share of the community property, worth $250,000.

Again, the details of the community property system vary from state to state, and you should be careful to notice that the system is operable in only nine states. The rest of the United States has a common-law property system, under which the other concepts discussed in this section protect a surviving spouse.

C.　Elective Share

The elective share, sometimes referred to as the "statutory share" or the "forced share," is designed to protect a surviving spouse from being intentionally omitted from the estate of a deceased spouse. Under these statutes, the survivor is permitted to make an affirmative election in the estate of the deceased spouse; if the election is made, the survivor receives a statutory percentage of the estate assets of the deceased spouse's estate, rather than the amount that the survivor would receive under the decedent's Will or the intestacy statutes. These provisions are designed to prevent the deceased spouse from leaving the survivor with nothing.

If the elective share is claimed, then the property of the deceased spouse is inventoried and the total value of the property that is subject to the elective share is determined. The court then calculates the value of the elective share and awards the surviving spouse property that equals the value of that share. The rest of the decedent's property is then disposed of pursuant to the decedent's Will or the intestacy statutes, with the surviving spouse being omitted for this purpose.

Originally, the elective share was based on the value of the deceased spouse's probate estate. As the use of trusts and non-probate property has grown, state legislatures have responded by broadening the base of the elective share to include items other than just the decedent's probate assets; this prevents the deceased spouse from arranging property so as to eliminate the value of the elective share to the surviving spouse. The amount of the elective share typically equals the amount that the surviving spouse would have received if the spouse had died intestate, but this varies from state to state.

D.　Homestead and Similar Rights

The family home is usually one of the major assets owned by a person, and it certainly represents the stability and security that the person covets. After all, your home is your castle. Most states have provisions protecting the family home from certain creditors during the lifetime of the owner, and they have restrictions on the ability of the owner to devise the family home to the detriment of the surviving family. These provisions, generically referred to as homestead protections, vary from state to state. Most states have restrictions on the size of the homestead protection from both an area and a dollar-value perspective. A few states, however, have no limit on the dollar value of the protected homestead.

If the owner of a home should die, survived by a spouse and child, the owner may be prevented from devising the family home to anyone other than then surviving spouse. If the owner is prevented from devising the house, then any attempt to do so would be void, and the law would provide for the disposition of the home. A typical result would be for the surviving spouse to receive a life estate in the family home, with the child receiving the remainder interest. These provisions enable the surviving family to remain in the home.

In addition to homestead, most states also have statutory provisions that protect certain items of property from the claims of the decedent's creditors. This "exempt property" consists of property that the legislature determined that the family would probably need in order to maintain its ability to function; it might consist, for example, of furniture, furnishings, and appliances in the house that do not exceed a stated value, and the decedent's automobile.

E.   Waiving Family Protections

The surviving family may waive the protections that the law provides for their benefit. Any person may waive his or her own rights, but may not waive the rights of another person. The most typical situation in which rights in this area of the law are being waived is that of the marital agreement. Most states provide that the rights to which a person would become entitled by virtue of being a surviving spouse may be waived via a prenuptial or postnuptial agreement.

Formality requirements are often imposed on these marital agreements. They are prone to litigation, and legislatures therefore want the terms of the agreement to be as clear as possible. The statutes often also require financial disclosure in order for the agreement to be valid, particularly if the agreement is being entered into after marriage. The parties to the agreement are in the confidential relationship of husband and wife at that point, and the law therefore acts to prevent any fraud or overreaching by either spouse.

VII. ADMINISTRATION OF AN ESTATE

As indicated at the beginning of this chapter, upon a person's death, the person's property is examined on an item-by-item basis to determine what happens to it. If the ownership of the property passes automatically, then the property is simply delivered to the successor; these items are described as non-probate property and are discussed in Part II of this chapter. The remaining items are classified as probate property, and they pass through the estate administration process to determine who the successor owner should be. That successor will be determined through either the language of the Will, discussed in Part IV of this chapter, or the application of the intestate succession statutes that are summarized in Part III.

The estate administration process is a judicially administered, in rem proceeding. The court monitors the procedure to ensure that everyone is treated fairly and that the appropriate beneficiaries end up with the property. The term "in rem" indicates that it is the property of the decedent that is being administered; the interested persons come into court only for the purpose of adjudicating their interests in the ownership of that property.

A.   The Basic Purposes of Estate Administration

The estate administration process, often referred to as "probate" or "probate administration," is very state-specific. Each state has special rules for the forms that are required and the procedures that must be followed. All of these procedures, however, are designed to achieve three basic goals.

First, the process appoints someone to gather together, manage, and protect the decedent's property. This person might be referred to as the personal representative, the executor or the administrator of the estate. Regardless of the terminology, this person is representing the decedent and the decedent's interests, and is answerable to the court.

The second goal of estate administration is to give the decedent's creditors an opportunity to be paid. Although it might be amusing, it certainly would not be fair to your creditors if the law provided that they could no longer collect on your debts after your death. Indeed, if that were the rule, then interest rates would be much higher! Notice the phrasing of this goal — we are giving creditors the opportunity of getting paid. They need to take some steps to protect their interests, and if they fail to do so, they might be precluded from receiving anything from the estate.

The final goal of probate administration is to distribute the remaining property of the estate to the appropriate beneficiaries. Creditors and the expenses of administration are paid out of the decedent's property, and the remaining property passes to the estate beneficiaries. If the decedent has a valid Will, then the beneficiaries are determined pursuant to the language of the Will. If the decedent's Will does not dispose of all of the decedent's property, or if the decedent does not have a valid Will, then the property that is not disposed of in the Will passes to the decedent's heirs, determined through the rules for intestate succession.

B.   The Estate Administration Process

The details of the estate administration process differ from state to state. The terminology used and the time deadlines that are imposed in each state are unique. There is virtual uniformity in what these procedures are achieving, however. The probate process follows three basic, overlapping tracks that serve to achieve the three goals outlined in the preceding section.

The first track in the probate process deals with the validation and determination of the decedent's estate plan. Here, we are determining whether the decedent had a Will and whether the Will is valid, notifying the people who might be entitled to the decedent's property, and identifying the beneficiaries of the estate. The validity of the decedent's Will would initially be determined by receiving the testimony of one or more of the witnesses to the Will, either in person or through an affidavit. This testimony would establish that the proper formalities were followed in the execution of the Will. If the decedent had a self-proving Will, then we already have the required affidavit and the Will is presumptively entitled to be admitted into probate. If the Will is not self-proving, then one of the attesting witnesses must be located to provide this testimony. If none of the attesting witnesses is available to provide this testimony, then other evidence may be presented to the court. The burden of proving the Will is on the proponent; if anyone contests the Will, then that contestant has the burden of proving the grounds for the Will contest. This process is described in more detail in Part III(D) of this chapter, discussing Will contests.

Once the court determines whether the Will is valid, the court appoints the personal representative of the estate. This is the person who is charged with the duty of administering the estate. If the decedent has a valid Will, then any person named to this position in the Will is entitled to preference in being appointed personal representative. If there is no valid Will, then the statutes give preference to a close family relative of the decedent. The person appointed as personal representative must be capable of doing the job and must be willing to do so. This position involves a fiduciary responsibility. There is an exposure to risk, therefore, and no one can be forced to undertake this role.

The personal representative then notifies those who might have an interest in the decedent's property. As indicated above, it is the decedent's property that is being administered, but we need to adjudicate the potential rights of people with respect to the property. We therefore bring them into the jurisdiction of the court by giving them formal notice of the estate administration process and giving them information sufficient to enable them to take steps to protect their interests. If the personal representative or some other person has a question as to whether an individual is a proper beneficiary of the estate, then that person can petition the court to determine the estate beneficiaries. This is how the court would determine issues such as the validity of a marital agreement, whether a potential beneficiary unlawfully killed the decedent, whether a beneficiary actually survived the decedent, and other issues such as family relationships to the decedent.

The second track in the estate administration process deals with the rights of creditors. As a matter of constitutional law, the personal representative is required to actively search for the decedent's creditors, and to give actual notice of the estate administration process to those creditors who are reasonably ascertainable. The personal representative also publishes a notice of the fact that the estate administration is proceeding in a local newspaper; this constructive notice is all the personal representative can provide to those creditors who are not reasonably ascertainable. The creditor is then given a relatively short time period, two to six months, usually, within which the creditor must file a claim in the decedent's estate. Once that time period has run, the personal representative can review the claims that are filed and determine whether they are valid. If a claim is valid, then the personal representative simply holds it until it can be paid. If the claim appears to be wrong, though, the personal representative must object to the claim. If the personal representative objects to a claim, then the creditor must bring an action against the personal representative to determine whether the claim is a valid obligation of the decedent.

Once all the valid claims have been determined, the personal representative can pay the creditors. The statutes provide a priority system under which the personal representative pays the expenses of the estate administration and the creditors of the estate. Generally, those statutes provide that the expenses of the personal representative are to be paid first, followed by any tax obligations and medical expenses of the final illness of the decedent, and so forth through all the estate creditors. The personal representative must be sure to fully fund the payment of each class of expenditure before moving on and paying anyone in the next priority class.

The final track in the probate process relates to the distribution of the decedent's property. At this point, the personal representative has paid or set aside enough money to pay the expenses of the estate administration and has paid all the estate creditors. The personal representative then reviews the Will or the intestacy statutes to determine what property should pass to each estate beneficiary. The personal representative then accounts to all the beneficiaries for all of the actions taken during the estate administration process and notifies the beneficiaries of the proposed distribution of the estate. The beneficiaries then have a short time period, usually one to three months, during which they can review all the documents. If no one objects, then the personal representative would distribute the estate assets, prove to the court that proper distribution was made, and then close the estate. If an objection is filed, then the objection would be resolved by the court before the distribution can be made.

The probate process generally takes six to twelve months. The personal representative is working on all three of these tracks throughout the process, but much of the time is spent waiting for claims to be filed by creditors. If the estate is relatively straightforward, then the personal representative should be prepared to begin closing the estate shortly after the creditors' claims period expires.

VIII. CONCLUSION

The transfer of property upon the death of an individual is an area of law that most individuals will be exposed to during their lifetime. A person who has engaged in pre-death planning will generally be able to distribute property according to their desires through the execution of a will, or trust, or the manner in which property is owned. However, in the absence of pre death planning, property is distributed under rules established by the legislature.

Chapter 14

FAMILY LAW: THE LEGAL ORDERING OF INTIMATE RELATIONS

By — Tanya M. Washington

SYNOPSIS

I. INTRODUCTION TO FAMILY LAW

In the United States, family law involves constitutional rights attendant to familial relationships and the extent to which those rights protect against certain government action within the private sphere of intimate relationships. These relationships include marital relationships, domestic non-marital relationships, and parent-child relationships. Much of family law doctrine (i.e., substantive law), practices, and policies govern the creation, substance, and dissolution of these relationships. A recurring theme that pervades the study of family law and policy is ascertaining the appropriate role of the State (i.e., government) in prescribing and limiting the ways in which spouses, domestic partners, co-parents, and parents and children organize themselves and interact with one another and the legal effect and status of their domestic arrangements. These are relationships that are at once private, for they involve intensely personal associations, and public, for the State has various interests in the continued existence of these relationships, in further-ance of the general welfare of its citizens. Some of these relationships, such as marriage, also have ecclesiastic (i.e., religious) origins. The varied and sometimes conflicting character of these relationships — personal, legal, institutional, and religious — creates a dynamic and fascinating area of study.

This overview of family law will explore the familial context within which the law operates: the creation and construction of the marital relationship; the creation and composition of families; divorce and its consequences for spouses and children; procreation issues; and state regulation of the parent-child relationship.

II. THE FAMILY LAW FRAMEWORK

Family law intersects with several distinct areas of law. Tort law governs private duties that arise within familial relationships and which may provide a basis for the assertion of a right of action by a parent on behalf of an injured child or spouse. Contract law governs the enforcement of agreements (e.g., premarital agreements or separation agreements) between relationship members. Property law dictates the ownership of assets upon divorce or separation of the parties. Criminal law governs the prosecution of spousal abuse and child and neglect cases, as well as other manifestations of domestic violence. Estate law governs inheritance rights upon the death of a family member. And constitutional law determines the legality of state interference with intimate associations, such as the parent-child relation-ship. In addition to common law, statutory law, and constitutional law, states' strong public policy interest in the regulation of the general welfare of its citizens allows for the enactment of laws that create, limit, or impact intimate relationships, within constitutional limits. Family law is largely regulated by state statutes that dictate the definition, scope, and rights of legally recognized familial constructs and relationships. These laws can vary substantially from jurisdiction to jurisdiction. In an effort to promote more consistent laws between states, uniform laws have been proposed that address child custody and support, adoption, marriage, premarital agreements, and jurisdiction to decide family law cases. Many states have borrowed liberally from these acts in fashioning the laws of their state in these areas, but the proposed statutes do not have legal effect until they are enacted into law by state legislatures.

Generally federal regulation of family law matters is limited; however, there are some federal laws that regulate child custody, child support and enforcement, domestic violence, and adoption by establishing eligibility requirements for receipt of federal funding that are conditioned upon state compliance. Despite the diminished legislative power of the federal government to prescribe family law rules and regulations, federal courts have jurisdiction (i.e., the power to render binding judgments) to determine the constitutionality of state laws that impair the protected fundamental rights of individuals that lie at the heart of family law. Such rights include the right to marry, the right to procreate, the right not to procreate, the right to create and participate in a family, and the right to raise and rear one's child according to one's beliefs.

While legislation can address the resolution of some family law issues, due to the fact specific nature of most family law disputes, statutory prescriptions are sometimes ill-equipped to respond to the particularities of each case. In response to this reality, many state statutes regulating family law issues allow judges and juries a great deal of discretion to achieve fairness in resolving family law disputes, within the specific factual context in which disputes arise. Generally, the judge's role in deciding family law cases is to use state, and in rare cases federal, laws governing families and family relationships to achieve equitable outcomes (i.e., fair results).

Family law, like all areas of law, must strike an appropriate balance between being structured enough to provide consistency and predictability of outcome, and flexible enough to accommodate the specific facts of the legal disputes the law exists to resolve. This tension is particularly acute in family law because at one end of the spectrum are shifting societal mores that inform greatly the content of the law and at the other end cases involving facts that reflect the variety of circumstances that characterize families and family relationships. For example, most state laws governing child custody determinations provide a general guideline, the best interest of the child standard, that leaves room for judges to exercise discretion as to which considerations are relevant to the operation of that standard. The variety of relevant considerations, and the relative weight given each one in the best interest framework, can produce inconsistent outcomes in cases across jurisdictions and between judges in the same jurisdiction.

In recent years, in the context of some controversial areas of family law, for example same-sex marriage, the question of institutional competency (i.e., which branch of government is best suited to make certain determinations) has become an issue. The question raised is whether the legislative branch or the judicial branch is the most appropriate branch to determine the rules by which family law disputes will be governed. Those who challenge the judiciary's competency to determine family law doctrine, charge that "activist judges" are making law, which is the function of the legislative branch, rather than engaging in the judicial function of interpreting the law.

The intimate character of family law disputes and the flexibility inherent in family law doctrine challenges the practitioner's ability to provide and predict satisfactory outcomes. The distinctive character of family law practice has enhanced the attractiveness and utility of alternative methods of dispute resolution (ADR) that depart from the adversarial processes inherent to litigation. The use of out-of-court processes (e.g., mediation and arbitration) affords parties greater flexibility in fashioning agreements related to marital conditions and expectations, child custody and support, and property division. This more collaborative approach to conflict resolution may diffuse hostilities that often accompany these highly emotive contests and facilitate constructive engagement between people who may have continued future interaction (e.g., where divorced parents will share physical or legal custody of their children).

Voluntary participation in ADR is encouraged, and in some states some form of ADR is mandatory. The most common form of ADR is mediation in which a neutral, trained professional mediator (a lawyer, retired judge, or psychological counselor) convenes the parties in an attempt to assist them in fashioning a solution to the issues in their divorce. The role of the facilitator is not to resolve the parties' disputes; rather, it is to bring the parties to a compromise of their own making. Parties can participate in mediation with or without their own attorneys. Once a settlement is reached, it will become the substance of an agreement that will be drafted and signed by the parties or a court order. Unresolved issues will be submitted to the court for litigation.

III. THE FAMILY: THE BASIC UNIT OF AMERICAN SOCIETY

Family law centers on the familial construct (i.e., the family unit), which American law regards as a fundamental unit of U.S. society. The shape and content of the American family has changed considerably, and the family in the U.S. has proven to be an incredibly diverse and dynamic social organism. It is most accurately described according to its many constituent aspects. It operates as an economic unit, as a societal institution (family as community), as a moral conception (an expression of family values); and as a unit of organized, legally recognized relationships.

A.   State Interests in Family Construct

The State's use of its governmental power to limit the definition of family to include or exclude certain organizational units serves several state interests, including: establishing and maintaining coherent community values that promote the well-being of all members of the community; creating peace and good order; promoting stability within the society and good citizenship; providing economic productivity; ensuring the continued growth and progress of the society and the population; establishing good moral standards; and allowing people to provide for their economic needs without state reliance. The achievement of these governmental aims is assumed to necessitate a specific familial composition. Accordingly, the law in most states distinguishes between those organizational units that are considered to constitute legally recognized families and those that do not.

B.   Family Composition

Family law does not dictate the ways in which groups of people may organize themselves or how they choose to self-define their organizational units; rather, it determines whether those units will be recognized by the law as a "family." Legal status as a family confers upon the unit and its membership certain legal protections, rights, obligations, benefits, and liberties.

The traditional family unit is most closely associated with the nuclear family (e.g., two married, heterosexual partners with or without children). The composition of modern family constructions may include non-traditional domestic arrangements (e.g., same-sex partners, co-habitating but unmarried heterosexual couples or single-parent family homes) as well the concept of the extended family (e.g., homes in which children are raised by grandparents, aunts, and uncles). There are also divergent cultural experiences and perspectives that influence the composition of a family. When culturally distinct definitions of family are at issue, they are often assessed according to traditionally held conceptions of family, and their status as a legal unit will depend upon the extent to which they mirror the traditional family model. More recent case law, however, reveals that an increasing number of judges are willing to adopt a more flexible standard for determining whether certain domestic arrangements, those that are distinct from the traditional model, qualify as legally recognized families.

State and federal legislation provide definitions of "family" for the purposes of determining whether a particular group is eligible for housing benefits, whether it may be subject to certain zoning restrictions, whether members of that unit possess property rights, or whether members have legal standing to make certain decisions for other members. Many of these definitions are rooted in traditional conceptions of family and limit familial status to domestic arrangements between co-habitating individuals related by blood, marriage, or adoption. While those whose domestic arrangement does not qualify as a legally recognized family can achieve some of these rights, privileges, protections, and benefits contractually, it is difficult, if not impossible, to draft an agreement that covers all of the potential contingencies inherent to the human experience. One of the primary benefits of the State recognizing a unit as a family is that this recognition confers the many legal protections and benefits inherent in that status.

C.   Characteristics of a Legally Recognized Family

In determining what constitutes a family, judges adopt either a formal definition (i.e., considering certain features of the organized unit to determine whether it "looks" like what has traditionally been considered to constitute a family unit) or a functional definition (i.e., considering the way in which members of the unit interrelate to ascertain whether the unit "operates" like a family). The latter definition may include domestic relationships that have not been considered to constitute traditional families (i.e., unmarried co-habitants with children or same-sex couples). In determining whether a unit constitutes a "family," a judge would consider some of the following characteristics of that unit: the domestic character of the unit (e.g., living arrangements); the permanence and cohesiveness of the unit; whether the members of the unit are related by blood, marriage, or adoption; the presence of children; the exclusivity and longevity of the relationship between the members; the nature of the financial and emotional investment in and commitment to the maintenance of the unit; and the way in which the members see themselves and present themselves to the society (i.e., how are they perceived by the community).

The composite of the American family continues to evolve and is characterized by increasing numbers of single parent homes, unmarried heterosexual and homosexual partners with and without children, co-habitating family members, and other non-traditional domestic units. Some characterize changes in the composite of the American family as an erosion of a valuable social and institutional structure, and some jurisdictions have enacted legislation and implemented curricular reform to reinforce a preference for the traditional, nuclear family model. However, fewer and fewer American families fit the traditional mold. Accordingly, courts face the challenge of interpreting the definition of family so that it is flexible enough to accommodate these new domestic arrangements, while still enforcing adherence to the character (if not the features) of the traditional family model, to ensure the achievement of important state interests.

IV. MARRIAGE: FAMILY BY LOVE AND LAW

The creation of a family with a spouse is regarded as one of the fundamental ways that one can achieve continuity and stability in American society. This revered relationship, with ecclesiastic roots, is at once a deeply personal relationship, a societal institution, a legal status, and an economic unit. Marriage is a specific category of family, and one to which the "traditional" conception of family closely adheres. Marriage confers legal status, creates a contractual relationship between two people, and is an institution for the distribution and acquisition of wealth in American society. While marriage is a contract between the parties to the marital union, the State's presence as a "shadow" party to the marriage contract is evinced by both the requirement of state sanction to create the legal relationship and the fact that the marital contract can only be terminated pursuant to state action. The character of marriage as a creation of the State, despite the deeply intimate nature of the relationship between marital partners, subjects it to state regulation and involvement.

A.   State Regulation of the Right to Marry

The Supreme Court recognizes the right to marry as a fundamental liberty secured by the Due Process Clause and the Equal Protection Clause of the Fourteenth Amendment of the U.S. Constitution. The intensely personal nature of the marital choice situates marriage within the protected scope of privacy liberties and qualifies marriage as a fundamental constitutional right. The constitutional status of the right to marry provides protection against state regulation of marriage, but the right is not absolute.

States can and do enact laws that limit or regulate marriage, but the applicable constitutional standard of review depends upon the characteristic (e.g., race, age, kinship) that provides the basis for the state regulation. State regulations which substantially interfere with the right to marry may be subjected to heightened scrutiny to satisfy the Equal Protection Clause. Application of this constitutional test focuses judges on both the nature and the aim of the restriction and requires an assessment of the extent to which the restriction serves the asserted end and the significance of the end to be achieved.

Specific formal marriage requirements vary by jurisdiction, but most states have licensing requirements and require a ceremony to effectuate the marriage performed by a religious or state official. Many jurisdictions require that both parties submit the results of a blood test and a few jurisdictions require testing for sexually transmitted diseases. Unions that do not comply with the dictates of state marriage statutes may be considered *void ab initio* (void) or voidable.

An annulment is the proper procedure for dissolving a void or voidable marriage. Each state establishes what deficiencies render a marriage void or voidable. A void marriage (e.g., one that is invalid because the partners were of the same sex, or were brother and sister, or because one of the parties was married to another person) does not require a formal annulment proceeding, although a party may petition the court for the judicial record to reflect that the marriage was in fact void. A voidable marriage (e.g., one that can be invalidated because it was entered into under duress or as a prank) can only be terminated pursuant to a formal annulment proceeding. Some states have adopted prescribed time limits for the initiation of an annulment action. If a party fails to annul a voidable marriage in a timely manner, he or she may be determined to have ratified (i.e., consented to) the marriage. Some states require the parties to obtain a divorce where there are children born into the void or voidable marriage. Historically, parties to annulled marriages were not entitled to court ordered support or property awards. Currently, however, some states have enacted legislation that confers rights to "spousal" support and marital property, pursuant to an annulment.

The doctrine of common law marriage allows the state to recognize a union that has not been effectuated in adherence to proscribed formalities. Recognition of these marriages has declined significantly across the U.S. The few states that still embrace the doctrine usually require that a couple satisfy an intent requirement expressed in terms of the extent to which they regarded themselves and others regarded them to be married. Some jurisdictions that do not recognize common law unions created within their state will recognize common law marriages effectuated in other jurisdictions that do allow for the creation of such unions. While some of the formal requirements for marriage are relaxed for common law marriages, jurisdictions that recognize them still impose limits related to the sexual orientation, age, and blood relationship of the parties involved.

B.   Same-Sex Marriage

Traditionally and historically, marriage has been limited in the U.S. to one man and one woman. In the face of a growing call for a definition of marriage that includes same-sex couples, an increasing number of States are enacting marriage bans to preserve the historical and traditional definition of marriage. To that end, many jurisdictions have also amended their state constitutions to expressly prohibit same-sex marriage. To date, these amendments have not been determined to violate the federal U.S. Constitution. Efforts to amend the U.S. Constitution to include a definition of marriage limited to two persons of the opposite sex have not been successful, but the debate surrounding that proposal is alive and well.

The family is regarded as the building block of American society, and marriage is regarded as the foundational unit of the American family. Accordingly, the State claims a significant interest in promoting and regulating marriage. Amplifying the State's interest in marriage is the presumption that marriage is the most appropriate context for sexual relations and for the creation and effective rearing of children. They identify the safety and well-being of children as a legitimate justification that supports the State's prohibition of same-sex marriage. Opponents argue that in light of the biological impossibility of conceiving children by traditional methods, same-sex couples should not be permitted to marry. They also charge that the idea that marriage between individuals of the same sex threatens the traditional ideal of marriage and, in turn, the strength of the family and the health of the society.

Proponents of same-sex marriage assert an equality-based challenge to these marriage bans, arguing that they are overbroad (they encompass same-sex couples who, through adoption and new reproductive technologies, can conceive and raise children within their relationships) and under-inclusive (they exclude heterosexual couples who do not want to or cannot conceive children by traditional methods).

Proponents of these bans argue that these laws amount to an infringement upon the fundamental right to marry and discriminate against homosexuals. They further charge that the State's justifications for prohibiting marriage between homosexuals are neither compelling nor legitimate.

The presumed relationship between marriage and procreation brings sex within the scope of state regulation. However, the U.S. Constitution, which at one time was interpreted to allow state prohibition of the sale of birth control to unmarried persons and permitted states to criminalize sodomy, now embraces consensual sexual activity between adults within its protective sphere, without regard to the sexual orientation of the persons. The 2004 Supreme Court decision in *Lawrence v. Texas*, where the Court announced this liberty interest, was decided on narrow grounds and did not sanction the constitutionality of same-sex marriages.

Some scholars and commentators suggest that one way to mitigate the inequality that characterizes the exclusion of homosexuals from the institution of marriage is to separate legal unions from religious unions and allow civil unions for all couples and treat marriage as a religious covenant that may be limited to heterosexual couples. They present the civil union as a constructive compromise which avoids the word marriage and all its attendant religious connotations. Those who advocate for "equal marriage" argue that this compromise may achieve formal equality while sabotaging substantive equality because it still perpetuates the idea that same-sex partnerships should not be considered "marriages" within the traditional meaning of the word. Those who oppose the idea of "civil unions for everyone" contend that it perpetuates differential treatment on the basis of sexual orientation.

In 2004 Massachusetts became the first state to recognize same-sex marriage. In 2008 California became the second state to recognize same-sex marriage. At this time, a same-sex marriage effectuated in Massachusetts or California, unlike heterosexual marriages, is not likely to be recognized in other states as valid and enforceable. State enactments prohibiting same-sex marriages operate as an impediment to the legal status of same-sex marriages. The Defense of Marriage Act ("DOMA"), a federal enactment, provides that no state is required to recognize the legality of a same-sex marriage created in another state. Some commentators question the constitutionality of DOMA, arguing that it may violate principles of full faith and credit — the concept that urges states to give effect to the laws or judicial decisions of a sister state. They challenge DOMA on the grounds that it represents a dramatic departure from the general rule that a marriage that satisfies the requirements of the state where it was effectuated will be recognized in all other states as valid, unless it violates a strong public policy of that state. Defenders of DOMA retort that states with strong public policies against the creation and recognition of same-sex unions as legitimate legal marriages can constitutionally decline to give legal effect to same-sex marriages created in other states.

V. DIVORCE

While marriage enjoys the status of being a fundamental protected constitutional right, its correlate, divorce, does not. The fact that the marital contract cannot be terminated without the involvement of the state confirms that marriage is a creation of the state. The command, "till death do us part," is part of the traditional litany recited during the marriage ceremony. In the past it imposed a requirement that made divorce virtually impossible under American law. Because marriage was regarded as a foundational society unit, divorce was regarded as a threat to American society. It was also perceived to reflect the moral deficiency of those who participated in it, particularly women. In light of the perception of marriage as the most appropriate relationship within which to conceive and rear children, state restrictions on divorce were also motivated by a desire to protect the interests of children who would not receive the same economic, and emotional support as a result of the dismantling of the family unit. By severely circumscribing one's ability to obtain a divorce, the State was able to secure the perceived social, economic and political benefits derived from the institution of marriage, safeguard the interests of children, and protect against an additional drain on state resources.

A.   Types of Divorce: Limited vs. Absolute

Some states recognize two types of divorce: limited and absolute. The limited divorce is a judicial decree ordering the separation of the parties (i.e., they may not live together) but does not change their marital status (i.e., they remain legally married) and neither spouse is free to remarry. Some states that allow limited divorces authorize courts to divide marital property, enter child custody and child support decrees, and award alimony (i.e., spousal support). Absolute divorce, by contrast, represents a complete termination of the marital relationship, freeing both parties to remarry.

B.   Traditional Fault Based Grounds for Divorce

American law first relaxed the prohibition against divorce by allowing fault based divorces — granting divorces to the spouse who was not responsible for the demise of the marriage. Fault based grounds for divorce, which persist in most states, include, but are not limited to: cruelty (personal violence or reasonable fear of violence or treatment that endangers one's life, safety, or health); adultery (engaging in sexual intercourse with someone other than one's spouse); desertion (physical or emotional abandonment of the marital relationship); incurable impotence (the inability to perform sexually); insanity (mental incapacity); conviction of a felony; imprisonment; habitual drunkenness; drug addiction; unnatural sexual acts; fraud (inducing marriage by means of material misrepresentation); duress (inducing marriage through coercive means); and extended absence indicating death of spouse. The spouse seeking a divorce on fault grounds must present evidence supporting the alleged basis for the divorce.

In response to a divorce action asserting fault based grounds for a divorce, the defendant spouse raises defenses that challenge the allegations of fault. States that allow fault based divorce recognize some or all of the following defenses: recrimination (a charge that the party seeking the divorce is guilty of contributing to the demise of the marriage); connivance (the complaining spouse consents to or facilitates the commission of a marital offense by the other spouse); collusion (the parties conspire to present false evidence to the court as a basis for obtaining a divorce); condonation (the spouse expressly or impliedly forgave the marital offense with the understanding that the offense would not be reported); justification (the asserted marital offense was an appropriate response to the misconduct of the party seeking the divorce); and insanity (the spouse lacked the mental capacity to appreciate the wrongfulness of the conduct asserted as the marital offense). With the emergence of the no-fault divorce and its comparatively relaxed evidentiary requirements, the fault based divorce and defenses to fault based divorces are less common than they used to be. However, a spouse may seek a fault based divorce because it may position them well for a successful bid for spousal support payments and property division under state statutes which consider fault in deciding alimony and property awards.

C.   No-Fault Divorce

The exclusivity of fault based divorces eventually gave way to no-fault divorces, which significantly eased the difficulty of obtaining a divorce. Married persons are now permitted in most jurisdictions to assert non-fault based grounds as a basis for divorce. The impact of the relatively recent convention of no-fault divorce (it has only existed for about twenty-five years) has been a significant increase in the number of U.S. divorces. Presently, fifty-one percent of all U.S. marriages end in divorce. Some observers note that no-fault divorces allow individuals to free themselves from unstable or unsatisfying relationships, mitigate the conflict inherent to ending the marital relationship, and enhance judicial efficiency in handling divorce petitions. Even in the no-fault divorce context, many states impose durational residency restrictions that require that the marital parties remain separate and apart from one another for a prescribed period of time before being eligible for divorce. If the parties resume cohabitation or engage in sexual relations during the prescribed time period, it interrupts the period of separation and eliminates the basis for the divorce. The time prescriptions for these residency requirements vary from state to state and can be as long as three years or as brief as sixty days. Pursuant to the principle of full faith and credit, sister states must give valid divorces granted in another state the full effect of the law.

D.   The Economic and Non-Economic Implications of Divorce

The character of marriage as an economic unit produces financial challenges upon dissolution of the marital relationship. It is in the context of those challenges that courts must balance a myriad of equities (i.e., fairness considerations) to fashion a financial settlement that reflects an equitable division of resources acquired during the marriage and keep parents and children from becoming financially dependent upon the State. The financial settlement generally has three aspects: property division, alimony awards (i.e., spousal support), and child support. Devising an equitable financial settlement is challenged by both the reality of the finite nature of monetary resources and the fact that it is generally more expensive to finance two separate households than one. States enact statutes that set forth factors that courts should consider in making these determinations; however, given the variety of economic circumstances, laws have historically left a great deal of discretion to judges to act as justice requires. The discretion and flexibility that judges have in making these decisions often produces conflicting and divergent decisions as to property division, alimony, and child support awards.

1.   Property Distribution

a.   Marital Property

The first step in the distribution calculus is to determine what constitutes marital property. Historically, marital property was defined in terms of real property (e.g., land, houses) or personal property (e.g., cars, jewelry) acquired during the marriage and distributions favored those who purchased the property or held legal title to it. This construction of marital property substantially disadvantaged a non-working spouse who made non-financial contributions to the marriage, which were not valued in the distribution calculus. Generally, the disadvantaged spouse was a woman. In recent years, states consider non-monetary contributions (i.e., maintaining the home, acting as primary caregiver for children) and intangible property, such as graduate degrees, professional business practices, and pensions and retirement earnings, when deciding both property distribution and spousal support awards. The law in this area has evolved away from a preoccupation with purchase and title toward considerations of contribution to the marital unit. Some state statutes exclude gifts and inheritance to one spouse from consideration as marital property, even though they may have been acquired during the marriage. Once the marital property at issue is identified and valued, courts must then turn their attention to how it will be divided between the spouses. The separate property system, where the division of property was determined according to the title holder of the property, has been abandoned in favor of more equitable marital property systems of distribution.

States are generally classified as either community property jurisdictions or common law jurisdictions. The community property approach to distribution subscribes to a partnership based principle and generally divides marital property evenly between spouses. This approach relies on fixed rules, from which judges have little discretion to depart, that result in consistent decision making. By contrast, the common law framework subscribes to an equitable distribution principle and generally divides property based on the respective contributions, financial and non-financial, made by the parties. The equitable approach invites greater inconsistency between judicial decisions because it leaves to judges a great deal of discretion in balancing relevant equities and assigning monetary value to the various contributions of the parties. While guidelines exist to direct the judge's attention to certain fairness factors, there are no rules governing how a judge should weigh the totality of considerations relevant to the distribution determination. It is important to note that division of marital property is often only one aspect of the court's overall approach to devising an equitable financial settlement between divorcing spouses. Other aspects of this financial composite include spousal support and child support. A few community property jurisdictions adopt an equitable approach to the division of marital property.

b.   Resolving Financial and Property Issues Upon Dissolution of Domestic Partnerships

Despite the pervasive hostility to a definition of marriage that would include same-sex couples, there is a burgeoning trend among some state courts to resolve property and financial disputes that arise between unmarried co-habitants according to the same principles that govern the resolution of dispute arising within marital relationships. These states remain in the minority, and judicial approaches to resolving disputes between unmarried cohabitants are marked by considerable variety. Domestic partners will often enter into detailed contractual agreements that define the terms and substance of their relationship and spell out the economic and non-economic consequences upon dissolution of the relationship. Most courts interpret and enforce these agreements according to the strict dictates of contract law, without regard for the personal nature of the domestic partnerships within which they were formed and operate, as they do when construing marital agreements. In the absence of an agreement, few courts regard domestic partnerships as the functional equivalent of marriages. Most courts do not adopt an equitable approach to interpreting the obligations and rights of the parties upon dissolution of the partnership.

Some state legislatures have enacted domestic partnership statutes and ordinances or amended their state constitutions to include common benefits clauses. These enactments and amendments operate generally to guarantee the same benefits and protections for domestic partners that are automatically conferred by the state upon married persons. Such entitlements include insurance coverage, the ability to transfer property, retirement benefits, family and funeral leave, property rights and standing to bring wrongful death and loss of consortium actions. The issue of the legal status of domestic partnerships presented itself in the context of the 9-11 Disaster Relief Fund when it had to be determined whether domestic partners were entitled to receive funds for the loss of their partners during the attacks in New York and Washington, D.C. Many surviving domestic partners received some monetary relief despite laws in New York and D.C. that do not recognize same-sex marriages.

2.   Alimony (Spousal Maintenance Awards)

The prevalence of the no-fault divorce signaled a decline in alimony awards but spousal support awards are still, though infrequently, awarded to entitled spouses without regard to gender. There are three types of alimony: pendent lite (an award for the duration of the divorce litigation); temporary alimony (an award for a prescribed period of time); and permanent alimony (an award that lasts until the death or remarriage of the recipient spouse). The policy justification for alimony awards is to provide temporary or (in very rare instances) permanent economic support for spouses who are not, nor capable of becoming, self-supporting. The chief concern of alimony awards is fairness, and statutory guidelines that govern alimony involve a variety of factors such as age, education, disparity of earning power between spouses, physical ability, years out of the workforce, any agreements reached between the parties during the marriage, and work history during the marriage. Statutory considerations vary from state to state but most statutes grant courts broad discretion to engage in a balancing of equities (i.e., fairness considerations) in making alimony decisions. In making these decisions, the exercise of judicial discretion is guided by a focus on how soon or whether the spouse seeking the award will be able to become financially self-sufficient.

3.   Child Support

All states, pursuant to a Congressional directive (the Federal Child Support Enforcement Amendments of 1984), have to establish non-binding guidelines for determining child support awards. In response to this legislation and in an effort to normalize child support decisions, all states have enacted laws that utilize specific formulas for calculating child support obligations and deprive judges of the discretion to depart from these formulas. Formula based calculations of child support mitigate inconsistency between support determinations because judges are no longer challenged by a determination of "need" to guide their decisions; however, they may fail to accommodate the specific circumstances presented by each child support case.

Where there is a change in circumstances, such as an increase or decrease in salary, a change in the child's needs, and in some jurisdictions remarriage, modification of an existing child support order may be necessary. States want to ensure that parents, and not the State, assume responsibility for providing for a child's financial needs. To this end, most states offer a variety of remedies for enforcing support obligations. These methods include, but are not limited to: civil and criminal contempt proceedings, liens on real property, and garnishment and attachment of property.

E.   The Impact of Divorce on Children

1.   Child Custody

Upon the separation of the parents and absent agreement between the parents, the State is charged with making a child custody determination. The best interests of the child standard is used almost universally by American judges to determine what custody arrangement best secures the physical and emotional well-being of a child. Though all jurisdictions embrace the best interests standard, there is substantial variety in terms of what constitutes a child's best interest and what considerations are relevant to securing that interest. When both parents are seeking custody of a child, the judge must make a fitness determination. In other words, the judge must determine, as between the two parents, who is the most competent to provide parental care that will serve the child's best interests.

In making this determination, courts will consider the importance of continuity in the child's life (i.e., not having to move or change schools) and the extent to which a custody determination will facilitate or challenge stability in the child's life. Considerations relevant to the best interest of the child include: parental preferences; the child's preference; whether a parent has served as the child's primary caregiver; the relationship between the child and each parent; the ability of each parent to establish and maintain a healthy living environment for the child; the gender of the parents and the age of the child; the stability of the proposed custodial home; continuity with respect to child's home and school; the quality of the respective neighborhoods; parental conduct that reflects ability to provide competent parenting; parental lifestyle choices; sexual orientation of the parents; the mental and physical state of the parents; the moral character of the parents; and the child's cultural and religious background. It is important to note that these considerations are value laden and the discretion that custody statutes afford judges allows them to use their own judgments in determining what constitutes appropriate parenting and the most appropriate environment for the raising of children.

State custody laws are gender neutral and no longer offer favored status to the mother as more fit to care for a child than the father. However, the primary caretaker presumption, which remains in effect in a few states, often confers favored status to mothers in custodial disputes because of the reality that women in American families continue to assume primary responsibility for the care of children. In other jurisdictions, primary caretaker status is a consideration but does not create a presumption that the parent who has acted as the primary caretaker will be granted custody of the child.

a.   Different Types of Custody

Courts can award parents sole or shared (i.e., joint) physical or legal custody of their children. In making the determination as to the most beneficial custodial arrangement for the child, judges are guided by the best interest of the child standard. The physical custodian is the parent with whom the child will reside primarily, with the other parent enjoying reasonable visitation with the child. Where the parents do not live close to one another, shared physical custody is less feasible because it may disrupt a child's sense of stability.

Legal custody refers to the authority of a parent to make important decisions on behalf of the child that relate to their health, education, and well-being. A parent can have sole physical custody and share with the co-parent legal custody of the child. Generally, courts are unwilling to grant joint legal custody where the parents demonstrate that they are unable to work together to provide for the best interest of the child. Many states have enacted laws that establish a presumption of joint custody unless there is evidence that a shared custodial arrangement will not serve the child's best interest.

b.   Modification of Custody Determination

Most statutory modification provisions, which allow a parent to petition for a change in the custody arrangement, require a precipitating change in circumstances that threatens the child's well being. Such an event might be a change in the age of the child or the proposed relocation of the custodial parent to another state or country. In deciding whether to reopen a custody order and modify its terms, the best interest of the child remains controlling, and the petitioning parent must establish that the child's interest is best served by the modification and that the benefit to the child outweighs any harm that may result from the change in custody.

2.   Visitation

Where one parent has been awarded physical custody, the non-custodial parent is entitled to reasonable visitation. Considerations relevant to the visitation determination are similar to those at issue in the custody context, and the decision is guided by that which serves the child's best interests. Some state custody statutes provide non-custodial parents with statutory and/or judicial means for the enforcement of visitation rights. In extreme cases, persistent interference with visitation by the custodial parent can result in a change of custody. Most jurisdictions do not condition visitation upon satisfaction of child support obligations.

F.   Visitation by Grandparents and Other Third Parties

While common law deferred to parental authority to decide whether third parties (e.g., grandparents, siblings, stepparents) would be permitted to visit their child, a number of states have passed laws that allow grandparents and other nonparents to petition for visitation rights and authorize courts to grant visitation where it is determined that doing so serves the child's best interest. The constitutionality of statutes allowing grandparents to petition for visitation was considered by the Supreme Court in a case where the Court struck down a Washington statute as unconstitutionally broad, reasoning that the statute interfered with parental rights to make decisions concerning the care, custody, and control of their children. The Court's decision was limited to the case before it and its holding did not determine the constitutionality of all nonparental visitation statutes.

G.   Mediation of Child Custody and Visitation

Several states have enacted statutes that allow courts to mandate mediation of child custody and visitation support and custody issues. These laws are thought to facilitate a less conflicted decision-making process for determining the specific custody and visitation arrangements that will serve the child's best interests and to inspire and enable co-parents to work collaboratively toward that end. In some states which do not have mandatory mediation statutes, judges, in their discretion, can order mediation where they determine that it would advance the interests of children. Even where parents have reached a mediated custodial agreement, the court is not obliged to ratify it if it determines that it does not serve the child's best interest. The court will give the parents's agreement due consideration but is not bound by it.

VI. MARITAL AGREEMENTS AND CONTRACTS

Prenuptial agreements operate to settle potential disputes as to the distribution of property and financial award entitlements in advance of a divorce. In addition to the designation or exclusion of certain property as marital property, these agreements allow the parties to privately control many substantive aspects of their marriage. Traditionally, these agreements were not enforced in most jurisdictions because judges believed that they promoted divorce. Presently, valid prenuptial agreements are enforceable in most jurisdictions. However, some provisions related to child support and maintenance may not be enforceable to the extent that the needs and interests of the child are different at the time of separation than they were at the time of the formation of the agreement.

Postnuptial agreements are private contracts between divorcing spouses that allow the parties to reach financial and property division settlements upon divorce, outside of the judicial system. Sometimes postnuptial agreements refer to agreements entered into during the marriage. For a prenuptial or postnuptial agreement to be valid and enforceable in most states, there must be full disclosure between the parties, and the agreement must be conscionable (i.e., fair to both parties in light of their respective circumstances). The validity of these agreements is assessed on a case-by-case basis, with the enforceability of each contract being determined based on the specific terms of and factual circumstances surrounding that agreement. Agreements satisfying the formal requirements will be construed according to general principles of contract law; however, given the unique status of the marital relationship, some judges will also assess the overall reasonableness of the contract in determining its enforceability. Traditional contract defenses (e.g., duress, fraud, or misrepresentation) are available to protect parties against the enforcement of invalid marital agreements.

Some observers identify America's increasing divorce rate as a catalyst for the rise in prenuptial agreements among Americans across socioeconomic lines. While these agreements have always enjoyed acceptance among wealthy Americans, more middle-class and working-class Americans, who seek to protect their existing or anticipated wealth, are entering into prenuptial agreements. Women, in particular, are initiating these agreements in greater numbers to mitigate the likelihood of the precipitous drop in their standard of living that generally follows divorce.

VII. PROCREATION

The choice to have or not to have children is regarded as one of the most fundamental privacy choices an individual can make; however, there is no express language in the U.S. Constitution that offers protection to this important liberty interest. Nevertheless, a right to privacy in matters of procreation has been interpreted to exist as an emanation of other express privacy interests, and is recognized as a fundamental right. This right of privacy provides for some freedom of choice in the controversial contexts of contraception, sterilization, artificial conception, and abortion.

A.   Abortion

Despite the Supreme Court's 1973 decision in *Roe v. Wade* making abortion legal, abortion continues to be a battlefield for rhetorical wars over state and federal regulatory power over abortion and women's rights to bodily and personal autonomy and integrity. It is in the context of abortion that the often competing rights and interests of the mother, the state, the unborn fetus, and the father intersect with scientific knowledge, biological realities, and spiritual, moral, and religious beliefs. Abortion law is also challenged by the difficulty inherent in reconciling conflicted perspectives on basic questions about what constitutes life and when life begins. State statutes that regulate and limit abortion may not unconstitutionally infringe upon the rights of the mother to choose to terminate her pregnancy.

The *Roe* majority situated a woman's privacy interests within the category of protected, personal liberty interests falling within the scope of the Fourteenth Amendment Due Process Clause of the U.S. Constitution. In a seven to two decision, the Supreme Court struck down a Texas statute banning abortion except when it was necessary to save a mother's life, holding that the statute unconstitutionally infringed upon the mother's privacy rights. The Court did not characterize the right to terminate one's pregnancy as absolute; rather, it treated it as a constitutionally protected interest to be balanced against the State's competing interest in the protection of potential life. The majority adopted a balancing test to guide the relative weight to be accorded the State's interest and the mother's rights, within the context of the relevant stage of pregnancy. The majority held that for a state regulation to be constitutional it had to survive strict scrutiny (i.e., be narrowly tailored to achieve a compelling state interest).

The *Roe* majority determined that during the first trimester of the pregnancy, the State's interest is minimal and the decision to terminate a pregnancy is relegated exclusively to the pregnant woman and her doctor. During the second trimester, the *Roe* majority determined that the State's interest in preserving the health of the mother authorized limited regulation of abortion to that end. During the third trimester, which the Court identified as the point of viability (i.e., the point at which a fetus can potentially live outside the womb), the State's interest expands to include protection of the fetus' constitutional right to life, and the State can prohibit abortion, unless the mother's life is at stake.

In the aftermath of *Roe*, the Supreme Court has continued to decide the constitutionality of state statutes regulating abortion. On balance, Supreme Court decisions have narrowed substantially the privacy rights of pregnant women and correspondingly broadened the authority of the State to regulate abortion. The Supreme Court has struck down state abortion statutes requiring spousal consent and notification, on the grounds that the potential father's rights are outweighed by those of the mother. In recognition of the constitutional rights of minors, the Supreme Court has held that statutes imposing parental consent and notification requirements for minors to obtain abortions must provide a judicial bypass option, which affords an alternative process by which a minor can demonstrate that the abortion serves her best interest and that she is competent to make the decision to terminate her pregnancy in consultation with her doctor, without parental notice or consent.

The Court has struck down state regulations limiting the performance of abortions to certain medical facilities as frustrating the ability of economically disadvantaged women from obtaining abortions. However, the Court has upheld statutes limiting eligible state funded medical treatment to exclude non-medically necessary abortions, which arguably adversely impacts women who cannot afford to finance an abortion. The Court has also upheld the imposition of a twenty-four hour waiting period as a constitutional exercise of state regulatory authority. Until 2007, Supreme Court decisions mandated that state abortion statutes limiting abortions include a health exception for the mother, which would allow an otherwise unauthorized abortion if the procedure was necessary for the health or life of the mother. In the Court's most recent abortion decision, however, *Gonzales v. Carhart*, the Supreme Court upheld a federal law banning partial birth abortions (an abortion procedure where the fetus is removed from the woman's womb partially intact) for women beyond their first trimester, notwithstanding the absence of such a health exemption.

Despite the replacement of the trimester framework with a reasonableness test and uncertainty as to the appropriate level of judicial scrutiny for testing the constitutionality of states' abortion laws, the *Roe* decision continues to offer some constitutional protection for a pregnant woman's liberty interest in choosing to terminate her pregnancy against state infringement. The scope and content of that protection continues to be a source of emotionally charged debate.

B.   New Reproductive Techniques

The area of new reproductive techniques is one of the most dynamic areas of family law and is an area of law which some scholars believe would benefit from federal regulation. There is considerable variety among state statutes and how judges are resolving disputes that arise in this area of law. New developments in medicine, science, and technology are allowing couples who have been unable to have children via conventional methods to experience parenthood. There are three artificial insemination methods. AID occurs where sperm from an unknown donor is injected into a woman's womb to fertilize the egg. AIH entails the use of sperm from the patient's partner or husband. CAI entails the injection of a mixture of sperm from both a partner or husband and an unknown donor into a woman. Artificial insemination is the longest practiced alternative reproductive method. The Uniform Parentage Act has provided guidance for state statutes that govern issues related to the relative parental status and rights of the mother and the man whose sperm was used to fertilize her egg. The Act provides that if a married woman is artificially inseminated with a third-party donor's semen under the supervision of a licensed physician and with the consent of her husband, the child will be considered to be the natural child of the husband. The Act does not address parentage issues when artificial insemination is used in less formal settings, outside the supervision of a licensed physician.

Surrogacy, another form of assisted reproduction, involves the solicitation of a surrogate mother who agrees to become impregnated and carry the child to term for another couple or individual. Generally, the surrogate mother and the couple or individual for whom she is carrying the child will enter into a surrogacy contract that sets out the terms of the agreement. State statutes governing the enforceability of surrogacy agreements vary considerably; however, most do not allow for the payment of money for the termination of parental rights. Issues arise in this area when the surrogate mother decides that she does not want to relinquish the child. While it is often clear that the man who provided the sperm that fertilized the egg is considered the natural father, there is often confusion as to the identity of the natural mother, particularly if the surrogate mother did not provide the egg for fertilization.

The newest reproductive technology is in vitro fertilization (IVF), where a woman's ova (egg) is fertilized by sperm outside of the womb and preserved. In the context of this method of assisted reproduction, the law struggles to respond to the unique realities of cutting edge medical advancements. Central questions that state enactments have answered in different ways in the context of in vitro fertilization are how to classify frozen preembryos (are they property or life or the subject of a contract agreement) and how to resolve disputes where one party wants to destroy the preembryos and one wishes to have them implanted. In vitro fertilization facilitates new methods of collaborative reproduction, allowing couples and individuals to purchase embryos, adopt embryos, or use them to facilitate surrogacy. These possibilities raise considerable legal issues as to parental status, parental rights, and right to life issues that arise at the intersection of medical technology, constitutional law, contract law, and property law.

VIII.   THE PARENT-CHILD RELATIONSHIP

The parent-child relationship enjoys significant constitutional protection against state infringement. The right of a parent to rear a child according to his or her own values and beliefs is regarded as a privacy interest of constitutional significance. Children's rights, which are difficult to discern and define, are often eclipsed by the rights of their parents, but parental rights are not absolute. States are authorized to invade the protected sanctuary of the family to protect children's best interests when they are threatened. Most states have enacted laws that allow for the involuntary termination of parental rights in instances of abuse and neglect. Abuse and neglect are generally defined in state statutes as conduct that causes physical, moral, mental, or emotional harm to a child and which impairs that child's best interests. Parents can also voluntarily relinquish their parental rights when they are unable to adequately care for their child. Once parental rights are severed, pursuant to a termination proceeding, the child becomes a ward of the state and the state assumes legal and physical custody for the child in its *parens patriae* authority (i.e., power of the state as parent). The child is placed in a foster home or a state institution and awaits adoption. Federal legislation establishes the primacy of permanent placement (i.e., adoption) over temporary placement (i.e., foster care or institutionalized care) for children who have been removed from their homes.

Adoption can be facilitated by state agencies or state licensed private adoption agencies. The few adoption eligibility requirements contained in most state statutes relate to age and require that where a couple is adopting, both husband and wife consent to the adoption. Placement agencies, private and state, use a long list of criteria to determine whether a prospective adoptive parent will provide a suitable environment and care for a child. In addition to the completion of lengthy applications, prospective parents are often subject to interviews and evaluative in-home visits.

Some states have enacted statutes prohibiting adoption by same-sex couples and gay and lesbian individuals. These statutes, like the Florida statute, allow gay couples and individuals to provide foster homes for orphans but prohibit children from being permanently placed in these homes. There are also states that prohibit same-sex couples from providing foster care for orphans. State statutes prohibiting same-sex adoption and limiting placement opportunities for orphans have not been deemed unconstitu tional. However, federal legislation has been enacted to discourage states receiving federal funding for adoption processes from delaying or denying placements to achieve race-matching (i.e., ensuring that the race of the orphan and the race of the prospective adoptive parents is the same). The legislation even authorizes a right of action by prospective adoptive parents on behalf of a child whose placement has been delayed or denied on the basis of a racial difference between the child and the prospective parents. Limitations on placements confine children available to adoption to foster and state institutional care.

IX. CONCLUSION

Family law is a dynamic area of law focused on a broad range of institutions, interests, and realities that shape and inform intimate relationships between people. The law in this area attempts to strike a balance between establishing uniform standards while accommodating the variety of circumstances characteristic of human relationships and the human experience. Family law must also walk the tightrope between privacy interests and the State's interests which sometimes converge, but often conflict, in the arena of personal relationships.

It is in the context of this area of law, characterized best by flux and ambiguity, that the family law practitioner must make strategic and legal decisions that best serve the interests of the client. This area of practice requires an understanding of governing legal frameworks and the ability to discern how judges will exercise their discretion within those frameworks and sometimes depart from them to reach equitable decisions. It also requires an appreciation for the concerns, expectations, and emotions of clients who are endeavoring to resolve conflicts centered on relationships and circumstances of the utmost importance.

Chapter 15

FUNDAMENTALS OF U.S. ADMINISTRATIVE LAW

By — William R. Andersen

SYNOPSIS

I. INTRODUCTION

Today's U.S. society is complex, economically sophisticated, and composed of highly interdependent elements. Even in a government that prizes freedom of private action, this complexity requires substantial public intervention. That intervention is needed to assure fulfillment of the private economy's goals, to restrict practices and structures that impede accomplishment of those goals, and to provide goods and services that a private economy tends not to produce in sufficient magnitudes or does not allocate in socially desirable ways.

Accordingly, the U.S. regulatory process has become a substantial activity with responsibilities for standard setting, enforcement and direct service provision in a range of activities that includes agriculture, commerce, education, energy, welfare, labor, transportation, environment, consumer affairs, maritime matters, workplace safety, communications, taxation, monetary policy, etc.

In each of these areas, a body of *substantive* law will be generated (tax law, labor law, securities law, environmental law, etc.), and the typical U.S. law school will have courses in such substantive areas. The typical law school course in administrative law, by contrast, treats the common *procedures* the agencies must follow in carrying out their substantive tasks. In addition, administrative law covers judicial review of agency action — the judicial role raising especially delicate interbranch issues, since the job of the courts is both to insure that the legislative branch complies with the Constitution and that executive and independent agencies comply with requirements set down by the legislature.

Regulatory bodies in the U.S. are staffed by officials who are probably best seen as members of the executive branch — though as we'll see in the next section, for practical and legal reasons some of these officials can be considerably independent of the executive. Somewhat similar arrangements are made for regulatory bodies at the state and local level.

The structural variety of these bodies is immense, the tasks assigned to them are enormously varied, and the statutory systems and mechanisms which empower and control them span an impressive range. The law which regulates procedure in this variety cannot be simply stated. But there are some general principles common to most systems, principles growing out of common functions, histories, and attitudes. With such principles in mind, navigating any complex regulatory structure will be greatly facilitated. It is a brief sketch of these general principles that we will essay in the following pages. To put some limits on our inquiry, we will focus here on federal agencies, but as indicated, the principles will be highly salient in state and local regulatory systems as well.

We will begin with a look at the constitutional placement of the regulatory process in Section II. We will then look at two typical forms of agency action that have special procedural requirements, adjudication and rulemaking, in Sections III and IV, respectively. Finally Sections V and VI look at the principles relating to the availability of judicial review and the scope or intensity of that review. In the Conclusion, we attempt to summarize all of this in one sentence. If you read it now that sentence will seem dense to the point of opacity. After reading the chapter, it should carry a little more meaning — a measure of what new perspectives this chapter may have opened up for you.

II.   CONSTITUTIONAL CONSIDERATIONS

We will begin with a look at the basic question of how the administrative process can be fitted into the separated power model of U.S. constitutional structure. Beyond that, we will discuss briefly a couple of other provisions of the U.S. Constitution that bear importantly on the procedures employed by regulatory bodies.

A.   Separation of Powers

1.   The Basic Plan — Three Separate Branches

The framers of the U.S. Constitution in 1787 concluded that while significant power had to be delegated to the new national government, government power should be divided into different branches. The reasons for this design included the perceived abuses of centralized power the colonists suffered under the British monarch. With power divided into separate branches, it would be difficult for a single individual or faction to gain control of the entire government. In addition, there is a sense in the framers' discussions that separated powers can be exercised more fairly — e.g., judges should not be interpreting laws they have written, prosecutors should not be judging guilt or innocence of those they are prosecuting, etc.

The nature of the division was based on the knowledge many of the framers had of political history as well as experience they had had with existing state constitutions. From at least the time of Aristotle, it was thought there were basically three distinct kinds of government power. In simplified form, there was, first of all, the power to promulgate general rules governing the society — we call this power *legislative*. Second, there was the power to implement or carry out these general rules — we call this power *executive*. Finally, there was the power to resolve disputes arising in the formulation and implementation of the rules — we call this power *judicial*.

The framers divided the government into three branches roughly on this pattern. Thus, Article I of the Constitution vests legislative power in Congress, Article II vests executive power in the President and Article III vests the federal judicial power in a Supreme Court and other federal courts Congress may provide. Many state constitutions today follow similar patterns.

It is clear from both text and context that the framers intended these three fundamental types of powers to be kept separate — that is, branches were not supposed to exercise the core powers of another branch or even to impede the other branches in the exercise of their core powers. Separation insured that powers were widely dispersed and that any changes to the status quo would require broad consensus. In addition, separation sought to achieve the fairness mentioned earlier which could be prejudiced by commingling inconsistent powers.

The design goes two steps further in its complex distribution of powers. First, the three branches are differently structured, their officials serve for different terms and answer to different constituencies. Thus, the executive branch is headed by a President elected nationally every four years. The legislative branch is made up of two chambers — the House, composed of 435 representatives elected from local electoral districts of roughly equal population who serve for 2-year terms, and the Senate, composed of 100 senators elected from states (2 senators from each state, irrespective of differences in population) and serving 6-year terms. Collectively, these two chambers make up Congress. The judicial branch is made up of life-tenured judges nominated by the President and confirmed by the Senate.

Second, there are a number of places where the powers of the branches overlap — where action by both branches is necessary (e.g., the Senate must ratify treaties negotiated by the President) or where some coordination is required (only Congress can declare and fund war, but the President is Commander-in-Chief). This system, with its so-called "checks and balances," supplements the division and separation of powers described. In all, it is a complex arrangement for empowering the functions of government.

2.   Fitting the Administrative Process Into This Plan

But the framers, for all their brilliance, all their insight, and all their wisdom, did not foresee the complex, economically interdependent society we were to become. For that reason, they had no way of anticipating the size and complexity of the regulatory functions such a society would require. Hence, there is no place in the framers' exquisite scheme for the administrative process. And today, that is something of an embarrassment, since that process has become larger and, on a day-to-day basis, more consequential for many of our citizens than the traditional three branches.

How can we permit agencies to administer vast programs (which seems like the exercise of executive power), to make multitudes of rules (which seems like the exercise of legislative power), or to adjudicate millions of individual cases (which seems like the exercise of judicial power) and still remain faithful to the framers' design? And how can we permit a single agency to exercise all three types of power despite the framers' sensible commitment to power separation as an aid to fairness?

The solution is not so much the result of an elegant political theory as it is a practical settlement that delegates power to the regulatory agencies to function as needed, with varying levels of supervision by the traditional branches. It is in these two ways — the traditional branches empowering regulatory agencies and then controlling them — that the U.S. administrative process is constitutionally legitimated. Let's take a little closer look at how needs of the real world and constitutional doctrine were brought into some semblance of accord.

a.   Empowering the Agencies

As the need became more apparent for more machinery to carry out government regulatory needs, Congress responded by creating governmental units variously styled bureaus, departments, agencies, commissions, boards, etc. Virtually all these agencies derive their power from a congressional grant. That means that decisions about which powers an agency is permitted to exercise are made by accountable branches of the government — the Congress which enacts the law, and the President who signs it.

Still, constitutional objections to this strategy are not hard to find. For example, to the extent agencies are given rulemaking power (most of them have been given this power), legislative power has been delegated to the agencies. But the text of Article I says that "all" legislative power is vested in the Congress. An obvious inference is that Congress must do all the legislating, that it cannot delegate that important power to other units of government. In the 1930s, there was a brief period when the so-called non-delegation doctrine was applied by the Supreme Court, invalidating a couple of New Deal legislative delegations. But since 1937, the principle has not been in fashion, and no statute since that time has fallen on the basis that it has improperly delegated power to a regulatory agency. The Court seems to have been satisfied that if Congress provided some guidance to its delegee (the agency), the true legislative function had been exercised by Congress, the agency just being the device that dealt with the details of implementation. This is generally recognized as a fiction today, since the kind of congressional "guidance" that satisfies the Court can be stated in almost cosmic breadth (e.g., a statute provides enough guidance if it authorizes the agency to act "in the public interest"). Pretty clearly, the Court has made its peace with the inevitable: the framers didn't foresee the shape and magnitude of government that was to come, and some accommodation to that circumstance was required. The nondelegation doctrine remains, however, as a tacit reminder that the legislature is the source of agency power and that the legislature can and sometimes does use that power to conform agency policies to legislative preference.

Something similar has occurred with statutes that empower agencies to exercise judicial power. Article III of the Constitution plainly vests this power in the courts. There are major protections in the federal courts, most notably their independence from political pressure and their life-tenure appointments. The deciding officer in an agency adjudication, by contrast, is an agency official, and perhaps a political appointee serving at the pleasure of the President. Is fair adjudication possible in such a system?

Practical needs to adjudicate millions of cases well beyond the capacity of the courts have resulted in substantial accommodation. Congress has granted, and the courts have approved, a very wide exercise of agency adjudicatory power. Independence and fairness in agency adjudication has been the subject of a number of special statutory protections, some of which we will examine below.

b.   Controlling the Agencies

Since most federal agencies are "placed" in the executive branch, that branch exercises considerable control over them. First of all, Article II, Sec. 2 of the Constitution gives to the President the power (subject to Senate confirmation) to appoint most high-level agency officials, and this power gives the President considerable control over agency conduct and policies. Similarly, most of those appointed by the President serve at his pleasure — the exception being the dozen or so "independent agencies" whose heads are appointed by the President but who serve fixed terms beyond the reach of the presidential removal power. For all the rest, the power to remove officials is another important element of executive control. Still further, the President has, by a variety of internal executive orders — notably through the Office of Fiscal Management — sought to integrate and coordinate agency action and to conform that action to presidential substantive and budgetary policies. These controls have been increasing in recent years and have important impacts on executive agencies and in some places even on independent agencies.

Congress also exercises significant controls over the administrative process. This can be done directly by amending agency statutory authority or controlling agency budgets. The Senate plays a role in staffing agencies through its power to confirm presidential nominees. In addition, the legislature has, and frequently exercises, the power of oversight — hearings, investigations, and other inquiries about administrative behavior. Supplementing all these formal measures — as anyone who has experience inside a federal agency will attest — are a variety of informal measures which in a variety of ways make agencies very much aware of congressional preferences. The accumulation of all these devices makes the legislature a powerful control force in the administrative world.

Finally, the judicial branch is part of the general system by which agencies are controlled. As we will see, most agency action is reviewable by the courts both as to the factual and legal adequacy of the agency's conclusions. The courts police agencies to insure that constitutionally required procedures are followed and that legislatively expressed preferences are respected.

c.   The Settlement

The resulting picture, then, is of a "branch" of government which was not anticipated by the framers, but which was made necessary by the growth of complex modern government and which was fitted into the framers' structure uneasily but with sufficient executive, legislative, and judicial controls to meet much of the framers' concerns about accountability.

d.   A Caveat

A final note on the constitutional placement of the administrative process. A typical modern agency will combine legislative powers (the ability to make general binding rules), executive powers (the ability to investigate and prosecute violators of those rules), and judicial power (the ability to resolve disputes about the application of the rules). If the framers put these powers in different branches in part to promote fairness, what can we say of administrative agencies which exercise all three kinds of power within one organization?

For example, can a commercial pilot expect fairness in a license revocation proceeding against her if the "judge" in her case is part of the same agency that wrote the rule she is said to have violated, that investigated her, and is now prosecuting her? As we will see, the solution to this problem is the task of procedural requirements which seek some degree of separation of inconsistent agency functions. Whether there is enough protection is a matter of continuing debate.

B.   Other Constitutional Requirements

Beyond these structural requirements, there are procedural requirements laid down by other parts of the Constitution that bind all government units including administrative agencies. In the administrative law field, the principal constitutional constraints lie in the Fifth Amendment's injunction to comply with due process of law (we will focus here on so-called procedural due process), that Amendment's prohibition of self-incrimination, and the Fourth Amendment's limits on government searches and seizures. We will look briefly at each.

1.   Procedural Due Process

The Due Process Clause only limits government, not private action, though this "state action" requirement is seldom a problem in administrative law, as the agencies involved are usually clearly governmental actors.

At the core of the procedural due process idea is the notion that when government is taking harmful action against an individual based on the conduct or circumstances of that individual, the individual should have some opportunity to be heard before the action becomes final.

Notice that the clause comes into force not on the occasion of harmful governmental action generally, but only from harmful action based on an individual's unique characteristics (think of a taxi license not being renewed because of the driver's poor driving record as distinguished from a nonrenewal occasioned by a general economic judgment that there were too many taxis in the city). When the government acts in ways that affect individuals as members of groups (such as setting general licensing standards), due process does not typically demand much in the way of individual opportunity to be heard. So when a legislature sets licensing standards — which may be very harmful to those who cannot meet the promulgated standards — due process does not require that affected individuals be given any notice or hearing whatsoever. As Section III below will show, there may be some statutory obligations to allow affected individuals to participate in the setting of general standards, but they are not rooted in due process.

When one is trying to determine what interests the clause protects, the language of the clause is critical. The courts have held that the clause protects only what it says it protects: "persons" whose interests in "life," "liberty," and "property" are threatened by government action. Courts have typically given a broad definition to the word "person." It includes individuals, corporations, aliens facing deportation, etc. The outer limits (aliens not within the U.S.) are being tested as we write.

Interests in life are not involved in administrative law, as agencies are usually not empowered to threaten that interest. Most of the litigation in the administrative law field has explored the range of interests that can be fitted into the "liberty" and "property" categories.

a.   Defining Property

The U.S. Supreme Court began with a definition of property that provided protection only for deprivations of interests to which the claimant had a "right." Thus, a landowner has a right to possession of his property; government action could not limit that right without providing a due process hearing. Today, the protection of the clause has been broadened to include things to which a claimant may not have a right but has a "legitimate claim of entitlement." In the setting of modern welfare benefits, for example, while a citizen may have no abstract right to have a welfare program established; if it *is* established, citizens who meet its qualifications are entitled to its benefits. If one is denied those benefits on grounds special to the beneficiary (e.g. on an agency claim that the beneficiary does not meet the statutory qualifications) due process will require an appropriate opportunity to be heard on the question of the beneficiary's qualifications.

b.   Defining Liberty

The Court has struggled with defining the liberty interest protected by due process. Deprivation of one's physical liberty would clearly qualify. Beyond that, the principle today is extended to reputational harm if the government action at the same time deprives the person of something of tangible value. A common example is terminating an individual's employment on publicly stated grounds of serious misconduct. Since both harm and stigma are involved, due process would usually allow the individual an opportunity to be heard on the question of misconduct.

c.   Identifying the Process That is Due

Remember that in cases of both property and liberty deprivations, due process does not prevent the government from imposing the deprivations; the clause only obliges the government to provide a meaningful hearing on any disputed issues. What is a meaningful hearing?

The basic principle of due process is this: the claimant should be given adequate notice of the action to be taken — including the reasons for the action — and afforded an appropriate opportunity to respond. The procedural requirements the courts have imposed are aimed at implementing this basic principle. Since the job of formulating detailed procedures has fallen to judges, it should not be surprising that the procedures required are very like procedures with which judges are familiar. The fullest list (discussed in judicial opinions and comment) might include such things as:

- an unbiased tribunal
- notice of the proposed action and the reasons for it
- the right to be present in person
- the right to be represented by counsel
- the right to introduce evidence
- the right to present arguments
- the right to cross-examine witnesses supporting the agency action
- the right to have a record compiled
- the right to have the decision made exclusively on the basis of the record
- the right to an explanation of the agency's final decision
- the right to internal and external appellate review

Not all these procedures are required in all cases. The sheer number of cases (in the millions) in any year preclude making each of them elaborate trials with all these protections. Instead, the Court has taken a more flexible approach, trying to identify places where a claimed procedure will be useful and can be provided at reasonable expense.

Currently, the Court uses a three-factor formula to test the due process adequacy of an agency procedure. The Court looks at (1) the interest of the claimant — including the degree of harm the government action might have on claimants of his type, (2) the extent to which the procedure claimed will increase the accuracy of the administrative determination — e.g., cross-examination might not be of much value in a case turning on documentary evidence — and (3) the public interest — which includes the cost of providing the procedure. Since these factors are very broadly stated, it is not possible to predict outcomes with any precision. But the factors are functionally relevant and give counselors, advisors, and litigators useful information about the approach to defining due process that a judge might take. As can be seen from the formula, successful claimant arguments for requiring a particular procedure will show that harm to the claimant will be substantial, that the procedure urged is the kind of procedure that will enhance accurate determination of the disputed issues in the case, and that the procedure can be provided with small cost in terms of time and other resources.

d. At What Time Is the Process Due?

If due process applies, and if it requires particular procedures in the case, the last question is "at what time" must the procedure be afforded — before or after the deprivation? While having a hearing before the deprivation would normally be preferable, the Court has held that fairly limited pre-deprivation procedures may satisfy the clause if more elaborate procedures are available later. Again, the Court has used the three-factor formula discussed above to govern its assessment of the time at which the protections must be available.

2. The Fifth Amendment and the Rule Against Self-Incrimination

The administrative process runs on information. Some of it is produced internally by the agency (studies, reports, etc.) and some of it is provided by regulated parties (required reports, etc.). But much of it comes from agency investigations of the papers and places of business of the regulated companies. The health department may inspect a restaurant; the drug agency may inspect a pharmaceutical plant; the aviation agency may inspect an airframe manufacturing facility, etc. Since regulatory infractions may be discovered in such inspections, the question has arisen whether the Fifth Amendment's privilege against self-incrimination protects regulated parties from such agency inquiries. The need for information is so great that the privilege has been narrowly construed in the administrative context. Whatever the power of the privilege in criminal proceedings, in the normal administrative context, the privilege offers limited protection to regulated parties. The privilege applies only to natural persons (i.e., it does not protect corporations), and even as to natural persons, it only protects against potential incrimination — not mere undesired regulatory outcomes. And in any event, it does not usually protect a company's records if those records were required by the agency to be kept.

3. The Fourth Amendment and Administrative Investigations

The Fourth Amendment prohibits unreasonable searches and seizures and places some limits on the issuance of search warrants. The obvious criminal law context of this amendment might suggest that it was not intended to apply to inspections by administrative agencies or to agency requirements that private information be disclosed. But for most businesses, the U.S. Supreme Court has held the amendment *does* apply in administrative contexts. For practical reasons, however, the Court has defined the required reasonableness in ways that seldom limit the investigative reach of the regulating agency. Thus, while agency search warrants may be a necessary condition of agency inspection of private premises, warrants can be obtained from a court with a showing that the search is random or part of a general pattern of industry inspection — "probable cause" that a violation is suspected (required in the criminal law context) is not required. Agency demands for information are routinely authorized by statute, and even if compulsory process is required (in the form, say, of a subpoena), judicial generosity in issuance and enforcement is typical.

III. RULEMAKING

A.   The Rulemaking and Adjudication Distinction

We need to begin our look at administrative law proper by getting comfortable with two central concepts: *rulemaking* and *adjudication* — perhaps unfamiliar terms for some readers, but basically simple concepts. We touched on them briefly when we talked about due process; we'll go into a little more detail here as they are fundamental to administrative law. Many statutes which prescribe procedures for agencies use these terms frequently, and, of course, courts and commentators use them to describe agency activity. So let's get comfortable with them.

In simplest terms, you can think of rulemaking as similar to what a legislature does and adjudication as similar to what a court does.

1.   Rulemaking — What Does a Legislature Do?

Usually when we speak of legislative action, we are talking about the adoption of a *general* principle to be applied to a defined *group*, to be applied in the *future*, and usually turning on questions of *policy*.

For example, a law might provide that "all airline pilots must have 20/20 vision." Such a law doesn't mention the eyesight of any particular pilot (it is *general*), but rather it applies only to pilots as a *group*. And a decision to adopt this standard will usually be applied only to the *future*. The kinds of matters that are considered by the lawmaker may include a general sense of the appropriate level of air safety that is desired, the reasonableness of the 20/20 requirement given what we know about flying and eyesight, and the general costs of enforcing such a standard, etc. These we would tend to describe as *policy* considerations, and they bear on the issue of whether the standards should be imposed, not on the circumstance of any particular pilot.

When a legislative body adopts a standard of this sort, we call it legislative action, and the product will be a statute. When an administrative agency promulgates standards of this kind, we will say it is engaged in rulemaking, and the product will be a rule.

2.   Adjudication — What Does a Court Do?

Now shift gears. Suppose enforcement agencies suspect that the eyesight of pilot Joseph Green is not up to the required standards. The agency may begin a proceeding to revoke Green's license. To revoke the license on the basis of the 20/20 rule, enforcement officials will have to show that Green's eyesight is not 20/20. Notice how different a process this is. The decision will now turn on facts peculiar to a particular named individual; the visual quality of pilots generally will be irrelevant. The proceeding will be based on what past eye examinations tell us about Green's eyesight. Finally, the proceeding need not consider the policy issues about the appropriateness of the 20/20 standard as that has been settled by adoption of the regulation.

When a court conducts a proceeding of this kind, we call it an "adjudication" and the same word is used to describe an individualized proceeding being conducted by an administrative agency.

It only remains to be said that there may be more specific definitions of rulemaking and adjudication in relevant statutes. Thus, the federal Administrative Procedure Act (APA), which spells out minimum procedural requirements, has a definition of "rule" which is very like the concepts we have been discussing. The same is true of many state administrative procedure acts. Of course, a lawyer dealing with these statutes will consult them directly and in detail.

B.   Choosing Between Rulemaking and Adjudication

An agency cannot engage in either rulemaking or adjudication unless it has statutory authority to do so. Many modern agencies have both kinds of power. For example, the Federal Trade Commission (FTC) has authority to promulgate general principles to limit consumer fraud (rulemaking). It also has power to prosecute companies that violate those rules (adjudication).

When would an agency choose one way of proceeding over the other? The question turns on the nature of the regulatory problem. Suppose an aviation agency is considering how best to assure that all pilots have adequate eyesight. Would it be better to adopt a general rule ("all pilots need 20/20 eyesight") or to proceed against individual pilots whose eyesight is problematic?

If the agency has had enough experience with the problem to have developed some confident views about the appropriate level, rulemaking has some great advantages. It can be quick, it can be comprehensive, it can be fair (applied consistently to all pilots), it can give the entire industry the opportunity to participate by commenting on the proposed rule and, since the rule would apply only from the date of promulgation, it can avoid any problems of retroactivity. And a rule may be easier to enforce; if the rule sets the standard for eyesight at 20/20, it can be enforced against a pilot merely by showing the pilot's eyesight is not 20/20; no showing of reduced air safety by reason of the pilot's vision need be shown.

On the other hand, if the agency has not had much experience with the subject, it may not be ready yet to adopt a general rule, and may prefer to decide claims of inadequate pilot eyesight on a case-by-case basis until some more general knowledge and experience is accumulated. Or, it may be that variations in individual circumstances are such that the problem is one that is not suitable for disposition by a general rule.

If under some logic of this sort the agency decides to proceed against a pilot only by adjudication, the agency will be required to show that the pilot's eyesight has implications for air safety (or whatever general statutory standard the agency is enforcing). This may make the agency's case more difficult and may benefit the pilot who is free to show special circumstances that make his or her eyesight perfectly acceptable. But the tradeoff is that the pilot may be faced at the end with what is essentially a retroactive decision — an agency decision against him applying a principle that couldn't have been foreseen.

Courts have generally permitted agencies freedom to choose whether to proceed through rulemaking or adjudication, though it is very clear from the opinions that courts are aware of the benefits of proceeding by general rule. An occasional state statute requires agencies to proceed by rulemaking because of the fair notice it gives all, and some states encourage (but don't require) rulemaking where it is feasible.

C.   Rulemaking Procedure

In important senses, a properly issued agency rule has the same force of law as a statute passed by the legislature. In practical terms, this means that one charged with violating the rule can argue that it doesn't apply to him or her or that he or she did not in fact violate it. But, as with legislation generally, all arguments about the wisdom of the rule have been foreclosed by the rulemaking process. Let's take a look at the procedures usually required before an agency can issue a rule with this powerful effect.

1.   Constitutional Requirements

As usual, we begin with questions of constitutional requirements, then look at statutory, regulatory, and judicially imposed requirements. The constitutional requirements are not onerous. As we have seen, due process does not entitle a citizen to any special opportunity to participate in the formulation of an agency rule, any more than it requires a legislature to give citizens a hearing before legislation is passed. So long as the measure applies to groups or classes — as most legislative-type action does — the U.S. Supreme Court has long held that the impracticality of giving all affected citizens hearing rights argues against such a principle. And even beyond the impracticality argument, it is probably true that the policy issues disputed in a legislative-type proceeding may not be suited for resolution by the sort of trial-type hearings we usually think of when we talk of adjudications.

2.   Statutory Requirements

Congress has prescribed important minimum procedural requirements for rulemaking by federal agencies. The most generally applicable are the provisions of section 553 of the Administrative Procedure Act (APA). Section 553 describes what we call "notice and comment" rulemaking. Subject to some exceptions (for rules concerning military, foreign affairs, and internal matters), section 553 provides that an agency publish in the Federal Register the gist or the text of a proposed rule, including enough detail to enable citizens to determine if such a rule would affect them. By judicial interpretation, this requirement for notice has been expanded to require agencies to disclose important studies, reports, and other research which was considered by the agency in formulating the rule. Today, most agencies publish a full draft of a proposed rule for citizen comment.

Citizens are then entitled to submit written comment on the proposal. After the close of the comment period, the agency is required to "consider" (but not necessarily "follow") these comments in its decision on the final rule issued.

In issuing the rule, the agency is required by the APA to include a concise general statement explaining the purpose of the rule. By judicial interpretation of this requirement, agencies are today required to respond to major comment received during the comment period which was not followed in formulating the final rule. As we will see in Part VI below, courts today require that in this general statement, the agency must explain clearly the rationale of the rule.

Today, much of this public comment on rules is done electronically. The reader can easily access the process by going to www.regulations.gov, where hundreds of pending proposed rules can be seen and where one can comment quickly and efficiently.

3. Other Rulemaking Procedure Requirements

It has turned out that agency rulemaking has been so pervasive and so intensive that Congress and the President have added some procedural requirements to the process beyond what is required by the APA. These additional requirements need to be examined by the lawyer interested in affecting a rulemaking process on behalf of a client. A number of statutes require that agencies adequately consider the impacts of their rules on special parties or situations (i.e., on the environment, on small business, etc.). Other laws and executive orders seek assurance that the product of agency rulemaking is adequately coordinated, is appropriately reflective of executive branch views, and is likely to produce benefits that exceed costs.

Beyond the APA and these supplementing statutes, remember that any procedural rules the agency itself has adopted must be complied with.

D. Interpretive Rules and Policy Statements

Some rules issued by agencies are expressions of agency opinion rather than being strictly regulatory. Interpretive rules and policy statements may be in various forms: rule-like documents, letters, manuals, etc. They are expressions of agency views on questions of policy and law and thereby provide important guidance to regulated parties and to agency staff. They are very valuable components of the process.

There is no statutory requirement that interpretive rules and policy statements be the subject of public comment before being issued, but they must be published when complete. Because these rules are not issued pursuant to the agency's rulemaking authority, and since they have not gone through the public comment process, they are said not to have the "force of law." But they may have great practical impact on regulated parties who, learning of an agency's interpretation of an agency statute, may have to alter their practices to avoid later agency prosecution. How to encourage agencies to give this kind of advice without depriving those affected of an opportunity to participate in their formulation is a continuing puzzle in the administrative law field. Recent executive branch orders have sought to increase public involvement in the formulation of significant guidance documents of this sort, to improve public access to them and to bolster their reliability.

IV ADJUDICATION

Turning to the other characteristic activity of the administrative process, let's consider adjudication. This may be more familiar to many of us because, in some sense, adjudication resembles what courts do.

A.   Is a Formal Hearing Required?

To determine what the Constitution or statutes may require in the way of adjudicative procedure, we need first to be sure we are dealing with an adjudication. The word "adjudication" can apply to a broad range of proceedings, sharing little in common except that they usually concern named, specific individuals, and have the task of determining the legal effect of certain past conduct and events. In our example above, this is the process by which we resolve the dispute between Mr. Green, the pilot, and aviation agency about the quality of Mr. Green's eyesight.

Section 551(7) of the APA Act defines adjudication as any final disposition of an agency "in a matter other than rulemaking but including licensing." So we essentially have to go back to our rulemaking definition. In our discussion of rulemaking, we said that the basic rulemaking definition involved statements of general applicability, and this case doesn't seem to fit that definition; it involves only Mr. Green. So we can conclude that the proceeding is not rulemaking. Hence, it must be adjudication.

Of course, there are many agency actions that are not within the definition of rules which cannot be adjudications in any reasonable sense (e.g., agency investigations, agency research projects, etc.). But in the case of Mr. Green, the adjudication concept seems to fit tolerably well — we need something like a judicial trial to hear evidence from the agency and from Green which will enable us to resolve the dispute.

How much formal process is Green entitled to? As we have seen in Section II, above, the Due Process Clause of the Constitution lays down some minimum requirements. We need to look further to see whether statutes or agency rules have added to these minima. Again, the most comprehensive, basic statute to look at is the APA. The APA doesn't itself require any particular adjudicative procedures, but it does provide a set of procedures which must be used if *another* statute calls for a formal hearing. In the language of section 554, the formal hearing provisions of the Act apply to "every case of adjudication required by statute to be determined on the record after opportunity for an agency hearing." The phrase "on the record" is lawyer-speak for a hearing resembling a trial in which the outcome must be based on evidence in the hearing record. (Contrast that with the rulemaking provisions of the Act which, as described above, require an agency to "consider" but not necessarily to follow comment from those affected by the proposed rule.)

This sends us to the aviation agency's statute which authorizes the agency to revoke licenses, and our question is, does this statute require a hearing "on the record"? Congress has not always been careful in its drafting of authorizations to engage in adjudications. If it were careful, it would specify whether a hearing "on the record" was to be required. But many such authorizations sometimes say nothing about hearings. Sometimes, they say only that a "hearing" is required without specifying its nature. For all we know, the legislative use of the word "hearing" may have been a reference to a public meeting or a legislative sort of hearing.

The courts have struggled mightily with this issue. For our purposes, let us summarize by saying that formality is not to be lightly assumed. Unless the legislature uses the specific "on the record" language in describing the hearing required, the agency will have considerable discretion to choose an appropriate procedure. If the agency is free under its own rules to choose an informal approach (i.e., a hearing short of APA requirements), many courts will defer to that agency judgment, provided always, of course, that constitutional minimum procedures are provided.

If the agency is allowed to proceed informally, there is little in the APA of relevance. Section 555 does include some general matters about appearances, representation and the need for some brief explanation of the agency action but beyond that, it is silent.

B.   What Procedures Must Be Provided in a Formal Hearing?

If the statute says (or is interpreted to say) that the hearing is to be on the record, the formal requirements of APA sections 556 and 557 will control. An ideal formal adjudicatory hearing would include measures to insure *accuracy* in fact finding, appropriate opportunity of those affected to *participate* in the decision, and impartiality and *objectivity* in the resolution of the dispute. Most of the provisions of sections 556 and 557 have these objectives in mind.

1.   The Hearing

Perhaps the most important protection in a formal adjudication is that the hearing will usually be presided over by an independent official, not just an ordinary agency employee. In the federal system, this usually means a hearing conducted by an Administrative Law Judge (ALJ). The ALJ is, in some sense, an agency employee, but the ALJ is independent in the sense that the agency does not control the judge's compensation and cannot fire the judge except for cause, which must be established in a separate proceeding before another agency. Importantly, the ALJ is not just a reporter with the task of compiling the record and sending it along to the agency head for decision. The ALJ is a judge in fact not just in name. The APA provides that if no appeal is taken from the decision of the ALJ, it becomes the agency's decision.

Like a judge in a normal judicial proceeding, the ALJ will have power to control the hearing, to issue subpoenas, to receive evidence, to take depositions, to dispose of procedural requests, and, finally, to make the initial decision in the case. The judge's initial decision must include findings of fact and conclusions of law with respect to all issues in the case, as well as rulings on any exceptions presented by the parties.

Section 556 includes provisions on technical, legal matters such as who has the burden of proof (usually the proponent of any assertion has that burden), what kind of evidence can be received (more liberal than the rules of evidence in judicial trials since there is no jury present in administrative hearings), when oral presentations are required (usually, unless the proceeding is formal rulemaking or initial licensing, when written submissions may be sufficient), when cross examination is required (when necessary for full disclosure), and the quality of evidence needed to support an order ("reliable, probative, and substantial evidence").

The section requires that all the testimony and exhibits constitute the exclusive record for decision — the essence of the "on the record" requirement discussed earlier. This means that the facts an agency uses to support its conclusion must have been admitted into the hearing and thus tested by cross-examination and rebuttal if needed.

2.   Internal Appeals

Where an appeal is taken from an initial ALJ decision (by a disappointed party or by disappointed agency prosecutors), the case will usually be heard by the head of the agency sitting in an appellate role. Usually that means the case will be submitted on briefs and oral argument, without the necessity of hearing the witnesses again.

Are the findings and conclusions of the ALJ binding on the agency head? The general answer is, no. APA section 557 is quite clear that on appeal, the agency has "all the powers which it would have in making the initial decision." This clearly means that the agency is not bound by ALJ conclusions of *law* or *policy*, and is accordingly free to substitute its views for that of the ALJ. While this bothers some lawyers representing private persons in agency hearings, it is consistent with the concept that politically accountable agency heads (not independent ALJs) should have the final power to set agency policy.

What about the ALJ's findings of *fact*? The APA makes no distinction, so the agency is technically free to overrule the ALJ on factual issues — perhaps subject, as we'll see, to some later judicial evaluation of the overall agency performance in the case. Some courts have imposed a weak requirement that an agency cannot wholly ignore findings based on "demeanor" evidence — evidence the fact finder can get from seeing and hearing the witness as contrasted with reading the testimony in the record. The notion is (some call it a fiction) that the ALJ's opportunity to see and hear the witness gives his findings of fact some special weight that should not be wholly ignored by the agency.

3.   Protecting the Integrity of the Process

A clear implication of the exclusive record requirement is that the decision should not be influenced by communications between the ALJ or other agency decisional officials and third persons outside the hearing and hence without knowledge of the parties. But communications from third persons may be important. For example, if an ALJ wants to confirm technical details with experts in the agency, may he contact them outside the hearing? If the agency head (on an internal appeal) needs some technical information to better understand the implications of the decision, may he privately contact agency experts? If public officials outside the agency want to insure that the decision is politically acceptable, may they communicate with those in the agency who are deciding the case? If the exclusive record notion is too strictly interpreted, much may be lost in terms of agency expertise and in terms of agency political accountability.

The APA provisions regulating ex parte communications (i.e., communications not made in the presence of the parties) are difficult to parse, as they must seek to limit the most distorting forms of these communications without totally shutting the door to any communication at all. Consider communications from within the agency. Subject to some exceptions, section 554 says the ALJ may not "consult a person or party on a fact in issue" unless all parties are present. That apparently leaves the ALJ free to consult on any matter that is not a "fact in issue" (e.g., a matter of enforcement policy). Further, seeking to insulate the ALJ from any communication with agency employees thought to have too committed a mind-set to be objective, the section prohibits agency personnel engaged in investigation and prosecuting functions in the case (or related cases) from participating or advising in the case at any stage, except as witnesses in public proceedings.

As to communications from outside the agency, section 557 prohibits an "interested person" from contacting the ALJ or any agency employees involved in the proceeding if the ex parte communication is "relevant to the merits of the proceeding." This prohibition seems to make sense with respect to efforts of private parties to influence the outcome in the case. But what about communications from public agencies or officials? Suppose the President wants to remind the person he has appointed to head the agency of some important policy? Suppose a member of Congress with oversight responsibility wants to be sure the agency understands the intent of Congress when they authorized the action? In such cases, we have a direct conflict between the values of fairness (which would prohibit the communication) and accountability (which might require it).

The courts have not settled all these issues, but it seems safe to bet that outside communications from public officials — even those with legitimate public interest in the proceedings — should not be allowed to deprive the parties of the opportunity to know the full case against them and to have an appropriate opportunity to respond. Due process may even be called into service in an especially egregious case. There are ample opportunities for the President and the Congress to communicate policy preferences to agencies without contaminating formal adjudications.

A final complexity is the problem of remedy. Suppose a violation of an ex parte prohibition in a case in which the government is seeking to terminate the license of airline pilot Green for alleged incompetence. Imagine a phone call from the president to the head of the FAA (who serves at the pleasure of the president), the communication suggesting that a finding in favor of pilot Green will set a bad policy and could cost the agency head her job. If we grant the impropriety of the communication, what remedy seems useful? We can hardly tell the agency head to forget the presidential message and proceed as if she hadn't heard it. And we can hardly conclude that the contamination so infects the agency proceeding that the case against Green must be dismissed, like we might dismiss a criminal case tainted by illegally seized evidence. That would leave Green in the cockpit of a commercial airliner in spite of our concern with his eyesight. These difficulties led the drafters of the APA to limit themselves to rather mild sanctions for violations of the ex parte rules. Basically, improper communications must be put into the record, and parties affected must be allowed to respond to them.

Practitioners in this field also must remember that agency rules may be much stricter than the APA in these matters. And for a company facing continuing regulation by the agency, violating agency rules today — even if the sanction may not seem too serious — may earn a party the ill will of the agency, which could be very costly in one's dealing with the agency in the future.

V.   AVAILABILITY OF JUDICIAL REVIEW

As we have seen in Section II, above, it is central to the constitutional legitimacy of the administrative process that judicial review be generally available to test the validity of agency action. It is one of the functions of the judicial branch in our system to assure that the agencies stay within the boundaries set for them by the Constitution or by action of elected representatives and, within those boundaries, that agency action is reasonable, somehow defined. But this commitment to the rule of law does not mean that courts are available to review all issues, at the instance of all persons, and at all times.

A series of largely judge-made rules limits judicial review so as to avoid undue interference with agency discretion, to assure that issues presented are appropriate for judicial resolution, to conserve judicial resources, and sometimes for other countervailing reasons (e.g., national defense). We will briefly summarize these doctrines by asking *what* agency action can be reviewed, *who* can seek review, and *when* review can be obtained.

A.   What Agency Action Can Be Reviewed?

Since U.S. federal courts can only act if they have statutory authority to do so, the person seeking judicial review must find some statutory foundation for the review sought. Usually, this is not a serious problem. Statutes either provide specific jurisdiction to review particular agency action, or, for agency action not so identified, there are statutory provisions granting jurisdiction to the federal courts to consider cases "arising under" federal laws — a standard not difficult to meet in a case challenging federal agency action.

1.   Preclusion of Judicial Review

The courts have often stated that there is a presumption of reviewability, which means that in most cases review is available. Presumptions can, of course, be overcome. One way to overcome the presumption is for the legislature, in aid of some policy it thinks important, to preclude, limit, or postpone judicial review.

For example, at one time, Congress felt that judicial review of agency decisions about veteran's benefits would be intrusive and complicating and that the Veterans Department itself could be relied on to make fair and prompt decisions without imposing on veterans the need for costly and drawn out legal proceedings. Congress provided (in a statute now repealed) that Department decisions on benefits "shall be final and conclusive and no . . . court of the United States shall have . . . jurisdiction to review any such decision. . . ." Another example is in the Selective Service area, where Congress felt that pre-induction judicial review of military draft classifications could interfere with rapid buildup of necessary military forces. Courts have not treated such statutes generously. For example, while these two statutes have been upheld, they do not usually preclude review of veterans benefits and selective service cases which raise constitutional issues.

As this text is being written, the law is in flux. Courts are considering various forms of preclusion seeking to limit judicial review of action involving suspected terrorists. Some new law may be emerging here in the near future.

2.   Commitment to Agency Discretion

Sometimes the agency action is so inherently discretionary that there does not seem to be anything for a court to review. In the language of the APA, review is not available if a matter has been "committed to agency discretion by law." For example, if a statute authorizes an agency head to act "when he deems it necessary or advisable" there would appear to be little point in judicial review; agency action cannot be tested against any standard or principle — there is no "law to apply."

Courts have generally respected such statutes, but again, they only narrow — do not preclude — all review. The courts have looked hard for objective standards by which agency action could be tested. A complaint that the agency head deemed it "necessary or advisable to" take action which violated a person's First Amendment rights would be reviewable, as the Amendment itself is "law to apply." And a statute authorizing an agency, in its discretion, to select a highway location through a park after considering alternatives and planning to minimize damage to the park did not commit the choice wholly to agency discretion as the court could still examine whether alternatives had in fact been considered and whether planning to minimize impacts had in fact taken place. Failing such standards, however, the courts generally respect the wish of Congress that agency discretion be exercised without undue interference by the courts.

3.   Review of Agency Refusals to Act

Sometimes courts are asked to review an agency's failure or refusal to act. Such cases are especially difficult, as a decision not to act may reflect an agency judgment about priorities and how it wishes to allocate its scarce resources among those priorities — surely such agency choices deserve great respect and should not often be subjected to second guessing by courts.

Responding to such concerns, the courts have held that there is a presumption of *un*reviewability for some cases of agency failure to act. The exact contours of the presumption are not clear, however. Decisions of an agency not to prosecute a case, e.g., will very seldom be reviewed by courts. Beyond such clear cases, there is judicial language suggesting that a court could review an agency's failure to act in the face of a statute commanding (not just authorizing) the action or in cases where the failure to act represents an abdication of the agency's responsibility. And the Supreme Court in 2007 held reviewable an agency decision not to initiate a rulemaking proceeding in response to a petition. This is another area where the law is still developing.

B.   Who Can Seek Judicial Review?

If judicial review is in fact one guarantor of lawful agency action, it might seem odd that there should be any limits on who can seek review. After all, if an agency is acting illegally, shouldn't any citizen interested in (and willing bear the considerable expense of) bringing the agency to book be permitted to invoke the judicial power?

However logical that may seem, the fact is there are important limits on who can qualify as plaintiffs in suits to review administrative action — the judicially created doctrine of "standing" outlines what those limits are.

Of course, when the agency acts directly against the plaintiff (e.g., revokes pilot Green's license) serious standing issues don't arise. Plaintiff is injured, the injury is caused by the action challenged, and victory for the plaintiff will redress the injury. But in an era where governmental action can have broad ramifications and can affect many (think of the impact of economic rulings, environmental measures, or social welfare programs), challenges will often face standing obstacles. And because so much is at stake in policy and practical terms, the law of standing has been one of the most difficult to describe with any certainty.

There are two basic reasons for the standing requirements — one having to do with the nature of agencies, and a second having to do with the nature of our courts. *First*, the range of persons qualified to challenge governmental action can have dramatic policy implications (to what groups must an agency be responsive?) and substantial practical effects (how many judicial challenges is an agency staffed to meet?). Standing doctrine seeks to provide workable limits on the nature and number of these challenges.

Second, our judicial system grew out of a system of common law courts to whom private parties presented concrete personal disputes for resolution. Judicial mechanisms are best suited for such issues, are less effective for resolving far-reaching generalized complaints about action that affects many. Standing doctrine tends to favor plaintiffs who, like common law suitors, have concrete personal disputes with another individual or organization.

For a variety of such reasons, Article III of the U.S. Constitution (which limits the judicial power to resolving "cases and controversies") has been interpreted by the courts over the years to lay down three requirements: (1) the plaintiff must himself or herself be individually and concretely injured by the agency action challenged; (2) the plaintiff's injury must be caused by the agency action; and (3) and the injury must be redressable by a judicial decree in the case. And since these are laid down as matters of constitutional interpretation, the ability of the Congress to alter them is limited.

The courts have troubled over such matters as how direct and how imminent the injury must be; whether it matters that many, many others also suffer the same injury from the agency action (courts are reluctant to entertain what they call "generalized grievances"); when is an injury sufficiently connected to agency action that one can say the action caused the injury; when will victory for the plaintiff truly redress the injury; and how far can Congress go in so-called citizen-suit provisions (which authorize "any citizen" to bring actions against allegedly unlawful agency action) before it crosses a line forbidden by Article III. Needless to say, there are no simple answers here nor, outside the easy cases, are there many predictable answers. The reader can only take the three basic constitutional conditions for standing (injury, causation, and redressability) as the starting, not ending points of standing analysis.

C.   When Can Review Be Obtained?

Repeated judicial intrusion into ongoing agency proceedings would be inefficient — the issues might not be clarified yet, and the parties may succeed in internal appeal opportunities, obviating judicial review altogether. Before all that work is finished, of course, interlocutory rulings and developments may sometimes have significant, immediate impacts on parties. In recognition of this, there are several doctrines which seek to affect the timing of judicial review. The three principal doctrines are finality, exhaustion of administrative remedies, and ripeness. These doctrines overlap, and courts sometimes use them interchangeably. They all seek to allow the agency to finish its work before a court is asked to review the legality of the work. But where a justiciable issue can be carved out of a proceeding and an early court ruling can, as a practical matter, avoid an injustice, the three doctrines may give way and permit early review. But it is an uphill battle in federal courts. Let's look at each of the three doctrines.

1.   Finality

A requirement that agency action be final before it is reviewable makes obvious sense, but in the administrative world, many agency actions may be final in the sense of incorporating a completed agency judgment on a matter — and thus potentially have practical impact on the behavior of regulated parties — yet are not contained in the usual formal dress (rule or order) we call "final." This might be because the formalizing process is still under way (the agency has issued a complaint against a party as a first step in formal process), because the agency judgment will never appear in formal dress (e.g. interpretive rules or policy statements with wide impact will never be "final" in the sense of being promulgated rules), or because the agency decision is a decision not to act.

The case law in this area is difficult to summarize, but there is an unmistakable judicial reluctance to review non-final agency action. The courts have granted review to completed but not formalized agency action only where there is a credible showing that the action does, in fact, incorporate a final agency judgment of the agency's top officials, that the judgment will be relied on by the agency in its regulatory work, and when early judicial review seems an efficient way to resolve the matter before harm is done.

2.   Exhaustion of Administrative Remedies

This doctrine (developed by the courts, but sometimes appearing in statutory form) tells a party complaining of agency action that the complaints must first be presented to the agency; if there are agency remedies available (e.g., internal appeals), they must be exhausted before judicial review is sought. While this might seem like just another version of finality, it has been singled out for separate statement by the courts. The classic example: a company is charged by an agency with violating one of the agency's rules, and the company believes the agency has no jurisdiction over it. Can the company get a court to rule on the jurisdictional issue in advance of what may be a long and expensive agency proceeding? An appealing argument, no doubt, but generally this is an unsuccessful one. In working with agency decisions, courts do not see themselves as deciders so much as reviewers. As such, courts want the benefit of agency fact finding and the use of agency expertise before they are called upon to resolve the dispute. And there is an efficiency argument, too — there is always the possibility that the company will prevail before the agency and save the court the trouble of any review at all.

Like most common law rules, of course, there are exceptions. First, the agency must require exhaustion (and stay the effective date of the action while the remedy is being exhausted). Secondly, there are the rare cases where (a) the impact on the parties of delaying review is especially severe (think prison sentences), (b) the issue presented can be resolved by the court without agency fact finding or expertise (e.g., plaintiff presents a "pure" question of law), or (c) plaintiff persuades a court that the agency's mind is so firmly made up that further internal appeal is futile. In such cases, an occasional court might permit a party to obtain judicial review even though there are agency remedies that have not been exhausted. Federal courts do not favor these exceptions, however; exhaustion is usually required.

3.   Ripeness

As we have seen our discussion of standing, in a system of judicial institutions built on a common law foundations, one might expect courts to be leery of working with cases which have not come to focus in a concrete controversy, with all the details and specificity that informs common law dispute resolution. A common problem is seeking to get judicial review of a promulgated but as yet unenforced agency rule. There is no finality issue here since, as published, the rule is as final as it's going to get. Nor is there an exhaustion issue as there are no likely remedies to exhaust. The impact of an unenforced rule could be substantial, as regulated parties may need to take drastic or expensive action to avoid prosecution should the agency decide to enforce the rule. But in advance of enforcement in a particular case, the issues may lack the concrete specificity the common law system relies on for careful analysis. Should a court nevertheless review the rule in advance of its enforcement?

The doctrine properly used here is the doctrine of "Ripeness." The courts have sometimes been sensitive to the practical impact of an unenforced rule and have attempted to balance the hardship to the parties against the practical needs of the judicial enterprise. For example, in a 1967 foundation case, the Supreme Court held an as yet unenforced rule could be reviewed at least for facial validity. The Court said preenforcement review was appropriate since regulated parties would either have to go to great expense to comply with the rule that they thought illegal or to risk very serious penalties if they didn't comply and ultimately lost their argument about the rule's validity. Since plaintiff's claim raised a "pure legal issue," review at this time was appropriate.

This decision has had a major impact on the administrative process. It has vastly increased the number of rules that are subject to judicial review. As the number and size of these proceedings continues to grow, there are some signs of dissatisfaction with a liberal ripeness doctrine. However it turns out, it seems safe to guess that the Supreme Court is not likely to increase further the generosity of today's ripeness doctrine.

VI. SCOPE OF JUDICIAL REVIEW

Assuming a plaintiff has surmounted all of these obstacles to judicial review, what attitude should a court bring to the process of reviewing agency action? Consider two possibilities:

> **Judge A.** "I believe judicial review should be highly deferential. Congress has conferred power on this agency to decide this case initially, and Congress is an elected, accountable body. As a judge, I am not accountable in that sense. Moreover, I do not possess the expertise that may lie within the agency members and its staff. So as long as the agency has followed the congressionally prescribed procedures and has come up with a result that is not totally zany, I feel I must affirm the agency. A high level of judicial

deference is thus the correct stance in aid of both legitimacy and competency."

Judge B. "In a society premised on the rule of law, agency action which is to have the effect of law must be carefully examined to insure it is lawful in a full sense. That means two things. *First*, the agency must have fully, not just nominally, complied with required procedures (e.g., in rulemaking, the agency should not only publish the proposed rule but in addition should disclose any reports and studies that it relied on in preparing the proposal). *Second*, the outcome must be both fully explained and rational to insure that the result is law and not mere politics appearing in the guise of expertise. I concede that this approach gives unelected judges some ability to second guess the agency on policy questions, but on most of those questions, Congress can always have the last word if it chooses."

As you can see, these two judicial attitudes towards review are very different, and the differences can have very serious consequences in the power allocation among the various branches of government. The attitude of Judge A expands the power of the executive and legislative branches, while the attitude of Judge B expands the power of the judicial branch. Whenever significant shifts of power from one branch to the other are produced by using different standards — standards inevitably expressed in words — you can expect fierce political battles to erupt over the words chosen to express the standards. That has been the fate of the verbal formulas which attempt to describe the appropriate intensity or scope of judicial review of agency action.

Let's look at some of these verbal formulas and see if we can get a feel for their meaning. To begin, you might think of scope of review as being a spectrum — we could call it the Intensity Spectrum. At one end — the low intensity end (where Judge A would feel most comfortable), we'll put formulas that suggest that a court should be highly deferential to agency views. At the other end — the high intensity end (where Judge B might feel most comfortable), we'll put formulas that suggest that a court can more freely substitute its view for that of the agency. Between these extreme places on the spectrum, there are various middle levels of intensity.

How does a judge determine the correct place on the intensity spectrum? The judge first looks for statutory guidance, as most judicial review statutes will include a formula identifying in a general way what the correct level of intensity is. While these statutory formulas are not crystal clear, they are words and phrases which have accumulated some general and roughly predictable meanings over the years. For example, statutory words like "de novo" signal the most intensive form of review: the judge simply decides the case according to his or her own view of the matter with no deference to the agency's view. At the least intensive end of the spectrum, by contrast, words like "minimum rationality" signal that an agency rule or order is to be accepted by the court if any conceivable rational basis can be found to support it.

In the middle of the spectrum is where the battles have been fought. Let's examine three of the typical agency actions that are subject to judicial review and see what formulas are in use.

A.　　　Reviewing Agency Factual Determinations

The APA says that if a court is reviewing a formal adjudication and the factual sufficiency of the agency's order is challenged, the judge is to see if the agency fact findings are supported in the record by something called "substantial evidence."

Well, that phrase alone doesn't tell a judge what to do, does it? But there are many cases in which the phrase has been explained and applied and the short summary of all this discussion is that "substantial evidence" exists when the judge finds that a reasoning person starting from the evidence in the record could have reached the fact findings the agency reached. That is, the judge is not supposed to see if the agency's fact findings are correct, only that they are reasoned in this sense. So we can place the "substantial evidence" test somewhere in the middle of our intensity spectrum.

Can a judge really distinguish between reasonableness and correctness? That is, can you imagine a judge saying, "Well, I wouldn't have made these findings on the basis of what is in this record, but a reasoning person could have done so, so I will affirm the agency"? Judges seldom talk that way, but in fact, in the common law system, a judge frequently has to make that distinction — as in reviewing jury verdicts, for example. So we assume it can be done.

B.   Reviewing Agency Determinations of Policy and Exercises of Discretion

The substantial evidence test seems to fit review of agency resolution of factual disputes, since the formula refers to evidence. Suppose there are no disputed facts, but the agency, as matter of policy or as an exercise of discretion, arrives at a conclusion that is challenged. Suppose all agree that, in this day of sophisticated airplane cockpit displays, 20/30 eyesight is comparable to 20/20. Nevertheless, the agency rule requires 20/20 eyesight, explaining that, as a matter of policy, passengers are entitled to an extra margin of safety. If the rule is challenged on judicial review, how intensive should the review be?

The APA says that when the court is reviewing something other than a formal adjudication, the court should "set aside agency action . . . found to be arbitrary, capricious, [or] an abuse of agency discretion." Again, those words do not carry a very fixed meaning, but over the years, some significant meaning has been imputed to them by judicial explanations and applications. In the 1930s, the Supreme Court found this test very deferential — agency rules were given the same presumption of correctness as statutes passed by Congress — meaning that they would be upheld if there was any conceivable rationale in their support. But by the 1970s, the Court was using words suggesting that more intensive review was contemplated by the test. The Court said the test required review that was "thorough," "probing," and "searching." Lower courts have said the judge's job in applying the "arbitrary and capricious test" was to insure that the agency took a "hard look" at the problem it was working with.

As of today, then, the arbitrary capricious test has moved up toward the middle of the intensity scale. Under the test, a judge must examine the agency product and affirm it if it is adequately explained, involves no errors of judgment, shows no significant gaps in reasoning, takes into consideration the factors Congress wanted considered, and avoids the use of improper factors. Those who like counting the number of angels that can fit on the head of a pin enjoy speculating on whether the arbitrary capricious test is more or less intensive than the substantial evidence test. But the better thinking is they are apples and oranges — different tests for reviewing different kinds of agency action.

C.   Reviewing Agency Legal Interpretations

Finally, what is the correct formula when a judge is asked to review not an agency finding of fact or a determination of policy but instead an agency's legal determination? For example, the agency argues that under its interpretation of its statute, the rule or order challenged is perfectly valid. Here, we have a complex problem. On the one hand, a two hundred year old tradition affirms that however we allocate the power to decide various types of issues, it is the duty of courts to decide questions of law. And the APA says courts "shall decide all relevant questions of law, and interpret constitutional and statutory provisions." Taken at face value, these statements would suggest that judicial review of agency law interpretation would be at its most intense, with the judge making the decision with little or no deference to agency views.

On the other hand, that position hasn't always felt comfortable for many judges. After all, as Judge A in this section's opening paragraphs indicated, Congress empowered the agency to act under the statute, and surely Congress understood that embedded in *any* agency application of its statute is an interpretation of that statute. So empowering an agency to apply the statute must have contained an implicit authority to interpret it. Shouldn't judges recognize the rather plain legislative signal that agency legal interpretations are entitled to significant judicial respect?

Moreover, it is not always easy to tell a finding of fact from a conclusion of law. How would you characterize an aviation agency's determination that Pilot Green did not meet the statutory standard of "medically qualified"? A finding of fact as to Green's eyesight as to which deference might be appropriate, or a conclusion of law about the meaning of the statutory phrase which tradition says should be decided independently by the judge? Surely, it is in some sense both a factual and a legal determination, and this insight muddies the water considerably.

These complications have produced unruly and not always dependable doctrine. Courts give generous and frequent lip service to a formula derived from a famous 1984 Supreme Court case (*Chevron*): if the statute is ambiguous — does not clearly reveal its own meaning on the issue to be decided — reasonable agency interpretations of the statute must be accepted by the reviewing court. On the other hand, if the statute is clear, the court will apply it as written, ignoring any contrary agency interpretation.

The *Chevron* doctrine is an acceptable starting point; it does recognize the propriety of some judicial deference to agency legal interpretations. But the formula is only a starting point. Its impact on a particular case will be hard to predict because of the considerable uncertainties in the language used to state the standard. For example, does the test apply to all agency legal interpretations or just those implicit in notice and comment rulemaking and formal adjudications? How is a judge to decide when a statute is ambiguous enough to warrant deference? (What guidance does a lower court take from a five-to-four Supreme Court decision that a statute is ambiguous, or not ambiguous?) If the reviewing court finds the statute ambiguous enough to require deference to a reasonable agency interpretation, when are agency interpretations reasonable? The plain fact is, *Chevron* probably raises as many questions as it answers. Certainly, it leaves the reviewing court with a wide range of discretion about whether and to what extent to defer.

It is probably safe to predict significant judicial deference to agency legal interpretations in cases where the interpretations are authoritative (i.e., accepted by the highest levels of agency officials), where the interpretation is informed by relevant agency expertise, and where there is evidence of care in the agency's formulation of the interpretation. On the other hand, expect less deference when these conditions are absent, when the legal question is of the sort courts deal with routinely, or — as with interpretations of broad statutory terms or constitutional provisions — the interpretation has impacts beyond the responsibilities of the acting agency.

VII. CONCLUSION

The legal foundations of the U.S. administrative process are not tidy. They are a complex of measures, made up of explicitly adopted legal terms, provisional arrangements, innovative structures, creative settlements, historical accidents, and political compromises — all developed within an insistent, pragmatic concern that the system must work today and must continue to work tomorrow. At a very high level of abstraction, what is suggested in this chapter can be summed up in the following sentence. Take it home.

If in compliance with relevant procedural requirements, an administrative agency is permitted to exercise executive, legislative, and judicial powers, with the understanding that this exercise is subject to selective control by the executive, plenary control by the legislature and — when judicially reviewable issues are timely presented by appropriate parties — measured judicial evaluations of the factual and legal bases of the agency action.

Chapter 16

CHOICE OF LAW & ENFORCEMENT OF JUDGMENTS

By — Michael S. Finch

I. INTRODUCTION

In the United States, there are more than fifty independent legal systems or "jurisdictions." They include the United States as well as the fifty individual states. Each jurisdiction has independent power to make laws and to enforce those laws through its courts. But whose law applies when a legal dispute involves parties or events from *two* jurisdictions? The subject called "choice of law" addresses this and related questions.

Choice of law can easily become confusing, because it involves many abstract concepts. We will try to lessen the confusion by examining choice of law in the context of a hypothetical legal dispute. Consider the following fictionalized but realistic dispute between two friends:

Lily and Chloe are friends who live in Tampa, Florida. In the spring of 2008, Lily invited Chloe to attend a harp festival in Atlanta, Georgia. Chloe, an accomplished harpist, gladly accepted the invitation. Lily explained excitedly that her father, Mr. Michelson, had agreed to loan his new car for the trip.

The young women attended the festival in Georgia and then began their return trip to Florida. In southern Georgia, they encountered a fierce thunder storm, and Lily lost control of the car on a rain-slickened highway. The car struck a bridge abutment resulting in injuries to both women.

Chloe has now retained a Georgia lawyer to file suit in a Georgia state court located near the accident scene. Chloe's lawyer decides to name as defendants (1) Lily and (2) Mr. Michelson. At this point, choice-of-law problems enter into the litigation.

Chloe asserts that Mr. Michelson is responsible for Lily's negligent driving because, under *Florida* law, a car owner is liable for the negligence of any person to whom he entrusts his car. Mr. Michelson disagrees and argues that the law of *Georgia* should apply, because that is where the accident happened. Under Georgia law, an owner is not liable for the negligence of persons who use his automobile.

The defendants also argue that Georgia law should apply to determine the consequences of Chloe's own failure to wear her seatbelt at the time of the accident. According to *Georgia* law, Chloe's damages should be reduced because of her negligence. Chloe argues, in response, that *Florida* law should apply. Florida law does not permit reduction of damages based on the victim's failure to wear a seatbelt.

What law should the Georgia court apply — Georgia law or Florida law?

Choice-of-law problems like this one occur increasingly often. Any time events occur in different jurisdictions, or parties come from different jurisdictions, a court may have to choose which jurisdiction's law should govern the dispute. In the twenty-first century, legal disputes regularly involve events or parties in different jurisdictions. Think of the last time you completed some on-line computer transaction like purchasing a book, video, or CD. You likely dealt with a party in another jurisdiction, and probably the item you purchased was shipped from another jurisdiction. If a dispute were to arise from your transaction — say, the item you purchased was damaged while being shipped and the seller refused to replace the item — you might face a choice-of-law question concerning which jurisdiction's law governs the seller's responsibility.

Our main goal in this chapter is to become familiar with some of the principal approaches American courts use to solve choice-of-law questions. We examine these approaches and how they have evolved over time. As we shall learn, despite the growing importance of choice-of-law problems in both national and international litigation, there are usually no straightforward, predictable "rules" to apply. But if we understand some of the important principles courts use in resolving choice-of-law questions, we are in a better position to predict how courts might resolve these questions.

Our second goal is to address a second issue that can arise when two or more jurisdictions are involved in a legal dispute: Once the plaintiff wins a judgment in the courts of one jurisdiction, must courts in other jurisdictions enforce the judgment? For example, if a Nevada casino successfully sues a Texas gambler in a Nevada court for failure to pay a gambling debt, must a Texas court honor the Nevada court's judgment when the casino tries to enforce it by seizing the gambler's assets in Texas? As we shall learn, the answer to this question is simpler than answers to choice-of-law questions. The U.S. Constitution usually *compels* one state court to enforce the judgment of another state court, like it or not. But when states are asked to enforce a judgment coming from the courts of a foreign nation, they retain much greater discretion in deciding whether to enforce the judgment. Likewise, when a state court issues a judgment that is taken abroad for enforcement, foreign nations usually enforce the judgment, or not, in their discretion.

II.   THE NEED FOR CHOICE-OF-LAW RULES

A.   The Setting for Choice-of-Law Problems

Fortunately, courts are not required to resolve choice-of-law problems in routine civil litigation. Why? Because most legal disputes involve parties and events centered in one jurisdiction. For example, it is statistically more likely that two Floridians like Chloe and Lily will have an accident while driving on Florida roads. When local residents are involved in a local accident, no one questions that local state law governs liability issues.

But an appreciable fraction of disputes are not "local." People frequently cross jurisdictional borders by car or plane, and accidents sometimes happen when persons are away from home. Further, much modern business involves parties or events in several jurisdictions. For example, a product may be produced in one state, shipped to another state, sold in yet another state, and eventually used in still another state. Which state's law applies if an injured consumer sues the various businesses that had some involvement with the product? As you can imagine, problems like this have multiplied with globalization of the world's economy. Many important transactions and occurrences today involve several states or nations, whose different laws could be applied to resulting legal disputes.

B.   The Law of the Forum

You might wonder why choice-of-law problems don't have a simple, obvious solution — just apply the law of the jurisdiction where the suit has been *filed*. For example, why doesn't the Georgia court simply apply Georgia law to the suit between Chloe and Lily? After all, Georgia judges are part of the same state government that enacts Georgia tort laws. Shouldn't Georgia judges apply their own forum law, or what is traditionally called *lex fori*?

Actually, most courts *will* apply their own forum law unless some party raises the choice-of-law issue. Even if all the parties are from another jurisdiction, and all events related to a suit occurred in another jurisdiction, courts assume forum law governs the suit unless someone argues differently. This simple solution has an obvious advantage for both the judge and the parties' lawyers, who have been specifically educated to understand forum law (this is required before they are admitted to practice law in the forum state).

But courts have long recognized that it can be unreasonable or unfair to always apply forum law even when a dispute has inter-state elements. Recall from

Chapter Five that plaintiffs usually have the power to select the forum for the lawsuit. If plaintiffs know that whatever forum they select will automatically apply its own law, they can more or less "pick" the law that governs their suits. For example, Chloe knows that Florida law permits her to recover damages from Lily's father because he owns the car Lily was driving. In contrast, Georgia law does not permit her to recover damages from the car owner. If Chloe knows that a forum court will automatically apply its own law, Chloe will sue in Florida so she can recover from Mr. Michelson. Does it seem fair that Chloe gets to *choose* whether Mr. Michelson is liable for Lily's negligence?

There are other problems with the automatic application of forum law. Imagine that, two years before the young women's accident, the Georgia legislature enacted a law requiring that all new cars sold after 2006 have a very expensive, but injury-reducing, air bag system. Car retailers who fail to comply with this requirement are liable for both compensatory and punitive damages. Chloe knows that Mr. Michelson's new car was sold in Florida, which does not require the safer air bag system required by Georgia. So, Chloe decides to sue the Florida car dealership that sold Mr. Michelson his new car in a Georgia court. Under Georgia law, the dealership will be required to pay substantial damages, including punitive damages, for its "negligence" in not selling cars with the safer air bag system.

If a Georgia court applies its air-bag requirement simply because it is forum law, consider the implications. First, is it fair to the Florida dealership? Second, won't Georgia's application of its air-bag requirement tell auto retailers throughout the southeastern United States (and perhaps beyond) they had better comply with Georgia law or risk substantial tort liability if they somehow get named in a Georgia lawsuit? Doesn't this give Georgia the power to regulate auto safety standards well beyond its borders, even though other states like Florida disagree with Georgia's policy?

In sum, automatic application of forum law can have very undesirable consequences for the parties, for persons and businesses in other states, and for the regulatory power of other states. It is consequences like these that give courts a reason to develop choice-of-law principles that permit application of the law of another state.

C.   The Ideal Solution — A "Super" Choice-of-Law Theory

Courts develop choice-of-law theory to rise above parochialism and sometimes apply the law of other jurisdictions. But wouldn't it be better to have a single "super" choice-of-law theory that must be applied by all states? Why doesn't the United States Congress devise such a single, uniform theory? After all, Congress is a "neutral" body that can better weigh all the relevant concerns and announce a choice-of-law theory that works best for all states.

Congress has such a power but has not exercised it. Nor have the states conferred together and voluntarily negotiated a single set of choice-of-law rules to govern all states. Consequently, in the United States, each state must come up with its own choice-of-law rules, based on its own assessment of what is fair and reasonable. This approach contrasts with that in some parts of the world — the European community, for example — where nations have begun cooperating to develop rules to govern disputes that cross national borders.

D.   The Historical Context for American Choice of Law

American courts were not the first to address choice-of-law problems. Such problems were first presented to European courts asked to decide which nation's law to apply when a dispute presented international elements. European legal scholars proposed solutions to these problems, some of which were eventually borrowed by American courts. The subject Americans call "choice of law" is referred to in most of the world as "private international law," reflecting the subject's international origins.

Early American courts often had to address a unique set of problems when choosing what law to apply. As you learned in Chapter Seven, when the United States was formed, its Constitution shared legal power between the new national government and the many state governments. Consequently, disputes heard by American courts could present at least four different "choices" of law:

- a choice between U.S. (federal) law and an American state's law;

- a choice between U.S. law and a foreign nation's law;

- a choice between an American state's law and a foreign nation's law; and,

- a choice between an American state's law and the law of another state.

The choice-of-law problems we focus on in this Chapter are the last two, i.e., when there is a choice to be made between (1) a state's law and (2) the law of another state or a foreign nation. (The first two problems are ultimately resolved based on the United States Constitution, which makes federal law "supreme" to that of any state or foreign nation.)

From the beginning, courts in America had to develop choice-of-law rules with little help from state legislatures. Even today, state legislatures seldom enact choice-of-law rules, and these usually address a limited set of problems. Consequently, most choice-of-law rules are "common law" rules, i.e., rules developed by the courts. This can make a difficult task even harder, as we must sometimes sort through numerous court opinions to construct an understanding of state choice-of-law theory.

We begin our examination of choice-of-law theory by considering an approach that prevailed in American courts for more than a century and still prevails in a minority of state courts — territorialism.

III.   THE TERRITORIALIST APPROACH TO CHOICE OF LAW

Perhaps the essence of what it means to be a state is the power to control conduct within the state's *territorial borders*. We are all familiar with this notion, even if we don't attach the label "territorialism." We know that when we cross state borders we must pay attention the laws of the state we are entering. For example, if the state we are entering requires that we drive with our lights on, or wear a seatbelt, we comply with its law. We intuitively know that, when law enforcement confronts us for failing to comply with local law, it is no defense to argue, "we don't do it that way where I come from!" As the saying goes, "when in Rome, do as the Romans do."

The notion that each state has sovereign control over conduct within its territory is the basis for the first choice-of-law theory to gain dominance in American courts — territorialism. Territorialism takes the idea that a state has the power to regulate conduct within its borders and transforms it into a body of choice-of-law rules. There is also a sophisticated jurisprudence that historically supported territorialist rules, but we leave that for another occasion.

The key to applying territorialist rules is to identify a *critical act or occurrence* that occurred within a state's borders. Each subject of the law usually has its own peculiar critical acts, as we illustrate below. Once you identify *where* that critical act occurred, you have identified which state's law governs legal issues arising from the act. Let's explore this theory by seeing how it applies to several important legal problems.

A.   Tort Problems

The territorialist rule governing torts looks to the *"place of the wrong."* The law of the state where the "wrong" occurred governs (*lex loci delicti*). To simplify, the place of the wrong is usually the place where the plaintiff suffered her injury, which is the "last act" needed to create liability (after all, if the plaintiff suffers no injury, he or she has little reason to be suing). For example, Chloe was injured when Mr. Michelson's car hit a bridge abutment in Georgia. Under the territorialist approach, Georgia law applies to all issues arising from the accident — including whether Mr. Michelson is liable as the car's owner, and whether Chloe's failure to wear a seat belt reduces the damages she can recover.

Application of the "place of the wrong" rule is usually easy, particularly when the plaintiff has suffered some physical injury or property damage. But sometimes the rule is more challenging to apply. For example, what is the place of wrong when a person is defamed by libelous or slanderous statements? Assume the New York Times publishes an article falsely stating that a prominent politician had sex with a prostitute while on vacation in Aruba. What is the place of the wrong? Aruba, where the alleged act occurred? Washington, D.C., where the politician lives? New York, where the article was written and printed? Or some other state?

The traditional answer is that the place of the wrong is *any* place where the libelous statement was "communicated." This is based on the concept that the defamed person suffers a "wrong" each time a person hears or reads a defamatory statement, thus injuring the defamed person's reputation with the listener or reader. In the case of a nationally-circulated newspaper like the New York Times, the "wrong" occurs in every state where someone *reads* the libelous article. There are, in essence, numerous "wrongs" occurring in numerous states. In theory, the defamed person could sue under Washington D.C. law for injury to his reputation among Washington readers, under New York law for injury to his reputation among New York readers, etc. Eventually, states devised solutions to the problem of interstate and international defamation, which we will not explore. The point is, sometimes the place of the "wrong" is not so apparent.

B.   Contract Problems

The traditional territorialist approach to issues in contract is the *"place of contracting"* rule (*lex loci contractus*). To understand this rule, reflect on your study of contracts in Chapter Two. There, you learned that the most conventional method for creating a legally enforceable contract is for one person to make an "offer" and another person to "accept" that offer. In ordinary situations, the acceptance of the offer results in a lawful contract that courts will enforce. According to the territorialist rule governing contracts, the state where the offeree is located when he or she accepts the offer is the "place of contracting," and that state's law governs legal issues arising from the contract.

We can illustrate the "place of contracting" rule by playing with the facts in the Chloe-Lily dispute. Assume that, while Chloe and Lily were in Georgia attending the harp concert, Chloe said to Lily, "You know, I've wanted to play the Irish harp for some time. I think I'll sell my pedal harp and buy an Irish harp." Lily responds, "What a coincidence, I've been thinking of buying a pedal harp. Why don't you sell me yours?" Chloe eagerly accepts Lily's offer to buy her pedal harp, and they shake hands to seal their agreement. When the two return to Florida, however, Chloe has second thoughts and tells Lily, "I'm sorry but I just can't sell my pedal harp; it means too much to me." Lily is at first saddened, and then angered by Chloe's change of mind. "We had a contract," Lily argues, "and I have already borrowed money to buy the harp. I expect you to keep your bargain."

When Chloe still refuses to sell the harp, Lily sues her in a local Florida court. But Chloe's lawyer defends against Lily's contract suit by pointing out that, under *Georgia* law, any contract to sell goods worth more than $5,000 must be *in writing*. Because the harp's selling price is $15,000, under Georgia law the young women's oral contract is not enforceable. Lily's lawyer responds by pointing out that such oral contracts are enforceable under Florida law. The result? Under the territorialist approach to contracts, the Florida court will probably apply Georgia law because Georgia was the "place of contracting" (i.e., where Lily purported to "accept" Chloe's offer to sell the harp). The so-called contract is unenforceable.

The next time you have occasion to read a contract, you may notice it contains language (probably toward the end) saying something like, "this contract shall be deemed made and entered into in the state of X." This language is intended to take advantage of the "place of contracting" rule by expressly stating what that place is. If you know that, you likely know more than many lawyers who include such language in contracts based largely on tradition.

One interesting application of the "place of contracting" rule is to marriage. Many of us conceive of marriage as a relationship officially endorsed by government. We know, for example, that marriages are dissolved by courts of law. But a marriage is fundamentally a contract, albeit a contract that must satisfy certain legal formalities required by the state. All states impose some restrictions on who may be married. Common restrictions include minimum-age requirements, prohibitions of marriage between close family members, prohibitions of polygamous marriage, and prohibitions of same-sex marriage. Does the "place of contracting" rule imply that two persons can pick a state in which to form the marriage "contract" and circumvent restrictions imposed by their home state? The answer is "maybe." The traditional rule is that the law of the place of the marriage "celebration" (i.e., where the marriage contract is consummated) determines the validity of the marriage. But, as we briefly discuss below, states also traditionally retain the power to refuse to enforce the laws of other states (and contracts made under those laws) which offend the state's "public policy." Consequently, two citizens may elope to another state in an attempt to evade home-state restrictions on their desire to marriage, but when they return, their home state has the option of refusing to recognize their marriage.

C.   Problems Involving Real Property

Nothing is more "territorial" than real property. And with rare exceptions like earthquakes or major floods, real property stays put. As a consequence, the most venerable rule in territorialism is the "*situs*" rule, which states that legal issues that directly concern real property are governed by the law of the state where the property is located (the situs). In the case of real property, notice that it is the location of property and not the location of some "act" that dictates the choice-of-law result.

The situs rule has many implications. If a person wants to execute a deed transferring property, the person must follow the requirements of the situs state. If a person wants to execute a will that disposes of his real property when he dies, he must follow the will execution requirements of the situs state. And if a person dies without a will, the situs state will have final say about who inherits the real property.

To illustrate the situs rule, let's return to Chloe and Lily. Assume that while Chloe and Lily were in Georgia, Chloe offered to sell Lily one of her vintage pedal harps — valued at $125,000 — in exchange for a small parcel of property in North Carolina that Lily recently inherited from her grandfather. Lily agrees. She just happens to have the deed to the property with her, and so she signs the deed and hands it over to Chloe.

Upon returning to Florida, Lily learns that her parents strongly object to her sale of Grandpa's land in North Carolina. Lily calls Chloe and asks for the deed back. But Chloe insists that they go through with their exchange, and she offers to deliver her harp to Lily immediately. Lily declines the offer and demands that the deed be returned. Eventually, Lily contacts a property law expert, who reviews a copy of the deed Lily gave to Chloe (Lily had made a copy at a local copy store). The expert breaks into a smile when he reviews the deed copy. "I have good news for you. The deed is no good. Under North Carolina law, the deed is ineffective unless two witnesses and a notary public sign it. You have no witnesses to your signature. The transfer of deed is invalid. The property is still yours."

Consequently, astute lawyers know that, when real property is involved in a legal transaction, they should always consult the law of the situs. One interesting application of the situs rule occurs when someone executes a will in one state disposing of an estate that includes property in another state. For example, assume a lifelong citizen of California executes her last will and testament disposing of all her worldly assets. Most of those assets are in California (e.g., her home and bank accounts), but one asset consists of a vacation home in Lake Tahoe, Nevada. If she fails to comply with the will-execution requirements of Nevada law, her bequest of the Nevada property may fail. And the result may be that Nevada law dictates who inherits the Nevada property, even though the will validly disposes of non-Nevada property. This is a phenomenon known as "split succession." A lawyer who commits such a costly error by ignoring "situs" law may find he is the defendant in a malpractice suit.

D.   Some Exceptions to Territorialist Rules

There are many exceptions to territorialist rules, and many ways to evade the results dictated by those rules. They are too numerous to review in this Chapter. We examine, instead, two important limits on territorialist rules, one that applies to contracts and another that applies to all types of legal issues.

1.   Party Autonomy and Contracts

As we discussed above, the "place of contracting" rule is the single most important of the territorialist rules governing contracts. However, for most of the nation's history, courts have recognized an important exception to the place of contracting rule. This is the principle of *party autonomy*, permitting contracting parties to *choose* the law that governs their contract.

A contract is a voluntary arrangement between parties, who have great freedom to decide the terms of the bargain they make and where they make it. The parties could, for example, travel to another state, sign the contract there, and thus make that state's law applicable under the "place of contracting" rule. But since the nineteenth century, American courts have given parties a simpler option — they can include a "choice of law" provision in their contract.

A "choice of law" provision can be written as simply as, "the parties agree that all disputes related to this contract shall be governed by the law of X." By including such a clause in their contract, parties know from its inception whose law will govern. Barring exceptional circumstances, the parties can be confident that any court will enforce their choice and apply the law of state X.

Choice-of-law clauses are now extremely common in contracts, especially contracts between businesses. Around the world, choice-of-law clauses are generally enforced because they bring predictability to commercial transactions. You probably have been a party to contract containing such a choice-of-law clause without knowing it. When you do business on the Internet — for example, when you purchase a product or a service — you typically are required to "click" a box indicating that you have read the terms of the contract and consent to them. The next time you are asked to click your consent, take a look at the contract (few of us do). Toward the end, you will probably find a choice-of-law provision. When you agree to the contract, you have made a choice of law whether you know it or not. Sometimes you unknowingly make an even more significant choice — agreeing to resolve any dispute with the business in the courts of some other state. These "forum selection" clauses can make it very costly to litigate against the business.

The increasing tendency of internet businesses to insert choice-of-law and forum-selection clauses in on-line contracts has prompted some states to object when those clauses are used against consumers. For example, some states have invalidated choice-of-law clauses when they are used to deprive local consumers of the protections of local law. And some states object when a consumer is forced by a forum-selection clause to file legal action in a distant state. In the future, we will likely see greater scrutiny of choice-of-law and forum-selection clauses in consumer contracts.

2.   The "Public Policy" Exception

As mentioned, American courts applied territorialist rules for more than a century. Some courts still do. Yet, the consequences of applying territorialist rules are sometimes simply unacceptable to a court. For example, a court (the forum) might be asked to apply the law of another state — like the state where a contract was made — even thought it is directly contrary to the strong policy of the forum. When asked to apply another state's law that offends important "public policy" of the forum, a forum court has the option of refusing. For example, a forum court might refuse to enforce a contract based on gambling debts if forum law prohibits gambling. Or a court might refuse to recognize the validity of a marriage between minors, even though the marriage is valid in the state where the marriage was consummated.

A court that invokes public policy and refuses to enforce the law of another state is taking a big step. For this reason, courts used the public-policy exception sparingly, most often to protect a citizen of the forum in matters thought "fundamental" to local legal policy.

IV.   A SHIFT IN CHOICE-OF-LAW THEORY FROM TERRITORY TO CITIZENSHIP

A.   "Governmental Interest Analysis"

The territorialist approach to choice of law seems properly deferential to other states. If critical acts occur in a state (e.g., injury, contracting), the courts of other states usually apply the law of the state where the critical acts occurred. This seems to show respect for the authority of other states to regulate conduct occurring within their borders. But is territorialism as deferential as it seems? Take, for example, the hypothetical suit of Chloe and Lily. Sure, the accident occurred in Georgia, and the territorialist rule requires application of Georgia law. But other important conduct occurred in Florida. For example, Mr. Michelson loaned his car to Lily in Florida. Shouldn't Florida have some say in whether Mr. Michelson's loan makes him liable for Lily's negligence? By requiring that courts apply the law of the place where the "wrong" occurred, doesn't territorialism arbitrarily select one fact and ignore other relevant facts? This is one of many criticisms of territorialism that helped undermine its authority.

Perhaps the most trenchant criticism of territorialism was that it seemed to ignore the *citizenship* of the parties, and a *state's* interest in protecting its own citizens by applying its law to their disputes. After all, state legislatures are elected by citizens of the state to make laws that promote the citizens' welfare. Aren't legislatures most interested in having their laws applied to their citizens, regardless of whether an accident occurs within the state's territorial borders? Doesn't territorialism overlook this interest by narrowly focusing on the place where the accident occurred, often a fortuity?

In the mid-twentieth century, a new approach to choice-of-law problems emerged. It was known as "*governmental interest analysis*" (or "interest analysis" for short). The critical question asked under interest analysis is, "does state government truly have an interest in having its law apply to a legal dispute?" Whether a state is interested in having its law applied requires examination of two things: (1) the *policies* underlying a state's law, and (2) the *facts* of a dispute, especially the citizenship of the disputing parties.

Interest analysis primarily developed as a method to resolve tort disputes. Given our limited time, we will focus on tort suits in exploring interest analysis. According to many courts, state tort law usually serves one of two main purposes: (a) *compensating* victims of a tort, or (b) *immunizing* tortfeasors from the burden of compensating tort victims. In a crude way, we might say that tort suits are "all about money." For example, when states permit the victims of negligent driving to recover damages from the wrongdoer, they primarily intend to compensate victims. Of course, negligence law might also deter future negligent conduct; but according to interest analysts, this is not the principal goal of negligence law. Sometimes state law shows greater concern with the tortfeasor's plight, as when it immunizes the tortfeasor from liability. A state that limits or eliminates a tortfeasor's liability is not, of course, declaring that it doesn't care whether persons negligently harm others. Rather, the state has identified a special reason to relieve the wrongdoer of the economic risk of liability despite the possible costs to the victim. The best example is *charitable immunity* law. A state may decide that, if charitable organizations are to be encouraged to perform their services within the state, they need to know they will not risk legal liability when some employee of the charity is negligent.

In other words, most courts applying interest analysis emphasize the *economic* consequences of state law for either the victim or the wrongdoer. Equally important, courts typically conclude that a state is concerned about the economic consequences of liability law for *its citizens*. They justify this view by pointing out that state lawgivers represent their citizens, not those of other states; and the economic consequences of an accident will usually be felt within the state where a litigant lives. If an accident victim does not receive compensation from the wrongdoer, the state may ultimately have to take care of the victim through state-funded medical care or welfare. So the argument goes.

B.   "True" and "False" Conflicts

To understand how interest analysis might be used to solve a choice-of-law issue, let's return to the dispute between Chloe and Lily. Recall that Chloe is seeking to recover damages from Mr. Michelson because he owned the car that Lily negligently operated. Under Florida law, Chloe is permitted to recover from a car owner; under Georgia law she is not. The court must now ask, "does the state of Florida have an actual interest in having its legal policy applied to the dispute between Chloe and Mr. Michelson? What is that policy?"

Most courts would immediately conclude that Florida in interested in applying its law. The reason Florida imposes liability on auto owners is to compensate its citizen-victims of auto accidents. Florida has concluded that tortfeasors (like co-defendant Lily) may sometimes be unable to fully compensate an accident victim for her damages. To improve the odds of the victim's receiving full compensation, Florida imposes liability on the auto's owner (with the expectation that owners will procure insurance to cover the negligence of people permitted to drive their cars).

Continuing with its interest analysis, the court will conclude that Florida has a *true interest* in applying its auto-owner liability law for the protection of its citizen, Chloe. The court must now consider whether Georgia has an interest in applying *its* law, which immunizes auto owners from liability. Georgia has decided that it wants to protect (immunize) auto owners from financial responsibility for accidents involving their autos. But does Georgia have a true interest in protecting Mr. Michelson? The answer is "no," since Mr. Michelson is a Floridian. (Notice that Mr. Michelson's home state of Florida has chosen not to protect him. That's the price he pays for choosing to live in Florida. If Florida doesn't choose to protect its own local auto owners, Georgia will not step in and protect them under Georgia law.)

According to interest analysis, the apparent conflict in Florida and Georgia law is a *"false conflict"* because only one state, Florida, has a genuine interest in the outcome of the dispute between Chloe and Mr. Michelson. Consequently, the court will apply the law of Florida, the only "interested" state. One of the most important contributions of interest analysis is the solution it provides when the plaintiff and defendant are citizens of the same state. When the disputing parties share a *common domicile*, courts applying interest analysis usually apply the law of their home state regardless of where the tort occurred.

But if we change one party's domicile, a problem arises. Assume that, when Chloe and Lily were attending the harp concert in Georgia, Mr. Michelson's car broke down. The young women had the car towed to a local auto dealership, where they rented a car to get them back to Florida. When the accident occurred in southern Georgia, Chloe sued the *Georgia* business that owned the car.

Because the car owner is a Georgia citizen, Georgia now has an "interest" in applying its law that protects owners from liability. That means both Florida and Georgia are "interested" in applying their laws. The court must resolve a *"true conflict."* But how? Even today, there is no agreed-upon answer to the question of how to resolve a true conflict. Some courts try to "balance" the interests of Florida and Georgia and select the state that is "most" interested. Other courts fall back on the territorialist rule, and apply the law of the place of the injury (Georgia). Still other courts figuratively throw up their hands and simply apply the law of the forum (Georgia). In other words, there is no obvious solution when two states really do have an interest in applying their laws. This is one of the principal shortcomings of interest analysis, which makes the application of this theory a bit unpredictable.

V. A NEW IMPROVED SYNTHESIS, OR A MESS?

Today only a handful of state courts use interest analysis as their choice-of-law theory. More than a dozen states continue to use territorialist rules in some form. But the prevailing approach to choice-of-law problems today is the Restatement (Second) of Conflict of Laws (1971). The Restatement (Second) is the product of the American Law Institute (ALI), a group of legal scholars, judges, and lawyers who purport to "restate" American law. In truth, however, the Restatement (Second) does not always restate the law applied by American courts; instead, it often espouses its members' views of what choice-of-law theory American courts *should* apply.

The Restatement (Second) was drafted in response to a belief that, as American courts entered the second half of the twentieth century, choice-of-law theory was badly in need of revision. Critics' special focus was the unsatisfactory state of theory applied to resolve *tort* conflicts. Territorialist theory was criticized because it sometimes led to arbitrary, unfair results based on the pure happenstance of where an accident occurred. Interest analysis, which a few bold courts had attempted to implement, seemed to be an improvement on territorialism but had its own problems — including how unpredictable it could be when applied by courts.

The drafters of the Restatement (Second) aspired to create a new approach to choice of law that would serve many purposes. These included (1) promoting the policies of state law, (2) insuring greater fairness to the parties involved in a dispute, and (3) providing the legal community better guidance and greater predictability in the resolution of choice-of-law questions. To accomplish these sometimes conflicting goals, the Restatement (Second) attempted to blend the "best" of many different approaches to choice of law, including territorialism and interest analysis.

The resulting Restatement (Second) is a *very* challenging document. The rules and guidelines for resolving choice-of-law problems can be interpreted in many different ways. In fact, one legal scholar believes that state courts have interpreted the Restatement (Second) in *nine* distinct ways! This makes it almost impossible to achieve a consensus on how a court should resolve choice-of-law problems under the Restatement (Second). But let's consider how a hypothetical court might apply the Restatement (Second) to the dispute between Chloe and Lily.

The Restatement (Second) provides a starting point for determining which state's law to apply to personal injury actions like that of Chloe and Lily. Courts are told they should apply the "local law of the state where the *injury occurred . . . unless . . . .*" Restatement (Second) of Conflict of Laws § 146 (emphasis added). In other words, the Restatement (Second) begins with a territorialist presumption — the law of the "place of the wrong" should be applied. This is a nod to traditional choice-of-law theory. It also gives an element of predictability to resolving choice-of-law problems in personal injury actions, a very prominent setting for choice-of-law disputes. But the law of the state of injury can be replaced if some other state has a more "*significant relationship* . . . to the occurrence and the parties." *Id.*

The most challenging question presented to courts is, how do they determine if some other state has a more "significant relationship" to the dispute, thereby rebutting the territorialist presumption? Courts have not agreed upon an answer to this question. Many courts conduct some form of interest analysis, examining the different states' legal policies and whether they might be implicated by the facts (e.g., whether a state's citizen is a party to the dispute). Other courts try to determine whether some state has greater factual contacts with the occurrence and the parties, a process derisively called "contact counting."

Most state courts would probably apply the Restatement (Second) to Chloe's claim against Lily in the following manner. First, because the accident occurred in Georgia, a court would assume that Georgia law applies. It then becomes Chloe's burden to convince the court that Florida has a more "significant relationship." Chloe might attempt to show Florida has a more significant relationship to the dispute by pointing out that (1) both parties are Floridians; (2) Florida law permits Chloe, its citizen, to recover full damages even though she failed to buckle her seat belt; and (3) Georgia, which limits Chloe's damages because she failed to buckle her seat belt, has no interest in applying its law to protect a Floridian defendant (Lily). In most states, Chloe would probably have a very good chance of convincing the court that Florida has the most "significant relationship," thereby rebutting the presumption that Georgia law applies.

The Restatement (Second) contains dozens of rules and guidelines to govern specific issues that arise in tort, contract, property, and many other legal disputes. Many have an element of territorialism built in. But almost always, a court's principal task is to figure out which state has the most "significant relationship" to this dispute. This is a major reason the Restatement (Second) can be difficult to apply, leading to unpredictability. Despite its shortcomings, however, most state courts appear to prefer the open-ended approach of the Restatement (Second) to alternative approaches like territorialism and interest analysis. Whether yet another, improved approach will emerge in the future is impossible to predict.

VI. CONSTITUTIONAL LIMITS ON CHOICE OF LAW

To this point in the Chapter we have considered how state courts develop their own solutions to choice-of-law problems. Before leaving the subject, one question deserves mention. Are there any *constitutional* limits on a state's power to choose the law that governs a dispute? The short answer is "yes," but the limits are not great.

Historically, the need for constitutional limits on choice of law arose from one main problem — the tendency of state courts to apply their own (forum) law to occurrences having modest connection to the forum. State courts have a natural propensity to apply forum law. For one thing, state courts are often the *source* of state law, as when they develop common law. When state courts develop a particular common-law rule, they tend to think their rule is superior to differing rules adopted by other states. When forced to choose between their own rule and that of other states, courts are predisposed to select forum law.

The propensity of state courts to choose forum law gives plaintiffs an advantage. Plaintiffs have incentive to file suit in a state whose law is favorable, even if the dispute has stronger connections to another state. In other words, they have incentive to forum shop. The problem is magnified when the defendant is a national corporation that can be sued in virtually any state — General Motors and Nationwide Insurance are examples of such companies. In theory, plaintiffs have considerable power to shop for a forum with the most plaintiff-friendly law.

Recognizing this propensity, the Supreme Court has announced constitutional limits on the power of state courts to apply forum law. The Court's most recent statement on these limits was given in *Allstate Insurance Company v. Hague*, 449 U.S. 302 (1981). In *Hague*, the Court held that "for a State's . . . law to be selected in a constitutionally permissible manner, that State must have a significant contact or significant aggregation of contacts, creating state interests, such that choice of its law is neither arbitrary nor fundamentally unfair." *Id.* at 313. The Court's standard is very general, using ambiguous concepts like "significant contacts" and "state interest." Application of the *Hague* standard often requires a case-by-case analysis of specific facts and laws. But the *Hague* standard clearly presents the worst form of forum shopping, where a plaintiff chooses a forum having nothing to do with the parties' dispute simply because the plaintiff prefers forum law. *Hague* makes clear that the mere fact that a state has the power to hale a nationwide defendant into its courts is not alone a sufficient "contact" to justify applying forum law.

VII. CHOICE OF LAW — AN INTERNATIONAL PERSPECTIVE

In a short chapter like this, we must use *very* large generalizations about choice of law. The subject of choice of law is one of the more complex subjects in the law, and generalizations are inevitably imprecise and often misleading. Our goal has been to give you some sense of what a choice-of-law problem is, and how American courts have struggled to develop solutions that will stand the test of time. If you wish to understand — really understand — choice of law, you must be prepared to do a lot more study.

As noted at the beginning of this Chapter, American choice-of-law theory originated in Europe. In recent decades, as European nations have joined interests in the European Union (EU), the EU has attempted to develop modern solutions to the same kinds of choice-of-law problems with which American courts have grappled. The EU's experience echoes that of American courts — choice-of-law solutions almost always involve an unsatisfying compromise of values.

For example, in 2007 the EU adopted a regulation called "Rome II," which specifies choice-of-law rules to govern "non-contractual obligations" like torts. *See* Symeon C. Symeonides, *Rome II and Tort Conflicts: A Missed Opportunity*, 56 Am. J. Comp. L. 173 (2008). As Professor Symeonides explains, Rome II aspired to develop choice-of-law rules that were both certain and predictable (like territorialist rules) and yet flexible and fair (like interest analysis). But as he laments, Rome II ultimately elevates the value of predictability over the value of flexibility because of the perception that the EU needs rules that can be applied uniformly throughout member states.

Excerpted below is Rome II's general rule governing torts (also called "delicts"). See if any of its provisions look familiar to you:

4. General rule

1. Unless otherwise provided for in this Regulation, the law applicable to a non-contractual obligation arising out of a tort/delict shall be the law of the country in which the *damage occurs* irrespective of the country in which the event giving rise to the damage occurred and irrespective of the country or countries in which the indirect consequences of that event occur.

2. However, where the person claimed to be liable and the person sustaining damage both have their *habitual residence in the same country* at the time when the damage occurs, the law of that country shall apply.

3. Where it is clear from all the circumstances of the case that the tort/delict is manifestly more closely connected with a country other than that indicated in paragraphs 1 or 2, the law of that other country shall apply. A *manifestly closer connection with another country* might be based in particular on a pre-existing relationship between the parties, such as a contract, that is closely connected with the tort/delict in question. (Emphasis added.)

As you can see, paragraph (1) adopts the "place of wrong" rule (i.e., where the "damage" occurs) that is the classic underpinning of American territorialism. At the same time, this rule can be displaced under paragraph (2) if adversaries "reside" in the same country. Does this remind you of the "common domicile" rule of interest analysis? Finally, observe that paragraph (3) permits displacement of the law of the place of wrong when another country is "manifestly more closely connected" to the wrong. Does that remind you of the "significant relationship" standard in the Restatement (Second)?

Perhaps it is only fair that American courts, having borrowed from Europe when developing choice-of-law theory to govern the nation's new courts in the eighteenth century, now give back to the newly-confederated nations of Europe. In any event, Rome II illustrates how the values that underlie choice-of-law theory may not be all that different whether one is addressing interstate or international disputes.

VIII.   ENFORCING JUDGMENTS ISSUED BY COURTS OF ANOTHER JURISDICTION

Modern litigation is expensive and time consuming. Many years often elapse between the filing of a suit and its conclusion. When plaintiffs succeed in such a costly endeavor, and obtain a "final judgment," they expect that the judgment will be worth something. Often their expectations are met, as the defendant satisfies the judgment. But if the defendant does not fully pay, plaintiffs may need the help of the same court system that issued the judgment to seize control of the defendant's assets — a process known as "judgment enforcement."

But what happens when a successful plaintiff — now called a "judgment creditor" — cannot find sufficient local assets to satisfy the judgment? Sometimes, the judgment creditor may simply abandon efforts to collect the judgment. But there may be another option — going after the defendant-debtor's assets in *another* jurisdiction. When a judgment creditor pursues a debtor's assets in another jurisdiction, he or she must usually employ the assistance of that jurisdiction's court system. The important question then arises: *must* that court system enforce judgments issued by another jurisdiction?

A.   Full Faith and Credit

In colonial America, judgment creditors often had trouble collecting from defendants. A Massachusetts plaintiff might win a judgment in Massachusetts court, only to discover the defendant-debtor had fled to another colony — along with whatever assets he possessed. The Massachusetts creditor might pursue the debtor to the courts of another colony, say the courts of Connecticut, but he or she encountered a sometimes costly problem — the Connecticut court could require that he or she re-file a lawsuit against the debtor and re-prove the merits of the original case. In re-proving the case, the Massachusetts creditor could submit into evidence the judgment previously obtained in Massachusetts court, but the debtor usually had the right to challenge the judgment. In other words, the debtor could ask the Connecticut court to re-try a case already tried in Massachusetts court. *See* Michael S. Finch, *Giving Full Faith and Credit to Punitive Damages Awards: Will Florida Rule the Nation?* 86 MINN. L. REV. 497, 512–13 (2002).

Eventually, the new United States developed a constitutional solution to the problem of inter-state judgment enforcement. Article IV of the Constitution now provides: "Full Faith and Credit shall be given in each State to the public Acts, Records, and judicial Proceedings of every other State." The Full Faith and Credit Clause generally *prohibits* a court in one state from reconsidering the merits of a dispute already litigated in the courts of another state. Provided the state court that rendered an earlier judgment had lawful authority to adjudicate the dispute, the judgment must be enforced by *any* state or federal court in the United States. A successful plaintiff may take the judgment to any state where the defendant-debtor has property and ask local courts to both recognize the judgment and seize the debtor's property.

In the centuries since adoption of the Full Faith and Credit Clause, defendant-debtors have raised a host of objections to enforcement of "sister state" judgments. Almost all have failed. We consider a few of the failed objections, for they reinforce how important the Full Faith and Credit Clause is.

One objection that defendant-debtors have raised is that significant errors occurred in the state court that issued the judgment a creditor seeks to enforce. For example, the first court may have considered improper evidence, mistakenly interpreted applicable law, or even made a ruling that violates the United States Constitution. But the Supreme Court has steadfastly refused to permit debtors to "reopen the merits" underlying the judgment of another court. If the first state court commits an error — even a constitutional error — it is up to the defendant to *appeal* the state court's decision within its own court system (and occasionally to the U.S. Supreme Court). Unless a judgment is corrected on appeal, it must be enforced by other state courts. Other state courts lack the authority to correct errors that could have been corrected in the courts of the state that issued the judgment.

Another objection some debtors raised when their creditors sought to enforce the judgment of another state court was that it offended "public policy" of the state where enforcement was now sought. You will recall that, when discussing territorial choice-of-law rules, we observed that a state court can refuse to enforce the *laws* of another state when they offend local "public policy." (The same objection can also be asserted under other choice-of-law theories.) We mentioned, for example, that a state court may refuse to enforce a gambling contract even though it is lawful in the state where the contract was made.

The public policy defense loses its force when another state has issued a monetary *judgment*. Even if the law underlying another state's judgment is offensive to the state asked to enforce the judgment, Full Faith and Credit requires that the judgment be enforced. To illustrate, assume that a Nevada casino loaned a Texas gambler the cash with which to gamble at the casino. The loan is a form of "contract" that is perfectly lawful under Nevada law where it was made. But the casino's lawyers know that a Texas court (where we assume gambling contracts are unlawful) will not enforce the gambling debt. The casino has another option, however. The casino can sue the Texas gambler in *Nevada* state court and win a judgment based on the enforceability of gambling contracts in the forum. The casino then takes its Nevada judgment to a court in Texas, where the Texan keeps his assets. At this point, the Texas court has no choice but to enforce the Nevada judgment, even though it finds the law underlying the judgment highly offensive. In other words, Full Faith and Credit does not require that one state enforce the laws of another state, but it does require that one state enforce the judgments of another state.

The Full Faith and Credit Clause can sometimes be used by plaintiffs to win an important advantage in litigation. We can illustrate this advantage by returning to the legal dispute between Chloe and Lily. You will need to pay close attention because the illustration quickly becomes complicated. But that is often the nature of choice-of-law problems.

Recall that Chloe has sued Lily's father, Mr. Michelson, because he owns the car Lily was driving. Also recall that Florida law permits Chloe to recover from Mr. Michelson, while Georgia law does not. Chloe's lawyer initially thought she would sue in a Georgia court. But she changes her mind when she thinks through the implications of suing in Georgia. Georgia follows the "territorialist" approach to choice of law when resolving tort disputes (this is actually true). That means Georgia will apply its own law to Chloe's claim against Mr. Michelson since Georgia in the "law of the place of the wrong." On the other hand, Florida follows the Restatement (Second) approach (this is also true). Based on the Florida court's interpretation of the Restatement (Second), Chloe's lawyer is convinced a Florida court would apply its law because Chloe and Mr. Michelson are both Floridians.

Where should Chloe's lawyer file the suit against Mr. Michelson? The answer is pretty obvious, isn't it? She has no chance if she sues in a Georgia court. She has a great chance if she files in a Florida court. What is more, any judgment a Florida court issues based on Florida law will be enforceable against Mr. Michelson anywhere in the nation. So, if need be, Chloe can enforce a judgment against Mr. Michelson in Georgia (where, for example, he may own a vacation home) even though Georgia courts would never have recognized Chloe's claim against Mr. Michelson had she originally tried the case in a Georgia court.

Whew! As we noted earlier, choice of law is complicated. But you can see how critical the understanding of that law may be for practicing lawyers.

We have seen that Full Faith and Credit prevents a court from re-litigating the merits of a dispute previously litigated in the court of another state. But a court asked to enforce a sister-state's judgment still retains the right to provide the judgment debtor some protection. In particular, the enforcing court can apply its *own* law to determine which assets of the debtor can be seized. For example, the enforcing court can apply local law placing limits on garnishment of the debtor's wages. Similarly, the enforcing court can apply local law protecting the debtor's "homestead" from forced sale. Some states gain a reputation as "debtors' havens" because of the liberal protections they provide debtors. For example, the state of Florida protects a debtor's homestead no matter what its value. Consequently, a debtor may be able to place all his assets in an expensive homestead and so avoid payment of judgment debts.

B.   Enforcing Foreign-Nation Judgments in State Court

The Full Faith and Credit Clause compels courts in America to enforce the judgments of state courts. This constitutional clause does not apply to foreign-nation judgments. Congress has the authority to enact laws, or enter into international treaties, that would require enforcement of foreign judgments. But at present, Congress compels enforcement of foreign judgments in only limited settings. By and large, the states have discretion whether to enforce foreign judgments based on their own notions of "comity" and cooperation.

In an age of globalization, American courts have greater incentive to enforce the judgments rendered by foreign courts. After all, American courts want their own judgments to be enforced when they are taken abroad. Consequently, an increasing number of states have enacted laws facilitating enforcement of foreign judgments. *See, e.g,* Uniform Foreign Money-Judgments Recognition Act.

Nonetheless, most states still retain the right to refuse enforcement of foreign judgments based on grounds they could not assert if they were asked to enforce a sister-state's judgment. We briefly examine a few of these grounds.

First, state courts will refuse to enforce a foreign judgment that results from judicial procedures considered fundamentally unfair. While sister-state courts must operate within the framework of the "due process" requirements established by the U.S. Constitution, foreign nation courts are obviously not subject to these requirements. As a consequence, state courts may scrutinize the procedures used in foreign courts to ensure that the court was impartial and its procedures more-or-less compatible with American notions of fairness. At the same time, American courts appreciate that all foreign courts use procedures that vary from our own, and so they do not insist that foreign courts play by the identical rules used in American courts.

Second, most states refuse to enforce a foreign judgment that is "repugnant" to public policy. For example, a state court might refuse to enforce a foreign libel judgment against a newspaper that fails to give the press the same protections given by American law when the libeled person is a "public figure."

Third, most states refuse to enforce the "penal" judgments of other nations. A penal judgment might include a judgment ordering the defendant to pay the plaintiff "punitive" damages for violating foreign law. A penal judgment might also include damages recovered by a foreign government entity as a means of enforcing its laws (e.g., a "civil" penalty).

Finally, some states follow a rule of "reciprocity," agreeing to enforce a foreign nation's judgment if that nation will similarly enforce the state's own judgments. This rule has been criticized, and many states refuse to follow it. The practice of "reciprocity" can prevent a state from making the type of overture needed to expand the international enforcement of judgments. If each jurisdiction takes the position, "I'll enforce your judgments as soon as you start enforcing mine," a stalemate may ensue. In comparison, if one jurisdiction unilaterally volunteers to respect the judgment of foreign nations, this benevolent gesture may inspire reciprocity.

In summary, the states continue to retain wide discretion when deciding whether to enforce most foreign nation judgments. That said, the states' record on enforcement is one that deserves compliment. As one commentator recently observed, "[t]he United States is one of the most hospitable countries to foreign judgments." A. Parrish, *Sovereignty, Not Due Process: Personal Jurisdiction Over Non-resident Alien Defendants,* 41 WAKE FOREST L. REV. 1, 53 (2006).

C.   Enforcing American Court Judgments in Foreign Nations

When a judgment creditor seeks to enforce an American court judgment in a foreign nation, matters become even more complicated. Foreign nations usually enjoy unlimited discretion in deciding whether to enforce American judgments, and they exercise their discretion in different ways.

One problem that may prompt a foreign nation to refuse enforcement of an American court judgment is the substantial variation between American judicial procedures and those of most foreign nation courts. American lawyers often do not appreciate how much our court procedures differ from those in other nations. American courts are exceptionally liberal in, for example, (1) permitting laymen juries to decide important, complex cases that are decided by judges in most foreign nations; (2) permitting a state court to exercise jurisdiction over defendants with quite limited connections to the state; and (3) permitting very large numbers of plaintiffs to band together in "class actions," sometimes resulting in exceptionally large awards of damages. Differences like these may prompt foreign nations to refuse to enforce American judgments, in part because these nations believe American court procedures go too far.

Similarly, foreign nations may resist enforcement of American judgments based on laws that offend their "public policy." For example, many foreign nations disagree with aspects of American anti-trust policy, which forbids businesses from agreeing (we might call it "conspiring") to limit business entry into certain markets. Especially when American courts have applied American law resulting in a judgment against the foreign nation's own business interests, the prospects of enforcing that judgment in the foreign nation's courts may be dim.

IX. CONCLUSION

Despite the advent of globalization, we still live in a very decentralized world of judicial authority. In the United States, greater centralization has been achieved through the constitutional command of Full Faith and Credit. In the international world, limited centralization has been achieved through treaties and conventions, especially among nations having shared interests (like member nations of the European Union).

While there is something to be said for greater cooperation among nations, there is also something to be said for permitting nations to develop legal policy that better reflects their own history and sense of justice. If this sometimes results in difficult choice-of-law problems, perhaps that is the price that must be paid for giving sovereign states the freedom to choose.

Chapter 17

THE PRACTICE OF LAW

By — Charles H. Rose III

I. INTRODUCTION TO THE PRACTICE OF LAW

Legal representation requires both an attorney and a client. The client turns an academic exercise into a real world situation with consequences tied to each decision the attorney makes. The formation of the relationship between the attorney and the client is the starting point. The first thing necessary for that relationship to exist is consent. The client must agree to representation by the attorney. The initial client interview is normally the place where the attorney-client relationship forms. The client's consent transforms him or her from a prospective client into a current client. That transformation serves as the starting point for the practice of law.

At its most fundamental level, practicing law is about representing clients who have a dispute or issue with another party. Those disputes often wind up at trial, and a review of the trial process serves as an excellent tool to introduce students to the practice of law from an adversarial perspective. This Chapter is designed to introduce you to the practice of law as conducted by attorneys in the United States on a daily basis. We will discuss the practice of law through the examples of what attorneys do when they get a client and must prepare to represent that client in an adjudicative proceeding — trial. The trial process in most U.S. courts is at its core a dispute resolution process that has a long and abiding history in the United States, and when finished with this Chapter you will have a fundamental understanding of how our courts structure and control this dispute resolution process through the eyes of the attorney that is engaged in the practice of law. This understanding will allow you to identify the procedural rules and substantive law that generally apply in most circumstances, and begin to forecast the steps that an attorney involved in the trial process would need to consider when representing his or her client.

The trial process in the United States is based upon an adversarial model. It is a fundamental precept within our court system that disputes at trial are best resolved when each side is completely committed to the representation of their client, bound only by their ethical responsibilities to the profession of law and their duties as officers of the court. This focus on the client ensures that each side is represented to the fullest extent allowed by law. The focus is on the relationship between the client and the attorney. That relationship is the engine that drives the representation for the benefit of the client. This same relationship also exists on the opposing side. The trial process is a means of controlling disputes between parties that are both represented to the fullest extent possible. Our system believes that this adversarial relationship between the parties creates the greatest opportunity to ensure the rule of law and the resolution of disputes based upon a search for the truth within the construct of a legal process. You have already studied the general makeup of the U.S. legal system. The issues discussed there apply here as well. We are now going to focus more narrowly on the resolution of disputes within the U.S. legal system. This is referred to within the United States as the trial process, and it breaks down into three general sections: pre-trial, trial, and appeal. This Chapter focuses primarily on the trial process, but where appropriate we will reference those portions of the pre-trial process and appeals process that impact on or are impacted by the trial process. Unless otherwise specifically identified, all courts referred to within this Chapter are trial courts. You should you remember from your earlier readings that the trial court is the first level of the court process in the United States.

There are two primary types of trials in the United States — civil and criminal. While both rely upon the same judges, the same court rooms, and similar rules of procedure, they deal with very different issues. Civil trials primarily address private disputes between parties where one or both parties have turned to the civil court system to provide final resolution. Normally they address legal issues that arise out of contract law, tort law, or some other statutory relief under a statute that establishes a civil remedy. Criminal trials, on the other hand, serve an entirely different purpose. Criminal trials are a process used by the government to take the liberty, and sometimes the life, of any individual subject to the jurisdiction of the court. Criminal trials deal with crime and punishment, and they form the stuff of television shows, movies, and popular fiction. Civil and criminal trials have similarities and differences that are determined by their unique functions and the specific rules of procedure that govern their individual process.

While the actual pieces of a trial and its investigative stages are always heavily influenced by the local rules of court, rules of procedure, and the attitudes of the judiciary in your jurisdiction, we can identify certain elements of the trial process that are relatively similar regardless of the issue before the court or the local court in which the action is found. This Chapter divides the trial process into the following general areas: (1) the attorney's client becomes involved in a situation that leads to litigation (pre-trial process); (2) the attorney begins case analysis, preparation, and investigation of the issues; (3) the attorney files motions based upon that case analysis; (4) the court rules on the motions, and the attorney either settles, pleads, or sets a trial date; (5) jury selection occurs if appropriate; (6) opening statements are made; (7) direct and cross-examinations are conducted; (8) closing arguments are made and jury instructions are given by the court; (9) the jury deliberates, and a verdict is rendered. We will use these general categories to drive our discussion of the trial process in the United States

II.   CLIENT NEEDS A LAWYER

Clients come into the office in a variety of ways, depending upon the size of the firm, the nature of the firm's practice, and advertising strategies employed. Frequently, the first contact between the prospective client and the advocate may be a telephone call or, reflecting our current technology, an email in which the prospective, current, or former client contacts the law firm about a problem and seeks to speak with a lawyer. Whether this initial conversation is with the advocate or his or her office staff, there are some useful, if not essential, things that can be accomplished during this brief exchange. Advocates should create systems within their office to maximize information gathering from that first contact.

The beginning of every dispute from the attorney's perspective occurs with the formation of the attorney-client relationship. The client has a legal problem and is looking for help in resolving that problem. The pre-trial process includes: (1) formation of the attorney-client relationship, (2) case analysis and preparation, (3) pleadings, and attacks on pleadings/review of the indictment, (4) formal and informal discovery, (5) motions practice, (6) settlement or plea agreement, and (7) trial preparation. Let us briefly consider each of these portions of the pre-trial process.

A.   Formation of the Attorney-Client Relationship

The formation of the attorney-client relationship is governed, as are most major issues for attorneys, by the rules of professional conduct that have been promulgated by the bar. Each attorney practicing in the United States has his or her conduct governed by the rules of professional conduct passed, implemented, and policed by the state bar and/or supreme court of the state where the attorney practices. These rules are designed to set a floor for ethical behavior that allows the profession of law to remain a self-regulating entity. The American Bar Association has promulgated model rules of professional conduct that often serve as the baseline starting point for many of the professional rules of conduct adopted by state bar associations. These rules govern how the attorney-client relationship is formed; the duties of the attorney to the client, the court, and others; the regulation of fees; and the controlling of advertising. Most lawyers practicing law in the United States are confronted with issues of professional ethical conduct on a daily basis. These rules form the bedrock of professional conduct for practicing attorneys.

Almost every case begins with a meeting between the prospective client and an attorney. If an attorney-client relationship forms, the attorney must take special care during that first meeting to gain the necessary information from the client and to convey the appropriate advice to the client based upon the goals of the representation. This is the beginning stage of representation that ultimately prepares the way to successfully navigate the rest of the trial process. Time spent during this point in the process is always time well spent. Without sufficient planning and communication between the attorney and the client, the other side will have the ability to set the tone and the focus of the litigation. Good attorneys quickly learn that if they do not set the direction of the adversarial process, the other side will.

The attorney sets the parameters for the representation in the form of a retainer or fee agreement, particularly in a civil case. In a criminal case, this applies as well, unless the attorney has been appointed by the court system to represent the defendant without charge to the defendant. Even when the defendant does not pay the attorney's fee him- or herself, the attorney-client relationship remains the same as in the other instances where the client does pay the fee. When a fee agreement is properly prepared and executed, both the attorney and the client will have a clear idea of what is expected — it helps to prevent future misunderstandings and to establish goals and expectations. Once this relationship is properly formed, the rest of the representation can continue. The formation of the attorney-client relationship is the bedrock upon which the representation of any client is built within the U.S. legal system, and it is the starting point of any trial process, although it occurs long before the trial begins.

B.   Initial Case Analysis, Planning, and Preparation

Case analysis is a continuing task at all stages of the pre-trial process, trial process, and appellate process. It is one of the most important tasks during the early planning stages of litigation because the analysis performed during that time sets the stage for the trial if and when the pre-trial process leads to that point. Case analysis is a systematic process that combines law, facts, and morality into an inclusive approach that empowers the attorney to represent the client to the best of his or her ability. It must be done continuously, particularly during the pre-trial portion of the trial process. The attorney uses case analysis to organize the file, develop the facts of the case, and identify the applicable law. Many of the most important facts of the case are learned through informal discussions, interviews, formal depositions, and the use of interrogatories in civil cases.

After obtaining as much information as possible about the factual underpinnings of the case, the attorney must begin serious case planning and preparation based at least in part upon whether this case is a civil or criminal case. If the case involves the representation of a plaintiff or defendant in civil case, the attorney must consider fundamental questions such as who are the parties to the litigation, where the case can and should be filed, which type of court is appropriate for hearing the case, and other practical considerations. The rules of civil procedure for that jurisdiction will give the attorney the answers to these questions, and they must be consulted prior to proceeding. If the case is a criminal case and the attorney is representing the defendant, they have to look at the offenses that the government alleges were committed by the defendant, potential defenses, and the procedural steps that protect the rights of the defendant throughout the process. These are found in the rules of criminal procedure relevant to that particular jurisdiction.

C.   Pleadings and Attacks on Pleadings/Review of the Indictment

In a civil case, the plaintiff is the party that brings the lawsuit against the defendant, the party that defends. The plaintiff begins the process by drafting and filing pleadings. Pleadings identify the issues in controversy and become the blueprint for how the case will be handled throughout the litigation. Claims and defenses are framed by the pleadings and nothing else in the life of the case happens without reference to these claims and defenses. Careful consideration as to what, when, and how various claims and defenses should be pled is required of the prudent attorney when representing a client during a civil case. The rules of civil procedure provide a baseline for the drafting of pleadings, but the art of pleading requires much more than these bare essentials. The defendant responds to the pleadings, and the interplay between the pleadings and response is used by the court system to identify the issues in controversy that cannot be settled without trial. This allows for the trial to be focused and creates a dispute process that is manageable when the case finally makes it into the courtroom.

In a criminal case, the representative of the people, usually referred to as an assistant district attorney, can bring charges against a member of society using an indictment process that is run through a grand jury hearing or by the filing of an information where the defendant is charged based upon information that the assistant district attorney, sometimes known as the prosecutor, has available. In either case, the State brings the charges against the defendant and it is the state that has the burden of proof in a criminal proceeding. The United States Constitution has a direct impact upon the way in which criminal trials occur, to include not only the standard of proof, but the right to a jury trial, the right of the defendant to remain silent when questioned by the state, as well as the right of the defendant to confront the accusers against him. All of these constitutional rights have a distinct and well developed body of law that directly impacts what can, and cannot, be done by counsel at trial. Criminal practice is both practical and constitutional, and by placing constitutional rights at the core of the adversarial process in criminal proceedings, the federal government as an entity has a constitutional watchdog in the form of the criminal attorney. This creates transparency in the judicial system and some degree of acceptance of the process by defendants. It also protects certain fundamental constitutional rights, regardless of the particular crime being prosecuted.

D.   Formal Discovery: Written and Oral

Although informal fact investigation is perhaps one of the most important tasks of an attorney, it is equally important for an attorney to fully grasp the various formal procedures for obtaining discovery from one's adversary under the auspices of the rules of procedure for that jurisdiction. Vehicles for accomplishing this include initial disclosures, interrogatories, requests for admission, and requests for production of documents in civil cases. Each of these tools is governed by separate rules of procedure and separate practical considerations. Each type of formal discovery has strengths and weaknesses, advantages and disadvantages, and the attorney must carefully choose from among this arsenal of weapons when going through the discovery phase of a civil lawsuit. One of the most useful, though expensive, forms of discovery is the oral deposition. The attorney can depose his or her own witnesses as well as those of the adversary and even seemingly neutral third parties not named in the lawsuit. This is a process where the witness testifies under oath and subject to cross-examination before a trained specialist normally called a court reporter. The reporter takes down every word that is said in the hearing and transcribes it for later use. There are different styles, methods, and variations of oral depositions. Both the law and the art of taking and defending depositions is an entire course of study at many law schools. Taken together, these varied forms of formal discovery become the tools used by counsel to identify possible resolutions of the case — to include assisting in predicting what may happen during the course of a trial. Discovery often facilitates disposition of most civil cases through motions practice or settlement. Some still make it to trial despite the fact investigation and discovery phase.

This same discovery process occurs in different formats during criminal cases, but the degree to which discovery occurs between the State and the defendant is unique for each jurisdiction. In each instance, however, there are specific rules of discovery that mandate disclosure of exculpatory information to the defendant, as well as requirements that information about witnesses called by the State and in the State's possession must be given to defense prior to the beginning of cross-examination. In some jurisdictions, criminal practice requires "open discovery," where the State is required to provide the defense access to all relevant information within the control of the State as long as it is not privileged. In other jurisdictions, the rules of discovery are more complex. As long as the discovery rules of the State do not impact a constitutional right, state legislatures have the ability to fashion rules of procedure that accurately reflect both state and applicable federal law as it applies to the discovery process.

E.   Motion Practice

Motions for summary judgment play prominently in most civil lawsuits. These motions are used to discover the meritorious claims amongst those that are lacking in substance. They are often employed by the plaintiff as a sword to establish a claim without the need for trial — or as a shield by the civil defense attorney to obtain dismissal on the merits of all or a portion of the plaintiff's claims. At one time, most judges in U.S. courts frowned upon motions for summary judgment, and they were rarely used or granted. The complexities of practice, as well as many other different factors, have increased not only the utility but also the occurrence of motions for summary judgment. Their use has reached the point now that it is uncommon for a civil case to arrive at trial without the defense attempting a motion for summary judgment during some point in the pre-trial process. The filing of a motion for summary judgment by the defense is often a last-ditch attempt to avoid paying money to the claimant either through settlement or a possible adverse judgment at trial. Plaintiff attorneys view summary judgments as a trap to be overcome. The defense, on the other hand, often falls asleep at night dreaming of ways to craft successful motions for summary judgment.

The criminal trial has a similar process called the motion to dismiss. A motion to dismiss the case against the defendant is brought by the criminal defense attorney and is normally based upon an earlier ruling that a violation of the defendant's constitutional rights occurred that requires suppression of evidence acquired by the State based upon that constitutional violation. When evidence is suppressed to the point that the judge can determine that the State could not prove its case or when allowing the trial to proceed would be fundamentally unfair, then the judge has the ability to dismiss the case either with prejudice or without prejudice. If the case is dismissed with prejudice, then the State cannot later bring another prosecution for those offenses. This is a remedy of last resort and is rarely granted by the judge. Usually the State is allowed to proceed while not being allowed to rely upon the evidence that has been suppressed.

F.   Settlement or Pre-trial Agreements

Often the last step before a civil case goes to trial is a voluntary settlement by the parties. These are normally done through both informal and private settlement negotiations or through mediation conducted by a neutral mediator. Most cases that survive a motion for summary judgment end up settling prior to trial. For this reason, attorneys must consider possible settlements as part and parcel of their trial preparation. Settlement becomes attractive to the parties once a motion for summary judgment has been denied because it allows for predictability and damage control.

The criminal trial's version of a settlement agreement is a pre-trial agreement. In a pre-trial agreement, the defense agrees to plead guilty to an offense or offenses in exchange for which the government agrees to a limitation on the sentence that can be imposed, or in the case where the judge determines the sentence, the government agrees to make a lower sentencing recommendation. Normally when the government accepts a pre-trial agreement, there is a benefit for the government that outweighs the loss of a potentially heavier sentence. Often that benefit can be one of time saved, costs reduced, or the ability to get additional evidence that can be used against other defendants. One of the maxims of criminal defense work is that it is always better for your client to be a witness as opposed to a defendant. A defendant can never be forced into a pre-trial agreement, but the realities of his or her situation often lead defendants to search out pre-trial agreements in an attempt to limit their prison sentence or to avoid incarceration altogether.

G.   Trial Preparation

If the case does not settle, it proceeds to trial. Most activities done by the attorney during the pre-trial stage are done in a fashion that also supports proceeding to trial when necessary. Most attorneys realize that the only way to make certain that the pre-trial process weeds out those cases that should not go to trial is to prepare at a sufficiently deep level that they are ready to go to trial if necessary. Taking this tack places the attorney in a position of power, making him or her able to negotiate a more favorable settlement if he or she chooses or, when called for, move for judgment as a matter of law. The pre-trial process is in a very real sense nothing more than a form of trial preparation. If the attorney's case has not been resolved by a pre-trial motion as a matter of law and the parties are not inclined or able to reach a compromise settlement of their dispute, how should the attorney get his or her case ready for trial? What final steps must be undertaken, what final case analysis should occur, and what additional motions and pleadings must be prepared for presentation to the court? These issues lead the attorney back to where he or she began — case analysis and case preparation.

III. CASE ANALYSIS

Although case analysis is an ongoing process that is not complete until the jury returns with their verdict, it is particularly important when the attorney first begins to prepare for trial. That period of case analysis is important because the decisions made then have a long-term impact on the case. A good attorney takes the time to carefully consider a number of factors in concert with one another to maximize the chances of getting off on the right foot. The decisions that attorneys make during this initial period of case analysis include an analysis of existing facts and the extent to which the law will allow the attorney to offer those facts at trial. These initial decisions about facts and law are important because they guide the attorney's decision-making process throughout the trial. When properly done, case analysis forces the attorney to identify a factual theory — what he or she believes happened, and a legal theory — how the law impacts the facts, and a moral theme — why his or her side should win. Attorneys develop and refine their approaches to case analysis throughout their careers. It is an organic process that never quite reaches completion.

During case analysis and preparation, the attorney routinely reviews evidence, investigates issues, interviews witnesses, prepares exhibits, and then compares the results to see if they are on the right track based upon their analysis of the law and facts. Attorneys follow this process in a cyclical fashion until the case is complete — modifying as required based upon the portion of the trial in which they find themselves. The goal is to develop a cohesive presentation that is supported by the facts that can be presented persuasively to the jury and that is admissible under the rules of evidence and procedure that govern the trial. Attorneys are also concerned at the same time with developing a moral theme that identifies an injustice the jury can rectify. Trial attorneys combine these three elements of case analysis because they create a presentation that effectively deals with the major portions of the trial in a way that ensures the attorney has properly targeted these issues to maximize the possibility of success.

Attorneys use case analysis to develop opening statements, direct examinations, cross-examinations, and closing arguments. Failure to take the time to conduct a proper case analysis at the outset can result in an ineffective presentation throughout the trial. Case analysis is also a crucial component that drives the jury selection process in that it allows the attorney to identify those issues that the juror must be able to consider. If a juror is so biased that he or she will not be able to consider a fundamental fact or legal requirement of the case, then identifying that juror during voir dire is a crucial step to removing unfair bias. Successful attorneys realize that case analysis is the structure before and during trial that drives every decision. Every case generates paperwork that must also be organized and referenced during the trial. In conjunction with their case analysis, attorneys must also organize their case file in a way that is understandable and usable.

A.   Understanding and Organizing the Case File

The initial papers that must be organized into a case file come to the attorney in myriad ways, depending upon type of trial, the firm at which the attorney works, and the client. Regardless, the attorney must know and apply the law that addresses filing procedures and reporting requirements for the court as well as his or her internal office requirements. This information should be understood before the attorney begins to delve into the depths of a particular case file, and failure to identify and comply with the unique procedural requirements of a particular jurisdiction could result in dismissal of the case. When organizing the case file, the attorney must: (1) gather together all relevant documents and evidence, organizing the information, (2) develop a systemic approach that may include timelines, trial notebooks, witness folders, and computer management software, (3) list all evidence without regards to admissibility, and (4) identify all legal issues while addressing procedural issues (evidence and procedure), substantive issues (applicable statutes and the common law), and constitutional issues (both state and federal). Once the attorney has properly organized the case file, they can begin to use it to support the representation of their client.

Most attorneys begin by reading through the entire file, setting aside their preconceptions as a lawyer and considering the information in much the same manner in which a jury will consider it when presented to them. The initial impressions that the attorney forms about the case from reading the file are usually the same sort of impressions that jurors will have when hearing the case. After reading the file, attorneys next take the time to identify any questions that come to them based upon their reading of the file. They record these questions for additional review and analysis later in the process. It is important to note that the attorney is not producing materials for filing with the court when performing case analysis. These materials are designed for the use of the attorney and are unique to each individual advocate. The goal through this process is not the write the perfect brief, but instead to develop a process that captures the information and issues before the attorney.

It is only after all of the relevant documents, legal pleadings, and other information have been gathered together and organized in a systematic way that the attorney can see the "conceptual whole" of the case. This allows the attorney to identify strengths and weaknesses and potential moral themes and legal theories. The ability to correctly identify the underlying moral themes is crucial. Morality, right and wrong, black and white, good guys and bad guys — this is the language of the jury. The public is fascinated with the process of assigning moral blame and imposing legal judgment. If the client's story falls into an archetype that the jury understands, the case will benefit immensely from a persuasive perspective. The initial step in deconstructing the case file is systematically organizing the information so that the attorney identifies and understands the relationships between factual and legal issues within the case. Organization in a systematic fashion is the key to successfully understanding a case file. Once the information is organized, it is analyzed using the three main steps of case analysis — identifying and analyzing the legal issues, identifying and analyzing the factual issues, and developing a moral theme and legal theory.

Case files are organized regardless of the forum in which the dispute will ultimately be adjudicated. These steps apply equally for trials to a judge, a jury, an arbitration panel, or any adversarial dispute resolution proceeding. Examples of where to do this include identifying closing argument topics, preparing direct, cross and redirect examinations, conducting discovery, deposing witnesses, creating juror profiles, choosing jurors, and selecting opening statement topics. This list is not exhaustive, but does provide a sense of the various portions of a trial to which the attorney applies the three main steps of case analysis and organization.

B.   Identify and Analyze the Legal Issues

A systematic approach is necessary to ensure that all of the possible legal issues are identified and covered. Before an attorney can identify the appropriate legal issues, they must understand not only the law, but the specific area of the law that applies in their particular case. Procedurally, the attorney must identify admissibility issues while also substantively looking for strengths and weaknesses where the law intersects with the facts. Attorneys look for both substantive and procedural legal issues because either can be case dispositive. After identifying the important legal theories, the attorney next tries to convince the judge that their interpretation of the law should apply in this particular instance. That discussion normally occurs in a pre-trial motion or in a motion in limine, a motion asking a judge to exclude specific evidence or statements during the trial.

These arguments about which law applies are normally made by counsel before the judge and outside the presence of the jury. When the issue is solely a question of law, it may be possible to argue motions without the need for evidence, but that is rarely the case. Attorneys must be prepared to offer evidence as requested by the court — whenever a court is talking about evidence, it is really talking about facts placed before the court through the testimony of witnesses. The first thing a judge asks counsel for when arguments about the law are being made is what facts support their position and what evidence will be proffered for the judge's consideration. Counsel can make a proffer of what the evidence will be, but that proffer is only counsel's opinion and not substantive evidence that the judge may rely upon when ruling. Evidence may take the form of testimony, previous stipulations, or previously admitted evidence. Trial judges are not bound by the normal hearsay rules found in the Federal Rules of Evidence when determining most motions, and they can rely upon written documents or other out of court statements for the limited purpose of ruling on a motion raised by an attorney.

C.   Identify and Analyze the Factual Issues

The skill of identifying and analyzing those facts that are case dispositive is a difficult one for attorneys to master. The identification of dispositive facts is, however, an outgrowth of the types of legal analysis taught in law schools around the world, and once an attorney understands this, they are readily able to use their ability to identify the relevant legal issues needed to assist them in finding the most important factual issues. There are always more facts available than there are relevant ones from a legal perspective, and deciding which factual issues are important for legal purposes can only be accomplished after the attorney has developed a clear grasp of the appropriate legal issues presented in the case. The facts of the case determine whether the law applied by the judge assists or hurts the theme and theory chosen during case analysis.

The essence of effective persuasion is the ability of the attorney to identify the ruling legal precedent, develop case dispositive facts, and then explain the relationship between them to the jury so that they are not only accepted but relied upon when deciding the case. The legal and factual theory is the application of the relevant law to the specific facts of the case. It forms the basis for the legal or procedural reasons that the attorney's client should prevail. When properly done, the legal theory, factual theory, and moral theme empower the jury to decide the case for the attorney and is derived from a complete case analysis as discussed previously. Once the attorney has completed his or her legal and factual analysis, the attorney must next address how to identify and develop a sound moral theme.

D.   Identify and Develop a Sound Moral Theme

The theme is the moral reason that one party should prevail over the other. It provides the "why" to the jury — making them want to decide the case in favor of one side over the other. A good moral theme identifies an injustice that is being committed against the client and empowers the jury to right that wrong. Themes are omnipresent in life, and attorneys look to a variety of sources to assist them in choosing themes that will resonate with the jury. Those themes are as varied as the people, places, and situations they are designed to represent. They provide the moral force that brings the case to life. A powerful theme not only brings the jury to one attorney's side, but it also creates a feeling of comfort about deciding the case a certain way.

When an attorney successfully identifies the legal and factual issues present in the case and has chosen a moral theme, he or she is ready to properly choose which motions to file either prior to the trial beginning or during the trial itself. Motions can be used to further define the facts that may or may not be admissible in accordance with the rules of procedure, substantive law, and the rules of evidence. They are used to prevent the jury from receiving evidence not allowed by law and to produce a story that is supportive of the moral theme that has been chosen to tie the case together. This process is referred to as motions practice. Motions practice is an attempt by both sides to limit the admissible facts supporting the legal positions of opposing counsel while expanding the available admissible facts that support their own legal position.

IV.   MOTIONS

A.   Generally

Motions practice is the vehicle that trial attorneys use to get a sense of how the judge will rule on the specific legal issues present in the case. As previously discussed, one part of case analysis involves choosing a legal theory of the case that is best for a particular position. The legal theory chosen must be supported by the law in the jurisdiction where the case is to be tried. This means that the legal theory should be supported by the rulings of the judge on issues of the admissibility of evidence, which instructions will be given to the jury, and what the controlling law will be on substantive issues. Trial lawyers use motions practice to further refine their legal theories in order to develop the greatest degree of determinacy when dealing with the unknown of trial. The actual process includes notice of motions to opposing counsel and the court, the service of motions and the service of responses to the motion, a motions hearing, and finally a ruling by the court.

B.   The Motions Hearing

Once the burden of proof is identified, the judge is ready to hear the motion. Most judges give both sides an opportunity to briefly state their position before the presentation of evidence. Normally the moving party has the burden and presents its evidence first. The opposing party then presents its evidence, if any. Afterwards, rebuttal and surrebuttal evidence, if any, is presented. The attorneys then argue their positions to the judge. The judge deliberates on the motion and ultimately makes a ruling, either orally or in writing. This sequence varies slightly from judge to judge, but such a procedural variance has no effect on the validity of the ultimate ruling. A judge is typically more proactive and inquisitive during motions practice than in open court session before a jury. It is not uncommon for the judge to attempt to focus counsel on the pertinent issues. While counsel's argument must be tailored for motions practice, the basic concepts of persuading the judge apply. A good motions argument initially states the position, moves to the facts, presents the law, applies the law to the facts, and, finally, restates the position on the requested relief. Attorneys understand that this is an area of the trial that is driven by local practices, and they must be proactive in knowing the judge and the local rules when developing the general scheme for the motions argument.

Rules of evidence for both the state and federal courts establish that the judge has the authority to decide questions of admissibility in a motions hearing. The judge may make such decisions without regards to the limitations on admissibility that the other evidentiary rules might place upon the offered evidence. The only limitation on what evidence the judge may consider is found in the rule on privileges. Privileges do apply during motions, and if the information is the result of a protected communication, it may very well not be admissible in a motions hearing. The courts have determined that we will not destroy the privilege protections when deciding motions because the policy considerations behind privilege doctrine support their exclusion from motions practice. The rule also allows for the conditional admissibility of evidence even though counsel has not yet established that it will be relevant. Conditional relevancy exists so that the court can control the flow of the trial and keep cases moving forward in a timely manner. It also reflects the modernization of trial process as part of the adoption of codified rules of evidence. The rule also allows the accused to testify for the limited purpose of addressing the subject of the motion without otherwise waiving his right to silence in a criminal case.

C.   Issues to Consider During Motions Practice

Superior motions practice either results in summary judgment, limits evidence that will be admissible against the client, or establishes precedents that will shape the entire trial process. Motions allow the attorney to set the stage from a factual perspective through the application of law. Although many facts may seem to be logically relevant, they must also meet the test of legal relevancy before they can be admitted as evidence at trial. The extent to which an attorney effectively learns how to use motions impacts directly on their success at trial. In addition to pre-trial motions attorneys also have the ability to respond to issues at trial by making motions before the court when the issues arise. These motions may be as simple as a request for an advance ruling on evidentiary issues, or as complex as determining the admissibility of key evidence that may very well be case dispositive. Finally, the attorney can also re-address motions filed prior to the start of the actual trial if some additional fact or issue raised at trial might impact on the earlier ruling of the judge. The decision to re-address an earlier motion where the judge ruled against you is one that must be made in light of the court's earlier ruling and the predicted impact of addressing that issue in the presence of the jury. Rulings on motions impact the facts presented. The superior attorney uses motions to shape the courtroom persuasively.

When engaging in motions practice, a competent attorneys know the local rules for filing deadlines according to the legal issue when appropriate and according to timeliness. They also take the time to draft motions in writing that use law, facts, and inferences to their advantage. Attorneys that are prepared have identified the source of their evidence for the motions hearing and have it available in an appropriate form to admit before the judge. In U.S. courts, the judge is able to consider evidence that might not normally be admissible when he or she is doing so for the limited purpose of ruling on a motion. Attorneys must be careful to not forget to balance the law, facts, and moral theme, even when dealing with motions. They should be prepared to identify for the judge the reason for the legal protection authorized. Sometimes the judge must be reminded of that necessity — good attorneys are ready to do so when necessary. Part of motions practice is also laying the groundwork for appeals if the case is not won at the trial level. Attorneys must know when the ruling of a judge preserves an issue for appeal and when they must raise it during the case-in-chief to secure the record. There are both tactical and strategic reasons behind any decision to raise such issues during the trial itself.

It is only after case analysis has been completed, motions have been argued, and the judge has ruled that the case is now ready to go to trial. In the next section, this text addresses the three fundamental sections of the trial process in the United States. Each of these sections is applicable to both civil and criminal trials, although in some instances the case may be decided by a judge without a jury. For purposes of discussion, we will address those cases where a jury will be present.

V.   THE THREE FUNDAMENTAL SECTIONS OF A TRIAL

Attorneys at trial must select the jury, make opening statements that preview the facts of their case, call witnesses to provide evidence, and finally make closing arguments to the jury. This process is generally followed in every jurisdiction in the United States, with local rules of court impacting the manner in which the jury is actually selected in each jurisdiction. As discussed previously in the section on motions practice, legal issues do arise from time to time during the trial itself, and attorneys may object and make motions to the court to exclude evidence or to stop the proceedings. The possibilities of an objection being made or of a motion being filed exist throughout the trial and continue into the post trial or appellate process as well. The trial itself can fairly be said to break down into three main sections: (1) jury selection and opening statements, (2) the case-in-chief where evidence is offered through the testimony of witnesses, and (3) closing arguments where attorneys bring together the facts of the case and the relevant law to persuade the jury to decide the case in their client's favor.

A.   Jury Selection and Opening Statements

1.   Jury Selection

Selecting a jury is called voir dire in most jurisdictions. It is a series of procedural steps controlled by the judge, with the participation of counsel, which is designed to identify which members of the venire (a pool of potential jurors) will serve as jury members for that particular case. It normally includes pre-trial questionnaires, initial questions posed by the judge, and questioning by advocates in those jurisdictions that allow advocates to question jurors. Some jurisdictions, most notably federal courts, no longer allow advocates to conduct voir dire and require instead that all questions be provided in writing to the judge who poses them to the potential jury pool. Regardless of how it is done, jury selection is one of the first things that an attorney does during the trial where there is direct contact with people who will actually decide the facts of the case. Attorneys attempt, as best they are able, to identify the members of the prospective jury that they believe have a bias that will prevent them from deciding the case in their client's favor. The process is not about choosing jurors that like the attorney, but rather about identifying those who don't like the attorney or the client and won't change their mind — those are the jurors the attorney must remove if possible. The attorney is only prepared to do that if they have sufficiently analyzed the case beforehand. They attempt to identify problem jurors with a bias based upon their legal theory, factual theory, or moral theme.

The primary purpose of voir dire is to obtain information about potential jurors that is used to challenge (a process that eliminates them from the jury) potential jurors who are prejudiced, biased, or inflexible. Attorneys also have a discreet number of peremptory challenges that they must intelligently exercise. Peremptory challenges allow an attorney to remove someone from the potential jury even if that person is not biased. It is a long standing tradition in the United States to allow peremptory challenges, but they have come under attack in recent years and are much more limited now than previously in the history of the courts — still they are a part of jury selection and an attorney must be aware of them, the relevant law that controls them, and the manner in which they may be used. Attorneys also use the voir dire process to educate potential jurors on the particular factual and legal issues in the case, eliminate shock and surprises, obtain promises of fairness, and develop a rapport with the jury pool. It may be used to preview the legal and factual issues in the case, even to the point of foreshadowing opening statements and closing arguments.

Attorneys must choose voir dire questions carefully, refraining from asking questions which insult the intelligence of potential jurors, and that are carefully tailored to the facts of each case. While doing so they must also be sensitive to the various education levels of the potential jurors and the practice requirements of the trial judge. Some judges will review written questions before trial, some will not. Others require written questions, especially in very serious cases. It is worth noting that in jurisdictions where judges are elected, voir dire is one of the few instances where judges are allowed to "campaign" their voting base. Smart attorneys are sensitive to this potential issue — when in doubt, they never embarrass a potential juror unless the needs of the client absolutely require it.

Attorneys must also take care to not use questions that are accusatory, reproaching, or cause embarrassment, especially during group voir dire. When confronted with a potentially embarrassing topic, attorneys should always review the questionnaires filled out by the jury members first, developing questions that probe into those questionnaire issues by using non-leading and open-ended questions in voir dire. Attorneys do not address sensitive issues during the group session, being careful to avoid going into detail with a potential juror on an issue that might ripen into a challenge for cause or an opportunity for embarrassment. They do not want to taint the other members of the group on that issue. When a response in general voir dire establishes a ground for a challenge for cause, counsel may ask the other potential jurors if they agree with the response. If others agree, then the number of potential jurors that could be challenged for cause has increased. These potential jurors are queried further during individual voir dire. During individual voir dire, the tone of the attorneys' questions may change, with a shift to the use of leading questions to nail down the potential challenge for cause identified during group voir dire.

One common source of potential challenges that attorneys routinely pursue is whether any potential juror had previous contact with counsel, witnesses, or the defendant or has heard something about the case. If so, the potential juror may have either favorable or unfavorable opinions that may affect their ability to be fair and neutral. This is not always the case, however, and just because they may have heard something about the case they are not per se disqualified. When this issue comes up, attorneys focus on whether the potential juror can set aside what they heard and make their decision solely on the evidence presented in court. The judge will expect potential jurors to state on the record how they would be able to set aside what they heard earlier as an affirmative promise to be fair and impartial.

Superior attorneys use the jury selection process to accurately reflect the issues they identified during case analysis. This is a crucial point. The final step of which voir dire questions are asked is the attorney's, and it should be made under the rubric of case analysis. The only way to effectively do this is to marry them to specific legal, factual and moral issues. The selection of an appropriate legal theory, factual theory, and moral theme assists the attorney in finding not only the right voir dire questions substantively, but the right means of delivering them to the jury.

2.   Opening Statements

Unlike many other portions of a trial, the opening statement is not governed by the rules of evidence in U.S. courts. Instead the law that applies varies greatly from state to state, as well as within the federal court system. A review of the case law in those jurisdictions establishes certain fundamental concepts that attorneys can rely upon when creating effective, passionate, and persuasive openings. Those concepts include the following: (1) the judge sets the guidelines, (2) no arguing — tell the story, (3) no vouching for the credibility of witnesses, (4) no personal opinions — lawyers are advocates, not witnesses, (5) no mentioning evidence that was excluded during pre-trial proceedings, (6) no referring to evidence in opening if there is not a good faith basis to believe it will be admitted, and (7) never violate the "golden rule" by asking the jurors to place themselves in a party's shoes. The opening statement should communicate the legal theory, factual theory, and moral theme to the jury in a fashion that persuades.

While the opening statement is one of the first things an attorney does once the trial starts, it is actually one of the last things prepared for presentation. Attorneys view opening statements as the beginning point of the jury's journey. The attorney sees him- or herself as the tour guide that the jury relies upon to reach their final destination. Opening statement actually occurs after jury selection. The judge instructs the jury and empanels them to hear the case. The attorneys then give opening statements. This is a storytelling opportunity that creates drama, forecasts issues, and previews solutions. An opening statement is a statement of what the attorney believes the facts of the case to be; it is not an argument about what those facts mean. The attorney is not able at this point to argue to the jury that facts have certain significance when they have not yet received those facts into evidence. Opening statement is the time to tell the jury what the attorney expects the facts will be, and to tease them with the promise of how their side will explain what those facts mean in closing argument. It is also a time to establish a moral theme — that sense of injustice that the jury can fix, the wrong that human nature calls upon them to right.

Attorneys identify the local rules of court and review the relevant case law in the jurisdiction in which they practice when preparing openings. The seven basic legal principles for opening statements discussed above apply in most, if not all, jurisdictions. Most courts expect advocates to make powerful and persuasive opening statements that relay the facts, establish moral themes, and forecast legal issues. Beyond that there is relatively little uniformity between the various jurisdictions. Most will let attorneys use exhibits — both tangible objects and documents — during opening if they have been either pre-admitted or there is a good faith basis to believe they will be able to admit them at trial. Judges not only have the discretion in controlling the manner and substance of opening statements, but they also instruct the jury about opening statements by letting them know what they mean and how to weigh them. The use of jury instructions is ubiquitous in the United States; it is the vehicle by which the judge explains the law and the responsibilities of the trial to the jury.

B.   The Case-in-Chief

Once the opening statement is complete, the production of evidence begins. During the case-in-chief, evidence is received by the jury through the testimony of witnesses. This normally occurs during direct examination and cross examination. The party bearing the burden of proof presents evidence first, this is called direct examination. In a criminal case, that is the prosecution; in civil cases, it is the plaintiff. Every question that is asked on direct or cross examination is designed to admit evidence, exclude evidence, or explain the amount of weight that should be given to a particular piece of evidence. A lot happens during the case-in-chief, and attorneys are judged by their ability to conduct directs, cross-examine, object to evidence, and ensure rulings from the judge that support their factual theory, legal theory, and moral theme.

Witnesses are the vehicle used at trial to admit evidence, either testimonial or otherwise. The route to the closing argument outlined in the opening statement is filled with the sign posts of relevant witness testimony. The testimony of witnesses is the primary means available to introduce evidence at trial. For every fact that the attorney intends to argue in closing, they must have a witness to introduce that fact. The legal theory and moral theme chosen by the attorney determines which witnesses must be called to testify and to a great extent what they will say. Each witness is a piece of the puzzle before the jury. This includes not only the attorney's witnesses, but the opponent's as well. Attorneys connect testimony to the closing argument, increasing not only their persuasive ability, but more importantly, the believability of their case.

When witnesses are called by one attorney, they testify in a portion of the trial that is called direct examination. Because the witness was called by that attorney, the form of the questions that can be asked is controlled by the relevant rules of evidence. In most jurisdictions, the attorney must ask their witnesses open-ended questions that do not suggest a particular answer to the witness. Attorneys normally focus on questions that include who, what, when, where, why, and how. They are not normally allowed to suggest the answer to the witness, although the judge has the discretion to let them do so if he or she wishes.

Attorneys use direct examination to place the facts of the case before the jury. They must use open-ended questions unless laying a foundation or dealing with a witness that allows them to lead because of an infirmity. Direct examination should showcase the witness. It presents a clear and logical progression of witness observations and activities in a way that persuades. Attorneys rely upon checklists for each witness to identify the facts and exhibits needed to make an effective closing argument that complements the opening statement. The foundation of that checklist are found in the case analysis and developed further by the attorney when preparing and conducting direct examinations.

Once an attorney has questioned the witness, the opposing counsel is then given an opportunity to question that same witness. This process is usually referred to as cross-examination. Because the attorney did not call this witness, the rules allow them to ask leading questions that suggest the answer and require an affirmative or negative response from the witness. Cross examination is designed to expose a lack of truthfulness or bias on the part of the witness that calls into question the reliability and credibility of their testimony in the eyes of the jury. Cross examinations occur when examining an opposing counsel's witness. They happen after the opposing counsel has completed direct, but may occur during the direct examination when dealing with expert witnesses. During cross, the attorney controls the witness, establishes facts that build to a theme and theory, and establishes facts that build up the credibility of their own witnesses while diminishing the credibility of the opponent's witnesses. The attorney must know more than the witness in order to be effective — case analysis makes that possible. Attorneys identify and list the legal issues in the case and adapt their theme and theories to support them when preparing for cross.

Witness testimony is a double edged process, and attorneys must be careful to not only identify those issues their witnesses will testify about, but they must also identify the issues that opposing counsel will address during the cross-examination, as well as the issues they will bring up when questioning opposing counsel's witnesses. The rules require each side to give advance notice to opposing counsel of the witnesses they intend to call at least in part to facilitate this process. Attorneys that prepare this way test the validity of their theme and theory and also identify the crucial testimony they must plan to get out of witnesses on direct and cross. When properly done, this type of case analysis produces a template that guides selection of witnesses, questioning of witnesses, and selection of topics for cross examination. The jury does not realize this is happening, and instead merely hears the witnesses saying things supporting the attorney's legal theory and moral theme.

This process is not limited to factual issues during the case-in-chief. The judge also rules upon motions and objections during the trial. During the trial, the attorney is constantly seeking to produce questions that support the admissibility or suppression of testimony or physical evidence. Since instructions are the vehicle used by the judge to control and assist the jury, the attorney uses that knowledge to identify certain instructions they want the judge to give the jury before deliberations. This helps the attorney mold witnesses' testimony in a manner that supports the instructions on the law and the facts they will request from the judge. When properly done, this foreshadows the judge's instructions during the closing argument. The jury hears the attorney say that the law is a certain way, and then the judge confirms that prediction, increasing the credibility of the attorney in the eyes of the jury when he or she instructs the jury on the law in accordance with the attorney's promise.

Case analysis and preparation drive the entire trial process. Direct examinations and cross-examinations are focused inquiries that highlight those facts and support the legal issues identified. Directs and crosses that are not focused on the ultimate goals of case analysis waste time, confuse issues, and are opportunities lost. Using case analysis as the organizational template for preparation engenders success.

C.   Closing Arguments and Jury Instructions

1.   Closing Arguments

Once the case-in-chief portion of the trial is completed, it is time for the dramatic moment immortalized in fiction and film — closing arguments. The attorneys make closing arguments to the jury after the defense has rested. The party with the burden of proof argues first and last. In between, the party defending the case presents their closing argument. This is when the advocates argue about what the admitted evidence means. Now is the time when comments on evidence, the believability of witnesses, and calls to common sense prevail. It is the attorney's moment to sway the jury, through logic, emotion and morality, to decide the case in their favor.

Closing argument is the final destination. If case analysis has been done properly, the court has arrived at the point where the jury can be led to make the decision that favors the client. While the law of closing arguments varies slightly from jurisdiction to jurisdiction, the following general legal principles apply: (1) the attorney is confined to the record, if evidence is not admitted it cannot be argued, (2) the trial court has supervisory authority over the scope and direction of closing argument, but should give deference to counsel unless the law is misstated, (3) prosecutors cannot argue merely to inflame or arouse passions, and courts will consider whether a substantial right of the accused was violated when reviewing this issue, (4) advocates cannot intentionally misstate evidence or attempt to lead the jury to draw improper inferences from admitted evidence, (5) personal beliefs and opinions of counsel are forbidden, (6) reasonable inferences are permissible and expected, and (7) it is improper to refer to evidence which was either successfully objected to as to admissibility, stricken from the record, or otherwise excluded.

Closing argument is the destination of the trial. The case-in-chief is the route taken, and the opening statement was the departure point. The closing argument contains the words that empower the jury to decide the case. It joins the facts and the law of the case, casting them in a moral light. A good closing argument demands, sometimes loudly, sometimes quietly, sometimes reluctantly, but demands nonetheless, that the jury do nothing other than what has been asked by counsel. If the attorney has properly identified the legal and factual issues and chosen the right theme and theory, the closing argument will come to him or her as an organic expression of what that hard work has shown to be true. If the attorney did not properly analyze the case, he or she will struggle to find a closing argument that makes sense and fits the facts and the law of the case. When the wrong argument is chosen, it does not ring true and will not be believed. It must come organically and spring from the facts and the law.

2.   Jury Instructions

Once closing arguments are completed, the judge charges the jury by instructing them on the law. The evidence is collected, and the jury retires to deliberate. Jury instructions are chosen and given to the jury by the judge. Instructions are practical statements drafted to reflect the current status of the applicable law and are designed to accurately represent what the bar currently believes that current applicable law to be. In most jurisdictions, there are committees of respected members of the legal profession who draft pattern jury instructions that are provided to the judiciary for their use. These instructions are made available to all members of the profession, and attorneys even file motions requesting that certain instructions be given to the jury based upon the facts and issues in their particular case. They are written in a way to make them understandable to the lay jury member and are designed to educate jurors on the proper application of the law to a factual situation. Jury instructions also assist the judge so that he or she does not incorrectly inform the jury as to the current status of the law.

3.   Deliberations and Verdict

Jury deliberations occur in private and are not normally subject to scrutiny by the legal system. The number of votes necessary for the jury to reach a verdict varies depending upon whether the case is a civil case or a criminal case. In most jurisdictions, a unanimous verdict is required for conviction in a criminal case, while findings for a plaintiff in a civil case can vary from two-thirds majority to unanimity. The jury deliberates in accordance with the instructions provided by the judge. Once they have reached a verdict, the jury returns to court, and the verdict is announced. Normally, the side that wins will seek enforcement of the verdict, and the side that loses may or may not file an appeal. If they do, then next begins the post-trial advocacy process, including appeals, settlements, very rarely the granting of a new trial, and usually finality based upon the verdict.

It is helpful to consider the relationships between the three basic portions of a trial when reviewing the practice of law in the United States. If one understands that attorneys approach the trial process in this interconnected way, it assists one in grasping the fundamental practice of law in the United States. The attorney creates coherent messages for the jury this way, and it also reiterates the point

420 THE PRACTICE OF LAW CH. 17

that representation of clients when dealing with issues in controversy may very well be determined by the organizational and analytical skills of involved counsel. Although trials are planned in reverse by beginning at the end, they play forward when presented. The jury hears the attorney tell them where they are going and how they will get there in the opening statement. They then go to the final destination through the testimony of witnesses, and the attorney reminds them of what it should all mean in closing argument. To the juror it seems as though the attorney told them what they were going to do, did it, and then reminded them it had been done and explained what it means. The attorney has credibility in the eyes of jury. They are seen as an ethical, straight-shooter who can be trusted. More importantly, the attorney will actually be an ethical advocate that has done the ground work to ensure success, the ultimate goal of any trial process.

VII. CONCLUSION

This chapter has discussed the practice of law through the lens of dispute resolution after the formation of the attorney-client relationship. It is important to note that many lawyers engage in transactional and business practice and never see the inside of a courtroom. The practice within a civil law system and a common law system are relatively similar when dealing with transactional work and business clients. The fundamental differences between a civil law system and a common law system are found when one compares the trial processes of both institutions. The discussion of the trial process and how it impacts upon the practice of law for those attorneys that engage in this form of dispute resolution in a common law system illustrates the mind set and reasoning process of common law attorneys practicing law.

INDEX

[References are to pages.]

A

ADMINISTRATIVE LAW
Generally . . . 355; 356; 380
Adjudication
  Generally . . . 367
  Formal hearing
    Generally . . . 368
    Appeals, internal . . . 370
    Integrity of process, protecting . . . 370
    Procedures, generally . . . 369
Constitutional considerations
  Generally . . . 360
  Fifth amendment and rule against self-incrimination . . . 363
  Fourth amendment and administrative investigations . . . 363
  Procedural due process
    Identifying process that is due . . . 362
    Liberty, defining . . . 362
    Property, defining . . . 361
    Time considerations . . . 363
  Separation of powers
    Controlling agencies . . . 359
    Empowering agencies . . . 359
    Settlement . . . 360
    Three separate branches . . . 357
Judicial review
  Generally . . . 372
  Agency discretion, commitment to . . . 373
  Exhaustion of administrative remedies . . . 375
  Finality . . . 375
  Preclusion of . . . 372
  Refusals to act, review of . . . 373
  Ripeness . . . 376
  Scope of
    Generally . . . 376
    Determinations of policy and exercises of discretion, reviewing . . . 378
    Factual determinations, reviewing . . . 377
    Legal interpretations, reviewing . . . 379
  When obtained . . . 374
  Who can seek . . . 373
Rulemaking
  Adjudication distinct from . . . 364; 365
  Constitutional requirements . . . 366
  Interpretive rules and policy statements . . . 367
  Procedural requirements, other . . . 367
  Statutory requirements . . . 366

ADMINISTRATIVE REGULATIONS
Source of law in U.S. legal system, as . . . 20

ARBITRATION
Generally . . . 37

ATTORNEYS' FEES
Tort actions, in . . . 103

B

BUSINESS ASSOCIATIONS
Generally . . . 257
Closely-held businesses
  Close corporations . . . 274
  LLC governance . . . 276
Conclusion . . . Generally
Development of corporate law . . . 262
Extraordinary transactions
  Friendly transactions . . . 279
  Hostile takeovers . . . 281
Federal securities law . . . 284
Fiduciary duties
  Due care . . . 268
  Good faith . . . 271
  Loyalty . . . 269
  Shareholder derivative suits . . . 272
Forms of
  Limited liability company . . . 261
  Limited liability partnership . . . 261
  Partnership . . . 258
  Sole proprietorship . . . 258
Structure of corporation
  Generally . . . 267
  Directors . . . 264
  Officers . . . 265
  Shareholders . . . 266
Third-party liability
  Defective incorporation . . . 278
  Limited liability . . . 277
  Piercing corporate veil . . . 277
  Promoter liability . . . 278

C

CASE LAW
Reading and briefing
  Generally . . . 23; 25
  Facts of case . . . 26
  Holding . . . 27
  Issue, determining . . . 25
  Procedural history . . . 26
  Purposes of reading . . . 24
  Reasoning of court . . . 27
  Rule, determination of . . . 26
  Sample case brief . . . 28
  Skimming case . . . 24
  Style of case . . . 25

CHOICE OF LAW
Generally . . . 381; 384

I-1

[References are to pages.]

[References are to pages.]

[References are to pages.]

[References are to pages.]

[References are to pages.]

[References are to pages.]

[References are to pages.]